Thinking with Whitehead

THINKING WITH WHITEHEAD

A Free and Wild Creation of Concepts

ISABELLE STENGERS

Translated by Michael Chase

FOREWORD BY BRUNO LATOUR

Harvard University Press
Cambridge, Massachusetts, and London, England

This book was originally published as *Penser avec Whitehead: "Une libre et sauvage création de concepts,"* copyright © Éditions du Seuil, 2002

This book was published with the support of the French Ministry of Culture — National Book Center / Cet ouvrage a été publié avec l'assistance du Ministère de la culture — Centre National du Livre

First Harvard University Press paperback edition, 2014

Library of Congress Cataloging-in-Publication Data

Stengers, Isabelle.
[Penser avec Whitehead. English]
Thinking with Whitehead : a free and wild creation of concepts / Isabelle Stengers ; translated by Michael Chase.
p. cm.
Includes bibliographical references and index.
ISBN 978-0-674-04803-4 (cloth: alk. paper)
ISBN 978-0-674-41697-0 (pbk.)
1. Whitehead, Alfred North, 1861–1947. I. Title.
B1674.W354S8413   2011
192—dc22   2010047153

To all the students who, in the course of the last few years, have taken my classes on Whitehead. It is thanks to them that I have become convinced that, for better or worse, this book could be, and therefore should be, written.

Contents

What Is Given in Experience?

Bruno Latour

Every synthesis begins "anew" and has to be taken up from the
start as if for the first time.
— Isabelle Stengers

I T COULD BE ONE of those little games journalists play on televi-
sion talk shows about books: "Who was the greatest philosopher
of the twentieth century whose name begins with *W?*" Most
learned people in America would answer "Wittgenstein." Sorry. The right
answer is "Whitehead"—another philosopher whose name begins with
W, to be sure, but one who is vastly more daring, and also, unfortunately,
much less studied. Among his many misfortunes, Alfred North Whitehead had the very bad one of provoking too much interest among theologians and too little among epistemologists. His reputation in America
is thus skewed toward his theological innovations to the detriment of his
epistemological theories. He also suffers from the terrible stigma of having indulged in metaphysics, something one is no longer supposed to do
after the edicts of the first "W," even though those who think that metaphysics is passé know usually much less science than Whitehead and
swallow—without an ounce of criticism—hook, line, and sinker the en-
tirety of metaphysical beliefs about nature that one can easily derive by
lumping together the least-common-denominator views of geneticists
and so-called cognitive scientists. As Isabelle Stengers says in her recently

The Foreword is excerpted from my review of the French edition of this book,
Isabelle Stengers, *Penser avec Whitehead: Une libre et sauvage création de concepts.*
The review was published as Bruno Latour, "What Is Given in Experience?," in
boundary 2, Volume 32, no. 1, pp. 223–237. Copyright © 2005 by Duke University Press. All rights reserved. Reprinted by permission of the publisher. I thank
Lindsay Waters for his valuable comments on earlier drafts of this essay. Cita-
tions to *Penser avec Whitehead* appear in parentheses, and, unless otherwise
noted, all translations are my own.—B.L.

published masterpiece about Whitehead, "critical consciousness admits so many things without criticizing them" (74).

What makes Stengers's book *Penser avec Whitehead*—in English, "to think with Whitehead"—such an important work for Anglo-American philosophy is that in it the greatest philosopher of the twentieth century is finally studied in great detail by someone who is one of the most innovative philosophers of science of the present time. Now we finally have, in other words, after years of embarrassed commentaries in which people had eulogized Whitehead's God and disparaged Whitehead's science, a book in which Whitehead's science and Whitehead's God are each given their rightful place. This development is not going to put process theology on a new footing. After having worked for years on the physics of time with Ilya Prigogine,[1] and then after having written her seven-volume treatise laying out her own version of *Cosmopolitcs*,[2] Stengers has dedicated 572 pages to her favorite philosopher, retranslating herself many pages of this most difficult of authors for the sake of her analysis in French.[3]

For people who have read both Stengers and Whitehead for years, the prospect of reading the prose of the first commenting on the prose of the second might be somewhat daunting. And yet, one gets exactly

---

[1] Because of this long and friendly collaboration, Stengers has been associated with the physics of complexity pioneered by Ilya Prigogine. In her own work since, Prigogine's influence is important not because she tried to prolong some more elaborated naturalism but because she learned from Prigogine's experience to which extent scientists would go to ignore something as crucial as time. Hence her admiration for science and her deep-seated suspicion for some of its sleight of hand.

[2] From *Cosmopolitiques—Tome 1: La guerre des sciences* (Paris: La Découverte—Les Empêcheurs de penser en rond, 1996), to *Cosmopolitiques—Tome 7: Pour en finir avec la tolérance* (Paris: La Découverte–Les Empêcheurs de penser en rond, 1997).

[3] Isabelle Stengers teaches philosophy in Brussels. Only a small part of her works is available in English: *Power and Invention,* with a foreword by Bruno Latour (Minneapolis: University of Minnesota Press, 1997); *The Invention of Modem Science,* trans. Daniel W. Smith (Minneapolis: University of Minnesota Press, 2000); Bernadette Bensaude-Vincent and Isabelle Stengers, *A History of Chemistry,* trans. Deborah Van Dam (Cambridge, Mass.: Harvard University Press, 1996); and Leon Chertock and Isabelle Stengers, *A Critique of Psychoanalytic Reason: Hypnosis as a Scientific Problem from Lavoisier to Lacan,* trans. Martha Noel Evans (Stanford, Calif.: Stanford University Press, 1992). I have attempted to present Stengers's epistemological principle in "How to Talk about the Body? The Normative Dimension of Science Studies," in Part 3: Body Collective of "Bodies on Trial," ed. Marc Berg and Madeleine Akrich, special issue, *Body and Society* 10, no. 2–3 (June–September 2004): 205–229.

the opposite result: Stengers illuminates the most obscure passages of Whitehead in *a* style that is supple, often witty, always generous. So readers should not be put off by the surprising subtitle, which Stengers actually borrowed from Deleuze: there is nothing "wild" in this book, except as that word might be used to characterize the freedom and invention of the author. Of those virtues the book is stuffed full.[4]

Following Whitehead, Stengers has been able to turn around many of the metaphors usually borrowed from critical thinking: "To think with Whitehead today means to sign on in advance to an adventure that will leave none of the terms we normally use as they were, even though none will be undermined or summarily denounced as a carrier of illusion" (24).

Whitehead is thoroughly put to the test here, and yet I have no doubt that, had he lived, Deleuze would have celebrated this book as a major event in the geopolitics of philosophy: a great but neglected Anglo-American is reimported into France through Belgium, and the event is taken as the occasion to reinterpret pragmatism, Bergsonism, and empiricism. What a wonder! What an interesting ecological "inter-capture"!

Although the book is a close reading, in chronological order, of the major books of Whitehead, and although it makes good use of the body of existing scholarship, it does not simply try to explain or popularize the history of Whitehead's thought. As the title indicates so well, the aim is to think *with* Whitehead. Because she is herself a philosopher of science who has explored minutely many of the same fields as Whitehead—chemistry, physics, Darwinism, ethology, and psychology (but not mathematics nor logic, although she takes very seriously the fact that Whitehead thinks as a mathematician)—Stengers's book can be seen as an effort to test out Whitehead's most daring concepts on new materials and in new examples. But contrary to the rather cavalier way in which Whitehead treats his own predecessors, Stengers is very precise and follows with great attention Whitehead's own hunches. Have no doubt: when we read this book, we are thinking *with* Stengers and *with* Whitehead all along; we are not thinking with Whitehead about what is on Stengers's mind.

The whole book turns around the most arduous question of Whitehead, without making any attempt either to avoid the difficulties or to obfuscate his philosophy by bringing in new irrelevant conundrums. The basic question is to decide whether or not empiricism can be renewed so that

---

[4] The choice of the subtitle is even more bizarre, since on page 307 Stengers reveals a clear contrast between the positivity of Whitehead and the exaggerated tropism of Deleuze for chaos and organicism.

"what is given in experience" is not simplified too much. Against the tradition inaugurated by Locke and Descartes, then pushed to the limits by Kant until it was terminated by William James, Whitehead offers another role for the object of study to play: "The object [for him] is neither the judge of our production nor the product of our judgments" (93).[5]

What has been least critically considered by the philosophical tradition, and especially by the anti-metaphysical one, is the feature of Western thought that occupied Whitehead for most of his career, what he calls "the bifurcation of nature," that is to say, the strange and fully modernist divide between primary and secondary qualities.[6] *Bifurcate* is a strange and awkward word, strange to the tongue and ear, but what it betokens is something even worse for our thinking. Bifurcation is what happens whenever we think the world is divided into two sets of things: one which is composed of the fundamental constituents of the universe—invisible to the eyes, known to science, real and yet valueless—and the other which is constituted of what the mind has to add to the basic building blocks of the world in order to make sense of them. Those "psychic additions," as Whitehead calls them, are parts of common sense, to be sure, but they are unfortunately of no use to science, since they have no reality, even though they are the stuff out of which dreams and values are made.[7]

---

[5] "It is because William James has refused to give to reflexive consciousness and to its pretensions to invariance, the privilege to occupy the center of the scene, that James has explicated so well [for Whitehead] what human experience requests from metaphysics and, more precisely, to what it requests metaphysics to resist" (230). Far from psychologizing everything, Whitehead sees in James—and especially in his celebrated essay on consciousness—the thinker who has ended all the pretensions of the mind. If the "actual occasion" is depsychologized, it is thanks to James.

[6] Here is a standard definition of the problem: "However, we must admit that the causality theory of nature has its strong suit. The reason why the bifurcation of nature is always creeping back into scientific philosophy is the extreme difficulty of exhibiting the perceived redness and warmth of the fire in one system of relations with the agitated molecules of carbon and oxygen with the radiant energy from them, and with the various functioning of the material body. Unless we produce the all-embracing relations, we are faced with a bifurcated nature; namely, warmth and redness on one side, and molecules, electrons and ether on the other side. Then the two factors are explained as being respectively the cause and the mind's reaction to the cause" (Alfred North Whitehead, *The Concept of Nature* [Cambridge: Cambridge University Press, 1920], 32).

[7] On the political dimension of this divide, see my own footnote on Whitehead's argument in *Politics of Nature: How to Bring the Sciences into Democracy*, trans. Catherine Porter (Cambridge, Mass.: Harvard University Press, 2004).

If I could summarize Stengers's version of Whitehead by a sort of syllogism, it could be the following one: modernist philosophy of science implies a bifurcation of nature into objects having primary and secondary qualities. However, if nature really is bifurcated, no living organism would be possible, since being an organism means being the sort of thing whose primary and secondary qualities—if they did exist—are endlessly blurred. Since we are organisms surrounded by many other organisms, nature has *not* bifurcated. Corollary: if nature has never bifurcated in the way philosophy has implied since the time of Locke, what sort of metaphysics should be devised that would pay full justice to the concrete and obstinate existence of organisms? The consequence of considering this question is radical indeed: "The question of what is an object and thus what is an abstraction must belong, if nature is not allowed to bifurcate, to *nature* and not to knowledge only" (95; my emphasis).

Hence the roughly three equal parts of the book (although Stengers divides her book in two): How to overcome the bifurcation of nature? What is an organism of a creative sort? What sort of strange God is implied for this new philosophical business?

[...]

I think it is with Whitehead's God that Stengers's book reveals its ultimate power. Commentators have often tried either to drag Whitehead in theology seminars—forgetting that his God is there to solve very precisely a technical problem of philosophy, not of belief—or to get rid of this embarrassing appendix altogether. Stengers does not hesitate to go all the way in the direction of Whitehead's argument: if nature can't be seen as bifurcated, if actual occasions are the stuff out of which the world is made, if "negative prehensions" are the only way actual occasions have to envisage the world, to apprehend it, if eternal objects are there as guardians against the shift back to substance and foundations, then a God-function is *implied* in this philosophy.

But, of course, everything now turns around the word *implied*, or *implicated*. Taken superficially, it shifts the concept of God into one of a king who sits on a throne or some great plant ensconced in a sort of flowerpot, holding this position in order to close a book of metaphysics—the equivalent in philosophy of the Queen of England in politics. Or else, taken as a belief, God gives some philosophical luster to parts of the creed of some church, becoming what you confide in when you have lost confidence in the world and especially in science. Without disregarding those possibilities, Whitehead means something else altogether. *Implied* is not only a logical function—who is less a logician than the Whitehead of the famous team "Russell and Whitehead"?—but a thoroughly ontological *involvement* into the world. God is the feeling for positive, instead of negative, prehensions. After years (or should I say centuries?) of associating God with negativity—think, for instance, of Hegel—it will take some time to see his role as consisting of a positivity, but that would be a welcome change! "Divine experience is, in that sense, conscious but also incomplete. God does not envisage what could be. His existence does not precede nor predict future actualizations. His envisagement comes from the thirst for some novelty that this thirst is going to induce but which, by definition, will go beyond it" (525).

In a way, it is not surprising that theology has found Whitehead so congenial, since innovations in theology are few and far between. But Stengers redresses the usual imbalance and places Whitehead's invention of a God implicated squarely inside the world—and unable to "explicate" it, nor to "extricate" himself out of it—as the most daring but also the most indispensable consequence of his early refusal to let nature bifurcate. No more than you can choose in nature to eliminate either primary or secondary qualities can you choose, in Whitehead, between his epistemology and his theology. And, of course, it would be impossible to say that the modernist philosophy has "no need for God," as philosophers are so proud of saying and say frequently. Their crossed-out God—to use my term—is always there but only to fill gaps in their reasoning. By taking Whitehead's God as seriously as Whitehead's epistemology, Stengers is leading us in the first systematic attempt at finding a metaphysical alternative to modernism. The reason why her attempts are so beautifully moving is that Whitehead has a gift of the most extraordinary rarity: he is not a creature of the culture of critique. "He knows no critique," as one could say of a saint "she knows no sin."

What does it mean to "speak Whiteheadian"? Amusingly, Stengers's book begins with some of those long Whiteheadian sentences that Grendel, the dragon hero of John Gardner's remake of Beowulf, thunders when he wishes to frighten his human victims out of their wits. Stengers's book is a frightening one, no question about that: five hundred pages of purely speculative metaphysics. But Grendel, as we learn when we read the story, is not there to eat all of us up. On the contrary, he is there to remind us of our lost wisdom. How can it be that America, nay, the Harvard Philosophy Department, provided a shelter to the most important philosopher of the twentieth century and then has utterly forgotten him? Why has it taken us so long to understand Grendel's moaning? Probably because it does not offer the easy grasp of the usual domesticated philosophical animals presented in zoos behind bars, always there to be inspected and endlessly monitored. Maybe this is what Deleuze meant by "a free and wild invention of concepts." "Wild" does not mean "savage," but out in the open, as when we go searching for some elusive wildlife.

I have always felt that Whitehead-watching had a lot to do with whale-watching as it is practiced, for instance, on the coast of San Diego in the winter. You stay on a boat for hours, see nothing, and suddenly, "There she blows, she blows!" and swiftly the whale disappears again. But with Stengers at the helm, the little ship is able to predict with great accuracy where the whale will emerge again, in a few hours. Come on board, prepare your binoculars, and be confident in the captain's watch.

Abbreviations and References

[*Works from which passages are cited in the text*]

AI Alfred N. Whitehead, *Adventures of Ideas* (New York: Free Press, 1967).

ANW Victor Lowe, *Alfred Whitehead: The Man and His Work,* vol. 2, ed. J. B. Schneewind (Baltimore: Johns Hopkins University Press, 1990).

CC Gilles Deleuze, *Critique et clinique* (Paris: Minuit, 1993).

CN Alfred N. Whitehead, *The Concept of Nature* (Cambridge: Cambridge University Press, 1964).

DANW *Dialogues of Alfred North Whitehead,* as recorded by Lucien Price (Boston: David R. Godine, 2001).

DD William James, "The Dilemma of Determinism," in *The Will to Believe, and Other Essays in Popular Philosophy, and Human Immortality* (New York: Dover, 1956), pp. 145–183.

DFT Steven Weinberg, *Dreams of a Final Theory* (London: Vintage Books, 1993).

DR Gilles Deleuze, *Différence et répétition* (Paris: PUF, 1969).

EWM Lewis S. Ford, *The Emergence of Whitehead's Metaphysics, 1925–1929* (Albany: State University of New York Press, 1984).

Gr John Gardner, *Grendel* (London: Robin Clark, 1991).

I Stuart Kauffman, *Investigations* (Oxford: Oxford University Press, 2000).

IM Henri Bergson, "Introduction à la métaphysique," in *Œuvres*, édition du centenaire (Paris: PUF, 1970).

LdS Gilles Deleuze, *Logique du sens* (Paris: Minuit, 1969).

LP Gilles Deleuze, *Le Pli* (Paris: Minuit, 1988).

LWL William James, "Is Life Worth Living?" in *The Will to Believe, and Other Essays in Popular Philosophy, and Human Immortality* (New York: Dover, 1956), pp. 31–62.

MEOF Étienne Souriau, "Du mode d'existence de l'œuvre à faire," *Bulletin de la Société Française de Philosophie,* séance du 25 février 1956, pp. 4–24.

MP Gilles Deleuze and Félix Guattari, *Mille plateaux* (Paris: Minuit, 1980).

MPML William James, "The Moral Philosopher and Moral Life," in *The Will to Believe, and Other Essays in Popular Philosophy, and Human Immortality* (New York: Dover, 1956), pp. 184–215.

MT Alfred N. Whitehead, *Modes of Thought* (New York: Free Press, 1968).

PAF William James, "The Place of Affectional Facts in a World of Pure Experience," in *Essays in Radical Empiricism* (New York: Longmans, Green and Co., 1912; repr., Lincoln: University of Nebraska Press, 1996), pp. 137–154.

PP William James, *The Principles of Psychology* (New York: Holt, 1890; repr., London: Macmillan, 1891).

PR Alfred N. Whitehead, *Process and Reality,* corrected edition by D. R. Griffin and D. W. Sherburne (New York: Free Press, 1979).

QPh Gilles Deleuze and Félix Guattari, *Qu'est-ce que la philosophie?* (Paris: Minuit, 1991).

RAT William James, "Reflex Action and Theism," in *The Will to Believe, and Other Essays in Popular Philosophy, and Human Immortality* (New York: Dover, 1956), pp. 111–144.

RM Alfred N. Whitehead, *Religion in the Making* (New York: Fordham University Press, 1996).

SMW Alfred N. Whitehead, *Science and the Modern World* (New York: Free Press, 1967).

SPP William James, *Some Problems in Philosophy* (New York: Longmans, Green and Co., 1911; repr., Lincoln: University of Nebraska Press, 1996).

SS David Abram, *The Spell of the Sensuous* (New York: Pantheon Books, 1996).

Th Gottfried W. Leibniz, *Essais de théodicée* (Paris: Garnier-Flammarion, 1969).

WJEP David Lapoujade, *William James: Empirisme et pragmatisme* (Paris: PUF, 1997).

WPE William James, "A World of Pure Experience," in *Essays in Radical Empiricism* (New York: Longmans, Green and Co., 1912; repr., Lincoln: University of Nebraska Press, 1996), pp. 39–91.

Other References Used Explicitly in the Text

[*References whose object should not give rise to any difficulties of identification have been omitted.*]

Andy Clark, *Being There: Putting Brain, Body, and World Together Again* (Cambridge, Mass.: MIT Press, 1998).

William James, "Does 'Consciousness' Exist?" in *Essays in Radical Empiricism* (New York: Longmans, Green and Co., 1912; repr., Lincoln: University of Nebraska Press, 1996), pp. 1–38.

Gottfried Wilhelm Leibniz, *Confessio Philosophi,* trans. Robert C. Sleigh Jr. (New Haven, Conn.: Yale University Press, 2006).

Raymond Ruyer, *La Genèse des formes vivantes* (Paris: Flammarion, 1958).

Donald W. Sherburne, ed., *A Key to Whitehead's Process and Reality* (Bloomington: Indiana University Press, 1966).

Daniel Stern, *The Interpersonal World of the Infant* (New York: Basic Books, 1985).

There are concepts wherever there are habits, and habits are made and unmade on the plane of immanence and radical experience: they are "conventions." This is why English philosophy is a free and wild creation of concepts. Once a proposition is given, to what convention does it refer, what is the habit that constitutes its concept? This is the question of pragmatism.

—Gilles Deleuze and Félix Guattari, *Qu'est-ce que la Philosophie?*

Whitehead Today?

A Discreet Philosopher

He glanced at me, suspicious. "You're not paying attention."

"I am!" I said, joining my hands to show my seriousness.

But he shook his head slowly. "Nothing interests you but excitement, violence."

"That's not true!" I said.

His eye opened wider, his body brightened from end to end. "*You* tell *me* what's true?" he said.

"I'm trying to follow you. I do my best," I said. "You should be reasonable. What do you expect?"

The dragon thought about it, breathing slowly, full of wrath. At last he closed his eyes: "Let us try starting somewhere else," he said. "It's damned hard, you understand, confining myself to concepts familiar to a creature of the Dark Ages. Not that one age is darker than another. Technical jargon from another dark age." He scowled as if hardly capable of forcing himself on. Then, after a long moment: "The essence of life is to be found in the frustrations of established order. The universe refuses the deadening influence of complete conformity. And yet in its refusal, it passes toward novel order as a primary requisite for important experience. We have to explain the aim at forms of order, and the aim at novelty of order, and the measure of success, and the measure of failure. Apart from some understanding, however dim-witted, of these characteristics of historic process . . ." His voice trailed off (Gr, 57–58).

How does a dragon talk? Such is the problem John Gardner had to solve when he undertook to reinvent the epic poem *Beowulf,* a poem that, as every English-speaking student has learned, is the oldest European literary work written in a vernacular tongue to have come down to us. In the original work, slow and somber, Beowulf is the hero who fights against the forces of evil: the monster Grendel, whom he kills in the first part of the poem, and the dragon whom he will likewise kill in the second part, but who will mortally wound him. In Gardner's fiction, however, it is Grendel who tells his story, for the question of knowing how one gets to be a monster produces a more interesting viewpoint than the one defined by the good. One thus discovers that if Grendel kills men, it is because he is simultaneously the witness, judge, and impotent voyeur of the strange power fiction has over them, and confers upon them. He has seen them build themselves a destiny, a heroic past, a glorious future, with the words invented for them by the *Shaper,* or the Poet in the strong sense of giver of form. Grendel is aware of the lies in these words, but this knowledge excludes him from what is taking shape before his eyes: his lucidity brings him nothing but hatred and despair. Thus, he chooses, forever solitary, to be the Great Destroyer for human beings, or more precisely the Great Deconstructor. He will derive a bitter, monotonous pleasure from the proof he never ceases inflicting on humans of the impotence of their Gods, the senseless character of their lives, and the vanity of their heroes.

Hatred is a choice, not a consequence. Before becoming the scourge of humankind, Grendel met a being much older than himself, the dragon that Beowulf was to fight one day. This dragon is "beyond good and evil," beyond both the passion for constructing and for destroying illusory constructions. For him, nihilistic rage is just as absurd as belief, for everything is tied together, everything goes hand in hand, creation and destruction, lies and authenticity. And he knows that Grendel will choose excitement and violence, despite his advice, the only one he can give: seek out gold and sit on it . . .

The homage of fiction to philosophy. It is fairly easy to give voice to a denouncer, an idol-smasher, a denier of all belief. Yet it is much harder to give voice to a nonhuman knowledge, more ancient than humankind, able to see farther than the insignificant ripple they create in the river of time. To escape the human point of view, and to do so with the calm self-evidence that is appropriate, as if the workings of the universe belonged to what is given, beyond all conquest and hypothesis, Gardner turned to the philosopher Alfred North Whitehead, copying out entire passages from Whitehead's last book, *Modes of Thought.*

In what follows, Grendel was to encounter Whitehead a second time. It happened in the course of an incursion that took him toward the circle of the Gods, those statues that terrorized men ask in vain for protection against him. Grendel meets the blind Ork, the eldest and wisest of the priests. He decides to have some fun and, before killing Ork, he asks him to confess his faith, and say who is the King of the Gods. This time, in breathless succession, it is the God of *Science and the Modern World,* the principle of limitation, ultimate irrationality, then that of *Process of Reality,* with his infinite patience, his tender concern that nothing may be lost, that come from the blind man's lips. Grendel, bewildered, lets his prey get away.

The words of a dragon, surging forth from the depths of the ages, associated with the neutrality of one for whom epochs, importances, and arrogances succeed one another, but also words of trance, come from nowhere, able to rout Grendel, who has declared war on the poet's tale-spinning: the reader has now been warned. It is a strange tongue that will gradually be elaborated here, a language that challenges all clear distinctions between description and tale-spinning, and induces a singular experience of disorientation in the heart of the most familiar experiences. It is a language that can scandalize, or else madden, all those who think they know what they know, but also all those for whom to approach the non-knowing at the heart of all knowledge is an undertaking that is meticulous, grave, and always to be taken up again.

And yet, of the philosophers of the century that has just ended, the one who proposes this strange test was the quietest, the most gentle, and the least anxious to shock. For most of those who know it, the name of Whitehead has, until very recently, merely called up an image of the couple "Russell and Whitehead," authors of the *Principia Mathematica,* a monumental attempt at the axiomatization of mathematics. Nor is anyone supposed to be unaware that Gödel's famous theorem sounded the death-knell for this undertaking. The name of Bertrand Russell, initially Whitehead's student at Trinity College, Cambridge, and then, between 1901 and 1910, his collaborator, is associated with many of the century's adventures. Whitehead's name, in contrast, has escaped the "Russell-and-Whitehead" association only gradually, and in the aftermath, to vibrate with its own resonance: first in the United States, and then, gradually, in other regions of the world, as translations of his great work *Process and Reality* were published.

Whitehead's personal life was not only without stories, but it has left very few traces behind. He answered the letters written to him only rarely, and at his death his personal papers were destroyed, as he had requested. This is why his biography, by Victor Lowe, is extremely sober, especially with regard to the second part of his life (volume 2, 1910–1947): there is nothing here to arouse the appetite of the fans of biographical-intellectual speculation, in search of the "man" behind the work. To my knowledge, only Bertrand Russell, who always found ways to denigrate what he did not understand, ventured such an interpretation of the philosophical turn taken by his friend: it was, he suggested, the death of his son Eric, a fighter pilot, in 1918, that led Whitehead to reject a purely mechanistic universe and turn toward philosophy. No comment. For the rest, what can we say, except that Whitehead's life was that of a gifted student, a respected university professor, a happy husband, and an attentive, affectionate father ...

Whitehead was born in Kent in 1861, the son of a schoolmaster, later an Anglican pastor, who took personal charge of his education until the age of fourteen. His youth, which was happy, was that of a student as gifted for studies as he was for sports. Upon his admission to Cambridge in 1880, he was offered the rare choice of a scholarship either for classical or for mathematical studies. He chose mathematics, which he then taught at Trinity College from 1885 to 1910. Yet he did not devote himself to mathematics alone. Whitehead often said that his philosophical ideas originated from questions he had pursued throughout his life. This pursuit was reflected, in particular, in a rather astonishing historical, philosophical, theological, and literary culture, of which he was to make free use throughout his works. Yet Whitehead was no scholar. According to Victor Lowe, when he received his students on Sunday evenings near the end of his life, "what he talked about really concerned him" (ANW, 302). Whether in philosophy, theology, science, or literature, his goal was neither to inform nor to cultivate himself, but always and above all to understand.

In 1911, at the age of fifty, Whitehead went into action. Far from the protected rhythms of Cambridge, he taught at University College London, then at Imperial College, and occupied a series of administrative positions. The mathematician was henceforth associated not only with an educational thinker—which, for him, is the same thing as a thinker of human nature—but also with a philosopher of nature, thinking the space-time of relativity with and against Einstein.

This life "within the world," divided between public responsibilities, reformist activities, and personal research, should have yielded to peace at the age of retirement, but two years before the fateful date, Whitehead was to receive the invitation that would change the course of his life: to cross the ocean and go teach at Harvard. To teach his own ideas there, which he could finally develop in the living, risky way that, for him, every educational process implies.

Whitehead set sail at Liverpool on August 16, 1924, and arrived at Boston ten days later. As early as September 23, he gave his first philosophy class, which, as he was to observe, was also the first one he ever attended. For thirteen years, Whitehead was to "think" in front of surprised, fascinated, and disconcerted students. For them, with them, and in front of them, he was to discover and explore the unexpected implications of the questions on which he had meditated all his life. Perhaps, moreover, it was the commitment that all teaching constituted for him that inspired what my book will try to follow, a mutation without equivalent in the history of philosophy. In a few years, the logician and philosopher of nature was to transform himself into a metaphysician, the creator of a strangely audacious speculative philosophy.

A homage of philosophy to fiction, John Gardner grasped the strange character of this audacity quite precisely: it is bereft of all excitement, of all appetite for destruction and scandal, simultaneously the word of a *Shaper*, or a creator of forms who might perhaps be able to disarm Grendel's hatred, and of the dragon who, with his immemorial knowledge, knows the vanity of arguments that try to fixate time, found the order of things, refute or justify.

Whitehead died in 1947. At the time, his influence in the United States was swept away by the rising tide of analytical thought. As far as England was concerned, *Process and Reality* had gone out of print. For years, in fact, it was through the teaching and the books of the philosopher and theologian Charles Hartshorne that a thread of transmission was maintained. The God conceived by Whitehead, and affirmed by the blind man Ork, thus earned him an improbable survival through the intermediary of American theology. And the consequence of this intermediary was an initial mode of reading that was rather peculiar: that of a theism that sought to elaborate, by rational arguments alone, the definition of a God conceived as "perfection," but which often looked favorably upon convergence with Christian doctrine (there are even Whiteheadian theological constructions that confer a philosophical foundation upon the Trinity).

For a European like me, a stranger to the theistic tradition, the true interlocutors make their appearance with Ivor Leclerc and William A. Christian. It is not that these philosophers rejected proximity with theistic concerns, but that their interest focused on the conceptual coherence proper to the work, not its contribution to theology. Thus, the question for them was not to renew the ideal of perfection associated with God, but to grasp the reasons and the extent of the conceptual creation Whitehead names God. One of these philosophers' ambitions was to restore Whitehead to philosophy, and more particularly to European philosophy, which constitutes the nourishing soil of his concepts (although today it is in Korea and Japan that Whitehead's thought meets with its greatest success).

Henceforth, American "Whiteheadians" are recruited among both philosophers and theologians, and the palette has been enriched by practitioners from the most diverse horizons, from ecology to feminism, practices that unite political struggle and spirituality with the sciences of education. This forms a world that is astonishingly disparate from a European viewpoint, in which a New-Age type of thought can rub elbows with metaphysicians discussing Plato, Leibniz, and Kant: a strange drop of water in the amazing American multiplicity, but which affirms itself in a singularly lively and tenacious way.

This is a "slightly secret school" as Deleuze wrote in *Le Pli* (LP, 103), and here the secret is not associated with a desire for mystery, quite the contrary: Whiteheadian philosophers are passionately attached to technical controversy, to explaining conceptual difficulties, and to evaluating possible or necessary modifications. The secrecy derives from the legacy of a philosopher who, discretely and without polemics, without ever asking his readers to thrill to the audacity and radicalism of the risk or to the threat of isolation, but with an obstinate tenderness, undertook to forge a conceptual language that forces those who acquire a taste for it to think.

Whitehead was a mathematician, and it is no doubt because he was a mathematician, because he knew and loved the way mathematics forces mathematicians to think, but also knew the rigorous constraints to which every mathematical definition must respond, that he never thought that mathematics could constitute a model that was generalizable. The kind of necessity proper to mathematical demonstrations cannot be transferred to philosophy. Philosophical reasoning that tries to be demonstrative in this sense could only produce an imitation unworthy of the adventure that, for mathematicians, is constituted by the production of a demonstration. What is more, in order to conform to the logical-mathematical model, such reasoning would require the goodwill of the readers, their submission to definitions that are simplistic compared with the extraordinary subtlety both of the situations and of the usages of natural language as it confronts these situations. Such simplistic definitions, which mutilate questions, would be the price to pay for an approach that would finally be rational. As a mathematician-cum-philosopher, Whitehead transferred from mathematics to philosophy not the authority produced by demonstration, but the adventure and commitment to and for a question, the "bad faith" with regard to every "as is well known," all consensual plausibilities.

If Whitehead's work is hard to approach, it is because it demands, with utter discretion, that its readers accept the adventure of the questions that will separate them from every consensus. Of course, one could say that this is the case for all "great" philosophers, those who do not limit themselves to asking a "classic" question: that of human freedom, or that of the validity of our knowledge, or of the relation between facts and values, for instance. When philosophers transform the landscape of questions, their readers cannot limit themselves to "taking cognizance" of what is proposed, or to evaluating, as "connoisseurs," the way certain well-known arguments are formulated and used, and whose authors situate themselves, construct alliances, introduce new distinctions that others will then have to discuss, conserve, or reject. Even when an argument is taken up again, its meaning changes, and the readers must accept the experience of this change. Yet even when philosophers innovate in this way, the novelty is usually introduced in a way that offers readers another kind of stability, the one that can be associated with progress. If they dare, they will be the ones to topple the present into an obsolete past, a past in which "people still believed that . . ." They will be united by the audacity of what they deny, and what they no longer need. And even a philosopher like Nietzsche, who thought he was writing for no one, because no readers could bear to situate themselves "beyond good and evil," supplied, no doubt involuntarily, the formula for a new consensus: not, of course, to live what is unlivable, or to think what is unthinkable, but to refer to the unlivable and the unthinkable, to criticize or deconstruct that in which others still "believe."

If Gardner's monster Grendel flees, helpless, instead of killing the blind priest, it is because his hatred is fed by the way human beings are situated in a history that he cannot share, a history that is the work of the *Shaper,* who transforms their lives into epics. And to disarm Grendel's hatred, it is not enough to deny progress, to reject human greatness. Time and again, the monster will perceive that negation and refutation are equally the affirmation of the superiority of those who have become capable of denying and refuting that in which others believed. Time and again, he will discern the work of the *Shaper,* and he will kill. Gardner needed Whitehead to give voice both to the priest and to the dragon because he needed statements that, in two different modes, separate Grendel from what makes him a monster. The dragon is extra-epic, but the priest, for his part, makes Grendel's powers of discernment redundant. How could one discern a mendacious construction where nothing claims to be authorized by the facts, where no argument ever claims the power to bring into agreement those who will prove, by this agreement, that they are worthy of what is demanded of them? The priest's speech is "laughable," as Whitehead's ambition may seem laughable in the eyes of contemporary philosophers: to construct a philosophy that is openly and systematically speculative.

One of the tests Whitehead reserves for his readers thus concerns the question of what is philosophically "serious," or what every serious philosopher knows today: it is illusory to deal in a positive way with the truth of God, or of the universe. This seriousness is marked at the division between the questions that belong to the history of philosophy, and those that designate its contemporary territories. Historians of philosophy can devote hundreds of pages to Plato's Ideas, the Hegelian Spirit, the Leibnizian monads, the Cartesian God, or the vision in God of Malebranche, and they can experience the efficacy proper to these concepts, and even succeed in transmitting them. They will not be asked how they situate themselves with regard to these philosophical propositions, because they are doing the job of a historian. They are protected by their distance. Yet Whitehead is a quasi-contemporary philosopher. He wrote at the same time as Heidegger, Husserl, and Wittgenstein, who are still cited today as references for thinking about our epoch. It is thus impossible to keep him "at a distance." And yet he seems to be unaware that there is a "before Kant," when philosophers considered themselves free to speculate about God, the world, and the human soul, and an "after Kant," in which, except for a few old-fashioned naifs, they have learned the lesson of human finitude, have accepted the consequences of the fact that they do not have the benefit of a direct intuition of these ultimate realities, and have admitted that "thoughts without intuitive content are empty."

Taking a Speculative Philosophy Seriously?

How can we take seriously a book like *Process and Reality*, which opens with a chapter devoted to that speculative philosophy that we are supposed to have relegated to history? All the more so in that Whitehead does not undertake to defend the conditions of possibility of such a philosophy, or to answer the condemnation that has been decreed against it. He limits himself to lining up, in a way that is perfectly serene, as if they were so many self-evidences, statements liable to plunge serious philosophers into abysses of indignant perplexity, if they do not close the book after two pages, not even seeing how one could attack a thought that is disarming in its naivety and its dogmatism. And how could one take seriously, as a quasi-contemporary, a book that ends with the grandiose vision of a perpetual cosmic process such that "the love in the world passes into the love in heaven, and floods back again into the world" (PR, 351)?

The difficulty is all the greater because it is impossible to maintain that Whitehead, as a mathematician, was naive and ignorant in philosophy, or to classify him among those who attempt a "return" to a philosophy of the "pre-Kantian" type. Does he not himself explicitly deny the possibility of such a return when he writes that "philosophy never reverts to its old position after the shock of a great philosopher" (PR, 11)? Of course, Whitehead reads Descartes, Spinoza, Leibniz, and even Kant as if they were his contemporaries, but he knows that he asks them questions that are not theirs, he knows that he does not respect what matters for them, or what made them think.

Perhaps one had to be a mathematician to realize that it is not appropriate to take seriously, for one instant, the unavoidable dilemmas and the insurmountable alternatives that philosophers produce in order to give their demonstrations a necessity that also enables them to criticize and denounce. Yet a humor of thought was also necessary in order not to overestimate this knowledge, so as not to transform it into an instrument of judgment, to know that, unlike mathematical definitions, definitions in philosophy are just as interesting by what they deny, judge, or refuse to think, as by what they affirm. Philosophical statements must generally be heard twice: in the mode of creation, they find their necessity in the problem that set the philosopher to work; in the mode of judgment, they designate what the philosopher has undertaken to silence and disqualify, that is, also the transformation of what gave rise to the problem in polemics against rivals and imposters.

Whitehead's speculative philosophy is indeed situated "after Kant," after the shock constituted for philosophy by the Kantian prohibitions, because this philosophy does not communicate with a "right to think." Thus, Whitehead does not infringe upon any prohibition, for prohibitions presuppose such a communication. The question for him is not what we can know, but what we know. If he became a philosopher, it is because questions to which, as an empirical fact, he felt that his epoch demanded an answer situated him in that tradition known as philosophy.

Reading Whitehead is a test, for he demands of his readers not only that they accept these questions, but also, and above all, that they accept the possibility that such questions are not destined to remain without an answer, the object of a meditation on the human condition, its paradoxes, and even its tragedy. More than any other philosopher, Whitehead was permeated by the vertiginous distance between the possibilities of the universe and our human abilities to apprehend them. Yet he never bowed down before a question, for every question is a human formulation, and none, as such, transcends the human adventure. The way we formulate questions always comes from somewhere, and can always lead somewhere: not, certainly, to an answer that would be definitive at last, but rather to new ways of formulating them, in a way that no longer communicates with an insurmountable enigma, but with a problem. If there is one position that denies the finitude of the human condition, it is the one that claims to put a stop to the adventure of thought, and supposes that we know what is imposed by that condition.

If reading Whitehead means accepting to commit oneself to an adventure whose starting point is always the formulation of a problem, without the legitimacy of the problem being well-founded, without the possibility of answering it being justified in terms of the right to think, one may rightly wonder if the formulations he attempted are still able to engage us today. Such a question could, of course, be raised with regard to every philosopher, and it is the greatness of the history of philosophy that it succeeds, sometimes, in giving what one could call, with Gilles Deleuze, a "portrait of the philosopher with his problem." Even when the problem is no longer ours, the way it forced the philosopher to think, create, and reject can then become ours, in the sense that it creates the experience of the movement of thought proper to philosophical creation. Deleuze was well aware of this, he who discovered that philosophy would be his life, would be what would make his life worth living, after a first class on Plato's Ideas—even if many consider him as the anti-Platonic philosopher *par excellence*. The surest way to "kill" philosophy is to transmit it in the manner of a science: one does not need to enter into contact with Newton's problem to learn rational dynamics—the equations of Lagrange and Hamilton define what must be retained of it—but to deal with Plato without first sharing his problem is somewhat analogous to studying butterflies on the basis of a collection of pinned butterflies, without ever having seen one fly.

Yet *Thinking with Whitehead* does not belong, properly speaking, to the history of philosophy. In it, to be sure, Whitehead will never be separated from his problem, and more precisely from the way in which he never ceased formulating and reformulating his problem. Yet this is no "portrait," for what is at stake in this book is also, and inseparably, to present Whitehead as a philosopher who belongs to our epoch. Unlike the portraitist, whose task is to make the viewers feel, to transfer what was lived and created, but without personally taking over from it, my approach to Whitehead cannot be dissociated from the importance of his work in my life. In this sense, I am part of the motley crew of "White-headians," of those ecologists, feminists, educators, theologians, and so on, who have discovered that Whitehead helped them to imagine and to fight against "ready-made" models, and above all not to despair.

The discovery that Whitehead helped me in this way is inseparable from my practical situation more than thirty years ago: that of a young philosopher who had come from the experimental sciences to philosophy because she did not accept the way researchers in science are trained, and who was trying to figure out how to situate herself with regard to these sciences. The goal, for her, was to be able to think about the creative power of these sciences—the path of critical epistemology was henceforth closed—but also about their catastrophic indifference to what they judge "non-scientific." The path that ratifies this judgment by making the sciences, in one way or another, an "access to reality" beyond our illusions was therefore closed as well.

It could, however, be maintained that Whitehead failed, if not in his diagnosis, then at least in his prognosis with regard to science. For an important aspect of what engaged his philosophical adventure was his conviction that what is called modern science had reached a turning point, which demanded a new philosophical thought. The period when modern science had developed by repudiating philosophy had been fruitful, but as he wrote in 1925, the threat was henceforth that science might degenerate into a "medley of ad hoc hypotheses" (SMW, 17). It will be said that this threat has not materialized, and that physicists have, without the help of the philosophers, transformed the foundations of their science, and have accomplished what seemed impossible to Kant: to interrogate the origin of the Universe, of matter, and even to place in debate the question "why is there something rather than nothing?" It will also be said that biology has accomplished its revolution, and that we have learned more about living beings in a few decades than throughout the preceding centuries. Others could also say that if science is threatened today, it is rather by the way in which its traditional allies, the State and industry, have undertaken to enslave it directly through what is called the economy of knowledge, and that Whitehead's propositions ignore what should be thought about today: not a science that is still a cousin of philosophy, trying to confer an intelligible order on what confronts us, but a technoscience for which to understand is to be able to transform, and which blindly serves those who actualize that power to transform the world.

Of course, Whitehead was only laterally interested in this last question, although one could say that the way he designated the "method of training professionals" (SMW, 196), as one of the great and most redoubtable discoveries of the nineteenth century, has lost none of its power. Yet his goal was not to denounce professionals or to bring them culture, the "supplement of soul" they lack. Whitehead belongs to our epoch because he asks a question that is ours, that of our lack of resistance to the way in which, since the beginning of the nineteenth century, what has been called progress has redefined the world. From this viewpoint, one could say that today, at a time when it has become impossible to ignore the consequences of this progress, worrisome to say the least, Whitehead's thought finds an actuality it lacked in its own day. To be sure, there has been innovation, but also rarefaction of those who, still in Whitehead's time, took the time to think. Instead, we have to do with a veritable "cult of the scientific revolution"—a new revolution will come along to solve the questions raised by the preceding one. One must "wait for genius," and meanwhile nothing must slow down the race, the process of accumulating results by researchers who are defined, in the first instance, by competition.

Yet what, one will ask, does Whitehead suggest? Are we to believe that his concepts, formulated so long ago, miraculously conserve their relevance in a world he could not imagine? Is he the genius we were waiting for? By no means, and I must confess that the way some physicists who have withdrawn from the race to speculate have become interested in Whitehead, and have found among the "process philosophers" the sympathetic and attentive ear their colleagues refused them, does not convince me. For this interest affirms what Whitehead refused: that the questions that issue from the specialized adventure known as physics are the "big questions" that deal with reality as such. Much more positive in this regard is the interest of certain chemists or biologists, who do not aim at a summit meaning between their science and metaphysics, but discover that the Whiteheadian concepts make aspects of the situations they study interesting and significant; they do not illustrate the power of theoretical approaches that are habitual, but imposed by experimentation.

However, for a philosopher like me, interested in science, what is no doubt most important is the way Whitehead suggests putting things in perspective. It allows us to resist the identification of the question of science with that of knowledge. Confronted by science, philosophy does not have to think of human knowledge, either to make this science the accomplishment of human rationality, and extract from it epistemological or normative norms in order to diagnose, in the manner of Bergson, the limits of rational knowledge, or, like Heidegger, to denounce science as "that which does not think." Beyond their contradictions, all these philosophical problematizations turn science into an accomplishment or a destiny that, beyond itself, speaks of something human, and of the knowledge to which this something human may lay claim. For Whitehead, in contrast, science must be understood as an adventure, and an adventure never enables us to draw a general lesson. When the adventurer is perplexed, when the adventure turns out badly, the question to ask is rather "what has happened to us?"

The Chinese, it is said, smiled at the naiveté of the Jesuit missionaries who reported to them the triumphs of seventeenth-century science, but all the words we have available today are laden with this "fact": "we," for our part, did not laugh. The community picked out by this "we" is the one Whitehead is addressing in the first instance. We are those who, for instance, have accepted and continue to accept the separation, proposed since the Galilean origins of modern science, between the "why" and the "how." Such a separation is always what prevails when a public question highlights what scientists propose (we know "how" to go about this . . .), and what is to be decided according to values defined as "purely human," alien to a nature supposed to be defined by the scientific "how." Such a separation gives rise to, and presupposes, an inability to resist, for as soon as it is staged and accepted, it is too late. The roles have been distributed, with the scientists on the side of innovation, and those who dispute their proposition on the side of inertia, habits, and what will eventually give in, for "you can't stop progress." And yet, we have not learned to laugh at this scenario. We are the ones who ask the question of our lack of resistance to what, in the name of progress, dismembers thought.

One does not need, however, to benefit from Chinese wisdom to question the separation between the why and the how, in particular to show that it has in fact no stable identity, and that the "how" never stops mutating. Yet this criticism will not go far, for scientists will be happy to admit it: for them, the "how" follows the advance of scientific territories and designates the "why" as what is left over, what is not scientifically demonstrable but is relative to the tastes and passions of an epoch; and it will pass, like the epoch. This was the sense in which Galileo proposed to distinguish between what he had succeeded in demonstrating, "how" bodies fall, and the question of "why" they fall in that way, a question which, as he remarked, there was "no great use" in asking: this is the domain of the imagination and of undecidable fiction. The dice are thus loaded from the outset, and the distribution unequal, implying as a previous proposition the relegation of what does not pertain to the territories conquered by scientific objectivity to the realm of fiction, human, all too human as it is.

In other words, for one who learned to think with Whitehead, the confrontation, which a few years ago inspired so many passions under the name of the "science wars," was not at all surprising. If the "objective" sciences can relegate to undecidable fiction what has not undergone a redefinition that would finally be scientific, why would representatives of the humanities deprive themselves of transforming this fiction into a counteroffensive category to show that the so-called "hows," finally objective, conceal the "whys" of human undertakings? As Whitehead wrote with regard to the duality between free, entrepreneurial individual spirit and regular, submissive matter bequeathed to us by the seventeenth century, "There is Aaron's rod, and the magicians' serpents; and the only question for philosophy is, which swallows which; or whether, as Descartes thought, they all live happy together" (SMW, 142–143).

History has proved Descartes wrong. Each "advance" of an objectivity reputed to be scientific has been acclaimed by some as a gain in rationality, and condemned by others as an attack on the subject. In fact, one could almost say that provoking denunciation has become a favorite rhetorical trick in certain scientific fields. The scandal stirred up bears witness to the conquest. The barking dogs constitute in themselves the proof that the caravan is passing, transporting the first fruits of the irresistible conquest. And the dogs are all the more useful in that the caravan in question is transporting only goods that are not very interesting at all: that is, the pretensions of "evolutionary psychology."

What has happened to us? One of the unique aspects of Whitehead's suggestion is that is does not contain any "bad guys," nor an explanatory construction of continuity that refers to something we "couldn't help." That "adventure" is the first and the last word implies that all continuity is questionable, and that no principle of economy should prevail that allows us to forget that the resumption of a seemingly similar theme takes place in circumstances that are different every time, and with stakes that are always different. The question "what has happened to us?" is therefore not the search for an ultimate explanation, but a resource for telling our stories in another way, in a way that situates us otherwise—not as defined by the past, but as able, perhaps, to inherit from it in another way.

Whitehead's contemporaries could, with amusement, perplexity, or scandal, wonder whether one should really incur the risks of a speculative operation, moving Heaven and Earth, God and matter, to remedy difficulties that are ultimately secondary: does not modern "progress" bear witness to the fact that, despite everything, "we" have succeeded in distinguishing ourselves from those peoples who, in fact, profited at the time from the benefits of civilizing colonialism? Times have changed, and what may have seemed to be "excess" may be worthy of playing a role in the apprenticeship that today imposes itself with regard to ourselves. For good intentions and a conciliatory spirit are not enough. Visions of the world that pacify contradictions by weakening them will always be at the mercy of one of the terms that will transform the fragile bridge of resemblances that has united it with the other as a means of passage and conquest. And they allow us, in all good conscience, to propose to the rest of the world a thought that is finally consensual. The speculative operation attempted by Whitehead could well be more relevant today than it was in his day, because it breaks with the claim to anonymity that inhabits us and constitutes us, still and again, as "the thinking head of humanity." To learn to resist, with regard to the "us" that made the Chinese smile, is also to learn that our adventure can indeed make people smile.

Thinking with Whitehead

Thinking with Whitehead today therefore means accepting an adventure from which none of the words that serve as our reference points should emerge unscathed, but from which none will be disqualified or denounced as a vector of illusion. All are a part of the problem, whether they refer to the whys of human experience or to the hows of "objective reality." If compromise solutions do not suffice, it is because they try to circumvent the problem instead of raising it; that is, they try to mitigate the contradictions and to make compatible that which defines itself as conflictual. Whitehead was a mathematician, and mathematicians are they who do not bow down before contradictions but transform them into an ingredient of the problem. They are the ones who dare to "trust" in the possibility of a solution that remains to be created. Without this "trust" in a possible solution, mathematics would not exist.

This truth is the one William James called faith or belief, his only answer when confronted by those who have declared that life is *not* worth living, "the whole army of suicides (. . .) an army whose roll-call, like the famous evening gun of the British army, follows the sun round the world and never terminates" (LWL, 37). It has nothing in common with what I would call, to underline the difference, "to be confident," that is, to continue, to carry on in the mode of "everything will work out fine." The mathematician's trust is inseparable from a commitment not to mutilate the problem in order to solve it and to take its demands fully into account. Yet it implies a certain deliberate amnesia with regard to the obviousness of obstacles, an active indetermination of what the terms of the problem "mean." Transferred to philosophy, this indetermination means that what announced itself as a foundation, authorizing a position and providing its banner to a cause, will be transformed into a constraint, which the solution will have to respect but upon which it may, if necessary, confer a somewhat unexpected signification.

To illustrate this indeterminization, I will refer to a well-known fable. There once was an old Bedouin, who, sensing that his death was imminent, gathered together his three sons and signified his last wishes to them. To the eldest, he bequeathed half his inheritance, to the second one quarter, and to the third one sixth. As he said this, he died, leaving his sons in perplexity, for the inheritance in question consisted of eleven camels.

How were they to respect the old man's will? Should they kill those of the camels whose division seemed prescribed, and share the meat among them? Was this the required filial piety? Did their father really want them to prove their love by accepting this loss? Or had he made a mistake, distracted or weakened by his imminent death? In fact, at least one error was obvious, because one-half plus a quarter plus a sixth do not make one. Yet to inherit on the basis of an interpretation that disqualifies a last wish, is this not to insult to the dead? And in this case, moreover, how could one divide? Who would take away the remainder of the division? All the ingredients were there for a fratricidal war. The three brothers nevertheless decided to try to avoid the war, that is, to wager that a solution could exist. This means that they went to see the old sage who so often plays a role in such stories. This old sage, on this occasion, told them that he could not do anything for them except to offer them what might perhaps help them: his old camel, skinny and half-blind. The inheritance now counted twelve camels: the eldest took six of them, the second three, the youngest two, and the old camel was returned to the old sage.

What did the twelfth camel accomplish? By its presence, it made possible what seemed contradictory, simultaneously obeying the father's wishes, discovering the possibility of respecting their terms, and not destroying the value of the inheritance. All this because it made it possible to bring to existence that which remained discretely undetermined in the paternal statement, the question of what it means to "share an inheritance." It is usually divided into parts, and this is what the statement seems to command. Yet this norm is only one way of answering the problem. What is required is that once the allocation has been made, the contents of the inheritance are distributed, but nothing determines what the allocation must deal with. The content of the inheritance is a given that acts as a constraint, but the role of this constraint belongs to the solution, and the question of the allocation can thus be plunged within a wider field of possibilities. Thus, the solution does not entail submission to the problematic statement, but the invention of the field in which the problem finds its solution.

The fable of the twelfth camel illuminates the meaning of what Whitehead was to call "speculative philosophy." First, it illustrates the difference between "trusting" and "being confident in." If the brothers had gone no farther than to wonder whether they could be confident in their father's intentions, their situation would remain without issue. It is only because they accepted the paternal will as an unknown, because none of them claimed to know what their father "meant," that they went to consult the old sage. And the "trust" presupposed by their procedure is not directed to the old sage himself, for the goal is not to yield to his authority rather than to the paternal authority. It is directed to the possible as such, to the possibility of a solution on the basis of which the unknown of the paternal will might find its meaning. As far as the twelfth camel added to the inheritance is concerned, it illustrates the efficacy proper to the speculative proposition. This camel will not benefit any of the brothers. It makes the division possible, in conformity with the father's will, but it is not distributed itself and is not added to any share.

The specificity of the concepts proposed by Whitehead is that, like the twelfth camel, once they have done their job, once they have transformed the way in which a situation raises a problem, they disappear without leaving a trace other than this transformation itself. This is why Whitehead can write that the interest of the speculative scheme he has constructed resides in its applications, in the transformations it carries out in our ways of explaining or characterizing our experiences. It is these transformations that are to give rise to the experience Whitehead associates with the goal of philosophy, an experience of "sheer disclosure" (MT, 49) rather than the concepts themselves. The concepts are required by the transformation of experience, but it is this disclosure that has, and always will have, the last word. For instance, the question raised by the speculative construction of God, required by Whitehead, does not imply the existence of this God. The only question is that of knowing which experiences would have been relegated to illusion—how the problem would have been mutilated—if what Whitehead names God had not been included in the conceptual arrangement constructed by Whitehead.

Yet the fact that Whitehead was able to discover that his conceptual arrangement needed God implies an aspect of his speculative philosophy that the fable of the camels does not allow us to describe, because this fable has the form of a riddle that allows one path to a solution, and only one. In the case of speculative philosophy, the role of the dying father, whose last wishes define what the solution to the problem of definition must achieve, is not played by anyone. This is why one cannot say that the Whiteheadian proposition constitutes "the answer," finally discovered. Quite the contrary, this proposition is inseparable from the constraints that Whitehead had to impose upon himself in order to formulate the problem to be solved, for it is these constraints that make him a creator: in other words, they confer upon the solution being sought the power to oblige him to create. This is why the speculative answer formulated in *Process and Reality* is itself coherent with what it tries to bring about: "sheer disclosure." It is inseparable from an adventure in which the problem of philosophers, that is, the constraints that must be satisfied by the solution they construct, have not ceased to be reformulated.

If Whitehead is the one who brings adventures into existence, where what we seek are reasons and justifications, or what is supposed to transcend and authorize our choices, it is crucial not to conceive of this adventure as reducible to what is arbitrary or contingent. What is at stake here enables me both to characterize Whitehead's approach as "constructivist" and to defend the constructivist position against the curse that weighs it down today, a weight it transfers to the situations in which it intervenes. There are social, cultural, linguistic, neurophysiological, historical, and political constructivisms, but their common feature is demystification. In a way that bears witness in itself to the polemical power of our categories, to affirm "it's a construction" is to affirm "it is a mere construction," and it will then most often be a matter of affirming the arbitrary nature of what others believe they can justify. In particular, the reality to which the sciences claim to have access must fall silent, unable to make a significant difference between the interpretative constructions that concern it. Such claims are themselves "mere" constructions, or "narratives."

Where polemics unmasks, Whitehead addresses adventures. In *Process and Reality*, he speaks of rationalism as an "experimental adventure" (PR, 9) and of metaphysics as an "adventure of hope" (PR, 42), but he also defines, in a speculative mode, all continuity as an "adventure in change" (PR, 35). For him, then, the term "adventure" is valid simultaneously, both on an empirical level—to characterize what we are dealing with, but which also situates us—and on a speculative level. And the choice of this term accentuates a question that polemical constructivisms render secondary. There is no adventure without a risky relation to an environment that has the power to complicate this adventure, or even to doom it to failure. Likewise, there is no construction that does not raise the question of "how it holds together," or how it is affected by its environment and how it affects it.

That a bridge may hold throughout its "adventure of change," through the multiple trials that its environment imposes upon it, is the achievement that matters in its case. And no one will say, with regard to a century-old bridge, "it's only a construction." However, it will be objected, if no one says this, it is because no one claims the contrary: no one claims that the bridge is "objective," or independent of human knowledge. Yet this answer, albeit legitimate, provides a good translation of the curse that weighs upon constructivism, that is, on its capture by a polemical network. If the notion of construction is used in a pejorative way, it is because it was initially mobilized by scientists to characterize what is not scientific, then catastrophically preserving its same connotation of arbitrariness, by the "deconstructivists," to show that scientific knowledge cannot escape the same judgment.

The fact that all continuity must be described as an "adventure" creates the possibility of escaping polemics. Instead, a set of notions organizes itself around the notion of adventure, and particularly that of a construction that "is able to hold," which, following Whitehead, and in the mathematical sense, we will call "generic." When Whitehead uses the word "generic," and also when he speaks of "generality," he is not thinking like a logician and is not giving the term the power to define a class of particular cases (all men are mortal; Socrates . . .). The generic notion does not authorize any definition. It suggests a way of addressing a situation whose eventual success will be the relevance of the questions to which it gives rise. Generalities in the logical sense authorize classifications, with each particular case exemplifying the general characteristic that defines a set of notions. Whiteheadian philosophical generalities, and the notions he calls "generic," make the wager that the questions to which they will give rise will shed light on features that are important for each situation.

Importance is a Whiteheadian generic notion. It enables no classification, yet nevertheless does not condemn it: to classify may be what matters, for instance, for a botanist. This is not a matter of psychology, for if one questions botanists, they will speak of vegetal proliferation, of the thorny questions raised by each type of classification, in short, of an adventure that confronts one with plants. Every adventure thus calls forth the generic question "what does it make matter?" which can also mean "how is the contrast between success and defeat defined for it?" and this question will call forth others in turn, which will imply the trials, risks, and type of environment required for success, and so on.

As an example, but also in order to introduce myself, I will allow myself to sketch here the way I have tried to characterize modern experimental science. I have practiced an approach that could be called constructivist, but not in the sense of a theory of knowledge or an epistemology that affirms that not reality, but human activities alone are responsible for our knowledge. The constructivist question I have asked is "what makes these human beings, these producers of the knowledge we call 'experimental,' become active?" In other words, "what is the uniqueness of the adventure in which they have become engaged?" "what matters to them?" "what does success mean to them?"

Of course, many things are important for individuals, but here the question bears not upon them but on the way they define an achievement, and the way this definition engages them. In *The Invention of Modern Sciences,* I suggested that what unites experimenters, what forces them to become active and to think together, is a question that can only be asked in the laboratory: did this experimental arrangement provide the phenomenon being questioned with the ability to bear witness in a reliable way, concerning the way what is made observable about this phenomenon must be interpreted? Has it succeeded in conferring upon the phenomenon being questioned the role of "respondent" for the interpretation that is given to it?

The ability to resist the accusation of "being a mere construction," in the sense of a merely human (social, linguistic, technical, subjective) fabrication, is thus no longer the privilege of the experimental procedure, but its key element. It is what defines the demands of the environment on which the success of an experimental suggestion depends, and this ability does not exclude the human beings who become active, discuss, and hesitate, but solicits them and mobilizes them around the eventuality of this achievement. And this is an achievement that no theory of knowledge, no epistemology could justify, for it belongs to the order of the event, of what can happen but is not deserved, and does not correspond to any right. It is an achievement that is rare, extremely selective, and radically situated. What situates it is not the world, objectively deciphered at last, but the experimental apparatus, for the questions that matter are established around the experimental apparatus. It is here that human beings become active, and that an art of testing and of consequences is practiced, whose correlation is the signature of the event. The tests of an experimental proposition's reliability are not a goal in themselves; the true verification of a proposition concerns its consequences or the new possibilities that it makes conceivable and which, if they are fruitful, will gather researchers together, whatever epistemologists may say.

That this type of success could become the model of a theory of general knowledge, containing the disqualification of what is "merely subjective," is the sign of a propaganda operation. The event "here we can do something!" is transformed into a norm (most often emptied of what, for experimenters, "makes an event," so as to extend it to the totality of what is recognized as "scientific"), and everything that escapes this norm is placed in the same sack, defined by the "why" of human subjectivity. The success story of this operation is part of the question "what has happened to us?" but in order to resist it there is no need to "deconstruct" the experimental achievement. On the contrary, it is by accepting it in its selective and rare uniqueness that we can understand that it is not "nature" that makes an experimenter think. Heidegger was right: in this sense, indeed, "science does not think." What matters to experimenters are the objections and the tests to which their proposition will be subjected, and the future it makes it possible to envisage.

Such an approach offers a certain analogy with the fable of the twelfth camel, because it limits itself to adding an ingredient liable to produce a "sheer disclosure": the confrontation only seemed inevitable because this ingredient had been left out of the problematic landscape. This obviously does not solve the very concrete problems raised by the role of science and of scientists in our society, but it separates these problems from what, for the experimenters, can only be a declaration of war: the judgment that produces agreement between them is nothing more than a purely human construction. One can listen to scientists tell the story of their achievements without having to challenge them, for they are situated in, and belong to, an adventure that has nothing to say about what does not answer to its demands. The questions that issue forth from this adventure are added to the other human questions and may complicate them, but if they appear to take the place of questions that matter in other adventures, as constituting the "finally objective" version of them, there is no need for confrontation, and it is enough to search with trust for how the story has been transformed into propaganda.

However, this camel—which I would call "practical," since the ingredient it adds designates what matters for experimental practices—does not accomplish the miracle of instantaneous reconciliation proposed by the original fable, any more than Whitehead's "speculative" twelfth camel does. Instead, it proposes a way of addressing those who are divided into two antagonistic poles.

Thus, one can certainly ask scientists many things, but not to renounce what matters to them, and particularly what resonates in the question "is it publishable?": the primacy of the objections of "competent colleagues," the only objections that can place their proposition in danger, because they are the only ones capable of detecting a fault, an over-hasty hypothesis, a possible counterinterpretation. Quite the contrary, one would discern the possible destruction of the experimental adventure if the knowledge economy were to prevail and transform competent colleagues into complacent colleagues, because they share the same dependencies. On the contrary, one will wish that the link between reliability and the presence of those liable to object may be maintained "outside the laboratory": that is, that all those who are competent to put every proposition to the test should actually be gathered around it.

In our academic world, however, where publication has become a question of life or death and where everyone henceforth depends on "competent colleagues," particularly when gathered in reading committees or evaluatory committees, questions also arise for those who have gathered around the other pole, which could be called the "critical" pole. They too are situated by the question of success, and of what success renders important. Is your success that of Grendel? That of the justice-dealers, working in the name of a general truth, which demands the destruction of those who do not bow down before it? Or else, what are the questions that make you think, around which the demands that define what matters for you are organized?

And it arises, in particular, for me. Who are my colleagues? What definition of what matters do I share with them? To what tests shall my proposition be subjected? The person who raises this question is intensely aware of the fact that, if her publications had depended on most of her "competent colleagues," that is, on those who mimic the sciences by demanding that an argument present itself as capable of forcing the agreement of all competent philosophers, she would have been professionally condemned. To think with Whitehead is also to affirm that the success of a philosophical proposition is not to resist objections but to give rise to what he himself calls a "leap of the imagination" (PR, 4)—and the point is to experiment with the effects of that leap: what it does to thought, what it obliges one to do, what it renders important, and what it makes remain silent.

Unlike French, English does not allow the word "experiment" to be used for an experience that implies an active, open, and demanding attention. No more than laboratory experimentation can be reduced to careful, systematic observation, can experience or the transformation of experience brought about by a scientific proposition be reduced to a new way of seeing. In both cases, a reciprocal influence is implied, that puts to the test both what brings about and what is brought about. This is the type of test that this book, which is written "with" Whitehead, demands. What is at stake in it is not to share a vision, nor to provide a definitive interpretation of Whiteheadian thought, but to experiment/experience in the present what it means to ask the question "What has happened to us?" in the way he suggests.

Choices of Writing

To try to render a philosophical proposition "present" means first of all to try to avoid the form of commentary that is suitable for the exposition of an author's beliefs, of what he or she thinks. It is to make thought inseparable from the problem of "how to think" that obliges this thought. This is why I have chosen an approach that has the look and feel of a narration, accompanying Whitehead over the course of a few years (from *The Concept of Nature,* published in 1920, to *Process and Reality,* published in 1929), in which an itinerary is accomplished from nature to metaphysics, and from metaphysics to cosmology. This is not a real story. As I have already emphasized, we have practically no biographical testimony that allows us to tell the story of how the person of interest experienced this itinerary. It is in the text itself (with one exception: "April 1925") that I have tried to follow the construction of the problems and the way they mutate and ricochet by colliding with the questions and demands for which they open the way.

The narrative form indicates that the person who is reading *The Concept of Nature* or *Science and the Modern World* is not reading them as a contemporary of their writing, but with the knowledge of what was going to happen. This does not, I hope, mean a finalized reading, imposing upon the texts an end that was not theirs, but a reading that tries to decipher the paths of an adventure that has the nature of a riddle. At the beginning of *The Concept of Nature,* Whitehead emphasized the extent to which it would be hard for his readers to accept that he would indeed confine his problems within the narrow limits he had just described, whereas it is precisely beyond these limits that things usually start to get exciting (CN, 48). At the end of *Process and Reality,* the same author seems to have exploded all the limits that modern good manners impose upon thought.

Another approach would have been possible: it would have started out from the questions raised by this world, and would have sought the way they arise in Whiteheadian terms, as opportunities for "applications" of the conceptual scheme proposed by Whitehead. In particular, it would have been possible to give more space to contemporary questionings, that is, to "bring Whitehead up to date," and to affirm his relevance today. One of the reasons that turned me away from this possibility is the ease with which relevance can become a model, that is, a source of answers. Whitehead's proposition does not address itself to knowledge in the sense that it could be detached from the situations in which it is operative. It does not constitute a vision of the world or a "new paradigm"—indeed, this is probably the worst confusion that can occur with regard to it. It is addressed to our "modes of thought," in the way a tool addresses our modes of action, modifying the relation that provides their identity relative to those who act and to that on which they act, by redistributing what is proposed as doable or not doable. In other words, it addresses the thinker *qua* situated, in the way that the thinker defines his or her situation.

I had the great good luck to experience the efficacy proper to Whitehead's thought on the occasion of a twice-annual course, which had the particularity of gathering senior students in philosophy and other senior students who had never done philosophy before. Each time, an experience took place, both collective and individual, that suppressed all hierarchy between philosophers and non-philosophers, but gathered them together in a sheer discovery that is different for each, because it is relative each time to their area of competence: "one can think like that!" Faced by the problem of a book to be written, my concern was to rediscover, by other means, what the interventions, questions, and astonishments contributed to the oral exercise of the class. Or else, to use an expression dear to Gilles Deleuze, to provide myself with the constraints capable of forcing me to "think Whitehead down the middle" in the twofold sense of the term: without a "beginning" from which the rest could be deduced, and face to face with the problems to which it gives rise. How could one fashion a textual apparatus that could introduce the unforeseen nature of the objection that hinders the unfolding of a sovereign intentionality?

It is said that Whitehead hated to be bored, and elaborated his thought in the presence of his students. Most of his philosophical writings have their origin in lectures, which he later worked up. Perhaps the procedure I have chosen is in response to this peculiar character of theirs: I chose it first of all as an experiment, "just to see," and then with a surprised interest in its effects, which stripped me of an author's position without thereby constraining me to disappear, quite the contrary: "to let Whitehead" (and a few others) "do the talking" in long fragments which, rather than quotations, are interventions, and to make my own text the soliloquy of a person who is exploring in her way, always in her way, what the intervention makes happen for her.

Some of these interventions will be "cries," others elaborations, in which thought is "put to work" in real time, but still others are genuine operators of brutal bifurcation. To let Whitehead do the talking at some length always means exposing oneself to the risk that he may play the nasty trick of derailing the orderly train of an explanation toward a seemingly incongruous horizon. And that is precisely what students do when a class awakens their thought, incites their objections, their "but thens," their "in that cases." Perhaps, as well, this is the way Whitehead himself functioned when the presence of his students provoked the risk of thought "in real time," re-creating at every step the meaning or the necessity of the next step. I do not know to what extent the solution I have experimented with will suit those who will read this book. What I can say is that it has made of its writing an adventurous and demanding itinerary, in which "what I already knew" has not ceased to produce new consequences and also the most close-fought work of negotiation with syntax and composition I have ever known.

The reader will note that I have, moreover, made the somewhat acrobatic choice of avoiding all footnotes. This is not the easy solution, but instead, once again, a constraint: the text should "hold" as it is, and above all should not have the appearance of an exhaustive exposition. A note, in general, refers either to a direction that the textual itinerary could have taken, and which the author decides not to take any further, or to a technical discussion that the author believes would overburden the text. The former type of note implies that the number of decisions about the itinerary is limited, but here it is not, for at every step other directions could have been taken, since each step is in fact a decision in the heart of a labyrinth. As far as the "technical" notes are concerned, most of them would have referred to the network of discussions and controversies that weave the links between process philosophers. But this book was written in French, that is, for readers who are foreign to this network, largely unknown in Francophone lands. I am aware that translation transforms this aspect of situation, but it does not transform the conception of the book itself, which is also the situation of the person who conceived it and who did not encounter "process philosophy" until well after her encounter with Whitehead. With the crucial exception of the reading proposed by Lewis Ford, which I adopt, it is the baton of Whitehead's text that I have wished to take up, and not of the discussions that concern him, for the question for me was not—above all—to claim to hold the "right interpretation," that is, to discuss other possible interpretations as well. What matters to me is to inhabit the movement that Whitehead proposes for thought, and, without stopping this movement, to experience and put to the test the way in which it is or is not able to receive questions that Whitehead did not ask because they are not those of his time. In other words, my choice is not to interpret but to try to transmit, that is, also, as every lover of Whitehead knows, to take up again in my way, tying it in to my questions, that which has no other truth than the set of resumptions to which it will give rise.

Another testimony to this choice is the absence in the index of the "great Whiteheadian concepts." They intervene "everywhere" (for instance, "event," "object," "nature," or "organism" in the first part, "to feel," "concrescence," "actualization," "society," "subject" in the second part), and taking them up again in the index would have produced something monstrous. I have, however, privileged certain transversal themes that characterize the way I have inhabited the Whiteheadian movement. Some, such as interstices and infection, are not even included in the Whiteheadian indices, while others are not properly Whiteheadian. Yet they have imposed themselves upon me as themes, in the musical sense of the term, and I thought that the index might help those who might encounter one of these themes in the manner of "well, here it is again" and would wonder where it has already intervened.

By another aspect, the index bears witness to the way this book tries to prolong the Whiteheadian movement outside of the usual categories of philosophy: the heading "social roles or types" brings together names of practitioners (mathematician, physician, chemist, biologist, psychologist, etc.) and names of animals (rabbit, fly, bacteria, etc.). I have taken my inspiration in this regard from Bergson who, in the index to his *Evolution créatrice,* juxtaposed the names of those who, for him, translated the culmination of two divergent paths of evolution: philosophers, on the one hand, parasites and insects on the other. Except that the point here is not to propose a scale of beings, distributing to each that to which it may lay claim. What interests me is the adventurization of the experience that philosophies of the subject have too often "domesticated" under the categories of the reflexive consciousness.

It is the task of ethologists, and all those who live in attentive contact with animals, to question, specify, and enrich what animals make us feel and think. It is the job of scientific communities to test the relevance of the problematic definitions that make them work. But it belongs to speculative thought to fight against the impoverishment of experience, particularly against its confiscation by the great theoretical debates that oppose mankind, "endowed with consciousness," to all the others supposedly deprived of it. Obviously, speculative adventurization does not produce miracles: I do not claim to speak for flesh and blood physicians, psychologists, and sociologists any more than I claim to have access to the experience of a butterfly or a rabbit. When I refer to practitioners and to animals, then, the goal is not to penetrate their own experience but to think on the basis of the "habits" that enable us to say "a rabbit" or "a sociologist," that is, to evoke a style or experience or adventure that is endowed with a certain stability.

Alongside the Whiteheadian references, I have therefore added a few others, faithful in this regard to the nomadism proper to British philosophy, as it has been characterized by Gilles Deleuze and Félix Guattari: not to build nor to found, but to inhabit. "A tent is enough for them [...] The concept is a habit acquired by contemplating the elements from which one proceeds (hence the very special Greekness of British philosophy, its empirical Neoplatonism). We are all contemplations, and therefore habits. *I* is a habit. There is concept wherever there is habit, and habits are made and unmade on the level of immanence and radical experience: they are 'conventions'. This is why British philosophy is a free and savage creation of concepts. Given a proposition, to what convention does it refer, what is the habit that constitutes its concept? This is the question of pragmatism" (QPh, 101).

"A free and savage creation of concepts," perhaps: but one can only "think with Whitehead" if one is willing to separate the adjective "free" from the noun "freedom," in the sense of absence of constraints, and the adjective "savage" from the noun "savagery," in the sense of an appetite for destruction. Free and savage creation, therefore, but not, especially not, ferocious, not defining that with which it deals as a prey to be attacked. The point is not to declare war on the conventions that bind us, the habits that enable us to be characterized. Instead, it is merely to place on the same level— that is, in adventure—all of our judgments, or our "as is well knowns," and thus to separate them actively from what gives them the power to exclude and to disqualify.

In closing this introduction, I would like to offer my apology to the readers who might be shocked if they encounter a physician or a poet "in the masculine." Insofar as they are figures of thought, I would have liked to place them in the neuter, as I would have liked to place in the neuter that God who, for Whitehead, is a "he." But I could not bring myself to associate them with this kind of a problem, for they would then have designated real persons. I hope these excuses will be accepted, for I feel deeply indebted for the attention that American thinkers have taught us to devote to the way in which words influence thought.

PART ONE

From the Philosophy of Nature to Metaphysics

CHAPTER ONE

The Mathematician and the Sunset

This is going to be about nature.
But how can we define nature?
It is what we are aware of in perception (CN, 28).

WHITEHEAD HAS PROPOSED a starting point that seems to be quite innocent. A bit too general or simplistic, one might say, although it attributes a most interesting role to "awareness," a word that we French-language philosophers have some reasons to envy our Anglophone colleagues. All we have available is the word "conscience," which is a trap here because of the reflexive dimension that is often associated with it. That is why I chose, when writing in French, to use the word "expérience" *(la nature est ce dont nous avons l'expérience dans la perception)*. My goal was to point out that awareness designates a mode of experience that includes a contrast between a "self" and "that of which there is experience," but without duplicating it by reference to an "I" or a "me": a contrast, not an opposition. The question then arises: who is this "we," who is aware of nature, and what does it include? Most ethologists will say without hesitation that a chimpanzee, a dog, or a rabbit are "aware." Their perceptual experience, without implying reflexive consciousness, must give meaning to the possibility of an exploratory activity, bearing witness to the fact that that "that which" is perceived may raise the question of meaning: when a rabbit turns its head in the direction from which a noise comes, it is exploring that noise's meaning. Yet the discussion may begin with the idea that bees also "explore." Does it not conceal a much more radical difference by means of a handy metaphor? Hesitation thus comes into play for bees, ticks, ants, or spiders. And it disappears when we have to do with thistles or mignonette.

Whitehead's starting point, which leads us so quickly into ethological speculations, thus seems highly indeterminate, too indeterminate to be able to guarantee a selection of what can testify, in a reliable way, for that nature whose concept is to be constructed.

We must beware, however, as we conclude, that we will certainly have to go beyond this starting point. Whitehead is a mathematician. For a mathematician, a starting point is not what enables one to go beyond. It is what commits us. It is that to which one must succeed in holding fast.

To restrict ourselves to what we are aware of in perception: this is the archetypal Empiricist decision. Yet we must immediately forget the clichés that often follow that decision, and which Whitehead knows well, because they are those in which his former collaborator Bertrand Russell henceforth indulges.

If Whitehead had written "nature is what we perceive," a version seemingly close to the initial statement, what would have followed was almost automatic. What do you perceive? A grey stone. What does what you perceive authorize? The affirmation that "this stone is grey." In contrast, the question "what are you aware of in the perception of this stone you call grey?" blocks the pedagogical series of explanations. A contrast insinuates itself, between the words immediately available for saying "what" we perceive, and the question, open for its part, of what we are aware of "in perception." An indefinite constellation of components becomes perceptible, which "that stone is grey"—that statement apparently so simple and transparent—had skipped.

First of all, however, when would I express such an apparently simple statement? Perhaps I might say it to a painter, if I am scandalized by the lack of faithfulness of his reproduction of the stone? Or else, upon receiving them, if I had ordered ochre-colored stones? In this case, however, the contrast between what I perceive and what I am aware of in this perception becomes intense, for my experience will be dominated by the risk of challenging the painter's choice, or by the prospect of entering into an unpleasant discussion with a distracted or even dishonest merchant.

As a starting point for philosophical reasoning, what we are aware of in the perception of the printed phrase "this stone is grey," is not, moreover, any simpler. The work of mourning to which readers are going to be obliged is already announced to them. They will be asked to limit legitimate statements about experience to those that designate a "pure" perceptual experience. The stone might, moreover, as the case may be, become a "grey patch," if readers are constrained to admit that the visual data do not let them affirm anything more.

Thus language habitually sets before the mind a misleading abstract of the indefinite complexity of the fact of self-awareness (CN, 108).

The empiricist decision to limit ourselves to what we are aware of in perception, could thus be called resisting what language proposes, trying to stick to the indefinite complexity of this "what." In this case, however, one must immediately add "succeeding in sticking to it." Without surreptitiously moving from the selection of the "what" to another selection, dealing this time with the case we choose. Without privileging the "pure cases," whose false simplicity designates not nature, but a theory of knowledge or subjectivity that remains to be founded. Whitehead was a mathematician. If he said "what," his statement commits him: the goal is to understand "everything" we are aware of. If he said "perception," this means any situation in which perception comes into play. And if nature is (all) we are aware of in perception, then:

[. . .] *everything perceived is in nature. We may not pick and choose. For us the red glow of the sunset should be as much part of nature as are the molecules and electric waves by which men of science would explain the phenomenon* (CN, 29).

"We may not." But of course we may, and in fact we do nothing else. Nor is it a question of criticizing those who pick and choose. When men of science describe the interaction between electromagnetic radiation and the suspended molecules that inhabit the atmosphere, linking the red glow to atmospheric pollution, they do not insult the poet. Unless they want to, unless they want to confer upon the relation they are studying the power to reduce nature to the terms of scientific explanation.

The "we" to whom this "we may not" is addressed does not exist prior to the demand posited by Whitehead, the demand that the "concept of nature" to be constructed must be bereft of the power of dividing, and declaring that one type of experience is right and another wrong. It is the "we" of the problem when a mathematician takes charge of it, simultaneously bringing into existence the problem and the constraints that the solution will have to satisfy. Here, moreover, this "we" affirms the most artificial demand: not to take advantage of the power to choose as we wish, however theoretically well-founded this wish may be.

Yet the problem must still be well formulated, that is, formulated in terms that do not surreptitiously confuse the characterization of a situation with a ready-made solution that commits the approach before it has even begun. For instance, if we were to accept as well-founded the scientists' affirmation that electromagnetic radiation provides an explanation for the red glow that poets try to celebrate, the matter would be understood from the outset, and the problem of affirming both the red glow and the molecules together would be "missed": what we are aware of in perception would indeed have to be called molecules, radiation, and so on. The point is therefore to state the terms of the problem in a way that resists the pretensions of solution included in the usual modes of formulation.

For example, the fire is burning and we see a red coal. This is explained in science by radiant energy from the coal entering our eyes. But in seeking for such an explanation we are not asking what are the sort of occurrences which are fitted to cause a mind to see red. The chain of causation is entirely different. The mind is cut out altogether. The real question is, When red is found in nature, what else is found there also? Namely we are seeking for an analysis of the accompaniments in nature of the discovery of red in nature [...] In other words, science is not discussing the causes of knowledge, but the coherence of knowledge. The understanding which is sought by science is an understanding of relations within nature (CN, 41).

Whitehead does not hesitate to speak of radiation, molecules, and electrons. The construction of his problem does not need to presuppose the epistemological discussion of the well-foundedness of our specialized statements, even if they mobilize beings that we cannot perceive directly. It affirms itself as superbly indifferent to all technical and theoretical mediations that enable scientists to construct their explanations. In contrast, what matters to him is the trick to which scientists would have recourse if they claimed to have explained "that which" causes perception, that which explains the fact that we "see red." These scientists can affirm that radiation has caused the excitation of such-and-such retinal receptors; they can, if their science has invented the means for such a procedure, follow the repercussions of this excitation in the great population of neurons. And they will probably succeed in reconstituting a continuous series of relations: if they were to be surprised, it would be by the eventual brutal interruption of that series, that goes from the perception of the red coal to everything that can accompany that perception within nature. Yet from explanation to explanation, from experimental situation to experimental solution, the "mind" remains in brackets, in the sense that the characterization of the experimental relation does not include the person for whom it constitutes an explanation. To claim to explain the "perceived red" is to claim that there will suddenly surge forth, like a rabbit pulled out of a magician's hat, a term that designates not what the scientists have succeeded in perceiving but that which all their achievements presuppose.

For Whitehead, when scientists claim that their approach should "some day"—because you can't stop progress—come to "explain" that which, in fact, it presupposes, one will not speak either of "scientific spirit" or of "materialistic persuasion." There is nothing to accept, nothing to negotiate, nothing to respect. The rabbit will not come out of the hat. The explanatory ambition translates and prolongs a problem that has been badly formulated, an arbitrary distribution, in the midst of what we are aware of, between what is supposed to pertain to objective nature, independent of knowledge, and what pertains to the mind. That this badly formulated problem should finally wind up as the ultimate mystery, the dizzying question of the possibility of a "materialist" explanation that would no longer even limit itself to "that which is perceived," red, but would deal with perception or consciousness, is neither surprising nor interesting for Whitehead. The problem has been badly tackled from the outset, as soon as the selection has been made, both of what explains and of what must be explained.

Will the mind then appear as the place of irreducible mystery, that which science will always fail to explain? Does Whitehead demand that the scientist bow down before the inexplicable? Not in the least. What Whitehead asks them to admit is not at all that their questions will always fail in the face of the problem of the mind. There is no defeat, insoluble problem, or mystery. There is the simple fact that the scientists' questions do not enable them to formulate the problem of the "mind" because these questions and their answers presuppose it.

The distinction between an insoluble problem and a badly tackled problem might seem insignificant to those who decide to understand, first and foremost, that Whitehead imposes limits on science, and will immediately oppose their "materialist" convictions to this shameful "spiritualist." For Whitehead, however, it is not a question of limits to be respected. It is rather a question of "behavior," in the sense in which "to behave badly" would here mean to insult one's own work, to expect from it something entirely other than what gives it its own value. It is impossible to describe the scientists' work, the creation of ever more unexpected and inventive experimental apparatuses, without taking for "granted" the possibility of knowing, that is, a reference to a mind, as presupposed by all the questions to which they seek an answer. Everything to which scientists could refer, insofar as they are aware of it in perception, including the electromagnetic radiation witnessed by "that which" their specialized instruments give them to perceive, is indeed a part of nature; that is, like the concept of nature itself, it designates the mind *qua* presupposed and bracketed.

Whitehead's approach is thus not that of a judge, imposing limits on the approach to explanation. It is, once again, that of a mathematician. An art of problems, and of the creation of their possible solutions. Whitehead is not afraid of the scientists' materialism; he is afraid of badly formulated problems. And every problem will be badly formulated which, dealing with the knowledge we can have of nature, forgets what it presupposes, namely, that there is knowledge.

Knowledge is ultimate. There can be no explanation of the "why" of knowledge; we can only describe the "what" of knowledge (CN, 32).

There is nothing dizzying, here, about what is ultimate; it simply corresponds to the question raised. It does not forbid any dream, but designates the path by which dreams can become nightmares, because it denies the dreamer, the path by which the construction of explanations can become the construction of the best way of dissimulating, of making a paradox or a fascinating mystery out of what goes without saying. There is nothing mysterious, nothing paradoxical about what is ultimate. Its designation corresponds to the difference between the problem of what Whitehead calls "metaphysics," which must imply both what is perceived and what perceives, and that of a philosophy of nature or of science. When it comes to science, all metaphysical questions must be excluded.

The recourse to metaphysics is like throwing a match into the powder magazine. It blows up the whole arena (CN, 29).

Yet to limit oneself to nature itself, as Whitehead demands of scientists but as he also demands with regard to the construction of his "concept of nature," does not at all mean to take the first step toward reducing nature to the question of knowledge, as it would, for instance, in a philosophy of the critical type. It is the mind that is bracketed, not the mind, always identical to itself, that brackets nature, *qua* a function of its own operations.

No perplexity concerning the object of knowledge can be solved by saying that there is a mind knowing it (CN, 28) [...] *In making this demand I conceive myself as adopting our immediate instinctive attitude towards perceptual knowledge which is only abandoned under the influence of theory. We are instinctively willing to believe that by due attention, more can be found in nature than that which is observed at first sight. But we will not be content with less* (CN, 29).

The true problem that confronts the concept of nature, the challenge that constrains us to invention, is thus not the "bad behavior" attested by certain explanatory pretensions. The point is to succeed in maintaining oneself at the level of what we are instinctively willing to believe, to resist the theories that do violence to what we cannot help but believe. Nature is by no means nature insofar as we know it, in the sense of any kind of a theory of knowledge; it is the nature we deal with, with which we establish many relations, and it is therefore also all that is presupposed, as far as "it" is concerned, by these multiple relations.

Later on, in *Science and the Modern World,* Whitehead was to speak of "instinctive faith," and, in *Process and Reality,* he would use the expression "animal faith" of the philosopher Santayana, his contemporary (diverting it from its original meaning). Yet the reference will always be to the same movement, the same demand: to recognize that our "immediate instinctive attitude" irresistibly exceeds the limits assigned by such-and-such a critical theory, and to adopt what this attitude presupposes as a constraint to be satisfied.

When empiricist philosophy undertakes to fixate its reader on the statement "this stone is grey," it does violence to this instinctive attitude. If this stone really does attract our attention, for one reason or another, we know that we can go look at it more closely, pick it up, weigh it, feel its roughness, try to break it into pieces. In sum, we can multiply "what" we are aware of in perception. And attribute all of it to nature, instinctively.

In contrast, when scientists express their trust in the experimental approach and proclaim its lack of limits, they prolong our "instinctive attitude" according to which, if we pay what is "due," that is, the appropriate attention to it, we will find more in nature than what we observe at first glance. And it is not empiricist prohibitions that will force them to give up introducing unobservable entities, if the latter enable them to articulate their questions and hypotheses, nor, in case of success, will they prevent them from affirming that these entities do indeed belong to nature rather than to the knowing mind.

It is only when scientists undertake to judge, in the name of these unobservable entities, what we are aware of in perception, when they try to convince us that electromagnetic radiation constitutes the only kind of entity that belongs to nature, that they contradict our instinctive attitude: they have found "more" in nature, but they propose to reduce it to "less."

What men say with words has no importance as long as their activities are controlled by well-established instincts. Words can ultimately destroy instincts. But until that happens, words do not matter (SMW, 4).

The concept of nature that Whitehead undertakes to construct thus does not have the vocation of taking its place in a process of purification, whether existential or epistemological. As long as a human activity exhibits its trust in the possibility of finding "more" in nature than what is observed in it at first glance, what it finds will be part of the constraints that the concept of nature must satisfy, not of what is to be judged in the name of any kind of norm. In contrast, the words that will be mobilized by the concept of nature have the vocation of resisting the power of words that either contradict this trust, convicting it before the tribunal of criticism, or promoting an asymmetrical version of it, a trust in this against that.

The vocation Whitehead assigns to his concept of nature is situated historically. It is primordially associated with "modern thought," haunted as it is by the distinction between "primary" qualities, those that one thinks legitimate to attribute to nature, and "secondary" qualities, those that are referred to the mind (tastes and colors, about which one is not supposed to argue, precisely because they are the subjects of endless discussions).

To the positive definition of the problem—the construction of a concept of nature such that everything we are aware of in perception belongs to it—there thus corresponds a negative definition, the determined rejection of any theory that makes "nature bifurcate." And nature "bifurcates" as soon as, in one way or another, the mind is called to the rescue, *qua* responsible for "psychic additions," to explain the difference between what we are aware of and what is supposed to belong to nature.

The theory of psychic additions would treat the greenness [of grass] *as a psychic addition furnished by the perceiving mind, and would leave to nature merely the molecules and the radiant energy which influence the mind towards that perception* [. . .]

What I am essentially protesting against is the bifurcation of nature into two systems of reality, which, in so far as they are real, are real in different senses [. . .] *Thus there would be two natures, one is the conjecture and the other is the dream. Another way of phrasing this theory* [. . .] *is to bifurcate nature into two divisions, namely into the nature apprehended in awareness and the nature which is the cause of awareness. The nature which is the fact apprehended in awareness holds within it the greenness of the trees, the song of the birds, the warmth of the sun, the hardness of the chairs, and the feel of the velvet. The nature which is the cause of awareness is the conjectured system of molecules and electrons which so affects the mind as to produce the awareness of apparent nature* (CN, 29–31).

To resist all those theories which, in one way or another, make nature bifurcate: such is the challenge Whitehead imposed upon himself when he provided himself with his initial definition, "nature is what we are aware of in perception." The value of this definition by no means depends on its neutrality or its plausibility, its precision, or its consensual character. It depends on the commitment to which it constrains whomever accepts it, and on the definition of what will then constitute failure or achievement for that person. Every statement that makes nature bifurcate will be a defeat.

In other words, Whitehead does not in the slightest propose to "prove" that we should abandon the great modern divide between primary qualities, attributed to the entities that constitute nature, and secondary qualities, relative to our perception. He does not even bother to name those who prolong and repeat this division even today: he knows that is it you and I, the philosopher or the scientist, all those who have accepted this division as important or as an unquestioned matter of fact. He defines this division as the absurdity that his concept will have to escape.

The absurdity here does not resemble the one utilized by a mathematical demonstration. Mathematical absurdity is defined by the fact that at the end of a process of reasoning, one is obliged to conclude that $1 = 3$, or else that a number is both odd and even. These are obvious contradictions, to which no hesitation or possibility of negotiation corresponds: the reasoning must be abandoned. Except, of course, when the feeling of the absurdity of mathematics invades a student to such a point that he or she is ready to accept anything ... Whitehead, as a philosopher, knows that the power of mathematics, exhibited by the possibility of ending up in a contradiction, and of organizing a demonstration around this fixed point, has little to do with philosophy. Philosophical absurdity is not consensual: it commits philosophers but does not enable them to constrain all beings who respect logic to adhere to their commitment. This is why Whitehead does not base his refusal on an argument intended to be authoritative for all. He will not undertake to criticize the theories that make nature bifurcate, nor will he demonstrate that the traditional opposition between primary and secondary qualities leads to a contradiction that would be recognized by any being of good sense. He knows that it is precisely the slope of good sense that he must climb, that he is faced by what contemporary good sense suggests that we accept without blinking, and even to celebrate it as a decisive progress of thought. He will limit himself, without adding anything, to exhibiting the consequences of bifurcation, what it imposes upon us to affirm.

Thus, nature sees itself credited with that which, in fact, should be reserved for ourselves: the rose for its smell, the nightingale for its song, and the sun for its brilliance. The poets are entirely wrong. They should address their songs to themselves, and should turn them into odes of self-congratulation for the splendor of the human mind. Nature is a stupid business, bereft of sounds, odors and colors; it is only matter in a hurry, without end and without meaning (SMW, 54).

If this consequence, that the poets must be said to be mistaken when they celebrate the smell of the rose, does not make the absurdity of the theory that imposes it perceptible, then, for Whitehead, nothing will do so. And if, today, some scientists and some philosophers identify without the least hesitation any questioning of this "stupid nature" with a worrisome manifestation of irrationality, a return of ancient beliefs, a denial of the universal value of physical laws, and so on, no argument will make them change their minds. Later, in *Science and the Modern World*, Whitehead was to ask the question of the history we inherit, which has turned the absurdity in question into a kind of consensual self-evidence, the rejection of which entails the greatest risks. For the moment, as in every demonstration by the absurd, the rejection of the theories of the bifurcation of nature is a principle of construction. The problem is not to polemicize but to accept the risk, to try the adventure, to explore what the rejection of a bifurcation of nature obliges us to think.

All we know of nature is in the same boat, to sink or swim together (CN, 148).

The fact that the statement of the problem raised by Whitehead can be understood as a veritable cry attests to the convergence, in this cry, of all the registers usually distinguished by argumentation. It is not a matter of negotiating in a finer way what will be "saved," attributed to nature. Everything is going to have to be saved together, at the same time, and by the same means. What engages Whitehead may be stated just as well in terms of intellectual obligation, as in terms of one that is aesthetic or ethical. Every line of division, whatever its plausibility, will refer to misbehavior: it will translate the transformation of a defeat, for which the philosopher bears responsibility, into a disqualification of what has resisted the invitation to take its place in the boat this philosopher formulated.

Correlatively, the concept Whitehead is going to try to construct will be neither true nor false. For truth and falsity, when they are attributable to a statement—*no, that's not Oliver's car*—imply a hesitation that refers to the demands of a particular mode of knowledge—*I was sure I recognized it*. But the point here is to construct a concept that satisfies the most artificial demand, that is, the one that requires the highest power of invention: not to privilege any particular mode of knowledge. This is why, in Whitehead's vocabulary, the terms "general" and "generality" will never have the meaning given to them by logic. They will never provide the power to forget particularities, but, on the contrary, will point to the ambition to affirm all of them together.

Sense-awareness is an awareness of something. What then is the general character of that something of which we are aware? (CN, 28–29).

All men are mortal. Socrates is a man. Therefore . . . This "therefore" means: whether you like it or not, Socrates, I have here the power to talk about you, even if I have never met you, even if I know nothing about you except this general property: "you are part of the set of human beings." The power of defining sets, of choosing them in a way that enables one to decide what will be included or excluded, is the best-shared thing in the world. Whitehead does not denounce this power, any more than he denounces specialized languages. Philosophy, for him, is not denunciation. Yet it can indeed be said to be resistance, internal resistance to the properly philosophical temptation to found this *de facto* power *in iure*.

Neither true nor false, Whiteheadian generalities expose their author to a wholly different risk: their success or their failure will always depend on whether or not they succeed in not giving any power to the person who constructs them, in not founding any judgment that will enable him or her to transcend the multiplicity of experiences, or to tame this multiplicity by defining the norms to which all experience must respond.

The Concept of Nature, however, does not yet deal with experience in general, but with what we are aware of in perception. This choice of the question indicates that Whitehead takes his place within the English Empiricist tradition, and this is indeed the challenge he will try to take up, that haunts this tradition since Berkeley, Locke, and Hume: the challenge of an articulation to be made explicit between perceptions and that paradigmatic knowledge called mathematical physics, which has been focused since Newton on the questions of space and time.

When Whitehead comes to ask other questions, when he becomes interested no longer in what scientists perceive but in what they seek, when he no longer recognizes "Cleopatra's needle," standing in the center of London, every time he sees it, but asks himself how to understand the story that insists through it, that of ancient Egypt or that of the rapine of colonial England, he will have moved from the question of "what" we are aware of in perception to the "how" of this awareness. From the exploration of what we are committed to by the refusal to make nature bifurcate between percepts, on the one hand, and a reality that is essentially spatio-temporal and functional on the other, to the exploration of what is required by the way we relate to experience. He will not modify the concept of nature then, but will abandon it, for it is no longer adapted to the problem, since the problem must henceforth include what the concept of nature designates as ultimate: knowledge.

CHAPTER TWO

Events and Passage

W E KNOW LITTLE ABOUT Whitehead's life in the sense that excites the curiosity of historians of philosophy: what did he read, and when? What is more, Whitehead by no means respects the academic rule according to which one cites the authors by whom one is inspired. There are not many footnotes in *The Concept of Nature,* nor any precise discussion of the way he introduces concepts that come from elsewhere without warning. We can, however, already hear genuine "cries" in it, in which what can be negotiated only gradually, in the close struggle with what is demanded by a concept once it is posited, and what may force the concept to be reworked or even abandoned, is concentrated and explodes all at once. Cries that have not been smothered by the construction of concepts, and that are remembered by those who have heard them, whether students or visitors.

Thus, on December 15, 1939, when he was quietly discussing the Bible with Lucien Price, Whitehead

[. . .] *suddenly* [. . .] *stood and spoke, with passionate intensity, "Here we are, with our finite beings and physical senses in the presence of a universe whose possibilities are infinite, and even though we may not apprehend them, those infinite possibilities are actualities"* (DANW, 111).

How can one address experience in the sense in which it resonates in this exclamation, that is, before it is invaded by the words that judge and distribute what belongs to the subject and what belongs to the object? How can one bring to life the difference between (all) we are aware of in perception and the object eventually perceived, associated with the ready-made words that designate it? Whitehead shares the question of the "return to experience itself" with a multitude of other modern philosophers. And it is obviously possible to attempt parallels, and even comparisons, with some of them, and in particular with the phenomenological approach of his contemporary Husserl. Yet there is a risk of losing the movement and neglecting what philosophers seek to bring to life, thanks to their concepts, and especially what they are trying not to lose, what they are afraid to lose, that which, as the case may be, they cry out. Whitehead will not ask, will never ask of experience that it admit its finitude. Any resemblance between one Whiteheadian statement and another coming from elsewhere will be declared null and void if the latter orients thought, in one way or another, toward a mode of judgment that turns the infinite possibilities that haunt our experience into a temptation that must be resisted.

If thought must carry out a judgment, it is not about experience but about itself, about the power it can assume of judging that experience in terms of what it captures of it in a way proper to explanation. But neither does judgment mean contrition, or the self-critique of a thought that betrays the experience from which it proceeds. Whitehead will not, will never ask thought to condemn itself. Any resemblance between one Whiteheadian statement and another coming from elsewhere will be null and void if it orients thought, in one way or another, toward a nostalgic relation with what escapes it, with that to which, through original sin or wandering, it has lost access. Whitehead's philosophy has nothing to do with a culture of dereliction. It simply brings into existence the importance of not confusing the "what" of thought, or its terminus, and "what we are aware of in perception."

To sum up: the termini for thought are entities, primarily with bare individuality, secondarily with properties and relations ascribed to them in the procedure of thought; the termini for sense-awareness are factors in the fact of nature, primarily relata and only secondarily discriminated as distinct individualities.

[...] The transition from the "red" of awareness to the "red" of thought is accompanied by a definite loss of content, namely by the transition from the factor "red" to the entity "red." This loss in the transition to thought is compensated by the fact that thought is communicable whereas sense-awareness is incommunicable (CN, 12–13).

Whitehead's ambition is not to oppose but to distinguish, in a way that confirms what we know instinctively. The goal is not to define a nature that is "knowable" in the philosophers' sense, that is, where the point would be to define nature and the legitimate mode of knowledge, in one way or another, but always correlatively. Instead, the goal is to confirm that it is indeed nature that is at stake in knowledge, the multiple modes of knowledge, whereas as soon as we state "what" we perceive, a transition occurs for which "nature" cannot account. In other words, the point will be to approach "what we are aware of" simultaneously as what awareness "offers" to the transition, as that about which the transition takes place, and as that which must be characterized in such a way that "what" we perceive does indeed designate nature rather than the perceiving mind. In still other words, whatever relations may be between "words" and "things," no theory can make Whitehead change his mind: we are not the prisoners of a closed circuit between perception and denomination. As soon as we pay "due attention" to it, we are grappling with "nature."

To construct the concept that answers this ambition obviously requires words, or, more precisely, names. From the names Whitehead will associate with "what we are aware of," one will not expect anything other than a dynamics of evocation, creating an experience of contrast, constituting the contrast as an experience for thought. This was already the case when Whitehead "named" the transition from factor to entity: denomination functions not as the starting point for a process of reasoning but rather as a point of accumulation around which other names will come to be added. Like a proper name uttered when we meet a person who is dear to us, the function of the Whiteheadian name is to celebrate, and in this case to celebrate a factor that belongs to what we are aware of, in a way that prevents us from confusing it with an object of thought.

"Event" is the first of the names Whitehead associates with what we are aware of in perception.

What we discern is the specific character of a place through a period of time. This is what I mean by an "event." We discern some specific character of an event. But in discerning an event we are also aware of its significance as a relatum in the structure of events (CN, 52).

The verb "to discern" is interesting, because it is indeterminate. It can be used in an active sense, which refers it to the discerning subject. Yet Whitehead thwarts this usage. The factor discerned is a part of what I am aware of in perception. Activity begins when, for one reason or another, I become interested in what is then selected as "what" I have perceived. In addition, what I am aware of is not defined by the character "that is discerned." We discern a character *qua* factor *of* something, which Whitehead names event. What is more, this event itself does not present itself in an isolated mode. What I have auditory experience of testifies to the fact that other events, although they are not discerned, include the event of which the sound is a factor, while this event itself includes others. The name "event" celebrates the "fact" that what we discern always has a beyond.

It is very important, even at this early stage, not to block the movement that Whitehead invites us to experience by questions that are overly hurried. Above all, not to demand a more precise definition of the event. What Whitehead meant is what he said, however disappointing his answer may seem to be: the event is that of which we discern a specific character, whereas, "as we know instinctively," this event is linked to other events. The cry of a bird. The refrigerator motor starting up. A laughing exchange between two passersby beneath my window. All this took place while I wrote these lines: specific characters, tending to be auditory since my visual attention was fixed upon my screen, but which cannot be reduced to a sound. I did not discern a sound but a specific character, sonorous, of events whose meaning I am "well aware" is not exhausted by this character. I know that if I go to my window, I will see the laughing people continue their conversation or go away, and I know that if I had been at my window two moments earlier, I would have witnessed their meeting. I have awareness of all that in the perception of their laughter, which is why, moreover, I do not jump as I would if I heard a desperate screeching of brakes: *some day one of these idiots is going to kill a child instead of a cat.*

Whitehead thus affirms that a discerned event is connected to other events within a structure. Yet structure, here, must also function as a name, celebrating, of course, as one might guess, what will be required by the definitions of space and time, but not being confused with them. In contrast, the term "extension" will be a primary term for characterizing the event *qua* connected. A discerned event always has an extension because it includes or comprises others, and it testifies to the extension of other events that include or comprise it. This is part of its meaning, as we are aware of it in perception.

A discerned event is known as related in this structure to other events whose specific characters are otherwise not disclosed in that immediate awareness except so far as that they are relata within the structure (CN, 52).

This complete general fact is the discernible and it comprises the discerned. The discernible is all nature as disclosed in that sense-awareness, and extends beyond and comprises all of nature as actually discriminated or discerned in that sense-awareness (CN, 50).

One can speak of the noise of the city, but where does the city end? Whitehead was a mathematician. If what is discerned has no power to define what is discernible, to assign limits to it, there are no limits. That which, in the mode of the discernible, is disclosed or is signified in a sensible experience is then "all of nature."

The need to translate the verb *disclose* into French raised a problem for me that was all the more acute because the word is important for Whitehead. Was he not to write later, much later, that "The aim of philosophy is sheer disclosure" (MT, 49)? The most usual French translations for "is disclosed" are "est dévoilé" or "est révélé," or "est rendu manifeste," which might give the impression that the philosopher's goal is to experience something hidden, latent, and implicit, which would be more "true," in one way or another, than our usual perceptions. French translations of Whitehead have yielded to this temptation all the more easily in that the influence of Heidegger and of phenomenology are strong in France. I had to counteract this influence, that is, affirm the fact that Whitehead belongs to the Empiricist tradition, in which the goal is never to go "beyond" usual experience but rather to transform it, to make what usually "goes without saying" matter. Consulting Harrap's dictionary, I found "déclarer" among all the possible translations of "disclose," and I adopted it, because it can be placed in communication with a situation that has nothing phenomenological about it: when a customs officer asks a traveler, "Have you anything to declare?"

The officer would be surprised if, in response to his question, the traveler began to spout an interminable list of everything he might be liable to declare . . . To declare, here, refers to a specialized situation, stable enough for any deviation to be surprising. Of course, the custom officer's surprise would not bear upon the discovery that a traveler is indeed capable of declaring something other than the merchandise he or she is transporting, but only on the fact that in these circumstances, this traveler should undertake to demonstrate such a capacity. The customs officer discerns— that's his job—the traveler *qua* potential bearer of merchandise liable to be taxed, but he also knows, when he asks his question, that the declaration he anticipates does not define the traveler. What he is charged with discerning could, moreover—and will be, when the fraudulent and relieved traveler returns to his family or his accomplices—be declared in a very different modality: "Whew!"

The event that constitutes the traveler's arrival, discerned in the experience of the customs-officer-who-sees-a-traveler-arriving-who-might-have-something-to-declare, is thus known by the customs officer *qua* connected to other events which, for their part, are only declared/disclosed in the mode of the discernible. He does not know these other events, but he knows that, if he gave himself the means to pay due attention to them, he could discern many other things. The customs officer's experience can no more be reduced to the purity of what such an officer has as his mandate to discern than the event "traveler's arrival" can be reduced to the purity of the specific character that discerns it. In other words, the experience of the meaning of the event *qua* connected to other events which are "signified" is not a "psychic addition" to the event. It is the event that, in the customs officer's experience, declares itself to be linked to other events: it is the traveler's answer "no, nothing" that declares itself as passing over in silence an indefinite number of possible declarations.

What such and such a traveler might say, how the event is linked to others, is an entirely different problem. Thus, at its simplest, the event of the "traveler's arrival" may engage other modes of discernment, in the specialized sense of the term, and in particular that of the policeman who might appear beside the customs officer and drag the traveler, suddenly transformed into a suspect, away to an office where he will have to answer a few questions. In this case, perhaps, the traveler's face, which the customs officer had not inspected, was the specific characteristic of the event, unless it was his "facies," the fact he did not look Caucasian enough, or his bearing.

Of course, the event of the "traveler's arrival" lends itself rather poorly to the type of specialized knowledge that the physicist sets in motion in the quite different context of a laboratory. The physicist's goal is to explain the meaning of an event—this uranium salt has left an impression on a photographic plate—and in this case the question of the structure to which this event must belong will be explicitly raised. If a policeman is lying in wait behind the customs officer, it is not in order to explain, but to spot. This difference is not, however, the starting point of a hierarchy. In general, "structure" in Whitehead's sense neither promises nor guarantees any explanation, although it is exhibited by any explanation that succeeds in the experimental sense, that is, by any experimental staging that succeeds in making the event a reliable witness with regard to relations more general than itself.

In other words, what Whitehead names has nothing to do with truth, whether it is objective, veiled, or transcendent, a truth toward which one would have to turn, in one way or another. We are not invited to judge the customs officer or the policeman in the name of the truth of the traveler. Nor, above all, are we urged to return to the condition of all possible knowledge, the traditional approach of philosophers when they undertake to separate the problem of knowledge as such, "the problem," from the teeming multiplicity of ways of knowing. To speak of meaning does not authorize us to define anything, does not found any judgment, does not call for any purification. It will never be a matter of access to the intelligible beyond confusion. Or else, such access will have to be understood in its irredeemably selective and partial dimension: on the basis of what is "offered," this rather than that, by taking advantage of the possibility, never warranted by any principle, of abstracting from this. To speak of meaning, however, commits us. Insofar as the meaning of an event, *qua* linked to other events, is a factor belonging to what we are aware of in perception, the question of meaning engages the way in which the question of knowledge will be raised, that is, of the meanings that each type of knowledge will select, privilege, and render explicit.

There is obviously nothing neutral about Whitehead's strategy, but this is to be expected, since the concept he is trying to construct is not neutral but has as its vocation to resist the bifurcation of nature. This is what is indicated by the importance of the term "to exhibit," which is and remains crucial in Whitehead's thought. This term must be understood in the sense of mathematics: according to the language used in the course of the adventure of mathematics, the circle has exhibited in different ways what makes it a circle, and has thus been an ingredient of distinct adventures. A philosopher's description is not neutral, any more than that of a circle is for a mathematician. It starts out, of course, from what is concrete, and for Whitehead concrete experience will always be its touchstone, what puts it to the test, that whose test it must accept. Yet philosophers are responsible for the way they describe or define what a concrete fact "exhibits," that is, also which obligations it entails. In the present case, the adventure Whitehead is attempting in *The Concept of Nature* commits him to ask the concrete fact to exhibit the way it allows the proscribed maneuver, the recourse to psychic addition, to be avoided. If the "mind" is to be responsible for something, it is in terms of selection and simplification, not of addition, that this responsibility must be defined, and if "what we know instinctively" is to be confirmed, selection and simplification—in short, abstraction—must not define "knowledge," but always such-and-such a way of knowing, which may be modified if we choose to try to explore how to pay due attention to what we are dealing with.

In somewhat more technical terms, this commitment implies that what Whitehead asks sense awareness to exhibit must be stated in terms of "requisites." The concept of nature will have to be such that what we instinctively know is justified, as well as what is presupposed by the explanations attempted, at their own risks and perils, by our specialized branches of knowledge. It must therefore satisfy what knowledge requires: that by due attention more can be found, that is, learned.

It is important to distinguish "requisites" and "conditions." To this distinction corresponds the question of the plural nature of the specialized branches of knowledge that we can produce with regard to nature, and the lack of a guarantee with regard to their respective achievement, as is, moreover, indicated by Whitehead's formulation "due attention." The kind of attention we must pay is a question, as scientists are well aware, that gives its interest to the adventure of science.

In fact, when philosophers speak of "conditions," the point is emphatically not to relate knowledge and adventure, but instead to define the conditions that must be answered by a description that is purified of all interpretative overload. The conditions are thus the vehicle of the ambition to move from fact to justification, from a description that is more or less arbitrary to a description exhibiting guarantees of its reliable character. And the satisfaction of this ambition will enable the selection of the kind of knowledge that best satisfies the conditions that have been made explicit. The conditions thus enable us to sort branches of knowledge, to determine which of them are illusory, which of them are "subjective," and which are worthy of defining an "object."

Correlatively, conditions are supposed to answer a fundamentally anonymous problem, which anyone could raise, the answer to which will therefore be valid in principle for anyone. This is where the crucial distinction between conditions and requisites lies: requisites, for their part, are immanent to the problem raised; they are "what this problem needs for a solution to be given to it." In this case, the point will be to name what is required from nature if "all that we are aware of in perception" is to be able to be "placed in the same boat," instead of being judged and sorted in the name of "additions" for which the perceiving mind alone is held responsible.

We have already encountered this kind of distinction with regard to "mind." If mind is what is ultimate as soon as the problem of the concept of nature is raised, it is, for Whitehead, the ultimate that corresponds to this problem, and not the ultimate that dominates this problem, with regard to which this problem would be a simple path. Both the requisites and the position of the ultimate thus engage the responsibility of the person who formulates the problem.

In addition, the distinction between condition and requisite is obviously parallel to the distinction between "knowable" nature and the nature which we instinctively think is "worth knowing," but of which we do not by any means demand that it declare how it must be known, or that it be subject to any principle that would guarantee the well-foundedness of a particular branch of knowledge. What is required by our instinctive knowledge, far from leading to a foundation of knowledge, as conditions would do, instead refers each mode of knowledge to its operations, its choices, its ambitions and priorities. Without a beyond. At its own risk.

Of course, the distinction between condition and requisite is relevant only insofar as there are candidates for the function of "condition," that is, a privileged mode of knowledge, judged to be capable of transcending all the others and raising the question of its conditions. Here, we must abandon the customs officer, the policeman, and the noises in my street to confront the physico-mathematical characterization of space and time that appears as such a candidate since Newton and, in Whitehead's time, with Einstein. If a theory of space-time, whichever it may be, Newton's or Einstein's, were to be recognized as rendering explicit the conditions of sense-awareness, these conditions would "found" this theory, which, reciprocally, could boast of transmitting, in a finally purified way, what every experience has to declare.

The classification into discerned and discernible events is not enough to confront this question, for, as we have seen, it designates an event as linked to "all of nature." Other characteristic features of what we are aware of are necessary, which enable us to name other factors in the fact of nature. First of all, the point will be to exhibit what is declared by these events that happen "at the same time," that is, "now."

These are the events which share the immediacy of the immediately present discerned events. These are the events whose characters together with those of the discerned events comprise all nature present for discernment. They form the complete general fact which is all nature now present as disclosed in that sense-awareness. It is in this second classification of events that the differentiation of space from time takes its origin. The germ of space is to be found in the mutual relations of events within the immediate general fact which is all nature now discernible, namely within the one event which is the totality of present nature. The relations of other events to this totality of nature form the texture of time. The unity of this general present fact is expressed by the concept of simultaneity (CN, 52–53).

The differentiation of space and time. The germ of space. The texture of time. Simultaneity. The key terms are here, which do indeed seem to promise a theory of space-time. Yet the point, quite the contrary, will be to exhibit the labor of elaboration necessary for such a theory, that is, the contrast between what this theory puts on stage and the "complete general fact," "nature that is now discernible," which is required if our knowledge is not to be illusory. In particular, the point will be the contrast between the unity of "now present" and the temporal identification supposed by "in the same instant."

It is important to distinguish simultaneity from instantaneousness. I lay no stress on the mere current usage of the two terms. There are two concepts which I want to distinguish, and one I call simultaneity and the other instantaneousness (CN, 56).

The notion of an instant communicates with that of continuous time, that can be decomposed into an infinite succession of instants. Mathematical physics gave this time the status of a condition for its definitions. From Galileo and Newton, the point was to describe the state of a system in a given instant. Since Einstein, the situation has become complicated because the point henceforth has been to avoid characterizing two distant events as occurring "in the same instant," independently of the person characterizing them. There is nothing to criticize about all that, unless this mode of definition is presented as a simple explication, the production of a purified definition, of the "now" proclaimed by experience. For the knowledge elaborated by mathematical physics would then have the privileged status of being directly authorized by experience, even if it means that this knowledge then turns against the experience that authorizes it and declares it to be relative.

There is no such thing as nature at an instant posited by sense-awareness. What sense-awareness delivers over for knowledge is nature through a period. Accordingly nature at an instant, since it is not itself a natural entity, must be defined in terms of genuine natural entities (CN, 57).

What experience declares, what must belong to nature, is not what conditions the definitions of the physico-mathematical sciences. A new name is required, evoking the contrast between the instant, which conditions an exact definition of simultaneity, and what we are aware of in the perception of the nature that is "now" discernible. This name is "duration."

A duration is a concrete slab of nature limited by simultaneity which is an essential factor disclosed in sense-awareness (CN, 53).

We can therefore return to the customs officer. A traveler approaches, his gaze crosses that of the customs officer, a negative, scarcely perceptible nod of the head, the traveler goes away. If nothing interrupts the routine, if no educated or wild guess has made the customs officer decide to do what he knows he can do, direct upon the traveler the attention that will turn him into something more than an anonymous baggage-carrier, this customs officer may have experienced this interaction as similar to a thousand others, the opposite of an event. And it is precisely because nothing has disturbed his routine, because nothing has distracted his attention toward other adventures, that the traveler's passing before his eyes can be said to be limited by simultaneity. If he is later asked to describe this passage in detail, the customs officer could probably break it down, but only by appealing to his knowledge of the fact that the traveler must have approached, slowed down or stopped, and gone away, hastening his pace but not by too much. But the concrete event, the "that of which" there has been awareness, the "now" that it declares, if they can be broken down, have not in fact been broken down: a-traveler-passes. A concrete slice of nature, such that all the components of the customs officer's experience, his aching foot, the low roar of the airport, the movements of travelers in the background, must be said to occur "at the same time," "simultaneous to this duration."

Once the traveler has passed, he has passed, and will not return. Or else, if he returns, for one reason or another, it will be a whole other experience. Duration, as a concrete fact, can be characterized by this statement of the highest generality: it happens and passes.

It is an exhibition of the process of nature that each duration happens and passes. The process of nature can also be termed the passage of nature (CN, 54).

Insofar as it happens and passes, each duration exhibits the passage of nature, but no duration provides a privileged testimony with regard to this passage. Every Whiteheadian passage is qualified insofar as it contains other durations and is contained in other durations. Thus, the duration of the experience of the customs-officer-in-front-of-whom-a-traveler-passes could have been broken down into shorter durations. In fact, it was not, and if it had been, it would no longer be the same, routine, experience but a series of distinct experiences, whose "that of which" would have mutated several times. Yet we know it "instinctively," and this is what is designated by "would have," the fact that there was an experience that was not broken down, a-traveler-passes, qualifies a particular experience, that of the customs-officer. The traveler's passage could, quite obviously, have been broken down by someone else who, for one reason or another, observed the scene: a policeman or a manager of human traffic, on the lookout for unnecessary slowdowns. Even a gesture positively experienced as non-decomposable by the person accomplishing it can be broken down into smaller units, as, for instance, when experts in ergonomics discreetly time a worker's activity. The duration of the customs officer's experience thus discloses other distinct durations, which are part of its meaning.

In contrast, what no duration discloses is the fact that it is made up of durations without thickness, or instants that happen and pass. Every duration has a thickness. The passage to the limit of this thickness toward the instant, which has none, is therefore not the passage from an imperfect, approximate knowledge to an exact knowledge. It is an abstraction that is constructed, and that is constructed only when it *can* be constructed. For this abstraction presupposes the choice of the properties that make this passage to the limit possible. It therefore imposes the active selection of what will be retained, the elimination of what, in what we are aware of, is lost when we take the path of the ever-more-exact.

Exactness is an ideal of thought, and is only realised in experience by the selection of a route of approximation (CN, 59).

The instant responds to an ideal of thought. Whether it is Newton's time, affirming absolute simultaneity, or Einstein's time, which makes it relative to the observer, what physicists take as the starting point of their reasoning, a moving object, or a dynamical system, or an event, each time in an instant, corresponds to a demand for exactness that does not belong to the concept of nature because it does not correspond to any experience. The same holds true for the point, corresponding to the definition of an exact position in space, and Whitehead will show that its construction is very much more complex than that of the instant, since it presupposes the ideal of an instantaneous space.

This is obviously not a matter of denunciation: the ideal of exactness to which the instant and the point respond conditions the specific risks of physics, but the condition must not be confused with what is required by every process of knowledge, including this specialized knowledge.

Whitehead will devote long pages to analyzing the procedure of "extensive abstraction," which enables the characterization of the "paths of approximation" leading from authentic natural entities, "what we have perceptual experience of," to physico-mathematical determinations, spatial and temporal. The definition of instants, of measurable space, of lines, and of the spatio-temporal metric includes its own risks, which are those of axiomatics. It entails defining a starting point such that no stage of the reasoning may be convicted of having given an implicit role to a property that has not yet been demonstrated. Here, we are at the threshold of Whitehead's great work in the philosophy of the natural sciences.

Whitehead was never to abandon this work. Some chapters are still devoted to it in *Process and Reality* (Part IV, "The Theory of Extension"), which take up the work carried out in *The Concept of Nature* (and in *An Enquiry Concerning the Principles of Natural Knowledge*), but with a renewed starting point. For, as he explains,

[. . .] *the "method of extensive abstraction" developed in those works was unable to define a "point" without the intervention of the theory of "duration." Thus what should have been a property of "durations" became the definition of a point. By this mode of approach the extensive relations of actual entities mutually external to each other were pushed into the background; though they are equally fundamental.*

Since that date Professor T. de Laguna has shown that the somewhat more general notion of "extensive connection" can be adopted as the starting-point for the investigation of extension; and that the more limited notion of "whole and part" can be defined in terms of it. In this way, as Professor de Laguna has shown, my difficulty in the definition of a point, without recourse to other considerations, can be overcome (PR, 287).

It is not because Whitehead will soon judge unsatisfactory the method of extensive abstraction set forth in *The Concept of Nature,* a path of approximation based on the part-whole relation, that I have chosen not to venture further in this question. It is simply because this project pertains to what Whitehead himself calls the "philosophy of the natural sciences," which he sometimes, as in *The Concept of Nature,* treats as equivalent to the "philosophy of nature" or "natural philosophy," but which seems to me to be distinct from the construction of the concept of nature as "that of which" we have awareness.

To carry out a separation, as I am in the process of doing, between two components of a work or of a book is always debatable. It might, moreover, give rise to the only objection that would really matter to me: the objection that would produce the "sheer disclosure" of the actual inseparability of the two components, thus modifying the way I understand them. My choice thus conveys a wager that I would be glad to lose: that of a possibility of distinguishing two regimes in Whitehead, of intellectual and affective functioning. When Whitehead prolongs or undertakes the labor of axiomatization that was, if not the first of his passions, at least the one that nourished his main professional work, he worked as a mathematician in a world inhabited by his colleagues, such as Professor Laguna, who were perfectly capable of sharing, evaluating, and questioning his method and his choice. In contrast, the construction of the concept of nature subjects the author (and the reader) to a very different test, for the question does not concern methodology first and foremost. Here, Whitehead may have friends, students, successors, but he no longer has colleagues who share with him a terrain that exists prior to all of them. He is a philosopher.

It is difficult for a philosopher to realise that anyone really is confining his discussion within the limits that I have set before you (CN, 48).

Indeed, the questions that many philosophers would ask a genuine philosophy of nature, if not to solve, then at least to approach, are excluded, for instance, the question of values in nature, that of its historicity, that of its self-constructive activity or its dynamics of emergence. Whitehead does not reject any of these questions, but for him they pertain to what must be called "metaphysics," since they point in a direction where, in one way or another, the mind will no longer be defined as "ultimate" but as that which may eventually and perilously "emerge from nature." This is a different problem, and it implies other concepts.

Duration, which has a thickness and which exhibits the passage of nature, insofar as it happens and passes, and nature, as that which is always passing (always moving on): these are what Whitehead limits himself to. Not without consequences, for it allows him to affirm at the same time that the ideals of exactness conveyed by our measures do not belong to the concept of nature, and that physics can nevertheless find within nature what its specialized operations require.

I definitely refrain at this stage from using the word "time," since the measurable time of science and of civilised life generally merely exhibits some aspects of the more fundamental fact of the passage of nature. I believe that in this doctrine I am in full accord with Bergson, though he uses "time" for the fundamental fact which I call the "passage of nature" (CN, 54).

It is rather seldom that Whitehead explicitly names a philosopher, and when he declares himself to agree with a philosopher, one must always pay "due attention" to this agreement.

In this case, it is fairly obvious that Bergsonian time is metaphysical in Whitehead's sense. This, moreover, is why Bergson fights with, or against, the definition of measurable or "spatialized" time, whereas Whitehead wishes to construct a meaning of it that renders explicit the way in which it is extracted or abstracted from sense-awareness. The difference is important: it does not merely convey what some call Bergsonian "anti-intellectualism," but above all a divergence with regard to the articulation between concepts and the experience that these concepts must be able to think. What is foreign to Bergson, "what is hard for a philosopher to understand," is that Whitehead's concepts respond to what is required by the problem he raised, and that none of them has meaning independently of such a problem (any more than complex numbers have meaning independently of mathematical problems).

"Everything must be in the same boat." Bergson wants the boat to change captains, wants us to recognize that our true experience is an experience in duration. This is why he must oppose busy experience, consisting entirely of projects and discontinuities, to this experience of true duration, a duration that is continuous and indivisible like a melody whose notes may succeed one another, but without it being possible to break it down into a before and an after. Whitehead, for his part, does not privilege any experience, for all of them affirm just as much the passage of nature, from the most unremarkable to the most extended, from the most specialized to the most purified of any practical interest, to "the one most deeply embedded in real duration," as Bergson would say.

Whitehead therefore does not oppose to intellectual knowledge the profound truth of duration, whose experience the Bergsonian texts try to induce in their readers. For him, the experience of a duration is the most widely shared thing in the world, and the most "democratic." What matters is not to confuse "what" we are aware of in perception and "what" we perceive. Whitehead by no means criticizes the fact that we pay to certain relations the attention appropriate for actively interpreting their signification . . . that is, for producing specialized knowledge. As long as we are not mistaken about what belongs to nature and what pertains to human approximation. As long as we keep in mind that it is the definition of measurable time and the notion of an instant that, as translations of an ideal of exactness, are obtained by approximation. The durations that happen and pass are the concrete fact, the "terminus" of sense-awareness (it is what I am aware of), what awareness offers to knowledge, and what knowledge requires.

However, the allusion to Bergson also conveys the risk to which White-head's enterprise is exposed here: to restrict oneself to nature alone, or to what we are aware of in perception. For Bergson would certainly agree that "the immediate data" of awareness itself matter, but he would ask Whitehead how he distinguishes between awareness and "what we are aware of," knowing that as soon as we try to think of awareness, the mind is no longer ultimate, but it is the problem.

Thus not only is the passage of nature an essential character of nature in its rôle of the terminus of sense-awareness, but it is also essential for sense-awareness in itself. It is this truth which makes time appear to extend beyond nature. But what extends beyond nature to mind is not the serial and measurable time, which exhibits merely the character of passage in nature, but the quality of passage itself which is in no way measurable except so far as it obtains in nature [. . .] In passage we reach a connexion of nature with the ultimate metaphysical reality. The quality of passage in durations is a particular exhibition in nature of a quality which extends beyond nature (CN, 55).

The passage of nature thus leads Whitehead to a zone of indecision, in which the meaning of the initial problem—the characterization of "that of which" we have sense-awareness—is indeed at risk. It cannot be denied that the meaning of the "now" belongs to experience itself, not only to its "that of which." Although Whitehead does not think in terms of time but of durations, he has just rediscovered the "big question," where the maximal divergence between philosophers is played out: is time the "number of motion," that is, a relation between motions belonging to the world, or does it not rather refer to the subject who "relates" things? Kant took this step, affirming time to be an internal sense. For Whitehead, this is the most complete example of the bifurcation of nature: time owes its passage to the human mind! As far as Bergson is concerned, he did not refuse duration to things, but he accorded it to them cautiously. Insofar as he opposes the melody in multiple continuities, intertwined and indivisible, that is our awareness, to the practical interest that carries us toward things and leads us to conceive them from the viewpoint of action, the awareness we have of things is always suspect. Of course, the world itself must be understood as "in the making" as our life is, and this is the project of the metaphysics to which he appeals. To do so, however, mind will have to install itself definitively within the mobile reality of this world, become capable of following it in its curves, in short, adopt "the very movement of the inner life of things" (IM, 1422).

For Whitehead, busy knowledge does not betray, but takes its own kind of risks. Nevertheless, for him, too, the question arises on which the very project of constructing a concept of nature outside of metaphysics depends. How can one limit oneself to this problem? How can one celebrate the fact that the passage extends "toward" the mind, without, however, including the mind in the passage of nature, without ending up by confusing nature and thought in the same "fact," which would henceforth be metaphysical?

CHAPTER THREE

The Foothold of the Mind

W E MUST LIMIT OURSELVES to the problem that has been raised, and trust our problem: such is the ethics of a mathematician. The passage of nature is exhibited by what we are aware of, and is required by our instinctive attitude. The problem to be solved does not concern the "mind," but the theories that make nature bifurcate and disqualify this instinctive attitude, and the concepts that will constitute its solution are not neutral, but they respond to the problem, conveying the imperative from which the problem proceeds. It is necessary and sufficient to characterize "that of which" we have awareness in the mode required by our instinctive attitude. We must confirm the "trust" that is actually presupposed by any demanding investigation, any specialized knowledge, even those that claim to disqualify this "trust." And all this without exaggerating the risk: critical consciousness admits so many things without criticizing them! Whether this is a pipe or this is not a pipe, the adopted stance ignores with the greatest of ease the abysses of presupposition that logicians discover with terror when they try to "clarify" it. "Animal faith" in a presence of things, emotion, and trust can be hunted down by radical doubt, examination, or tests of legitimacy. In fact, the logical process that intends to hunt them down still testifies, by its self-assurance, to this faith, like the movement of a cat chasing its own tail testifies to the unity of a body from which its pursuit makes abstraction. For if what words appeal to really does turn out not to answer, if the miserable cat, driven mad by the sufferings we are liable to inflict upon him, chews on his tail in his cage, this is no longer a game, whether logical or feline, nor is it a laughing matter.

Commitment to an experimentation capable of freeing the question of nature from its habitual formulations associated with our specialized branches of knowledge, and of succeeding in creating a plan able to welcome, without privilege or hierarchy, the plurality of what we are aware of, presupposes a trust that needs neither guarantee nor foundation. On the contrary, it conveys the difference between two modes of "trusting": the implicit one presupposed by our certainties and habits, and the riskier one, which exposes the thinker to adventure.

Unlike habit, which is carried out in a determinate world, trust is paradoxically exercised in a world of indeterminacy, what James calls the "plastic zone, the transmission belt of the uncertain, the meeting point of the past and the future." It is indeterminacy that makes us need trust, but it is also because we have trust that we take the risk of the indeterminate [. . .] *The feeling of trust makes experience a field of experimentation. It is therefore the condition for every form of creation* (WJEP, 87).

Bergson is cited only once in *The Concept of Nature,* but William James is never cited, although terms appear unexpectedly, without commentary, which point out that Whitehead is thinking "with James." *Terminus* is one of these terms, *stream* is another. But the term that will emerge in this moment of delicate negotiation imposed by the passage of nature, between the concept of nature and the metaphysical question, this moment when it comes to escaping the temptation, designated by Bergsonian thought, of a psychology leading to metaphysics, in order to take the risk of the indeterminate, is *specious present.*

A duration retains within itself the passage of nature. There are within it antecedents and consequents which are also durations which may be the complete specious presents of quicker consciousnesses (CN, 56).

William James's specious present designates the extension of the duration that we experience as "present." Here, extension does not designate an external, clocked measure, but a concrete range, thick with the number of events it includes in a way that is divisible but undivided.

[. . .] *The practically cognized present is no knife-edge, but a saddleback, with a certain breadth of its own on which we sit perched, and from which we look in two directions into time. The unit of composition of our perception of time is a duration, with a bow and a stern, as it were—a rearward—and a forward-looking end. It is only as parts of this durationblock that the relation of succession of one end to the other is perceived. We do not first feel one end and then feel the other after it, and from the perception of the succession infer an interval of time between, but we seem to feel the interval of time as a whole, with its two ends embedded in it* (PP, I, 609–610).

Specious present is often translated into French as "présent apparent," which indicates how much the notion of appearance is a powerful attractor, dangerous in this case since it induces a stereotyped confrontation between two possibilities. Either the experience of the present is judged to be purely relative to consciousness, and hence a deceptive appearance which it is the psychologist's task to describe in the well-known mode of *"you think that* x ... *but experimental psychology shows that* y ... *"* or else consciousness *qua* what bestows the present confers upon appearance the status of ultimate reality. For whoever tries to "think with Whitehead," both possibilities are equally catastrophic, since the first one makes nature bifurcate, and the second one eliminates nature in favor of "what appears." It is therefore important to recall that specious, like "spécieux" in French, first signified "of beautiful appearance," about which there is nothing negative in and of itself. The suspicion that "this beautiful appearance" is only apparent, intended only to deceive, took hold of the term at the beginning of the eighteenth century. Such an etymological itinerary, which brings about the triumph of suspicion, discloses the worry that may be inspired by what, for William James, was of the order of radical indeterminacy.

What, for instance, does it mean to be "captivated" by the beauty of an image? If we are moved, is it the situation that is moving, or our emotion that makes it so? And if we say that an idea is "suggestive," does this come from it, or from the way we have appropriated it? William James made this hesitation the very thing that experience forces us to think. Of course, the responsibility for such experiences can be attributed either to the world or to the subject, but this will always be an attribution after the fact, when we ask ourselves, after the fact, the question of what happened. The specious present, that block of duration upon which experience is "perched" and which testifies to a quality of the passage that extends "beyond nature to mind," could be the subject of the same radical hesitation, whereas we can, of course, learn more about it by paying it due attention.

William James introduced the "specious present" in the context of a "psychological" analysis, but he took care not to relate this present to consciousness as its producer. In fact, it is rather consciousness that will be qualified, related, shown to be dependent on what one might call "cerebrality." The specious present cannot be defined directly, in the sense that one would "become aware of" it, but it may be subject to variation, both ethological and pharmacological: the variety of animal species or the variety of human experiences, as they can be modified, for instance, by taking drugs.

In hashish-intoxication there is a curious increase in the apparent time-perspective. We utter a sentence, and ere the end is reached the beginning seems already to date from indefinitely long ago. We enter a short street, and it is as if we should never get to the end of it (PP, I, 639–640).

William James interprets this kind of disturbing sensation on the basis of a twofold hypothesis. On the one hand, hashish intoxication gives rise to a finer discrimination of events, that is, augments the quantity of events of which we have experience *qua* liable to be distinguished. On the other hand, whether intoxicated or not, we (human beings) preserve the same subjective sensation of time, with the specious present always including in an undivided way about as many successive events that are liable to be distinguished. Everything thus seems to be normal, except that the "range" of the present is more reduced, which entails, for one and "the same" episode (coming to the end of a sentence, crossing a street), an increase in the number of successive "presents." This is why the hashish-smoker must often deliberately remember the beginning of the phrase begun: not only is this beginning not included in the present, but it is "very far away," separated from the present by a completely incongruous number of shifts from the present to the past.

It is important to emphasize that, according to James, the experience of hashish intoxication is not abnormal but strange, a vector of strangeness, because it includes a contrast. The modification of the specious present is only perceptible, or knowable, when the intoxicated experience is accompanied by the contrast with similar habitual experience: *But this is a short street! But I usually know without effort how I began a sentence!*

From this viewpoint, there is a big difference between the characterization of the specious present and the study of optical illusions, which also pertains to experimental psychology. In the case of optical illusions, what is studied is "what" the subject perceives, the interpretative part of perception, and psychologists have the means to judge and know that, whatever their subject may say, the parallel lines are "really" parallel, and the line segments are "really" of equal length: this is why they can speak of an illusion. In the case of the specious present, we have to do not with knowing interpretation, but rather with what experience offers to knowledge, and the reference to "really" cannot work: no one can objectively measure what I testify to when I say, *"This street seems to have no end!"*

Thus, if "specious" means "of deceptive appearance," those who are deceived are those who have gone so far as to define experience in terms of a succession of instants without thickness. And it is indeed in this sense that the specious present can be involved in Whitehead's problem, enabling him to negotiate the connection between nature and "ultimate metaphysical reality" without, however, slipping into metaphysics. The specious present, which happens and passes, which can be subjected to variation by drugs and can be the subject of speculations with regard to the animal variety of experiences, does not designate the perceiving mind *qua* creator or responsible for experience. It designates what experience delivers to perception, whether animal or human. It can only be defined if we pay due attention to variety, and it therefore pertains to the concept of nature, that is, to what must be restored to nature if it is not to bifurcate.

Such a restitution is not, however, without consequences, for it introduces William James's indeterminacy into the heart of what we are aware of as "passage." *"There is a passage,"* but this passage henceforth includes the passage of awareness, what we are aware of as "passage of the present": it has passed.

Are we really so far from Bergson? No longer quite that far, for the "indeterminacy" of what we are aware of as passage coincides, if not with the vocation of Bergson's text, at least with the means this text sets in motion in order to transform its reader. It has often been noted how hard it is to "summarize" Bergson, to present his theses, and to discuss his positions. One may be tempted to abstract from the highly meticulous, critical description his text offers of the ways in which our languages define the self, the will, freedom, in order to go straight to his conclusions, to what he "wanted to demonstrate," for instance, his definition of intuition, memory, or duration. And one realizes that the definitions in question are then so many betrayals. Bergsonian concepts are not made to enter into a relation of force with others, which they oppose. They are inseparable from a practice of writing and from the practice of reading to which writing appeals. If Bergson's meticulous descriptions cannot be eliminated, it is because they produce what they describe. The Bergsonian text first functions as an operator for inducing variation, a modification of experience, and the truth of the duration to which he refers is "specious," for it captivates his reader.

Bergsonian inner life may well refer to music, to the melodic quality of the descriptions that succeed one another in a mode that is deliberately resistant to division, but the experience inspired by Bergson's text, for its part, makes one think of William James's hashish intoxication: the creation of contrasts that induce indeterminacy. Bergson fashions a "trance reading," and asks the reader what all hypnotizers ask their subject: to agree to slow down, to let oneself be penetrated by the words, to release the grip that makes us think we know what they mean. Bergson names and describes duration, but his text induces the experience of it, induces the trust that transforms experience into experimentation on duration.

And it is precisely at this point that he coincides with Whitehead, for the concept of nature also depends on a "literary" apparatus liable to induce a perception of what we are aware of in the mode that this concept has the task of exhibiting.

The purpose of a discussion of such factors may be described as being to make obvious things look odd. We cannot envisage them unless we manage to invest them with some of the freshness which is due to strangeness (CN, 107–108).

One of the ways of conferring a bizarre appearance upon any kind of experience, without recourse to the particular experience provided by hashish, listening to music, hypnotic induction, or the philosopher's meticulous description, is to call attention to the "constant factors," those we neglect because they inevitably belong to all experience, but which no experience exhibits in particular. The point is thus to create a contrast between what I say I perceive and what is always exhibited by what I am aware of.

It is because of this habit of letting constant factors slip from consciousness that we constantly fall into the error of thinking of the sense-awareness of a particular factor in nature as being a two-termed relation between the mind and the factor. For example, I perceive a green leaf. Language in this statement suppresses all reference to any factors other than the percipient mind and the green leaf and the relation of sense-awareness. It discards the obvious inevitable factors which are essential elements in the perception. I am here, the leaf is there; and the event here and the event which is the life of the leaf there are both embedded in a totality of nature which is now, and within this totality there are other discriminated factors which it is irrelevant to mention (CN, 108).

Not only does experience include the "now" as a constant factor, but also the "here." And this "here" raises the same problem as the "now": it is an aspect of experience that questions the difference between nature and mind, and therefore includes the threat of making the philosophy of nature slide into metaphysics.

Here we are touching on that character of the passage of nature which issues in the spatial relations of simultaneous bodies [. . .] Passage in this aspect of it also seems to extend beyond nature to mind (CN, 56).

Like the specious present, the "here" must therefore be plunged into indeterminacy. To do this, it is no longer the idealization of instantaneousness that must be surmounted, but that of reversibility. When we think of "here" and "there," we may be tempted to affirm the interchangeability of the terms: I am here and you are there, but the relation is reversible, and you might just as well be here, and I might be there; to define "here," moreover, any kind of body would do just as well instead of me. What then counts are spatial relations, measured by distances.

Once again, the point is not to denounce or to deny that the notion of distance may derive from what we are aware of, and be made explicit as "what" we perceive. The point is to attribute to nature not what we perceive, but what we are aware of in perception. The apparent simplicity of a space in which "simultaneous" bodies would be located, including the one that perceives, conveys the specious character of what we are aware of. It is not those who have relied on their instinctive knowledge who have been deceived, but those who have sought to pass from the contrast between "here" and "there" to a more precise definition. This contrast must not be stated in terms of space or in terms of distance.

Against the abstract ideal of a reversibility guaranteeing that what is "here" could have been "there," we can appeal to a cat, when he has not been driven mad by our mistreatment, but offers himself to us as a marvel of perceptive experience. A cat on the hunt, making perceptible the vibration of what is not a distance but the release that will cross an interval, or else a contemplative cat, never situated just anywhere in a room, always in a location around which the room seems to be arranged. Experience, for Whitehead, is always situated and always includes a *locus standi*, or a perspective, or viewpoint. And he is bold enough to call this point of view "event here," included in what we are aware of.

This locus standi *in nature is what is represented in thought by the concept of "here" namely of an "event here." This is the concept of a definite factor in nature. This factor is an event in nature which is the focus in nature for that act of awareness, and the other events are perceived as referred to it. This event is part of the associated duration. I call it the "percipient event." This event is not the mind, that is to say, not the percipient. It is that in nature from which the mind perceives* (CN, 107).

That this *locus standi,* perspective, or "focus for that act of awareness," is an event in nature, a factor belonging to what we are aware of, not a condition for awareness or a subjective principle of all possible awareness, is vital for Whitehead's construction. If, in one way or another, the perspective had been that of the percipient mind rather than "for" the percipient mind, the door would have been left open for the bifurcation of nature. "How" one perceives would have referred to the mind, which would then be a command post, constructing according to its categories "that of which" it has experience in perception. The fact that this perspective must be understood as an "event," in contrast, implies that the neutral and impersonal statement "there is a passage" will constitute an ultimate generality belonging to the concept of nature, which thus includes the percipient event as a factor of experience offered to knowledge.

Like all events, the percipient event happens and leaves, and when it is gone, it is gone. It is relative, of course, since every event declares itself to be related to other events, a part of some and made up of others. But it is not relative to anything, and especially not to a subject. And it refers the delights of introspection—by which the subject declares itself to be able to explore its own perceptions, place them in doubt, explore their meaning, go back to their eventual principle—to indeterminacy, that is, to the passage of nature, which the transformation of points of view is the first to testify to. You think you are free to explore your experience, like one explores a given landscape, to vary points of view and meanings, to render implicit meanings explicit. But you are not the author of this variation. The passage is neutral, and the standpoint does not belong to you unless it is in your quality as occupant, but it is what occupies you, much more than you occupy it. The variation of standpoints is not what you decide but what happens, and you interpret it in one way or another, and, for instance, in the way that puts you in charge. The event that provides you with a point of view belongs to the great impersonal web of events. Your standpoint testifies to the whole of nature, is connected to the whole of nature, even if it takes on the particular meaning that is required by the interpretation of perception as yours. This interpretation may be specious, but that does not make it illusory. But what we "know instinctively" is not that our consciousness possesses a point of view, but rather that the "here" of this viewpoint is ours.

Our "percipient event" is that event included in our observational present which we distinguish as being in some peculiar way our standpoint for perception. It is roughly speaking that event which is our bodily life within the present duration [. . .] The distant situation of a perceived object is merely known to us as signified by our bodily state, i.e., by our percipient event [. . .] In the course of evolution those animals have survived whose sense-awareness is concentrated on those significations of their bodily states which are on the average important for their welfare. The whole world of events is signified, but there are some which exact the death penalty for inattention (CN, 187–188).

Like the specious present, the declared signification of the percipient event offered to knowledge does not have to be explained, since it is of the order of the fact. The fact is that, most often, what sense experience delivers to knowledge allows itself to be interpreted in a way that lets me dissociate the permanence of my body, "here," from a world in which things happen, "there." The point is to pay attention to these things, the kind of attention they are due, on pain of death. But the "death penalty," through which the question of biological evolution now emerges, does not explain the "here" of perception, any more than the tests to which scientists submit their statements explain what these statements say. Just as resistance to such tests is what is required for a scientific statement to survive, attention to certain events "there" is required on pain of death, but the relation between the "here" of attention and the body does not have the status of a general fact. We can therefore, without fear of denying "what we know instinctively," take into account experiences that subject our routines to adventure.

Thus, those who testify to the well-known out-of-body experiences testify that the "here" of the percipient event is not always defined by a coincidence between standpoint and the body, since, in this experience, this body is suddenly signified as distant. The distinction then imposes itself between the permanence of the body and what Whitehead calls "roughly speaking" bodily life. These unusual experiences are associated not with the mind's decisions but with the adventure of this bodily life, since they occur at the onset of death, or on the occasion of taking drugs, or else thanks to the cultivation of that bodily life implied by spiritual techniques. All are situations in which "survival" and its pragmatic urgencies do not play a dominant role.

Biological evolution would thus only explain a habitual correlation, also attested by the plausibility of the (metaphysical) temptation to which we yield when we affirm that our mind perceives "on the basis of our body," or that this body, as it is localized by biology, would be its "seat," its "prison," or its "production site." Likewise, biological evolution would explain not the specious present as such but perhaps the type of conservation that James hypothesizes, which could well extend to all animal experiences (including human). The fact that flies seem to experience the motion of my hand, fast as it is, as a slow arrival that allows them plenty of time to fly away cannot be assimilated to the experience of an intoxicated person since the fly has actually had the time to fly away. Is the fly aware? Does it have a percipient experience in the present? In any case, whatever may be the way in which the approach of my hand affects it, its experience probably integrates, as does our "specious present," a correlation with events that exact a death penalty if its reactions are too slow.

Whitehead has thus succeeded in avoiding a twofold danger: he has taken away from the mind its responsibility for the "here" and the "now" of all experience without referring this explanation to biology, that is, without subjecting the concrete fact of passage to specialized knowledge. What seems to extend from nature to the mind has been referred to the register that no one can claim to appropriate: the event.

The complete foothold of the mind in nature is represented by the pair of events, namely, the present duration which marks the "when" of aware-

ness and the percipient event which marks the "where" of awareness and the "how" of awareness (CN, 107).

Here, "foothold" does not designate the act of taking hold but what the mind, or knowledge, requires from nature, what it needs to be offered by nature if its operations are not to be illusory, if the trust that leads us to speak of a knowledge about nature is to be confirmed. And insofar as what nature "offers" articulates a pair of events as "constant" factors, the mind's foothold in nature does not found any judgment that goes beyond the concrete fact: "there has been a foothold." Hence the image of the mountain-climber evoked by the term Whitehead chooses: "foothold." The mountain-eer's climb depends, and counts, on a ledge found by her hand or foot. If the vertical wall were completely smooth, there would be no mountain-climber: the mountain-climber's mode of existence requires that of the ledge that offers her a foothold. It is not the job of the mountain-climber, who takes advantage of the foothold to exist *qua* mountain-climber, to justify that foothold's existence. Nor, moreover, is it up to her to turn this existence into that which, in one way or another, could justify the mountain. The "nature that offers a foothold to the mind" indeed designates the percipient mind as ultimate, for its concept is relative to the mind's mode of taking hold. A perfectly smooth wall, giving the mountain-climber no foothold, poses no problem for a fly, and could be ascended (but not climbed) by someone who obtains an adequate system of suction disks. The possibility of a foothold is the requirement immanent to the problem to which the term "mountain-climber" constitutes a set of risky solutions. Likewise, the present event and the percipient event are the "footholds" required by the problem of "due attention," a problem designated by the term "awareness," and to which all perceptual specialization, whether it refers to biological evolution or to practical life, brings a risky solution.

What I now want to discuss is the special relation of the percipient event which is "here" to the duration which is "now" [. . .] Within the short present duration the "here" of the percipient event has a definite meaning of some sort. This meaning of "here" is the content of the special relation of the percipient event to its associated duration. I will call this relation "cogredience" (CN, 108).

What I want to bring out is that the preservation of a peculiar relation to a duration is a necessary condition for the function of that duration as a present duration for sense-awareness (CN, 109).

The present snaps into a past and a present when the "here" of cogredience loses its single determinate meaning. There has been a passage of nature from the "here" of perception within the past duration to the different "here" of perception within the present duration (CN, 108–109).

For Whitehead, then, the preservation of cogredience has the status of a "condition," and this condition designates a duration, "a concrete slab of nature limited by simultaneity" (CN, 53). Conditions and limits can play a role in this case because they do not deal with experience but with the way knowledge can appeal to experience, not, this time, with regard to the "here" and the "now" but to the simultaneity "I and my world at the same time," to the "here and now" that designates the present.

Once again, the point is to resist the theories that presuppose that we can base ourselves on what we perceive. In this case, what Whitehead has in view is the specious character of the "here and now" that proposes itself as a stable, reliable starting point from which it seems possible to interrogate all possible experience. To make the preservation of cogredience a condition evokes what the specious character of experience may make us forget: the "here and now" is not that which, belonging to all possible experience, also enables us to "think of experience." It creates neither right nor access, because it is itself conditioned by "it holds together." What counts in the "here and now" is the "and," and this "and" conveys a fact: the preservation of a relation of which we can only observe, once it has "passed," that it has ceased to hold true. And it certainly ceases to hold true as soon as the mind seizes hold of experience to call it as a witness.

The duration may comprise change within itself, but cannot—so far as it is one present duration—comprise change in the quality of its peculiar relation to the contained percipient event. In other words, perception is always "here," and a duration can only be posited as present for sense-awareness on condition that it affords one unbroken meaning of "here" in its relation to the percipient event. It is only in the past that you can have been "there" with a standpoint distinct from your present "here" (CN, 110).

Whereas the usual "here and now" treats space and time symmetrically, the "and" of the relation of cogredience breaks this symmetry. The thickness of the present, that indivisible compound of multiple durations that constitutes "nature now," has as its condition and limit the duration of the percipient event that it includes. The experience of the passage, the shift of the present into the past, is primordially the passage of the percipient event, the passage of the "here," but also, and perhaps above all, of the "how." For the percipient event not only marks the "where" of experience but also its "how," and whereas the "here" can refer in a somewhat specious way to the body's permanence, the "how" raises the question of the "bodily life inside present duration" constituted by this percipient event. A sudden noise attracts my attention: it is the "how" of the experience that has changed when an event "there" is suddenly discerned. The cat's ears stand up. It is utterly approximate to say "I am where I am while time passes," but the specious character of the approximation is interesting. It designates an "I" that is first and foremost "bodily life," a set of multiple correlations unified by the series of "here-how" that pass in such a way that "the standpoint is always here."

Events there and events here are facts of nature [. . .] *cogredience has nothing to do with any biological character of the* [percipient] *event which is related by it to the associated duration* (CN, 110).

The relation of cogredience belongs to what is required. It is crucial that it cannot be explained by specialized knowledge such as biology, for it is what is required by all our explanations, whether biological or other. One will therefore certainly not say that it is "subject" to bodily life, but perhaps one can say that it is what makes bodily life crucial for perception. Every living being the biologist can compare with other living beings would thus constitute a specialized response to the questions organized around the preservation of the relation of cogredience, an answer that presupposes this relation itself as a fact belonging to the concept of nature. It is *qua* stratified, stabilized answer, proper to a living species, that the sense organs in particular should be described, and that we should characterize the way these organs discern, sift, and capture what, for them, "makes an event," that is, breaks the relation of cogredience.

All the descriptions produced by neurophysiology, all the experiments of experimental psychology aiming to measure the extent of the "specious present," all the comparisons between living beings of different species, all the body's adventures, whether intoxicated or spiritualized, then begin to sing in harmony with the positive definition that Whitehead has given of nature: we know that if we pay it due attention, we will find more in it than what we observe at first glance. The sense organs testify to the importance of paying due attention to nature, on pain of death. Each one proceeds from a wager on what is due. And the body is therefore not what explains but what testifies.

Attention itself would thus be that aspect of bodily life that testifies to a risky solution, to the choice of the events capable of "attracting attention," or breaking the relation of cogredience. For survival depends on the relevance of what this choice offers to knowledge, and especially on the irrelevance of all that is signified without thereby making the present slip into the past. The cat lying in wait for its prey, immobile and vibrant, is probably living through an experience such that what for her prey has the quality of an undivided "here and now" is for her a succession of presents that happen and pass. Attention explains nothing: the testimony concerns the solution by which the problem exhibits itself but does not explain the problem.

William James's "specious present" belonged to psychology, because James was trying to characterize it. But the relation of cogredience, in its factuality, refers instead to what James, in his *Essays on Radical Empiricism*, calls "pure experience."

The instant field of the present is always experienced in its "pure" state, a plain unqualified actuality, a simple "that," as yet undifferentiated into thing and thought, and only virtually classifiable as objective fact or as some one's opinion about fact [...] *Only in the later experience that supersedes the present one is this "naïf" immediacy retrospectively split into two parts, a "consciousness" and its "content" and the content corrected or confirmed. While still pure, or present, any experience—mine, for example, of what I write about in these very lines—passes for "truth"* (WPE, 74–75).

James's pure experience is "true," but unlike Descartes' "I am thinking," its truth does not authorize anything. It is up to the experience that follows and supersedes it to give this truth its consequences, perhaps to judge it, always to restore it in a different way, according to the different "hows" associated with a different standpoint. What William James proposes is nothing other, and nothing less, than to betray every "and therefore" that would undertake to transcend the facts: it is in this way, and in no other, that this present has appropriated this past. Pure experience is "plain," that is, mute with regard to what it will signify retroactively. The experience that slips into the past may well be appropriated by an experience dominated by reflexivity: "I" have this experience. But that means that the experience has changed. The new "reflexive" experience is a "reflection on" the one that has slipped into the past, in the sense of a resumption rather than of an outcome or an elucidation. James thus proposes a version of experience, including the experience dominated by the "I" of reflection, which exhibits that this "I" always comes later, included in a new experience. And the experience of the "I" appropriating the past, making this past "its" experience, is again plain, mute with regard to the consequences that will be produced concerning it. The continuity of the "I" is one construction among others, which only holds as long as the resumption in the mode of reflexive appropriation is continued.

William James's pure experience functions as a proposition that readers must accept to inhabit, that they must take the time to inhabit. And Whitehead certainly took the time to inhabit it, for his characterization of the percipient event operates in the same way as that of pure experience: it induces an experience in which the event is always "this" event, which happens and passes. Nevertheless, we should recall that for Whitehead the "mind," bracketed in *The Concept of Nature*, must stay that way: experience itself is not in question, and the percipient event is not experience, only that factor of experience that testifies to the "passage" that is the ultimate concrete fact.

Already at this point, however, Whitehead and James agree at least on one thing: all the reasons we can give with regard to the passage, with regard to experience insofar as it passes, come later. My attention was distracted by that birdsong; I suddenly thought of the chicken in the oven; in spite of your glance, I did end my phrase, to be sure, but without believing in it any more, and so on. We attribute responsibilities to elements of experience that we can name, we construct reasons, and these reasons are not false. They are simply abstracted from what (specious) experience offers to consciousness, and are presented in a manner that translates the way it has seized hold of them: in this case, by inverting them, by confusing the interpretation that has come afterward with the reason why the present has slipped into the past and has become a past signified by the present. This must not be denounced, for it is one way of paying due attention to certain factors of our experience.

Even today, many readers of Whitehead encounter this difficulty: he seems to deny "self-consciousness," or the possibility of an immediate relation such that we can feel and feel ourselves feel at the same time. Likewise, he seems to deny the possibility of saying, "I see my child there, smiling at me," two beings in direct contact. Yet, the person who mobilizes this example will protest, it is indeed at me that my child is smiling, I feel it at the same time that I see her, that her smile is directed at me, and this smile testifies to a genuine contact between us and therefore testifies for me, for the ultimate truth of my awareness of being me. Any way of complicating the description of this situation would be a form of cheating with regard to the truth of this experience.

We must take this protest seriously, because there can be no question, there can never be any question, either for James or for Whitehead, of transforming experience that is indeterminate with regard to the way it will eventually be appropriated into an instrument of judgment or disqualification of an experience. What the statement "I see my child there, smiling at me" intends is an experience. Yet a slight variation may make us feel that it is neither the same experience as "my-child-is-smiling-at-me" nor its truth. Let us imagine that this smile is fixed, that the child's gaze is suddenly turned away, or that she suddenly winces. The "I" that was mobilized to turn the smiling child into a privileged case of "interpersonal" relations (for instance) will then have little chance of appearing, or coming to reinforce the initial experience, giving it an interpretation that transforms it into an argument or an objection. What happens does not place the veracity of the experience "my-child-is-smiling-at-me" in doubt, but the capacity of this experience to play the role of a foundation, which the argument had assigned to it. What happens "passes for truth," but the content of this truth does not belong to it.

To attribute to William James the inauguration of a new period in philosophy would make us neglect other contemporary influences. In any case, however, it is still relevant to compare his essay, Does Consciousness Exist?, *published in 1904, with* The Discourse on Method, *published in 1637. James clears the scene of the accessories of the past: more precisely, he gives the scene a completely new illumination* (SMW, 143).

It remains, of course, to explore this renewed scene, to construct what it obliges us to, and Whitehead will do so later when he will ask not William James but the problem created by James how to construct the concepts imposed by a succession of experiences, each one of which takes the preceding one for an ingredient while conferring a meaning upon it. In no case, however, will the point be to transcend the scene illuminated by James toward a higher truth. When Whitehead became a metaphysician, conscious experience became a creature of passage, which itself has become creativity.

CHAPTER FOUR

There It Is Again

AVE WE SUCCEEDED in escaping the bifurcation of nature? One might think so, and take the experience induced by Whitehead's proposition as a sign of this success.

The experience of passage, always composite, ceaselessly decomposed, in an infinite spectrum of modalities, exhibiting other characters according to other standpoints on each occasion. Even a mystic in prayer, whose experience should exhibit the most focalized continuity, is, it is said, unable to recite a *Pater* to the end without experiencing a non-negligible number of incongruous, parasitical thoughts.

The experience of letting go, of suspending the automatic interpretation that makes me attribute either to an external cause or to a reason of mine the fact that an experience has passed, that it has *de facto* slipped into the past of a new experience. The passage is neutral, and the slippage of the present into the past always comes first, ready to be mobilized in terms of a cause or a reason.

The experience of placing all continuity in a series, with no term in the series having the power to explain this continuity to which it belongs, even if each one can "explain itself," that is, interpret what it proceeds from as explaining what it is.

An experience with no fixed authority, essentially pathic. It happens, offering, if need be, to the activity of knowledge what it requires to explain that it happens, the specific character that discerns the event perceived "now." Yet this now must already be said in the past tense, for its mobilization for purposes of explanation conveys a change in standpoint. Interpretation prolongs the series.

An experience that may have become disconcerting, no doubt, but not opaque, for it does not act as a screen for anything. It has probably become indeterminate, but it does not lack anything except, of course, for what is demanded by its mobilization in an argument in which it is to act as proof or foundation.

In the letting go to which nature incites us, in its pure, shimmering mobility, how could one fail to experience the sign that we are indeed upstream of the bifurcation that presented nature to us as colorless, odorless, and mute?

You cannot recognise an event; because when it is gone, it is gone (CN, 169).

A brutal stoppage. Pure, shimmering mobility is not enough. The possible seduction of letting go which I have just deliberately tried to induce, sought to render perceptible, for whomever has experienced it and has been tempted to adhere to it, the ease with which we adhere to what judges us. A strange hostility, so often attested, if only by the history of philosophy, toward everything that can be suspected of instrumentalizing the truth, of staining what is pure by interests that are thought to sully it. Including the vile interest of survival, something that is hard to conceive in the pure mobility evoked by the passage of nature.

Whitehead's project by no means includes condemning our multiple interests or judging our busy, mobilized, greedy consciousnesses in the name of the nonmobilizable character of what they nevertheless never cease to mobilize. He does not have the project of making us forget the meanings we never cease affirming with regard to nature, in terms of which we stratify it, but of constructing what they require, what is required by the "trust" they presuppose and declare.

Whitehead demands that the redness of the sunset find its respondent in nature, but so must the sun as described by the astronomers and astrophysicists. His concept of nature is not constructed in order to condemn the possibility of identification, for this is indeed a part of experience. Of course, to name the event, duration, the now, he has recourse to the evocative power of language, to the induction of an experience capable of turning us away from the strange idea that words have the power to define what they designate. Yet to call this power into question does not justify limiting oneself to the celebration of a nature that is always different, from which words distance us further. Such a celebration, to which the poetic exaltation of the event seems at first to invite us, an event that is never the same, new and ineffable each time, may satisfy Romantic thinkers, or those who assign the first priority to defending Being against their busy inspection; but for mathematicians, whose problem is preventing nature from bifurcating, it would be a sign of defeat. For the mind would find itself at the command post, even if this command is mendacious. It would be responsible for the fact that we recognize "the same," whereas one event is essentially distinct from every other event. It would be responsible for any stability that stratifies the pure mobility of nature, the one that—arbitrarily, because nature does not offer it any respondent—carves, fashions, distinguishes, categorizes, compares, and recognizes.

I use recognition for the non-intellectual relation of sense-awareness which connects the mind with a factor of nature without passage [. . .] *I am quite willing to believe* [. . .] *that there is in fact no recognition without intellectual accompaniments of comparison and judgment. But recognition is that relation of the mind to nature which provides the material for the intellectual activity* (CN, 142).

Things which we thus recognise I call objects (CN, 169).

Objects are the elements in nature which can "be again" (CN, 144).

"*Say, there it is again.*" Cleopatra's Needle, for instance, which rises in downtown London. What we are aware of in the perception of the Needle, *a fortiori* because we can designate it by a name, certainly implies those intellectual faculties known as memory and judgment. No matter what those terms refer to, moreover, knowledge is ultimate, that which the concept of nature must refrain from explaining. But if nature is not to bifurcate, with the mind then being held responsible for everything that "is again," for everything that acts as a landmark, it must offer a foothold for memory and judgment. The concept of nature must include what is required by the experience of "recognizing Cleopatra's Needle." "Object" is the name Whitehead gives to this requisite, which is presupposed by knowledge but does not explain it.

The object is a requisite immanent to Whitehead's problem of avoiding the bifurcation of nature, and therefore has nothing to do with a condition guaranteeing the objectivity of knowledge. It is required by comparison, judgment, definition, but it cannot give anyone the power to establish a hierarchy, a foundation, or a discrimination, and it also takes away the power to interpret these operations on the basis of a psychological type of analysis. The Whiteheadian object is neither judge of our productions nor the product of our judgments. It thus calls for evocative statements, inducing the experience of the contrast between the required object and any objective definition of what is perceived. This time, however, the contrast involves the multiplicity of definitions, that is, the diversity of abstractions exhibited by all definitions.

Day by day and hour by hour we can find a certain chunk in the transitory life of nature and of that chunk we say, "There is Cleopatra's

Needle." If we define the Needle in a sufficiently abstract manner we can say that it never changes. But a physicist who looks on that part of the life of nature as a dance of electrons, will tell you that daily it has lost some molecules and gained others, and even the plain man can see that it gets dirtier and is occasionally washed [. . .] *The more abstract your definition, the more permanent the Needle* (CN, 166–167).

For the passerby, the Needle is always there, every morning. For the person in charge of London monuments, it is also always there but needs many more words to be characterized, because the point is to ensure its good conservation and decide when it should next be cleaned. Yet the Needle does not pass, nor do any cracks it may have, nor the soot whose accumulation is evaluated by the official in charge, any more than do the electrons or molecules of which the physicist knows that the Needle consists. As far as the event itself is concerned, or the most concrete fact that could be attested, for instance, by an artist who affirms that the Needle is never the same—that the experience of it is different at each hour of the day and in every season, escaping words, a pure sensation, constantly renewed, light, the great noise of the city, the intensive depth of space—it does not allow the denunciation of the abstraction of the reference to that which does not pass. This abstraction is presupposed by the testimony, for the artist knows that she is bearing witness as an artist, in contrast to her own daily experience: it happens to her, too, when she is passing by, to "recognize the Needle."

Between the most concrete experience and the various abstractions, there is no hierarchy for Whitehead. The artist's perception is not more authentic, it is different; and, what is more, it testifies to a trained eye. Nor is there anything painfully paradoxical about the very fact that, when testifying that "it" is never the same, she must say "it," implying the stability that she nevertheless denies. The artist's testimony concerns the experience of a contrast but does not provide weapons to a contradiction.

Similarly, it is quite possible that the description of certain modes of experience deriving from spiritual techniques may evoke the "pure" passage of nature, and that the way these techniques present themselves may evoke their own success in terms of purification, or access to a truth which, in one way or another, transcends the experience of "recognizing." Yet these very techniques, it should be noted, presuppose the deliberately cultivated and labored abandonment of what they transcend. "Purification," as a demanding technical practice, does not give us the power to denounce the parasites of daily experience. Rather, it incites us to think about the way we experience the event, the multiplicity of these ways and their possible variation.

In fact the character of an event is nothing but the objects which are ingredient in it and the ways in which those objects make their ingression into the event. Thus the theory of objects is the theory of the comparison of events. Events are only comparable because they body forth permanences. We are comparing objects in events whenever we can say, "There it is again" (CN, 143–144).

What we discern is the character of an event, that birdsong, for instance, whereas, of course, other events, and even all of nature, are signified in experience. The event, or the most concrete fact, can be named; but as soon as we talk about it, we are referring to something much more abstract. Of this song, I can say, "There it is again"; I can recognize it even if I have no words to describe it. But the possibility of recognizing must belong to the concept of nature; otherwise, the latter would immediately bifurcate. Knowledge and words do not create abstraction, but they require the abstraction constituted by the discerned character.

Recognition and abstraction essentially involve each other. Each of them exhibits an entity for knowledge which is less than the concrete fact, but is a real factor in that fact. The most concrete fact capable of separate discrimination is the event. We cannot abstract without recognition, and we cannot recognise without abstraction (CN, 189–190).

How can a concrete fact exhibit entities that are abstract compared to it and nevertheless belong to it? We cannot really say that the object solves this problem in *The Concept of Nature*. Instead, it affirms it in its generality, exposing it in the radical character conferred upon it by the rejection of the bifurcation of nature. If nature is not to bifurcate, the question of the object, and therefore of abstraction, belongs not to knowledge alone, but to nature. Knowledge can be made responsible for many things, and in particular for theories that give primacy to abstraction or explain it in abstract terms. But it is not responsible for the fact of abstraction. The latter must find its respondent in the concept of nature.

In *The Concept of Nature*, knowledge is what is ultimate, and the question of the abstract is therefore merged with that of the object as the requisite of knowledge as recognition. Later on, the category of the ultimate will mutate along with the problem, and the object we are aware of will then disappear correlatively as a requisite. Yet the question of abstraction, for its part, will not disappear. For Whitehead, it cannot disappear.

The explanatory purpose of philosophy is often misunderstood. Its business is to explain the emergence of the more abstract things from the more concrete things. It is a complete mistake to ask how concrete particular fact can be built up out of universals. The answer is, "In no way." The true philosophic question is, How can concrete fact exhibit entities abstract from itself and yet participated in by its own nature? In other words, philosophy is explanatory of abstraction, and not of concreteness (PR, 20).

Could Whitehead have been unaware that by defining the work of philosophy in this way, he was taking his place in the heritage of what historians of philosophy have called the "quarrel of universals"? Was he familiar with those medieval authors who took up again and again, ceaselessly repeating and reinventing it, what imposed itself on some of them as a dramatic alternative bequeathed by their Greek masters? Those beings that we all recognize as "horses," for instance: do we recognize them because they all exhibit a universal, such as horseness? Is the universal that which, while remaining identical to itself, is in many things? Or else, is it only what is *said* of many things, thus relative to our utterances and to the generalizations in which we indulge? Does "the Horse," distinct from every particular horse, refer to being or to our knowledge?

Whitehead never announced any explicit interest in the medieval thinkers. When he cites philosophical lineages, he often jumps directly from Plato and Aristotle to Descartes. But this proves nothing, for nothing is more alien to Whitehead than the profession of historian of philosophy. When he cites a philosopher, it is not at all to discuss the correct interpretation, but, most often, to point out a connection that he will, as the case may be, transform into a surprising contrast. What is more, he is liable to shower praise upon the lucidity of an utterance which, within the work in which he captures it, has the status of a semi-involuntary regret: the greatness of Descartes, Hume, or Locke may consist in the fact that, despite their systems, they were unable, in this specific paragraph, to avoid affirming that . . .

Once again, Whitehead is a mathematician: it is the problems that count, not the authors. Nevertheless, it is not poor taste to recall the Middle Ages here. Although Whitehead does not cite medieval authors explicitly, he does insist amply, in contrast, on the fact that the modern faith in an ultimate material reality, blind and bereft of meaning, against which he struggles, is indicative not of a "progress of reason" but of an anti-rationalist movement, playing facts against reasons.

Of course, the historical revolt was fully justified. It answered a need. More than a need, an absolute necessity for healthy progress. For several centuries, the world asked to contemplate irreducible and obstinate facts. It is hard for man to do more than one thing at a time, and that is what they had to do after the rationalist orgy of the Middle Ages. It was a most normal reaction, but it was not a protest in the name of reason (SMW, 16).

For Whitehead, the struggle against the bifurcation of nature is an integral part of a new era that closed this revolt, which may have been healthy but was heavy with consequences. For the contemplation of obstinate facts will also mean that "science repudiates philosophy," and remains superbly indifferent to the demonstrations of the philosophers who have followed one another since Berkeley and Hume, each of them establishing to their own satisfaction the impossibility of what science claims to accomplish—to shed light on the order of nature, on the basis of obstinate facts. How could one rise back up to an order of things from particular facts, however numerous they may be? One can only rise back up to generalizations, which are never authorized by the facts and always refer to operations of consciousness! In other words, the medieval quarrel is not dead, and it still continues today, particularly with the quarrel between physicists and sociologists of science. Yet it now opposes only the proponents of two rival slogans: the "nominalist" slogan gathers together those for whom all knowledge exceeding the individual description of cases must be assimilated to a more or less convenient, more or less fruitful convention, always mendacious if it claims "to have made the facts speak"; while the "realist" slogan gathers together those for whom scientific knowledge, however abstract it may be, must convey what "reality is in itself," on pain of being a vulgar fiction.

Whether or not Whitehead cites them, the medieval thinkers are indeed present in his work, in the sense that philosophy, as he defines it, must once again go through the questions about which they indulged in a "rationalistic orgy," those questions that the modern period had decided to avoid, only to find them again in the form of watchwords. Indeed, in *The Concept of Nature*, Whitehead seems to me to come close to the man his contemporaries named the "doctor subtilis," Duns Scotus.

Subtle indeed was the position of Duns Scotus, who, faced by the alternative that either "universals" are relative to knowledge or else they belong to reality, refused to choose. For Scotus, all abstract features that fit a multitude of different individuals, all the distinct "quiddities" that allow me to describe them at different levels of abstraction, do indeed belong to what is described. Yet when I enumerate them and define them *qua* attributes of this individual, I treat them as if they were actually, that is, numerically, distinct (a horse is an animal, a mammal, a herbivore, an ungulate . . .) whereas ontologically they are only "formally" distinct, composing the individual as a unique, concrete being. The same is true of Whiteheadian objects: like the subtle doctor's plurality of "forms," they are the "respondents" of "that which" we recognize, name, judge, and compare: that is, what these operations answer to and also what can eventually answer for them. Yet although they exhibit themselves as abstract or permanent, they cannot be isolated from the concrete event, which, for its part, passes without return.

The Whiteheadian object may also make one think of the signs of Charles Saunders Peirce, which is rather appropriate since Peirce placed his undertaking under the banner of Duns Scotus. Indeed, Peirce's sign is real, although its meaning requires an interpreter to make it signify. It is real because the person who interprets does not fashion signs in a mute or "insignificant" world: she requires signs in the way Whiteheadian recognition requires objects. Signification is ours, no doubt, but the fact that there is a sign liable to signify is not the product of a "psychic addition" alien to what we call reality.

Nevertheless, Whitehead did not take as his starting point either Peirce's signs or the formally distinct attributes of Duns Scotus, but what we are aware of under the name of the "passage of nature." The concrete fact no longer bears the name of an individual, as it did in the Middle Ages, nor does it evoke the situation of interpretation. It is evoked by the name "event." In other words, what raises problems is not the contrast between "this" individual horse and the abstract composition of attributes that make a horse in general. What is problematic is what we are aware of while perceiving this individual horse itself: *"Say! There it is again!"*

One might think that the question has been radicalized, since it places the very permanence of the individual in doubt. But it has also (apparently) become more modest: Whitehead is not seeking either to found or to oppose abstract knowledge on the basis of what an individual allows us to know. He asks that nature, what we are aware of, be conceived as liable to deliver to the mind what the possibility of abstraction requires, what is required by the indefinite set of abstractions already required when we recognize this horse. Or when we recognize ourselves in the bathroom mirror every morning.

Our body itself is the palmary instance of the ambiguous. Sometimes I treat my body purely as a part of outer nature. Sometimes, again, I think of it as "mine," I sort it with the "me," and then certain local changes and determinations in it pass for spiritual happenings (PAF, 153).

Whitehead would retranslate this utterance by William James by distinguishing the body I recognize—*"There it is again, what bags under the eyes this morning!"*—and bodily life as a factor of experience, that is, insofar as the percipient event is "bodily life within the present duration." I will never exclaim *"Say, there I am again"* with regard to the percipient event, and if an event must be said to be spiritual, it is not in the sense that the spirit is said to be opposed to the body, but in the sense in which the event is opposed to any confusion between the bodily life that passes and what is there once again as an object. Whitehead would thus adopt the ambiguity underlined by James, to transform it into a "generality": every experience is ambiguous, and if the body wins the palm of ambiguity, it is because it brings about the coexistence, with the same intensity, of two modalities of experience which, when it comes to nature, are cultivated in divergent specialized ways. On the one hand, there is objective nature, stratified into objects about which we ask ourselves "abstract" questions, and on the other "spiritual" nature, multiple passages in unison.

What could be more "spiritual" than the expression of a face? You avoid my gaze, and I become disillusion and bitterness, a plaintive cry to the possible as it fades away. But we are also genuine prodigies, acrobats in the field of recognizing faces: *"It's him, it really is him, I recognize him."* The way the technique of robot-portraits has evolved, seeking to capture in an analytic way the "what" of recognition, gives a good indication that a face is not the sum of a nose, a mouth, a chin, on so on, but a set of stable relations "between" these features. All these relations imply this face, to whose description the features seem to lead. Unlike our body, the face of the other wins the prize not for ambiguity but for the most extreme twofold specialization: it is the paradigmatic object, and it is also the expression of a possible world, a world with which we become in unison.

How can we articulate these distinct components of what we are aware of in perception, without opposing them or placing them in a hierarchy? For Whitehead, every question begins with a name, the name of the problem that is to be constructed. We have already encountered the name of our problem at the turn of a phrase: "ingression."

The ingression of an object into an event is the way the character of the event shapes itself in virtue of the being of the object. Namely the event is what it is, because the object is what it is; and when I am thinking of this modification of the event by the object, I call the relation between the two "the ingression of the object into the event." It is equally true to say that objects are what they are because events are what they are. Nature is such that there can be no events and no objects without the ingression of objects into events (CN, 144).

A pseudo-definition, if ever there was one: the event is what it is because the object is what it is, and objects are what they are because events are what they are. Yet this pseudo-definition simultaneously prohibits and incites.

It prohibits us from waiting, hoping for, or anticipating conditions that explain why and how an object can perform ingression into an event. Objects and events are in strict reciprocal presupposition, and one cannot, in all generality, ask for more. It is not because the event is more concrete that it has the power to explain the object. To attribute this power to it would be to suppose that one can start out from the "pure" event or from the "pure passage of nature" to then ask how, from what is never repeated, there can emerge what, in one way or another, we are aware of in the mode of "once again." At the risk—and nature would obviously take advantage of the opportunity to bifurcate—of using the answer to this question to sort between what truly belongs to nature and everything else, the product of psychic additions.

In contrast, we are incited to pay attention to the diversity of the objects gathered together by this common feature, *"There it is again."*

Ingression is a relation which has various modes. There are obviously very various kinds of objects; and no one kind of object can have the same sort of relations to events as objects of another kind can have (CN, 145).

That birdsong I recognize, even if I have no words to describe it, has carried out an ingression. I don't know where the bird is, I don't even know if there *is* a bird—it could be a human imitator or else a recording. I don't ask myself the question, because I am busy writing a text, not on the watch, living an adventure in which the bird's song might mean the presence of allies or of menacing intruders. If I had been an ornithologist lying in wait, able to relate the bird's song to the songbird I am trying to locate, if I had had the experience not of a birdsong but of the immediately recognizable cooing of a dove, my experience would have been different. "What I would have been aware of" would have exhibited the song as a characteristic feature, signaling the presence of such a bird, whether rare or unexceptional. The event would have declared the bird's permanence, it would have signified the physical presence of that dove, there, somewhere in that tree. Perhaps I would have approached the tree to carry out a verification and a comparison. Here, I have continued to type on the machine, without the song making my experience of writing shift into another one, dominated by the "there" of the bird, by its localization in the landscape.

The song has made ingression as a sense-object, in this case a sound. The bird can be there, on the branch, but the bird's song, as a sound, is not "there" in the same sense. One can say *"there it is"* (again) of any object, but when it comes to a birdsong, to say *"there it is"* does not at all mean it is "out there." The respective ways in which the song and the bird make ingression are thus different.

The contrast upon which my example is intended to attract attention deals with what Whitehead calls "relation of situation," and more precisely with the plurality of relations of situations. What we are aware of in the respective perception of the song as a sound, and of the song as indicating the bird's presence, "situates" these two types of object differently with regard to the event that is their situation, the event in which they make ingression. And this difference matters, for it opposes the general ideal of "localization." In *Science and the Modern World,* Whitehead was to speak of localization in terms of misplaced concreteness. Localization responds to an "abstract" question, demanding the abstraction constituted by space, and this question may of course be fruitful, but it cannot under any circumstances relegate to appearances the concrete plurality of the "theres" designated by the "situation."

In discussing the relations of situation in particular and of ingression in general, the first requisite is to note that objects are of radically different types. For each type "situation" and "ingression" have their own special meanings which are different from their meanings for other types, though connexions can be pointed out (CN, 148).

A plurality of objects, such is the first requisite immanent to Whitehead's problem, to the imperative of avoiding the bifurcation of nature, and in this case, avoiding the kind of opposition on which the intellectual activities represented by discrimination, comparison, or judgment undertake to base their pretensions. Sound, color, odor, in short, what Whitehead calls "sense-objects," would then be opposed to "scientific objects," for instance, those molecules whose overall behavior explains the propagation of what we perceive as sound (at least in principle, for the matter is not simple). At the risk that this opposition between "secondary" qualities, referred to the intimate experience of the percipient subject, and "objective nature" may be complicated by the question of what Whitehead was to call "perceptual objects," for instance, that singing bird, there, on its branch.

To affirm "sense," "perceptual," and "scientific" objects at the same time is to refuse any principle of sorting. I know it is this bird that is singing: what I am aware of not only declares itself as a succession of sounds but as a "song," and this song is produced by a living being, not by a material body vibrating, and this being also inhabits this world in which I am; I perceive it *qua* declaring that I am not alone in it. I am a part of the world of this being, as it is a part of mine. The poet who celebrates the bird's song, and the world this song celebrates, are not wrong. And ethologists testify against the bifurcation of nature when they trust their experience and seek to exhibit the meaning of the song for the bird, a call to its female or a territorial announcement *"this is my tree."*

There are, I think, an indefinite number of types of objects. Happily we need not think of them all. The idea of situation has its peculiar importance in reference to three types of objects which I call sense-objects, perceptual objects and scientific objects [. . .] These three types form an ascending hierarchy, of which each member presupposes the type below.

The base of the hierarchy is formed by the sense-objects. These objects do not presuppose any other type of objects (CN, 149).

Plurality as the "ultimate fact" of nature, of what are aware of in perception, might thus communicate with a hierarchy. Yet could this be so without making nature bifurcate? Certainly, as long as this hierarchy is of a "logical" type, that is, is pragmatic as well. If it is appropriate to differentiate and articulate sense, perceptual, and scientific objects in a hierarchical way, it will be in the biased and partial way suggested by the very different ways in which we have to do with them from the viewpoint of the situation, that is, the very different ways in which objects can be said to be "there." In other words, the hierarchy does not concern "what we are aware of in perception," but it answers the logical question of the different, and abstract, meanings presupposed by our modes of characterizing what we discern. This hierarchy will have to enable the articulation of what every critical doctrine leads us to oppose, beginning with the doctrine according to which everything that "really exists" is localized in space and time. It will therefore constitute the arena in which the plurality of requisites will accept the risk of a direct confrontation with critical thought, both the one that summons us to recognize that the singing bird is never anything but an inference constructed from perceptual "facts," and the one that summons us to forget the bird, the sound, and the color in favor of "scientific" molecules in their stupid interaction. Nor should this confrontation itself result in a critique of criticism, but in a new construction of requisites. What every form of critical thought privileges unilaterally must also have a "respondent" in nature, if the plurality of significations and anticipations we associate with an object is not to be the result of psychic additions. Critical thought, when it succeeds in paying due attention to nature, can also find "more" in it.

CHAPTER FIVE

Attention to Objects

HITEHEAD NEVER TIRES of emphasizing that a sense-object is not an attribute or a property. We cannot solve the problem by returning, short of bifurcation, to the quiet world of utterances of an Aristotelian type, affirming a plurality of existents endowed with properties: the bird "is" a songbird, song is attributed to the bird. Yet neither must we disqualify the operations of the attributive intellect, defending the "pure" sonorous song against the busy activity of the person seeking to identify the bird that is responsible for it. Nor, moreover, are we to defend the bird as a living source, actively conditioning the song, against questions addressed to the modes of vibration of the air and their propagation. The point is, first, for us to remember that the song, like everything we are aware of, signifies the totality of nature into which it makes ingression. Even when we are aware of a vibrating sound in its haughty, solitary singularity, this sound is situated, is in a relation of situation. Nor is it enough to say that hearing a birdsong presupposes a relative situation between the "there" where it is emitted and the "here" of the percipient event, a two-term relation. If the sonorous object has a singularity, it is precisely the irreducibility of its situation to any localization. This is well known to those who build concert halls. Whatever the hall, the musician will be inside it, but the sound, for its part, will testify to a sonorous quality that is nowhere in particular.

It is not, therefore, because of a fundamental simplicity that Whitehead places the sense-object at the base of his hierarchy, but because the way this object makes ingression into nature does not require us to identify its source, or its function, or what it relates to. It is an object—*there it is again*—it does not, as such, take part in the passage of nature, and it is not itself—unlike the blackbird there on that branch, who is singing, a small black silhouette with a yellow beak and a shining eye—a relation among other factors of nature.

[...] *A particular sort of colour, say Cambridge blue, or a particular sort of sound, or a particular sort of smell, or a particular sort of feeling. I am not talking of a particular patch of blue as seen during a particular second of time at a definite date. Such a patch is an event where Cambridge blue is situated. Similarly I am not talking of any particular concert-room as filled with the note. I mean the note itself and not the patch of volume filled by the sound for a tenth of a second. It is natural for us to think of the note in itself, but in the case of colour we are apt to think of it merely as a property of the patch. No one thinks of the note as a property of the concert-room* (CN, 149).

Why is the mention of a musical note or of a birdsong more effective in slowing down the almost automatic movement that leads us, when it comes to color, to make it the property, for instance, of a piece of cloth? We shall attribute to the artist's interest and training the possibility of seeing "blue" where others see a flannel coat that happens to be blue. But we shall also attribute to the piano tuner's interest and training the possibility of turning a specific sound into the property of a chord that is more or less tightly stretched. Or to the interest and training of the connoisseur in architecture the ability to turn it into a property of the room in which the note resounds. For Whitehead, the question cannot concern a difference between sense-objects. This difference designates our practices, including those that are stabilized by what we call "sense organs." And in fact, while the literature is filled with cases of "optical illusions," exhibiting the deceptive differences between "what" one sees and "what is there to be seen," one speaks rather of "sound effects," as if the possible unreliability of "what" one hears, as compared to "what is emitted" or produced in an identifiable way, caused us fewer problems.

Correlatively, if objects as different as a bird, Cleopatra's Needle, or a "Cambridge-blue"-colored flannel coat are gathered under the common category of perceptual object, it is because they raise, for their part, a common problem that is not raised by the sense-object: the pragmatic problem conveyed by the question of whether a given perceptual object is "illusory," for instance, as a reflection in a mirror, or whether it is an "active condition" in the ingression of the sense-objects we perceive.

In general the situation is an active conditioning event; namely the coat itself, when there is no mirror or other such contrivance to produce abnormal effects. But the example of the mirror shows us that the situation

may be one of the passive conditioning events. We are then apt to say
that our senses have been cheated because we demand as a right that the
situation should be an active condition in the ingression (CN, 153).

Once again, the hierarchy among events has nothing to do with a question of value, whether aesthetic or epistemological. It exhibits the diversity of materials required by our judgments, our comparisons, and our
discernments if the practices to which they respond are to confirm the
trust that by paying due attention we will find more in nature than what
we observe at first glance. In this case, whereas the empiricist tribunal
has the vocation of pursuing all claims to find in nature anything other
than "what" we perceive—that is, again and again sense-objects—the
concept of nature constructed by Whitehead is not to found or to guarantee this claim but to provide it with a respondent that constitutes it as
a legitimate risk. As legitimate as the risk taken by a mountain-climber
whose foot seeks the foothold it needs on the rock-face.

It is a law of nature that in general the situation of a sense-object is not
only the situation of that sense-object for one definite percipient event,
but is the situation of a variety of sense-objects for a variety of percipient
events [. . .] *Furthermore this concurrence in the situations of sense-*
objects has led to the body—i.e., the percipient event—so adapting itself
that the perception of one sense-object in a certain situation leads to a
subconscious sense-awareness of other sense-objects in the same situa-
tion. This interplay is especially the case between touch and sight. There
is a certain correlation between the ingressions of sense-objects of touch
and sense-objects of sight into nature [. . .] *I call this sort of correla-*
tion the "conveyance" of one sense-object by another. When you see the
blue flannel coat you subconsciously feel yourself wearing it or other-
wise touching it [. . .] *The perceptual object is not primarily the issue*
of a judgment. It is a factor of nature directly posited in sense-awareness
(CN, 154–155).

I see this "Cambridge-blue" coat, but the words that make blue an attribute of the flannel do not state what I am aware of. They make my
perception communicate with a judgment about which questions of exac-
titude could be raised—*no, it's a jacket*—or of legitimacy—*what you call*
a coat is only a blue patch; it could, moreover, be a hologram. It may be a
jacket, and nothing guarantees that it is not a hologram, but what I am
aware of in my perception of this blue flannel coat did not have much to
do with these questions, except for particular circumstances. The blue
conveyed the touch of the cloth, a gentle sensation of flannel, the supple
fluidity of the draping on my body, the comfortable warmth of the wool.
Not the abstract possibility of touching it, feeling it, wearing it, in case my

judgment is legitimate, but the very sensation of touching it, wearing it, feeling the folds of the wool accompany the motion of my body. And if my trusting fingers encountered only the void, my shocked surprise would testify to the fact that the point was not to verify, but to prolong. A brutal interruption: the hologram was perfect, and the trust that was declared in the correlations conveyed by the visual object has been disappointed.

One may be tempted to judge that this correlation, which Whitehead names conveyance, is quite incapable of justifying the coat's "objective" existence. However, the experience of worry, admiration, or amusement, according to the situation, that occurs if my hand encounters the void where I had seen a blue coat bears witness: the mode of ingression of the "blue flannel coat" into the event declares itself to be different from that of blue. The perceptual object is what is required by this difference, what is demanded by this experience whose declared meaning is called seeing-a-blue-coat, the experience exhibiting the coat as an object.

Yet one can still insist: would nature bifurcate if we made conveyance a "psychic addition"? Whitehead himself, moreover, writes as follows:

The perceptual object is the outcome of the habit of experience (CN, 155).

That the blue coat results from a habit seems to bring us straight back to the empiricist tribunal: conveyance is a mere habit, what we add, as a result of past associations, to visual perception. Shocked surprise is merely disappointed habit.

But why should we say "merely," as if habit did not need a respondent, as if it did not itself exhibit a "fact of nature," its existence testifying to its usual verification? Habit presupposes a world in which a sense-object often signifies a perceptual object: it indicates a wager concerning such a world, and is not added to it like a fiction for which the mind alone would be responsible. At the limit, the problem is reversed: why are there sense organs if what is discerned has as its respondent only the shimmering, noisemaking, and odor-emission of a nature in which no situation is an active condition for anything at all? Even if we speak of an "aggressive blue," no one dies from it, but the little match girl, for her part, fed only by the fumes of the Christmas feast, died of hunger.

Habit thus testifies to nature, just as the existence of a mountain climber testifies to the fact that in general, the side of a mountain offers reliable footholds. Of course, habit corresponds to a risk with no guarantee, to a "law of nature" that is only valid "in general," but it cannot be questioned by an intellectual judgment that makes it "merely a habit." Quite the contrary, it is the fact that the habit does, most often, pay off that must be affirmed by the concept of nature. And it is this fact that is the requisite of the intellectual judgment providing it with its material: after all, when judgment is not transformed into a tribunal, demanding in a maniacal and systematic way guarantees that habit is quite unable to provide, it typically intervenes when habit is disappointed, together with what we call "interpreting," "trying to understand," or "taking a closer look." Correlatively, one can describe disappointment but not a satisfied habit. The maniacal tribunal is always a simulation, tacitly accepting an entire tissue of trusts and habits to stage an eventual disappointment, which it would not even have words to designate without the tissue itself.

Some works dealing with the ethology of newborns provide quite appropriate nourishment for Whitehead's thesis, more precisely the distinction between "habits of experience" and their empiricist translation "habits constructed by the subject on the basis of her experience." Daniel Stern claims that a newborn's sense-experience may be transmodal or amodal, with one "sense-object" always conveying another, whereas the experience of the senses as distinct (seeing is not touching, touching is not tasting, etc.) does not come until later. Indeed, among other objects of various forms, a newborn visually "recognizes" (preferentially fixes her gaze upon) an object she has felt without having seen it. In other words, if there is a habit when we sense the possibility of a "soft touch" at the sight of a "blue flannel coat," this habit is not constructed on the basis of experience, but is indeed a habit of experience.

The conveyance of some sense-objects by others might one day, of course, be given neurophysiological descriptions. It would be miraculous if it did not, and if the neuronal processes that accompany "seeing blue" were not themselves accompanied by activities "elsewhere" in the brain, perhaps akin to the experience of "touching" or even "tasting." The crucial point is that conveyance does not explain the perceptual object, but celebrates it as a "factor of nature." The fact that the situations of distinct sense-objects concur, or co-occur in a regular way, which relates them to the same object as their active condition, is the ultimate fact that the habit of experience indicates and exploits.

Whereas the sense-object can only be a term in a relation, the perceptual object is that which exhibits a relation whose terms are sense-objects. It is this ultimate fact of nature that is ratified by the attributive judgment, which makes every sense-object the property or attribute of a perceptual object. A ratification which, because it transforms what is a requisite into a right, takes on a certain exaggeration. It is as if the fact that the slopes of a mountain usually provide reliable footholds were established as a property defining the mountain. Whitehead often comments on intellectual abstractions in this way: it is not that they are false, but they are somewhat exaggerated in their claims. Even the identification of sense-objects with the terms of a relation is a bit exaggerated. This leaf is green: so be it. But at the same time as my experience exhibits the materials of this intellectual judgment, a mass of distinct or indistinct sounds, odors, and variations in ambient luminosity haunt my concrete experience. A sudden silence, and "nature falls silent": it is terrifying, even if the thousand noises of nature that have just fallen silent did not declare their source. But I also know that multiple smells that I do not recognize, whose active condition I cannot localize, are the material required by the dog's passionate activity, without which he would be a poor, bewildered thing. And I also know that the rhythm impressed upon the female spider's web by the male spider who ventures upon it to copulate corresponds to a crucial sense-object, which must turn the mode of existence of she who experiences it upside down, making her change from predator to female: a trust that constitutes the male, and is most often legitimate, but only most often.

Sense-objects, in their indefinite multiplicity, are so many signs, a limited number of which exhibit a meaning for a living being, always a specific living being, and among these, some, in an even more limited number, exhibit themselves as conditioned by an object of another type, by a perceptual object. Are they really such? Whereas many living beings are incapable of not letting themselves be fooled by appearances, as is attested by the ease with which ethologists can identify the habits of their specific experiences by setting lures for them, humans know they can be wrong. To this knowledge corresponds the possibility of doubting, being wary, that is, the trust that by experimenting, by taking a closer look, one will know whether one can trust: in particular, one will know whether the object is illusory or not. Whitehead calls what has emerged victorious from this trial a "physical object." The situation, the "there" of the sense-object, has been confirmed as the situation of a physical object: the situation of the sense-object was indeed indicative of the active condition for the ingression of this sense-object. It was indeed a coat, it is blue, and not white but bathed in a blue light, I can touch it, I can manipulate it, my suspicions are appeased, and my criteria are satisfied. "Substantialist" philosophers ratify this with some exaggeration when they make sense-objects the attributes or properties of physical objects.

There is a great difference in the rôles of the situations of sense-objects and physical objects. The situations of a physical object are conditioned by uniqueness and continuity (CN, 157).

To recognize a coat, placed immobile on a chair, a leaping tiger, or an iridescent, precarious soap bubble . . . in three seconds, the coat will still be there, the tiger may have killed me, and there will be no more soap bubble. And yet there exists a duration short enough for the tiger to be said to be "there where it is": the uniqueness of the situation. And there exists a passage of events, a passage of nature, such that I recognize the same bubble situated in distinct events, such that the bubble belongs simultaneously to my past and to the experience that has just slipped into the past: continuity in passage.

Uniqueness and continuity are what is usually attributed to a "substance," or to that which, as soon as nature bifurcates, is assigned to what is "really there," "localizable," as opposed to what depends on the subject. Uniqueness and continuity are also what is required by the extremely sophisticated operation that leads us to "locate" an object, to define it by assigning to it a position in an instant. The relative confidence we can have in our attributions and our definitions bears witness to uniqueness and continuity as factors of nature, but these are prerequisites, what these operations take advantage of, at their risks and perils, as mountain climbers take advantage of what offers them a foothold. As for the notions of space and time, on the basis of which we transform into a right the possibility of locating an object in reality, since we demand of an object "if it really belongs to nature" that ideally it should be at a determinate point at each instant, they do not by any means render explicit what we are aware of, but only what conditions our definitions. They testify, first, to the fact that science and philosophy take their abstractions too seriously. In particular, they reduce the question of ingression to that of situation.

Science and philosophy have been apt to entangle themselves in a simple-minded theory that an object is at one place at any definite time, and is in no sense anywhere else. This is in fact the attitude of common sense thought, though it is not the attitude of language which is naively expressing the facts of experience. Every other sentence in a work of literature which is endeavouring truly to interpret the facts of experience expresses differences in surrounding events due to the presence of some object. An object is ingredient throughout its neighbourhood, and its neighbourhood is indefinite [. . .] we are driven to admit that each object is in some sense ingredient throughout nature; though its ingression may be quantitatively irrelevant in the expression of our individual experiences (CN, 145).

In *The Concept of Nature*, Whitehead will make no other allusion to literature as a testimony that is at least as reliable as science, as far as the general problem of ingression is concerned. Here, however, the allusion suffices. It evokes what we could so easily forget when we limit ourselves to the situations that have inspired the bifurcation of nature. When we deal with birdsongs, or with birds perched on branches, we forget that what we are aware of in perception can also be called "presence."

Who could ever define in limitative terms the multiple ways in which the sudden presence of my neighbor in this room, where I was working alone with Whitehead, modifies my experience? In any case, the ingression transforms my experience, which is no longer primarily in this room, alone in front of this screen. Correlatively, far from being there in the doorway, and therefore located relative to me, my neighbor, smiling or annoyed, friendly or hurried, is first of all a presence that de-localizes me and signifies a world from which I have suddenly ceased to be protected.

Presence is not a simple matter of psychology, making the mind intervene as a responsible promoter. Quite the contrary, if we can believe studies of the ethology of newborns, it is what we call "psychology" that requires this experience of presence. According to Daniel Stern, a newborn, well before memory or operations of intellectual judgment can be attributed to her, "reacts" in differentiated affective modes to the facial features presented to her. As if the features of faceness were the primordial requisite for human young to construct the twofold correlative emergence that will make them human beings, endowed with what we call a "psychology": that of a sense of self, and that of a sense of others, not as "there" but as "present." Of course, "presence," like perceptual objects, might then result from a habit of experience, but there would be nothing "merely psychological" about this habit, which would define what is required by what we call psychology: what must become an important factor of experience for human young, on pain of death, if not biological then at least affective.

"Presence," of which we cannot give an abstract definition, would thus be the requisite for sophisticated intellectual operations, which, as the case may be, will end up denying what they take advantage of: what provides a foothold for the mind in nature.

This kind of hypothesis would have interested Whitehead all the more in that the infant's testimony with respect to what, for her, as early as her first weeks, constitutes a smiling-human-face, seems to exhibit what he calls an "object in the complete sense." In the infant's experience, the ingression of a smiling face must no doubt be said to be "a specific set of correlated modifications of the characters of all events," whose center is designated by the situated smile.

An object of one of these types has relations to events other than those belonging to the stream of its situations. The fact of its situations within this stream has impressed on all other events certain modifications of their characters. In truth the object in its completeness may be conceived as a specific set of correlated modifications of the characters of all events, with the property that these modifications attain to a certain focal property for those events which belong to the stream of its situations [...] The conventional limitation of the object to the focal stream of events in which it is said to be "situated" is convenient for some purposes, but it obscures the ultimate fact of nature. From this point of view the antithesis between action at a distance and action by transmission is meaningless. The doctrine of this paragraph is nothing else than another way of expressing the unresolvable multiple relation of an object to events (CN, 189–190).

Soon, in *Science and the Modern World,* Whitehead was to listen to the poets testifying to the somber and heavy presence of the ancient hills. Of the hill, the poet does not say "there it is again," but "it's still there." The continuity of the perceptual object will then have become endurance, an endurance we can be aware of in a way that exhibits the communication between perception and affect, that gives meaning to a "complete fact" exceeding the definition of the hill as a geographical or geological entity.

In *The Concept of Nature,* however, Whitehead will ask so-called scientific objects to testify to the ultimate fact of nature, which is obscured by the conventional construction of a well-defined identity of the situated object. No doubt we can see in this a reflection of the limits of the problem that Whitehead has set for himself in this book: to construct the "concept of nature" against the threat of a bifurcation of that nature. For a mathematician, the limit of a problem is neither a weakness nor a defect. What is a weakness or a defect is to forget that limit: to forget that a problem has a price, to forget that the concepts created respond to a question, not to a vision.

CHAPTER SIX

The Ingression of Scientific Objects

HERE, THE CONSTRUCTION of the concept of nature must confront the risk of bifurcation, for nature, "what we are aware of in perception," will become populated by "objects" that declare themselves to be "independent of the percipient event"; those very ones that, as the case may be, will be evoked to "explain perception." Electromagnetic radiation would constitute the objective explanation for what you are subjectively aware of as "red." To deal separately with the question of the mode of ingression of scientific objects does not mean to confer upon them a "fundamental" character: the singing bird or the leaping tiger are just as important. Once again, what is at stake is not to explain everything we are aware of. In this case, as we remember Whitehead has emphasized, ingression should be declined according to an indefinite number of distinct modes, all of which exhibit multiple relations. The discrimination between the three types of mode, corresponding to sense-objects, perceptual, and scientific objects, responds to the need to prevent nature from bifurcating. The goal will be to show that "scientific objects," far from designating a nature that is "independent of perception," imply, like sense-objects and perceptual objects, that nature has "given a foothold" to the mind. They too thus belong to nature, as respondents to this foothold that refer to the mind, which is what is ultimate.

By the time Whitehead undertook to think of "scientific objects," the point was no longer merely to articulate with the concept of nature statements explicating the regularities proper to observable phenomena. Physics and chemistry have succeeded in transgressing the limits that tied them to the generalizations articulating measurable factors (pressure,

temperature, and so on) in various roles. These sciences actually identified, beyond the phenomena, the "tiny bodies" supposed for centuries
by the bifurcators of nature, but which others denounced as the perfect
example of dubious speculative constructions, menacing the rational
identity of the scientific enterprise. But Whitehead is happy to accept this
event. He who was trying to construct a concept of nature affirming what
we are aware of in perception did not harbor any nostalgia toward what
remained possible until the end of the nineteenth century: to assign limits
to scientific descriptions that affirm the indisputable primacy of what we
are directly aware of, what we can observe and measure.

Physicists and chemists, it is said, have succeeded in "going beyond the
phenomena," but this expression has many meanings. There is one that
Whitehead would reject: identifying the phenomenon with what is illusory. Thus, when astronomers make fun of astrologers, they oppose the
constellations, "appearances" on which the astrologers have relied, to their
knowledge that constellations designate groups of stars that are completely unconnected, some of them close, others very far away. The group
exists only for inhabitants of the earth, for only the terrestrial viewpoint
can thus unite stars that do not have the least privileged relationship
among themselves. However, this opposition is polemical, in that it rests
entirely on an abstract resemblance: astronomers, like astrologers, contemplate the heavens. But the astronomers' heaven is "scientific," insofar
as they are interested in the luminous points they observe in a mode that
defines them as "physical objects," that is, playing the role of active conditions for the emission of light. The astronomical tradition has diverged
from astrological practice, insofar as it has devoted itself to discovering
what attention is due to these physical objects, how one "finds more" in a
sky which, by this very fact, finds itself practically defined as bereft of any
other meaning.

It is also on the basis of the attention devoted to what has a role, to
what actually plays the role of active condition for the ingression of (measurable) sense-objects, that the difference can be stated between the electrons, atoms, and molecules that henceforth populate physics, and the
atoms of ancient hypotheses. Physicists and chemists have thought of the
atom, and other unobservable entities, as actors, that is, on the basis of
their roles in "events" (collisions, chemical associations, emissions, de-
compositions, and so on), and they have conferred upon these events the
hypothetical role of "situations," the active conditions of certain experimental observations. Their success means that these hypotheses have allowed
them to "find more," that is, to produce specific experimental situations in
which a precise and "falsifiable" reference to those unobservable actors is

necessary to explain what can be observed. This is the paradigmatic experimental achievement. The experimenter is now in a position to affirm that atoms are not a mere interpretative hypothesis, since no one can interpret what she has observed without recourse to them: they are the respondents to which the difference between an interpretative hypothesis and a fruitful hypothesis refers.

Whitehead can thus serenely celebrate the atoms of the physicists and chemists because they have nothing to do with the "tiny bodies" associated with the bifurcation of nature. These atoms are by no means active participants in an operation of distribution between what pertains to "us" and what pertains to nature. They are a response to the kind of attention associated with the experimental effort. "Going beyond the phenomena," here, does not at all mean going "beyond" secondary qualities toward a nature "independent" of our perceptions; it is to prolong the test already pointed out by the distinction between perceptual object and physical object. It is not merely a matter of verifying, like a rabbit turning its head in the direction of a noise, the conveyance "noise-movement of a predator," but of explaining the multiple significations that can be assumed by the term "active condition." Nor is it a matter of limiting oneself to multiplying experimental regularities and to defining the distinct roles of each measurable factor that plays a part in the corresponding situations as active conditions for observation. The scientific object responds to an additional achievement: these "roles" no longer respond only to the first experimental question *"What's going on?"* They can also be related to the presence of "objects" which, for their part, do not pass.

The origin of scientific knowledge is the endeavour to express in terms of physical objects the various rôles *of events as active conditions in the ingression of sense-objects into nature. It is in the progress of this investigation that scientific objects emerge. They embody those aspects of the character of the situations of the physical objects which are most permanent and are expressible without reference to a multiple relation including a percipient event [. . .] In fact the whole point of the search for scientific objects is the endeavour to obtain this simple expression of the characters of events. These scientific objects are not themselves merely formulae for calculation; because formulae must refer to things in nature, and the scientific objects are the things in nature to which the formulae refer* (CN, 158).

The question of the active condition is central, both for the scientific undertaking and for living beings. If nature were made up only of sense-objects, ghostly contacts, floating odors, sounds, luminous shimmerings, all without an identifiable source, the scientific enterprise would not have been possible. But neither would there have been any physical object nor any living beings, for living beings testify to a world where, like the little match girl, we die if the odor does not announce, at least sometimes, a nourishing encounter with what is its active condition. This is true whether the living beings are aware or not. Thus, we may think that a butterfly does not really have the perceptual experience "of a world," and that its flight responds to what we would call "detection," not to the experience of the signs of the world that sense-objects represent for us. Yet when its flight is oriented in the direction in which what is detected increases in intensity, there most often occurs, fortunately for it, an encounter with what we call a flower, what we, for our part, identify as an active condition for the ingression of the odor, and what, for it, will be a concrete, delectable experience, the eventuality of which was presupposed by its life as a butterfly.

To cite the example of the butterfly as an experience involving detection rather than perception does not mean to designate it as an automaton, but to call it to witness to understand a "scientific object" that declares itself to be independent of the percipient event. The butterfly, whatever its own experience may be, testifies to the flower as a physical object. A specific flower, in the sense in which we recognize it as an object—*say, there's that rose again!*—may well be illusory—*another hologram!* And what attracts the butterfly may be a lure set by an entomologist. Yet the butterfly, human disappointment, and the very notion of a lure celebrate the trust that, "by going to take a closer look," we will most often discover what plays the role of an active condition in the ingression, both of what the butterfly detects and of what we perceive as odor and color.

The scientific enterprise, like living beings themselves, like common sense itself, requires a world in which sensible signs signify in a generally reliable way; in which, when discerning a sense-object, we can anticipate, without being wrong too often, certain features of what only declares itself in experience as discernible. The butterfly's mode of existence requires that the detection of what is for us a specific color or odor authorize anticipation that is often enough confirmed and verified by its consequences, by what we can characterize as a satisfying *"nectar!"* encounter. Human beings, gardeners, naturalists, perfume makers, and creators of new, fragrant floral species, have addressed themselves to flowers as physical objects with some success, and have studied the various roles of the events that contribute to the active conditions of the ingression of the object "odor." They have confirmed the well-founded nature of what is presupposed by the distinction between the flower, as a physical object, and the flower as a habit of percipient experience: the flower responds for the habit, and, by paying it due attention, we can find even more in it that what it offers to an insect. Yet it is the ambition proper to chemists to succeed in defining, and then to synthesize an "object" common to human beings and butterflies, a molecule whose presence plays a determinant role both for what we call "odor" and for the detection attested by the butterfly's flight.

Such an achievement would have no meaning independent of the physical object, "fragrant flower," from which perfume makers have long since learned under what conditions the "principle" could be extracted in a way that could conserve it as an active condition for the ingression of the sense-object "odor." Nor would it have a meaning independent of that organ we baptize "nose," or else of insects that could be assimilated to "detectors." Scientific objects presuppose physical objects, at the same time as they declare themselves to be independent of the percipient event. They are indeed at the summit of the logical ascending hierarchy, in which each member presupposes the lower type, and whose base designates sense-objects. However, this hierarchy can be stated in another way, and this is where the risk of the bifurcation of nature resides.

Quite obviously, there is a relation of contemporaneity between the scientific enterprise and the great theme of bifurcation: both confer a crucial importance upon entities that declare themselves independent of the percipient event. For Whitehead, however, this feature is not the privilege of a truth that would finally be "objective," naked, beyond the motley trappings of sense-experience. It is because it reflects an achievement, a "reliable foothold" of the mind in nature, that the scientific object is important, and as such this object may reveal its usual association with the general theme of the bifurcation of nature, and be together with, or placed "in the same boat" as, other objects, particularly sense- and physical objects. Just as "sense-objects" testify to a world in which their ingression signifies, in a way that is sufficiently regular to be reliable, a physical object that is worth paying attention to, certain physical objects testify to a world in which it is worthwhile to vary their situations, to extract the factors that play a role in this situation as "active conditions," in order to set the spotlight on them. This is not always the case, far from it: a chirping bird can be described as a function of the various roles played by the events that contribute to its chirping, but it will always be events (nightfall, the approach of a female or of an intruder) that presuppose a bird that is quite alive and involved in its business. No experimenter has succeeded in "extracting" from the bird the "active principle" of the ingression of the sonorous objects for which its situation is the active condition, but only in identifying and imitating these objects, in describing their roles for other birds.

The great theme of the bifurcation of nature is thus not the statement of a general truth that could be confirmed by experimentation. It marks the forgetting of what constitutes the value of experimental achievement: "here," nature has offered a new kind of reliable foothold to the "mind." It is this forgetting that allows it to be said that scientific objects "explain" sense-appearances or constitute their hidden objective truth. The scientific object is then no longer the respondent required by the experimental foot-hold, but explains what we perceive in general, in a way that claims to be independent of all perception.

For Whitehead, then, the molecule obviously does not explain the event "smelling that odor" which it accompanies. Yet its privilege is two-fold. On the one hand, it has a permanence that the event in question lacks. Each time I uncork a jar containing a solution of synthetic vanilla, I will smell once again that odor that resembles that of vanilla. On the other, unlike "natural" vanilla, extracted from pods, synthetic vanilla can be described and produced without reference to the sense-object "odor," and therefore imposes itself as associated with a vast multiplicity of events and objects to which the type of attention designated by our sense organs is not appropriate. The privilege of synthetic vanilla is not that of explanation but of abstraction; and unlike the abstraction of perfume makers, which succeeds in extracting an active principle from vanilla pods, this is not an abstraction with regard to the physical object. When I note, "*Yes, that's about the same smell,*" I celebrate the relative success of the set of risky abstractions employed by the practice of syn-thetic chemistry, which presupposes the ingression, in these events we call "chemical reactions," of those actors with differentiated roles we call "molecules."

The molecule of synthetic vanilla is "really" in nature, but it does not explain nature: what is abstract can never explain what is concrete. It is abstraction that must be explained. The molecule has no meaning inde-pendent of nature, independent of the various types of events in which it makes ingression. Precisely because it seems self-sufficient, its definition exhibits its abstraction, exhibits the rare achievement constituted by the definition of scientific objects, the possibility of relating to them what we are aware of, of bracketing or leaving aside the percipient event.

Undoubtedly molecules and electrons are abstractions. But then so is Cleopatra's Needle. The concrete facts are the events themselves [...] to be an abstraction does not mean that an entity is nothing. It merely means that its existence is only one factor of a more concrete element of nature. So an electron is abstract because you cannot wipe out the whole structure of events and yet retain the electron in existence. In the same

*way the grin on the cat is abstract; and the molecule is really in the event
in the same sense as the grin is really on the cat's face* (CN, 171).

Sense-objects, as soon as they are defined as "what" we perceive, "that
sound," "that smell," which we recognize "quite apart" from the passage
of nature, are abstractions. Here, abstraction implies what are called the
sense-organs, but it refers to the ultimate authority constituted by the
mind, in its guise of the extraction of what is perceived, separated from
the event we are aware of in perception. And abstraction is, of course,
not arbitrary: it indicates a foothold that is generally reliable, and in this
sense its respondent must be a "fact" of nature. To be sure, both the discernible and the discerned differ from animal species to animal species,
but each time they constitute a wager with regard to what matters, with
regard to that whose neglect entails the death penalty. And the modes of
abstraction, the conveyance of certain sense-objects by others, testify to the
importance of the abstraction constituted by the perceptual object, that
Cleopatra's Needle, for instance, with which I would collide, to my preju-
dice, if I reduced it to a simple visual image.

Likewise, the successful abstraction constituted by molecules implies
the modes of detection made possible by laboratory instruments, and
refers to an experimental tradition, which may be as rich in presuppositions, imagination, and technical, economic, and intellectual ingredients
as we may wish, but in a way that defines as what really matters the production of a mode of abstraction independent of the percipient event. Yet
abstraction is not arbitrary in this case, either. It has nothing to do with
the abstraction proposed by metaphysical statements that seize upon scientific abstractions as if they were achievements due to them, generalizing
them in a way that testifies to their indifference to the risk of failure. What
matters is the vocation of the experimental apparatus, that independently
of which it would not exist: to produce a testimony to the role of scientific
objects that must accept and resist the risks of controversy, to be recognized as benefiting from a "reliable foothold," authorizing the abstraction
which, in return, will make scientific objects in nature its respondents.

In a way, the one that is proper to experimental innovation, the definition of scientific objects is thus situated in the tradition of the definition of
physical objects, verifying the reliable character of perceptual objects. And
the latter, deriving from the habits of experience, designate in turn the trials
associated with biological evolution. The only difference is that the risk
and importance at stake do not concern the well-foundedness of a perception or the survival of a living being. What is at stake is the survival of the
"mind's" new "foothold," and of what is supposed to be that foothold's
respondent in nature, that is, the twofold passage to existence of the ex-

perimental apparatus *qua* reliable, and of the object to which it refers *qua* belonging to nature, or to what we have to do with in awareness.

Some scientific objects exist, however, whose importance for the concept of nature is of a different type. In their case, the work of mathematical physics, which organizes and articulates a set of different experimental testimonies to relate them to an object, winds up approaching the properly conceptual problem of what Whitehead has called "ingression." The point is then no longer to identify a molecule as a function of the "role" it plays, but to describe this role itself in terms of activity. When "laws of nature" are enunciated, exhibiting the "passage of nature" in an explicit way, objects are defined as inseparable from the events in which they make ingression, whereas events are defined as "being what they are," because molecules, atoms, and electrons "are what they are."

But in science we have found out that when we know all about the adventures amid events of material physical objects and of scientific objects we have most of the relevant information which will enable us to predict the conditions under which we shall perceive sense-objects in specific situations [. . .] The analysis of these adventures makes us aware of another character of events, namely their characters as fields of activity which determine the subsequent events to which they will pass on the objects situated in them. We express these fields of activity in terms of gravitational, electromagnetic, or chemical forces and attractions (CN, 170).

The gravitational force proposed by Newton created a scandal because it "acted at a distance." It might, perhaps, have sufficed to impose the abandonment of localization, of the idea that the primordial scientific characterization of the sun, and of the earth as well, is to be where they are. The historical fact is that physicists have instead made do with a mathematical formulation that affirms, at the same time, that a massive body is defined by precise spatial coordinates, and that nevertheless other bodies, defined by their mass and their distance, intervene in the calculation of its motion, a double definition that does without the notions of adventure or activity. As far as "chemical forces" are concerned, they, in contrast, were deduced from the activity of a mixture of reagents as such. Yet their activity is attributed not to a scientific object, a particular molecule, but to a global mixture. Chemical forces say nothing about the molecule's adventures; they qualify "relations" specific to two chemical reagents, but this qualification, since it is independent of the localization of the molecules, does not allow this localization to be questioned. Since Faraday, however, the electromagnetic field has exhibited properties irreducible to those of a force "between" two charged and localized bodies. And, as a second surprise, this field has, since the end of the nineteenth century, been associated with the presence of electrons in motion, capable of being localized and endowed with a charge. In this case, the problem is fully deployed at last. The mode of ingression of the scientific object "electron" questions localization as a primordial, "objective" property.

A scientific object such as a definite electron is a systematic correlation of the characters of all events throughout all nature [...] The electron is not merely where its charge is. The charge is the quantitative character of certain events due to the ingression of the electron into nature [...] the electron is the systematic way in which all events are modified as the expression of its ingression [...] We may if we please term the mere charge the electron. But then another name is required for the scientific object which is the full entity which concerns science, and which I have called the electron (CN, 158–159).

Unlike its charge, the electron does not let itself be localized, any more that the cat whose Carrollian grin I can see. Not only does mathematical physics thus testify against the ideal of simple localization associated with the theme of the bifurcation of nature, but it confirms what ingression obliges us to think: the event is what it is because the object is what it is, and objects are what they are because events are what they are.

The conception which most fully expresses the character of nature is that of each event as modified by the ingression of each electron into nature (CN, 160).

To be sure, the dream of some physicists would have been, and still is today, to deduce the particle from the field, and to make it a local expression of the field. Why, for instance, could we not think of the particle in the manner of a wave wrinkling the ocean? It would of course have a behavior all its own, but we would also know that it is nothing other than a local expression of the ocean, than this aspect "here" of the ocean "everywhere." Many physicists have tried their hand at this, and field theory today is inhabited by this hypothesis when it suggests turning particles into "excited modes" of a field that is, in principle, coextensive with the universe. At the risk of making the possibility of talking about an electron depend on the existence of the detector that is to localize it. Just as the wave affects us, the particles would affect our detectors. But the only "objective reality" would be the ocean or the field, which explains without being explained.

If Whitehead were among us today, perhaps he would have objected: the wave is what it is because the ocean is what it is, to be sure, but doesn't this metaphor incite us to formulate the question of ingression in a way that is too unilateral? Perhaps the ocean is expressed in the wave, but how does the presence of the wave affect the ocean? The challenge associated with the concept of ingression would thus be to succeed in formulating the idea that the ocean, too, is what it is because the wave is what it is. This is the kind of objection some physicists oppose to contemporary field theory: the adventure of the particle in a field should not be reducible to a mode of expression of that field.

In other words, the question of how to represent the electron's ingression into its field, favored by Whitehead, has indeed become generalized, but the only sure point in this experimental and intellectual adventure today is the abandonment of the master idea of the bifurcation of nature: the identification of the relation of situation with that of localization. For the rest, the least one can say is that this representation is still under construction, trying to take into consideration and order the multiple and ever-proliferating aspects of the "field of activity" in an attempt to define the type of attention that is due to them.

The fact that mathematical physics intervenes to deprive the doctrines of the bifurcation of nature of their most prestigious support is, of course, utterly crucial. The fact that, for a century, physicists have been confronted by the question of how to articulate local and delocalized, particle and field, are just as important. Yet it would be catastrophic to transform the testimony contributed by mathematical physics today into an authority. This is so whether it be to "rectify" the Whiteheadian notion of ingression, that is, to affirm triumphantly that the particle is indeed what it is because the field is what it is, but that, contrary to what Whitehead thought, the converse is not true; or whether it is to acknowledge that he was right. Even if mathematical physics one day came to confirm what ingression affirms, if some day a theory should be formulated that really does articulate particles and fields, that is, redefines these two physico-mathematical notions on the basis of the problem of their articulation, this would be a matter of science, not of the generality Whitehead called "ingression." For this new theory, whatever may be its interest, would deal exclusively with situations where the ideal of the exactness of mathematical physics is relevant, in particular the ideal definitions of point and instant. Such a theory would still be an abstraction: there is no such thing as nature at an instant, all events have a duration, and all durations have a thickness.

The temptation to identify the Whiteheadian event with the mathematico-physical notion of a field must therefore be resisted, even if they both share certain features, precisely those features that have prevailed against good sense, first with the scandalous notion of forces "acting at a distance," then of a field that is irreducible to these forces. Correlatively, the general concept of ingression cannot by any means be assimilated to the problem raised by the inseparability between electron and field. However complicated it may be, for physicists, to construct what nature obliges them to accept, the very possibility of defining this complication reveals the abstraction of the definitions whose relations are to be articulated.

The aim of science is to seek the simplest explanations of complex facts. We are apt to fall into the error of thinking that the facts are simple because simplicity is the goal of our quest. The guiding motto in the life of every natural philosopher should be, Seek simplicity and distrust it (CN, 163).

CHAPTER SEVEN

Interlude

A Pragmatics of Concepts

WHITEHEAD HAD WARNED US: perhaps what is hardest to understand in *The Concept of Nature* is the limits assigned to this concept, and more precisely what these limits exclude. For what is excluded are all questions capable of exciting philosophers of a metaphysical bent, but also—and today, perhaps, above all—the cohort of those who define as the final frontier for science the question of the emergence of conscious experience as such from neuronal mechanisms. To the questions raised by the thinkers who call themselves "Naturalists" in the United States—those who present themselves as modestly, or even pragmatically, adopting the path opened up by the "natural sciences"—Whitehead would not only answer "that's beside the point, for it would be metaphysics." He would speak of badly framed questions, to which there is no possible answer. Of course, neural mechanisms belong to nature, in the sense that they are part of what we have learned by paying it due attention. They are really in nature, in the sense that the grin of Lewis Carroll's cat is really on the cat's face. Yet they are successful, relevant abstractions, or "scientific objects," and as such they presuppose what naturalist philosophy would have them explain: "mind" *qua* "knowing." When it comes to nature, knowledge is the ultimate.

Framing the problem in this way will meet with the assent of phenomenological philosophers, and there is certainly a kinship between phenomenology and the Whiteheadian generalities known as the passage of nature and the object "that is there once again." And yet Whitehead was no phenomenologist, for these generalities have nothing in common with a "phenomenological reduction," with the ambition of thinking of pure phenomenality, the donation presupposed by everything given. The threat of confusion, very present in France where phenomenology is extremely influential, concerns the meaning of this word "ultimate." The ultimate in the phenomenological sense is both what is to be thought and what imposes upon thought a distortion that has something to do with a conversion, since the point is no longer to think "about something" but to address an experience purified from any particular interest in any particular object. The Whiteheadian ultimate, for its part, is only ultimate with regard to the problem raised, and it is defined by its function—to avoid false problems—not by an order of truth that transcends our habitual modes of thought. It does not demand the suspension of what testifies to the certitudes of common sense. On the contrary, the distinction Whitehead proposes between "factors," belonging to sense experience, and "entities," implying the transition toward thought, has as its first effect to vindicate common sense, our habits in the world, and everything we "know," even if our theories of knowledge do not give us the right to know it. Although the ultimate is "mind," when it comes to the concept of nature, this is so not in the sense that everything refers to it or proceeds from it, but in the sense that nature is to be thought as capable of "giving a foothold" to knowledge.

Nature is thus neither knowable—definable, for instance, as a system of relations between entities—nor unknowable, the famous "mute reality" upon which we project human, linguistic, or social categories. This binary alternative, which nourishes so many philosophical discussions, is fatal for common sense. Nature is that about which relevant knowledge may be produced. If we pay due attention to it, we can learn, discern relations, and multiply entities and ratios. Contemplative subjects wondering whether they are the authors of what they see, or whether their vision gives them access to a reality independent of them, is a disastrous philosophical fiction. To ask such a question, one must already have eliminated, as unworthy of being thought, all those who bustle about, inquire, and carry out tests and experiments: from those who, in the darkness of time, learned how to track an animal or discern plants with curative virtues, to scientific experimenters in their laboratories. And one must ignore that one is oneself part of all those who learn, every day, what attention must be paid to in a world that ceaselessly demands attention. "Pay attention," says the parent to the incautious child.

Knowledge as ultimate does not designate a "knowing subject," but corresponds to a problem of a pragmatic kind: the concept of nature must give meaning to the world with which we deal, a world we can learn about, but which is also capable of tricking us and placing us in danger. In short, a world that demands our attention. It is to this pragmatics that the "hierarchy" of objects responds, as does the intermodality of our senses, for each type of object corresponds to a type of demand and a possibility of verification, that is, also a way of paying attention. From this viewpoint, experimental science, as a producer of "scientific objects," by no means carries out a break with common sense. It designates the surprising discovery that it is possible, in some cases, to "ask even more." In this case, the object, which is always "situated" and cannot be abstracted from the events in which it makes ingression and that actively condition it, provides a foothold for questions addressed to an entity whose behavior is a function of determinate interactions with other entities. The signature of the pragmatic approach, here as elsewhere, is to link the production of such an "objective" definition with an achievement, with the fact that in some cases the mode of attention proper to experimental science is found to be a "due" one, not the general definition of knowledge finally freed of its subjective attachments.

Whiteheadian generalities are themselves inseparable from a pragmatics, a pragmatics of the concepts that participate in the concept of nature, and must also be evaluated in terms of eventual success. On the one hand, they must succeed in constituting knowledge as an ultimate, not as central. In other words, the concept of nature must be such that nature provides a "foothold" for knowledge, but it must not legitimize any particular form of knowledge; it must not duplicate, by any kind of justification, the empirical fact of the eventual success of certain ways of paying attention. The question of the type of attention that is due in each case is a question for which there is no conceptual shortcut. They must, moreover, succeed in situating the mode of attention that gave rise to the bifurcation of nature in a way that verifies that it is always possible to discover more in nature, but without ever discovering in it that which would enable what is known to be "explained."

Did Whitehead succeed, from this last point of view? To verify this, I will address two technical terms introduced to help think of the passage of nature, the continuous and relational multiplicity of events, and the qualitative multiplicity of objects: ingression and cogredience. The goal will be to show that these two terms, which remain indeterminate at the end of *The Concept of Nature,* are so in the positive sense of the term, that is, in the sense that every scientific explanation that targets them would restore the bifurcation of nature. And the point will be to raise the question of the way this indeterminacy resists, or fails to resist, certain contemporary modes of explanation.

The primary function of an object's ingression is to affirm that the abstraction required by the judgment of recognition, memory, and comparison is not reducible to these intellectual operations. When it comes to what is abstract, to the entity as an object of thought, it must be said both that it is the product of an abstraction and that this abstraction may respond—although this remains to be verified—to an offer for which nature is the respondent. The respondent, not the cause: it is not because "the same objects" have made ingression that we perceive them "again." The criteria that render explicit our definition of "the same" do not define the object in the sense that it belongs to nature and does not exist independently of the event in which it makes ingression.

It is here that the developments of neuroscience, of cognitive psychology, and of the "connectionist" models seem to be able to contribute something new. For some, they enable us to envisage an explanation, scientific at last, of the emergence of the perceived object, that is, of the experience associated with the Whiteheadian object: *there it is again.*

Let us take the case of the networks of coupled automata that serve as references for the connectionist models of neural mechanisms. They were considered momentous, since an ability for "artificial recognition" can be associated with them, as if the network were able to abstract an object, that is, to adopt a specific form of behavior that may serve as a signal: a given object, of which no one has produced an abstract definition, is detected. Of course, when the connectionist networks function as a technical apparatus, the technicians know what is to be detected, and they also know how to act on the connections in a way that stabilizes and specifies the detection. Technical success is the ultimate. Yet when it comes to the brain, the person who knows "what" is detected is absent. Could we not say, then, that such a mechanism "explains" the abstraction of what we call an "object," and that the latter is therefore merely a product of neural mechanisms, not of a generality belonging to the concept of nature? Ingression would then be replaced by a process of emergence, explicable in terms of connected neural networks, and nature would bifurcate, for the perceived object would not be abstracted but produced as such by detection.

As the neurophilosopher Andy Clarke points out, however, such an explanatory hypothesis features a cerebral machinery that works on itself and by itself, and a world that appears on stage only in as insignificant a way as possible, carefully stripped of all that might constitute a landmark and hence complicate the question of responsibility. It is important for the stage-managers that the network's behavior can be described as explaining an emergence that has no correspondent in nature, as responsible for an emergent *"there it is!"* Like the networks used by engineers, although in a different mode, the network is thus situated by what is at stake. The staging in which it plays the role of what is responsible for emergence proposes a confrontation between two abstractions: the "neuronal brain" and a reality conceived as "mute," like an illegible text or image. In contrast, when the stage becomes crowded, when the brain receives an acting body and this body is itself situated in a world whose patterns are important, and some of which must be detected "on pain of death," the brain is no longer that which explains, but just as much that whose workings are explained on the basis of the activity of living beings capable of recognizing, but also of exploiting, and even creating; what matters for their activity. This does not mean that the question of the eventual relevance of the connectionist model loses its interest, but it does lose the power to make nature bifurcate. It confirms that when the brain is addressed *qua* belonging to nature, one can learn more from it. What one will learn will not, however, enable us to surmount the indeterminacy affirmed by Whitehead with regard to the object's ingression, unless the kind of answer we seek is the ultimate, that determines the staging.

As the reader will recall, cogredience, for its part, alludes to what exceeds the concept of nature, that is, to metaphysics. It designates the question of what constitutes the meeting point between the two "realities" we call "nature" and "mind," respectively: the question of what constitutes an event for the person perceiving. As a concept, it points out that neither nature nor mind is in command here. The interruption of the relation of cogredience is a fact for which not explanation but notice is appropriate, even if it can "explain itself" if we can always later—but only later—explain it. We then give to what has been associated with the interruption the power to explain that interruption. In contrast, what can be affirmed is that the precarious stability of the cogredient relation—the sorting process that differentiates between what constitutes an event and makes the present slip into the past, and what "escapes notice"—is itself something that is at stake. At stake for survival, for lack of attention may entail the death penalty. At stake for spiritual techniques, that aim at the mind through work on the body. At stake for magical practices, and for experimental psychology—although today, the latter knows a great deal less than the magicians on the subject. Yet cogredience is itself the common requisite for these stakes; it is what they all presuppose, and what turns all our explanations into commentaries.

Today, the science of dynamic attractors allows us to make sense of "phase transitions," and of bifurcations or tipping-points where a system changes its behavior without there being any need to assign a cause responsible for this change. Could we not imagine that the specious present, the duration of a here "and" now, might be explained in these terms? Once again, the goal will not be to deny that, oriented by the models of systems with attractors, the attention we pay to the brain may make us better able to learn more about it. Yet once again, the explanatory ambition, which would make nature bifurcate since what "constitutes an event" would be determined by the dynamic system, is reflected by the fragmentation of what must be thought of together.

The explanatory power of systems with attractors is determined by the possibility of separating what explains—a system governed by a limited number of variables whose relations remain fixed—and what is to be explained, the qualitative changes in behavior that characterize this system. Yet the explanation loses its power if the model deals with a brain that is not isolated, but an integral part of what Whitehead called our "bodily life," a life that is never the same twice, that is never there "once again." In this case, the explanatory model requires what it does not explain: what could be called "a viewpoint on bodily life" from which would follow the definition of the variables required by the landscape of dynamic attractors. Once again, the stage is repopulated, preventing nature from bifurcating, for such a viewpoint, far from being fixed once and for all, must include, in one way or another, what it is important to pay attention to in a concrete situation. The question of what constitutes an event, far from being solved, then constitutes the crucial element presupposed by the definition of the variables required by the model.

Obviously, in neither of the two cases I have just envisaged is there any question of designating a "mind" that makes cerebral complexity its instrument. The mind as ultimate plays no role when nature is concerned: its role is to avoid false problems that emerge as soon as the brain, described as a set of entities in relation, is rendered unilaterally responsible for what we are aware of, like mountain climbers capable of producing a hold by their own means and climbing up a smooth wall. When the brain becomes an integral part of what, with Andy Clarke, one could call an ecologically realistic situation, the mind is no longer the ultimate, since the question exceeds the limits of the problem answered by the concept of nature. We no longer have to do with generalities, or attributing responsibilities, but with the impassioned and fascinating adventure of living beings in environments that are always already partially fashioned, in ways that matter and signify.

It is remarkable that in *The Concept of Nature,* ingression has the very limited role of resisting the philosophical disaster entailed by the lack of distinction between different types of object, different types of situation, and between localization and situation. If, of course, instead of identifying that bird as a perceptual object associated with this sound, I was moved by the vibrating corporeality of its song, and if I did not restrict myself to recognizing this face, but felt when I saw it that the discussion will be stormy or painful, the temptation to deny that the object affects its environment would be much less seductive. But I would twice have exceeded the limits of the concept of nature such as Whitehead constructed it. As a living being, the bird testifies to a world in which beings sensitive to its song exist. The expression on the other person's face raises the question of emotion: not what I perceive, but how what I perceive affects myself.

Whitehead was soon to cross the ocean, and on American soil he was to provide himself—was to dare to provide himself?—the means of becoming what, in *The Concept of Nature,* he had challenged himself not to be: a metaphysician. There is no contradiction here, for the metaphysics he wanted to avoid was the one that is done without knowing it—when nature is asked to explain knowledge—or without accepting what it commits us to—when "mind" is introduced to explain what does not enter into the definition of nature one has provided oneself. When Whitehead becomes a metaphysician, neither nature nor mind will subsist, and knowledge will no longer be the ultimate. The point will no longer be to construct a nature to which this flower, whose scent I recognize, may belong, but a world in which this enjoyment vibrates: "how nice it smells."

We may imagine that Whitehead, in 1920, did not suspect the adventure on the threshold of which he found himself. No one can know, for there is no trace left of his feelings in this regard. It remains that the operation of reading I have attempted certainly does not correspond to the effect that *The Concept of Nature* had on contemporary readers. I have accentuated the wholly mathematical freedom with which Whitehead defines the problem of nature, whereas for many readers, no doubt, the two sources he privileges—the scientific definition of objects and sense experience—were the two normal poles of the problem. What I have chosen to exhibit is Whitehead's gesture, the way he decided to establish the concept of nature as the answer to a problem, that is, on the edge of the bifurcation that traps thinkers as soon as they to approach it, by attributing responsibilities to subject or object. In so doing, I have presented *The Concept of Nature* as the beginning of an adventure, and I have placed this adventure under the banner of mathematical audacity: not to search for some negotiated solution, evaluated according to its plausibility or its capacity to provide a minimum of satisfaction to the various parties, but to tackle a problem *mano a mano* and go as far as that problem will demand. In this case, to accept fully and without restriction what we are "instinctively willing to believe," but without trying to prolong, found, or generalize the justifications or interpretations we give to this "instinct." A subjection to adventure, not to judgment: the point is not to discuss the general question of the extent to which "nature" is the respondent of our knowledge about it, but to take an interest in what testifies to the importance of this question for those concerned by it, in the processes of verification that include the rabbit staring at the spot from which a noise is coming, and the experimenter's art of consequences—*If I'm right, then I should, in such-and-such conditions, be able to* . . .

The importance of William James for Whitehead's transformation into a philosopher cannot be overestimated. Not only are the *Essays in Radical Empiricism* as well as *The Principles of Psychology* present in *The Concept of Nature,* but one could say that the very construction of the concept of nature accomplishes a junction, which had remained rather implicit in James, between radical empiricism and pragmatism, between nature as what we are aware of, and nature as providing a foothold. In particular, unlike Bergson, it is at the level of this foothold, and not of experience in its immediacy, freed from what makes us calculate, verify, and hesitate, that a relation with evolutionary thought is established. This is why the question raised by Whitehead will never be that of knowledge faithful to the truth of that experience. From this viewpoint, Whitehead is, after William James, one of the very rare philosophers of the twentieth century to have fully envisaged the consequences of the Darwinian evolution for the classical problems of philosophy, that it, to have situated questions of truth not on the side of right, legitimacy, or authenticity, but on the side of its consequences. Nature neither explains nor justifies anything, but it is pragmatically implied in the consequences that verify, or fail to verify, the relevant or important character of a landmark or a generalization, the appropriateness of a kind of attention. Perception implies the risk of trusting what is perceived, a trust whose practical consequences may entail the death penalty for impertinence.

However, Whitehead will not generalize this pragmatic type of approach. At first glance, the speculative adventure upon which he will embark even reflects an abandonment of pragmatism. Yet only at first glance: that is, when pragmatism is reduced to the sad morality of the businessman: what is true is what is profitable. The fact that William James's expression "cash value" sufficed to justify such a reduction is not only indicative of the philosophers' laziness, but also of the continuing power of bifurcation, this time bearing upon what "really counts" and what is insignificant or illusory. And evolutionary biology itself testifies to the same power, when it transforms selective advantage into an explanation and can then serve as the base for a psychology or an anthropology that seeks to define a universal human nature, forged by biological selection. In other words, the link between pragmatism and evolutionary thought may easily become a new instrument of judgment, once again testifying to the power of abstractions when they function in a polemical mode. Whitehead, for his part, never broke with the pragmatic art of consequences, which he no doubt learned from James, because he did not stop for an instant at the idea that what counts, what matters, might pertain to a generality. If he changed his approach, it was because his problem had changed.

Whitehead was no longer to limit himself to a pragmatics of concepts aiming to avoid the false problems to which our abstractions give rise, because, for him, the point was no longer to "civilize" our abstractions, to separate them from their polemical power, but to transform them. In *Science and the Modern Word,* the question of bifurcation was given a new name: "*the fallacy of misplaced concreteness.*" A fallacy, not a vice proper to the intellect. As an art of consequences, pragmatics forbids any position of truth whose consequence would be to transform the problem into an insurmountable horizon of the human condition. A fallacy is first and foremost an exaggeration, an exaggerated impact attributed to an undeniable success.

The advantage of confining attention to a definite group of abstractions is that you confine your thoughts to clear-cut definite things, with clear-cut definite relations. Accordingly, if you have a logical head, you can deduce a variety of conclusions respecting the relationships between these abstract entities. Furthermore, if the abstractions are well-founded, that is to say, if they do not abstract from everything that is important in experience, the scientific thought which confines itself to these abstractions will arrive at a variety of important truths relating to our experience of nature. We all know those clear-cut trenchant intellects, immovably encased in a hard shell of abstractions. They hold you to their abstractions by the sheer grip of personality (SMW, 58).

In cauda comes not *venenum* but humor: there is nothing abstract about the power of abstraction. Whitehead was probably thinking of Bertrand Russell, but we may think of Richard Dawkins or Daniel Dennett, honorable men, passionately devoted to the service of humanity. To undertake to transform the abstractions that impose themselves upon them, and which they try to impose in the name of reason, demands a trust that will not be shaken by the cold logic of deductions, and humor that does not denounce but knows that such coldness always has the poignant will to convince as one of its ingredients.

CHAPTER EIGHT

Science and the Modern World

A Strange Book

WITH *SCIENCE AND THE MODERN WORLD,* the reader will be exposed to difficulties that are not presented by *The Concept of Nature.* First of all, there is the difficulty of grasping the very subject of this book.

Apparently, it is a work that belongs to the register of the history of ideas or of civilizations. This, at any rate, is what one might think after reading the statements that open and close the book.

The progress of civilization is not wholly a uniform drift towards better things. It may perhaps wear this aspect if we map it on a scale which is large enough. But such broad views obscure the details on which rests our whole understanding of the process (SMW, 1).

The moral of the tale is the power of reason, its decisive influence on the life of humanity. The great conquerors, from Alexander to Caesar, and from Caesar to Napoleon, influenced profoundly the lives of subsequent generations. But the total effect of this influence shrinks to insignificance, if compared to the entire transformation of human habits and human mentality produced by the long line of men of thought from Thales to the present day, men individually powerless, but ultimately the rulers of the world (SMW, 208).

Whitehead thus presents his book, if not as history, then in any case as a meditation on the history of Western civilization. And at the conclusion of the book, there appears that to which these "details," hidden by a large-scale vision, alluded: the disproportionate influence of a line of "powerless" thinkers. This, of course, inspires a slight discomfort on the part of the suspicious reader. Undoubtedly, Whitehead, the mathematician-philosopher, is to be situated in this lineage. On the way he will analyze the influence of his precursors depends the way he envisages his own influence, and often, when one explains the way philosophers situate themselves by means of the terms of their analysis, one reaches the triviality of a story of progress: history as a long path leading toward "me" (or us, when the authors allow themselves to speak in the name of their epoch). Bergson himself fell into this trap, since the intuition of which he is the philosopher accomplishes the exploit of reconnecting intelligence, whose power and excesses can be understood thanks to the long line of philosophers, and instinct, whose perfection and closed nature can be explicated thanks to the long line of insects and parasites.

If Whitehead's story differs from many other meditations on the progress of civilization, it is precisely because, as he will make fully explicit in *Adventures of Ideas,* what interests him is not the great story of the progressive revelation of the truth of history that inevitably makes the West the thinking head of humanity. What interests him is an "adventure of reason," and it is this adventure that creates its subject. Reason is thus defined as what is ventured in the course of this history. In other words, what is sought is not a definition of reason, but a particular description of the historical process that exhibits what we call "reason" as one of its questions. The meaning of that "rule" that the long line of thinkers, from Thales to Whitehead, has impressed upon the world, also depends on this process.

In the present case, if Alexander, Caesar, and Napoleon were victors over identifiable enemies, strength against strength, it was the highly unheroic victory of persuasion over strength that the adventure of Whiteheadian ideas was to describe in 1933. Here, the power of ideas must be said to be suggestion rather than truth, for, like what we call suggestion, it travels along roads that do not have much to do with deduction, reasoning, logical necessity, or the principle of reality. What was originally an extravagant ideal, transported by a visionary thought, by an individual bereft of social or political power, became a "habit" or "routine," stabilized by institutions, laws, and professional regulations. If ideals are victorious, then, it is without glory or glamour, by all the practices that are indeed invented by men but that also fashion them in return, creating the social environment from which new risks, new experimentations with ideas become possible.

Whitehead's great example, in *Adventures of Ideas,* is the complete implausibility of the saying of Jesus, calling upon men in the midst of a civilization based on slavery, to recognize each other as the children of God. The history that fashions us today, "respectful of the rights of man," in the name of which slavery can be routinely condemned, had the Christian ideal as an ingredient, but it also constitutes a betrayal of this ideal. We know this today even better than Whitehead. The adventure continues, he would have said: in each new social environment, ideals judged to be utopian by the new norms will express the new formulation of the problem these norms claim to have solved.

This "pragmatic" conception of a story woven by experimentation with the ideas and routines of habit refers to a conviction, an aesthetic, and an ethic that were Whitehead's well before his philosophical adventure. They are, for instance, already perceptible in the articles collected under the title *The Aims of Education*. And it is remarkable that the concepts created by Whitehead in *Process and Reality* did not constrain this conception to new risks but merely conferred on it a new amplitude, with the apotheosis of the fourth part of *Adventures of Ideas*, in which beauty, truth, adventure, and peace acquire the power to define all civilizations.

This, moreover, is a difficulty proper to the reading of *Adventures of Ideas*: the concepts are present without the problems they answer, like a quasi-poetic duplication of what is narrated. It is therefore tempting not to pay attention to them and to confuse what is narrated with one history of ideas or of culture among others: it is simply more grandiose, or naively audacious, than most. In contrast, there is no temptation of this kind in *Science and the Modern World*. Here, the concepts seem to intrude, interrupting the narrative, brutally widening a perspective, ceaselessly imposing upon the reader the question of whether she has to do with a delirious eruption or an inspired thought.

To be more complete, let us describe the surprises this very strange book has in store for its reader.

Right from the first chapter, Whitehead raises the problem of faith in an order of nature, without which the flourishing of modern science would have been inconceivable. There follows a rather original reading of the origin of that science which, as we shall see below, places it under the banner of a historical revolt against rationality. The reader, seduced by this originality, is nevertheless, like many scientists, ready to make faith in the order of nature a mere psychological adjuvant, a simple vision guaranteeing the legitimacy of the quest: reality is determinist, or causal, or written in mathematical characters. At the end of the chapter, however, Whitehead will suddenly unfold all that this faith implicitly requires:

There is no parting from your own shadow. To experience this faith is to know that in being ourselves we are more than ourselves: to know that our experience, dim and fragmentary as it is, yet sounds the utmost depths of reality: to know that detached details merely in order to be themselves demand that they should find themselves in a system of things: to know that this system includes the harmony of logical rationality, and the harmony of aesthetic achievement: to know that, while the harmony of logic lies upon the universe as an iron necessity, the aesthetic harmony stands before it as a living ideal moulding the general flux in its broken progress towards finer, subtler issues (SMW, 18).

The succession of "cola" marks the equivalence of the propositions, each of which, however, seems more stupefying than its predecessor. Whitehead has done nothing other than explain the faith or trust of the scientist, and especially of the practitioner of the theoretico-experimental sciences, but he has explained it completely. Whereas scientists often express themselves as if the order in which they have faith were already there waiting for them, what they "discover" is inseparable from their shadow, from their own presence in the landscape they describe. In order to come into being, the logical harmony they make explicit and celebrate required a living ideal of aesthetic harmony, without which the "scattered details" could never have become themselves and found their logical place. Whitehead thus restricted himself to explaining this living ideal, without which scientists would not rack their brains over a detail that resists, would not expect their statements to be able to predict the result of a new experiment, nor that their theories, appropriately formulated after an eventful itinerary, could come to exhibit a form of beauty and simplicity without which they would not be satisfied. Yet unprepared readers might well conclude that the author is not only original, but endowed with a solid poetic verve.

Other surprises await our readers. They will realize, for instance, that Whitehead never confines himself for very long to historical narrative. Thus, in the course of Chapter 4, when one might think the subject was an interesting evaluation of the practical successes that marked the eighteenth century, from the invention of English parliamentary government to that of the steam engine, the story suddenly stops. We suddenly learn (p. 64) that space and time have two characteristics in common, "separative" and "prehensive." For several paragraphs, the reader will attempt to follow the elaboration of what a prehensive unity of volume means, but this analysis, suddenly qualified as deceptively simple because it induces the idea that space-time is a self-subsistent entity, independent of perception, is in turn interrupted. And Whitehead turns to Bishop Berkeley to ask what perception is. He seems to accept the answer . . . except for one simple substitution: where Berkeley speaks of the mind, Whitehead will speak of a process of prehensive unification and generalize it to all that exists . . .

Here, the reader who is a bit familiar with the history of philosophy (I dare not imagine what has become of the others) is seized by a slight dizziness. To call upon Berkeley to resist a "ready-made," self-subsistent space-time is to call upon the man who affirmed that "to be is to be perceived." One might therefore have expected all notions implying a reality "independent of perception" to be suspended. Yet Whitehead has just transformed "being perceived" into a model on the basis of which this reality can be thought. An original and poetic author, no doubt, but also endowed with a strange sense of humor . . .

The reader, more and more dumbfounded, can certainly hang on, perhaps at the cost of proceeding to a selective reading. By the time she reaches chapters 10 ("Abstraction") and 11 ("God"), however, all possibility of selection collapses: the history of ideas has yielded to a metaphysical construction, and a construction that seems, moreover, to require a reference to God as the "ground" of all limitation. Our reader then runs the risk of abandoning *Science and the Modern World:* originality, poetry, and humor, perhaps; delirium, certainly.

What I have just described was my first experience with Whiteheadian reading, years ago. In other words, this reading was a defeat. Later on, once I understood that Whitehead was not a historian of ideas liable to delirious surges, but a metaphysician, I came to a "non-reading" of *Science and the Modern World,* situating this work, as Whitehead himself seemed to invite his readers to do in the preface to *Adventure in Ideas,* within a continuity. *Science and the Modern World, Process and Reality,* and *Adventures of Ideas,* writes Whitehead, all express one way of understanding the nature of things, but in a complementary way, supplementing each other's omissions and compressions. I thus accepted the idea that these three books had the same author, who chose, according to the perspective adopted, to put forward his ideas in a specific way. A "non-reading": the bizarre mode of composition no longer counted, because at any rate I "knew" what Whitehead meant, and what he said, moreover, much more explicitly in *Process and Reality.*

It was then, in the early 1980s, that I heard Lewis Ford present the results of his work for the first time, work without which, I believe, I would never have envisaged to attempt the present essay. According to Ford, *Science and Modern World* (like *Process and Reality* later) was the result of a genuine work of montage, not only in the sense that some chapters come not from the Lowell lectures, whose publication the book officially constitutes, but from other lectures (the chapters on mathematics and in science and religion). In fact, one should read the two chapters, on abstraction and on God, as well as what Whitehead in his Preface calls a few "slight" amplifications inserted in other chapters, as if they had been written by "another author," introducing ideas that the former neither possessed nor foresaw. This is confirmed by the analysis of the notes taken at Whitehead's classes given at Harvard by one of his students: reading them, as we shall see when the time comes, one can follow "in real time" a radical change that took place in April 1925, two months after the Lowell lectures.

Lewis Ford's great book, *The Emergence of Whitehead's Metaphysics, 1925–1929,* will constitute a permanent reference for my reading. I thus unequivocally take a stand in the midst of the controversy that divides Whiteheadian philosophers today, between partisans of the analysis called "compositional" or "genetic," and partisans of the "systematic" analysis, according to which a single system is, as Whitehead himself wrote, expressed in various modes by all the "American" books. Yet my problem is not the same as Ford's: it is not to reconstitute the various strata that make up a book; I accept the results of his analysis. It is to bring to existence that Whitehead who, in June 1925, when he signed his preface to *Science and the Modern World,* knew what had just happened to him and nevertheless insisted that the reader accept this book as representing "one train of thought."

Was Whitehead hiding the truth? Did he think that if the transformation to which this book bears witness were known, he would be asked to rewrite the whole thing, which bored him in advance (Whitehead apparently hated being bored)? Or else, without excluding this first hypothesis, can we not understand that we have to deal, despite everything, with one train of thought? In that case, Whitehead will have said nothing but the truth, albeit not the whole truth.

As I will not tire of emphasizing, Whitehead was a mathematician. My reading of *The Concept of Nature* has tried to show a mathematician engaged by the definition of the problem he assigns himself. My reading of *Science and the Modern World* will try to bring to life a mathematician seeking how to formulate a problem and learning from his problem what it obliges him to. A unique train of thought, so be it, for the problem is one, insofar as it refers to a unique imperative, its "having to be thought." Yet this unique character does not contradict the possibility of brutal transformations in the formulation of this problem, with regard to the construction of its possible solutions.

A philosopher never stops reshuffling his concepts, and even changing them [. . .] (QPh, 26–27). *A concept is bereft of meaning as long as it is not connected to other concepts, and is not attached to a problem it solves or contributes to solving* (QPh, 76). *Problems and solutions are constructed of which one can say "A failure . . . A success . . . " but only gradually and according to their coadaptations* (QPh, 79).

The mode of reading I propose to adopt implies an active staging, the creation of explicit distinctions where, as Ford has shown, Whitehead proceeded with the most radical indifference, making coexist what I will bring to existence as distinct. One way of specifying this contrast would be to say that Whitehead seems to have tried to induce a transformation in his reader by setting up a kind of "total spectacle": he trusted brutal transitions and unexpected coexistences to carry out a destabilization of all the habits that had to be surmounted, deliberately jarring thought out of its ruts. My reading, for its part, is addressed to the creator of this spectacle. And perhaps it is due to the fact that the defeat of my first reading means that I resisted the spectacle itself, and that, in any case, I was not the only one to do so. From the viewpoint of the effect sought, it must be said that Whitehead missed his mark, and my mode of reading tries to draw the consequences from this.

However, this reading also translates a obstinate, irreducible fact: at the same time as I was learning to read Whitehead, I was also learning to inhabit the "image of thought" Gilles Deleuze calls into existence in *Difference and Repetition*. From the outset, therefore, I thought Deleuze with Whitehead and Whitehead with Deleuze, two distinct and inseparable explorations. Yet these two explorations made the compositional analysis proposed by Lewis Ford something quite other than a useful survey: what Ford had discovered had already been described by Deleuze, and conversely, what Deleuze described had been experienced by Lewis Ford's Whitehead.

Problems or Ideas emanate from imperatives of adventure that present themselves as questions. This is why the problems are not separable from a deciding power, a fiat, which, when it traverses us, makes us semi-divine beings. Doesn't the mathematician already claim to belong to the race of the gods? In the two fundamental processes of adjunction and condensation, this power of decision, based on the nature of the problems to be solved, is exercised to the highest degree, since it is always with regard to an ideal body added by the mathematicians that an equation turns out to be reducible, or not to be so (DR, 255).

If my reading of *Science and the Modern World* does not "miss its mark," the enigmatic terms of adjunction and condensation will come alive for the reader, and if they come alive, what Whitehead tried to transmit will be transmitted by other means. As a sign, no longer of a wager of reading, but of a commitment to reading, I propose an initial presentation of it here.

Adjunction: Deleuze takes his inspiration here from the method of solving algebraic equations inaugurated by Abel, then Galois. Algebraic equations such as "$3x+5=14$," for instance, capture the features of the problem in such a way that it becomes explicated *qua* liable "in itself" to provide the missing information, in this case the solution "$x=3$." However, in the general case, the goal is to complete the problem by adjoining to it elements, dimensions, expectations that do not belong to its original formulation (such as the "twelfth camel" of my introduction . . .). The "ideal body" that is to be adjoined means that the solution no longer corresponds to an item of information contained implicitly in the problematic situation, and which is to be explicated. It can be called "ideal" because it designates the "idea," the imperative of the problem to be solved, which intervenes explicitly in the new formulation conferred upon the problem. It therefore reflects the learning process of what the solution obliges. The mathematician, working simultaneously on the formulation of the problem and the determination of the path that will lead to its solution, does not limit herself to organizing the description of a situation: adjunction designates her as a creator, prohibiting this mathematician from separating the "fact," "the problem has found its solution," from her shadow, that of the mathematician, whose trusting intervention—*the problem must have a solution*—has created the path toward this solution.

Between the first lines of *Science and the Modern World* and the two chapters added by Whitehead after April 1925, plus the minor "amplifications" inserted in other chapters, the train of thought can then indeed be said to be "unique," responding, moreover, to a problematic situation which Whitehead more than probably meditated upon long before he crossed over to America. If one admits that the problem did not dictate his solution, the "additions" nevertheless mark a turning point, the one at which Whitehead "makes a decision": decides that the process of explanation in which he trusted is insufficient, and makes up his mind to construct what the solution demands. It is then, and only then, that he commits himself to a creation of concepts that will make him the most audacious of twentieth-century speculative thinkers.

Condensation: Deleuze takes his inspiration from Charles Péguy's *Clio:* a difficulty one encountered suddenly passes through a point of resolution that is almost physical in the sense of critical points of physics, such as condensation, fusion, and so on. As a liquid condenses brutally, the possibility of a path of solution bursts forth, and both the thought and the way in which what was to be thought presented itself, all at once, determine one another as if in a new beginning of the world. A new beginning, not an illumination, nor new, instantaneous evidence. Everything begins (again), for the difficulty, having become the principle of solution, will oblige us to go through once again what seemed to be stably acquired, and this itinerary will ultimately decide what the principle demanded.

And indeed, everything will begin again, but in *Process and Reality*. For in this case, the strata of composition will no longer concern only chapters or paragraphs, but sometimes sentences that transform the meaning of the paragraph when they are inserted. It will no longer be a matter of a strange book, but of a labyrinth-book, a book about which one no longer knows whether it has an author, or whether it is not rather the book that has fashioned its author, in an incessant hand-to hand combat between what has been written and that to which what has been written will oblige the writer. Whitehead was "traversed" by a "decision," a *"fiat,"* which redefined both thinker and problem, both of whom are subject to a series of questions that henceforth no longer belong to one or the other.

Questions are imperatives, or rather questions express the relations of the problems with the imperatives from which they proceed. *Should we take the example of the police to manifest the imperative nature of the questions? "I'm the one who asks the questions," but in fact it is already the dissolved ego of the interrogated that speaks through his executioner* (DR, 255).

The commitment to read has been made, and it remains to answer it. And first of all, to avoid going straight to Whitehead's *fiat*. We must start by exploring the initial formulation of the problem, in this case the thought of the organism Whitehead intended to propose, since it is this thought that must summon the adjunction through the discordant separation between the perceived possibility of a solution and the means to construct it. And before this, once again, it remains to perceive something of the imperative from which Whitehead's adventure proceeds: the "trust" that enabled him to create the modern epoch, that is, his epoch, as a domain of experimentation.

CHAPTER NINE

A New Epoch?

I N A GENERATION *which saw the Thirty Years' War and remembered Alva in the Netherlands, the worst that happened to men of science was that Galileo suffered an honourable detention and a mild reproof, before dying peacefully in his bed* (SMW, 2).

A certain tone has been struck, the history of what we call modern rationality will not be placed under the banner of heroism. It was in vain that Galileo, not without arrogance, mounted an assault on the Roman fortress: he will not figure in Whitehead's story as a martyr breaking with a tradition, but far rather as the herald of a change in mentality.

This new tinge to modern minds is a vehement and passionate interest in the relation of general principles to irreducible and stubborn facts. All the world over and at all times there have been practical men, absorbed in "irreducible and stubborn facts"; all the world over and at all times there have been men of philosophic temperament who have been absorbed in the weaving of general principles. It is this union of passionate interest in the detailed facts with equal devotion to abstract generalization which forms the novelty in our present society (SMW, 3).

The multiple, intricate event constituted by the appearance of "the modern mind" has, of course, caused many gallons of ink to flow, and every analysis, every transformation into a story, every transformation into thought is inseparable from the diagnosis given by the author to the world in which she lives: from the great song of progress, the decisive moment when Man emerges from darkness, down to prophetic imprecations against technology, calculation, or reason. Whitehead's story is, of course, no more veridical than any other, but it is original in that his goal is neither to celebrate nor to denounce. Whitehead thought he was living at a key moment, he thought he was telling the story of an epoch that was slipping into the past. He was certainly wrong in this, for what he describes still constitutes the dominant mode of thought today. Yet it is precisely this optimism, factually unjustified, that gives his prose its actuality: today's reader can share, if not his optimism, at least his diagnosis. And this very diagnosis fashions a form of "non-factual" optimism, the possibility of breathing, laughing, separating the quite justifiable fear, inspired in us by our history, from any duplication making that history the justification for a judgment. It may be a very bad story, but it is no more than that.

In any case, it is an astonishing story. Whitehead's goal is not to judge but to shake our judgmental routines, particularly those that feature "a modern mind" in harmony with itself. A harmony supposed to manifest itself in particular by the convergence between the progress of science and the new turn taken by philosophy: the world must henceforth be described in terms of possible knowledge, and the "cosmos," that which one does not decipher without learning to inhabit it, must be relegated to the storehouse of illusions. Thus, right from the first chapter, it is amply emphasized that the dominant philosophies of science have not been and are still not in the least participants in the adventure of that science, which they nevertheless claim to understand and even to found. Of course, modern scientists and philosophers all testify just as well to the new authority of facts, but in an antagonistic way.

David Hume is paradigmatic in this regard. Does he not claim, to his greater satisfaction, that the link between cause and effect can only be arbitrary, since no fact can establish it? By so doing, he disqualifies the faith attested by scientists in an order of nature that it is their role to decipher. Whitehead admits, of course, that some aspects of Hume's doctrine were taken up verbally by some men of science, but, as we already know, words don't count for him. What matters is that

[. . .] *scientific faith has risen to the occasion, and has tacitly removed the philosophic mountain* (SMW, 4).

The relevance of Whitehead's proposition, rather shocking for those who chalk up the critical spirit to science, is of course partial. It concerns only "realist" scientists, not those—I have in mind many specialists in the so-called human or social sciences—who limit themselves to identifying or constructing regularities, while boasting of not going any farther. And it concerns only the critical philosophers, be they the descendants of Hume or, like Kant, those who were awakened by Hume from their dogmatic slumber. Yet it is also these philosophers who took charge of promoting the rationality known as modern. And the way they promoted it is indeed, even today, capable of inspiring in scientists the reaction described by Whitehead. Let us listen to Stephen Weinberg, one of those physicists who dream today of a "final theory," closing the search for the laws of nature and imposing itself as the starting point for all rational questions about all that exists:

Ludwig Wittgenstein, who denied even the possibility of explaining the slightest fact by reference to another, affirmed that "at the basis of every modern conception of the world lies the illusion that the alleged laws of nature are the explanations of natural phenomena." Such warnings leave me cold. To tell a physicist that the laws of nature are not explanations of natural phenomena is to tell a tiger in search of its prey that all flesh is grass. The fact that we scientists do not know how to state in a way that would garner the approval of philosophers what we do when we search for scientific explanations does not mean that we are indulging in a vain activity. Professional philosophers could help us to understand what we are doing, but with or without them, we will continue to do it (DFT, 21–22).

For Whitehead, the conflict is modern insofar as it opposes two types of protagonists united by the respect for "facts": philosophers, who ensure that the facts are not asked for more than they can deliver, and scientists, who undertake to ask those facts to explain themselves, to explain reality, even ultimate reality. And this conflict places modernity under the banner not of a progressive history, but of a revolt: a "historical revolt" against medieval rationalism, against which "observable, irreducible" facts became a weapon. The historical fact is that modern science repudiates philosophy, without thereby repudiating the trust in an order of the world to be deciphered, whereas modern philosophers, for their part, are devoted to repudiating this trust, which they associate with an uncritical past, and to betting on the individual mind, which alone can be rendered accountable for the well-foundedness of the reasons associated with an order, whatever it may be.

Thus the evolution of thought in the seventeenth century coöperated with the enhanced sense of individual personality derived from the Middle Ages. We see Descartes taking his stand upon his own ultimate mind, which his philosophy assures him of: and asking about its relations to the ultimate matter—exemplified, in the second Meditation by the human body and a lump of wax—which his science assumes. There is Aaron's rod, and the magicians' serpents; and the only question for philosophy is, which swallows which; or whether, as Descartes thought, they all lived happily together (SMW, 142–143).

The modern epoch is thus placed under the banner of a recurrent difficulty, not of a progress of reason to be interpreted. Yet this difficulty might perhaps not be very important if it affected only such specialized thinkers as scientists and philosophers. For Whitehead, the true problem is that we—and this "we" includes all those who accept the image of a reality ruled by laws—have fallen into the habit of thinking in an incoherent way.

This radical inconsistency at the basis of modern thought accounts for much that is half-hearted and wavering in our civilisation. It would not be going too far to say that it distracts thought. It enfeebles it, by reason of the inconsistency lurking in the background. After all, the men of the Middle Ages were in pursuit of an excellency of which we have nearly forgotten the existence. They set before themselves the ideal of the attainment of a harmony of the understanding. We are content with superficial orderings from diverse arbitrary starting points. For instance, the enterprises produced by the individualistic energy of the European peoples presuppose physical actions directed to final causes. But the science which is employed in their development is based on a philosophy which asserts that physical causation is supreme, and which disjoins the physical cause from the final end. It is not popular to dwell on the absolute contradiction here involved. It is the fact, however you gloze it over with phrases (SMW, 76).

Whitehead's analysis is diagnostic, and the diagnosis still holds true. Suffice it to think of the ineptitude of the propositions induced by the postulate that Darwinian selection must suffice to explain the evolution of living beings because it acts as a barrier against the irrationality of final causes. The transmission of genes and their selection give meaning to the only way of accommodating our own "finalized" enterprises (including science) to a world in which physical causality reigns supreme. In the name of this "holy war" against final causes, all human activities are summoned to affirm their submission to selective logic. As a result, the intellectual and artistic capabilities of human beings, whose problem is that they appear to be somewhat excessive with regard to strict survival needs in these mammals, have been related by some contemporary spokespersons of Darwinism to sexual selection. This means, whatever circumlocutions may be used, that the person who summons us to accept this sober truth is also in the service of the only thing that really matters: the transmission of her genes. Nor is it a matter of becoming indignant at the idea that one's ardor responds to a project of seduction, copulation, and recruitment of as many vehicles as possible for one's own genes. The point is simply to note the imaginative poverty, the "enfeebled thought" of those who expose themselves in such a deliberate way to the oldest argument in philosophy, the retorsive argument, which can be expressed as follows: as a test, apply to yourself the statement you just made, what your statement affirms about everybody else: turnabout is fair play.

Whitehead does not denounce the modern epoch, but speaks of it as of something that must, and will, pass. His diagnosis is also a prognosis. He identifies the weakness, the hesitation, and the confusion concealed by the successes that allow this epoch to be identified with progress, but this weakness, hesitation, and confusion are described in a way that affirms trust: the adventure continues; that is, the incoherence is temporary and "epochal."

Whitehead's great thesis in *Science and the Modern World* is that science can play an important role in the epochal change called for by the adventure of ideas. This is why, in the same book, the goal may be to justify, against the philosophers, the scientists' faith in an order of nature, and, against the scientists, to place the history of modern science under the banner of what he calls "the fallacy of misplaced concreteness." A concrete character has been "misplaced," that is, conferred upon abstractions whose success is that of modern physics. Yet Whitehead diagnoses that this very success is henceforth impeded by its own abstractions. The physicists' matter can no longer be understood on the basis of the motion of masses susceptible of "simple localization" (an instant without thickness, a point without extension).

At any epoch the assumptions of a science are giving way, when they exhibit symptoms of the epicyclic state from which astronomy was rescued in the sixteenth century. Physical science is now exhibiting such symptoms (SMW, 135).

The reference to astronomy saved from the epicycles designates the history that runs from Copernicus to Kepler, more than sixty years later. And it was Kepler who took what may have been the most difficult step, rejecting the epicycles to which all scientists before him, including Copernicus, had recourse to make mathematical description and observation converge. Kepler dared to demand the secrets of planetary motion from observational data themselves.

Far more than Copernicus or Galileo, Kepler enters the lineage of those powerless visionaries about whom Whitehead wrote that they have ultimately guided the world. It is impossible to know to what extent Whitehead compared quantum physics, whose birth he witnessed and which, from his viewpoint, "exhibits" epicyclic phenomena, to such pre-Keplerian systems as that of Copernicus, who maintained the postulate of circular motion, or that of Tycho Brahe, who tried both to keep the earth at the center and to make the planets rotate around a sun that itself rotated around the earth. Yet the parallel, that is, the anticipation of a "new Kepler," can hold (it was proposed by Arthur Koestler, who explicitly took his inspiration from Whitehead in *The Sleepwalkers*), and it is all the more interesting in that Kepler affirmed a new faith in the order of nature. Not a faith in the power of the facts "in themselves," brute and obstinate, but in the possibility that a detailed examination of the facts may lead not to arbitrariness, but to harmony: the living ideal of aesthetic harmony. For it is precisely this faith that Whitehead was to associate with the notion he placed at the center of *Science and the Modern World*: the notion of organism.

However, the parallel must be drawn cautiously, for we must distinguish Kepler's "faith" from his theory as astronomers have inherited it. The mathematical construction of planetary ellipses responds to a quite determinate field of data, those of astronomy, which this construction enables us not only to reproduce but to organize in an intelligible and economical way. Correlatively, the "new Kepler," who Whitehead possibly anticipated, would be a working physicist, not a visionary inspired by her faith in nature's harmony. With regard to the organism, in contrast, it is better to speak not of a scientific concept but of a "doctrine," "thought," or "philosophy." For Whitehead, the organism, "as the complete expression of what takes place," is a "generic" notion, which means that it cannot designate a privileged field of ideas. The questions that will be articulated around the notion of organism must concern all those who are interested in a particular aspect of the order of nature, but they must not take the place of their specific questions. The success of the "philosophy of organism" would be to have each of them situate its own specificity in a positive way, and not, like the "materialist theory," mutilate their questions.

One might of course think that the biological connotation of the term chosen by Whitehead entails a privilege, but the privilege in question is strategic: it has to do with the particular situation of the life sciences. For Whitehead, they offer the interesting particularity of having been handicapped, rather than rendered fruitful, by what he calls "scientific materialism," that is, the explanation of all change in terms of changes in "external" relations between beings that do not change in themselves. This handicap has even become a pure and simple contradiction with the modern doctrine of biological evolution, which should be enough to impose the abandonment of "scientific materialism."

The aboriginal stuff, or material, from which a materialistic philosophy starts is incapable of evolution [...] Evolution, on the materialistic theory, is reduced to being another word for the description of the changes in the external relations between portions of matter [...] *There can merely be change, purposeless and unprogressive. But the whole point of the modern doctrine is the evolution of the complex organisms from antecedent states of less complex organisms. The doctrine thus cries aloud for a conception of the organism as fundamental for nature* (SMW, 107).

As I have already emphasized, the contemporary leading lights of Darwinian theory glorify this theory for ensuring the compatibility between the "complexity of living beings" and a "materialist," or more exactly "physicalist" theory, which limits itself to defining such complexity as highly improbable, with reference to the omnipotence of selective sorting. Whitehead did not have to deal with the poverty of contemporary propositions, but he knew that in any case selective explanation was doomed to substitute one and the same monotonous, "epicyclic" answer (in this case, "adaptionist") for the multiple questions that arise for those who study living beings. Hence the crying need for another starting point. Yet this starting point must not constitute a direct answer to the crying need: Whitehead is no "vitalist" in the sense that he would claim to know "what is life," or what the notions of goal and of progress mean for living beings. What is demanded of the thought of the organism will not be an explanation of life but a characterization of the order of nature itself.

The first appearance of a reference to the organism in *Science and the Modern World* does not, moreover, concern biology but physics itself, and more precisely quantum theory as it had been organized around the model of the atom due to Niels Bohr. This model seems to indicate that the electron—*there it is again*—does not have a continuous motion but is liable to occupy a series of discrete positions in space during successive durations in time. It is as though the permanence of the electron must be understood not as the permanence of something that remains "the same," but as the permanence of a self-repeating pattern. Indeed, this interpretation would make it perfectly normal that the description of a continuous motion, presupposing a continuous succession of instants, is not appropriate for the electrons that orbit around the nucleus in the quantum atom. The electron "does not exist" in a given moment. What exists "takes the time" required by a vibration or a succession of contrasts. And it is when he describes what would be an "organised system of vibratory streaming of energy" that Whitehead suddenly speaks, without the least warning, of a "vibratory organism," only to conclude abruptly, in a mode that is as hyperbolic as it is out of place (officially, the chapter deals with mathematics in the history of thought).

The field is now open for the introduction of some new doctrine of organism which may take the place of the materialism with which, since the seventeenth century, science has saddled philosophy [. . .] *Such a displacement of scientific materialism, if it ever takes place, cannot fail to have important consequences in every field of thought* (SMW, 36).

We need hardly point out that quantum mechanics has by no means taken the road Whitehead hoped for. For him, the description of the quantum atom could only announce a new realism, since science owes it to itself to try to elucidate the order of nature, a realism that would abandon the vision of a world described as a continuous succession of instantaneous material configurations. The quantum theory of Heisenberg, Born, Dirac, and von Neumann was to preserve continuity and let go of realism. As far as I know, Whitehead never commented on this turn taken by physics. Yet everything indicates that he would have maintained his judgment of 1925 concerning the epicyclic symptoms exhibited by physics.

It is important to emphasize once again that Whitehead does not envisage any "theory" enabling the definition of both the (quantic) vibratory organism and of the living organism. His proposition has no ambition to provide a unifying point of view, as was successively proposed by the notions of energy, system, or information. The organism does not designate a possible object of knowledge, it does not constitute an answer around which the sciences would converge, but it is rather, as we shall see, what should oblige us to think about the divergence of their questions as a reflection of the "living values" that constitute the order of nature. And the living value, here, is none other than the affirmation that refuses to be separated from its own shadow, simultaneously affirming what it has succeeded in producing and the ideal without which this success would not have been possible. As such, the thought of the organism is obviously itself a living value, inseparable from the project of articulating, in a finally coherent way, what the modern era has opposed in the mode of contradiction. In the vocabulary of *The Concept of Nature,* the organism is what will prevent nature from bifurcating and will articulate what modern thought opposes: the free subject, assigning itself goals that affirm the supremacy of final causes, and the indifferent objective world, which affirms the supremacy of physical causes. It is thus not a unifying vision of the world that is proposed with the organism, but what Whitehead designates as a new mode of abstraction, capable of reconciling science and philosophy.

You cannot think without abstractions; accordingly, it is of the utmost importance to be vigilant in critically revising your modes of abstraction. It is here that philosophy finds its niche as essential to the healthy progress of society. It is the critic of abstractions. A civilisation which cannot burst through its current abstractions is doomed to sterility after a very limited period of progress. An active school of philosophy is quite as important for the locomotion of ideas, as is an active school of railway engineers for the locomotion of fuel (SMW, 59).

The definition of "fuel" is obviously inseparable from that of the techniques that define motors, gears, and infrastructures. Coal, gas, and electricity only became resources thanks to the ceaselessly renewed invention of what a railway is. The huffing and puffing of a locomotive, the heroic ages of the railroad workers, can be called the victims of progress, but they testify to the inventiveness of railway engineers. According to Whitehead, our modes of abstraction have not benefitted from such creative and critical efforts, and ideas have become unable to catalyze a "healthy progress of society." We do not know when Whitehead began to conceive of the notion of organism in relation to the question of the order of nature. What seems to me certain is that the question of "social progress," that is, also of the diagnosis given of "progress" as defined by the modern world, is considerably earlier. The new mode of abstraction Whitehead names organism must therefore be approached twice. What it proposes to set in motion the ideas concerning nature, to be sure, but the proposed mode of setting in motion is inseparable from the possible setting in motion of many other things as well. To prolong Whitehead's analogy, a railway engineer is active in solving problems involving motion and fuel, but he also dreams of all that can also be set in motion thanks to this solution: not only travelers, merchandise, minerals, and soldiers, but also ways of living, ways of communication, modes of distribution of the possible and the impossible . . .

It is, however, hard to describe at the same time the technical conception of a new system of combustion and the dreams of those who conceive it, who themselves make the difference between what depends on them and what they must leave up to others. Likewise, when it comes to thinking of the organism with Whitehead, the question will be that of the order of nature. What is more, it will take us along on a metaphysical adventure in which the actors of the modern world, which Whitehead dreams of seeing transformed, will no longer have a distinct voice in the chapter. In *Science and the Modern World,* Whitehead has absolutely no concern for this kind of difference, but "thinking with Whitehead" does not mean authorizing oneself all the liberties that Whitehead took with his readers. This is why, before approaching the question of the organism as such, I have chosen to bring Whitehead's "dreams" to life, that is, to give all its importance to his reading of the modern world. The question of science is of course part of this reading, and the new type of movement Whitehead wishes to confer upon scientific ideas is the intended contribution of *Science and the*

Modern World to the new epoch that is to be brought about. But what we must leave behind is even broader, since it includes all the "superficial arrangements" to which we have become accustomed. In particular—this is where I shall begin, and this is what is most surprising—the habit of saluting as a progress religion's loss of authority, that is, the loss of religion as a living source of value.

That Galileo set out to attack the authority of the Church as far as the "positive" truth of the world is concerned is part of the classical history of the progress that leads up to us. To be sure, Galileo was a Christian, but progress, as it is narrated, holds that he participates in the history of the differentiation between personal faith and the public authority of religion, a history that (in European countries, at least) ends up with the contemporary self-evidence that religion must be confined to a strictly personal conviction, merely a particular version of the moral law inscribed in each person's heart, without any incidence on the "public" world. Galileo did not, of course, demand, against Revelation, the possibility that each person should determine in all freedom how the world works: rather, he preached the exclusive authority of science in this regard. But this public authority of science is also taken as part of progress as it is narrated. Galileo therefore participates in progress. He disqualified religion where we know henceforth that it was interfering in what was not its business, in what should concern only science.

Whitehead refuses to define this "privatization of religion" as progress, that is, to define the public authority of religion, by a retroactive judgment, as "a retrograde movement of progress," as what was to be eliminated. To tell the story of the modern world, for Whitehead, is also to tell the story of a degeneration. "Modern" religion boasts of being a testimony in the heart of the believer, without legitimate incidence on public life. In fact, it has been reduced to a kind of supplement of soul, embellishing a comfortable life.

[. . .] *For over two centuries religion has been on the defensive, and on a weak defensive. The period has been one of unprecedented intellectual progress. In this way a series of novel situations have been produced for thought. Each such occasion has found the religious leaders unprepared. Something, which has been proclaimed to be vital, has finally, after struggle, distress and anathema, been modified and otherwise interpreted. The next generation of religious apologists then congratulates the religious world on the deeper insight which has been gained. The result of the continued repetition of this undignified retreat, during many generations, has at last almost entirely destroyed the intellectual authority of religious thinkers* (SMW, 188).

It may amuse free thinkers that the succession of Catholic popes since Paul VI, instead of accepting the need to proceed to the retreat that everybody judges necessary and has, at any rate, come much too late as far as the marriage of priests, contraception, or abortion are concerned, hang on to these prohibitions against all comers. We think that what they do not concede, some successor will sooner or later yield. And no doubt they have foreseen it too, for they too belong to the history marked by the degeneration of religion, the undignified retreat from the positions it defined as vital. They undergo the epoch as if it poses no other alternatives than defeat or resistance to change.

Religion will not regain its old power until it can face change in the same spirit as does science (SMW, 189).

The author of these lines does not define himself as a Christian, nor even as a believer. He will soon find himself constrained to involve God in the conceptual construction of the order of nature, but he will never be tempted by any confusion between this necessity and a justification of religion as such, much less of any specific religion. The question of the future of religion is thus, for Whitehead, completely distinct from the metaphysical question of the order of creation, and the place of human beings in this creation. Whatever the doctrine may be of what God asks of human beings, this doctrine's destiny depends on the living values of which it constitutes an affirmation.

The power of God is the worship He inspires (SMW, 192).

The term "worship" is one of those that Francophones can envy the English language, for it unites when French fragments through such words as "culte," "adoration," and "vénération." For Whitehead, worship first signifies "surrender to the claim for assimilation," a claim whose motive force, he writes, is mutual love. The crucial point is that this definition operates in immanence. "That which" demands assimilation has no distinct identity. Of course, Whitehead speaks of a force, but this force, which he calls mutual love, is not the force of God's love, a God who might demand our surrender. This love belongs to the very experience of worship, and the effect called surrender is not explained by a cause, but characterized by a style. To evoke God's power does not imply, in Whitehead, the preliminary affirmation of His existence, for both the God of a religion and the *worship* that is framed by this religion derive, for Whitehead, from a fundamental experience of humanity: religious vision. A vision of which no religion can be the privileged expression, although each one develops and collapses, from epoch to epoch, according to whether its doctrine, its rites, its commands, or its definitions do or do not evoke this vision, revive it, or inhibit it, giving it or failing to give it an adequate expression.

Religion is the reaction of human nature to its search for God. The presentation of God under the aspect of power awakens every modern instinct of critical reaction. This is fatal; for religion collapses unless its main positions command immediacy of assent. In this respect the old phraseology is at variance with the psychology of modern civilisations (SMW, 191).

The modern critical spirit could indeed be called "religious" since it, like what it denounces, is a reaction to a proposition dealing with God. The problem is that its axis, "to believe or not to believe" in God, testifies in its way to the "weakening" of modern thought, and gives rather inadequate expression to the religious search to which it owes its passion. The question "Does God really exist?" is crucial only if God is conceived as demanding and forbidding, that is, if the statements that include Him claim to benefit from the authority to which the term "really" always alludes, whether this authority refers to political power, to reason, or to the truth of a revelation.

In other words, Whitehead is an agnostic, in the sense that the question "Does God really exist?" has, for him, no valid answer outside of a religious practice. Yet his agnosticism does not communicate with a simple "anthropology of the religious feeling," whose author would contemplate as if from nowhere, submitting to a neutral, objective, and in short scientific gaze a human feature from which he himself would be rather mysteriously free. His agnosticism is positively constructivist, that is, also pragmatic, for the way religion is described commits the person who describes it, implies a wager on what can "make a religion hold," on what the religious feeling might indeed be capable of. For Whitehead, the wager does seem to bear today upon a religion's ability to accept and affirm that the power of God it invokes can indeed be understood as the way this religion defines the kind of power it claims. God is the name for the efficacy upon human beings of the religious vision that they nourish, cultivate, and constitute as an ingredient of their life.

The twofold possibility of nourishing this constructivist conception of the religious vision, and of the religions that give it an expression, which is always "epochal," and of trusting the ability of those of his readers who adhere to a religion to accept this conception, must be understood as a testimony to the time. More precisely, it would be a testimony to the epochal change that Whitehead anticipates and tries to carry out. A constructivism squared: by providing a constructivist version of religion, Whitehead does not stop with the operation of demystification with which the statement "religion is a construction" is immediately associated, but he fights for the future of this construction, for the statements that will one day inspire a new immediate assent and provide religious vision with the words and practices capable of stabilizing their collective importance, irreducible to a question of psychological comfort.

Religion has emerged into human experience mixed with the crudest fancies of barbaric imagination. Gradually, slowly, steadily the vision recurs in history under nobler form and with clearer expression. It is the one element in human experience which persistently shows an upward trend. It fades and then recurs. But when it renews its force, it recurs with an added richness and purity of content. The fact of the religious vision, and its history of persistent expansion, is our one ground for optimism. Apart from it, human life is a flash of occasional enjoyments lighting up a mass of pain and misery, a bagatelle of transient experience (SMW, 192).

It is thus without incoherence, but, as he writes, "in all diffidence," that Whitehead ventures, with regard to the vision that nourishes all religion, the words that make him a witness to what he believes his epoch is capable of.

Religion is the vision of something which stands beyond, behind, and within, the passing flux of immediate things: something which is real, and yet waiting to be realised: something which is a remote possibility, and yet the greatest of present facts; something that gives meaning to all that passes, and yet eludes apprehension; something whose possession is the final good, and yet beyond all reach; something which is the ultimate ideal, and the hopeless quest (SMW, 191–192).

When he was writing *Science and the Modern World,* Whitehead did not yet know that this "something" would soon be situated at the very heart of a mode of abstraction aiming to "set in motion" an idea that he had not yet constituted as a resource, that of a "cosmos." The thought of the organism proposed in this book, for its part, has no direct incidence on the religious vision. It designates the question of the order of nature, not of what may be situated beyond it. The incidence is thus merely indirect, but it is clear: what Whitehead is undertaking, like a railway engineer, is to critically (re)set in motion ideas that are not themselves religious but which, beyond their contradictions, have settled into an agreement that defines as progress the denial of religion as an expression of living values.

Yet there would be nothing overly catastrophic in the privatization of moral worlds, God speaking in the intimacy of each person's heart, if other names than that of God had come to stabilize what matters to human life beyond itself.

Whitehead does not cite Max Weber, who had proposed to associate the rise of capitalism with the anguished question of salvation with which Protestants found themselves confronted, a question addressed to each individual alone and undecidable by definition. If he had done so, he would certainly not have been moved by the somber grandeur of habits of thought that make the accumulation of capital an end in itself, but would have read in it the best testimony to the barbarous imagination, featuring a despotic God and a nature that has bifurcated. The world is reduced to a scene bereft of meaning in itself, in which the only thing that matters, the individual's salvation, is won or lost. But Whitehead preferred to frame the question in a different way. The question that worries him, as always, is that of abstraction, and more precisely the lack of resistance characteristic of the modern epoch to the intolerant rule of abstractions that declare everything that escapes them frivolous, insignificant, or sentimental. We must take seriously the fact that the disasters of the modern world, its ugliness and its brutality, are part of what is called "progress"; what has been done was done in the name of progress. We must think of the widely shared and plausible character of this reference to progress as an "epochal fact."

In other words, Whitehead raises the problem starting out from those who have "sung along" with industrial development, while reserving the right to deplore its excesses. In particular, he wonders why so many remarkable people—and he cites some of his colleagues—have been able to accept and even approve, define as the price and even as the precondition of progress the "rationalization" that reduces workers to "mere hands, drawn from the pool of labour," and nature to a set of exploitable resources.

[...] *Self-respect, and the making the most of your own individual opportunities, together constituted the efficient morality of the leaders among the industrialists of that period. The western world is now suffering from the limited moral outlook of the three previous generations [...] A striking example of this state of mind is to be seen in London where the marvelous beauty of the estuary of the Thames, as it curves through the city, is wantonly defaced by the Charing Cross railway bridge, constructed apart from any reference to aesthetic values* (SMW, 196).

Here, Whitehead could be considered a precursor of ecology. For him, the ugliness of the Charing Cross railway bridge testifies to a catastrophic divorce, not from "purely aesthetic" values but from values that are aesthetic in the sense that they testify to the reverence of human beings toward their environment, and therefore to the intrinsic value they recognize in their environment. He might also be considered a Marxist without knowing it, for the domination of abstraction is what is presupposed and realized by the process of commodification, when all concrete production is reduced to its exchange value in a regime of generalized equivalence, and when the living labor of human beings is evaluated as "labor force." Yet there would be a risk of misunderstanding in both cases, because, for Whitehead, one should not attack one intolerant abstraction by another intolerant abstraction. When they turn the capitalist redefinition of things and of social relations, or its contempt for the environment, into the privileged key for a reading of the modern epoch, both the militant revolutionaries and the protectors of nature rely on an abstraction that is in danger of being intolerant. Indeed, whoever says "key" says "mode of reading that is blind to its own selectivity," for the key designates its lock as the door's only relevant element. And if they rely on such an abstraction, Whitehead would no doubt have insisted, however well-founded their interventions and however relevant their denunciations, their moral horizon risks being just as limited as that of their adversaries.

For Whitehead, the tale the modern world obliges us to tell is thus, in the first place, of how an affirmation of reason, of a vigorous and virile reason chasing away superstition, but also of a short-sighted reason lacking in-depth vision, was able to contribute effectively to the liberation of minds in the eighteenth century, but became fatal in the nineteenth century. What he calls the "history of thought" is a history that is above all collective and anonymous, which must be stated in terms of "habits of thought," that is, of the organizations that stabilize those habits as well, providing them with a protected environment in which they can be perpetuated even when their destructive consequences are obvious. As we shall see in what follows, whoever speaks of a "stable habit implying a protected environment" refers to the general notions articulated by the "philosophy of the organism." This means, in return, that the latter is indeed an abstract, not a salvific doctrine. Abstraction is necessary for setting resources in motion, but it does not dictate the direction this motion must take. In the present case, it does not define what must be done, because it is just as appropriate for the description of what has happened to us. Yet it obliges us to think of what has happened to us in a way that is not the fatality or routine refrain about the normal price to pay for progress.

In fact, what those visionaries of the origins—Galileo, Newton, Leibniz—could scarcely have dared to hope for has indeed become a daily routine in our universities. And this routine has also betrayed the trust that bore them, the trust in a global order to be deciphered in the detail of facts. Nevertheless, the certainties, value judgments, and blindnesses of their university heirs do not authorize any *a posteriori* requisition against these visionaries. Nor do they reflect an "ideology" in the sense that it could be separated from the active, inventive thought on which it would be parasitical. They reflect what happened to thought itself, the weakness with which it pays for the particular strength it has acquired, in the protected environments in which it has developed. The problem is not that the "vision" of the origins has become a habit, but that it has become a "professional habit." According to Whitehead, the greatest discovery of the modern epoch has been the "method of training professionals." This is what accounts for both its formidable strength and its eminent weakness: the organization of the problems and responsibilities of public life, as well as of school and university training, have been placed under the banner of "professionalization."

Each profession makes progress, but it is progress in its own groove. Now to be mentally in a groove is to live in contemplating a given set of abstractions. The groove prevents straying across country, and the abstraction abstracts from something to which no further attention is paid [. . .] *The remainder of life is treated superficially, with the imperfect categories of thought derived from one profession* (SMW, 197).

Professionalization has spread to all practices, including that of scientists. Whitehead makes it responsible, moreover, for a certain stagnation of science in the course of the last twenty years of the nineteenth century,

[. . .] *one of the dullest stages of thought since the time of the First Crusade* (SMW, 101).

Whitehead does not deny that the professionalization of science may be associated with the rapid progress of what have become "scientific disciplines." But this is no reason to find a justification of professionalization. Wherever it exists, this progress comes in the first instance from the fact that research, even if it did not have new ideas as motive forces, could benefit from technological development. As Whitehead emphasizes, this situation is particularly clear in physics: whereas from a technical viewpoint, Galileo could have performed his experiments in front of the family of King Minos, an experiment like that of Michelson, which resulted in the relativistic questioning of space-time, could not have taken place before the moment it was carried out. The possibility of envisaging a measure of the speed of light as compared to the ether testifies not so much to the inventive strength of a science that would have escaped professionalization as if by miracle, as to the direct symbiosis with technical innovation from which this science benefits.

The eighteenth century opened with the quiet confidence that at last nonsense had been gotten rid of. To-day we are at the opposite pole of thought. Heaven knows what seeming nonsense may not tomorrow be demonstrated truth. We have recaptured some of the tone of the early nineteenth century, only on a higher imaginative level. The reason why we are on a higher imaginative level is not because we have finer imagination, but because we have better instruments (SMW, 114).

If professionalization does not prevent us from speaking of a certain progress of science, it has, however, been catastrophic from the viewpoint of the way so-called modern society has been thought and transformed. For Whitehead, the builders of the Charing Cross bridge were genuine professionals, proud of not allowing any sentimental considerations such as harmony or beauty to enter into their calculations. Likewise, those who today manage what are called the "human resources" of corporations are proud to have the strength to abstract from the immediate, concrete consequences of their management in the name of the pitiless necessities of global competition.

We should not be surprised, therefore, if the last chapter of *Science and the Modern World,* entitled "Requisites for Social Progress," deals mainly with the question of education. In fact, this question had already occupied part of Whitehead's life, when he left Cambridge for London. From 1910 to 1924, Whitehead abandoned his "gown" and devoted himself to "the town." He took on heavy academic and administrative responsibilities, and he was also an active participant in movements for educational reform.

Of course, the way Whitehead raises the problem of education is not at all that of a professional pedagogue. His guiding idea is that children are lively and interested, and that the first problem in education is to nourish interest without killing life. What Whitehead calls education does not, therefore, in the first instance designate a reliable transmission of information, or a training in skills that could be evaluated, nor, moreover, the opposite slogan, the respect of differences and the autonomy of the "learner." In fact, education mobilizes all the themes that will oblige him to think as a philosopher: coherence, interest, importance, life, values, emotions, specialization, abstraction, and above all trust. All themes of which the thought of the organism will propose an initial articulation . . .

With the question of the organism, we thus come to the genuine epicenter of Whitehead's thought, at the point of articulation of the diagnosis he gave of the modern epoch and the philosophy of the organism he undertook to construct. If Whitehead, following William James, became so interested in the creator's trust and the power of habit, it is perhaps also because the educator must affirm them both just as much. Educators must trust the creative character of what they are charged with transmitting, and, although they are concerned with the difference between good and bad habits, they cannot denounce habit as such. They will never turn it into the manifestation of a regrettable tendency of the human mind, or a form of voluntary servitude. It was, moreover, on this point that Whitehead explicitly refused to follow Bergson, who proposed to identify the fascination with abstraction with a feature of human intelligence as such, or a trap into which intelligence falls almost necessarily. Whitehead was not fighting against habits, nor did he call for a future in which everyone would be a visionary. In the possibility of a transformation of habits, he had the kind of trust that the craft of an educator presupposes and requires.

For Whitehead, thinking about what social progress requires designates education as a crucial site, in which an epoch judges itself on the basis of the way it fashions those who will prolong its choices, strengths, and weaknesses. Education can create the habit of appreciating concrete facts, complete facts. It can also create the opposite habit, as is the case with the education that produces professionals, the habit of yielding in the face of what is unacceptable, of adhering to what is incredible. Because for Whitehead, the link is obviously direct between the blind way in which thinkers who stuck to secure and definite habits of thought, that is, professionals, have subscribed to the concrete unacceptable consequences of industrial development, and the way in which other thinkers, just as "serious," have prolonged, in a routine way, the incredible theses that made nature bifurcate and reduced reality to the agitation of stupid, insensate matter.

When you understand all about the sun and all about the atmosphere and all about the rotation of the earth, you may still miss the radiance of the sunset. There is no substitute for the direct perception of the concrete achievement of a thing in its actuality. We want concrete fact with a high light thrown on what is relevant to its preciousness. What I mean is art and aesthetic education [...] "art" in the general sense that I require is any selection by which the concrete facts are so arranged as to elicit attention to particular values which are realisable by them. For example, the mere disposing of the human body and the eyesight so as to get a good view of the sunset is a simple form of artistic selection. The habit of art is the habit of enjoying vivid values. But, in this sense, art concerns more than sunsets. A factory, with its machinery, its community of operatives, its social service to the general population, its dependence upon organising and designing genius, its potentialities as a source of wealth to the holders of its stock is an organism exhibiting a variety of vivid values. What we want to train is the habit of apprehending such an organism in its completeness (SMW, 199–200).

The "organism" has made its appearance, unexpectedly, in the context of a factory, its workers, its stockholders, its executives, and its environment, indicating the end of the diagnostic itinerary and the moment when it will finally become necessary to envisage what Whitehead understands by an organism. Today, when "rationalization," "competitiveness," and "flexibility" reign, this emergence at the end of an itinerary may raise a smile, and this may already have been the case in his time. The enjoyment of vivid values does not imply a praise of reality. It makes the difference, central in *The Aims of Education,* between "vivid" and "dead" ideas, the former setting the students' minds in motion, and the latter being synonyms of indoctrination and passivity.

Before we conclude, I offer a tribute to the person who, years ago, made this difference a vivid idea for me when he forced me to set in motion what I thought I knew well, in this case the equivalence between kinetic energy and potential energy as illustrated by the perfect pendulum. A dead, scholastic example, he objected to me, which silences what this equivalence does not say, but which is attested by the pendulum clockwork mechanisms: it is when the pendulum has fully unfolded its motion that it enters into the twofold contact, with the mechanism of the needles and with a falling weight (or a relaxing spring) that makes it a "timekeeper." This "technical detail" matters, whatever the claims of dynamic equivalence! Thus, an austere treatise on clock making, dealing with "escape mechanisms," finally came alive, a passionate and fascinating story of the multiple inventions that take advantage of what only a pendulum coming to the end of its ascent is able to do. An example of the aesthetic education mentioned by Whitehead: the pendulum clock no longer illustrated a law of motion without simultaneously nourishing speculation, poetry, and narration. A genuine "ecology" of abstraction, for the abstract law of the pendulum can then elicit the attention it is due without denying the rest, in a way that creates the possibility of a mutual aesthetic appreciation between specialists of precision and adventurers of generalization. The question is no longer of knowing "who is right," but of what each one of them has "done" with the vivid experience that nourished them all.

CHAPTER TEN

From the Concept of Nature to the Order of Nature

THE WHITEHEADIAN notion of organism is not, as such, scientific, unlike the definitions that each specialized branch of knowledge might be inclined to give to what this notion comprehends. It pertains to the philosophy of the organism to construct the abstract concepts that constitute each specialized version of the organism as "cases," exhibiting in a more or less partial way what these concepts, for their part, will designate as a "complete and concrete fact." In this sense, the common reference to the organism will also have to illuminate the divergence between the sciences, for this divergence will reflect the way in which the concern of each authorizes it to take into account only certain aspects of the "complete and concrete fact" in order to give them a determinable meaning. This means that "scientific reasons," as demanding determination, will still be theirs and will not be judged in terms of a more powerful philosophical reason to which they must submit.

In other words, Whitehead does not intend to return to the past. The origin of modern science was above all a historical revolt against inflexible medieval rationalism. Galileo played "the stubborn facts" against reason, always returning to the way things happen against those who try to understand why they happen, but the philosophy of the organism will not seek assistance from ancient reasons "against" Galilean abstraction. Quite the contrary, its job will be to confirm the trust in the facts that animates modern science. However, those who have recorded their dissatisfaction, as contemporaries of modern scientific facts and abstractions, must be listened to. In so doing, they have, each in their own way, exhibited aspects of the experience for which these abstractions, and the facts they privilege, did not account in a satisfactory way. Likewise, the fact that the "reasons" appropriate in physics and chemistry are an obstacle to the development of biology or psychology can and must be taken seriously.

It is important to emphasize that the obstacle in question is, in fact, less "conceptual" than social, as is attested by the interminable debates over the mind-body problem. Given that what we call "body" can be represented in these debates in terms of "state of the central nervous system," decipherable in principle as one physico-chemical system among others, while what we call "mind" is reduced to so-called question of the "qualia"—perceiving a specific frequency of electromagnetic radiation as "red"—implies first of all that everyone seems to be able to grasp with impunity what is designated by "body" and "mind" in order to caricature them in terms that repeat the bifurcation of nature over and over again.

Whitehead's procedure should be approached while keeping this aspect of the situation in mind: trust in ideas, to be sure, but above all in the possibility of a transformation of habits. From generation to generation, body and mind have found "defenders," protesting against scientific caricatures, but their arguments have been impotent against the habits of impunity of the scientists, who shrug them off with reactions of the type "Yes, I know, but nevertheless": nevertheless, you can't stop the progress of science, and what does not seem to us to be possible today will be so tomorrow.

This is why Whitehead will not base himself on dissatisfactions and obstacles, but will place them in the service of a strategy addressing imagination, the only eventual producer of a transformation in habits. The goal is neither to prove nor to refute, but to transform what was intended to be a proof that there is room for dissatisfaction, or a refutation based on an obstacle reputed to be insurmountable, into contributions to the "job specifications" that his conception of the order of nature will have to fulfill.

To speak of a "job specifications" is to avoid speaking either of "requisites" or of "concepts." Requisites were appropriate for the approach of *The Concept of Nature,* because they were immanent to the problem Whitehead had decided to raise in that book. Here, it is the epoch that raises its (nonphilosophical) problems, and the requisites will have to wait for the completion of the inquiry resulting in the "job specifications," for these requisites will reflect the way Whitehead defines, through the obligations imposed by these job specifications, what is required by the order of nature. As far as conceptual construction is concerned, it will begin with the transformation of what has been collected and affirmed into requisites immanent to the properly philosophical problem that is henceforth raised, and it will have to satisfy the demands of logical rationality and harmony presupposed by faith in the order of nature. The notion of organism is thus situated at the interface between an empirical type of inquiry whose terrain would be the history of ideas, protestations, and denunciations, and a conceptual construction, whose starting point will be the requisites extracted from the terrain by the inquiry.

It is already clear that the conceptual construction obliged by the notion of organism will have to aim at what was excluded by the approach of *The Concept of Nature:* since we are no longer dealing here with nature in the sense in which we experience it, but with that nature for which we suppose an order, the point will be to construct reasons; and therefore, also to determine the obligations to which our reasons must submit.

We have to search whether nature does not in its very being show itself as self-explanatory. By this I mean, that the sheer statement, of what things are, may contain elements explanatory of why things are. Such elements may be expected to refer to depths beyond anything which we can grasp with a clear apprehension. In a sense, all explanation must end in an ultimate arbitrariness. My demand is, that the ultimate arbitrariness of matter of fact from which our formulation starts should disclose the same general principles of reality, which we dimly discern as stretching away into regions beyond our explicit powers of discernment (SMW, 92–93).

Where scientific materialism postulates localized entities as the ultimate reference for all explanation, the philosophy of the organism will ask that the concepts to be constructed exhibit the way nature "explains itself." This demand formulated by Whitehead is a modified version of "all in the same boat, to sink or swim together," but it announces the need for a new position for the category of the ultimate. Since the problem will henceforth be the ultimate of our explanations, what is presupposed by all our explanations, we may take arbitrariness as a name for this ultimate, but here the arbitrariness does not correspond to a limit, imposing a renunciation: it is defined by a demand. Whitehead demands that the ultimate arbitrariness must be similarly concluded with regard to every explanation, even those concerning the states of things that are most familiar. And he demands, correlatively, that no aspect of reality should designate this arbitrariness in a privileged way.

As in *The Concept of Nature,* the designation of something ultimate thus goes hand in hand with conceptual construction, and they point to the same strategy of resistance to the lures of specialized thought. The concepts to be constructed presuppose, and enable us to resist, the facile solution to which all specialized thought yields: something ultimate often intervenes at the point when their clear categories, corresponding to what they privilege, cease to operate. This is the case when scientists affirm that they can explain the *how* of things, but invoke the unknowable character of chance, or of God's will, when their *why* is concerned. But also when critical thinkers demonstrate that all our knowledge has as its object phenomena not things as they exist in themselves, only to collide, as with an enigma, with the fact that when astronomers pointed their telescopes in the direction in which their calculations indicated the possible existence of an unknown planet, they did indeed find it. Or again, when theoreticians of the mind-body problem declare that the ultimate mystery is constituted by the emergence of *qualia*. The way in which a difficulty, which follows from the framing of a problem, is avoided by means of submission to the unknowable is just as unacceptable for Whitehead as the theory of "psychic additions": it corresponds to "rationality's great refusal to insist on its rights."

Concepts will thus ensure that rationality can affirm its rights, all its rights, but not the right to an ultimate and self-sufficient explanation. The very idea of such an explanation cannot seduce a mathematician: every explanation has its premises, and every premise designates the irreducible responsibility of whoever demands the explanation, this explanation and no other. The premises are part of the work. The right claimed by conceptual work is the right of not turning what is ultimate into a limit of thought, where it is a specialized thought that meets its limits. Like everything we are aware of in perception, therefore, all our specialized explanations will be "placed in the same boat": what we are directly aware of will have to refer to the same ultimate arbitrariness as the "depth" of reality that we cannot clearly grasp.

First, however, it is time to write down the job specifications, that is, to carry out empirical inquiry. Or, more precisely, the inquiry that will transform all those whom it addresses into empirical witnesses, bringing to existence one or another aspect of the concrete and complete facts of which the organism will have to take charge. Obviously, what will be retained is not always what these witnesses thought they were producing—far from it. Whitehead accords no importance to the intentions of the witnesses he provides for himself or the vocation they conferred upon their propositions. Whether they wanted to or not, they testify, and their testimony concerns the order of nature.

The most extraordinary example in this matter is certainly the one I have already cited: the treatment undergone by the thought of Bishop Berkeley. Whitehead is not concerned with Berkeley's doctrine, or his usual historical inheritance by Hume, then Kant. He intends to go back to what is, for him, Berkeley's key problem, the critique of the mode of abstraction that confers a misplaced concreteness upon simple localization. In so doing, he obviously goes back to the problem raised in *The Concept of Nature* as well. Berkeley asks why we confuse what we perceive "here" with real things that we suppose to exist at a distance, "there." But the point is no longer to fight against the bifurcation of nature, to construct the concept of nature required by what we are aware of: this castle, this cloud, this planet, that declare themselves to be "there." For what is at issue now is the order of nature, and experience will have to exhibit the way it participates in this order.

Whitehead therefore registers Berkeley's testimony among his job specifications, as a protest against reducing the concrete fact of perceptive experience to the abstraction of a space in which things "in themselves" are situated, a "reality" to which we could refer while forgetting the perceiving mind. He will therefore affirm, with Berkeley, that what constitutes the realization of natural entities, castle, cloud, or planet, is the fact of being perceived, but . . . on the condition of carrying out one small modification. The point is simply to avoid passing, as Berkeley did, from the idea that natural entities are "realized" in the unity of a perception to the idea that they owe their reality to that perception. And to avoid this, it suffices to "add" to Berkeley's testimony that what is realized is nothing other than the unity of the mind itself, or

[. . .] *that the realisation is a gathering of things into the unity of a prehension; and that what is thereby realised is the prehension, and not the things. This unity of a prehension defines itself as a here and now, and the things so gathered into the grasped unity have essential reference to other places and other times. For Berkeley's mind, I substitute a process of prehensive unification* (SMW, 69).

In *The Concept of Nature,* the perceptive event, associated with "corporeal life," provided all experience with its "here," and perception with its viewpoint. Whitehead had emphasized that what we are aware of exhibits itself as "providing a foothold" for mind: that is, the event declares nature's connection with the ultimate metaphysical reality, where "mind" and "nature" cannot be opposed. With Berkeley's doctrine, we jump feet-first into the risk, emphasized in *The Concept of Nature,* of making mind intervene in a way that blows up the entire powder keg. This is what Berkeley did, since his name is henceforth linked to the extraordinary questions associated with "solipsism," or the doubt that anything exists independently of "my" perception (or of yours . . .). Yet with the "minor modification" proposed by Whitehead, an entirely different kind of "leap" is announced, just as adventurous but with a quite different orientation. It is not a matter of arguing over "what is more real?" experience or that to which it testifies, this castle, these clouds . . . The point is to take experience, and what it testifies to about what is other than it, about other places and other times, as a mode of articulation to which the metaphysical language to be constructed will have to grant meaning.

The key term is, of course, "prehension." Prehension is a "taking into account," and this neologism indicates that Whitehead intends to free this term from all subjective or intellectual connotations, as well as from everything such a connotation implies. The statement "I take into account" presupposes the possibility of distinguishing the subject and the account carried out by this subject. If I take into account the possibility that it may rain at the moment I step outside, and stop to get my coat, I do not by any means have the impression that I am producing myself in this operation. Prehension, in contrast, should make the operation and the production of reality coincide. What prehends realizes itself in the process of prehensive unification, my hesitation "here," my coat "there," the threatening sky up above, and so on.

Prehension is thus a primary term, as was perception for Berkeley. It does not require explanation but must enable the exhibition of the common feature of all situations in which something makes a difference for something else, including the least "psychological" ones. For instance, the earth's trajectory "takes account" of the sun. The mathematical function with which celestial mechanics associates this trajectory testifies to a remarkably stable mode of prehension, referring to the sun *qua* endowed with a mass and situated at a determinate distance. The identification of the sun's distance and mass as variables of the earth's acceleration at each instant thus explicates, in an abstract way, this aspect of the "prehensive unification" that we call acceleration.

Perception is simply the cognition of prehensive unification; or more shortly, perception is cognition of prehension. The actual world is a manifold of prehensions: and a "prehension" is a "prehensive occasion," and a prehensive occasion is the most concrete finite entity, conceived as what it is in itself and for itself, and not as from its aspect in the essence of another such occasion (SMW, 71).

The breathless succession of utterances gives this passage the character of a veritable eruption of metaphysics, of the description of what is "actual," existing in and for itself, and Whitehead's readers might think they have to do with a meditation on the thinkers of the seventeenth century. Whitehead is not doing history of philosophy, however. He treats Berkeley, and soon Leibniz and Spinoza, as a mathematician treats his colleagues. Like Berkeley, Leibniz, and Spinoza, he attempts the paradigmatic enunciatory adventure: the inauguration of terms that will bring to existence both the thinker and the thought, terms which, in this case, must carry out the transition from the question of the concept of nature to that of the order of nature. To attempt this adventure, however, he, like all mathematicians, must distinguish, in the work that precedes him, between what can be respected and what will have to be generalized in another way. In this case, what is to be respected is the experience that has made the thinker and the thought exist, but what can and must be generalized designates the conclusions that Berkeley drew from them. This does not mean that these conclusions are wrong, but that they reflect a freedom and a risk that can, and must, be appreciated in a mode that is primarily that of contrast, experimentation of agreements and divergences.

The things which are grasped into a realised unity, here and now, are not the castle, cloud, and the planet simply in themselves; but they are the castle, the cloud, and the planet from the standpoint, in space and time, of the prehensive unification. In other words, it is the perspective of the castle over there from the standpoint of the unification here. It is, therefore, aspects of the castle, the cloud, and the planet which are grasped into unity here. You will remember that the idea of perspectives is quite familiar in philosophy. It was introduced by Leibniz, in the notion of the monad mirroring perspectives of the universe. I am using the same notion, only I am toning down his monads into the unified events in space and time. In some ways, there is greater analogy with Spinoza's modes; that is why I use the terms mode and modal. In the analogy with Spinoza, his one substance is for me the one underlying activity of realisation individualising itself in an interlocked plurality of modes. Thus, concrete fact is process. Its primary analysis is into underlying activity of prehension, and into realised prehensive events. Each event is an individual matter of fact issuing from an individualisation of the substrate activity. But individualisation does not mean substantial independence (SMW, 69–70).

It is hard, and no doubt futile, to know whether Whitehead thought he possessed the essential part of the solution at the time he wrote these lines. The proponents of a systematic reading, affirming the unity of his work from *Science and the Modern World* to *Adventures of Ideas*, can affirm that everything is already here, summarized in brief form. Like the Leibnizian monad, the individual prehensive event may lay claim to the features that Whitehead judges essential to any realism: "memory of the past, immediacy of realisation, and indication of things to come" (SMW, 73). Indeed, the event, as Whitehead characterizes it here, not only reflects in itself the modes of unification of its contemporaries, but also those of its predecessors, and finally those aspects that the present has determined with regard to the future. Yet one can just as well speak of "wishful thinking" or "betting on a comet." For the notion of a substrate activity that is individualized is a black box, a placeholder for a solution. Let us say, more positively, that it already designates what is refused, the substantial independence that corresponded to a world of individuals, and that it introduces an initial "specification" to be fulfilled, an initial constraint to be satisfied. The fact that an individual is thought of as an individualization implies that the question of the relations between individuals (conceived as substantially independent) is a badly framed question, in that it presupposes the possibility of conceiving of isolated, localized individuals. The well-formulated question must deal with the "how" of relations, not their existence. Yet these are still mere words, promising to be sure, but which have not undergone any of the tests capable of determining what they commit us to.

In fact, Whitehead is quite clear about the operation he has attempted. *In this sketch of an analysis more concrete than that of the scientific scheme of thought, I have started from our own psychological field, as it stands for our cognition. I take it for what it claims to be: the self-knowledge of our bodily event. I mean the total event, and not the inspection of the details of the body. This self-knowledge discloses a prehensive unification of modal presences of entities beyond itself. I generalise by the use of the principle that this total bodily event is on the same level as all other events, except for an unusual complexity and stability of inherent pattern* (SMW, 73).

The "psychological field" of which Whitehead speaks refers, in a fairly transparent way, to the analyses of William James, and particularly to his article "Does 'Consciousness' Exist?" to whose ambition Whitehead subscribes (SMW, 143), as we have already seen: James closes the philosophical epoch inaugurated by Descartes.

Whitehead, one might say, "starts out" from what is, for James, the riskiest speculation: consciousness does not exist, it is a fictitious unit; thoughts, however, are fully real, and are made of the same "stuff" as things. And with the term "self-consciousness," Whitehead also accepts James's proposition that consciousness "stands for" a "function," a function that thoughts "perform" and which is called "knowing." With the expression "self-knowledge of our bodily event," the question of consciousness as a "function" is thus raised. And the cautionary note is already struck: consciousness is not to be reduced to an "epiphenomenon," as is claimed by those who, as they inspect the "details" of neuronal functioning, undertake to "explain" it. The "total" bodily event is by no means the body as the object of scientific definition, but rather the unknown element of the problem James proposed, and which will have to be solved.

In *Process and Reality,* Whitehead will implicitly present himself as the one who "comes after William James." Implicitly, because it is precisely insofar as *Science and the Modern World* had turned William James into the inaugurator of a new philosophical epoch that a much more general remark by Whitehead, concerning the rhythm proper to the history of philosophy, assumes all its meaning.

Every philosophical school in the course of its history requires two presiding philosophers. One of them, under the influence of the main doctrines of the school, should survey experience with some adequacy, but inconsistently. The other philosopher should reduce the doctrines of the school to a rigid consistency; he will thereby effect a *reductio ad absurdum.* No school of thought has performed its full service to philosophy until these men have appeared (PR, 57).

Insofar as Whitehead always insisted on presenting himself as a part of the history of philosophy, rather than as its culmination, it is not prohibited to maintain that, as soon as he began to write *Science and the Modern World,* he considered himself to be trying to confer his "rigid coherence" upon the philosophy of William James, and more precisely on his position with regard to consciousness. There is nothing negative about this, coming from a mathematician: the point is to go "right to the end" of a proposition, to render its presuppositions and consequences explicit, to reconstruct everything on its basis, at the risk that this undertaking may render perceptible (to others) a potential absurdity of the system. And, by so doing, the service that will have been rendered to philosophy will be the dissatisfaction inspired, a motive for a new philosophical creation.

In this case, before going to the end of the proposition that turns consciousness into a function, its meaning must be constructed. What Whitehead must avoid is fairly clear: his entire construction would collapse if he accepted a consciousness that would be the subject of statements concerning experience, a consciousness that, as the master of its ship, could freely choose to address one or another aspect of its own experience. Consciousness cannot be a pure activity, capable, as the case may be, of asking whether it might not, after all, be responsible for all that it perceives. Yet that does not make it a "function" in the scientific sense, that is, explicable as the sum of the "details" brought to light by the scientific inspection of the body. For Whitehead, consciousness in James's sense obliges us to think of the "total bodily event," and, as he continues with rigid coherence, it obliges us to think of every event in the sense in which it exists "for itself." The production of a standpoint enabling us to speak of "self-consciousness" is not the privilege of the "psychological field." The only privilege of this field is to constitute the site where the twofold question "What is a function?" and "What is an event?" will find its most demanding terms.

James's philosophy could be, and generally was, confused with a philosophy of an opportunistic entrepreneur, for whom the pretences of consciousness are illusory, for whom the truth of an idea is identical with what it earns, with its cash value. No one would dare to disqualify *Process and Reality* in this way, where the demand that all that exists may be said to be both "cause of itself" and "function" was to find its full explanation. Quite the contrary, what characterizes Whitehead's great work is the incongruous effort demanded of the reader, to whom a set of concepts is proposed, none of which declares its cash value, and none of which, moreover, has any meaning independently of all the others. Whereas James's thought could be taken apart and simplified, Whitehead's writing "reduces" this supple and vulnerable thought "to a rigid coherence"; that is, it actively produces a strange inseparability between the experience demanded by reading and the experience proposed by concepts.

We have not reached that stage yet. Here, the point was to emphasize the commitment constituted by Whitehead's allusion to the psychophilosophy of William James. If the psychological field is ever to be a reliable starting point for a generalization that may eventually surmount the "territorial division between science and philosophy" (SMW, 145), it is to the extent that it obliges us to risk all that is presupposed by our descriptions centered either around the "subject" or the "object," either around what is "active" (explanatory) or around what is "passive" (explicable). At this stage, however, the division in question is far from having been actually surmounted. Whitehead is announcing an ambition that he still lacks the means to satisfy, for the problem as he frames it is situated in the strict prolongation of his position in *The Concept of Nature*. Nor is he unaware of this, since he takes care, on the contrary, to specify the continuity of his thought, to articulate the new notion of prehension with the old notion of an object making ingression.

I will say that a sense-object has ingression into space-time. The cognitive perception of a sense-object is the awareness of the prehensive unification (into a standpoint A, including the sense-object in question) of various modes of various sense-objects [. . .] I am merely describing what we do perceive: we are aware of green as being one element in a prehensive unification of sense-objects; each sense-object, and among them green, having its particular mode, which is expressible as location elsewhere. There are various types of modal location. For example, sound is voluminous: it fills a hall, and so sometimes does diffused colour. But the modal location of a colour may be that of being the remote boundary of a volume, as for example the colours on the walls of a room (SMW, 70–71).

So far, then, Whitehead has limited himself to repeating what we already knew: ingression is a relation that has various modes. But he has done so in such a way that observation is no longer connected with experience, but with "reality," or the process of realization. The multiplicity of modes of ingression will have to be understood on the basis of the new questions of realization and individualization. We no longer have experience of an event, but our sensible experience is a typical case of an event.

We are only at the beginning of the itinerary associated with the philosophy of the organism, for the point here is no longer to think of perception, but to confirm faith in the order of nature. A castle, a cloud, a green leaf have in common the fact of posing the question of perception, but insofar as they are united by this common feature, they are silent with regard to the way we perceive and feel, that is, also with regard to what is attested by what we perceive and feel. Here, Whitehead abandons those seventeenth-century thinkers who discussed the relation between perception and the spatio-temporal world. Their testimony does not suffice, for it is liable to treat a castle, a cloud, and the face of a loved one indifferently. It does not do justice to what I have already introduced as the question of "presence."

Whitehead now turns to the Romantic poets of the early British nineteenth century, toward those who "reacted" to scientific abstractions by celebrating a nature to which these abstractions fail to do justice.

"We murder to dissect," according to Wordsworth's accusation. Whitehead cites this indignation, this fury, and he chooses to understand it as a testimony not to the violence of the assassin, or to the pain of the victim, but to the inadequacy of the "materialist" scientific approach, as well as of the empiricist approach that was contemporary with it. The philosophy of the organism is first and foremost an epistemology.

It is important to ask, what Wordsworth found in nature that failed to receive expression in science. I ask this question in the interest of science itself; for one main position in these lectures is a protest against the idea that the abstractions of science are irreformable and unalterable. Now it is emphatically not the case that Wordsworth hands over inorganic matter to the mercy of science, and concentrates on the faith that in the living organism there is some element that science cannot analyse [. . .] It is the brooding presence of the hills which haunts him. His theme is nature in solido, that is to say, he dwells on that mysterious presence of surrounding things, which imposes itself on any separate element that we set up as an individual for its own sake (SMW, 83).

When I go for a walk, it is no longer a matter of saying of a hill, *"Say, there it is again,"* as was the case with Cleopatra's Needle. The hill, brooding and ancient, has a weight; it is a "presence" and not simply "there" for me, who perceives it "here." The experience of its presence imposes itself in such a way that I belong to it much more than it belongs to me: this is what a science focused on separability cannot express.

Nor, however, can it express what was celebrated by Shelley, who, unlike Wordsworth, loved science. For Shelley's poetry celebrates nature that is in a state of flux, of perpetual change, and it testifies not to presence, but to a "change that cannot die," an incessant shimmering, an elusive rustling.

Shelley thinks of nature as changing, dissolving, transforming as it were at a fairy's touch (SMW, 86).

The contrast between brooding, ancient presence and the shimmering of colors and sounds does not depend on the difference in the temperament of the two poets facing the "same" landscape. This would silence experience in favor of bargain-basement psychology. If a difference in temperaments does come into play, it is in the different sensitivity with regard to two "facts," both of which must appear among the job specifications. One of them testifies to what Whitehead will call "endurance," which includes change, the other to what he will call "eternality."

The mountain endures. But when after ages it has been worn away, it has gone. If a replica arises, it is yet a new mountain. A colour is eternal. It haunts time like a spirit. It comes and it goes. But when it comes, it is the same colour. It neither survives nor does it live. It appears when it is wanted. The mountain has to time and space a different relation from that which colour has (SMW, 86–87).

"A colour is eternal." Color already played a highly peculiar role in *The Concept of Nature*, as it is the paradigmatic hostage of the bifurcation of nature in the same way as *qualia* are today in the sempiternal controversies organized around the *mind-body problem*. Whitehead does not limit himself to confirming the answer he had given in *The Concept of Nature*: color is a sense-object, and all objects make ingression. Here, color appears endowed with an adjective, eternal, that topples us into a new world of questions. The sense-object is no longer defined on the basis of the empiricist question; what raises problems is no longer the relation between the set of sense data I can perceive and this "stone" to which I attribute them. The bifurcation of nature between primary and secondary qualities yields to the question to which the poets oblige us, the difference between modes of experience of the brooding mountain, always there, and of color, without age or memory, which appears when it is "called."

The adjective "eternal" has a rugged, and highly controversial, future ahead of it. When he was finishing writing *Science and the Modern*

World, Whitehead conferred a decisive role upon "eternal objects," a role that would not cease to be redefined in subsequent times, on the occasion of each technical transformation of his thought. What is important, at this point, is to eliminate any possibility of confusion. For the moment, the adjective "eternal" is connected with a contrast. One may baptize what endures with a proper name—each human being, of course, but also a dog, a mouse, or even a mountain, and Cleopatra's Needle—but proper names are not appropriate either for colors or sounds, or for the geometrical objects Whitehead also associates with the mode of experience designated by the adjective "eternal." When I say "it is blue," but also "it is a circle," I am not naming a blue object, or a circular one, but I testify to the ingression into my experience of an "eternal object."

Whitehead is not mad enough to calmly announce that "red" as we perceive it existed before the biological invention of the visual organs. This is why he speaks of "eternality," a neologism that enables him to avoid "eternity." "Eternality" designates a dimension of the concrete, complete fact that must belong to the job specifications. The testimony of the poets must be heard, but it does not say *how* it should be heard, what requisites correspond to it.

In the present case, the contrast between colors and mountains first calls into question the construction proposed by *The Concept of Nature.* The wonderful world of colors, the mystery of presence, the somber rumination of the mountain testify to the fact that, by the mere fact that it does not share the passage of nature, the object defined in *The Concept of Nature* is no longer adequate for thinking of the order of nature. Color was a sense-object, and the mountain a perceptual object, taken in a hierarchy that made it explicit that the mountain always has a color, whereas we can have the experience of a color independently of what it colors: the famous Cambridge blue. The poets contributed a testimony that raises a very different question, no doubt because their experience is not focused on the urgency of having to decide whether that yellowish shadow is or is not a tiger. And, in so doing, they also forced the experience Whitehead assimilated under the word "recognition" to diverge: *"it's the same color"* and *"that's my coat"* testify to experiences whose difference can no longer be referred to a hierarchy.

"There it is again" was appropriate for Cleopatra's Needle and a birdsong, because the main contrast took place between events that passed without return and objects liable to be recognized, both required by what we are aware of. What is happening, however, is no longer the event, but what is unification, gathering, in a twofold sense, passive and active. The event not only discloses itself as related to other events: it realizes this relation in and for itself. It happens and passes, of course, but we must first

say that, like the here "and" now of *The Concept of Nature,* its duration is that of an individualization, of the "holding together" of the gathering it constitutes. Correlatively, the part is no longer merely included in the whole, and the totality of events "linked" to a particular event is no longer merely "signified" by this event. The whole ruminates in every part, and the various parts are henceforth "presence."

As far as color is concerned, it is no longer there "again" but "once again," always the same but always new, for it is not worn out, does not live, does not endure. Eternal not because it is always there—it would never be anything but an indefinite endurance—but because experience testifies to color in the sense that it is what it is, without reference to a process within time. Color is eternal in the precise sense that it requires that endurance and change do not define in an exhaustive way what is required in the order of nature. Red testifies to something that, in nature, does not emerge from this order like all that endures and changes. Red appears "when it is called," although the sensation of red requires the endurance proper to the eye and the brain. In order to express this non-emergence, this appearance that does not testify to a process but rather to a call, Whitehead will henceforth reserve the term "ingression." Red does not emerge from the order to which the eye and the brain testify, but rather the eye and the brain must be understood on the basis of the possibility of the ingression to which the sensation "red" testifies. The fact of their existence testifies "for" the eternal object felt as red.

Both sensible objects and intelligible objects are "called," or gathered together, by the notions of eternal object and ingression. Yet this association designates our human experience, not a particular connection between sensible and intelligible, such as a particular legitimacy attributed to sense experience and to formal reasoning. Eternal objects are not there to found geometrical reasoning, or the indisputable sensation "blue." They are required by the contrast exhibited in a privileged way by the experiences that make us speak of sensible objects and intelligible objects. In the event constituted by my experience of the famous blue coat, blue qualifies another event which, for its part, endures: that more or less worn-out coat. The cloth may undergo wear and tear, but a color, for its part, will always be "that" color, whatever detergent commercials may claim to the contrary. Consider this circle clumsily drawn in the sand, perhaps to illustrate a process of reasoning. The wind is erasing its contours, but the "circle" that qualified my experience of the contour will not disappear with the wind.

Whoever considers that Whitehead is proposing eternal objects as a solution to the problem raised by geometrical forms and colors will rightly conclude that he has fallen into a trap identified by Gilles Deleuze: that of the "décalque" (tracing), or the concept "made to explain," in this case made to found the contrast, to which experience testifies, between color and mountain. And it is criticism that Whitehead would be the first to accept, since it would mean confusing job specification and concept. If experience is what raises problems, the way the problem is constructed belongs to the formulation of the requisites, that is, to the characterization of an organism as a complete, concrete fact, and it is in response to this formulation that eternal objects will, as the case may be, receive their concept.

For the moment, eternal objects merely oblige us to resist the idea that sensation or intellection emerge from the brain. In *Process and Reality*, these objects will be defined as "pure potentials for the specific determination of fact" (PR, 22), and Whitehead will then have completed the conceptual construction that transforms the experience of color into a "case." As indicated by the adjectives "sensible" and "intelligible," red or circle will then refer to our experience, not to direct access to a "pure" potential.

Let us return, now, to the mountain that "endures." Unlike eternal objects, which offer the temptation of a brutal continuity between the sense-objects of *The Concept of Nature* and the speculative scheme of *Process and Reality*, endurance constitutes a theme that is obviously new. The event had been that which passes. If an order of nature exists, it is because the event, henceforth understood as a unifying grasp, can also hold fast and endure through an environment that never ceases to change. And the poet's emotion when faced by the millennial mountain must be heard. Endurance is not only a fact: it is an accomplishment and an achievement. It requires that the order of nature integrate what we are accustomed to thinking as paradigmatically human, that is, value.

"Value" is the word I use for the intrinsic reality of an event. Value is an element which permeates through and through the poetic view of nature. We have only to transfer to the very texture of realisation in itself that value which we recognise so readily in terms of human life [. . .] realisation therefore is in itself the attainment of value. But there is no such thing as mere value. Value is the outcome of limitation. The definite finite entity is the selected mode which is the shaping of attainment; apart from such shaping into individual matter of fact there is no attainment. The mere fusion of all there is would be the nonentity of indefiniteness. The salvation of reality is its obstinate, irreducible, matter-of-fact entities, which are limited to be no other than themselves. Neither science, nor art, nor creative action can tear itself away from obstinate, irreducible, limited facts. The endurance of things has its significance in the self-retention of that which imposes itself as a definite attainment for its own sake. That which

endures is limited, obstructive, intolerant, infecting its environment with its own aspects. But it is not self-sufficient. The aspects of all things enter into its very nature. It is only itself as drawing together into its own limitation the larger whole in which it finds itself (SMW 93–94).

We are at a crucial point here, and the tone has changed. For value is what is required by the divergence between the experiences of Berkeley, Spinoza, Leibniz, Shelley, or Wordsworth. Value is required by an author capable of using the same term, whether in reference to an electron, a living organism, or an industrial firm. The organism has now come into contact with its requisites.

There is not the slightest allusion in Whitehead's text to subjects who would "have values" in terms of which they would evaluate, or to which they would conform. To follow Whitehead, then, we must obviously free the term "value" from any psychological connotation, as well as from any appeal to any kind of transcendence. Yet this demand is not gratuitous: it announces that what we call "value" will be put to the test in a highly interesting way. The obstinate preservation of a value, whatever happens, may be a heroic virtue: there can be no question of denying this. With typical British humor, Whitehead limits himself to giving a generic definition. If we, as humans, can claim to be different, it is not because we nourish values. Value belongs to the order of nature: it is what is realized by all that exists, in the sense that what exists succeeds in enduring, succeeds in maintaining its individual way of gathering together, that is, of making things hold together in a determinate way. Value indicates a success in and for itself.

The habitual economy of scientific explanations is turned upside down, as is that of subjective motivations. What is maintained without change is no longer the ensured starting point for understanding what changes. Don't ask me why I am distracted: on the contrary, be amazed that I am able to complete my phrase safe and sound. Above all, do not consider that it is "I" who am responsible for this exploit. "My" success, like that of an atom, has no justification higher than this fact: the experience of this phrase to be completed has succeeded in holding out in an environment that might have had a very different role: *"Wait, you've distracted me: what was I going to say?"*

The explanation of endurance is not an attribute of the individual who endures, but depends first of all on a dynamics of infection. All that succeeds in enduring has succeeded in infecting its environment in a way that is compatible with this endurance.

"Infection" is the term Whitehead chooses to designate, in a generic way, what the poets celebrate as "presence." Celebration refers to the fact that it is a poet's experience that is infected by the mountain, gloomy and ancient. "Infection" must be understood, not without humor, in a neutral sense, designating the success constituted by all endurance in a changing world. The interest of this chosen term is that it designates the specific character of this success. This infectious holding-together is not a fusion but a valorization, a determinate shaping, conferring a value—that is, a role—on what is prehended. The fact that the variables of a function, in the same way as the poet's experience, require a "value" thus ceases to belong to linguistic contingency. Far from being a mere quantity, the value of a variable presupposes the stability of the role that one thing plays for something else and measures the importance of that role. In addition, the term "infection" is there to remind us that there is nothing neutral about "attributing a role to something." The role you attribute to me drives me crazy.

Every entity that realizes itself in its mode of prehension of other beings also prehends the way in which it itself is prehended by those others, or the aspect of itself that is taken into account and valorized by these others. How will it prehend the prehension of itself that it reflected back to it? Such are the stakes of the "dynamics of infection," upon which the success of endurance depends. Infection designates the way in which the modes of prehension are reflected for each other, and success implies a co-adaptation of values. When a being endures, what has succeeded is a co-production between this being and "its" environment. This environment is nothing other than the totality of beings taken into account and valorized in a determinate way, and each of the valorized beings prehends the taking-into-account of which it has been the object, the role that has been assigned to it, in a way that is not incompatible with the maintenance of this mode of prehension, or of this role.

This time, the question of the organism is indeed raised, and it selects what will count as the concrete, complete facts. Farewell to Cleopatra's Needle, and even to the gloomy hill: for neither the perceptual object, nor weighty presence, enable the complete unfolding of the dynamics of repercussion and infection. The very notion of "due attention" becomes indeterminate, for the repercussion of attention upon that to which one pays attention can no longer be neglected. Henceforth, the favorable cases will be those in which the "interaction" must be called an inter-action, that is, the shaping of an attainment that exhibits its dependency by the way in which each of the interacting terms valorizes the other: for instance, the complex sexual parade in which a male and a female, from posture to posture, from approach to approach, gradually co-produce one another, as each one confers upon the other the role and the value corresponding to mating. Or again, the set of cases in which the role assigned to a being becomes an integral part of its individualization. For better or worse, as, for instance, in the case of the infernal dynamics of relations of dependency—when the gaze you cast upon me becomes an ingredient of my experience of myself, to the point of producing myself in the way you need, or at least in the way I sense you need, and so on. The result is sometimes a huge misunderstanding, but a remarkably enduring production of two beings whose respective modes of valorization call obstinately upon one another.

The fact that the dynamics of infection can find privileged examples in relations of dependency obviously does not mean that such relations become the truth of what makes human beings hold together. They are part of the way things may happen, of the adventures of individualization, in the same sense that the fact that human young need a human environment to become children, and that children dare to become, because they feel that one trusts they will, because their clumsy efforts are approved and encouraged. Such facts do not require any particular psychological explanation, in the sense that its goal would be to justify a departure from a norm of autonomy; for the idea of autonomy, for Whitehead, is obsolete. Relations of dependency can instead require fine-grained descriptions with regard to the way in which the environment, and perhaps particularly an environment infected by that norm of autonomy, participates in this selected mode of achievement.

All values presuppose a risk. The generic risk that corresponds to endurance *qua* successful infection must not be expressed in terms of a conflict—between autonomy and dependency, for instance—but rather of "clash." Conflict implies the existence of a negation—it is he, and then not I, or I, and then not he—and can only belong to a realization that gives meaning to the negation, or at least to its germ: to hesitate, to feel in conflict with oneself. A clash, for its part, is neutral and indeterminate in its result. It exhibits the fact that an "entity," realization, individualized mode of capture, can only succeed in holding fast if the way it "infects" its environment does not give rise to repercussions that make it lose its hold. Clash thus signifies that infection has failed. This is what happens, for instance, if I am talking to someone who abstains from all the semiautomatic signs of complicity that indicate that she is listening. I begin to stammer: how can I keep hold if the person I am dealing with provides no foothold, does not integrate within her own reality the aspect of herself I am proposing her—*yes, she is listening to me*—but realizes herself in a way that is incompatible with what my mode of holding together and evaluating proposes to her?

People say "our visions of life clashed," but Whitehead has written, "a clash of doctrine is not a disaster—it is an opportunity." His "trust" deliberately ignores hatred and anguish, polemical passion, or the feeling of having been abused. What counts is what happens. A clash can be an obstacle and a limit, or it can "evolve" into a durable, even symbiotic new harmony. Or else it can create problems. There is a clash between the desire of the person stretched out on the psychoanalyst's couch to get a reaction, and the latter's obstinate, irreducible silence, and this silence, this aspect of the psychoanalyst prehended by the analysand, infects the experience that prehends it and takes it into account. Unless, of course, the analysand succeeds in "prehending" certain other aspects, tenuous and involuntary: the rhythm of the psychoanalyst's breathing, his muscular tension . . . In which case the clash is between the psychoanalyst's doctrine and a mode of success which, for him, presents an obstacle to the analytical task.

The term "infection" is thus technical, that is, neutral with regard to the differences we attribute to what endures. In *Adventures of Ideas,* Whitehead will use it in particular to characterize the role played by Christian ethics, associated with the completely impracticable ideal proposed by the life and preaching of Jesus of Galilee.

A criterion of evaluation had now been created, expressed in concrete illustrations that resisted all perversion. This criterion is a gauge allowing us to estimate the defects of human society. As long as the Galilean images are merely the dreams of an unrealised world, they must continue to propagate the infection of a worried mind (AI, 17).

Whenever Whitehead uses the term "infection," his point is to deny that something has "in itself" a power over something else. The only power of the Galilean ideal was the obstinacy of concrete illustrations, vectors of contrast, and the worry inspired by this contrast.

The reader will have intuited that Whitehead is no critic of power as such: a nature in which nothing succeeded in infecting anything else would not be a nature, and the possibility of maintaining any kind of nostalgia toward a "powerless" society implies in itself an incalculable number of "social achievements." From this viewpoint, Whitehead is rather close—albeit in a whole other tone, since his goal is not to unveil human illusions—to the thesis of Michel Foucault, according to which power is not primarily repressive but inciting, inspiring interests, questions, and knowledge. This, indeed, is how infection in Whitehead's sense could be defined: not by the imposition of a role, but by the incitement, reflected in multiple and varied ways, to take up and prolong that role. In the generic sense, nothing imposes anything, for there is no authority that has, by itself, the power to impose. All "social power," unless it is purely and simply repressive (a rare and unstable case), designates first and foremost a dynamics of infection.

To allude here to Michel Foucault is to give myself the opportunity to emphasize the extent to which Whitehead is liable, and will become increasingly more liable, to disorient a reader for whom denouncing power is the very duty of philosophical thought if it is to serve human emancipation, including an emancipation that would have as its prerequisite the destruction of the human, all-too-human subject. Foucault himself never conformed to this obligatory figure. He affirmed that he merely "described," without reference to a transcendence that would authorize denunciation, and he has, moreover, been reproached with failing to "found" in reason that in the name of which he set forth his merciless diagnosis, that in the name of which the struggles that should follow from such diagnoses would proceed. To "think with Whitehead" exposes us to a rather different test, for not only does Whitehead not denounce, but he also does not attach himself specifically to a description of power as such. The twin poles of power that Foucault has taught us to distinguish—repressive and incitatory power—would not have surprised him, for they both belong to the definition of the dynamics of infection. Yet what interests him, what interests an educator, what will become a requisite for his conceptual construction, is not the analysis of the formations of power, but that of the link between power and adventure.

Let us take a somewhat speculative example. Some anthropologists have ventured the hypothesis that before human beings were speaking or thinking, they were "dancing"; that is, they were singularized by the power that sound exercised over their experience *qua* rhythmic. More precisely, by the power their experience conferred upon the rhythmic sound that infects it. The hypothesis of such a power, which would define us well before we define it, or specialize it before we construct its multiple consequences, before we exacerbate it or repress it, would no doubt have interested Whitehead, however adventurous it may be. As we shall see in what follows, he was to associate language and consciousness with doubt, with trial by consequences, but he would have found it interesting that this novelty should have intervened in a history already marked by another novelty: by the power already conferred upon rhythm to infect human experience and to produce a dancing group (or one marching in step) with individuals.

Dance, it is sometimes said, makes the dancer: a good testimony to the power eventually associated with rhythm. Yet we must immediately add that there does not exist any "dance in general" to which this power may be attributed, which would allow us to do without the multiple adventures that presuppose this power, but which this power does not explain. And we must also add that from "free" improvisation to faithful execution, from the singular act from which "a" dance emerges to codified body stances, the question is not one of freedom from power. All testify to the power associated with sound and rhythm by human experience, yet all do not testify to it in the same way. They do not all correspond to the same definition of the role, although, in any case, the dancer is "enrolled."

This example announces what is already engaged with the notions of value, endurance, and infection: a quite peculiar politics of explanation, articulating things that seemed to be made to oppose each other. The paleoanthropological hypothesis according to which a "cerebral innovation" was associated with those hominids from which humans are supposed to have issued, conferring upon rhythm the power to infect experience, is exemplary from the viewpoint of the position in which it places those who formulate it. On the one hand, of course, it expresses the futility of the temptation to define freedom "against" power, yet on the other hand it expresses the futility of the attempt to return to a determination "beyond" multiplicities, toward what would be common to all humans. For a "new fact," such as this hypothetical "cerebral innovation," if it ever took place, would certainly pertain to something "in common," but it would be something "common" that would be necessarily silent with regard to the divergent meanings mobilized by human practices with regard to it. Whatever the work of future neurophysiologists may be, their results will in fact be added to the long series of what, on this hypothesis, has already been created to convoke, capture, canalize, manipulate, socialize, and comment on a power that has no identity other than the series of roles that are constructed along with it. Somewhat in the same way that the force of gravity, as soon as we leave the domain of bodies defined as "heavy," has no other identity than the series of roles conferred upon it by far from equilibrium physico-chemical systems, by birds, by dancers, by mountain-climbers, and so on.

Even when, in *Adventure of Ideas,* the subject is human societies, Whitehead will refuse to oppose power and freedom, but will choose to place on stage two contrasting versions of power—persuasion and force—and will identify commerce as what marks the genuine "progress" of civilizations. Persuasion and commerce will refer to that other human innovation, the infectious power proper to "ideas," recalling the fact that one may speak both of the commerce of ideas and of the commerce of things. Of course, the persuasive character of an idea guarantees nothing: a loathsome idea can infect the mind, as powerfully rhythmic music can lead human beings into battle. Nevertheless, for Whitehead, the reference to the power of persuasion, in contrast to despotic power, is what is required by the very definition of what we call "ideas." And no "deconstruction," debunking the inciting infection where the illusion of free and transparent rational production prevailed, can abstract from the fact that it presupposes, requires, and prolongs the power associated with ideas, while describing it otherwise. Foucault's incisive laughter, the confusion he sowed in so many well-thinking minds, presupposes and mobilizes this power just as much as the knowledge-power he describes.

Infection in the Whiteheadian sense is neutral with regard to values, in the usual meaning we give to the term "value." On the other hand, it has the rather peculiar effect of communicating directly with the possibility that what is holding together may cease to hold together. An obstinate, intolerant value succeeds in infecting its environment, but this success is never a right, and it has as its correlate the fact constituted by the community of events that enables the organism to "maintain its hold."

Whether this permission is expressed in terms of more or less precarious tolerance, of a risky wager, of experimentation or of confirmation, and even of dependency, it always designates the success of a "trust." The image of mountain-climbers is radicalized; they exist—that is, they endure—only insofar as the patience of what they define as a "hold" is confirmed. The question raised by professionals, for its part, is generalized: the obstinate maintenance of their rut, the possibility of making judgments denoting the absence of any "aesthetic appreciation" with regard to what escapes this rut, presupposes the "patience" of their environment. If a general burst of laughter were to greet such judgments, professionals would learn prudence very quickly, and might even allow themselves to be infected by the difference between the questions with regard to which their judgment holds and those that make them lose their foothold.

The fact that endurance is a factual success without any higher guarantee may be expressed as follows: may those who are no longer afraid that the sky might fall on their heads be all the more attentive to the eventual impatience of what they depend on. Thus, it is not without interest today that the new figure of Gaia indicates that it is becoming urgent to create a contrast between the earth valorized as a set of resources and the earth taken into account as a set of interdependent processes, capable of assemblages that are very different from the ones on which we depend. In order to distinguish the endurance of Gaia—and of the multitude of bacterial populations that play an active role in its assemblages—from the precariousness of our modes of existence and of those of other large mammals, some speak of a Gaia's "shrug of the shoulders" capable of making us lose our foothold: "Gaia is ticklish, we depend on her patience, let us beware her impatience." The contemporary period is exploring the difficulty of a transformation of what are called "values" in a sense that corresponds well to the Whiteheadian use of the term: a particular way of shaping our attainments, presupposing the stability wagered upon by this way, while explaining itself in terms of habits.

In contemporary terms, we will say that endurance, value, clash, obstinacy, conflict, harmony, dependency, patience and impatience, and so on place the notion of organism under the banner of an etho-ecology: the approach that tries to connect the *ethos,* or the way, constitutive of a living being, that such a being takes its environment into account, and the *oikos,* or the vaster totality to which it belongs, and more precisely the many links, niches, and collectivities produced by the *ethos* that mutually imply one another, and on which each depends in one way or another. An organism does not explain itself *qua* having succeeded in conquering a stable identity, bearing its titles of legitimacy, but it explains itself in and on the basis of the patience on which it depends, a patience presupposed by the value of which it is the achievement. The organism exhibits a "trust," and this "trust" is etho-ecological, simultaneously a way of shaping that is always individual, limited, and obstinate, and a wager on an environment that confirms and nourishes it.

CHAPTER ELEVEN

Scientific Objects and the Test of the Organism

F OR WHITEHEAD, all that endures succeeds in enduring, every success designates inseparably both individual objects and their environment—that is, the concrete, complete fact to which the notion of organism corresponds—and every science of nature, insofar as it deciphers a reality in terms of the interplay of individual actors, concerns organisms. It is this third affirmation that we shall now put to the test. Can the notion of organism communicate with a new value for the divergent multiplicity of scientific undertakings, with shaping their successes in a manner that affirms, in a coherent way, the order of nature that each explores, according to its own means?

Whitehead appeals in particular to the possibility of a physics that would accept that its atoms, its molecules, and its electrons are organisms. And he tries to infect the usual narration of the development of science in the nineteenth century with this possibility. Thus, the same paragraph will witness the coexistence of scientists we are in the habit of separating: Bichat, Müller, Schleiden, and Schwann, associated with the cellular theory in biology; Pasteur and his micro-organisms; but also Dalton, who introduced atoms into chemistry. All of them conferred a new type of meaning upon the "individual." Of course, the idea of the atom goes back to Democritus or to Lucretius, but for Whitehead, who emphasizes the contemporaneity of physical atoms with the cells of microorganisms, the point is to accentuate their novelty, to open them up to a future in which they would no longer participate in the rhetorical success of "scientific materialism."

United in this way, physics, chemistry, and biology not only cease to share in a hierarchical vision in which molecules are made out of atoms, cells out of molecules, and out of cells . . . and so on, they break with every "world vision" in general. For it is by characterizing the respective practices of these sciences that the etho-ecology proper to their respective "atoms" can be approached.

Add a proliferating virus to your culture of microorganisms, boil your cellular culture, mix your molecules of oxygen with hydrogen and add a spark, heat your gas to the temperature of plasma, bombard your aluminum atoms using a radioactive source: in each case, what you study spotlights the contrast between "keeping hold" and "losing hold," which designate the organism from the viewpoint of its endurance and the limits of its endurance. The scientific practices Whitehead intends to unite have all abandoned in fact—that is, in practice—the idea of an atom, an element, or a part as self-subsistent individuals and principles of explanation of interpretation for everything else. They all derive their success from the fact that they have been able to characterize their "atoms" in a practical way, *qua* something "holding together," whose endurance must be evaluated on the basis of the trials this hold resists or fails to resist.

We shall not be surprised if Whitehead privileges his favorite example, the electron and the electromagnetic field that is inseparable from it. In *The Concept of Nature*, the electron as a scientific object was interpreted as the systematic correlation of the modifications of all events, insofar as these modifications express its ingression. Yet every event is now itself understood as a unifying grasp of a set of aspects of its environment. Henceforth, then, the possibility of identifying the electron as a charge first reflects the endurance of the mode of grasping that specifies it, the fact that this grasp succeeds in holding fast. The inseparability of the electron and its field thus becomes exemplary for Whitehead's thesis: the electron is what it is because of the way it prehends its environment, and its environment is what it is because of the way in which this prehension infects it. In this case, physical laws describe a mode of pattern under its twofold complementary aspect, implying the endurance of the electron and the patience of the environment. Their object is the way in which the electronic grasp modifies the environment, and in which this modification modifies this grasp itself.

Nevertheless, the assimilation of the electron to an organism is not a simple redescription of what physics already knows.

The concrete enduring entities are organisms, so that the plan of the whole influences the very characters of the various subordinate organisms which enter into it. In the case of an animal, the mental states enter into the plan of the total organism and thus modify the plans of the successive subordinate organisms until the ultimate smallest organisms, such as elec-

trons, are reached. Thus an electron within a living body is different from an electron outside it, by reason of the plan of the body. The electron blindly runs either within or without the body; but it runs within the body in accordance with its character within the body; that is to say, in accordance with the general plan of the body, and this plan indicates the mental state (SMW, 79).

Physicists to whom this text is presented usually develop a frankly phobic reaction: for them, the electron's behavior is a function only of physical variables, the living body is a physical environment like any other, and therefore the electron remains "the same" inside or outside the body. Whitehead agrees with this to some extent: even within a living body, the electron runs blindly, blind to the stakes of its behavior for the body. Yet only to some extent, for no environment is "like another," and the experimental environment from which our description of the electron's behavior derives is not, in any case, comparable with any other.

The question turns not upon a decidable experimental question but upon the way the experiment as an achievement is described. For the physicist, experimentation succeeds in addressing the electron in general, but in a particular way, in which it is capable of testifying reliably to its behavior, that is, of enabling the identification of the variables that determine this behavior. For Whitehead, such an achievement corresponds to creating a particular environment for the electron, and the experimental electron will be the electron that has solidarity with this environment. Quantum mechanics confirmed this, in its own way, when it forbade the attribution of properties to quantum entities independently of the experimental apparatus enabling the testimony that gives meaning to these properties. Yet old habits die hard, and physicists have so far preferred to see in this prohibition a dramatic limit upon objective knowledge, which raises problems for realism, rather than a perfectly positive testimony dealing with "quantum organisms."

For Whitehead, even localization, the possibility of being situated in space and time, is relative to endurance. This implies that space-time itself, far from being the common framework for events, constitutes an abstraction. The possibility of situating bodies with regard to one another in terms of distances or temporal intervals is not primary, but corresponds to the pattern of the environment that interacts with the etho-ecology of those enduring entities whose behavior can be characterized in terms of variables of space and time.

When he wrote *Science and the Modern World*, Whitehead had, of course, already elaborated the theory of space-time he envisaged as an alternative to Einstein's. Whereas Einstein proposed a unique space-time whose local properties of spatial curvature are affected by the (massive) bodies situated within it, Whitehead, between 1920 and 1923, constructed a theory of multiple space-times, a theory that never, in fact, really interested the community of specialists. When he presents it in chapter VII, moreover, Whitehead freely admits the legitimacy of this reaction: his theory is mathematically much more complicated than Einstein's because it is more general. Indeed, it relegates to the "empirical case" many of the properties that Einstein's general relativity defines *a priori* as belonging to the space-time metrics.

In particular, Einstein's theory allows the deduction of one and only one law of gravitation, and can therefore be presented as a generalization of Newtonian space-time, a generalization that is particularly satisfying because it realizes the dream of a purely geometrical behavior of heavy bodies, reflecting the metric properties of space-time. Whitehead's theory, for its part, starts out from the refusal of such a geometrization. It affirms that every body defines its own spatio-temporal stratification, its own discrimination of what space and time are. A body's spatio-temporal behavior in relation to other bodies thus becomes relative to the articulation between the spatio-temporal stratifications that each defines on its own account. Consequently, the universal relevance of the law of gravitation can no longer be either deduced or justified. It reflects one possibility among others, and the limits of its validity for our universe must be decided experimentally.

The version Whitehead proposes of the general theory of relativity thus unfolds a universe of possibilities, among which there appears, as a very particular case, the situation described by Einstein on the strength of Newtonian universality. Physicists have judged it as a useless complication, but sometimes I find myself daydreaming that, in view of the problems contemporary physics encounters when faced by the unification of the gravitational force with the other interactions, this complication might well open up interesting perspectives. In any case, it meant placing physics at risk, on the grounds of imperatives of intelligibility that indeed announce the theory of the organism. The metrical properties associated with space-time should not be defined *a priori*, but should characterize the pattern of the environment that is inseparable from enduring bodies *qua* enduring. Endurance should be the primary fact, presupposed by all physical descriptions.

The pattern is spatially now; and this temporal determination constitutes its relation to each partial event. For it is reproduced in this temporal succession of these spatial parts of its own life. I mean that this particular rule of temporal order allows the pattern to be reproduced in each temporal slice of its history. So to speak, each enduring object discovers in nature and requires from nature a principle discriminating space from time (SMW, 119).

Whitehead later called this most general fact, to which physics as well as biology or perceptive consciousness bear witness, the "extensive continuum": each in its own way bespeaks the solidarity we observe, and on which we depend, in the midst of the multiplicity of events.

Above all, the extensive continuum must not be confused with a "common place" existing prior to events, nor, more generally, with an explanation of their solidarity: it will instead have to explain itself once this solidarity has been granted its concepts. It is neither a reason, nor, much less, an *a priori* condition. It constitutes the most abstract characterization of the way events are situating themselves with regard to one another, of the relational complex that articulates with one another all the possible viewpoints of each with regard to others, quite apart from the way each one produces the concrete meaning, for it, of that from which it is inseparable. With regard to this abstraction, Einstein's space-time, endowed with a metrics intended to explain the motion of bodies, is already the expression of a specific mode of solidarity, presupposing masses and motion, that is, a specified mode of endurance.

Are Whitehead's propositions capable of finding the slightest echo within physics? The question remains open, but the very fact of raising it is important. For together with this question it is also the question of the "world visions" inspired by physics that is raised.

The fact that physical laws, by means of such "visions," including those that introduce the quantum void or virtual particles today, have not ceased to encourage the error of "misplaced concreteness," to introduce a reality doomed to make nature bifurcate, is by no means an accusation. It is simply the direct consequence of the kind of success that singularizes it, and is announced by the notion of physical "law": the situations that will be privileged are those in which the abstraction that separates an organism from its environment—that is, that defines the endurance of the former and the patience of the latter in terms of right, not of fact—will be operational and fruitful. Another way of describing this success is the reduction of all change to an explanation in terms of what Whitehead calls "external relations": the behavior attributed to each enduring entity is not relative to the way it realizes itself through the unification of its prehensions, but is a function of variables designating other entities *qua* responsible for the changes it undergoes.

If physicists presuppose endurance and patience, chemists, for their part, are primarily interested in the contrast between patience and impatience, that is, in the conditions of the chemical transformations by which molecules gain or lose their ability to hold and endure. Modern chemistry has learned to characterize the ethology of molecules, or the way they hold together; more recently, it has also learned some aspects of their ecology, or the kind of pattern this holding-together imposes upon the environment. Yet here we run into a difficulty, in which the philosophy of the organism is put directly to the test. If the interests of physicists and chemists diverge, how can we explain the fact that they agree in describing "the same atoms" or "the same molecules"?

Something is certainly put to the test. It remains to be determined, however, who puts whom to the test. It would be tempting, here, to evoke the complications of high-energy physics. Physicists who study the proton observe that this particle, on whose identity the identification of the variety of atomic nuclei relied, is a "soup." They even go so far—and this, for a physicist, is a terrible condemnation—as to speak of a "chemistry of the proton"! Yet it is not appropriate for the philosophy of the organism to derive an argument from the perplexities of a science, for the point is not to take one's rivals down a peg, at the risk of beating an undignified retreat once these rivals succeed in deciphering the labyrinth in which they seemed to be hopelessly lost.

It is in their full maturity, and not in the process of their constitution, that concepts and functions necessarily cross one another, each being created only by its own means [. . .] (QPh, 152).

This statement by Gilles Deleuze and Félix Guattari has made more than one philosopher shudder, but it takes on an immediate meaning for the philosophy of the organism. No more than scientists should separate themselves and their achievements from their own shadow, should anyone take hold of those scientists' shadows independently of what they have achieved or the function they have succeeded in constructing, reflecting the way the variables that inseparably characterize a type of organism and its environment hold together. We must therefore turn to the exploit constituted, for twentieth-century physics, by the possibility of affirming that molecules remain "the same" throughout all the roles they play in physical explanations, whether these molecules belong to a gas, a liquid, a solid, or a situation of phase transition, and even the chemistry in which they enter into reaction.

To separate this exploit from its shadow, to make it rhyme with the "unified vision" of a world whose fundamental laws are deciphered by the physicists, is not to pay homage to physics, but rather to insult it. For it means relegating an achievement to an imagery that makes short shrift of the physicists' sophisticated, imaginative work. Here, in fact, what is called "explanation" has nothing to do with a deduction. To succeed in explaining has meant to succeed in redefining, in each case, what "molecules in interaction" means: that is, the way these interactions must be characterized in order for theoretical description to converge with experimental observation. The greatness of physics derives from the fact that the physicist's goal has been in each case to learn how to define molecules and their role, that is, how they "infect" their neighbors and are "infected" by them. And the exploit of twentieth-century physics is to have succeeded in producing a (more or less) coherent articulation of the definitions, different in each case, of its actors, including actors that are capable of entering into chemical reactions. It is indeed possible to affirm that it is "the same" atoms that enter into the characterization of various chemical reactions, but that the role "a same" atom plays depends upon the reaction, that is, upon the environment to which this reaction corresponds. Some atoms, however, particularly those of carbon or iron, have thus become veritable chameleons, unfolding many different properties according to their environments.

In fact, physics today has already begun to explore the limits of this achievement. This is not a question of reflexivity or of epistemology, but of pursuing the adventure and surprises reserved by its achievements. I am thinking in particular of those physicists who no longer study "matter" but "materials," which are no longer defined by "qualities" that oppose them to a homogeneous matter but by the fact that things happen to them. Correlatively, they are no longer characterized in terms of properties, flexibility, fragility, or various and diverse textures, as the questions now concern verbs denoting actions and passions. What makes glue stick, mayonnaise set, soap foam, or steel bend and then suddenly break? Corresponding to such questions, there is now a multiple wealth of models that negotiate how to co-define the relevant actors, their modes of coupling, the scales of description that enable us to approach the transformations, whether progressive or brutal, of observable properties.

How can one express the contrast between a remarkably stable whirlpool that can be engendered by a turbulent flux when it comes to strike an obstacle, and the clear, distinct sound produced by a solid when struck? In both cases, a gigantic number of particles participate in what is to be explained, be it whirlpool or sound. When the subject is sound, however, the multiplicity can be forgotten, since a few parameters suffice to characterize the solid's vibrant elasticity. When it comes describing the whirlpool, in contrast, one must yield to the obvious: the description of a liquid flux colliding violently with an obstacle does not deliver the whirlpool's secret unless it takes into account how whirlpools form on every scale, playing a role that cannot be smoothed over in terms of average values. As far as the "behavior" of a material is concerned, its ductility, its fragility, it will be the fault lines, their modes of propagation, their encounters with heterogeneous media, their entanglements with each other that will tell why it bends or breaks.

In the guise of what is called the "mesoscopic," situated "between" microscopic descriptions, whose actors are supposed to be definable independently of their environment, and macroscopic descriptions of the observable properties of the whole, physicists have thus discovered the need for an art of negotiating the in-between, the modes of existence of beings that should not be confused with mere intermediaries translating the microscopic into the macroscopic. They are genuine actors, interacting with one another in genuine intrigues, which we must learn to narrate if the intelligibility of observable properties is to be produced. Whereas sociologists may have been tempted to take the crystal as a model and to define society in terms of a finite number of variables, materials physicists know, when they deal with a piece of steel that consists only of iron, carbon, and a few impurities, that they are addressing a "pattern" whose singularity must be explored each time, and whose relevant constituents must be negotiated and characterized on each occasion. They thus prolong an exploration carried out for millennia by those who have learned the art of forging steel of ever-different properties.

Here, the goal is not to adduce physics as an example for sociologists, for the adventures of steel, in the last analysis, occupy only a few hundred pages in a treatise on metallurgy, and the fact that they could have been characterized by metallurgists as "properties" referring to well-defined processes of fabrication is enough to recall the pragmatic divergence between the two domains. The point is to celebrate a history whose success must, first and foremost, be described as relevance. The articulation, henceforth entangled, between questions that had—albeit for only a century at most—clearly separated what concerns physicians and what concerns chemists, may confirm the wager that the philosophy of the organism makes on the order of nature: "there are organisms everywhere," and each kind of organism is in itself, and without any beyond, an active, enduring production of what the scientist deciphers. But it confirms, first, that scientists, despite their simplifying slogans, are indeed those for whom nature is a source of innovation: by taking a closer look, one finds more in it.

However, it belongs to another science, biology, to unfold the totality of what the organism obliges us to think. Living beings have the privilege of exhibiting endurance *qua* achievement, in the midst of a risky environment. Indeed, although beings and their interactions, as characterized both by physics and by chemistry, may well have come to exhibit the inseparable character of the definition of an entity and that of its environment, the values to which they give meaning remain those of variables. Biologists, for their part, address the enduring organism insofar as its stability is at stake for this organism itself, insofar as it *matters*.

Biologists do not so much explain the living being as celebrate the living being's achievement: this might be the proposition that emerges from the philosophy of the organism, and this proposition can shed light on the contrast between "biological function" and "physico-mathematical function," a contrast that gave rise to the vitalist temptation to oppose the "how," which supposedly suffices for physics and chemistry, to the "why," whose relevance is imposed by the living being.

In fact, every time biologists identify the intricate, multiple roles of the various components of a cell, a tissue, an organ, or a body, they are subject to the temptation of explaining the totality in terms of goal-directed organization. They deal with the organism *qua* exhibiting, in an obvious way, its dependence upon a selective taking-together: certain entities are taken into consideration and not others, and in this way to the exclusion of other ways, while the overall regime wagers on such an environment and loses its hold if the confidence implied by this wager is betrayed. Also, when biologists are confronted by a pathology, they see the relative simplicity of functional relations—*this* is responsible for *that*—disappear in favor of an almost indescribable multiplicity of relations: the safe hold of reasonings gets lost at the same time as the biological function. In other words, descriptions of a "normal" living being did not explain its functional stability, but depended on it. And when, once they become biophysicists, our biologists study the various components of a living being separately in the context of an experimental environment, they discover how hard it is to make an isolated component have the type of behavior that characterizes it in the midst of a living organism. If the difference between an electron within a body and an electron in the laboratory is hard to determine, the three-dimensional folding that confers its "functional" properties upon the protein offers problems whose frightful subtlety is being discovered by contemporary science: the "functional" protein needs its living environment.

The term "organism" thus rightly indicates a privilege of living beings. In biology, the question "how?" exhibits itself as inseparable not from the why *(pourquoi)* but from the what-for *(pour quoi)*: it is inseparable both from the world *for (pour)* which a living being's functioning has meaning and from the wager *for* this world, and not another, that this functioning affirms. In other words, the privilege of a living being is to exhibit each biological function as risking itself "with regard to" the outside world, and "for" an external world.

Quite obviously, in the case of a living being, the problem of the "whole" and the "part," of the body and "its" parts is also raised, and raised in terms of functional interdependence. Both the whole and each part need the success of the other parts for their own success and for the endurance of their mode of "functional" behavior.

The question of the whole and the parts is an ancient one, which haunts biology. Is the whole anything other than "sum" of its parts? Is it "more," or is it not "less," in the sense that, in one way or another, it "binds" its parts, subjecting them to its own interests and thus depriving them of certain possibilities of behavior? Such questions also belong to the history of philosophy. Even Leibniz, who sought to understand a reality conceived in terms of monads, each of which deployed for itself its own viewpoint, was obliged at the end of his life to introduce the strange notion of a vinculum. As a nonsubstantial link, knot, or yoke, the vinculum answers the need for describing the crowd of monads that make up an individual body *qua* collected, or "subjected," variables of a function, although each one nevertheless conserves its autonomy. It was this kind of question that plunged embryology in the first half of the twentieth century into a crisis, before the triumph of molecular biology defined the entire field as "fallow," destined to be elucidated some day in genetic terms. Embryologists had discovered the failure of any attempt to explain the progressive differentiation of the embryo in terms of "abstract" mechanisms, identifiable independently of the totality in which they participate. They had to admit that in embryology no cause has within itself the power to cause or the power to produce a specific effect independently of a specific environment. At the limit, all causes designate the developing embryo as such as "the cause" responsible for their effect.

For Whitehead, the parts do not constitute the whole without the whole infecting the parts. In other words, the identity, or the enduring pattern, of the whole and the parts are strictly contemporary. This is why the same term, "infection," can be used both to designate the relations between the whole and the parts, and to describe the relations of a living organism with its environment. If the body exists for its parts, it is because its parts are infected by such-and-such an obstinate aspect of what we call the body, but which, for them, is a portion of their environment; if the parts exist for each other and for the body, it is because the respective patterns of each are highly sensitive to any modification of the environment they constitute for one another.

Thus the body is a portion of the environment for the part, and the part is a portion of the environment for the body; [the difference between the case of the body and its parts, and that of the living being and its external environment is] *only they are peculiarly sensitive, each to modifications of the other* (SMW, 149).

Some ten years later, in *Modes of Thought*, Whitehead was to say the same thing in a more poetic form:

In fact, the world beyond is so intimately entwined in our own natures that unconsciously we identify our more vivid perspectives of it with ourselves. For example, our bodies lie beyond our own individual existence. And yet they are part of it. We think of ourselves as so intimately entwined in bodily life that a man is a complex unity—body and mind. But the body is part of the external world, continuous with it. In fact, it is just as much part of nature as anything else there—a river, or a mountain, or a cloud. Also, if we are fussily exact, we cannot define where a body begins and where external nature ends (MT, 21).

The body is not made up of all its parts, and its parts are not part of the body. The parts have vested interests in each other and in the body, in the sense that these are the proximate environment required by their success. The only genuine totality is the event itself, each event realizing for itself the combination of its prehensions, the account of what it takes into account. Each part is grasped by the whole as an aspect of its own pattern, a variable of its functioning. And this aspect of itself, obstinately exhibited by the whole and by the other parts, infects the environment of each part, which thus exhibits itself as a part. For as long as it lasts.

To refer to a familiar situation, let us take the particular example of the "whole" constituted by a hospital, and of the "parts" constituted by doctors and patients. Doctors and patients enter and leave the hospital. Outside the hospital, the doctor is a normally courteous exemplar of humanity. In the hospital, having become a "part" of the hospital, he sweeps in, followed by a cohort of assistants, talks about the patient, to whom he scarcely says a word, and often leaves before he can be asked the slightest question. Nevertheless, still *qua* part, he is extremely sensitive, not, to be sure, to the suffering patient, but to the selected "aspects" of the patient that are addressed to his skill. As far as the patient is concerned, once she becomes a part, she accepts to be treated in this way, and accepts to anxiously await the verdict the doctor will issue on the basis of data whose meaning she, as a patient, is not supposed to share.

The endurance of the pattern named "hospital," as we know it, depends, of course, on the patience of the environment: if, for instance, users did not accept to be defined as "patients" as soon as they enter the hospital, that is, to renounce most of their rights, the "whole" and the other parts would lose their hold. As long as the hospital as we know it succeeds in infecting both patients and doctors, it will succeed in enduring.

Let us return to the biologists, who, for their part, are not confronted with a "social fact" but with a multiplicity of "natural" histories. Whereas the history of an atom or a molecule remains largely hidden to us, that of a living individual, of a population, of various populations in interaction, and of species, together constitutes the terrain on the basis of which the most complete and concrete testimony we have available on the subject of nature may be heard.

Among these histories, the Darwinian ones were radically innovative, as they brought with them a new mode of appreciating living beings, placed under the banner of a long, slow process, and of celebrating the "living value" associated with obstinate small causes that end up producing major effects. Today, the interpreters of Gaia are the heirs of this appreciation. In contrast, today as in Whitehead's time, most of those who profess allegiance to Darwin have produced a biased, abstract version of him, focused on competition. For Whitehead, this is the direct consequence of the concrete, misplaced character of the abstraction according to which an organism is what it is independently of its environment. If the identity of a living being had been recognized as a "living value" inseparable from its environment, the notion of a "favorable environment" would have been recognized as something crucially at stake in evolution. But an abstract role was conferred upon the environment, and the only responsibility assigned to it was that of selective sorting, where this term presupposes the possibility of defining independently the criterion of sorting and that which is sorted.

The givenness of the environment dominates everything. Accordingly, the last words of science appeared to be the Struggle for Existence, and Natural Selection. Darwin's own writings are for all time a model of refusal to go beyond the direct evidence, and of careful retention of every possible hypothesis. But those virtues were not so conspicuous in his followers, and still less in his camp-followers. The imagination of European sociologists and publicists was stained by exclusive attention to this aspect of conflicting interests. The idea prevailed that there was a peculiar strong-minded realism in discarding ethical considerations in the determination of the conduct of commercial and national interests. The other side of the evolutionary machinery, the neglected side, is expressed by the word creativeness. The organisms can create their own environment. For this purpose, the single organism is almost helpless. The adequate forces require societies of coöperating organisms. But with such coöperation

and in proportion to the effort put forward, the environment has a plas-
ticity which alters the whole ethical aspect of evolution [. . .] *romantic*
ruthlessness is no nearer to real politics, than is romantic self-abnegation
(SMW, 111–112).

Whitehead's proposition did not make history in biology, although it
did nourish the thought of one its most remarkable scholars, the embry-
ologist Conrad Waddington. Until his death in 1975, Waddington was "a
biologist on the watch." He did not limit himself to analyzing the question-
begging "errors of misplaced concreteness" that lead to reducing Darwinian evolution to a genetic sorting process. He sought out and tried to
gather together all those biologists, physicists, mathematicians, and philosophers who were liable to contribute to a "theoretical biology," or a
formalization that would enable biologists to resist the many pseudo-
dilemmas that harass the way living beings are thought: innate/acquired,
genetically determined/relative to the environment, individual/group, and
so on.

Nevertheless, quite apart from the question of his own influence, Whitehead was right to trust living beings and the interest they inspire. Abstraction has never encountered the same adhesion in biology as it has in
physics, and the dissatisfaction it inspires has not ceased to give rise to
new interpreters. Thus, the sociobiological abstraction, which constitutes
natural selection as the only thing responsible for the "values" attached
to the organism—if poets feel the beauty of the glow of the sunset, it is
because celebrating it has enabled hominids to seduce females, and has
therefore given them an advantage with regard to their less eloquent
colleagues—can certainly be presented as a triumph of scientific rationality. Yet this professional judgment, continuing as it does along the path of
an abstraction whose only value is the reduction of all values to selective
value, is the vector of more controversies than consensus in biology.

Whereas in physics, the idea of a law of nature does not give rise to
any particular impatience, it pertains to the life sciences to produce witnesses against the abstraction called "materialist." This is the case in ge-
netics, when Barbara McClintock, busy and precise, nevertheless affirms
the importance of "listening to what corn has say." It is the case in embryology, when Albert Dalcq is moved by the fact that the embryo's response to his experimental questions has "all the surprise and charm one
can find in the answer of an intelligent interlocutor." Also in evolutionary
biology, when Stephen Gould opposes to the nasty ugliness of all-terrain
selectivism the joy of a biology that would learn how to understand how,
when it comes to living beings, "the world outside passes through a
boundary into organic vitality within." And in ethology, when meticulous

study is joined to a link of respect, or even love, or else amazement, or again jubilation: all that is implied, along with astonishment, by the term "wonder." Each time, the sense of a presence that cannot be appropriated, an invitation to becoming, finds its witnesses, articulated without contradiction with the most meticulous investigative approach.

And theorists themselves try to respond to what is demanded by living beings in terms of formal descriptions, whether it be autopoiesis with Francesco Varela, or the great undertaking of René Thom that sought to characterize the type of mathematization that is relevant to living beings. And perhaps above all, the alliance between formal and dynamic models of etho-ecological co-construction Stuart Kauffmann is now trying to forge in his *Investigations*. As Whitehead had foreseen, each of them testifies, each in his own way, to living beings, implying and calling for a new conception of the order of nature. All are infected by the discovery, characteristic of the life sciences, that chains of cause to effect are never prolonged very far, and that, at each step, one must be ready for a mutation of the mode of description, a bifurcation of what is at stake, the intrusion of a new actor pointing to (without causing it) a radical transformation of the distribution of roles and significations.

Although the philosophy of the organism designates biology as its privileged field, its ambition is not limited to biology. We should recall that it was from objective perception, "I see a castle there," that Whitehead drew the correlative notions of event and prehension. Yet perception is henceforth a dangerous abstraction from the point of view of the organism, as are the notions of perspective, reflection, and viewpoint, which belonged to the contributions proposed by classical philosophy for the job specification. These notions will have to be generalized, in order to exhibit the features that now designate the organism: endurance as what is at stake, risky success, and the inseparability of what endures from its environment. In other words, they will have to be reformulated in a way that renders explicit what they require, and will have to undergo the same transformation as the "presence" celebrated by the poets, which has become a "dynamics of infection."

Perception and the spatio-temporal definition of the physical object were the two sources of "facts" privileged by *The Concept of Nature*, corresponding to this book's ambition: to resist the bifurcation of nature, whose justifications, consequences, and the possibilities of getting around it were explored, in one way or another, by the great classical philosophers. Henceforth, in contrast, the starting point constituted by the definition of the electron and the field associated with it no longer communicates directly with the question of the order of nature, for it presupposes the patient character of the environment constituted for the electron by the field. The electron's functional behavior, the stable definition of the variables that define it, is what is presupposed and confirmed by the experimental staging that enables it to be made explicit, but from the point of view of the order of nature this is not a generality, but only what is demanded by physics. In other words, the fact that physics succeeds in describing a world of stable entities in functional interaction speaks less of the order of nature in the generic sense than of those aspects of the order of nature that physics will recognize as its own, once experimentation has allowed their identification.

The question will arise in a similar way with the object of perception. We recall that, in *The Concept of Nature,* Cleopatra's Needle communicated with the possibility of saying "*there it is again*" and required an object. The object did not explain its recognition, but was required for recognition to have a respondent and not to make nature bifurcate. But perceptive experience, precisely because it exhibits this dimension of recognition in a dominant way, communicates with the abstraction of a staging that is neutral with regard to values, and makes us forget that concrete experience can very seldom be reduced to the observation that Cleopatra's Needle is indeed still there in its place. In other words, the fact that perceptive experience privileges permanent objects, defined as stable active conditions for the perceptions we have of them—I see the Needle, and I also know that you, who are on the other side of the square, see it too, but from another perspective—does not constitute a reliable generality from the viewpoint of the philosophy of the organism. It does not exhibit the risky character of the unification it presupposes. The notion of perspective, and more precisely the stable differentiation implied by the notion of perspective between the object and its spatial environment (space as the place of all the perspectives from which Cleopatra's Needle can be seen), speaks not of the order of nature but of that particular aspect of the order of nature that is called perception.

In *Modes of Thought,* Whitehead will explicitly question the concept of perspective he had accepted when the abstract question was to describe how we can perceive, "here," the Needle, castle, or cloud that are located "there." Perspectivism, that is, the identification of prehension with a form of "reflection," the event reflecting all other events from its viewpoint and being reflected from their viewpoint by all events, places the emphasis on a possible symmetry, an impartiality that conceals the concrete fact that what we perceive interests us and matters to us.

We may well ask whether the doctrine of perspective is not an endeavour to reduce the concept of importance to mere matter-of-fact devoid of intrinsic interest. Of course such reduction is impossible. But it is true to say that perspective is the dead abstraction of mere fact from the living importance of things felt. The concrete truth is the variation of interest; the abstraction is the universe in perspective (MT, 11).

The reflective mirror, whose various orientations exhibit the different ways of placing the same scene in perspective, communicates with the abstract ideal of neutrality with regard to values. It is the person who orients the mirror who decides what the mirror will reflect. The value of the mirror *qua* mirror is precisely to authorize the abstraction of its own role. If this role is to be taken into account, it will be insofar as it departs from the ideal: such a defect, such an irregularity, deforms the image. The notion of perspective thus has the weakness of its vulnerability to being reduced to a simple "effect" of the landscape. Unless, as Leibniz proposed, one makes the landscape an effect of the perspective. In both cases, however, what is missed is the risky affirmation of the person who perceives "for" a world. The point then is not dependence; what is affirmed is the way one is oneself the invention of the world on which one depends.

It might have been anticipated, however, that the link between perspective and importance would communicate not with "variation of interest" but with the question of value, as proposed by poets and imposed by biology. It seems that the philosophy of the organism ought to end up with a meaning of the term "perspective" that resonates in the affirmation "to each his own perspective," obstinate, selective, affirmative, intolerant. To hell, then, with the common world that collects perspectives, and with Leibnizian harmony, which turns this common world into a well-constructed illusion. Whitehead seemed destined to move from classic perspectivism, a Cleopatra's Needle perceived from different viewpoints, to a perspectivism of a Nietzschean or at least postmodern type. Yet Whitehead did not make this move. His thought was to bifurcate in a wholly other direction, without the least explanation.

Here, "thinking with Whitehead" obliges us to take the liberty of a diagnosis. What prevented Whitehead from carrying out the obvious generalization that would have led him to a psychology based on the biased and partial character of perceptions, thus putting an end to the exploration of the facts that exhibit the order of nature?

To attempt this diagnosis, I propose to tackle the problem from the other end. What would Whitehead have wound up with if he had transferred to psychology the notions of endurance and value, whose relevance is exhibited by biology? A rather formidable result: the praise of the professional. Indeed, what better example could there be of an organism than the professional described by Whitehead, he who boasts of the selective seriousness of his thought, that is, of its limitations? What better example of obstinately affirmed value than the professionals' trust in the well-foundedness of the rut they are following, of the routine mode of grasping that they are prolonging? What better example of endurance than a professional judgment, maintaining the separation between what should be taken into account and mere anecdote, whereas the anecdote in question may signify the despair of thousands of persons? What better example of successful infection than the creation of such professionals from "normal" beginners: those first-year students who will have to learn the differentiation between the "good" questions, those that will turn them into "true professionals," and the others, which inspire "impatience" of their teachers in the form of an explicit reprimand, or an inept answer, or a little smile that is mocking, condescending, or pitying? And what better example of the "patience" of the environment than the fact that this differentiation has been taken up: the good questions are objective, scientific, or rational, while everything else, even if it is what is most important, belongs to "values," to subjectivity, to sentimentality, to culture . . . ?

In other words, Whitehead's proposition, centered on the organism and on "value" as the outcome of limitation, is certainly not bereft of relevance with regard to psychological science, which, following William James, he wished to make enter the "order of nature." Yet it risks nourishing a psychology that defines as its normal horizon what Whitehead has precisely questioned. The professional's rut would be celebrated as paradigmatic success.

Physicists who describe the motion of a solid body take advantage of the endurance and the patience characteristic of what is called "physical reality." The possibility of making a mathematical function correspond to the motion of a planet, for instance, presupposes and reflects the fact that this motion testifies to a determinate mode of prehension that seems to have endured since the solar system has existed. Biologists, for their part, know that the way a living being "holds on" reflects a risky and successful sorting of what affects it, and their own description depends on this success. Biologists are "captivated" in both senses of the term: the success of their description depends on a success that precedes it, and has determined the terms of that description. For them, to understand means to "follow" this sorting process, but also to "appreciate" how the body distributes meanings, how the parts refer to the whole that infects them. In contrast, the psychologist's description, if it were similarly "captivated," would risk either edifying redundancy or cynicism. Thus, psychologists captivated by the professionals' quiet success would be led to celebrate the firm, self-assured way they "sort" what they have to deal with, relegating to the status of an anecdote all that anyone other than they might find important or worrisome. Starting out from this hypothesis, they could establish a cynical portrait of what it is to be human, beyond all illusions of lucidity. And they could also identify how the norms common to our societies infect everyone, such that the "development of the sense of morality" in the adolescent, for instance, would pertain purely and simply to the fabrication of a being that does not inspire impatience on the part of its social milieu.

This perspectivism might satisfy a professional psychologist, but it would neglect one small detail, or judge it purely anecdotal: by following the biologist's example in this way, the psychologist does not resemble a biologist at all. A living being's limitations celebrate its success, whereas whoever might undertake to describe me on the basis of my limitations would insult me. In contrast, whoever nourishes my "disquiet" (inquiétude)—a Leibnizian term that is to be understood without the slightest doloristic connotation—nourishes me: not in terms of a phobia of all limitation, but of an appetite for experimentation, for the consequences of variation of interest, for the exploration that plunges what I thought was given into the realm of the possible.

"It can cease to hold." For biologists or doctors, this means in the first instance the risk of illness or death. Yet whoever is interested in human experience must take this question as a primary term. This, moreover, is what the familiar stories do, such as the one of the king whose prestige infected his environment to such an extent that no one, prior to the impertinent child, had dared to say, "But he has no clothes!" Or those games that exhibit the ability of infectious dynamics to destabilize the relation to the "normal" world: "I've got you, you've got me by the chinny-chin-chin, the first to laugh . . ."[1] Irrepressible laughter reflects the impossibility of "staying serious" in an environment infected by reciprocal modes of prehension focused on only these aspects, a sparkling glance, pursed lips, frowns, that can both inspire and foretell laughter.

In The Concept of Nature, the relation of cogredience, the "and" in the "here and now" of all experience, exhibited the precariousness of the fact of "holding on": the specious present that Whitehead inherited from William James endures and succeeds in making those variations that do not make it slip into the past of a new present hold together, but it is fleeting

---

[1] In the French game of "Je te tiens, tu me tiens par la barbichette," two children hold each other's chin as they stare into each other's eyes. The first to laugh loses. —Trans.

at first. Once it has gone, it is gone, and the very attempt to hold it back makes it slip away, unless we have to deal not with a deliberate effort but with the result of spiritual techniques whose result is precisely the divorce between voluntary effort and accomplishment.

Since it is fleeting, William James's specious present thus forces us to conceive of the problematic character of holding-together, which may be concealed both by biological success and by objective perception designating an object—that castle, that cloud—that will still be there when I open my eyes again. Yet lived continuity, as James has described it, a succession of presents that appropriate their past, taking up once again what precedes them and assigning a value to it by making it a variable of their own function, not only designates an enrichment of the job specifications, leading to a new formulation of what is required by the philosophy of the organism. It also raises the problem of the communication between the "order of nature" and the metaphysical question, implying what we call "mind," or rather "soul," in the sense that the soul designates that which psychology should have to address if it is to address the experience of disquiet.

If it is not to make nature bifurcate immediately, the mode of holding together of lived continuity must be conceived as inseparable from the order of nature. If not, the soul would risk being identified with a feature that is fundamentally alien to this order: freedom, to be precise. In one way or another, this order itself will have be situated, and with it the notion of organism. Just as chemistry exhibits what physics accomplishes in abstraction, and biology exhibits what chemistry succeeds in abstracting, the question now arises of what psychology should exhibit so that the abstraction on which biological order depends may be situated and identified.

According to my diagnosis, we can foresee that when Whitehead takes up the question of the "specious present," the question should be decided of how the endurance of the organism may be articulated with "the disquiet of the soul." And the specious present will indeed appear in *Science and the Modern World* in a decisive place, that is, as an introduction to three paragraphs that constitute, according to Lewis Ford, an insertion added by Whitehead after April 1925.

The total temporal duration of such an event bearing an enduring pattern, constitutes its specious present. Within this specious present the event realises itself as a totality, and also in so doing realises itself as grouping together a number of aspects of its own temporal parts. One and the same pattern is realised in the total event, and is exhibited by each of these various parts through an aspect of each part grasped into the togetherness of the total event (SMW, 104–105).

We seem to be on familiar ground here, all the more familiar in that Whitehead was dealing with endurance in the preceding paragraph, and the obstinacy with which "the same thing for itself" is there in front of you, however you may analyze it from the temporal flux of its parts. One might therefore think that that he is prolonging this same question by specifying how the whole realizes itself by gathering together its parts, each according to the aspect that contributes to its own pattern. One might even suspect the role that psychological experience must have played in the philosophy of the organism. Whitehead no doubt intended to make it the terrain of conceptual construction that was to provide "rigid coherence" to William James's "adequate" exploration. For the psychological field, interpreted as "self-knowledge of our total bodily event," is indeed what imposes a fully deployed conceptual construction, since it implies, as a concrete fact, what biology certainly does not allow to be ignored, but from which the biologist may be tempted to make abstraction: the "for itself" character of the event.

Yet it was in fact another author who had taken his pen, according to Lewis Ford, who has dubbed what begins in this way the insertion of the "triple envisagement." What is being introduced is a notion to which neither physics, nor perceptive experience, nor the biological organism, nor the poets chosen by Whitehead, nor even William James has borne witness: that of the "possibilities of value," whose envisaging is a primordial aspect of "eternal activity." It is the birth of this other author, henceforth a metaphysician, that must be described before we pursue the reading of this insertion, one of the most obscure texts in *Science and the Modern World*.

Let us note, however, that at the moment when this other Whitehead undertakes to turn the economy of his own thought inside out, to plunge into the risks of metaphysics, whereas he had previously tried to conceive of the order of nature, that is, the enduring success of beings, it is a term deriving directly from William James, "specious present," that came to his pen.

CHAPTER TWELVE

The Event from Its Own Standpoint?

THE PATH I have followed leads to the question of the "psychological field" associated with the thought of William James, and the fact that I have introduced the term "soul" indicates the stakes I propose to associate with it. To describe the soul is problematic in terms of a theory that relates value and endurance; such a theory rather means insulting the soul. The concepts called for by our faith in an order of nature do not suffice, for they do not enable us to resist the blind version of this faith proposed by professionals. If unity is to be realized where subject and object are opposed, we must rise back up from the success exhibited and celebrated by organisms toward what is possible—which these organisms succeed in excluding. The concepts to be constructed cannot take advantage of the modes of intelligibility proposed by the "order of nature," but must risk the test of the metaphysical question in its full state of deployment.

This line of reasoning is entirely due to my imagination, to the way I am trying to accompany Whitehead's thought. *Se non è vero* . . . Yet other paths may be envisaged, which allow us to understand what happened to Whitehead in April 1925. Let us therefore follow another, complementary path. Let us consider human experience, the "psychological field" defined as "a bodily event considered from its own standpoint," as they force upon us questions that remain unsolved. In fact, the conceptual construction to which the thought of the organism obliges us has only just found its own locus and risks. For to the question "What is an event?" only concepts enable us to respond in a generic way, independently of the limitations that allow an organism to be characterized.

As Whitehead often repeats, the order of nature has as its subject "that which endures": that is, not the event, but the pattern realized by the event, which, in the case of success, is repeated from event to event. The point will therefore be to construct the distinction between this pattern and the event itself, which is "prehension," the unifying grasp of the aspects prehended according to a determinate mode. This is where the reference to the "bodily event" is crucial.

It is important to discriminate the bodily pattern, which endures, from the bodily event, which is pervaded by the enduring pattern, and from the parts of the bodily event. The parts of the bodily event are themselves pervaded by their own enduring patterns, which form elements in the bodily pattern. The parts of the body are really portions of the environment of the total bodily event, but so related that their mutual aspects, each in the other, are peculiarly effective in modifying the patterns of either [. . .] we can now see the relation of psychology to physiology and to physics. The private psychological field is merely the event considered from its own standpoint. The unity of this field is the unity of the event. But it is the event as one entity, and not the event as a sum of parts (SMW, 149–150).

To conceive the event as one entity thus means, at the same time, to try to construct the kind of "rigid coherence" appropriate for the innovative thesis of William James. For there can obviously be no question of consciousness "*qua* function" being consciousness "reduced to a function." This is why thinking of the event "for itself" is crucially at stake. What interests "psycho-philosophy" must be both distinguished from, and placed in relation to, the enduring patterns characterized by the so-called objective sciences, and on which these sciences depend, from physics to physiology. The "territorial division" between science and philosophy must not be "surmounted" by explanation, but the very possibility of explanation must have the status of a consequence from the perspective of a thought based on the event.

When Whitehead wrote the lines just cited, he seems to have thought he had constructed the terms of its solution. The event realizes and unifies, and it unifies "for itself," by producing its own standpoint. In other words, the reality of an event must be understood on the basis of "internal" relations alone. An event is not what it is because of other events, but because of the grasp it realizes of those other events, the way in which it "prehends" them, and the aspects under which it takes them into account as it produces itself. An event itself, as such, thus never has the power to define what its action will be, or its effect, or its influence on something else. The aspect of itself that will be taken into account, and thus contribute to the explanation of the account, did not, as such, preexist this taking-into-account. Action, effect, influence: all these terms that seem to designate "external" relations, in which a transformation is explicable by something external, are relative to endurance. They designate the type of taking-into-account, the role, or the "valorization" that an event's mode of pattern obstinately confers upon what is prehended. Of course, the transformation can "be explained" as a function of something external, but here the fact is disconnected from the "principle." What explains did not have the power to explain "in principle": it obtained this power in fact. Yet this fact is relative to the endurance of the pattern, to the mode of taking into account, insofar as it has succeeded in enduring.

In other words, we should not celebrate the sun as a source of life, but the endurance of a mode of pattern that makes the properties of solar light exist for the plant, these properties that henceforth infect us as well, since the mode of pattern proper to our experiential apparatus has produced its stable signification, which can be articulated in terms of a function. As a dynamics of successful infection required by the order of nature, the endurance of modes of pattern that refer to one another does not allow us to describe the way an event is prehension "for itself," even as it participates in a world from which it is inseparable.

As far as the taking-into-account as such is concerned, it raises a properly conceptual question. Indeed, the mode of taking-into-account, the aspect in which the various aspects "enter" into the constitution of an event—that is, just as much, the way this event testifies to the presence of other events beyond itself—must be so characterized as to enable the affirmation that an event "explains itself" with regard to others. And this affirmation must in no way be liable to confusion with the idea that one event is explained by others. To construct the concepts to which the event obliges us, it is therefore crucial to avoid all recourse to terms that imply a stable mode of valorization—*this has the value of a cause for that*—or that intervene in descriptions conditional upon the endurance of pattern. All these terms refer to the event as "pervaded" by a pattern, and define value as the outcome of the corresponding limitation. The point is to conceive of the event "from its own standpoint," as a "determinant," without any allusion to the questions of endurance, motion, or emergence.

It is here that the "eternal objects" will reappear, in a problem that is henceforth conceptual. Whitehead's "first metaphysical solution" consisted in bringing to conceptual power the testimony of "eternality" that colors and geometrical forms had led him to inscribe in his job specification. And this is easy to understand, for the point is to conceptualize the taking-into-account in a way that cannot be confused with an emergence, for what emerges is always an enduring being, never a taking-into-account. Eternal objects, however, were required precisely by that aspect of what we perceive that does not emerge from the flux of things. The fact that colors "come and go" requires that eternal objects make ingression. One might say that their ingression "makes an event," even though they themselves are not events. And this is precisely what interests Whitehead. The determination of each mode of taking into account requires an eternal object, because no mode of determination can be described as "emerging" from what is taken into account.

Wherever such objects have ingression into the general flux, they interpret events, each to the other. They are here in the perceiver; but, as perceived by him, they convey for him something of the total flux which is beyond himself (SMW, 151).

Color, always a specific color, or geometrical forms, a circle or a square, are no longer privileged as such, but because they exhibit the "twofold role," that is, the relational character, that Whitehead henceforth attributes to "eternal objects": green is what I perceive as belonging to that leaf, the circle is what I conceive as proposed by that wheel. We must insist on this point, for just as perceptive experience risks favoring the error of "misplaced concreteness" because of the privilege it confers on the relational contrast between the "here" of the percipient event and the localizable "there" of what is perceived, sensible and intelligible objects run the risk of dangerously centering the conception of eternal objects around "what" we, who are *here,* perceive *there.* But what is generalized is by no means the experience of sensible or intellectual certainty, the well-determined character of a "form" with the power of dictating how it must be perceived, the circle *qua* illustrated by all round objects, this green by the leaves of that tree. If eternal objects intervene in the thought of the event, it is in a generic mode, equally relevant for all perception. An eternal object is henceforth that which has ingression in the mode of "how" an event takes another event into account, that which allows prehension to be said to be the prehension of something else.

We must start with the event as the ultimate unit of natural occurrence. An event has to do with all that there is, and in particular with all other events. The interfusion of events is effected by the aspects of those eternal objects, such as colours, sounds, scents, geometrical characters, which are required for nature and are not emergent from it. Such an eternal object will be an ingredient of one event under the guise, or aspect, of qualifying another event. There is a reciprocity of aspects, and there are patterns of aspects. Each event corresponds to two such patterns: namely, the pat-

tern of aspects of other events which it grasps into its own unity, and the pattern of its aspects which other events severally grasp into their unities (SMW, 103).

Eternal objects thus ensure the distinction between the two types of pattern, that of the unification of the event "for itself," and that of its aspects that are grasped by other events. This is a crucial distinction, since it must enable us to speak of consciousness as a function, without affirming that consciousness "is merely a function," or is the mere result of something other than itself. More generically, it is the question of individualization that is at stake. If the "how" of the taking-into-account "did not make an event," the individual might be deduced from its community. Eternal objects thus give resonance to the difference between what Whitehead rejects: a "simple fusion" that gives no meaning to individuality, and what he aims at: a specific mode of taking into account, in this way and not otherwise. An event does not have the power to determine how it will be prehended, but it must be prehended, and it must be prehended "severally," in a determinate mode each time. Prehension and ingression thus cannot be defined separately. Prehension without ingression would be reduced to some determinate relation of cause to effect. As far as the ingression of an eternal object is concerned, if it were conceivable independently of prehension—always that prehension—whose "how" is to be determined, it would confer upon eternal objects a power of explanation that would relegate the concrete fact, the event that determines itself to be this event and no other, to the realm of appearances. We would then fall into what Whitehead defines as the paradigmatic philosophical error: trying to explain a particular fact on the basis of universals.

Philosophy is explanatory of abstraction, and not of concreteness (PR, 20).

It remains to be seen how these two registers, with regard to which the event is to be understood, are articulated, that is, the mode of unified grasp that is realized on the occasion of each individualization, and the contribution of each individual to other individualizations.

The answer to this question would have been the "solution," the crowning achievement of the construction of the concepts that gives its intelligibility to the order of nature. But the actual Whiteheadian solution, the one Whitehead was to propose in *Process and Reality,* is not the answer to this question. For in *Process and Reality,* the event will simply have disappeared, or, more exactly, will have lost its primordial conceptual status. Here, then, we have reached the critical point, the point at which, for Whitehead, there occurred what I have called an "adjunction," and we are also at the threshold of an adventure which, in approximately four years, would make him the most unique speculative thinker of the twentieth century. We are in April 1925.

We do not know what path Whitehead followed; no doubt he followed several simultaneously. What we do know, from the notes taken in his classes by one of his auditors, William Ernest Hocking, is that on April 7 he announced that he was in a "state of confusion." In front of students, who were no doubt somewhat confused also, he affirmed that science today needs an "atomic" theory of time. While he was at it, he affirmed the need for questioning a feature he had previously associated in a stable way with the event, that is, the relation of inclusion. We must, he insists, distinguish between inclusion, or the extension of events including other events, and temporality, which is associated with the "direction of time." Whitehead then refers to Hegel: extension is an abstraction that demands that one go beyond it. A fourth and fifth point follow, which directly associate the question of the event with two new themes that will become vital in *Process and Reality*: the "potential" and "becoming."

4. The temporalization of extension, via realization of the potential. The individualization of each event [is brought] *into a peculiar togetherness. The future,* qua *relevant to reality, is merely for something which is real. An event as present is real for itself. It is this becoming real which is temporalization.*

5. But here we bump up against the atomic view of things, also their subjective view. The subjective view has got to be expressed within the objective view. It is there—the psychological field. You have got to express the subject as one element in the universe [as there is] *nothing apart from that universe* (EWM, 281–282).

The "confusion" Whitehead displays thus has as one of its ingredients a vibrant connection between "atomism" and "subjective vision," where the latter designates the "private psychological field" of which William James is, for Whitehead, the privileged witness. Yet although Whitehead thought of himself as James's successor, it is here that the answer to the question "how to succeed?" is being played out. For the "subject" is now that element of the universe on the basis of which we can ask the question "what is an element of the universe?" That to which we are obliged by "subjective vision" must therefore be taken fully into account. Temporalization is not the unfolding in the course of time of real elements as a function of real elements, it is "real becoming," and as such requires that the universe also be characterized as "potentiality."

On April 4, Whitehead had already pointed out the following new theme, among other considerations:

Potentiality is so called in contrast to actuality. But a contrast implies a positive element (EWM, 280).

I have presented two paths leading to what happened to Whitehead at the beginning of this month of April 1925, and there is no way or reason to choose between these two paths. Whitehead's question may have been both to conceptualize the event and to construe the fact that there is no psychology without "disquiet," without "hesitation," without the sense that the future hesitates in the present. A future that this gesture, this word, this detachment engage in a way that may be still indeterminate, but from which there is no possible turning back. If deliberation and the hesitation deployed in calculations belong to the workings of consciousness, the possibility of hesitation must, for its part, belong to the "psychological field," that is, to the "bodily event," the only event of which we have experience "from its own standpoint." With regard to what is required by this possibility, the contrast between potential and actuality, it must be affirmed in a generic way; otherwise, we would ourselves ultimately be authors of what we experience when we do not limit ourselves to recognizing Cleopatra's Needle over and over again. We alone would be responsible for our anguish, our doubt, and our decisions in a world of "professional" values. And nature would immediately bifurcate, for "trust" would be "purely subjective," an agitation causing a ripple in the veil of ignorance.

In order for the philosophy of the organism to construe the way the universe responds to "trust," what is realized must make an irreducible difference. An irreducible meaning must be given to a "fact" as that which might not have been: that is, also, to what has not been as well as to what might have been. Yet the extensive tissue of the events included in one another implies that every event is a grasping of other events, and is grasped by other events. It affirms solidarity, but this solidarity risks making impossible what Whitehead will never cease, from now on, to demand for all that exists: *elbow room* for self-determination.

At first, Whitehead may have thought that eternal objects, whose ingression makes the difference between the determination of a standpoint and a standpoint as emergence or reflection, would suffice to affirm the primordial character of the fact that a grasp has taken place in this way and in no other, to deprive the continuous tissue of its power of explanation. Yet how was he to articulate ingression with the interwoven continuities? In any case, in April 1925, Whitehead carried out a choice, or had one carried out upon him. A decisive power that traversed Whitehead, and turned him into a "semi-divine being," or, more humbly, "a speculative philosopher." An adjunction was necessary: the atomic character of duration must be affirmed, against the idea of a temporal flux indefinitely divisible down to the fiction of an instant without thickness.

Here, thinking with Whitehead becomes difficult, for one is tempted to hurry, and to measure all the consequences of the addition. Yet Whitehead was to proceed in a completely different way. In *Science and the Modern World,* he limited himself to adding two chapters and a few insertions, so that, he may have hoped, what had just happened to him might pass almost unnoticed. In all probability, he put off for the future the task of exploring (one recalls the "condensation" Deleuze adapted from Péguy) some of the consequences of what he had just decided. The reader is thus in a state of tension: whoever knows what is coming can say "it was already there"; whoever does not, stops where Whitehead himself stops, that is, at the construction of an articulation between the continuous and the discrete, at the risk of getting lost, as I myself did. My choice is not to hurry, and even to slow down the pace, so as to learn, with Whitehead, to what one is committed by a conceptual adventure that accepts being obligated by its own concepts.

So far, I have emphasized the urgency of a thought of the event, and its connection with the question of experience, the only testimony we have to an event "from its own standpoint" (SMW, 150). Yet it was in no such terms that Whitehead introduced his "adjunction." It appeared in the form of a few paragraphs, added rather abruptly to the end of the chapter devoted to the physical theory of relativity. It was thus in connection with the theory of space-time as an extensive continuum that Whitehead chose to affirm for the first time the "atomic" character of duration, made up of "atoms," or of "epochs," which are themselves indivisible.

Whitehead's choice implies that the construction of concepts has no privileged locus. It can start up on the occasion of any question, as long as the philosopher knows to what obligations it responds. In the present case, if realization is to be conceived as the realization of a potentiality, rather than as reality in the course of becoming, it cannot be conceived in terms of continuous space and time. It is not enough to say that a realization "takes time," or that it "takes its time," as if it could be observed and characterized "from outside," with regard to a common continuous time. The terms of the problem must be reversed. If realization is primary, if it cannot be explained but "explains itself," then all the notions that enable us to explain something in terms of something else must be abandoned, as far as it is concerned. And among them is included henceforth, first and foremost, the notion of continuity.

Whitehead had already emphasized that the spatio-temporal coordinates to which physics attributes a determining role require the endurance of bodies, both those that locate and those that are located. Yet the point is no longer to think of the order of nature and its relation to endurance, but to think of realization, which is presupposed by all endurance but is neutral with regard to it. The concept of realization must designate what occurs for and by itself. Actuality is therefore not situated "in time": it situates itself, that is, it produces its situation. In short, it is "epoch-making," in the sense in which we use this expression when we designate an event *qua* creator of the possibilities of questioning and describing it.

In realisation the potentiality becomes actuality. But the potential pattern requires a duration [sc. to become actuality]; and the duration must be exhibited as an epochal whole, by the realisation of the pattern [. . .] Temporalisation is realisation. Temporalisation is not another continuous process. It is an atomic succession. Thus time is atomic (i.e., epochal), though what is temporalised is divisible (SMW, 126).

At this stage, the reader might be tempted to try to imagine this "atomic time," and perhaps more successfully than I have been able to. In any case, this is no intuition of time—quite the contrary. The impossibility of appealing to intuition with regard to an atomic time goes without saying, since we run into the "specious," constructed character of the intuition of continuity, as analyzed by William James. Whitehead's thesis does not have the vocation of leading us to an authentic relationship to lived time, but, here as always, of resisting the power of abstraction. It is therefore by using it to measure the power of the abstractions authorized by continuous time, and not by trying to inhabit it for itself, that we will explore the interest of this thesis.

In this case, as the site of the first insertion indicates, the thesis of atomic time allows us to construe the meaning of what Whitehead already affirmed in *The Concept of Nature,* that nature knows no such thing as an instant without thickness. Yet it also enables us to measure its impact.

In *The Concept of Nature,* Whitehead spoke of nature as what we are aware of in perception. He was thus free to associate an instantaneous quantity with an idealization, and with the path of approximation that carries out this idealization. The question raised by *Science and the Modern World* is that of the order of nature, and the confrontation is no longer merely with the measure of a quantity but with the order attributed to nature by physico-mathematical laws. In this case, the notions that refer to nature "in an instant," particularly those of position, velocity, and acceleration, are no longer derived from what we are aware of, and can therefore no longer be defined as idealizations. They are required by the equations that make motion a function of space and time, whether they are those of classical dynamics—motion as described by Galileo, Lagrange, or Hamilton—or those of relativity. The instant without thickness is thus an integral, and even central part of the functional order presupposed and described by mathematical physics.

The situation of the first insertion, testifying to the atomicity of time, thus reflects the fact that Whitehead finally has the means to specify in what sense physical laws, and, more generally, the extensive continuum, are indeed an abstraction. He can finally identify, in a positive way, the sense in which the concrete character conferred upon the notion of localization, implying the point and the instant, was misplaced. When this localization is relevant, it does not reflect the fact that the physicist may, unlike the chemist or the biologist, get "to the bottom of things," exhibiting nature's exact submission to spatio-temporal laws. What is exhibited by the abstraction of localization, where such abstraction is relevant, is the possibility of doing without the "atomic" character of realization. The notion of function, which is at the center of so-called modern physics, is thus by no means synonymous with supreme intelligibility. It is recognized and saluted as a judicious approximation, an approximation whose limits are no doubt pointed out by quantum mechanics.

I shall linger a bit over this relation to mathematical physics, because for me it designates one of the ways of expressing the importance of Whitehead's thought. The conceptual construction engaged in April 1925 may indeed be presented as the first philosophical proposition allowing both the celebration of the exploit constituted by "mathematization," that is, functionalization, that physics since Galileo has carried out, and the liberation of thought from the temptation to attribute a metaphysical significance to this exploit. The Galilean body in motion, endowed with an initial velocity and subject at each instant to gravitation, can indeed be described by a function, which defines its acceleration, that is, in Whiteheadian terms, its way of "taking account" of the earth's presence at each instant. And the history of dynamics, for its part, exhibits the multiple ways in which this taking-into-account may be represented. Far from being the simple description of a motion, a trajectory is a physico-mathematical entity whose definition depends on the choice of variables of which this trajectory will be a function. With general relativity, the earth's presence no longer makes a difference for an arrow's trajectory in terms of "force," or even of "gravitational potential," but through the structure of space-time itself. Of course, with Whitehead's alternative theory, space-times become multiple: the enduring body is no longer plunged within a structured space-time. Instead, the differentiation of space and time is one aspect of an enduring pattern. Nevertheless, all these theories share the same abstraction. In Newtonian physics, the function describes, at each instant, how a body's acceleration continuously composes, or "unifies," the totality of what Whitehead would call the external relations relevant to this body's behavior. And if the theory proposed by

Whitehead could have been fully developed, its success would also have been to explicate the differentiation of space and time under the banner of continuity, governed by a function. It would not have authorized a positive contrast between the potential and the actual, any more than the functionalization of motion from Galileo to Einstein.

In physics, however, it will be objected, functions and the equations that articulate them correspond to a form of potential. Real motion is therefore defined against the background of the possible. Moreover, doesn't the significance of the invention of the "field" in physics consist of the fact that it places potential at the center of the description? Of course, but this potential confers no meaning upon hesitation, provides no locus for the possibility that what is realized in this way could have been realized otherwise. More precisely, a motion could have occurred otherwise, of course, but only if the initial conditions of the trajectory had been different. And this, it should be noted, is still the case in contemporary theories of "dynamic chaos," insofar as these theories feature a "sensitivity to initial conditions": if the actual state of a chaotic system were determined with an infinite degree of precision, the solution of the equations would unfold the actual behavior of that system, instant by instant. Readers familiar with the subject will not fail to object that this is not the case in quantum field theory, but they will have to admit that in this case it is the notion of actuality that becomes indeterminate, or attached to the act of detection.

The strength, and also the limit, of the notion of function consist in the fact that it features a behavior *qua* unification, the articulation of distinct functional variables, but without making unification a "real" problem. More precisely, the problem only arises for the physicist, who must rise back up from observable behavior to the function, or must integrate the functional equations to deduce the observable behavior. The state of affairs to which the function corresponds, for its part, is defined not in terms of problems, but of solutions. The function, one might say, transforms the behavior it describes into a continuous succession of instantaneous solutions to the problem it enunciates once and for all. As long as this function enables us to take the pattern as given, that is, without functionalization, it matters little whether it brings into play relations that are external (the earth's presence is responsible for . . .) or internal; no possible meaning can be given to temporalization, to the positive contrast between potentiality and actuality.

Since Leibniz, the notion of function has presided over the symbiosis between mathematics and the order of nature, and it is this symbiosis that Whitehead is now interrupting, or, more precisely, restricting to the cases in which it is in fact relevant. There is no doubt that Whitehead knew that there must, in one way or another, be a break with such a symbiosis. One may imagine, however, that he did not know how to carry out this break, how to specify in what sense the functional physico-mathematical order is abstract, and what it does without. And this difficulty was intensified, or exhibited, by an ambiguity. Until April 1925, the two decisive terms represented by pattern and realization designated both a process and its end result, the event that realizes, and what it realizes. They could thus give the impression that process and product may be confused, which is precisely what is proposed by functions, as a continuous realization.

The character of an "epoch" or a "pause" must be conferred upon the "duration of an event," its "specious present." Such is the meaning of the insertion Whitehead added to his considerations on the theory of relativity. The ambiguity has now been raised, and the break with the functional physico-mathematical order has been consummated.

It is worth specifying the way Whitehead introduces his "atomic theory of time" into this insertion. He introduces it in the same mode in *Process and Reality,* as an answer to the same question. It is as if this question, that is, the question of the impossibility of motion, as demonstrated by Zeno, were for him attached inseparably to the event of this enunciation.

Let us take the movement of an arrow, for instance, but forget the laws of dynamics: we are among the Greeks. For Zeno, the arrow should never reach its target, because traversing the distance to this target implies successively traversing an infinite number of sub-distances, those that are obtained by dividing the total distance into two, then the first half into two, then the first quarter into two, then . . .

Since the invention of the mathematics of infinite series, the technique of "dichotomous" (into two) division has became a pedagogical introduction to the idea that the sum of the terms of an infinite series may be equal to a finite number: $1/2 + 1/4 + 1/8 + 1/16 + \ldots = 1$. For mathematicians, "Zeno's paradox" finds a satisfying solution with the notion of infinite series, since the contradiction between finite and infinite is resolved. The paradox is thus evoked to make this articulation between finite and infinite interesting, to make the contradiction vibrate before it is solved. Nevertheless, there is something bothersome, or insufficient, in this situation: it gives the role of a solution to something Zeno knew perfectly well, for he knew that the distance he broke down into an infinite series of dichotomous divisions was finite. In other words, the novelty of infinite series in mathematics is undeniable, but it concerns the new problems it allows to be raised, not the elimination of the original paradox, which dealt with the articulation between physical motion and divisibility in the mathematical sense. The paradox can therefore be considered as solved only by those who accept that the continuum, in the mathematical sense of what is infinitely divisible, is appropriate to the concrete motion of the arrow. It is therefore not surprising that Bergson saw both in the paradox and its alleged solution the illusion of a "spatialized" motion, divisible in the same sense as the distance traversed.

Like Bergson, Whitehead refuses the (dis)solution of the paradox, but for him Zeno's paradox obliges us to conceive, not the continuity of a concrete motion, but the question of continuity itself.

[. . .] *Zeno understated his argument. He should have urged it against the current notion of time in itself, and not against motion, which involves relations between time and space. For, what becomes has duration. But no duration can become until a smaller duration (part of the former) has antecedently come into being* (SMW, 127).

If the process of realization were to share the divisibility of what is continuously extensive, it could no more take place than the arrow's motion could, according to Zeno, enable it to traverse any distance whatsoever. One could always describe any duration as including shorter durations, or any realization as including a series of distinct realizations, or again, any adoption of a position as including a series of successive positions. And one would finally arrive at a continuous series that prohibits what is being realized from being said to be "epoch making," producing a present that "adopts a position," irreversibly, with regard to the future. No adoption of a position would finish happening, unfolding in expectations and sub-expectations, and the sole actuality would then be the continuity, indefinitely divisible, of change that the function in fact describes. Whitehead repeats this in *Process and Reality*:

The extensive continuity of the physical universe has usually been construed to mean that there is a continuity of becoming. But if we admit that "something becomes," it is easy, by employing Zeno's method, to prove that there can be no continuity of becoming. There is a becoming of continuity, but no continuity of becoming. The actual occasions are the creatures which become, and they constitute a continuously extensive world. In other words, extensiveness becomes, but "becoming" is not itself extensive. Thus the ultimate metaphysical truth is atomism (PR, 35).

The two registers on which the event had to be expressed—individual and community, unification "for itself" and "for each of the others"—are thus relegated to two disjunct questions: that of what becomes, and that of the continuity that is brought into existence (constituted) by becomings that are themselves "atomic." In other words, that which in 1927 presented itself as an adjunction, inducing the addition of two chapters and some insertions, has become, by 1929, an ultimate metaphysical truth, forcing what had seemed to be acquired to be gone over again. It is no longer the order of nature but becoming, and it is no longer the organism but the "actual occasion," that oblige us to think. But we have not reached this point yet.

In *Science and the Modern World,* Whitehead thus limits himself to making insertions, as if he were merely contributing a few specifications that might have gone without saying or that might follow from the doctrine he had set forth previously. His second insertion, explicitly introducing the atomicity of time, appears in the chapter devoted to quantum theory. In the course of this chapter, Whitehead had shown that the endurance of the structure with which physicists associate the atom must no doubt be said to be the reiteration of an elementary pattern understood as a "vibration," that is, an undivided succession of contrasts. He can now insert/conclude that corpuscular, or primate organization indeed requires the atomicity of time, as he had announced to his students in April:

Thus realisation proceeds via a succession of epochal durations [...] *one complete period defines the duration required for the complete pattern. Thus the primate is realised atomically in a succession durations* [...] *This vibration* [which constitutes the primate] *is not to be thought of as the becoming of reality; it is what the primate is in one of its discontinuous realisations* (SMW, 135–136).

However, is what is appropriate for a vibratory organism also appropriate for a living organism? In fact, Whitehead has not proceeded to any insertion here, and we can understand why. It is hard to move from atomic duration to the endurance of entangled patterns implying what we call "whole" and "parts." One consequence is clear, however: both the organism and the order of nature that the organism was to enable us to think, because they lend themselves to explanation and inspire us to think of a continuity of becoming, may henceforth be conceived as giving a partial and biased explanation of themselves. What was "value" henceforth affirms unilaterally, as its condition, the stable elimination of divergent possibilities.

The limits of the notion of organism are in fact similar to those of the notion of function: both define a being not "for itself," but insofar as it endures. What varies from science to science is the "insofar as." A biological function cannot be assimilated to a physico-mathematical function. It is not defined in terms of variables, but rather in terms of varieties that result from sorting operations, thresholds, and discriminations, in short, judgments. Thus, the definition of a sense organ constitutes a judgment with regard to what the organ defines as "sensible." This, moreover, is what constitutes its "value," the risky success that makes it an organ. Even if René Thom had succeeded in what he defined as his great work, exhibiting the mode of mathematization adequate to living beings, a mode that would organize biology as spatio-temporal functions have organized the way physicists address what is called physical reality, he would not, by so doing, have "explained" living beings in the way physico-mathematical functions seem to be able to explain physical behaviors. He would simply have rendered explicit the values that the living being carries out *qua* organism.

For some animals, of course, sorting processes, thresholds, and discriminations appear as "specific," and we do indeed have a tendency to speak of the members of these species as automata. Yet this does not mean that these animals can be defined as "sticking" to the definition of the organism, merely that this definition suffices for the relations we have with them. With others, however, we maintain relations that exhibit and imply what is generally called "learning." The functional identity of an ant seems to define it relevantly, but rats can learn, and accept taming. And how could one fail to celebrate the achievement attested by this kind of learning, including the possibility of domestication that is correlative to it, when we humans ourselves, independently of our "domus," are merely failed mammals? We thus return to Whitehead's trust in the possibilities of education. This term also designates a "function," except that this function cannot be approached *qua* enduring pattern, but only as the "becoming of a continuity." "Becoming conscious" is a functionalization of what was never an enduring pattern, as is required by the possibility of education, and as is attested by novels.

Endurance is the key term for the philosophy of the organism. It allowed Whitehead to hope for a coherent conception of the order of nature, enabling in particular the designation of the "misplaced concreteness" that "materialism" has conferred upon physical abstraction. Yet Pandora's box has now been opened, for with the atomicity of time it is henceforth the specious present that becomes the prototype of "what is realizing itself." In *Process and Reality,* moreover, it is right in the midst of the discussion of Zeno's paradox that William James makes his appearance.

The authority of William James can be quoted in support of this conclusion [the epochal theory of time]. *He writes:* "*Either your experience is of no content, of no change, or else it is of a perceptible amount of content or change. Your acquaintance with reality literally grows by buds or drops of perception. Intellectually and on reflection, you can divide these into components, but as immediately given, they come totally or not at all*" (PR, 68).

A new idea burgeons, lived continuity is prolonged, but drop by drop. In *Process and Reality,* the quotation from James allows atomic duration to be associated with an "act of experience," that is, it also enables the generalization of the notion of an act of experience to all that exists. We have not reached that point yet. However, we have reached the disjunction between what realization obliges us to think and what endurance allows us to define. This disjunction will relegate the description of organisms to the status of particular, special investigations. The "actual occasion" that is realized with a proper duration of an atomic nature belongs, for its part, to metaphysics.

CHAPTER THIRTEEN

Entry into Metaphysics

I N THE PRESENT CHAPTER, *and in the immediately succeeding chapter, we will forget the peculiar problems of modern science, and will put ourselves at the standpoint of a dispassionate consideration of the nature of things, antecedently to any special investigation into their details. Such a standpoint is termed "metaphysical"* (SMW, 157).

The way Whitehead introduces the chapter "Abstraction," the first of the two chapters written after April 1925, gives a good indication of the fact that we have left behind the question of the order of nature, as modern science trusts it and designates its problem. Scientific investigations are always particular in that, as mountain climbers envisage their wall from the standpoint of the foothold it offers or fails to offer, their questions presuppose, and reflect in case of success, specific modes of envisagement, associated with the specific way in which, on each occasion, "it has to work." Success thus designates reality by means of its enduring "relief," capable of patience with regard to footholds, capable of repaying due attention. Now, however, the subject is the "nature of things" in the most general sense, that is, without reference to the question of the success or failure of such-and-such a particular mode of envisagement. The metaphysical standpoint may be said to be "dispassionate" in that its (passionate) challenge will be to construct concepts that will not favor or found any particular approach but answer to what is required, both by the organism that endures and by the one that comes undone, both by success and by betrayed trust, both by electrons and by the person reading this sentence.

Subsequently, and particularly in *Modes of Thought,* it is the term "importance" that will be used to express that in which an organism succeeds, including the success constituted by a mode of succession such that each new occasion realizes the most intimate conformity with the past. The term "value," for its part, will pertain to metaphysics: all realization is value, the adoption of a position, thus and not otherwise.

Importance and function are obviously linked: the function as we construct it, mathematically or by discursive reasoning, takes advantage of a conformity maintained between the present and its past. It transforms this conformity as a function of the present, and the future is then exhibited as the mere reproduction of the same in different circumstances. Whether this function is physico-mathematical, biological (the organ as a wager on the importance of what affects it), or psychological (the past providing the present with its meanings) matters little. What counts is that the function exhibits the accomplishment constituted by making the present continuous with regard to the past.

Here we must open a parenthesis. Some have seen Whitehead's philosophy as a "panpsychism," a doctrine that attributes a "psychism" to all that exists. This usually inspires derision: *so you think electrons "think like we do"?* Yet the importance, which I have emphasized, of the role played for Whitehead by the type of psychology of which William James announces the possibility might reinforce this misunderstanding. In a sense, one might say that the specious present is the prototype of the actual occasion, which Whitehead is going to try to conceive as a metaphysician. Yet this does not mean that Whitehead attributes a "psychology" to the actual occasion. If experience in the sense of William James could serve as a prototype for the actual occasion, it is because James's description results from a deliberate project of "depsychologization" of experience in the usual sense of conscious, intentional experience, authorizing a clear distinction between the subject and its object. It is insofar as William James rejected reflective consciousness and its pretensions to invariance, the privilege of occupying center stage, that he rendered explicit what human experience requires from metaphysics, and more specifically what it demands that metaphysics resist.

Conversely, it is perhaps psychology, among all the special, particular investigations, that has the most vital need of the resources that can be contributed by metaphysics in the sense that Whitehead defines it. In fact, when James, followed enthusiastically by Whitehead, makes consciousness a "function," producing the specious continuity and the reflexive self-explanations that constitute us as subjects, continuous "authors" of our multiple experiences, he knew that philosophy was "also" necessary, because the situations in which the possibility may be experienced of dispassionately exploring what reflexive consciousness passionately claims raise questions that the "serious," "professional" psychologist would reject as "philosophical." This is why I like to use the word "soul," which, as the reader will have understood, I by no means intend in a religious or Kantian sense, as something involving the question of salvation or that of duty. It is with disquiet or hesitation, with wandering, and even the possibility of "losing one's soul" that I would like to associate this term. Those are also the types of experience which, it seems to me, forced Whitehead to conceive of reality as realization, on the basis of the contrast between potentiality and actuality.

If the soul forces its question upon psychology, it is clearly not at all because psychology, despite what its name indicates, has the soul as its object. As "psychological," experience does not as such impose metaphysical questions, which are neutral with regard to any special order. It pertains to the order of nature, in the sense that it is an experience whose point is to construct a shared knowledge, an experience that must therefore be able to be "named," "described," "discussed," in short, qualified, *qua* psychological. Psychologists, like each of us when we analyze ourselves from a psychological standpoint, never cease fabricating descriptions, interpretations, elucidations, in short, functions. The fact that these are motives or intentions, rather than causes, is secondary: what is crucial is that the possibility of describing these motives and these intentions presupposes their importance, in other words, obliges us to take an endurance for our axis of description. The "soul," in contrast, is not an object of description as such. The singularity of psychology, which psychologists can sometimes hardly bear, impatiently or with nostalgia for the successes of their more fortunate scientific colleagues, is that having to deal with the soul, it has to deal with that which can no longer allow the conjugation of endurance and success. A hard challenge, since it demands that psychologists rid themselves of the appetite for what might, by its endurance, be capable of being the "respondent" of its questions.

If an allusion to the "soul" may be vital for psychology, it is therefore not in order to arrive at the truth of a properly spiritual experience. It is rather a question of practical "appetite," appetite for what this particular science has to deal with. Here, metaphysical investigation in Whitehead's sense is relevant because it accepts the quite particular interpretative challenge of being neutral with regard to the possibilities of footholds implied by enduring success. It may therefore suggest a form of humor with regard to the success constituted by a foothold. And psychologists need this humor, for the image of the mountain climber and her wall does not work very well as far as they are concerned. One must imagine a ticklish wall, which offers or gives a foothold not, to be sure, as it wishes, but nevertheless without it being possible for psychologists to attribute their success with certainty to the relevance of their questions. What is more, this is a wall that outmaneuvers the very meaning of "climbing," for it is just as capable of submitting as it is of smothering the investigator in its embrace. Stop gritting your teeth in imitation of the mountain climber, trying to define what you have to deal with in terms that authorize you to judge it; instead, learn to commit yourself to becomings, even if, to do so, you must resist all those who demand the possibility of judging. If metaphysical neutrality could give psychologists the strength to accept what is suggested by their own experience, it will have answered the most crying need of a science that pays a heavy price for its modern definition, including its duty to repudiate philosophy.

The concepts articulated around the actual occasion thus have nothing to do with a metaphysical foundation of psychology, nor with a theory of the soul, unless, of course, it is in the Leibnizian sense in which every monad (every *res vera,* as Whitehead will say in *Process and Reality*) is a "soul." As intimately connected with a "dispassionate" (or generic) approach, these concepts would be deficient, badly conceived, if they could serve to found one mode of experience against others, to guide one mode of definition, to privilege one type of facts. Whatever the experience, definition, and facts they highlight, the point is to rediscover their possibility, *qua* immersed within other possibilities of feeling, experiencing, and thinking, in short, of becoming. In particular, metaphysical concepts will have to be neutral with regard to the distributions carried out by common sense between what we know perfectly well and what we cannot believe: they will have to constrain us to envisage everything that can be attested by experience, and that can be cultivated in various ways, as a testimony bearing upon "the nature of things." Experience is no longer "our" experience but the concrete fact, which forces us to metaphysical creation.

Of reality as such, we recall that Whitehead, commenting on Berkeley and the other speculative philosophers whom Kant reduced to silence, had affirmed that it is "process," and that we must understand the process in terms of an "underlying activity of prehension" and of "realised prehensive events" (SMW, 70). Whitehead seldom returns to his affirmations, but limits himself to proposing "elaborations" which, without contradicting them, sometimes completely replay their meaning. In this case, it is clear that the underlying activity with regard to which there is individualization should henceforth refer to potentiality, in contrast to which there is realization.

It is right in the midst of the chapter devoted to the nineteenth century, and to the notion of energy, whose conservation that century celebrated,

that Whitehead chooses to go more deeply into the question of the contrast between what is "underlying" and what is realized, or individualized; in other words, he chooses to replay the meaning of that contrast
with regard to the new contrast between potentiality and actuality. Whereas
the text was dealing with the articulation between energy defined scientifically, in a quantitative mode, and the theory of the organism, Whitehead inserts the three paragraphs that Lewis Ford called "of the triple
envisagement," to which I have already alluded. Suddenly, the subject of
discussion will be "energy" in the sense of "eternal underlying activity,"
of which each individualization is a realization.

One can speak of this energy, or this eternal activity, only in abstract
terms, Whitehead specifies immediately, for one must abstract from actuality, or what emerges as a real state of affairs. Eternity must therefore be
understood as what is presupposed by realization *qua* temporalization.
In other words, Whitehead is not trying here to construct a complete
definition of actuality, but merely to construe the contrast between possibility and actuality in a way that turns what is possible into "that which
underlies," that is to say, in a way that defines it as an abstraction. What
this abstraction omits, what defines actuality in contrast to potentiality, is
none other than "value." As Whitehead will never cease repeating, only
actuality has value.

Unlike Whitehead, who acts as though what he writes is clear, I will try
to approach the strange, obscure, and important text that describes the
"triple envisagement" in the manner of a commitment to still-indeterminate
expectations and consequences, a kind of conceptual wager that presages
a style, rather than a finished conceptual construction.

*The consideration of the general flux of events leads to this analysis into
an underlying eternal energy in whose nature there stands an envisagement
of the realm of all eternal objects. Such an envisagement is the ground of
the individualised thoughts which emerge as thought-aspects grasped within
the life-history of the subtler and more complex enduring patterns. Also in
the nature of the eternal activity there must stand an envisagement of all
values to be obtained by a real togetherness of eternal objects, as envisaged
in ideal situations. Such ideal situations, apart from any reality, are devoid
of intrinsic value, but are valuable as elements of purpose. The individualised prehension into individual events of aspects of these ideal situations
takes the form of individualised thoughts, and as such has intrinsic value.
Thus value arises because there is now a real togetherness of the ideal aspects, as in thought, with the actual aspects, as in process of occurrence.
Accordingly no value is to be ascribed to the underlying activity as divorced from the matter-of-fact events of the real world* (SMW, 105).

In the next paragraph, Whitehead, who claims to be summarizing, specifies that there are therefore three types of envisagement: what are envisaged are eternal objects, possibilities of value with regard to the synthesis of the eternal objects, and finally the actual matter of fact, "which must enter into the total situation which is achievable by the addition of the future." After this rather enigmatic characterization, Whitehead repeats once again, as if to hammer home his point, that in abstraction from actuality, that is, the realization of that envisaged matter of fact, eternal activity is divorced from value.

It can hardly be said that the way this "triple envisagement" works is intelligible. Whitehead's writing is a work in progress, precisely in the midst of the activity of envisagement. It is already possible, however, to think some particular points of his elaboration along with him, as it is to specify my wager of reading.

Clearly, the eternal objects have become a crucial metaphysical concept, the correlate of what Whitehead calls "envisagement," and they announce themselves in three distinct modalities. The first type of envisagement implicates "all" the eternal objects and their "realm," which Whitehead also calls "kingdom" or "domain." In the second type of envisagement, the eternal objects appear as united, together constituting "ideal situations." And in the third, it is the "aspects" of these ideal situations that are the object of an individualized prehension, and as such they participate in individual events, described as the real togetherness of ideal aspects with actual aspects. A rather enigmatic analogy is proposed: on the one hand, between "the real togetherness of ideal aspects" and thought, and on the other between the individualized prehension of aspects of the ideal situations and individualized thoughts.

Of course, when confronted by this perspective, as grandiose as it is obscure, the possibility of philosophical comparisons rushes to the forefront: with Spinoza's substance and its individualized modes, of course, as Whitehead emphasizes, but also with the Intellect of Plotinus, a rather good candidate for an envisagement without an envisaging subject. Not to mention the obvious comparison with a Platonic "kingdom" of Ideas: a threatening comparison, since it would define a relation of sovereignty of eternal objects with regard to actuality. If Whitehead had put a final point upon his career as a philosopher after *Science and the Modern World,* the need for such comparisons would no doubt impose itself, but it so happens that the perspective in question was to disappear in *Process and Reality.* I therefore choose not to treat the "underlying eternal activity" as a culmination of Whitehead's thought, which would call for a meeting with other thinkers, but as a moment in his path.

Let us begin with what is most simple. As I have already said, value is henceforth no longer associated with the organism insofar as it endures, but with actualization as such. "Value," henceforth an integral part of metaphysics, is indifferent to "importance," which, for its part, will be associated with every pattern that succeeds in enduring, and that may be privileged, as such, by a special investigation. On the other hand, value is now linked inseparably to the notion of envisagement. Envisagement is the precondition for there to be value, but there is no value independent of the actual "purpose" that will conclude this envisagement "by the addition of the future," independent of the individualization of what *will* be, in contrast to what might have been.

The choice of the term "envisagement" is in itself significant in this regard. In *Process and Reality*, it is the verb "to envisage" that will appear, implying the question of "who" is envisaging. We have not reached that point yet, and "envisagement" translates one aspect of a process without a subject. But the explanation Whitehead will give for his choice of the verb is already relevant for his choice of the noun. As he explains (PR, 33–34), to associate eternal objects with a "vision," or, worse yet, with an "intuition," suggests a contemplative activity, that is, one bereft of yearning after concrete fact. Eternity is not an object of contemplation, beyond the concrete: the concrete is the only value. Whitehead therefore chooses the verb "to envisage" as "safer," for this verb suggests an activity designating as its value the actuality to be promoted with regard to various possibilities, and therefore designates possibilities as "deficient," as bereft of value independent of their realization.

Whitehead thus rejects, rather explicitly, any contemplative ideal, such as the one that, in the post-Platonic tradition, made intellect, intelligence, and intelligible coincide. The ingression of eternal objects has nothing to do with a participation in a higher, sovereign reality. Instead, it is associated with a term that evokes a busy, hesitant, perhaps conflictual activity which all contemplative philosophies, or those which, in one way or another, establish a convergence between salvation, certainty, and coincidence of self with self, would characterize as the wanderings of a distended, disoriented soul, deprived of what orients it toward its authentic destiny.

Perhaps only Leibniz, another mathematician, has adopted a perspective on experience similar to Whitehead's. In his *Philosopher's Confession*, Leibniz proposes, as the only general piece of advice he has to give, to always ask the question *"Dic cur hic"* (say why here). The point is to "say," not to "know." Leibniz demands that when we have to define a "purpose," we not obey general reasons, a conformity indifferent to circumstances, a blind norm, but that we submit such generalities to the test of the *"hic."* In this case, one may use the verb "to envisage." Leibniz asks that we accept that the way we define a situation is "purposeful," and that we envisage this purpose as related to the situation taken as a "case," that is, in a mode that is as concrete and as explicitly situated in the here and now as possible.

Leibnizian envisagement is a piece of moral advice: it translates what is "best," since we cannot deduce our choices from any divine imperative. We have no access to the reasons that determined the divine choice of this world as the best one, but we can integrate into our decisions the fact that it is this world that God has chosen. This advice therefore means "exist for *this* world." Without promises or guarantees, it is "better" to adopt a stance that affirms this world, that exposes itself to this world, rather than to protect oneself by abstract generalizations, however noble they may be.

Whitehead is no Leibnizian: for him, envisagement translates what must be attributed to the underlying activity itself if actuality is to be value. And this concerns every actuality. It is quite obviously conscious thought, the experience of hesitation between abstract possibilities, that exhibits and requires a positive contrast between potentiality and actuality, but, as Whitehead specifies, every occasion, even the most tenuous, fugitive wrinkle differentiating general energy, has a value *qua* individualization of the eternal activity, that is, it constitutes an individual purpose.

Just as envisagement, in the metaphysical sense, confers no privilege upon human envisaging experience, "eternal objects" cannot be invoked to found any kind of privilege of those cognitive activities for which Plato required the Ideas—to judge, to sort, to evaluate in terms of legitimacy, of faithfulness, of resemblance—nor to appeal to any kind of a dynamics of elevation or conversion. And therefore, as we now turn toward "Abstraction," the first of the two new chapters entirely written by Whitehead after April 1925, we will have to bear in mind that the eternal object, or ideality, certainly designates what "transcends" actuality, but that transcendence is thereby stripped of any "eminent value," to which the things of this world would owe their legitimacy, or of any desirability orienting souls toward their salvation. Transcendence, as exhibited by the experience of knowledge, is nothing other than what is demanded by immanence, the concrete fact, so that none of the questions experience asks us may be reduced, denied, or disqualified. Here, Whitehead adopts the approach that will systematically prevail in the construction of concepts in *Process and Reality*: all the aspects of our most singular, most routine experiences, must be able to be described as exhibiting that which, from the metaphysical standpoint, is presupposed by all actualization.

In any occasion of cognition, that which is known is an actual occasion of experience, as diversified by reference to a realm of entities which

*transcend that immediate occasion in that they have analogous or differ-
ent connections with other occasions of experience. For example, a definite shade of red may, in the immediate occasion, be implicated with the
shape of sphericity in some definite way. But that shade of red, and that
spherical shape, exhibit themselves as transcending that occasion, in that
either of them has other relationships to other occasions* (SMW, 158).

It is thus on the basis of "cognitive occasions," that is, of the experiences that make us speak, describe, analyze, and reason about experience,
that eternal objects impose themselves, but the privilege of cognitive occasions is not metaphysical. Eternal objects are not required by knowledge;
above all, they are not synonymous with a "pure" intelligibility that finds
the opportunity to manifest itself in changing reality. They are, of course,
required by what we are aware of in knowledge, but, unless knowledge is
to be reduced to a phantasmagoria, they must be implicated in every realization. Even when they intend to ignore it in favor of the reassuring empirical statement "that red patch there," description, analysis, or reasoning irreducibly imply a transcendence, that is, a set of references that
exceed "this" red. I cannot say "red" without, at the same time, implying
that it might have been blue, that it is "something" that is red, that other
things may have the same shade of red, that this "same" red may, or
might, be the object of other experiences.

As I have already emphasized, a color is not, in itself, an eternal object.
It is the experience of color that testifies to the ingression of an eternal
object. Whitehead will call the type of eternal object whose ingression is
exhibited by sense experience a "sensum." For him, the sensa constitute a
particular class of eternal objects, and this particularity is due to the fact
that sense experience, for instance that of color, does not necessarily imply
the relevance of anything else. Here we find once again the characterization of the "sense object" in *The Concept of Nature*: the ingression of a
sensum does not imply that other eternal objects make ingression according to other specified modes.

As sensation, color makes no specific reference to the trees, the pond, or
the bushes over there; it belongs to the event of experience. And therefore,
once it has gone, it is gone, whereas the landscape lasts and endures. Of
course, one must, like Shelley, be a "poet of sensation" to celebrate shimmering and twinkling, the play of shadows and lights, without at the same
time describing trees or a time of day, but in such a case, if the contrast
between what is and what might be cannot be genuinely "envisaged," it is
not because it does not exist, but, quite the contrary, because it dominates
experience, like a fragile miracle, without guarantee or explanation. For
Whitehead, red is then accompanied only by the sense of color as possible: "this" red, different from all the others.

If, however, contemplating the yellow of a field of wheat, my experience implies other yellows already seen, or the yellow of Van Gogh's wheat fields, this experience exhibits the multiple relations that the eternal objects maintain with one another. The same holds true when it comes to the grey of those clouds, the chalky shade of the rocks of that castle, in short, colors that do indeed belong to the cloud over there, to that castle up on the hill. Or again, to cite Whitehead's favorite example, the touch of blue in that painting, necessary for the painting to be what it is, that makes it special: a sensation once again, but a complex sensation, not only inseparable from the play of forms and colors, but with a risky composition that signs "this" painting.

Only the injunction of empiricist censors can lead us to violently ignore the many propositions that are irreducibly articulated with the perception of this field, these clouds, or this castle. It is the unlimited character of this "many" that gives its meaning to the "realm" of "all the eternal objects." In *The Concept of Nature,* a discerned event was as though linked to other events defined as discernible, with the discernible being, at the limit, the whole of nature as it declares itself in an experience. Here, "realm" means that an eternal object will not be able to make ingression without all the eternal objects being thereby mobilized in one way or another.

How can one speak, in all generality, of an eternal object? Whitehead tries out two principles:

The first principle is that each eternal object is an individual which, in its own peculiar fashion, is what it is. This particular individuality is the individual essence of the object, and cannot be described otherwise than as being itself. Thus the individual essence is merely the essence considered in respect to its uniqueness. Further, the essence of an eternal object is merely the eternal object considered as adding its own unique contribution to each actual occasion. This unique contribution is identical for all such occasions in respect to the fact that the object in all modes of ingression is just its identical self. But it varies from one occasion to another in respect to the differences of its modes of ingression. Thus the metaphysical status of an eternal object is that of a possibility for an actuality. Every actual occasion is defined as to its character by how these possibilities are actualised for that occasion. Thus actualisation is a selection among possibilities. More accurately, it is a selection issuing in a gradation of possibilities in respect to their realisation in that occasion. This conclusion brings us to the second metaphysical principle: An eternal object, considered as an abstract entity, cannot be divorced from its reference to other eternal objects, and from its reference to actuality generally (SMW, 159).

The eternal object "is what it is." A strange definition, with highly singular consequences. The first of these consequences is that it is impossible to describe an eternal object, or even to talk about it, "for itself," that is, without reference to something other than itself. One will not rise back up from the color to the sensum according to a principle of resemblance or analogy, for the sensum would then be something other than "what it is"; it would also be the analogue or the model for something other than itself. And something would have happened to it: with the appearance of the sense organs, it would have acquired the current means to confer their finality on these organs. The eternal object would explain, or be explained by, the color-sensation. Likewise, the intelligible object "circle" would explain, or would explain itself in, the mathematical intellect.

It is important to emphasize that Whitehead will never change his mind on this point: an eternal object cannot equip any judgment, found any reasoning, confer its power on any privilege communicating with any "pure" experience. It is not the intelligible, nor is it even intelligible, for intelligibility refers to an actual experience. It neither guides nor orients. If it can itself be said to be "pure" or "transcendent," it is in the sense of being impassible, radically indifferent to its own ingressions, radically foreign to any discrimination between the pure and the impure, and even to any procedure of purification. And all this for the simple reason that it would then be something more than what it is, since it could be characterized on the basis of some of its privileged cases of ingression.

In the essence of each eternal object there stands an indeterminateness which expresses its indifferent patience for any mode of ingression into any actual occasion (SMW, 171).

We now come to the question of the relation of one eternal object to other eternal objects. In fact, in *Science and the Modern World,* the question is of its relation to all other eternal objects. Here we will reencounter the question of envisagement, for what there is envisagement of is never an eternal object, but always the eternal objects, and first of all the "realm" of all the eternal objects.

When Whitehead speaks of the realm of eternal objects, he is not talking about a static and ordered totality. This realm designates the systematically complete, uniform, nonselective relationality of each eternal object with all the others. Whitehead devoted a great deal of effort to an attempt to characterize this type of relationality, proper to eternal objects. He sought to define this realm in a way that would make possible the affirmation that the choice of a determinate mode of ingression of a particular eternal object implies a determinate mode of ingression for the complete totality of all eternal objects, which Whitehead calls an "ideal situation." Each ideal situation corresponds to a "gradation of possibilities," or an abstract hierarchy whose summit is occupied by the selected eternal object. The grades of entry of the others "can be expressed only as relevance of value" (SMW, 162). I will not follow him in these technical considerations, not only because this is one of those attempts in which Whitehead runs the risk of axiomatic formulation, rather than those of metaphysics, but also because what is at stake in this formulation, the abstract hierarchy that constitutes each ideal situation, will, as we shall see, raise a major problem, which may explain why this attempt was to be abandoned in *Process and Reality*. What matters here is what was to be formalized: envisagement *qua* eternal activity. The realm may be said to be eternal, in contrast to the temporalization represented by realization, because, like the eternal objects themselves, it is indifferent to what requires it. Nothing happens to the realm as such, which is eternally what it is, indifferently expressed by any of the ideal situations associated with the "second envisagement."

Each realization implies the selective actualization (third envisagement) of a "possibility of value" corresponding to an ideal situation, classifying all the eternal objects. Let us think of the experience: "you who are looking at me, but perhaps without seeing me," and of the number of propositions that can be articulated with such an experience, of the number of purposeful determinations with regard to the past, of the number of implications, of "ands," of "ors," of "and yets," of "and therefores," or of "and ifs": potentially, we have here the material for a novel (albeit not necessarily a good novel). The ideal situation generalizes, in the metaphysical sense, the thread of all the questions that can be raised by an experience henceforth placed under the banner of "presence," as is attested by novelists or psychologists when they celebrate experience instead of reducing it to triviality.

Of course, the perceptual experience "this red table" is clearly not as loquacious, but, as we have seen, it nevertheless conveys with it an indefinite number of possibilities: the possibility of touching, of leaning, of putting down, of admiring or displacing, and in *The Concept of Nature*, the "complete general fact" ultimately comprised "all of nature as actually discriminated or discerned" in a sensory experience. What was important in *The Concept of Nature* was that everything we are aware of should have a respondent in nature. Imagination explains nothing; it is what must be rendered conceivable. The important point here is the characterization of experience itself, *qua* realization: individual realization is not the same thing as substantial independence! (SMW, 70). Here, Whitehead seems very close to Leibniz, for whom it is possible to say that the whole world "conspires" in every state of each monad.

As we have seen, the fact that all eternal objects enter into the ideal situation does not mean that there is "equality" between these eternal objects. On the contrary, each ideal situation corresponds to a determinate hierarchical ordering among the indefinite multiplicity of orderings that the realm can tolerate just as well. Each occasion thus realizes what has been actualized as a particular, differentiated mode of ingression for each eternal object. Moreover, the ordering constituted by each ideal situation will not only classify the eternal objects according to their mode of ingression but also *qua* excluded. All eternal objects are included, each corresponding to its more or less relevant contribution to the value of the actuality, but some are included *qua* excluded, *qua* "not-being" with regard to that occasion. An actual occasion thus presupposes a synthesis, or a togetherness, of being and not-being.

By making exclusion a mode of inclusion, Whitehead distances himself from Leibniz, that is, from a perspectivism that can play only on the scale of differences between clear and confused. He has provided the ideal situation with the means to affirm itself as a "possibility of value," which should enable realization to be not a standpoint on the world, but involved in a world, thus and not otherwise. Thus, the experience of the "poet of sensation" exhibits an ideal situation such that the particularity of the sensa, the fact that they do not necessarily imply the ingression of other eternal objects, becomes a singularity: the eternal objects whose positive inclusion would imply the perception of a colored landscape are included *qua* excluded. Conversely, the insistence of the future reflects the inclusion of eternal objects in a mode that requires the passage to other individualizations, in which what is not-being may become being. All the questions that may be inspired by an experience, all the experiences that prolong and interpret an experience, or all the variations in interest exploring a felt contrast between the discerned and the discernible attest to modifications of the ideal situation, one eternal object succeeding another at the summit of the hierarchy, or an eternal object defined as excluded finding itself included. Each ideal situation thus defines in an abstract mode both a world and a "standpoint on the world," but the realized, concrete standpoint is stripped of any analogy with vision, reflection, or conspiration. The standpoint is "prehensive," taking and seizing as much as it rejects and excludes. It is "for a world," not "of a world."

We are not done yet, and I will now approach the question of envisagement in a way that will be somewhat peculiar. Indeed, I wish to emphasize that there is something in envisagement of the audacious movement by which a cat, in the midst of a free fall, twists itself around to land on its feet. Like this movement, the third type of envisagement cannot be described independently of the threat it enables Whitehead to escape. Even if the cat succeeds in escaping injury, it still experienced a fall. In other words, my approach will attempt to problematize the triple envisagement which constitutes, if one may say so, the "abstract" face of individualization properly so called. I will try to characterize this abstraction as a risky moment in Whitehead's thought, a moment in which Whitehead may be undergoing the consequences of this abstraction more than he creates them.

In fact, the following question arises: with regard to what is the eternal underlying activity an abstraction? I have insisted on limiting the eternal objects to the "how" of prehension in order to combat any confusion between this "how" and the concrete fact, or the entity such as it has actualized itself, thus and not otherwise. Yet it must be admitted that Whitehead's text is sometimes less clear, that it is not quite categorically opposed to the interpretation that would make actuality a simple passage to reality of the ideal situation itself.

It is perhaps here, in the importance I confer upon the risk to which this interpretation exposes Whitehead's thought, that I feel most intensely my debt to Gilles Deleuze. For every reader of Deleuze is, by definition, attentive to the difference between "virtual" and "potential." The "potential" is "made to explain" the real, and therefore places the explanation under the banner of resemblance or tracing. The "possible" in this sense calls for a realization that is in the first instance a selection: as such, each possible is well defined, and all it is missing is reality. Realization is therefore the selection of the one that will be realized. Of the virtual, in contrast, one must say that it is not actualized without changing "in nature" (taking on a different "mode of existence"), a thesis Deleuze took over from Bergson. This implies, first of all, that it cannot be conceived in the image of its actualization, and that the latter can be no means be assimilated to a simple selection.

When he tries to conceive of eternal objects as abstracted from all actuality, Whitehead is situated in the vicinity of the virtual: the "realm" of the eternal objects must be said to be a coexistence without hierarchy, an indifference to the disjunction "either/or," assembled without real togetherness, for all real togetherness indicates actuality. When, however, he defines "actualization" (not to be confused with Deleuze's) as a selection among possibilities (SMW, 159), Whitehead constructs the figure of an envisagement that appears as self-sufficient, whose result does indeed risk lacking nothing but reality, and which would have the power to explain that reality. This is also indicated by the notion of "possibility of value": it seems to be missing only realization in order to be "value." In other words, the aspect of "underlying eternal activity" constituted by the triple envisagement seems to leave to realization only the somewhat poor role of ratifying the selected possible.

One might say, of course, that this difficulty designates the absence of a theory of prehension, or taking into account. The problem is that the ideal situation does not create the "yearning" for such a theory in the reader, that it does not make its absence exist insistently, as that without which ideality would have no value. This is a serious objection, as is attested, moreover, by the need Whitehead feels to repeat, as if to force his readers to remember it, "no actuality, no value." In fact, when the theory of prehensions arrives, when, in *Process and Reality,* Whitehead provides himself with the means to go to the end of what this theory demands, the abstraction constituted by an "eternal underlying activity" will disappear.

It is not surprising that many contemporary Whiteheadians dream of ridding Whitehead's system of the eternal objects, or else of conceiving the possibility of making them emerge historically. As long as the distinction between actualization and realization in Deleuze's sense is not radical, that is, as long as Whiteheadian realization can be interpreted as the mere realization of a predetermined possibility, the envisagement of eternal objects risks reducing the difference between possibility of value and value to a ratification. And the question will become all the more crucial when, in *Process and Reality,* God becomes an actual being to whom the envisagement of eternal objects pertains. How can one prevent realization from being reduced to a mere choice between possible worlds that are already ideally determined from the standpoint of divine envisagement? How can one fail to detect the old slight of hand that prevails whenever one claims to respect the freedom of others, while leaving them only the freedom of choosing among solutions without participating in the construction of the problem?

If the eternal objects do not bother me in *Process and Reality*—quite the contrary—it is, here once again, thanks to the distinction Deleuze proposes between virtual and potential. It is because this distinction enables me to recognize the risk that it also allows me to grasp, in what might otherwise seem to be a thought in continuity, the extraordinary, problematic mutation that was to surmount this risk. In a nutshell, or as a foretaste, divine envisagement will take its place at the very point where realization risked being understood as mere ratification. More precisely, it will participate in the mode of existence that Deleuze, here following no longer Bergson but the philosopher Étienne Souriau, confers upon the virtual: that of a problem to be solved or a work to be accomplished.

I insist on this idea that as long as the work is in the workshop, the work is in danger. At each moment, each one of the artists' actions, or rather from each of the artist's actions, it may live or die. The agile choreography of an improviser, noticing and resolving in the same instant the problems raised for him by this hurried advance of the work; the anxiety of a fresco painter knowing that no mistake will be reparable, and that everything must be done within the hour left to him before the plaster dries; the works of the composer or the writer at their table, with the time to meditate at leisure, to retouch, to redo [. . .] *it is nevertheless true that all must ceaselessly answer, in a slow or rapid progression, the questions of the sphinx*—guess, or you will be devoured. *But it is the work that flourishes or disappears, it is it that progresses or is devoured* (MEOF, 13).

The insistence of the problem does not implicitly contain the means for its solution; the work's "idea" is not an ideal from which the artist takes inspiration. It exists only through the risk it brings into existence, by the fact that at every step artists know they are exposed to the risk of betrayal, particularly when, through laziness, ease, impatience, or fear, they believe they can decide on the path, instead of capturing, step by step, the question posed to them at that step.

Unlike the mythical Sphinx, the sphinx of Étienne Souriau does not know the answer to the riddle. The "deficiency" of envisagement is then no longer a lack, but designates the Deleuzian difference in nature between the virtual and the potential, connoted by a risk and by a wait. A risk has no determinate identity or stake before it is actually taken. A wait is a wait for what will answer, not for such-and-such an answer.

I needed to present the risk to which, from my (committed) point of view, his concepts expose Whitehead, before turning to the elucidation of the third envisagement, or the third aspect of eternal envisagement, for this elucidation will be the "last word" of *Science and the Modern World*. And I wish to understand this "last word" as a "twisting *in extremis*," a twisting which, as the reader will have understood, is by no means sufficient to solve the difficulty associated with ideal envisagement, the fact that it does not inspire the "yearning" for the concrete. It does, however, reflect the fact that Whitehead has already discovered the need to resist the slope down which his metaphysical construction was taking him.

I have emphasized that the ideal situation prolongs the thesis of *The Concept of Nature*, according to which the "general complete fact" of which we have experience is "all of nature." Yet what I did not emphasize is the consequence of this kind of prolongation: you think you have produced a local standpoint, thus and not otherwise, but it is a world that has been chosen. And it is this consequence that the third aspect of envisagement will "parry," at the cost of a conceptual invention that testifies by itself to what the concept of eternal underlying activity lacks: the "yearning" for actuality, which alone is value. For in order to preserve this individual value, Whitehead will dare to introduce, *in extremis* indeed, since nothing foretold it previously, a metaphysical "God."

Thanks to God, we may indeed say, between value such as it has meaning for experience and value such as it follows from the possibilities of value that derive from the second type of envisagement, a mode of characterization will be avoided that would have relegated the first one to a deficient approximation.

CHAPTER FOURTEEN

The Great Refusal

[...] *EVERY ACTUAL OCCASION is set within a realm of alternative interconnected entities. This realm is disclosed by all the untrue propositions which can be predicated significantly of that occasion. It is the realm of alternative suggestions, whose foothold in actuality transcends each actual occasion. The real relevance of untrue propositions for each actual occasion is disclosed by art, romance, and by criticism in reference to ideals. It is the foundation of the metaphysical position which I am maintaining that the understanding of actuality requires a reference to ideality. The two realms are intrinsically inherent in the total metaphysical situation. The truth that some proposition respecting an actual occasion is untrue may express the vital truth as to the aesthetic achievement. It expresses the "great refusal," which is its primary characteristic. An event is decisive in proportion to the importance (for it) of its untrue propositions* (SMW, 158).

Specialists are beginning to learn how to characterize, at the level of the recordings of cerebral activity, the qualitative difference between one and the "same" performance, according to whether it is due to a routine activity or to a mind that hesitates with regard to what it is to do. It should be possible to characterize many other differences: one walks "as one breathes," but the mountain climber's foothold, an "aware" experience characterized by due attention, exhibits a risk that is usually not consciously formulated: won't what this foothold trusts give way, will the relief on which it depends be patient to its exploitation? And one must also distinguish between this mountain climber's art, implying a trained body and concentrated attention, and other risky practices, which, for their part, imply conscious hesitation. Unlike the mountain climber's risky exploit, "aesthetic accomplishment" does not have as a stake the risk of "being wrong," of seeing the realization of what had been produced as "untrue"—it will not give way. What is at stake is the very contrast between true and untrue: each proposition produced as "true" vibrates with the "great refusal" of everything that, inseparably, will have been produced as untrue. "Pure" sensation, this red, vibrates with everything it does not include, that it is the red of this hood, worn by this little girl, who is carrying a big basket and is headed down there, toward the forest . . . The mountain climber risks falling, but the artist risks betrayal. It is insofar as aesthetic accomplishment exhibits the way that the untrue is produced as well as the true that this accomplishment exhibits actuality as value.

However, from the dispassionate viewpoint of metaphysics, the fascinating differences between routine, clumsy hesitation, concentrated attention, and aesthetic risk yield to the generic problem raised by all the propositions that every realization will render "true" or "untrue." And this is where the problem arises. The ideal situation corresponds to a complete envisagement of the eternal objects and their relations, that is, just as much to the determination of what is included as "being" as of what is excluded as "not-being." If one had to admit that true and untrue propositions realize the distinction between "being" and "not-being," what aesthetic accomplishment demands of metaphysics, the "great refusal" *qua* vital truth of an accomplishment would find only a rather ironic answer. This vital truth is nothing other than the truth of the ideal situation, a selective one indeed but hardly a "refusal."

But there is another answer, which demands that we confer all its weight upon a detail in the quotation where Whitehead affirms the great refusal as a vital truth of aesthetic accomplishment. Here, he speaks of untrue propositions that may be *predicated significantly* with regard to an occasion, of the *real relevance* of these same untrue propositions, and of their importance *for* the event. From the viewpoint of the ideal situation, the restrictions implied by these terms have no meaning: all the consequences and implications of actualization, as articulated by the ideal situation, are relevant, even if this relevance is graded. From the viewpoint of experience, however, the meaning of these restrictions is decisive. Adam chose to accept the apple offered by Eve and to disobey God, but he could not choose the drama of the Redemption. We may decide on a world, but the fact that we decide on a world does not correspond to any actual experience in any of the practices in which the question of aesthetic accomplishment arises.

It is here, of course, that the contrast between limited human knowledge and the infinite, divine viewpoint is usually proposed. The radical disjunction proposed by Leibniz between our experience, in which it is "as if" we decided, and the universe as God has evaluated and chosen it mobilizes this contrast. We think we can name the reasons for our choices, but these reasons are only the result of a multitude of tiny perceptions, which, for their part, refer to the choice of God, to the universe He has chosen, and not to "us." For Whitehead, however, this solution constitutes a defeat for metaphysics. Insofar as Leibnizian monads do not allow the formulation of an actual difference, belonging to the present, between what might be and what is realized, but merely reflect the difference chosen by God, they imply, as Whitehead denounces, a serious "incoherence." And in fact, what is denied in the name of a metaphysical system is what is presupposed by the very activity of thinkers, who must think that what they enunciate is capable of creating a difference for themselves and for others. However subtle Leibniz may be, the surprising effects, vectors of peace and of lucidity, to which his system is meant to give rise, are not included in this system.

It is precisely this incoherency that Whitehead intends to reject when he identifies value and actuality. If only actuality has value, it is value as our experiences can manifest it, with the sense of novelty, of risk, of purpose, all of which allude to what Whitehead calls "addition of the future," not a value that would reduce our experience to a fiction or an illusion—even if, as Leibniz was careful to show, this illusion were well constructed.

To combat this threat, to confer an irreducible character upon what is demanded by the propositions rendered "untrue" by an aesthetic accomplishment, their relevance, their significant character, Whitehead will have recourse to God.

The God of *Science and the Modern World* has nothing in common with a God of religion, and particularly with the God of the Christians. One of the very few anecdotes we preserve from Whitehead's life, moreover, is a sketch played out in his family, where he himself played the part, not without irreverence, of God, who suddenly has a new idea to invest a soccer ball with life. He then comments on what happens with his children (the Son and the Holy Ghost, of course), wonders whether the idea was really all that good, decides to delegate his son to Redemption, and so on. Everything concludes with a solid kick applied to the unfortunate ball: the case of creation is truly hopeless. More seriously, it is against the God of the metaphysicians that Whitehead unleashes his irony and his sarcasm: against the sad habit of addressing metaphysical compliments to him (SMW, 179), that is, constituting him as a "metaphysical reason," making him the supreme author of the play, who may be responsible for its success but also for its inadequacies. If Whitehead introduced God, it was indeed because the mode in which he needs what he calls God to intervene escapes this hypothesis.

In fact, God will only intervene at the end of the game, not as what imposes itself in an eminent way but as what is required by what imposes itself in an eminent way: the need to define a real difference between actuality as value and the unlimited totality of the determinations and implications that correspond to the ideal situation. In short, God will be explicitly required to characterize not envisagement in general but the third type of envisagement as Whitehead has characterized it, writing in his insertion of the triple envisagement about "the individualised prehension into individual events of *aspects* of the ideal situation" (SMW, 105).

*So far I have merely been considering an actual occasion on the side of its full concreteness. It is this side of the occasion in virtue of which it is an event in nature. But a natural event, in this sense of the term, is only an abstraction from a complete actual occasion. A complete occasion includes that which in cognitive experience takes the form of memory, anticipation, imagination, and thought. These elements in an experient occasion are also modes of inclusion of complex eternal objects in the synthetic prehension, as elements in the emergent value. They differ from the concreteness of full inclusion. In a sense this difference is inexplicable; for each mode of inclusion is of its own kind, not to be explained in terms of anything else. But there is a common difference which discriminates these modes of conclusion from the full concrete ingression which has been discussed. This dif-*ferentia *is* abruptness. *By "abruptness" I mean that what is remembered, or anticipated, or imagined, or thought, is exhausted by a finite complex concept* [. . .] *There is a limitation which breaks off the finite concept from the higher grades of illimitable complexity* (SMW, 170–171).

What has just been the object of a "great refusal," in which the risk proper to metaphysics vibrates, is the generalization of the thesis defended in *The Concept of Nature*. There, event and inclusion were conceived together. Not only was every event included within other events, but it declared itself to be such in experience: to discern an event is also to have the experience of the discernible, it is to have the experience of its meaning *qua* included within other events that do not declare themselves otherwise than *qua* signified. To state that the complete concrete fact is the totality of nature was to emphasize the way in which declared meanings and discerned objects cannot, as language might induce us to think, be isolated from what we are aware of as implicit or discernible. It was thus to create the contrast between concrete experience and the abstraction of the reasons, takings-into-account, and names in which we place our trust. This is the same contrast Leibniz had proposed when he described the multitude of indistinct little perceptions that contribute to the roar of a wave, and also the multitude of muffled thoughts that disquiet the thinker. For Leibniz, this is a pedagogical example of the way the whole world conspires in any experience, and it is also what Whitehead had accepted in *The Concept of Nature:* if there is no reason to set limits to what the event declares in the mode of the discernible, there is no limit to be set. Yet he has just concluded *in extremis:* what was not necessary for a philosophy of nature is necessary for metaphysics. Certain kinds of occasion exhibit, as their vital truth, a limitation, a form of "abstraction" that must find its meaning in the concept of "complete actual occasion." In fact, it is the occasion characterized as fully concrete that constitutes an abstraction, in the same way as "nature." The "vital truth" of the great refusal indicates that the mind is no longer "the ultimate," but that which obliges us to think.

To understand an explicit signification is also, of course, to experience everything to which it alludes implicitly, and logicians must sometimes be reminded of this, as must those scientists who study the order of nature and take advantage of the declared and stabilized modes of prehension that disclose the endurance of organisms. Yet it belongs to the metaphysics of the actual occasion to let itself be obliged by "aesthetic accomplishment" in order to construct the deployed totality required by the value of an occasion. This accomplishment exhibits an actual, decisive break in the unlimited network of implications, an abrupt difference that intervenes in the midst of the unlimited totality of what discloses itself only as signified. To put things in a grandiose way, the artist's gesture does not concern the great breath of the world; rather, it is the world that holds its breath as the artist begins her gesture.

This breaking off from an actual illimitability is what in any occasion marks off that which is termed mental from that which belongs to the physical event to which the mental functioning is referred [. . .] *the things apprehended as mental are always subject to the condition that we come to a stop when we attempt to explore ever higher grades of complexity in their realised relationships. We always find that we have thought of just this—whatever it may be—and of no more* (SMW, 171).

Here, mentality does not mean "subjectivity," but it indicates how Whitehead has undertaken to think of individualization as a value. And his solution is rather original. The difference between a "physical" event, an event *qua* "in nature," and the "mental functioning" that gives meaning to the complete actual occasion is none other than finitude. *Qua* physical, the event is on the side of the infinite, whereas the finite character of what is "just this and no more," as is required by the relevance of a decision, corresponds to the mental.

The relevance of mathematical physics thus depends on the possibility of ignoring the way the occasions oblige us to conceive of a "break": "just this . . . and no more." Although the spatio-temporal functions of classical physics say that one heavy body makes more difference for another the closer it is to that other, they do not say that after a certain distance it makes no difference, only that the difference becomes more and more negligible. It is the physicist, not the body, who is supposed to define what must be taken into account and what can be considered negligible, ignored by approximation. Henceforth, however, mathematical physics is no longer an adequate testimony. Where its testimony is relevant, this relevance signifies that "what is termed mental" matters little, makes no calculable difference.

As far as the way in which the living organism "holds" *qua* enduring is concerned, it certainly exhibits a selective character, as is indicated by the relevance of such technical terms as "detect," "react specifically to," "activate," and so on. Yet it is a selection that endures: we have to do here with what Whitehead henceforth calls "intermediate cases," which could be described as forms of routine mentality, dominated by the reproduction of a mode of foothold. In contrast, if one may speak of a "history of mentalities," what becomes crucial is the way in which the difference between implicit and explicit is defined on each occasion or in each epoch.

"They should have realized that. . . . Since it was an implicit dimension of the situation, why didn't they make it explicit?" All the scandal that the professional mentality may inspire, as well as the very problem of what may also be called the history of consciousness, consists in such questions. Both the challenge of education and the career of the historian must undergo their trial. Experienced teachers know the difference between the student's first encounter with a new kind of mathematical definition and what that definition "says" to them. Historians know how pay due attention to the difference between the questions they themselves, like each of us, may ask the past, are inclined to ask the past, and those that were relevant for the people who lived in that past. More generally, the process of "making explicit" may, of course, indicate a risk of contingent misunderstanding and then appear as productive of exactness; it may reflect the legitimate impatience inspired by the professional's ruts. Yet it may also be indiscreet or intrusive, giving rise to the embarrassment, anger, and even violence of the person whose gestures, implications, and meanings are being interpreted. Finally, it may also reflect a genuine innovation.

As the case may be, then, the implicit may be what might just as well be explicit, that whose rendering-explicit raises no other problem than that of a "call to order" that may be redundant or even malevolent, but it may also be that whose rendering-explicit constitutes a form of intrusion, and finally that whose "discovery" constitutes an event: *"I had not realized that ... "* When Einstein undertook to construct explicitly the conditions in which we may speak of simultaneity between two distinct events, it was to create a problem no one before him had thought about. When sixteenth-century chemists undertook to make explicit the difference between them and the alchemists, the creation was twofold. It concerned alchemy as well, as they defined it in explicit contrast to chemistry, an alchemy that did not, as such, exist prior to this operation. And for each student who encounters a new mathematical being, the point is to learn to take into account a set of distinctions that by no means went without saying beforehand.

In these cases, then, the contrast between the explicit and the implicit should be assimilated to a genuine horizon. It is in vain that Socrates acts as though Meno's slave "already knew" the irrational character associated with the measurement of a square's diagonal: the concrete fact is that the slave did not have the slightest idea of this fact. Socrates is well aware of this but does not care, because it is in fact to Meno that he wanted to show his power while he forced the slave, step by step, to admit everything his declared knowledge was supposed to imply "implicitly." This is why, after the last "You are right, Socrates," he coldly abandons his guinea pig, who has not, for all that, become a mathematician. If the slave had suddenly said "I understand!" it was with him that Socrates should have pursued the dialogue.

I term this abrupt realisation the "graded envisagement" which each occasion prehends into its synthesis. This graded envisagement is how the actual includes what (in one sense) is not-being as a positive factor in its own achievement. It is the source of error, of truth, of art, of ethics, and of religion. By it, fact is confronted by alternatives (SMW, 176–177).

Error and truth, ethics and religion are united, in that the value of the experiences corresponding to them also consists in what they do not take into account "in fact," and it is also in this that they oblige a reference to the ideality requiring the third mode of envisagement proposed by Whitehead: what makes ingression is an ideal ordering of a *finite* degree of complexity. What exceeds this finite degree is situated beyond its horizon, excluded from the purpose and value associated with actuality.

"My demand is, that the ultimate arbitrariness of matter of fact from which our formulation starts should disclose the same general principles of reality, which we dimly discern as stretching away into regions beyond our explicit powers of discernment" (SMW, 92–93). Whitehead is now in a position to satisfy this demand. The "great refusal" declared by our achievements must be the starting point for a formulation that extends to every occasion. We have no access to an electronic occasion as such, we do not know everything that counts "for it," *qua* positive factor in its accomplishment. Yet there is no metaphysical differentiation between a "physical" and a "cognitive" occasion, but rather a pragmatic one, responding to the pragmatics of our definitions. An occasion may be qualified as "physical" insofar as the becoming of the continuity to which it belongs confirms the pragmatic relevance of the definition Whitehead gave of nature: by paying it due attention, we find more in it. As we have seen, things get complicated when it comes to psychology. And when, in a typical domestic scene, the man, infuriated by the "attention" his wife pays to him, slams the door, his impatience exhibits and requires a "mentality." Yet if every occasion is characterized in terms of "purpose," *qua* related to a limited horizon—not only this and not that, but for *this* limited world, rather than for the indefinite world that "this" cannot help but imply—every occasion also discloses an "ultimate arbitrariness."

Thus as a further element in the metaphysical situation, there is required a principle of limitation. Some particular how is necessary, and some particularisation in the what of matter of fact is necessary [...] we must provide a ground for limitation which stands among the attributes of the substantial activity. This attribute provides the limitation for which no reason can be given: for all reason flows from it. God is the ultimate limitation, and His existence is the ultimate irrationality. For no reason can be given for just that limitation which it stands in His nature to impose. God is not concrete, but He is the ground for concrete activity. No reason can be given for the nature of God, because that nature is the ground of rationality (SMW, 178).

The God Whitehead has just introduced is simultaneously, and equivalently, a principle of limitation and a principle of concretion. He has nothing to do with the despotic God toward whom all explanatory chains go back: *It was God's will, God's will be done.* He answers to a need produced by metaphysics. Quite precisely, he is made necessary by the third type of envisagement. The ideal situation explains only the physical occasion, which is a mere abstraction. The concrete occasion requires a limited, individualized horizon. God does not provide the reason for this limitation, but he is named in order to express its "arbitrariness" in the sense in which the very notion of reason, and the possibility of defining "that" for which an account is being requested, imply a limitation. He is that without which the "great refusal" could only be an illusion.

The only alternative to this admission, is to deny the reality of actual occasions. Their apparent irrational limitation must be taken as a proof of illusion and we must look for a reality behind the scene (SMW, 178).

This is indeed what Whitehead reproaches Leibniz: to have proclaimed that "there is a reason for everything," even the choice of God, who has access to the sole genuine reality, to the infinite conspiration of the universe with each state of the monad, or, reversibly, to each state of the monad as a standpoint implying an entire universe. If Leibniz were right, the true meaning of our experiences would be unlimited, "behind the scene," and our choices would be mere appearances, with the divine choice of this world as their hidden reason. *Decision* must therefore be primordial, and our reasons must be relative to it. The possibility of invoking, like Leibniz, the "reasons of God," even defining them as unknowable, must become a metaphysical or a technical impossibility. The world cannot be deduced from a calculation, whatever the meaning of the divine calculation may be. It decides itself.

Here, then, we encounter once again Whitehead the mathematician, who has not the least patience for those who wish to ignore the fact that every question sets in place its "ultimate," that which cannot be questioned because the question presupposes it. It is henceforth the question of metaphysics that is under discussion, the question of the nature of things, that is, of their reasons, and of the ultimate presupposed by the construction of every reason, whatever it may be. Every search for a reason presupposes a problem, and every problem is a horizon. You may construct reasons, but not the reason for the limitation of what you envisage with regard to the indefinite labyrinths of envisageable relations. You can ask people to explain themselves, to explicate what they mean, or intend to do, or think that they should do, *dic cur hic,* but remember that your question demands from the other, and may inspire in the other, not a simple explication but a displacement of horizon. You can show as much as you want in what sense the (new) reasons on the basis of which you raise your problem transcend the particularity of the statements you intend to question: your reasons will still respond to the problem as you pose it, and therefore to a horizon that is also limited. Yet those who would take advantage of this limitation to deny the novelty of your reasons, to situate you within the "historical context" that would explain your proposition, could never help but take their place, *a posteriori,* within the enlarged horizon you have proposed. The "context" they would invoke to situate you would be none other than the one which your proposition has turned into its own situation, and which happens to have been "patient" to the novelty you proposed, or even susceptible of being infected by that proposition, henceforth accepted as plausible and interesting. Only endurance, not originality, has discernible reasons.

If there cannot be a metaphysical discourse that deals, by analogy or otherwise, with God's "reasons," this is not, therefore, a question either of ignorance or of inaccessibility but a question of coherent definition. God *qua* principle of limitation is that from which every reason derives, and he therefore cannot have a reason himself. This, Whitehead concludes, is why God is "categorically determined," required *qua* principle of limitation, but "metaphysically indeterminate"—again Leibniz is wrong.

Whitehead might have been able to "save" Leibniz, but his judgment is without indulgence. In contrast, he chooses to attenuate his difference from Spinoza. God, he suggests, might be conceived as "qualifying" a substantial activity analogous to Spinoza's infinite substance, with the attributes of Spinoza's substance being assimilated to the domain of the eternal objects, as expressed by individualization in a multiplicity of modes. Thanks to God, who is categorically determined by this "thanks to," Spinoza's modes can then be freed from the suspicion that they constitute mere "reflections" of the infinite. Of course, Spinoza finds himself slightly modified by Anglo-Saxon humor. Possibility is no longer an illusion but enters into the economy of infinite substance. As far as the idea of God is concerned, it is no longer associated at all with a knowledge "of the third kind," that of ideas that are finally adequate. Quite the contrary, it is called forth by the need for an envisagement of the third type, that makes "inadequacy" irreducible, that is, by the contrast between the ideal situation and "its" realization, whose value demands its limitation.

Whitehead's God, a speculative wonder, is therefore firmly bound to the refusal of a metaphysical speculation that denies what we are well aware of. The creation of the limited horizon allows the affirmation of what is implied by every purpose: the asymmetric character of relations. My prehension of you and your prehension of me cannot, from any standpoint, be redefined in a way that would make their hidden harmony explicit, two standpoints reflecting the same world with a common purpose. My thought is individualized, a thought of "that," not of all the implications and consequences of "that" as you may entertain them. This is the paradigmatic empiricist affirmation: there is no beyond to the fact that we clash against the irreducible, obstinate fact of a world which, far from espousing our variations of interest, may oppose to us the firm discontinuity of its angles—thus, and not otherwise, no further. Let us listen to Whitehead in the class he gave on April 16, 1925:

I enter a room. The room does not enter me, in any sense at all. Our experience is always that of entering into the world, not into the world as supported by oneself in any sense at all (EWM, 287).

It is also from this empirical standpoint that we can sense the possible instability of Whitehead's first fully metaphysical construction. Doesn't the break that makes the difference between ideality and the set of propositions true and untrue "for the occasion" place novelty under the banner of passivity? Endurance may depend on the set of *non sequiturs* that realize and are realized by a finite standpoint. Yet can originality be reduced to a modification of this set? In short, is the restriction really appropriate to what we understand by "value"?

This problem obviously has much in common with that of the abstraction risked by Whitehead: God, as a principle of limitation, is part of that abstraction, and does not, as such, enable a remedy for its primary defect, the fact that it does not inspire a "yearning" for a theory of prehension. On the contrary, he underlines this defect, because thanks to his intervention, envisagement seems to be able to do without the question of prehension to an even greater degree. Now that the cat has fallen on its feet, however, it is possible to inspire, against the movement proposed by Whitehead, the yearning for something else and to specify the sense in which this movement, which has been from the organism to the actual occasion, calls for another movement, which may, as the case may be, designate another ultimate.

The link between value and restriction was constructed in metaphysical terms, but it had first been formulated in the context of the philosophy of the organism, insofar as the organism's success is its endurance. An organism "endures" in the sense that it exhibits functions that are fundamentally asymmetrical to its environment: here, value is equivalent to judgment, and the "intolerant" organism maintains, as long as it is able to endure, a remarkably stable and simplifying judgment that defines what counts for it in its environment and how. Yet the fact that this connection was taken up again at the level of the metaphysical categories might well introduce the shadow of an "as if" when it comes to our subjective experience. What of our impression that "having a purpose" is of the order of "taking initiative"? What of our claim—it's called freedom—to be, in one way or another, "the cause of ourselves"? And "trust," for which the point, in this case, is no longer to find a respondent in the order of nature but which is presupposed every time experience takes the risk of experimentation: can it be supported by a reference to God as ultimate limitation?

Of course, if the point was to make metaphysical speculation communicate with wisdom, all these objections would collapse by themselves, becoming so many versions calling for the necessary "detachment from the self" that usually coincides with wisdom. The same would hold true if we had to do with that practical aesthetics proposed today by the so-called "sliding sports." To keep one's hold or to lose it: at each wave, surfers risk themselves, without any illusion of control, risking their possibility of enduring, of fitting with the wave, at the critical point where only the sensitive, exact insertion of one motion within another can earn the patience of a breaking wave.

However, to the world as a breaking wave corresponds the spiritualized body, the detachment from the ego, not the art of problems that orients the research of Whitehead the mathematician. Mathematicians do not seek to "endure," to stylize their bodies, gestures, or soul in a way that would enable them to provide a minimum hold to the trials susceptible of destabilizing them. Their trust is of a different type, not "they will not get me," this wave, this illusion as a vector of pain, this attachment that exposes me, but "what transformation do they demand of me?"—this possibility that would be so easy for me to ignore, this murmur of experience that I could easily disqualify, this incoherence I would have no difficulty in making people forget, or that I could elevate, with impunity, to the status of a riddle or a mystery before which reason must accept to bow down.

The speculation of Whitehead the mathematician, because it can be said to be "control" the construction of a coherent, adequate discourse, must provide a foothold, offer the maximum foothold to what might destabilize it. At no time may it be transformed into a vector of norms, a norm of sliding elegance or wisdom, because a norm, in this case, is too tempting a way to eliminate, to simplify, or to judge what might otherwise pose a problem.

This is why I was able to compare Whitehead's solution, the definition of the third type of engagement, to the desperate twist that a cat carries out in order to complete its fall on its feet. It may be this twist that enables Whitehead to adopt Spinoza's substantial activity, but one may also wonder if it is not the seduction of this substantial activity that had first inspired his wager: to risk the abstraction constituted by ideal envisagement. For ultimately, Whitehead is closer to Leibniz than to Spinoza, in the sense that Leibniz has not turned the "as ifs" with which he populates his metaphysics into a path toward wisdom. If there is a link between metaphysics and wisdom, for Leibniz as for Whitehead, this link cannot bypass trust in the possibility of a "peace" that must be fashioned actively, intelligently, not achieved by some process of conversion. Like Leibniz, Whitehead worked in this world, for this world, and in a way that any sage might judge "perverse": without bringing to existence a truth that would have the power of conquering idolatries, passions, and illusions, but in direct contact, without a beyond, with our polemical habits. Metaphysical experimentation, neutral with regard to what matters, has no other goal than to produce "elbow room" against the identification of passionate incoherence with a virtue, of the fight against error with a mobilizing slogan, and of thought with a deduction.

Yet if this wager, of making the prerequisite for peace not a purification that subtracts but a creation that constructs, that adds and complicates things, must be adequately described in metaphysical terms, limitation must not be the last word. If the activity of Whitehead, a mathematician who became a philosopher, is to find its meaning in the terms of his own metaphysics, realization cannot be described as a restriction.

Sometimes, in the course of this text, I have been unable not to anticipate, and to use the word "decision," which Whitehead was to use in *Process and Reality* to name the "breaking off" that turns the occasion into the affirmation of a "thus and not otherwise." When he named the "great refusal," Whitehead himself could doubtless not help but be inhabited by a syntax that makes the occasion the producer of its limitation. No doubt he was aware, when writing *Science and the Modern World,* that his concept of an occasion was merely a first approximation. And perhaps the use of the word "decision," in *Process and Reality,* indicates that he has henceforth provided himself with the means to fully affirm the meaning William James conferred upon this term: that of a living moment that produces its own reasons.

Decisions, for him who makes them, are altogether peculiar psychic facts. Self-luminous and self-justifying at the living moment at which they occur, they appeal to no outside moment to put its stamp upon them or make them continuous with the rest of nature. Themselves it is rather who seem to make nature continuous; and in their strange and intense function of granting consent to one possibility and withholding it from another, to transform an equivocal and double future into an inalterable and simple past (DD, 158).

With James, Whitehead refused to make continuity primary; that is, he also refused to allow the occasion to be deduced from the whole. Every continuity is a result, a succession of resumptions that are so many "purposes," deciding the way the present will prolong the past, give a future to this past and make it "its" past. Yet the way James characterizes decision, "granting consent to one possibility and withholding it from another," could not be adopted as such, for it contains too many unknowns. It had to be constructed, in a way that enables every production of existence to be characterized as a decision. It is the actual occasions themselves that will affirm, no longer merely "just this, and no more," but "thus and not otherwise."

Everything must therefore be redone. Everything will be redone in the course of the writing of *Process and Reality.*

PART TWO

Cosmology

CHAPTER FIFTEEN

Hic Circuli, Hic Saltus

E CAN and we may, as it were, jump with both feet off the ground into or towards a world of which we trust the other parts to meet our jump and only so can the making of a perfected world of the pluralistic pattern ever take place. Only through our precursive trust in it can it come into being.

There is no inconsistency anywhere in this, and no "vicious circle" unless a circle of poles holding themselves upright by leaning on one another, or a circle of dancers revolving by holding each other's hands, be "vicious."

The faith circle is so congruous with human nature that the only explanation of the veto that intellectualists pass upon it must be sought in the offensive character to them of the faiths of certain concrete persons.

Such possibilities of offense have, however, to be put up with on empiricist principles. The long run of experience may weed out the more foolish faiths. Those who held them will then have failed: but without the wiser faiths of the others the world could never be perfected (SPP, 230–231).

This text, a veritable profession of faith, is probably one of William James's last writings, and the way it connects trust, leap, and circle of faith no doubt constitutes the best introduction to what *Process and Reality* commits its reader to. Whatever path of approach to *Process and Reality* one chooses, this path presupposes a leap far from the solid ground of our self-evidence. It is a very curious leap, involving both mobilizing experience and putting thought to the test. A speculative leap.

Philosophers have long since learned that speculation is a temptation that philosophy owes itself to resist. We must reject any recourse to an "intellectual intuition" that assumes the possibility of a direct access to a higher order of truth, accepting the finitude of the human condition. This—after all, no profit is too small—enables us to hunt down in others the illusory beliefs that we ourselves have renounced. Whitehead is not unaware that he is swimming against the current: against the "progress" that has made the difference between (outdated) speculative philosophy and the philosophy that is finally modern. Right from the outset of *Process and Reality,* he assigns his undertaking the "first task" of defining the "speculative philosophy" he is going to practice, but the definition he gives it is not likely to reassure the sceptics.

Speculative Philosophy is the endeavour to frame a coherent, logical, necessary system of general ideas in terms of which every element of our experience can be interpreted (PR, 3).

An excessive program if ever there was one, whose totalitarian nature might, *a priori,* inspire fear. If a system were to be capable of deducing everything we are liable to be aware of, it would realize the wildest dreams of absolute knowledge. Except that when expressing this fear, I replaced "interpret" by "deduce," which means that I have attributed to the system the power of a theory, a power that Whitehead refuses to it. What he has just defined is not a power, but a demand concerning the general ideas that are to be assembled. They will have to succeed in not selecting, that is, in not judging, measuring according to a norm, or differentiating between experiences whose objects are legitimate or illusory. This does not mean, however, that the experiences involved with the production of measures, the creation of criteria, and the differentiation between the illusory and the legitimate must be denounced. However, for the "necessity" proper to the speculative system to have a sense, they must lose their privileged import.

Thus the philosophic scheme should be "necessary," in the sense of bearing in itself its own warrant of universality throughout all experience, provided that we confine ourselves to that which communicates with immediate matter of fact. But what does not so communicate is unknowable, and the unknowable is unknown; and so this universality defined by "communication" can suffice (PR, 4).

In a note—notes are rare in *Process and Reality*—Whitehead specifies that the "doctrine" he has just stated concerning "what does not communicate" is a paradox, and, in a rather atypical way, he allows himself a touch of irony: "Indulging in a species of false modesty, 'cautious' philosophers undertake its definition."

In *The Concept of Nature,* Whitehead had undertaken to put everything we are aware of in perception "in the same boat." The mind was

the ultimate then, that which is presupposed by all perception. The project is now prolonged; for the point will be that this scheme, by its very
working, affirms itself to be capable of interpreting "any element of experience" in the same way as long as the latter communicates with an
immediate state of affairs, that is, as long as there is an actual experience
rather than a possibility of experience *("if only we could . . .")*. However,
the subject of discussion is no longer perceptive experience, and the mind
is therefore no longer ultimate. What is in question is that of which we
have experience—joy, grief, freedom, responsibility, as well as swallow,
stone, or sun. And this raises a new problem, for here the totality cannot
be defined by reference to what does not belong to it.

Whitehead knows quite precisely what awaits every attempt at definition in this case: has he not, with Russell, encountered the paradoxical
class of beings who, like Epimenides, the Cretan who (truthfully?) defined
all Cretans as liars, belong to the set they define in a way that contradicts
the possibility of that definition? To define the set of experiences that
communicate with an immediate state of affairs in a way that opposes it
to anything else would again fall victim to the same paradox, for the mere
fact of producing that "anything else" *qua* having the power to assert itself as "other," escaping any possibility of actual experience, makes it fall
back into the set. There is a placing-in-communication with an immediate
state of affairs because there is an actual experience, the experience of this
very power. Hence the paradox: the set includes what claimed to define it
exclusively.

The speculative leap does not announce an entry into logical paradox,
but a farewell to the power of logical definition, for it is the power Epimenides the Cretan assumed to define "the set of all Cretans" that creates
the paradox. Likewise, it is the "prudence" of the philosophers who think
they can designate the class of what is knowable, or, as Wittgenstein said
in the *Tractatus,* of "that of which one may speak," that makes them slip
into an infinite labor of mourning in which "that of which one may speak"
no longer has much importance, compared with what one must learn to
keep silent about.

To interpret will thus not imply a definition of the set of what can be
interpreted, or of the conditions that authorize belonging to that set. On
the contrary, the system's necessity reflects a commitment that makes all
the constraints weigh on the interpretation itself, which takes up the
challenge of having actually to place all experiences on the same level,
whether or not they are able to define their object, that is, to affirm them
all *qua* obliging interpretation. By this commitment, Whitehead by no
means opposes to the philosophers' "prudence" a source of knowledge

whose necessity would transcend all definition. Right from the opening paragraph of his work, he limits himself to affirming that the knowledge produced by speculative philosophy as a method is "important."

No term would seem to be more vague that this one: important. And yet it practically constitutes the "cipher," or the trademark of the concepts proposed by Whitehead's "speculative philosophy," and it will confer its singular style upon the "leap" or jump of the imagination to which the reader of *Process and Reality* is invited. For this word in fact designates what cannot be defined by anything else; it is an "ultimate generality" proposed by its own system.

Importance is a generic notion which has been obscured by the over-whelming prominence of a few of its innumerable species. There are perspectives of the universe to which morality is irrelevant, to which logic is irrelevant, to which religion is irrelevant, to which art is irrelevant. By this false limitation the activity expressing the ultimate aim infused into the process of nature has been trivialized into the guardianship of mores, or of rules of thought, or of mystic sentiment, or of aesthetic enjoyment. No one of these specializations exhausts the final unity of purpose in the world. The generic aim of process is the attainment of importance, in that species and to that extent which in that instance is possible (MT, 1–12).

A circular situation: in order to present itself, the undertaking that begins with *Process and Reality* uses a term upon which it will confer a meaning without which its way of presenting itself is hard to hear. One must always begin a circle somewhere, but there is nothing dizzying about that. It is enough to accept that, in any case, no one ever really begins with the beginning. Even currents of thought that seem axiomatic "start out" from their principles only subsequently, and more to verify their formulation than to "discover" their consequences. No doubt because he knew the demands of a truly axiomatic construction, Whitehead does not try to save appearances. Serious readers may complain that they cannot make heads or tails of his approach. What matters is that at the end of the day one may finally go back to the beginning, that the snake can bite its tail. Here, indeed, is the final sentence of *Process and Reality*:

In this way, the insistent craving is justified—the insistent craving that zest for existence be refreshed by the ever-present, unfading importance of our immediate actions, which perish and yet live for evermore (PR, 351).

What has happened between the book's beginning and its end? The vocation of speculative philosophy *qua* productive of "important" knowledge has not been modified, but the phrase has been laden with all that is required by the seemingly obvious fact that certain objects of knowledge can be "important." It is the expression "to be important" that is primary, and it is on its basis that we may try to define why it is important, to what extent, and according to what criteria. And of course, these efforts are themselves "important"; there is no reason to denounce them, and especially not to disqualify those "species" constituted by ethics, logics, religion, art. . . . Yet it is important to strip them of their power of limitation, to fight against their clear propensity to denounce what, to speak with William James, is "repugnant to them." And so, speculative philosophy, for its part, will not be able to produce any limitation; it will not be able to "deal" with anything that can be defined as an "object," whether that object falls under the definitions of logic, ethics, religion, or art. The "zest for existence" will have been "refreshed," but not by the proposal of a special aim defining the meaning or vocation of that existence. What Whitehead hopes to have accomplished is, quite the contrary, to have eliminated the specific definitions which, by trying to explain what matters, that is, to found importance according to special categories, reduce our insistent, craving need that "it matter" to the triviality of the "guardianship" of a chosen definition.

This craving matters. It must therefore be justified, but as the reader will have understood, this cannot happen by contrast with something else. In particular, it cannot be retranslated in terms of value, ethics, or freedom, such that what happens to a rock, a swallow, or an electron may be said to be "without importance." Where *The Concept of Nature* demanded that everything we are aware of in perception be placed in the same boat, we can say that the "verification of the scheme," or the test of its necessity, will be that "all that communicates with experience" may matter. This, moreover, corresponds to the sudden halt imposed upon the definitional power of logic. Whatever may be the subtle delights of discussions of the relations between the statement "the cat is on the rug" and this cat that is on this rug, whether the state of affairs can verify the statement or remains separated from it by an impassable abyss, the fact is that "this" cat and "this" rug matter little. It is enough to have a cat, whichever it may be, and a carpet, whichever it may be, each one defined by its belonging to the sets designated by the words "cat" and "rug." Both cat and rug, because they present themselves as capable of being defined in isolation, in a way that authorizes belonging to a well-defined set, confer a privileged role upon logic and are therefore inappropriate for metaphysical statements. And the same obviously holds true of reasoning of a deductive type.

It has been remarked that a system of philosophy is never refuted; it is only abandoned. The reason is that logical contradictions, except as temporary slips of the mind—plentiful, though temporary—are the most gratuitous of errors; and usually they are trivial. Thus after criticism, systems

do not exhibit mere illogicalities. They suffer from inadequacy and inco-
herence. Failure to include some obvious elements of experience in the
scope of the system is met by boldly denying the facts. Also while a philo-
sophical system retains any charm of novelty, it enjoys a plenary indul-
gence for its failures in coherence. But after a system has acquired ortho-
doxy, and is taught with authority it receives a sharper criticism. Its denials
and its incoherences are found intolerable, and a reaction sets in (PR, 6).

The warrant of universality that a philosophical system bears with it is an effect of its working, which inevitably implies the question of what matters in a given epoch. When what a system has failed to include takes on enough importance for this failure to be experienced as intolerable, the necessity collapses, and the system becomes arbitrary. And the same holds true when its incoherencies become intolerable. As we have seen, Whitehead characterized his own speculative system by its ambition for coherence, logic, and necessity, an ambition that is obviously inseparable from the diagnosis he has just laid down with regard to what makes a philosophical system be abandoned. This does not mean, however, that his ambition is that his own system should never be abandoned. Indeed, unlike logic, neither necessity nor coherence can be defined in terms of well-specified demands. This is why logic is what one might call a "minor virtue," which certainly entails demands, but not obligations. As soon as there are specifications, arrangements can always be made. In contrast, coherence, like necessity, obliges thinkers to think against the assurances of language, against any meaning that presents itself as "going without saying," and their ability to do so cannot be abstracted from the way their epoch enables them to think.

"Coherence," as here employed, means that the fundamental ideas, in
terms of which the scheme is developed, presuppose each other so that in
isolation they are meaningless. This requirement does not mean that they
are definable in terms of each other; it means that what is indefinable in
one such notion cannot be abstracted from its relevance to the other no-
tions. It is the ideal of speculative philosophy that its fundamental notions
shall not seem capable of abstraction from each other. In other words, it is
presupposed that no entity can be conceived in complete abstraction from
the system of the universe, and that it is the business of speculative phi-
losophy to exhibit this truth. This character is its coherence (PR, 3).

Once again, a circle: we had started out from "ideas," but the quotation leads brutally to the "entities," taken to be in the "system of the universe." The ideas will, of course, have to allow us to define speculatively both what an entity and the "system of the universe" are, but they also define themselves as mere "entities" among others. Their relation of reciprocal presupposition merely exhibits what is, speculatively, to be thought. And once again, the circle is not logical, in the sense of those paradoxical statements in which thought "feels" that it is spinning its wheels. It is "pragmatic," in the sense that it brings the "matter" of speculative philosophy into existence, what it risks, that toward which it leaps "with both feet off the ground," with trust but with no solid certainty.

It is usually said that the measure of the solidity of an intellectual construction is the solidity of its weakest link. Yet this argument presupposes the possibility of putting each link to the test separately, and it is precisely against this possibility that Whiteheadian coherence affirms itself. Reciprocal presupposition replaces the image of linking by that of William James's revolving circle of dancers, which "makes true," or verifies, what an isolated dancer would have refuted. The circle enables each moving body not to fall, although the vertical projection of its center of gravity is situated dramatically outside of its sustaining base. Likewise, the ambition of speculative coherence is to escape the norms to which experiences, isolated by the logical, moral, empiricist, religious, and other stakes that privilege them, are subject. The point is to leave behind the solid ground designated by these stakes and take the risk of ignoring each dancer's center of gravity. Speculative philosophy must, in its very production, bring to existence the possibility of a thought "without gravity," without a privileged direction, that "neutral" metaphysical thought of which *Science and the Modern World* had already risked the adventure.

The dancers' spin is only possible because each of them trusts the others "precursively" at the moment when they accept that their own body is put off balance: they all accept to no longer define themselves by their own means but by supposing the others, in the precise sense in which, taken in isolation, these others would be quite incapable of giving what is asked of them. None is a guarantor, as a pillar would be. Each one presupposes the others. Likewise, the speculative concepts or "fundamental ideas," because they cannot be rooted in any privileged experience, must circle with each other. Taken together, they must affirm what speculative thought "trusts" to think "without support." Coherence is what creates the specific space of the speculative circle, what engages the "trust" without which there is no leap, and what demands of the leap that it leave with both feet the solid ground of our specialized interests. That toward which there is a leap must be expressed in neutral, "generic" terms, not with the clarity that our interests always confer on the statements that correspond to them.

The verification of a rationalist scheme is to be sought in its general success, and not in the peculiar certainty, or initial clarity, of its first principles.

In this connection the misuse of the ex absurdo *argument has to be noted; much philosophical reasoning is vitiated by it* (PR, 8).

In fact, the "first principles" articulated in the scheme Whitehead presents at the beginning of *Process and Reality* "do not speak of anything." The scheme "speaks itself," as the production of a thinker struggling with the question of coherence, a veritable abstract machine, carefully stripped of any reference to the privileged cases in which we expect every philosopher: truth, responsibility, freedom, mind, matter, and so on. The scheme is asignificant. To try to understand it "for itself" presents the same kind of difficulty as trying to understand an immobile machine, where one doesn't know from which end to look at it.

Yet coherence itself, which obliges the thinker and which the scheme makes prevail, would, if it were an end in itself, be bereft of importance, for what it cannot render explicit is precisely that in which it matters. If the principles must be stated in generic terms, no leap is generic. In order for imagination to leap, it needs to trust that something will come to meet it. The knowledge produced by the coherent scheme must be actually "important." Indeed, everything changes when the schematic machine is set in motion, when its multiple movements produce the twofold discovery of the articulation between its components and its effects on the situations and statements it transforms. A radical contrast, because, although the scheme is mute, the statements or applications it induces are the warrant of universality that Whitehead associates with necessity. And they will be such a warrant by separating abstractions from their claim to universality. Every abstraction, every right conferred upon a generality, will communicate with an immediate, concrete state of affairs. One never *has* a right, one *takes* it, and the question is not to criticize the taking but to correlate it with what it produces.

This is the case, for instance, with the "argument from the absurd," whose deplorable use in philosophy Whitehead criticizes, whereas it is an essential resource for mathematical creation. Its use presupposes the right, when faced by a contradiction, to try to find out which of the premises of the reasoning, or, most often, which of the premises laid down by the tradition that the thinker inherits, is "guilty," as if each one could be modified separately. It is not a matter of criticizing the right that philosophers thus claim but of correlating it with its predictable effect: each new philosophy becomes the one that was announced, despite, and even by virtue of, its defects, by the lame ensemble of its predecessors, until it, in its turn, is abandoned.

In *The Concept of Nature,* Whitehead himself had made use of the argument from the absurd, but the aim was not to lend his reasoning the authority of logic, or to confer upon it a consensual evidence. The aim was to make absurdity felt. *"That's absurd!"* is a cry that commits us, a "cause" that will force us to take the least prudent "risks." In *Process and Reality,* by contrast, there is no longer any "cause," or else everything has become a cause: every element of experience must be understood and interpreted. And, to the greater perplexity of his readers, Whitehead has put his own doctrine into action. Whereas in the course of writing his book, he varied most of his definitions, he never proceeded to the slightest self-criticism, or the least explanation of the contradiction to which a definition would have led if it had not been modified. He limited himself to "clarifying," by inserted additions, the way in which the function of a notion had to be understood because of its "relevance" for other notions. And this is so even if this "clarification" in fact modified the global economy of the system in formation.

According to Lewis Ford, the initiator of the compositional analysis of Whitehead's work, up to twelve layers of successive writing may be distinguished in *Process and Reality.* In contrast to what was the case in *Science and the Modern World,* we no longer have do only with more or less massive and countable additions, but also with raw, continuous interventions, the work of successive rereadings that wager on the possibility that a given insertion, here, in the middle of this paragraph, will suffice to make the text's meaning slide for the reader as it "slid" for the author when he reread: *"Yes, I agree, but . . . "*

And this time, the wager was won. Most readers and commentators have assigned to the work as a whole a meaning which, according to Ford, is that of the "last" layer, at the cost of wondering why Whitehead thought it well to create so erratic an itinerary, why a given expectation or consequence, which certainly had to be produced, will indeed be affirmed, but, perhaps, one hundred and fifty pages further on. Without doubt, no book has ever been more inseparable from its index. And as far as I know, it has not happened to any other book to undergo the strange treatment that the American philosopher Donald Sherburne reserved for *Process and Reality.* Tired of guiding his students through this labyrinth, he chose not to rewrite it but to sort it and organize it, and he published "another" book, *A Key to Whitehead's "Process and Reality,"* which is entirely made up of rearranged fragments of *Process and Reality.* Some of its pages constitute a mosaic whose pieces come from ten different pages of the original work.

Sherburne wanted to turn *Process and Reality* into a book with which one could "become acquainted," but the recomposition to which he proceeded entailed a rather surprising change of nature, both of the text and of its author. An author endowed with a well-defined thought, his own, sets forth his ideas, but what has disappeared is the back-and-forth between concepts, and between concepts and empirical experience, the movements of thought entangled in one another, one of which never becomes apparent without appealing to others that have not yet been deployed. What the readers miss is the test constituted for them by the perpetual implication of what is explained within what explains it. What has been erased is the author's incessant return upon his trade: Whitehead, rereading his own text, operating not by *yes* or by *no,* but always by *"yes, but."* Instead of an author discovering new, unforeseen problems, we must speak of an author in the process of becoming, fashioned by the text he is fashioning. The author has become anonymous, in the sense that he makes the distinction between author and reader undecidable. The hand that writes the insertion is not that of the author correcting himself, but that of the reader fashioned by reading, or else that of the author-reader undergoing the series of thought-events that happen to him more than he produces them.

If Whitehead is simultaneously the author and reader of his own text, the reading for which this text calls seems to me to be the one that turns the reader into author, inserting and prolonging, and zigzagging, like the author, from *"yes, but"* to *"but then."* Even Lewis Ford, that paradigmatic reader, seems to have undergone this highly particular effect. He could not learn to distinguish and place in chronological order the insertions, transpositions, reorganizations (here, the vocabulary of historians of the genome could be highly useful), without at the same time undertaking to prolong, that is, to modify. More generally, if the community of Whiteheadians is indeed, as Deleuze wrote, a "slightly secret school," it is because it cannot manifest itself publicly under the academically prescribed form of doctoral dissertations competing for the most exact reading or the tightest interpretation. As long as Whitehead's text remains alive, it will transform its readers into coauthors, accepting the adventure of the imagination to which the text calls us.

Unlike my choice in the case of *Science and the Modern World,* therefore, I do not see any great advantage in organizing my presentation around a tale of the succession of Whiteheads at work in *Process and Reality.* I will go even further, not hesitating to appeal to such later writings as *Adventures of Ideas* (1933) or *Modes of Thought* (1938). For the movement of a coherence that discovers itself by inventing itself cannot be narrated: it is pursued. And this is what I will try to do, even when, on several occasions, this pursuit will imply a "tale" of what has caused a mutation in a meaning or an articulation, a tale that will be my interpretation. In fact, when Whitehead went back to his work in the mode of *"yes, but"* that authorized him to carry out insertions without rewriting, he probably would often not have been able to "tell" what had made him "change his mind." He had become capable of "feeling" a new aspect of the indefinable, that is, just as much, by contrast and retroactively, to feel the definition of a notion as too "isolated" from the others, or too slanted, unduly privileging certain types of experience.

Philosophers can never hope finally to formulate these metaphysical first principles. Weakness of insight and deficiencies of language stand in the way inexorably. Words and phrases must be stretched towards a generality foreign to their ordinary usage; and however such elements of language be stabilized as technicalities, they remain metaphors mutely appealing for an imaginative leap (PR, 4).

In fact, the way I have just interpreted the composition of *Process and Reality* constitutes in itself an "imaginative leap." Whitehead never explained himself. He refused boredom, as Lewis Ford deplores, and considered it boring to "start all over again," to write in order to say more clearly what he had already understood. Yet as I have already emphasized, other reader-interpreters, such as Jorge Luis Nobo, wager on systematic unity, and become indignant at the fact that one could produce the hypothesis that Whitehead is lazy, deceptive, and even mendacious when he affirms in the preface to *Adventures of Ideas* the unity of the undertaking of his three books, *Science and the Modern World, Process and Reality,* and *Adventures of Ideas.* The differences, Whitehead affirms, reflect the fact that each of these books completes what was omitted or simplified in the other ones. Yet the argument is a bit weak. It is undeniable that there is continuity, and it goes back much further than the three books just mentioned. In the preface to *Science and the Modern World,* Whitehead specifies that this book is the product of thoughts and readings pursued for years, without any intention of publication (the author thus excuses himself for the absence of reference to his sources, which is indeed rather remarkable). But as I have already emphasized, to say continuity is not the same as to say "ready-made thought," reeled off as books provide the occasion, deliberately simplifying or omitting some questions to spare his reader. Whitehead never spared his readers, and my reading wager, including narrativizations of what happened to Whitehead in the course of his writing, is intended to present a "becoming of continuity."

My reading wager is thus that Whitehead was not lying when he spoke of the unity of his undertaking, but that, to an equal extent, he refused to lie by erasing the traces of his itinerary. The "boredom" he rejected is that which is the price of the production of mendacious fiction, which wants authors to establish the portrait of a world they claim to have understood once and for all. As far as possible from certain deduction, the text as I will read it will come to exhibit what Whitehead, as we shall see, understands by a "route of occasions": each occasion must be defined as "having to take into account," "heir," and "obliged," but each occasion has to decide, for itself and for everything that will subsequently have to take it into account, its own mode of account. Each has to decide how it will have been obliged by what it, *de facto*, inherits. *"Yes, but."*

To refuse to be bored when writing also means trusting the reader, that is, trusting the becoming, undecidable in any case, that will decide "how" the reader will read you, on the basis of what demands, that is, of what experiences. The readers, for their part, are thus called upon to leave behind the status of an ignoramus, faced by an author who says what it is appropriate to think. They have to head, in their turn, "down the road," a road on which thought stumbles at every step, and must invent itself all over again. Yet throughout *Process and Reality* the point is indeed to reinvent, and first of all to reinvent, while prolonging it, the tradition in which the book takes its place. A tradition which—and this is a test for the contemporary reader—Whitehead does not hesitate to identify with rationalism.

That we fail to find in experience any elements intrinsically incapable of exhibition as examples of general theory is the hope of rationalism. This hope is not a metaphysical premise. It is the faith which forms the motive for the pursuit of all sciences alike, including metaphysics.

In so far as metaphysics enables us to apprehend the rationality of things, the claim is justified. It is always open to us, having regard to the imperfections of all metaphysical systems, to lose hope at the exact point where we find ourselves. The preservation of such faith must depend on an ultimate moral intuition into the nature of intellectual action—that it should embody the adventure of hope. Such an intuition marks the point where metaphysics—and indeed every science—gains assurance from religion and passes over into religion. But in itself faith does not embody the premise from which the theory starts; it is an ideal which is seeking satisfaction. In so far as we believe that doctrine, we are rationalists (PR, 42).

The author who diagnoses the point where metaphysics passes over into religion is obviously not religious. Just as whirling dancers do not need to be reassured that they will not fall by sprouting a third leg, for instance, and restoring relevance to the laws of gravitation on each isolated body, philosophers do not need to appeal to religion in order to preserve their faith, unless they wish to found their hope, provide it with a guarantor, and constitute it as an exclusive premise. Thus, if rationalism becomes that on which hope in this world depends, it will justify imperatives and judgments: "We must, or else despair will reign." White-head, for his part, intends to trust movement as such, that is, at the same time, to confer upon it its maximum amplitude, freeing it from the limits always entailed by the concern for foundations. The hope of rationalism concerns experience, not any kind of religious Beyond. The beyond of experience is always merely insurance against the loss of that hope.

Philosophy destroys its usefulness when it indulges in brilliant feats of explaining away (PR, 17).

If we are rationalists, and because we are rationalists, we must also be empiricists, and take the demands of empiricism to their extreme: to accept as a constraint to deliberately abstain from the great resource of philosophy, "explaining away," that is, by eliminative judgment. This "exploit" is not only an act of violence committed against what we are aware of, but also a betrayal of the rationalist hope. The power of hierar-chizing, of reducing things to an illusion, of disqualifying, rectifying, in short, the power to judge that makes the "masters" of thought, then takes the place of the adventure of reason. The ideal no longer seeks satisfac-tion, at its own peril, but demands satisfaction.

The regime of reading and writing by which ideas are explained and transformed will thus oscillate between what Whitehead calls the "ratio-nal side" and the "empirical side," two sides that render explicit the obli-gations associated with coherence and necessity.

Logic and coherence express the rational side. As we have seen, the point is first to refuse all arbitrary disconnection between principles. It demands a refusal of the principles that would derive their authority from privi-leged cases, to which they apply so clearly and distinctly that they seem to be necessary and sufficient: that is, capable in and of themselves of defin-ing that to which they apply. This is the case, for instance, with the two substances, "extended" and "thinking," in Descartes: the authority of the principles that define each of them needs nothing other than itself to ex-ist, and, above all, they do not need each other. This makes a virtue out of what is, for Whitehead, a radical incoherence. "Cartesian dualism" is a failure of thought, for its principles are incapable of accounting for the reason why a world that would be either purely material or purely spiri-tual would be inconceivable.

What belongs to the "empirical side" is what provides verification for the scheme, the success against which Whitehead asks to be evaluated. From the viewpoint of his interpretations, the scheme must be applicable and adequate, and it is the practical coupling between adequacy and ap-plication that gives meaning to the need for a system "that bears in itself its own warrant of universality."

*Here "applicable" means that some items of experience are thus inter-
pretable* [in terms of the scheme], *and "adequate" means that there are
no items incapable of such an interpretation* (PR, 3).

The difference between applicability and adequacy is announced in
terms that evoke logic, but in a rather paradoxical way. Indeed, the statement that there is no case that escapes interpretation is logically equivalent to the statement that every case is subject to interpretation, which, it
seems, makes the affirmation that some cases are interpretable redundant.
The distinction between applicable and adequate is therefore not logical,
but practical.

The demand for adequacy is the aspect of the empirical side that is directly correlated with the rational side. It obliges philosophers not to invoke any cause allowing them to eliminate, forget, treat as an exception,
or disqualify an element of experience. In particular, the scheme must be
able to embrace the very thing that would be invoked in the mode of a
challenge, contradiction, or scandal: *but what do you do with "this"?* In
contrast, the affirmation *"there exists . . ."* is the aspect of the empirical
pole that is correlated with the success of the scheme and with its verification. Applicability demands that some elements of our experience actually
lend themselves to the imaginative leap to which the wording of the
scheme made a mute appeal, producing by that very fact the experience of
their relevance. The condition of applicability, when it designates a set of
cases privileged by a metaphysical system, is always fulfilled. It is fulfilled
equally well by any science, for every science makes the functions it proposes correspond to states of affairs that exhibit what the function defines
in terms of the articulation between variables. Yet when it comes to the
"rational adventure," the freedom with which each science "camps" on its
privileged examples, constituting them as a territory, becomes a trap.
Applicability cannot communicate with any normative or even pragmatic
privilege. It cannot correspond to the identification of situations that "lend
themselves" to application (as is the case, for instance, with the paradigms
described by Thomas Kuhn). Applicability must be verified by an inventive dynamic, which creates the transformations of meaning and the
stakes required by adequacy.

*The adequacy of the scheme over every item does not mean adequacy
over such items as happen to have been considered* (PR, 3).

Let us take, for instance, a statement that seems typically to make nature bifurcate: "atoms truly exist!" Here, one may be tempted to carry
out an act of censorship: "atoms, whether in the sense of Democritus or
in the sense of physics, are not an element of our experience, and must be
excluded." Yet by the same movement, the experience of all those who

actively implicate atoms in their reasoning, and have succeeded in bringing them to "explain themselves," for instance, in saying how many there
are in 5.92 gallons of hydrogen, would be censored. For physicists, chemists, engineers, the fact is that atoms henceforth "communicate" well
with their experience. It would be an attempt at disqualification, attempting to catch the speakers in the act: *they don't know what they're
saying, they believe what the scientists claim . . .*

In contrast, the statement "atoms truly exist" can and should be linked
to the pragmatic difference that its enunciation in a given situation is supposed to make, to the way it is intended to be taken into consideration. If
physicists are confronted by sociologists, who seem to them to shed doubt
on the objectivity of physical reality, the statement can, in particular, communicate with an experience of perplexity or shock, and atoms will surge
forth here not in the sense that they are implicated in a specialized reasoning, but in their capacity as representatives of an "objective reality": *"You
cannot deny that atoms truly exist, independently of human knowledge!"*
This challenge also communicates with an actual experience, but unlike
the chemist minding her own business, which relies on the possibility for
atoms to be counted, this experience reiterates the mode of differentiation
that made nature bifurcate, a mode which, with the "philosophical primary qualities," had made it bifurcate well before the physicists and
chemists found a way to make atoms intervene effectively and irrevocably
in their practice.

If the scheme is adequate, it is thus the link between *"you cannot
deny. . . . "* and *"independently of human knowledge"* that it will address
and constitute as an example of application. And what is then at stake in
this application is no longer the atoms of the physicists, the chemists, and
the engineers. Those atoms by no means exist independently of human
knowledge, since they have only been taken into account insofar as they
have surmounted the tests set up by these scientists, as they have satisfied
demands intended to make the difference that matters for scientists, between free interpretation and interpretation verified in a reliable way by
its consequences. Quite the contrary, the point will be to present the
situation—just as concrete, but completely distinct—that has given its
meaning and passions to the strict separation between that which, existing independently of human knowledge, should impose agreement between humans and that which, dependent on such knowledge, would
forever be a source of conflict and illusion.

Here, then, thinking with Whitehead means learning to celebrate atoms, but to celebrate them against the bifurcation of nature with which
they are associated, against the breakage of the constitutive link between

these atoms and the insistent, passionate urgency of the scientists who have succeeded in creating the possibility of transforming them into integral and reliable protagonists in their practices. These scientists were part of an adventure of hope, trusting the possibility of defeating skepticism: they and the atoms they succeeded in constituting as the respondents of their statements require a description that does not stop where habitual language stops. Whereas we usually have a choice between looking at the moon while forgetting the finger pointing at it, or looking at the finger and disqualifying what is designated as relevant merely to this designating gesture, the point is to succeed in affirming at the same time both the finger and what this gesture requires and presupposes, and what this gesture gives us to perceive.

Every science must devise its own instruments. The tool required for philosophy is language. Thus, philosophy redesigns language in the same way that, in a physical science, pre-existing appliances are redesigned. It is exactly at this point that the appeal to facts is a difficult operation. This appeal is not solely to the expression of the facts in current verbal statements. The adequacy of such sentences is the main question at issue. It is true that the general agreement of mankind as to experienced facts is best expressed in language. But the language of literature breaks down precisely at the task of expressing in explicit form the larger generalities— the very generalities which metaphysics seeks to express (PR, 11).

Philosophy is an experimental practice like physics, but it experiments on language, that is, it devises concepts that will have no meaning unless they succeed in bringing to existence those dimensions of experience that usual statements can ignore, since these statements are inseparable from specialized thought. Such dimensions are required by the generalities of metaphysics, as it endeavors to achieve neutrality with regard to any specialization. In both cases, scientific and speculative, experimentation makes "truth" and "productive practice" correspond. Whereas the existence of atoms, for physicists, chemists, and engineers, has been "verified" by a practice that produces situations in which those atoms have received the power to impose themselves against the hypothesis that they are a mere interpretative fiction, the "truth" of Whiteheadian concepts, from the events and objects of *The Concept of Nature* to the speculative scheme of *Process and Reality,* is inseparable from a transformation of experience. This is what Whitehead calls "imaginative rationalization."

We habitually observe by the method of difference. Sometimes we see an elephant, and sometimes we do not. The result is that an elephant, when present, is noticed. Facility of observation depends on the fact that the object observed is important when present, and sometimes is absent.

The metaphysical first principles can never fail of exemplification. We can never catch the actual world taking a holiday from their sway. Thus, for the discovery of metaphysics, the method of pinning down thought to the strict systematization of detailed discrimination, already effected by antecedent observation, breaks down. The collapse of the method of rigid empiricism is not confined to metaphysics. It occurs whenever we seek the larger generalities. In natural science this rigid method is the Baconian method of induction, a method which, if consistently pursued, would have left science where it found it. What Bacon omitted was the play of a free imagination, controlled by the requirements of coherence and logic. The true method of discovery is like the flight of an aeroplane. It starts from the ground of particular observation; it makes a flight in the thin air of imaginative generalization; and it again lands for renewed observation rendered acute by rational interpretation. The reason for the success of this method of imaginative rationalization is that, when the method of differ-ence fails, factors which are constantly present may yet be observed under the influence of imaginative thought (PR, 4–5).

The transformation of experience must always be produced. In other words, the applications of the scheme are always local. They designate cases which, at the moment when the plane lands, may seem to be privileged, but the privilege is nothing other than the possibility thereby gained of a new type of verification: the imaginative leap. "Imaginative rationalization" thus makes Whiteheadian necessity correspond to a dynamics in which, accord-ing to the expression of Deleuze and Guattari, "to penetrate is to create."

Correlatively, "reason" no longer corresponds here to any "principle of parsimony": the applications, as numerous as one may wish, will have to take place in the concrete mode of "one by one." Never, therefore, accord-ing to Whitehead, will philosophy give to thought what navigational satel-lites have given aviation: an exhaustive and neutral coverage of the field of experience. Deduction will never replace discovery, for the latter implies, each time, a becoming that transforms both the person doing the describing and what is described. The scheme does not dictate, but it "calls," and the call always requires the elucidation of the concrete meaning of the situation for the person exploring it, that is, an effective transformation by which the problem raised by this situation ceases to be general, referring to questions of right or legitimacy, to become "commitment," exhibiting the kind of im-portance it claims. The concepts devised by Whitehead are therefore in a re-lation of mutual presupposition with the "flight of experience," or the itiner-ary of an interpretation that constructs as it goes what is required by the dimensions of experience it becomes capable of discerning, and whose im-portance it becomes capable of affirming.

The primary advantage thus gained is that experience is not interrogated with the benumbing repression of common sense (PR, 9).

Whitehead's phrase is ambiguous: is common sense what represses or what is repressed? Most philosophers would opt for a repressive common sense, but for Whitehead, common sense is what is capable of affirming "what we know" without allowing itself to be bothered by the question that poisons modern philosophy: "What can we know?" (MT, 74). Speculative philosophy, which has the vocation of uniting imagination and common sense (PR, 17), thus pursues, with other means, the defense of common sense undertaken since *The Concept of Nature* against the repressive power of abstractions and the authority given specialized theories, which makes our knowledge bifurcate.

It goes without saying, however, that the "flight of experience" which *Process and Reality* tries to induce through, with, and against language has no critical or demystifying vocation with regard to the specialized languages. The point is no more to set up immediate experience against atoms than it is to establish the objectivity of the sciences against the zest for existence, as refreshed by the importance of our immediate actions. The point is to trace a "line of flight" with regard to these oppositions that are optimally expressed by philosophical language. In particular, the generalities at which Whitehead aims cannot, therefore, leave intact any "fact" that presupposes the great dividing line between subject and object, upon which most philosophical languages comment even when they seem to justify it. Yet this flight has nothing to do with the takeoff of an inspiration, with the efficacy of an emergent conviction that sweeps away oppositions by the power of a general "vision," be it mystical, poetic, or dialectical. To be sure, the Whiteheadian scheme is, for Whitehead, a "matrix," but here we must not understand matrix in a vital or fluid sense, as the spontaneous source of a living thought beyond dead oppositions. "Matrix" must be understood in the sense of mathematics: a device mute in itself, representing nothing, calling for a leap of the imagination, that is, having meaning only through the transformations, always "this" transformation, produced by its "applications."

The use of such a matrix is to argue from it boldly and with rigid logic. The scheme should therefore be stated with the utmost precision and definiteness (PR, 9).

Whitehead had defined the ambition of speculative philosophy by necessity, coherence, and logic. In the name of necessity and coherence, logic, as we have seen, was stripped of its power to define, that is, also to sort. Yet here it is in its rightful place, coupled with audacity. Logic only gives orders when it places thinkers in difficulty, when it obliges them to go farther, when it forces them to create, in cases where they thought they could prolong an already formulated situation. The adventure of rationality in Whitehead's sense, in the sense of an ideal seeking satisfaction, affirms the most radical divergence from the critical or logical positivist ideal, which, since the latter is judicial, does not seek but rather demands satisfaction. And this divergence will find its full unfolding in what seems to have been one of Whitehead's last conceptual creations in the adventure of *Process and Reality:* the audacious, logical transformation of God into an actual entity endowed with a "consequent nature." Another circle: the truth of Whitehead's God presupposes that upon which this God will confer his metaphysical justification, that is, the audacity and trust that may allow destructive contradictions to be surmounted. Here, speculative creation can be audible only in its very movement: in that it presupposes the realization of what is intended by its concepts, the elimination of the "benumbing repression" that suggests that we carry out a heroic sorting process, separating what is "rationally justifiable" from what is "vital." At the cost of eliminating that which we might need, but which, we should admit, is a matter of mere fiction.

One might nevertheless fear the totalizing character of the circle devised in this way: the philosopher would be the person through whom the reality of what exists finally accedes to itself or to a finally coherent explanation. Except that this explanation is openly factitious, fabricated in a philosophical way, and in an experimental mode. It is only important to the extent that it succeeds, where the multiple experiences whose scheme runs the risk of interpretation will patiently allow themselves to be infected by the translations it carries out of them, and will accept the contributions it proposes to them as important.

The circle never stops turning. As a generic notion, importance implies that the very meaning of what exists is proposed in pragmatic terms—the production of what matters. But the importance of this proposition can only claim a pragmatic justification—is the transformation of experience produced by this proposition important?

In literal terms, pragmatism thus proposes not so much a new definition of truth as a method of experimentation, or construction for new truths. To experiment is to consider theory as a creative practice. This is why it is no longer a question of knowing what is true, but how truth comes about. And this question is itself inseparable from another one: what does the truth do? A true idea, in the pragmatic sense, is an idea that changes something in a satisfactory way in the mind of the person thinking it. The true idea is not only what one believes, does, or thinks, it is what makes us believe, makes us act or makes us think (WJEP, 59).

Pragmatism as a method for the production of new truths is no doubt the key to the construction of Whitehead's cosmology; yet this construction is not the advent of the truth of the cosmos but merely one of its "exemplifications." The production of speculative philosophy belongs, in its constraints and its hopes, to a "particular human specialty," which is certainly important, but local: the adventure of rationalism. The starting point is thus "contingent" insofar as it designates its "milieu": both what obliges Whitehead to think and what enjoins hope. Of course, Whitehead seems to return toward a manner of thinking held to be irreparably outdated, but the movement he proposes, because it affirms itself to be an adventure, produces the mime of a return operation. The "flight of experience" reawakens and activates what modern philosophy had renounced in order to be able to attribute to truth the ability to defeat skepticism. It constructs "true ideas," but their truth is exhibited as relative to this flight and to the obligations (coherence, adequacy) that make it exist. Correlatively, the knowledge that the scheme should produce, and therefore the transformation of experience it should induce, are not a reencounter with a truth on which we have turned our backs but the production of a new truth. This implies, in a circular way, the paradigmatic case for which Whitehead's scheme will have to exhibit its applicable character: it should give meaning to the production of new truths.

A new exhibition of the circle: the scheme proposes the categories of a world, but the categories do not define a reality independent of the process that produces this proposition. What exhibits a reality is the proposition and its effect, that is, the working of the scheme, the flight that is at the same time that of experience and that which transforms experience, and the point is thus less to define them than to bring them to existence. The categories make us think in a way that exhibits the reality of which they propose the definition. Whereas reality becomes philosophical, philosophy becomes realization. Or, as Deleuze and Guattari proposed, philosophy in this sense is doing for thought what a synthesizer does for listening: "making audible the sound process itself, the production of that process [. . .] Philosophy is no longer synthetic judgment; it is like a thought synthesizer functioning to make thought travel, make it mobile, make it a force of the Cosmos" (MP, 424).

As the reader will have understood, when describing how Whitehead's scheme works, I have also presented my approach, the one dictated to me by an author who becomes a reader, returning indefatigably to what he has written in the mode of *"Yes, but . . . "* If the writing of *Process and Reality* entangled "flights of experience" by Whitehead himself, every reading of *Process and Reality* can constitute, in its own way, an entanglement of flights of experience, both experiencing and putting to the test the scheme that induces it. Each flight is singular. The ones Whitehead carried out as an author have the peculiarity of having produced, in their very itineraries, the scheme that should constitute the matrix for the totality of "Whiteheadian flights." Those we can attempt, more than sixty years after his death, should not have understanding what Whitehead thought as their primary goal, but rather experiencing and putting to the test what it means to "think with Whitehead" in our epoch, which he did not know.

This flight has already begun, for *The Concept of Nature* and *Science and the Modern World* are, in this perspective, certainly part of the same history, and they report the first "landings" of the Whiteheadian flight. We will, moreover, have occasion to revisit sites we have already explored: the question of living beings, that of bodies, that of perceptive experience, and, of course, that of the bifurcation of nature, for they designate what first incited me to think with Whitehead, the possibility of describing in a different way the terrains populated by the abstractions to which philosophical thought has granted the power to judge experience. Other stagings were certainly possible, in particular those that would have allowed a more systematic reference to the keywords of philosophical tradition or to the treatment to which Whitehead subjects his predecessors. But these would be other flights, produced by other readers, whom Whitehead had guided through other questions. No reading of Whitehead—such is my wager—can be "neutral." All must combine experimentation and putting to the test, thereby prolonging the adventure of an ideal seeking satisfaction.

CHAPTER SIXTEEN

Thinking under the Constraint of Creativity

N ALL PHILOSOPHICAL THEORY there is an ultimate which is actual in virtue of its accidents. It is only then capable of characterization through its accidental embodiments, and apart from these accidents is devoid of actuality. In the philosophy of organism this ultimate is termed "creativity" (PR, 7).

The ultimate, in Whitehead's sense, cannot, as we recall, by any means be identified with any form of transcendence, in the sense that any kind of sublime or intrinsically unthinkable character would be attached to it. If there is transcendence, it is a "technical" transcendence. The ultimate is not the judge of problems and opinions, but is relative to the way the problem is framed and therefore liable to change along with the problem. This is why the Whiteheadian ultimate, whatever its avatars, will always communicate with what is "without reason," not in the sense of the point of collapse of all reason but in the sense in which every reason is a solution to a problem and cannot therefore transcend the "fact" that the problem was raised in this way and not otherwise, communicating with some determinate designation of the ultimate, and not with another.

The Concept of Nature and *Science and the Modern World* already designated distinct "ultimates," presupposed by all the statements corresponding to the problematic space that was to be constructed. In *The Concept of Nature*, the ultimate designated the "mind," so that to nature had to correspond a concept that would make it the "respondent" called upon by each of the "accidental incarnations" of the mind, that is, by each of the footholds that succeeded, implying, at least at a first approximation, that due attention has been paid to this nature. In Whitehead's first metaphysical construction, at the end of *Science and the Modern World,* God appeared as the ultimate, the foundation of all concrete actuality, in the double sense of the ultimate arbitrary and of the ultimate principle of determination: that which is presupposed by any construction of reason, and which we therefore cannot define in terms of reason. The ultimate irrationality constituted by the existence of God was to be followed, in *Process and Reality,* by what is neither rational nor irrational as such, but has, with regard to this opposition, the neutrality of metaphysics. Whitehead baptizes this ultimate as "creativity."

Creativity was already presupposed by the definition of speculative philosophy: it is what is presupposed and exhibited by the "imaginative rationality" associated with the "flight of experience." As an ultimate, however, it is not what will justify speculative philosophy, nor what the latter must think. As is attested by *Process and Reality*'s subtitle, "An Essay in Cosmology," it is the cosmos that is henceforth to be conceived. Not, however—especially not—in the form of a "cosmic creativity." If Whitehead had made the reference to the cosmos his "ultimate," it would have constituted a genuine transcendence, that in the name of which the actual may be judged, that which demands that thought recognize the difference between cosmos and chaos, and place itself in the service of cosmos. The ultimate would then constitute, behind the scenes, the secret of reality. This is why "creativity" is above all not "cosmic." In itself, it has no discriminating character. With regard to it, everything that happens must be said in the same mode: that of the accident.

Creativity thus has the neutrality of metaphysics, and obliges the philosophy that defines it as "ultimate" to take the risk that is proper to empiricism: to affirm all that exists, all that happens, all that is created *qua* irreducible to a reason higher than the decision to exist, to happen in this and in no other way, to affirm and exhibit such-and-such a value and no other. And if everything we have to deal with at each instant, including ourselves, must be said to be first and foremost an "accident" of creativity, all that is to be thought, including the hypothesis that we have to do with a cosmos, must first be greeted with equanimity as a new and interesting exemplification of creativity.

"Creativity" is another rendering of the Aristotelian "matter," and of the modern "neutral stuff." But it is divested of the notion of passive receptivity, either of "form," or of external relations; it is the pure notion of the activity conditioned by the objective immortality of the actual world—a world which is never the same twice, though always with the stable element of divine ordering. Creativity is without a character of its own in exactly the same sense in which the Aristotelian "matter" is without a

character of its own. It is that ultimate notion of the highest generality at the base of actuality. It cannot be characterized, because all characters are more special than itself. But creativity is always found under conditions, and described as conditional (PR, 31).

In a sense, creativity as Whitehead has just presented it seems to prolong the "eternal activity" that *Science and the Modern World* had placed under the banner of a triple envisagement. Yet the framing of the problem has changed. Eternal activity presented itself as an abstraction, and as such was qualified by what it should give meaning to, by the possibilities of value, in contrast to the actuality that is value. Creativity, for its part, is bereft of qualifications. In particular, we must avoid associating it with an underlying impulse. Its "activity" has nothing to do with the power of a river, that always ends up destroying the banks that imprison it. Creativity is "activity," but activity affirms, simultaneously and inseparably, the river and the banks without which there would be no river, whether it overflows or not.

However, it will be objected, creativity, according to Whitehead, can only be described as "conditioned." And "condition" is never very far from "explication": the condition then allows the deduction of what is subject to it. The river's course can be deduced from the relief of its banks. If, however, in addition, what conditions creativity always entails "the stable element of divine ordering," how can we avoid reducing creativity to some kind of more or less tractable material, whereas intelligibility, legitimacy, rationality, and right refer to what conditions it?

Let us leave the "divine ordering" in indeterminacy for the moment, and limit ourselves to noting that it does not contradict what, in *The Concept of Nature*, was called "passage," both of nature and experience. Let us affirm right off the bat that the entire conceptual construction proposed by the metaphysical scheme of *Process and Reality* is an answer to this problem: to express in concepts what conditions creativity, in a mode that does not make the condition a principle of explanation; to create the concepts that make what is produced under a condition converge with what produces its own reason. And it is this problem that Whitehead begins to solve when he selects the terms that will intervene in the first of the four series of categories included in the scheme, the "category of the ultimate." This selection is risky, for these terms, if they came to communicate in a privileged way with specialized characteristics, including those that correspond to the cosmic hypothesis, would seal the defeat of the attempt.

"Creativity," "many," "one" are the ultimate notions involved in the meaning of the synonymous terms. These three notions complete the

Category of the Ultimate and are presupposed in all the more special categories.

The term "one" does not stand for "the integral number one," *which is a complex special notion. It stands for the general idea underlying alike the indefinite article "a or an," and the definite article "the," and the demonstratives "this or that," and the relatives "which or* what *or* how." *It stands for the singularity of an entity. The term "many" presupposes the term "one," and the term "one" presupposes the term "many." The term "many" conveys the notion of "disjunctive diversity"; this notion is an essential element in the concept of "being." There are many "beings" in disjunctive diversity* [. . .]

"Creativity" is the principle of novelty. An actual occasion is a novel entity diverse from any entity in the "many" which it unifies [. . .]

"Together" is a generic term covering the various special ways in which various sorts of entity are "together" in any one actual occasion. Thus "together" presupposes the notions "creativity," "many," "one," "identity," and "diversity." The ultimate metaphysical principle is the advance from disjunction to conjunction, creating a novel entity other than the entities given in disjunction. The novel entity is at once the togetherness of the "many" which it finds, and also it is one among the disjunctive "many" which it leaves; it is a novel entity, disjunctively among the many entities which it synthesizes. The many become one, and are increased by one [. . .]

Thus the "production of novel togetherness" is the ultimate notion embodied in the term "concrescence." These ultimate notions of "production of novelty" and of "concrete togetherness" are inexplicable either in terms of higher universals or in terms of the components participating in the concrescence. The analysis of the components abstracts from the concrescence. The sole appeal is to intuition (PR, 21–22).

As we can see, Whitehead proceeds with the greatest precaution. The creator of axioms is at work, demanding as general as possible an articulation between the primary terms of his system, those that are presupposed by metaphysical statements and will never be explained by them. At this stage, therefore, it is impossible to explain, for every explanation will imply the primary terms. It is nevertheless possible to accentuate, and, in the present case, to accentuate the contrast between the many, placed under the banner of disjunction, and the one, placed under the banner of conjunction (togetherness). The fact that we have to deal with primary terms means that one will never ask why there is a conjunction, that is, how it comes about that the many can become one. What will have to be characterized is the "how," which Whitehead relates directly, *qua* "relative," to the "one." This certainly indicates that there cannot be a general "how," that is, that every conjunction is, as such, "new."

Creativity is the principle of novelty, and all the primary terms Whitehead articulates have the vocation of giving meaning to this definition. Thus, the fact that the many are characterized by disjunction excludes a "together" that would explain the unity of their synthesis, or their togetherness produced by the new unity. And the fact that the latter, once produced, should be added to the many in the mode of disjunction excludes any dominant position of the synthesis with regard to what it synthesizes. Every synthesis is "new," and everything must be started all over again every time.

Novelty thus has no need of being defended: it is generic. All production, whatever it is, constitutes, by the same token as any other, an "accidental incarnation" of creativity. The "many" have become "one" in this way, and not otherwise. No higher universal will allow the resorption of this "fact." In other words, creativity, which is neutral, is not to be celebrated. On the contrary, it induces a rather peculiar humor. For both the "calculating thought" denounced by Heidegger as "forgetfulness of being" and its own meditative remembrance are testimonies to creativity. Creativity is just as much affirmed by the reasoning that Bergson condemns as the spatializing negation of duration as by the harmonic intuition of that duration.

Whiteheadian humor is formidable, and deeply annoying, because it cancels any dramaturgy of thought. In his terms, when Bergson writes, for instance, that "time is an invention or it is nothing at all," the invention of this grandiose alternative should be saluted as new, as a purely Bergsonian "cry." In contrast, the possibility of taking the alternative itself seriously, or of conferring upon it the ability to close the philosophical debate, may be ignored. It is the cry itself that bears witness and is added to the terms of the opposition it articulates. What Bergson calls "invention" is not creativity but creativity "on condition," the conditions that correspond to the specialized categories designating what he calls "intuition."

The fact that creativity, as an ultimate, cannot be conceived as such, that we can never characterize it "in itself" but always on condition, that we can describe it only as conditioned: all this by no means constitutes "limits of thought" in the sense that the term "limit" would imply the possibility of transgression or the evocation of *The One for whom such limits do not exist*. What is unknowable is unknown, and any pretended transgression will constitute another accidental "creature" of creativity, conditioned by the terms that define the limit that, in this case, matters. Instead of a limit, it is fitting to speak of an obliging constraint. As an ultimate, creativity obliges the thinker to affirm that all the verbs used, "to characterize," "to have to deal with," "to describe," themselves presuppose creativity. As soon as a situation matters enough for us to be tempted to see in it an "example of creativity," the generic terms "one" and "many" will have been specified, and thought will be conditioned by specialized categories, those that matter for this situation. Once again, this specification is not a screen, and does not separate us from an inaccessible truth. It is neither a source of nostalgia nor an object of denunciation, nor, above all, the instrument of a critique of the fallacious character of all explanation. If creativity intervened as a critical instrument, it would be characterized, enabling such-and-such a position to be defended against such-and-such another, whereas both are just as much its accidents. As a constraint, the neutrality of creativity thus has as its first effect to turn us away from the temptation always constituted for thinkers by a position that affirms itself to be "neutral," defining them as "not participating" in a debate, which they will then be able to adjudicate. In Whitehead's speculative philosophy, there is no position of adjudicator, or else every "creature of creativity" is the carrying out of an adjudication, and adjudicators themselves are the one as unifying the many.

Correlatively, creativity obliges us to think of conditions. There is not, nor can there be, any tension between creativity and conditioning, nor even between novelty and explanation, for novelty is inseparable from the way something is explained by something, the way a being is conditioned by what Whitehead often calls its "social environment." Nothing is more alien to Whitehead than the strategy of Descartes' "radical doubt," which undertakes to make a clean sweep of any inference that could be recognized as fictive or mendacious but forgets all that is presupposed by this very approach, including the fact that his decision and his research presuppose, at the very least, words to formulate the legitimate reasons to reject, one after the other, everything that is no longer to be believed. Descartes' doubt requires the specialized social environment which, most creatively, it undertakes to judge.

The data upon which the subject passes judgment are themselves components conditioning the character of the judging subject. It follows that any presupposition as to the character of the experiencing subject also implies a general presupposition as to the social environment providing the display for that subject. In other words, a species of subject requires a species of data as its preliminary phase of concrescence [. . .] The species of data requisite for the presumed judging subject presupposes an environment of a certain social character (PR, 203).

You think you are free to interrogate what you have to deal with, like a judge demanding an explanation. And you come to ask yourself if the explanations you constantly, and successfully, provide refer to a world whose reasons it renders explicit, or if they merely refer to your own interpretations. But it is you yourself who, by interpreting, produce yourself from this world which you interpret. And the very act that produces you *qua* judging bears witness, by itself, to the fact that the disjunct many you gather under the unity of a judgment were indeed (socially) liable to turn you into a judge.

"I'm the one who asks the questions": in fact, however, it is already the dissolved self of the one being questioned that speaks through his torturer (DR, 255).

Perhaps it is the experimental sciences that constitute the most dramatic example of this co-creation between judgment and social environment. It is in reference to these sciences that Kant celebrated as the "Copernican revolution" the "discovery" that it was not fitting to learn from nature as if it was a master, that the knowing subject was rather submitting it to the question, like a judge interrogating a prisoner according to the categories that allow offense and delinquent to be identified. Kant might well have believed he had stabilized the relations between subject and object, giving the sciences their horizon, that of a monotonous elucidation of the way in which the object is indeed, once and for all, determined by the categories of the subject, but scientists cannot, any more than judges or torturers, prevent their decree from being taken up into new adventures. Whatever may be the reasons mobilized by the judgment, or the claims that accompany it, these reasons and these claims will come to be added to the indefinitely proliferating cohort of the many available for a new unification, conditioning a new creation. The very justifications they will invoke in order to claim to transcend apparent diversity toward what conditions that diversity will condition the creative advance, adding to the disparate diversity that will constitute the problematic terrain for new syntheses.

In fact, Kant was extremely creative: he had to be, in order to turn Galileo, the prototype of the scientist who has carried out his Copernican revolution, into a "knowing subject" testifying to a generality. If there is one case that exhibits itself a vector of novelty, it is indeed the case of the twofold "production" of a Galileo discovering that he is capable of telling the difference between fiction and scientific statement, and a new type of data ("experimental") that confers this capacity upon him. The production of Galileo the experimenter, and of his data, is inseparable from the new environment constituted, as soon as they are produced, by "the experimental laboratory," that is, in this case the new type of apparatus that conditions this double production, the inclined plane that transforms the way a ball rolls into an ("objective") argument judging away what is then nothing more than Aristotle's "opinion." And the entire experimental adventure of physics, even if it can be placed under the banner of the ever-renewed "face-to-face" between "judge" and "nature," which this judge summons to answer his questions, also narrates the fabrication of the increasingly sophisticated social environments required by that face-to-face. In so-called high energy physics, the face-to-face in question needs years of preparation and demands a meticulous articulation between an indefinite number of instruments, the creation of languages intermediary between "data" and theories, the mobilization of hundreds of researchers, the invention of arguments suitable for convincing politicians and inspiring the public, and so on. Yet the most elementary judgment, the one carried out by a (conditioned) pigeon when it pecks at circular forms and not the others, also requires an indefinite and disparate number of stabilized relations, a hybrid social environment intermingling the pigeons and the psychologists who undertake to pass judgment on the pigeon's capacity to judge.

As a principle of novelty, creativity does not impose any limit on explanation but merely suggests that explanation not forget the social environment that simultaneously conditions it, and conditions what is proposed as explicable. This does not mean, however, that an explanation is "relative" in the sad sense in which relativism announces the ironic and disenchanted equivalence of all explanations, held to be equally fictitious. For this would still be to appeal—only to declare it impossible—to an ideal that cannot be stated by any language obliged by creativity, and that does not communicate with any actual experience. What is unknowable is unknown. "The only appeal," Whitehead concludes, "is to intuition": not to Bergsonian intuition, which resists intellectual constructions, but to the constructed intuition I have characterized as the "flight of experience." Yet this flight also exemplifies creativity in a way that is conditioned by a "social environment": the environment constituted by the scheme, and the demands for coherence to which it responds.

In *Process and Reality,* the call to intuition will be produced in a way that counteracts any confusion between creativity as an ultimate relative to the problem articulated by the scheme, and any romantic figure of emergent, spontaneous creativity "without a reason." To avoid such confusion, it is not enough, as I have emphasized, to affirm that creativity is always conditioned. The image of a pipe channeling the great creative flow, adjusting its emergent activity in a passive way, would still be possible. We must affirm the impossibility of distinguishing between passive conditioning and active production. And it is this affirmation that will be sounded by the "ontological principle," taking up the paradigmatic rationalist cry: "nothing happens without a reason!"

According to the ontological principle there is nothing which floats into the world from nowhere (PR, 244).

Officially, the ontological principle corresponds, within the scheme, to the eighteenth category of explanation. As its name indicates, however, it is by no means one category among others, and it receives, moreover, a large number of distinct formulations in the course of the text, conferring on it a differently accentuated relevance each time. The version I have just cited is opposed to the appeal to a "spontaneity" that comes from nowhere. This is also the aim of the formulation that appears in the eighteenth category, but this time it forbids, in a more explicit way, that creativity or any other generic principle be invoked by way of a reason.

This ontological principle means that actual entities are the only reasons; so that to search for a reason is to search for one or more actual entities (PR, 24).

Since an actual entity is always "this" entity, no reason can have a general value. The ontological principle thus implies that there is no stable difference between explanation and description, but only distinctions dealing with what matters, and with the environments required by what matters. Correlatively, other formulations emphasize, for their part, that what must "be explained" exhaustively in terms of "its" reasons, that is, the way in which "the many become one," is a "decision."

The ontological principle asserts the relativity of decision; whereby every decision expresses the relation of the actual thing, for which a decision is made, to an actual thing by which that decision is made (PR, 43).

The ontological principle declares that every decision is referable to one or more actual entities, because in separation from actual entitles there is nothing, merely nonentity—"The rest is silence" (PR, 43).

As a "category of explanation," the ontological principle may seem to concern "our" search for reasons, asking us not to refer to generalities, to abstractions, to anything that claims to transcend "this" world—or, at least, not to do so in ignorance of the fact that in no case will we arrive, in this way, "beyond empirical appearances." The ontological principle thus takes on an "epistemological" import, demanding that every explanation exhibit itself as a testimony to creativity, that is, to this extent, contingent, accidental, and properly "democratic." No explanation can lay claim to a higher instance of justification than what makes a difference for it, what matters for it. Yet when it comes to "decision," the principle takes on a truly ontological import, an import that will deprive the rationalist cry "nothing is without a reason" of all its epistemological power, as it will oppose any possibility of establishing communication between "reason" and "submission to a deduction." Everything has a reason, but everything is equally decision. Rationality is usually celebrated, or criticized, because it intends to subject everything that happens to reasons. Whitehead is fully rationalist, but he takes this rationality to the limit, and therefore makes it change its nature.

To ensure the divorce between reason and submission, however, it is not enough for reason and explanation to divorce, as is shown by the Leibnizian operation: the divorce between reason and human explanation did not prevent Leibniz from invoking a God to make reason and explanation converge. The divorce will be actual, however, if among the reasons that make a being exist, there appears the decision of this being itself. Among the actual beings that are the only reasons, the ontological principle will include the actual entity that "decides for itself": thus, and not otherwise.

The ontological principle can be expressed as: All real togetherness is togetherness in the formal constitution of an actuality (PR, 32).

For Whitehead, "reason" does not communicate with "submission." A being becomes determined by determining its reasons: such is the meaning of what Whitehead calls "the formal constitution of an actuality." Whereas the notion of submission implies that the "reasons" have in themselves the power of determining what they will be the reason of, this power, according to the ontological principle, must itself have a reason: only in the process of constitution of the entity of which they will be reasons are reasons articulated, "put together," in a way that confers upon each of them its determinate power.

Let us think, for instance, of a judge's decision. This decision must be based on multiple considerations, and yet the judge is anything but submissive, for it is the decision itself that has assembled these considerations, and presented them in a way that makes the judgment their consequence. Yet this does not make judge's decision arbitrary. It is "conditioned," but it is the judgment itself that determines the relation between the decision and what conditions it. Whitehead can therefore accept that everything has a reason, that nothing happens without a reason, that nothing "comes from nowhere": yet all the while specifying that, of course, nothing is a reason independently of the way in which a decision produces it *qua* the reason for this decision or this actuality.

Every decision is thus explained by its reasons, and as such it exemplifies creativity, the way in which "the many become one." Creativity has then nothing to do with a form of "supplement of soul," of "subjective evaluation" of what is given, adding a touch of originality to what already holds together. It is presupposed by this very "holding-together."

Nothing holds together independently of a decision, which is played over again each time with regard to the "how," with regard to the way it will hold together.

The ontological principle will place the rational pole of Whitehead's system under a constraint that forbids it any facility, any shortcut to the transcendence of what might claim to be indubitable, to go without saying, holding together by itself, without risk, without adventure. The principle will demand reasons, while forbidding that the slightest authority be conferred upon reasons. If you're looking for a reason, you are looking for an actual element that conditions creativity, but don't forget that the very way this element conditions creativity affirms this creativity just as much, for it is the decision through which what has produced itself as "one" has produced its reasons that has determined the actual role played by this conditioning.

In a sense, an actual occasion is causa sui (PR, 86).

Neither creativity as an ultimate, nor the ontological principle have assumed their full import independently of the process of writing *Process and Reality*. The smart reader, who has not forgotten the "divine ordering," a stable element conditioning creativity, will have already understood that this process of determination must have involved the question of God. If the ontological principle is to take on its full import, God will have to figure among the actual entities "that are the only reasons," for otherwise he would be metaphysically useless. What is more, like all other entities, God will have to "make a difference" without having the power to define the difference he will make. In fact, in the conceptual adventure constituted by the writing of *Process and Reality*, the ontological principle is inseparable from the construction of the concept of God, until the final decision, in which Whitehead will propose a divine experience that would be, in its way, the "consequence" of the constitutive decisions of the (other) actual entities. We will return to this point, but let us emphasize already that without this decision, an eventual "divine ordering" would have constituted an infraction against the ontological principle. In order not to correspond to a form of transcendental "togetherness," this ordering will have to have actual entities as its reasons; that is, these entities will have to be reasons for God. But this is possible only if God himself becomes, producing these reasons as "his" reasons.

Perhaps we can imagine Whitehead at the moment when he came to conceive of this major philosophico-theological innovation. He did not— and this is a constant element of his position—want any part of a creator God. Moreover, when he decided to make creativity the "ultimate" affirmed by his system, he had already been forced to abandon a possibility he had envisaged in 1926, in *Religion in the Making:* that of God as a "principle," "ideal entity," or "formative element," that is, an authority bereft of individuality, a name for an aspect of the creative advance of the world. Since creativity is the ultimate, none of its aspects can any longer be named, that is, privileged. God can no longer be a principle, and if Whitehead needs him, he will have to be conceived, like everything else, as an "accident of creativity."

Whitehead had thus arrived at the hypothesis, which subsists in many pages of *Process and Reality,* that God might be actual and not temporal, required as a "reason" for the actuality of new possibilities, and identified as such with the eternal envisagement of all ideal possibilities. Suddenly, however, he decided to take the decisive step.

Opposed elements stand to each other in mutual requirement. In their unity, they inhibit or contrast. God and the World stand to each other in this opposed requirement. God is the infinite ground of all mentality. The World is the multiplicity of finites, actualities seeking a perfected unity. Neither God, nor the World, reaches static completion. Both are in the grip of the ultimate metaphysical ground, the creative advance into novelty (PR, 348–349).

The very cry of coherence resounds here. Retroactively—for it is always retroactively that a position is sensed as incoherent—the nontemporal God who has just disappeared can indeed be diagnosed as a poor solution; a strong-arm move or an *ad hoc* response, since this God has no other role than to respond to a difficulty. For Whitehead, an actual but nontemporal God had no other "reason" than to act as a remedy for the confrontation between two kinds of reason: those designated by the ontological principle, referring to the actuality of decisions already taken, "objectively immortal," and those that imply a reference to what is possible, without which our experience could never be interpreted adequately but merely reduced—even if, according to Spinoza, such reduction is the path to wisdom. Coherence, however, is little concerned with wisdom, but it demands the reciprocal presupposition: if we need God, he must need us. The "decision" to endow God with a consequent nature will thus mark the passage from the voluntarist postulate to the positive articulation of reasons: confrontation becomes reciprocal presupposition.

God can no more be conceived independently of the World than the World can be conceived independently of Him. A moment of properly Whiteheadian decision, but also of perplexity: will everything have to be rewritten?

In the subsequent discussion, "actual entity" will be taken to mean a conditioned actual entity of the temporal world, unless God is expressly included in the discussion. The term "actual occasion" will always exclude God from its scope (PR, 88).

This "warning" brutally concludes a discussion (inserted late) of how the divine works. In the history of philosophical literature, it probably constitutes the most discrete signal of a major conceptual upheaval ever emitted. Whitehead refused to get bored, and no doubt renounced verifying every occurrence of the term "actual entity." For some of them, from now on, can bear just as much upon God as upon actual occasions, since God is no longer merely a nontemporal accident of creativity, but, like all other entities, a "creature of creativity." Rather than proceeding to an exhaustive sorting process, Whitehead thus limited himself, where it was important, to pointing out explicitly that God is included in the statement. In the other cases, "by default," it is better for the reader to think exclusively of the entities that belong to the "temporal world."

Not until the fifth part of *Process and Reality* will Whitehead deploy—freely, poetically, almost prophetically—what his own creation has made of him. We will get to this, but here the point was, first and foremost, to point out a spectacular example of creation, carried out under the twofold constraint of the ontological principle and the appetite for coherence. To make God a creature may constitute a revolutionary idea for theology. Here, this mutation imposes itself as a consequence of Whiteheadian speculative working conditions. It may be why Whitehead did not show off this innovation. Instead, we can easily imagine Whitehead perplexed, wondering whether he will be forced to intervene and make corrections every time God appears in a textual stratum dating from the time when he was a "nontemporal accident," then making up his mind in accordance with the "formula" of Melville's Bartleby, celebrated by Deleuze: *"I would prefer not to."*

Each original is a powerful, solitary Figure that overflows every explainable form: it launches flaming bolts of expression, which mark the obstinacy of a thought without images, of a question without an answer, of a logic that is extreme and without rationality. Figures of life and of knowledge, they know something inexpressible, they live with something unfathomable. There is nothing general about them, and they are not particular: they escape knowledge and defy psychology. Even the words they pronounce overflow the general laws of the language ("the presuppositions"), as much as the simple particulars of speech, since they are like the vestiges or the projections of an original, unique, primary language, and they carry all of language to the limit of silence and of music.

There is nothing particular about Bartleby, nothing general either: he is an Original (CC, 106).

An original never wants to be an original, unless we are to plunge into the masquerade of Oedipal conflicts. Creators should never wish themselves to be "creative," although it is sad to have to repeat this sometimes. It is probable that Whitehead-who-refused-to-be-bored, but who, every time he tried to explain himself, made the proliferation of *"yes, but"* and *"but then"* start up again at some point of his explanation, did not want to "defy psychology" or impose upon his reader the terror of an unfathomable experience. If he did not judge it to be important, or perhaps even desirable, to take his reader by the hand, it is probably because what he first wanted to communicate was the contrast between what "can" be communicated and what speculative language, because it must produce the generalizations which every specialized language does without, "must" communicate: the impossibility of ever defining what one "means."

The point is that every proposition refers to a universe exhibiting some general systematic metaphysical character. Apart from this background, the separate entities which go to form the proposition, and the proposition as a whole, are without determinate character. Nothing has been defined, because every definite entity requires a systematic universe to supply its requisite status. Thus every proposition proposing a fact must, in its complete analysis, propose the general character of the universe required for that fact (PR, 11).

It pertains to speculative propositions to "make us feel" what is, in fact, a generality that bears upon every proposition: it pertains to them to propose not a fact, opinion, state of affairs, or even a vision of the world, but the universe required by thought itself producing that proposition, a universe whose general, systematic character is none other than the very experience of thought as a "leap," productive both of the thinker and of what is to be thought. Speculative propositions do not designate a world that exists prior to them, but, quite the contrary, they bring into existence what Deleuze and Guattari call an "image of thought," in the sense that such an image coincides with a "thought without images," that is, without a stopping point that makes words and things communicate in a satisfactory way. No longer the thought of someone about something, but thought experiencing itself as anonymous, as if produced not by the thinker but by its very movement.

According to Deleuze and Guattari, an "image of thought" is not described but is produced in the very movement in which thought exceeds the images that fixate it, to itself become production-sensation, an "abstract machine" producing concepts that inhabit what is, in itself, neither thought nor thinkable, the "plane of immanence."

The plane is like a desert that concepts populate without dividing up. The only regions of the plane are concepts themselves, but the plane is all that holds them together. The plane has no other regions than the tribes populating and moving around on it. It is the plane that carries out conceptual linkages with ever-increasing connections, and it is concepts that carry out the populating of the plane on an always renewed and variable curve.

The plane of immanence is not a concept that is or can be thought but rather the image of thought, the image thought gives itself of what it means to think, to make use of thought, to find one's bearings in thought [. . .] The image of thought implies a strict division between fact and right: what pertains to thought as such must be distinguished from contingent features of the brain or historical opinions (QPh, 39–40).

"Creativity" would thus be a Whiteheadian name for what Deleuze and Guattari call the "plane of immanence." On this plane, an event as seemingly important as a radical mutation of the concept of God is merely a new linkage, of which Whitehead is not the author but the operator, who does not share his writing between before and after, but merely imposes the emergence of new folds in the ever-variable curvature of a chapter, a paragraph, or even a sentence. While the insertions populating the text multiply, thought loses the certainty of its images to experience what it means to think.

If philosophy begins with the creation of concepts, the plane of immanence must be considered prephilosophical, not in the way in which one concept may refer to others, but in the way concepts themselves refer to a non-conceptual comprehension (QPh, 43).

The plane of immanence designates the imperative—that which insists and demands to be thought by the philosopher, but of which the philosopher is not in any way the creator. The plane does not command concepts, and does not connect them without them making its curvature vary. This is why the appropriate name for the plane of immanence that haunts the philosophers' thought may mutate. It is not that what haunts them has "changed," like one changes one's mind; rather, the zone of connection that constituted the site for this name has been brutally introverted, imposing new operations of linkage, causing the emergence of new accentuations of what is insistent. Thus, we can affirm that "organism" was the first name for the Whiteheadian plane of immanence. It designates the moment in which "what pertains to thought" can be called "trust." The organism is inseparable from the diagnosis of the modern epoch, insofar as Whitehead trusted that this epoch was to pass away, and it does indeed carry out a new distribution of fact and right. Trust is inseparable from thought as such: it does not refer to an opinion, whether historical or subjective. Nor will it ever be reducible to some functioning of the brain. The brain will never explain trust, for every explanation, by the brain or by something else, first of all manifests in principle the trust of those who have undertaken to explain. Trust can be killed by disqualifying words, by dominant opinions, by the accidents of life, but trust itself is not accidental. Trust is on the side of "right," of what is presupposed by every explanation.

The organism is a way of expressing this trust, because it conjugates existence and success. Nothing is "no matter what," secondary, epiphenomenal, superstructure, anecdotal, with regard to something more general. Everything that exists, in the sense that we can undertake to describe it, or even to explain it, has first, and prior to any explanation, succeeded in existing. Our trust exhibits the success to which we owe our existence as thinking beings, a success that nothing guarantees. It has the character of a wager, but a wager with nothing beyond it, on the basis of which it could be dissected. The organism expresses the task of thought: not to judge, but to learn to appreciate.

And perhaps because it is the organism that made him a creative thinker, Whitehead will continue, in the first layers of the writing of *Process and Reality,* to baptize his philosophy as a "philosophy of the organism." Yet the concepts that, since April 1925, have come to populate the plane have produced what the distribution between fact and right known as "organism" could not realize. The plane has taken on a new and highly curious curvature. Henceforth, it must be impossible for the distribution between fact and right to communicate with a judgment, even if the latter merely affirms the wager of "trust." The speculative movement must refer every right to an accident of creativity, and celebrate every fact together with all that it implies, as the conditioning of the creativity to which it bears witness.

Retroactively, the organism could not be conceived independently of the universe that it required, but it required it in a way that was merely implicative and incapable of explaining itself. It may equip the thought of an educator inventing new ways to address thirsty young souls that school threatens to turn into professionals. All that matters then are the "good habits" to be acquired, those that should enable students to resist the dead abstractions that come from the disciplines. But Whitehead could not describe in terms of habits his own soul, which undertook to awaken the habit of aesthetic enjoyment in his students' souls. Nor could he apprehend these souls in the process of becoming, in the terms in which he taught them to apprehend the living, limited, and intolerant values that a factory succeeds in perpetuating. He could only trust them and teach them to trust, to dare the leap whose possibility the organism does not state. In short, Whitehead, for whom education was an adventure, could no more describe himself in terms of his educational project than Epimenides the Cretan could classify himself within the set of lying Cretans he defined. The concept of organism was meant to answer the challenge of education, but it was mute about why this challenge would make itself felt at all.

"Habit" was, however, never to assume a pejorative sense in Whitehead. Above all, the criticism to be addressed to the professional must not be confused with a critique of habits. And if the organism, because its inspiration is biological and proposes "keeping its hold" as what is at stake, is inadequate, it is because it does not seem to leave any other alternative in the face of professional habits than the project of making them "lose their hold," which is certainly quite tempting but ultimately catastrophic, for this is exactly what professionals think: if they "let go" of their abstractions, they are lost. Yet the "applications" to which the speculative scheme appeals are, again and again, questions of the habits to be adopted. The difference is that these habits exhibit a trust that is no longer paradigmatically that of an educator, but may be that of a participant in the adventure of mathematics, in which the art of an imagination obliged by coherence is cultivated as such.

In this case, *Process and Reality* demands, in the minor key of an (original) habit to be acquired, what Deleuze and Guattari describe in a somewhat dizzying way.

Thought "merely" demands motion that can be taken to infinity [. . .] What defines infinite motion is a coming and going, because it does not go toward a destination without already turning back on itself [. . .] It is not, however, a fusion, but a reversibility, an immediate, perpetual, instantaneous exchange, a bolt of lightning. Infinite motion is twofold, and there is only a fold from one to the other. It is in this sense that it is said that thinking and being are one and the same thing. Or rather, motion is not the image of thought without also being the matter of thought. When the thought of Thales leaps forth, it returns like water. When the thought of Heraclitus becomes polemos, it is fire that returns upon it [. . .] the plane of immanence has two faces, like Perseus and like Nature, like Physis and like Nous. This is why there are always a great many motions implicated in one another, folded up within one another, insofar as the return of one instantaneously relaunches another one, in such a way that the plane of immanence never stops weaving itself, like a gigantic shuttle (QPh, 40–41).

Each concept calls for a leap of the imagination, but none of them is privileged, none can be aroused or experienced without other motions surging forth, each of which may be at the starting point and/or at the point of arrival. Every starting point is contingent. Every point of arrival is a stage on the way. All that counts is the incessant weaving between the two faces that this motion brings into existence as it weaves itself: Thought and Nature, *Nous* and *Physis*. It perhaps belongs to Whitehead to have made reversibility—the immediate, perpetual, instantaneous exchange between what thought intends and its return upon itself, its becoming "matter for thought"—the very thing that is to be inhabited, of which the habit is to be acquired . . . by applying the scheme. The twofold wager of a transformation of the sciences of nature and of the aims of education has thus not disappeared, but constitutes one starting point, or else one point of arrival among others, for a motion that brings into existence simultaneously a "Physis" in which thought matters, and a "Thought" that no longer belongs to the thinker.

The ancient doctrine according to which "no one crosses the same river twice" is generalized. No thinker thinks twice (PR, 29).

Simultaneous contraction and dilation: if no thinker thinks twice, the two faces we call *Nous* or *Physis* are required to think a thought. God and the world, both under the sway of the gigantic shuttle of the creative advance.

However, is it possible to inhabit a thought in the form of a Möbius strip, where one cannot explore one face without finding oneself on the other? Can one live in the world of Escher, in which two hands draw one another? Anglo-Saxon humor: it is a habit to be acquired, it suffices not to allow oneself to be trapped by the paradox of thought thinking itself. For this paradox, inducing the experience of a dizzying, uninhabitable *mise en abyme*, by no means indicates a limit of thought colliding with itself, but is due to the inadequate abstraction of a reflection that claims to grasp its proper conditions. The fact that my itinerary takes me back to the other face, which it presupposed but to which it could not accede, the fact that my hand draws what is drawing it, are only dizzying for the third party I have introduced surreptitiously: the person who contemplates the opposing faces of the Möbius strip, or sees those two hands, each of which is drawing what draws it. There is no third party in Whitehead's system: there is only itinerary, flight, movements, or gestures. And the thinking experimentation on thought corresponds, again and again, to this pragmatic question: what difference in experience could be produced, what new regime of habit could be experienced if, in principle, I affirm that everything that pertains to thought, all the rights it claims, all the hopes it nourishes, are so many testimonies to the "reality" that is its problem, so many requisites for the construction of the solution to this problem?

The fact that habits to be acquired come up for discussion again and again is all the more important in that it is easy to confuse a philosophy that defines creativity as an ultimate, with a philosophy inhabited by what is attested by the adventure of creators. The image of Whiteheadian thought is not the image of Deleuzian thought. It does not place the creator under the banner of an imperative that irresistibly distances him from all the others, all those who are satisfied by opinion, by the securities of routine, by words as they are proposed to our perceptions: a world that is most often reassuring, saturated with cultural artifacts that orient us, giving rise to due attention without our even having to be aware of it. This is why Whitehead, the thinker of creativity, will never celebrate the creator in the heroic mode of radical risk and extreme solitude to which Deleuze sometimes yields.

Philosophy, science and art want us to tear open the firmament and dive into chaos. Only at this cost will we vanquish it. And I have thrice crossed the Acheron, victorious. The philosopher, the scientist and the artist seem to return from the land of the dead (QPh, 190).

From a Whiteheadian viewpoint, the proposition is slightly exaggerated. Creatures confronting chaos take for granted a respectable number of conditions: the endurance proper to electromagnetic regularities, to molecules, to cellular metabolism, and finally to the body, which, even when submitted to terrible trials, must maintain certain crucial habits . . . Not to mention an entire inheritance of things and items of knowledge, some of the components of which will eventually be subverted, but never all of them at the same time. Not to forget, finally, all that creators have learned that makes them able to "dive" without being swallowed. A dive cannot be improvised, but demands equipment. Unlike those who may happen to "sink" into chaos, creators are those who know that what they experience "matters," and that they will be able to recount something of what has happened to them, that is to come back . . . even from the land of the dead.

Madness, the destruction of consensus, the terrible and somber truth of chaos from which opinion tries to defend itself thus do not belong to the image of Whiteheadian thought. The fact that "I" is "another" will not, by its proximity to madness, make vibrate the thought of the man for whom "no thinker thinks twice" is perfectly inhabitable, for whom the "I" is an interesting habit, an ingredient of the link ceaselessly re-created by each act of thought, by each new distribution produced be-tween thinkers and what they think.

Correlatively, it is not so much the problem of risk as it is the impor-tance of the fact that one can "come back from the land of the dead" that will establish itself as what obliges us to think. What matters is not that a mathematician like Cantor "went mad"—such things happen—but that, unlike Cantor, other mathematicians have been able to find in their community those who have accepted to inhabit the new possibilities that they have brought back. The solitude and misunderstanding to which the creator may give rise are not a privileged testimony to creativ-ity, for creativity also acts as a constraint when it comes to thinking about rejection, misunderstanding, or else recuperation, the way in which what the solitary adventure has "brought back" from chaos is trans-formed into a consensual "acquisition."

As a mathematician, Whitehead was never tempted by the iconoclastic gesture that intends to make a clean sweep of the past. He knows the extent to which mathematical creation requires the past, even when it may present itself as a break. And the very adventure of writing *Process and Reality* introduces a process that exhibits the difference between in-tuition, or vision in the sense that Plato associated it with mathematical truth, and the work of fashioning concepts. Such concepts demand a leap of the imagination, of course, but none of them "make an image," none holds all by itself, because all are "conditioned" by a process that pro-duces its own trials, the questions that never cease reviving it, making new demands surge forth that impose a problem where an answer had been formulated. This process does not require the figure of a creator or a visionary, confronting what exceeds the categories of thought or of perceptions, but testifies instead to a practice to which philosophers may owe their existence. When Whitehead defined the philosophical tradition as a series of "footnotes" to the text of Plato (PR, 39), what he designated was indeed a tradition that requires reading and writing. What are phi-losophers other than those who read other philosophers? But they read them in a way that will communicate with writing, that will make them add, subtract, modify, and insert the "footnotes" that make a text mu-tate. Including, for instance, a little note "interpreting" the contemplative vision of ideas as a "leap of imagination."

When Whitehead makes creativity the ultimate, therefore, he does not particularly celebrate creators. Thinking under the constraint of creativ-ity has nothing to do with a heroic adventure, and creativity demands nothing. Whatever we do, whether we live in the most reproducible of routines or whether we cross the Acheron, each moment of our lives is equally and impartially the creature of creativity. But also, and perhaps above all, thinking under the constraint of creativity has nothing to do with the vision of a "creative cosmos" that might, as such, become the subject of our descriptions. Such a vision is not banished, of course, but it does not belong to the register of applications of Whitehead's scheme, of his "verification," for the visionary flight then seems to be the only thing that matters, and not its landing "for renewed observation rendered acute by rational interpretation" (PR, 5). Similarly, Whitehead's God, as an accident of creativity, cannot be isolated from the adventure of the successive revisions of the categoreal scheme that will end up in its definition. It neither expresses nor calls for a vision. It is the scheme, including God, that calls for verification, experimentation of the difference it produces upon our habits of thought, including those that are religious.

When he committed himself to the adventure of a speculative cosmology, then, Whitehead did not abandon the definition of philosophy he had proposed in *Science and the Modern World*: if we cannot think without abstraction, it is important to revise our *modes* of abstraction. And, for instance, it is important not to abstract creators from the equipment on which they cannot help but rely when they undertake to cross the Acheron, and from the equipment they provide themselves in order to be able to "come back."

Perhaps, then, humor is one of the ways of characterizing the transformation Whitehead intends to produce upon our habits. The habits of professionals are bereft of humor: what questions their mode of abstraction is either judged to be insignificant—reduced to ignorance of what is demanded by science or rationality—or as endangering civilization—many scientists speak of a "rise in irrationality" when they sense that the questioning of what they propose can no longer be rejected by a shrug of the shoulders. The habits to be acquired, what creativity appeals to as a constraint, would be, compared to professional habits, like a wall of dry stones compared to a cement wall. Cement rejects the interstices in which the weed grows that will one day crack it open. The dry stones, for their part, can of course be displaced, and the weed that displaces them might certainly be tempted to abstract from the fact that without the stone the earth in which it grows would not have held. But the wall of dry stones is not defined against the interstices; the latter belong to it just as much as the stones that make it up. Thinking what imposes itself as obvious under the constraint of creativity, Whitehead's wager is that we can learn modes of abstraction that enable us to celebrate together both the obstinate stones and the interstices that will transform them into preconditions for what will eventually displace them.

Thus, Whitehead will avoid all the words susceptible of disqualifying the type of order presupposed by opinion. The charge of contempt in these words, the absence of humor, and the somewhat misplaced heroism they suggest, add nothing to the risk taken by thinkers when it comes to *this* particular thinker who, at *this* instant, has produced *this* proposition that turns *this* opinion into that whose point is to experience its abandonment. Yet these words risk insulting the world, the immense, heterogeneous population of "opinions" that endure in the interwoven and precarious relations of "trust," or mutual presupposition. In the process, they risk cementing against them an alliance that will confirm that the historical truth they propose is unbearable to self-righteous people or to the "system."

Yet the point is not to condemn those by whom the scandal arrives. The words they use are not theirs, but those suggested to them by the modes of abstraction of our time. Whiteheadian humor, demoralizing the great oppositions, the binary choices between adherence and polemic, is addressed to our time, simultaneously dominated by professional modes of judgment and fascinated by heroic protests. This humor does not attack, for the point is not to know who the good guys and who the bad guys are. The point, impersonal and cosmological, is that of the "trick of evil."

Each task of creation is a social effort, employing the whole universe. Each novel actuality is a new partner adding a new condition. Every new condition can be absorbed into additional fullness of attainment. On the other hand, each condition is exclusive, intolerant of diversities; except in so far as it find itself in a web of conditions which convert its exclusions into contrasts. A new actuality may appear in the wrong society, amid which its claims to efficacy act mainly as inhibitions. Then a weary task is set for creative function, by an epoch of new creations to remove the inhibition. Insistence on birth at the wrong season is the trick of evil. In other words, the novel fact may throw back, inhibit, and delay. But the advance, when it does arrive, will be richer in content, more fully conditioned, and more stable. For in its objective efficacy an actual entity can only inhibit by reason of its alternative positive contribution (PR, 223).

My readers have now been warned. If they are fascinated by the heroic grandeur of refusal, and despise compromises; if they deplore the fact that the radical demands of every new position are recuperated by what was supposed to be subverted; if "to deconstruct" is a goal in itself for them, and scandalizing self-righteous people is a testimony to truth; if they oppose the pure to the impure, the authentic to the artificial; if they cannot understand how the most "unplatonic" of philosophers situated himself as a "footnote" to the text of Plato . . . let them close this book. Never will they see celebrated in it the power of a truth that is verified by the destruction of false pretenders. They will therefore find in it only disappointments and reasons for contempt.

CHAPTER SEVENTEEN

The Risks of Speculative Interpretation

*P*HILOSOPHY DOES NOT INITIATE *interpretations. Its search for a rationalistic scheme is the search for more adequate criticism, and for more adequate justification, of the interpretations which we perforce employ* [...] *the methodology of rational interpretation is the product of the fitful vagueness of consciousness. Elements which shine with immediate distinctness, in some circumstances, retire into penumbral shadow in other circumstances, and into black darkness on other occasions. And yet all occasions proclaim themselves as actualities within the flow of a solid world, demanding a unity of interpretation. Philosophy is the self-correction by consciousness of its own initial excess of subjectivity* (PR, 14–15).

Speculative philosophy must aim at neutrality, not in the sense that neutrality, objectivity, and rationality are associated in the experimental sciences, but as an immanent practical obligation that condemns it to the most risky interpretation. From this perspective, every statement that presents itself as "neutral," in the scientific sense of "authorized by a state of affairs," is not only eminently selective, but also specifically partial. The clarity of the reference is not only detached from darkness, but also reflects the excess of subjectivity that leads us to deny that darkness. When the subject faces the object, when, for instance, it defines itself as pure intentionality, it silences, with passion, violence, and purifying bias, the confused totality of what Leibniz called "little perceptions," indefinable but as inseparable from distinct perception as the cloth from the fold that qualifies it.

Correlatively, the neutrality aimed at by speculative philosophy bears witness to a cosmos to the same extent that, by its undertaking, it presupposes the possibility for consciousness of affirming the dark and the distinct, the cloth and its noteworthy folds. If consciousness must be corrected of its excess of subjectivity, the correction must not proceed in the name of a demanding imperative but in terms of a possibility which, as it is suggested, becomes inhabitable by this very fact. Otherwise, it might well become a new case illustrating the "trick of evil."

To speak of suggestion is not to speak of precautions, prudence, or slow, controlled progress. These are the characteristics of a practice articulating the hunter and the prey that is to be caught unaware or else to be directed toward the enclosure in which it will finally be held prisoner. It matters little if, at that moment, it panics, charges, tries to regain its freedom, or yields to the despair of the vanquished: it is too late. Whitehead by no means intends to oblige his readers, step by step, to admit that they are progressively reduced to submission, unable to object, summoned to accept without knowing any longer where they should have rebelled, where they could have escaped. By no means does he proceed like Socrates the dialectician, whom his adversaries compared to an electric ray, anesthetizing his adversaries and numbing their ability to resist. Quite the contrary, he never ceases to utter veritable enormities, leaving his reader, at each instant, the freedom to laugh, to smile, but also to experience what it means to be able to laugh or smile where a dramatic alternative held sway.

Thus, those who might be tempted to raise the question of the legitimacy of speculative thought will receive the following answer, cavalier to say the least:

The scheme is true with unformulated qualifications, exceptions, limitations, and new interpretations in terms of more general notions (PR, 8).

The scheme is "true": whatever the definition of truth may be that a philosophy honors, this affirmation is so "enormous" that it literally disarms thought. It is not until, and unless, the movement has been engaged that confers a meaning upon the affirmation that the import of this restriction becomes important. Whitehead appeals to a future when the limits of the scheme will make themselves felt, that is, when the speculative interpretations of which it is the matrix will become judgment, when application will impose silence, in short, when the generalities articulated will produce the experience of their inadequacy. In that future, the scheme will have rendered one of the most important services of which it is capable: to have brought about the disclosure of unformulated limitations, to have made perceptible the insistence and the interest of experiences that impose, in return, the qualification of this scheme, exhibiting its selective character.

In this way, moreover, Whitehead goes on to praise the philosophical systems of which he is the heir. It is true, for instance, that, as Kant maintained, the way concepts work constitutes an essential aspect of perceptual experience. Kant's analysis of experience, as a subjective process that produces objectivity, thus designates a general idea that makes Kant an important philosopher. Whitehead inherits the idea of experience as constructive functioning, but he calmly reverses the order in which this functioning works: the process he will describe produces subjectivity from objectivity, and not vice versa. This is a homage to Kant, for

The order is immaterial in comparison with the general idea (PR, 156).

It is highly unlikely that today's Kantians will appreciate the homage in question, any more than historians of philosophy will appreciate the "cavalier" perspective Whitehead adopts on this matter. Yet as we have seen, Whitehead is just as "cavalier" with his own thought, and with what was the truth of his intentions when he was writing such-and-such a paragraph. In fact, there is only one case in which he really points out a disagreement, and this, rather curiously, is when the philosopher in question is no doubt the one who was closest to him: Leibniz, a mathematician like him, and who, like him, gave primacy to coherence.

There is a book that should be written, and its title should be The Mind of Leibniz (MT, 3).

The way Whitehead condemns Leibniz, again and again, for what he describes as a genuine fault, a "magician's trick" (preestablished harmony) must be understood as that of one mathematician attacking another mathematician, reproaching him with being content with a "trivial" solution, in the sense of mathematics, to what should have been "the problem," that is, the question of the solidarity of all that exists. Yet in all the other cases, Whitehead accepts, and he prolongs "with a slight modification"—that is, in a way that makes the apparent casualness communicate with a genuine fabrication. He creates what can be associated with a "cavalier perspective."

One calls "cavalier perspective" a perspective that combines two contradictory properties: a scenography in relief, and the conservation of the principal dimensions of the object placed in perspective. The most distant parts will be "seen" as distant, and yet their size will not be reduced in comparison with that of the nearer parts. Whitehead superbly ignores the dilemmas of the history of philosophy, the attempt to understand a philosophical system from an immanent viewpoint contemporary with itself, while relating it to a historical filiation by which the stakes pursued by the philosopher are situated. The western "adventure" of rationality, as Whitehead inherits it, is not a "history" but a succession of "planes" that make ideas that matter surge forth, and whose importance must be preserved such as it is, independently of the intentions we may attribute to those who have produced them. The cavalier perspective, ignoring intentions, deliberately abstracts from what might impose a choice between faithfulness (return to the "real" Kant) and assignment to an obsolete past (in Kant's time . . .).

The freedom with which Whitehead captures and retranslates the "general ideas" of his predecessors, at the risk of making them undergo mutations of meaning, no doubt puts to the test the "excess of subjectivity" that can transform a philosophical work into "doctrine," with regard to which the question of faithfulness or opposition first arises. Yet this freedom is first and foremost that of a philosopher-mathematician, for whom philosophy, like mathematics, is creation.

Mathematicians celebrate their creations as "generalizations," which succeed in ridding a definition of its excessive attachments to a particular case. And this success is not a judgment upon what mathematicians of the past thought or believed, for in mathematics definitions do not translate intentions or convictions, but possibilities of operating, of raising problems, of producing new cases of solution. The cavalier perspective in philosophy thus suggests that philosophy, like mathematics, is adventure, but it does so in a way that leaves philosophers perfectly free to go their way with a shrug of the shoulders: how can someone be criticized who renounces so radically all the justifications in terms of which others defend themselves against the threat of disqualification? They will therefore not feel themselves constrained to dig defensive trenches around a threatened interpretation. Not only does Whiteheadian practice discourage this reaction, but philosophers who do not drop the book while concluding *"He's crazy, there's no use continuing"* have already undergone a modification that takes away their taste for becoming a censor. This is no doubt why Whitehead's work has remained marginal in the academic world, for readers find themselves "disarmed," deprived of that paradigmatic academic weapon, the critical commentary.

The risk of being rejected by the academic community does not raise a "cosmic" problem, to the precise extent to which such rejection is reflected by an indifferent shrug of the shoulders, not intensified by any justification whereby the rejecters would become worse than they were, more intensely dependent on a position demanding the destruction of what endangers it. But the risks of speculative interpretation become very different when Whitehead no longer has to deal with philosophers— that is, with interlocutors who are, in fact, rather used to shrugging their shoulders and to having their statements cause others to shrug theirs—but with interlocutors engaged by a conviction that rejects the possibility of indifference. In this case, the question of adequacy is raised in a completely different, much more risky way.

In fact, mathematical humor does not suffice when it can resemble ironic renunciation, when what Gilles Deleuze honored as the "truth of the relative," which it makes perceptible, can, predictably, be perceived as the cavalier affirmation of the relativity of all truth. A humorous reformulation can certainly retranslate any pretense while neutralizing it, but it can do nothing against the concern of those who, upon seeing their convictions retranslated, have the impression that they are being made fun of, that one refuses to hear them out, that they are being transformed into a bull driven mad by the pirouettes of the bullfighter's cape. And this concern may be transformed into hatred if no adequate response is made to the "cry": but all ways of unifying, all ways of becoming "one" with regard to the many are equivalent!

This cry can be "specialized," but for Whitehead, all specializations affirm one and the same thing. They all bear witness to the inadequacy of a thought that would reduce reality to chaos, to the pure multiplicity of disparate free acts, an absurd dream, a tale told by an idiot, full of sound and fury, and so on. Each cry demands the recognition that it imports, and there is a speculative obligation to give meaning to that demand.

However, the problem is not solved for all that. When it comes to correcting the excess subjectivity of creators who propose themselves as marginal or subversive, it is rather relevant to make the "cosmic importance" of their work communicate with the "social effort" that its reception will impose. Yet when it comes to convictions that irreducibly associate their importance with a pretense to exclusivity, such a "cavalier perspective" can no longer be placed under the banner of humor, contributing a small correction to the excess of subjectivity. It risks a frontal collision. What will collide is the fact that, as such, the cosmic perspective proposed by Whitehead cannot "verify" any cry in particular: all the species pertaining to a genus affirm that genus without a hierarchy. Both the anti-Dreyfusards, for whom the Army and the Nation were well worth the sacrifice of one innocent, and the Dreyfusards, for whom all that mattered was the triumph of Justice and Truth, affirmed and presupposed a cosmos. And also those who will say, it is important not to place these two affirmations on an equal level, to make explicit a difference between anti-Dreyfusards and Dreyfusards.

In other words, speculative interpretation must take the risk of disappointing. Discreet but without hypocrisy, Whitehead was to propose a test somewhat similar to the one imposed by the rabbi, who, according to the story, when confronted with two contradictory theses, declared each one right in turn, and answered his students, who had objected that both protagonists could not be right at the same time, that they too were right. This latter *"Yes, you too are right,"* apparently so cavalier, is a quiet test, offering students an opportunity, but also leaving them free to go away with a shrug of the shoulders, abandoning that cowardly impostor.

In *Religion in the Making,* published in 1926, Whitehead first took the risk of a speculative interpretation of what inspired passion for exclusivity much more intensely than philosophy or science. Philosophers are used to indifference, while scientists are interested only rather secondarily in "diffusing" their knowledge, the essential part of their passion being focused on the questions they share with their colleagues. In contrast, the question of religion, and more particularly the question of the Christian religion, is indissolubly linked to that of "conversion." Can one be a convinced Christian, and accept that faith in God "matters" in a way that is merely specific?

Religion in the Making is a transitional work, some of whose statements Whitehead apparently even regretted. Yet this work is very interesting, in that it allows us to "follow" the way Whitehead answers the challenge of circumstances. It consists of the text of four lectures given in February 1926 at King's Chapel in Boston, once again in the context of the Lowell lectures, as was the case for *Science and the Modern World.* This time, however, it was religion that Whitehead was to discuss before his audience.

In his preface, Whitehead does not omit to mention, as usual, that he is applying the same procedure to religion as the one that he had applied in 1925 to the sciences, in the lectures that gave rise to *Science and the Modern World.* Yet the "same," in Whitehead, should never be taken quite seriously. In contrast, the invariant that is to be taken seriously is that, addressing a new type of audience, it is the members of this audience he must address, and it is the primary terms of the practice that unites them that he must celebrate adequately . . . while reinventing them, of course. The risks to which the situation he has accepted will expose him are so many engagements.

The limitation of God is his goodness (RM, 153).

This statement, which occurs in the text almost without warning, is not compatible with the God of *Science and the Modern World,* for God, as a principle of limitation, cannot have any limitation. It could, however, have been signed by Leibniz, for whom God's choice of creating this world, and not just any other, must answer to a reason: if we do not want to insult God by attributing to him the arbitrariness of despots, He cannot, by definition, wish anything but the best. Coming from Whitehead's pen, it may well be that this statement signifies "taking up a hypothetical position," the kind of position he would like to construct, but the means to which he must formulate.

In fact, Whitehead's position will be articulated around the question of the moral order, that is, the distinction between good and evil. It is impossible to address people of Christian faith without insulting them if one cannot give this distinction an irreducible meaning, which cannot be dissolved into the humor of neutralization. The point is thus not only to make room for this distinction, but to give it its full import. Since God, as the unqualifiable principle of all limitation, could not qualify good and evil, it is the entire construction of *Science and the Modern World* that must be reassembled in a new coherence, at the cost of transforming the definition of God from top to bottom. This is indeed the "same" procedure of thought as the one that constrained Whitehead to atomize becoming, in order to give meaning to the possible.

Of course, the distinction between good and evil must be created, not accepted as is. In this case, Whitehead takes up the great rationalist tradition that refuses to believe that evil can be desired for evil's sake. All that exists produces its own value, and all values are positions, to be described positively. The distinction between good and evil cannot, therefore, be a radical opposition. It may, however, entail the consequences of a position for its environment: physical suffering or mental suffering, where it matters little whether they designate others or one's own person. Between people who cannot help doing what they feel they should not do and who suffer as a result, and people who make others suffer, the difference is entirely relative, concerning only the definition of the environment, according to whether it includes, or fails to include, the person who causes the suffering. If he read it, Whitehead would have approved the world of Erewhon invented by Samuel Butler, in which the sick are punished and the criminals cared for, as being perfectly reasonable. In any case, whether the subject is evil or illness, the problem is the same: how can they be understood without ending up in a position which, by making God responsible for good, should also lead to holding him responsible for evil and suffering?

The fact of the instability of evil is the moral order in the world.

Evil, triumphant in its enjoyment, is so far good in itself; but beyond itself it is evil in its character of a destructive agent among things greater than itself [. . .] Evil is positive and destructive; what is good is positive and creative [. . .]

This instability of evil does not necessarily lead to progress. On the contrary, evil in itself leads to the world losing forms of attainment in which that evil manifests itself [. . .] *For example, a species whose members are always in pain will either cease to exist, or lose the delicacy of perception which results in that pain, or develop a finer and more subtle relationship among its bodily parts.*

Thus evil promotes its own elimination by destruction, or delegation, or by elevation. But in its own nature it is unstable. It must be noted that the state of degradation to which evil leads, when accomplished, is not in itself evil, except by comparison with what might have been. A hog is not an evil beast, but when a man is degraded to the level of a hog, with the accompanying atrophy of finer elements, he is no more evil than a hog. The evil of the final degradation lies in the comparison of what is with what might have been. During the process of degradation the comparison is an evil for the man himself, and at its final stage it remains an evil for others [. . .]

There is a self-preservation inherent in that which is good in itself. Its destruction may come from without but not from within. Good people of narrow sympathies are apt to be unfeeling and unprogressive, enjoying their egotistical goodness. Their case, on a higher level, is analogous to that of the man completely degraded to a hog. They have reached a state of stable goodness, so far as their own interior life is concerned. This type of moral correctitude is, on a larger view, so like evil that the distinction is trivial (RM, 95–98).

Whitehead does not accept distinctions without transforming them. Not only does he not construct a distinction in content between "good" and "evil," but he risks a comparison between those who know what the good is, those in whom the question inspires no doubt, and those "completely degraded," who no longer even suffer from their debasement. The elimination of evil has destroyed "things greater than itself," but the judgment brought to bear upon these relative magnitudes is purely immanent: it is associated with the comparison between what is and what might have been. When the witnesses to what might have been disappear, it should be noted, this situation can be described in terms of the theory of the organism. If the good were to be defined by its endurance, "a stable state of goodness," it would depend, like a stable state of degradation, only on the patience of the environment: the maintenance of a unilateral position, insensitive to the possibly destructive character of the infection associated with it, alien to hesitation, that is, to what is possible.

God is not directly necessary for understanding the order of nature, what is affirmed as "good in itself," of which hogs, "good people of narrow sympathies," as well as the "professionals" of *Science and the Modern World*, constitute so many examples. He will, however, be necessary to affirm how a suffering being can develop "a finer and more subtle relationship among its bodily parts." It is this possibility that—like everything that matters—imposes a "cosmos" that is, at the same time, an evaluatory authority: in this case, God as the "measure of the aesthetic consistency of the world."

The kingdom of heaven is not the isolation of good from evil. It is the overcoming of evil by good. This transmutation of evil into good enters into the actual world by reason of the inclusion of the nature of God, which includes the ideal vision of each actual evil so met with a novel consequent as to issue in the restoration of goodness (RM, 155).

Whitehead's solution is not yet technically well constructed. For this to be achieved, it will be necessary for terms like "ideal vision," "consequent," and "so met with as to issue in" to be understood in such a way as to avoid attributing to God a form of "knowledge" that would guide creativity. In that case, indeed, what Whitehead always fought against would be restored: the figure of a God who "knows better," and who can therefore be judged responsible for the evil he allows, if only by abstention. The demand is already in place that this figure must be avoided: it is novelty, associated with relevance ("to issue in" . . .) that indicates the "kingdom of heaven," that is, that permits the affirmation of a "moral order," or a cosmos.

Whereas, one year previously, in *Science and the Modern World*, God was a principle of limitation, he has now become an actual but atemporal entity. He is part of the "formative elements" of the temporal world, in the same sense as creativity, which, for its part, is associated with the temporal passage toward novelty, and the domain of "ideal entities," not actual in themselves but exemplified in each actual occasion. God, like creativity and like the ideal entities, is required by the need to affirm not only the possible but also the insistence of the possible, that is, evil as what may be overcome. This is what is to be thought, and what Whitehead affirms, "as if it were done."

Nothing is done—and we will return to this point—but the "cavalier perspective" will be maintained, with its own risks. For it is not, in this case, addressed to those "adventurers of reason" known as philosophers, who are summoned to recognize themselves as such, to abandon the cult of any kind of power of reason in favor of the humor of an adventure of hope. In fact, the history of philosophy is so densely populated with bizarre risks, unusual positions, and unstable constructions, unanimously despised by real professionals, that it clearly exhibits that its mere endurance is the hope, constantly reborn, of overcoming incoherence, of making concepts hold together even at the cost of an edifice so implausible that it inspires only laughter on the part of the environment. Although they have dreamed of it, philosophers have never been excellent counselors to princes, and their concepts, in the final analysis, have caused little suffering. The same does not hold true of the Christian religion, and here Whitehead must hope that the "kingdom of heaven" testifies in his propositions. Will the Christians listening to him be able to accept that if God "knew" what the good is, in a sense that transcends the multiplicity of occasions of experience, if he constituted in this sense a stable measure of the good, a measure closed to progress, he would in turn be analogous to the man degraded into a hog, or to good people of narrow sympathies? This is the unknown of which Whitehead risks the question.

In fact, the suggestion of a moral order of the world implies a construction that has nothing religious about it. If the good is God's limitation, that is, the way that God can be qualified as an "actual fact in the nature of things," it is excluded metaphysically, that is, grammatically as well, that God should know what the good, which is his limitation, is. To know one's own limitation is not to be limited but subject, it is to be able to envisage evil even when one can will only the good. This may be an extrapolation, offering God the strange metaphysical compliment of being "like us, only better," free as we are, but "free for the good," a happy state which, according to Augustine, was promised to Adam if only he had resisted the trial of temptation. Above all, however, it is the fatal combination of the rational and the empirical that enables God to be fashioned in the image of man, by means of a passage to the limit that eliminates imperfection by making pretensions pass to the infinite. Whitehead, for his part, tries to think of the cosmos, not of man who, in one way or another, God would have made in his own image, a typical example of the excess of subjectivity that is to be corrected. And the cosmos, different from every state of affairs, does not correspond to any "image." In short, what is assigned to God is a role or a function.

The fact of "not knowing" is not a lack, but the characterization of a mode of working. Grammatically, God cannot have available an abstract definition, independent of the "actual world," opposing the good to the bad, because it is the very nature of his functioning to contribute to the immanent possibility, for each creative act, of creating that difference. God is that thanks to which each act of creation can integrate within its own process the important possibility of "overcoming" evil. Not evil in general, but always "this" evil here and now, or "this" destructive position, insofar as it cannot affirm itself without denying. Correlatively, the good has no identity in itself. It is never good that overcomes: it is evil that, because it is overcome, designates a good that has no other identity than this overcoming, that possibility of articulating what was destructively opposed.

Whitehead will articulate this metaphysical proposition in a more satisfactory way in *Process and Reality,* when he makes creativity his "ultimate." In *Religion in the Making,* however, the first point is to think of religion, and hence the adventure that we empirically inherit. And here, Whitehead, undeniably, belongs to his time. What he undertakes to describe is nothing other than *"the Ascent of Man"* (RM, 38), the emergence of what can be described as co-creation of the religious sentiment, and of the truth of consciousness for itself.

This doctrine is the direct negation of the theory that religion is primarily a social fact. Social facts are of great importance to religion, because there is no such thing as absolutely independent existence. You cannot abstract society from man; most psychology is herd-psychology. But all collective emotions leave untouched the awful ultimate fact, which is the human being, consciously alone with itself, for its own sake.

Religion is what the individual does with his own solitariness [...] *Thus religion is solitariness; and if you are never solitary, you are never religious. Collective enthusiasms, revivals, institutions, churches, rituals, bibles, codes of behaviour, are the trappings of religion, its passing forms. They may be useful, or harmful; they may be authoritatively ordained, or merely temporary expedients. But the end of religion is beyond all this* (RM, 16–17).

By religion, it seems we must understand what Whitehead called "religious vision" in *Science and Modern World,* to distinguish it from religion as an institution. This time, however, we should pause over this question of the religious vision, for here we are at the starting point of a speculative adventure, and no longer of the description of the modern world. Hasn't this adventure, which recognizes neutrality as its primary obligation and its first being-put-to-the-test, just emitted a somewhat "cavalier" judgment against what it calls "social fact," to identify it now with herd psychology?

There are two ways to understand such a text. If we understand it in a register that ratifies the judgment emitted against those who were unaware of the truth of their solitude, we will have to think that Whitehead, after Hegel and at the same time as the almost unanimous chorus of his contemporaries, is allowing himself to celebrate the appearance of monotheistic religions as participating in the emergence of a truth that transcends history. Yet it is equally possible to understand it on an empirical level, without which I would have to conclude that the speculative interpretation, in this case, has been blind to its own risks.

The risk associated with the link between religion and the feeling of solitude is to authorize a reading of human history as a site of the revelation of a truth endowed with the power of judging. And in this case, in the first place, to assign a "herd psychology" to all those peoples who have thought of themselves in terms of belonging. In such a case, there would indeed be "technical weakness," for what has been celebrated as the "disenchantment of the world," Man's discovery of his own solitude, has been and still is the basic reference for all the modes of presentation that link monotheism to the denunciation of attachments said to be idolatrous. Solitude, if it were an "ultimate fact" in this sense, would place speculation in the service of the most routine judgment possible against those who are protected by their "beliefs" from the terrible news: they will, after all, have to recognize, like us, that their ancestors are dead, that their fetishes have no other power than the one they lend it, that the world is deaf to their rites and indifferent to their superstitions. In short, Man's solitude cannot be expressed without destructive opposition, dooming those who cannot bear to live alone to the pain of awakening, for their greater good.

It is possible, however, to affirm that Whitehead here presents himself as the heir to an "empirical fact," precisely the one that is to be described in another way, to be produced according to a cavalier perspective that reveals the importance of novelty against the pretenses which, historically, have turned that novelty into the discovery of a preexisting truth. The novelty that constitutes the awareness of man's solitude, an ultimate fact as soon as it is felt, would then be separated from all coincidence, finally realized, between fact and right.

Usually, what one becomes aware of, in this case, solitude, is defined as preceding the acquisition of awareness. Solitude is then what "Man" primordially fled, taking refuge in the certainties of the group, until he found the courage to accept the hard truth. For Whitehead, however, "becoming aware" means to produce, to bring something new into existence in the guise of the interpretation of the old. No interpretation can claim to be a simple elucidation of something already there. And, in this case, even herd psychology belongs to the contrast produced by novelty: by tautological definition, what the solitary consciousness despises, against which its cry rises up when it seeks its respondent in God. Job dares to demand an account from God of the evils overwhelming him, dares to affirm that his cry finds an advocate before God, the witness and defender of a cause that no false friend could convince him to deny. But those he silences because they bear witness, from this new viewpoint, to a "herd psychology" are his own contemporaries. Their "conformism" belongs to the same epochal fact as his protest, and thus legitimizes it in a very normal way. All refer together to the same general dogma that God is just, to derive divergent consequences from it: Job to demand justice, his friends to ask him to return to the ranks, to accept his case as deducible, in one way or another, from the dogma.

In the book of Job we find the picture of a man suffering from an almost fantastic array of the evils characteristic of his times. He is tearing to pieces the sophism that all is for the best in the best of possible worlds, and that the justice of God is beautifully evident in everything that happens. The essence of the book of Job is the contrast of a general principle, or dogma, and the particular circumstances to which it should apply (RM, 48).

Here, of course, still and once again, the figure of a typically Whiteheadian circle presents itself. The contrast between principle and circumstance that raises the question of divine justice is new, associated with the monotheistic figure of an omnipotent God. Yet this contrast also belongs, typically, to the risks proper to the rationalist adventure, always liable to eliminate what does not correspond to the postulated reasons. In this sense, this contrast is part of what commits Whitehead to the construction of his cosmology. Job's cry rises up to the heavens and returns to earth in the form of the risks associated with Whitehead's speculative interpretation: how can we hear this type of cry while correcting the excess subjectivity it conveys, and avoiding the exacerbation of factual suffering by the feeling of injustice that tortures the solitary consciousness? How can we say that the words that make the difference between just and unjust *matter* but belong to an idiom and do not express an ultimate generality, without, however, joining the number of Job's false friends? Without having recourse to the Leibnizian trick named "the best of worlds"? The risk proper to Whitehead's cosmology, the wager of his adequacy, is not that Job is satisfied, but that he is transformed, and that the transformation of his experience bears witness to what is to be trusted: not the good *qua* more powerful than evil, but evil *qua* liable to be overcome.

No reason, internal to history, can be assigned why that flux of forms, rather than another flux, should have been illustrated. It is true that any flux must exhibit the character of internal determination. So much follows from the ontological principle. But every instance of internal determination assumes that flux up to that point. There is no reason why there could be no alternative flux exhibiting that principle of internal determination. The actual flux presents itself with the character of being merely "given." It does not disclose any peculiar character of "perfection." On the contrary, the imperfection of the world is the theme of every religion which offers a way of escape, and of every sceptic who deplores the pre-vailing superstition. The Leibnizian theory of the "best of possible worlds" is an audacious fudge produced in order to save the face of a Creator constructed by contemporary, and antecedent, theologians. Fur-ther, in the case of those actualities whose immediate experience is most completely open to us, namely, human beings, the final decision of the immediate subject-superject [. . .] is the foundation of our experience of responsibility, of approbation or of disapprobation, of self-approval or of self-reproach, of freedom, of emphasis. This element in experience is too large to be put aside merely as misconstruction. It governs the whole tone of human life. It can be illustrated by striking instances from fact or from fiction. But these instances are only conspicuous illustrations of hu-man experience during each hour and each minute. The ultimate freedom of things, lying beyond all determinations, was whispered by Galileo— E pur si muove—freedom for the inquisitors to think wrongly, for Gali-leo to think rightly, and for the world to move on despite of Galileo and inquisitors (RM, 46–47).

The freedom, in other words, for Whitehead, to perhaps "have made a mistake," to have transformed his reader, or the Christians listening to him, into enemies, ready for any kind of violence if they cannot affirm that, in one way or another, their truth has the power to emerge victori-ous against error. Job may well have been right to refuse the hypocritical consolations of his friends, but we must also imagine a Job suddenly furi-ous in the face of the "consolations" of a Whitehead telling him, "Yes, of course, the feeling of injustice to which you bear witness has a respon-dent," only to add, "and the same is true of what you denounce as resig-nation, indifference, or hypocrisy on the part of your friends, and also of the course of the world, which is free to reduce you to a wreck on a pile of manure, whether you like it or not, and whether your friends like it or not."

"But I demand that the injustice I have undergone be genuinely real, that no one in the world may say that what I am feeling is of the nature of a fact! And if you tell me that this demand is also of the order of fact, all I have left will be violence to make you understand that your tender-ness and your humor are unbearable to me—that I prefer, like Samson, to destroy the universe rather than admit the nonexistence of a beyond which, here and now, justifies me, me and me alone."

The suffering of this cry corresponds to what Whitehead calls evil, for what is affirmed proclaims its need for the destruction of what is greater than the cry. Was it provoked by metaphysical neutrality? Certainly, if the latter insisted on proposing itself "at the wrong season," which is a typical trick of evil. This is why Whitehead's text never exhibits, as I have just done, the test his categories constituted for our sense of the true and the just. His cavalier and artificial perspective then seems to describe, whereas it is betting on a transformation that it does not describe. My commentary, just as cavalier, implies a change of epoch and a change of risk. The empirical fact is that what I experience as "what is to be avoided" is the possibility of constituting human solitude as an ultimate, and that what I feel as "what is to be anticipated" is the possibility that my reader may consider "the death of God" to be an irreversible fact, with regard to which any hesitation is regression.

The vast causal independence of contemporary occasions is the preservative of the elbow-room within the Universe. It provides each actuality with a welcome environment for irresponsibility. "Am I my brother's keeper?" expresses one of the earliest gestures of self-consciousness. Our claim for freedom is rooted in our relationship to our contemporary environment (AI, 195).

"Am I my brother's keeper?" This cry of Cain comes, rather curiously, to interrupt a technical development in which Whitehead was discussing the past, present, and future in reference to the physical theory of relativity, as is indicated by the term "contemporary." For Whitehead, two occasions are contemporary if neither belongs to the past of the other. In usual relativistic terms, what does not belong either to the past or the present of an event (for those who might be reminded of something by this, what is situated outside Minkowski's double cone) belongs to its "elsewhere." And this is indeed what Whitehead is attempting: to raise to the power of metaphysics the independence of the *here* with regard to the contemporary *elsewhere*. Our contemporary environment does not doom us to say "we can't believe it any more." I am not the guardian either of what my epoch defines as an "ultimate fact" or of what it defines as an "irreversible acquisition."

Whitehead no more takes the side of Cain, claiming irresponsibility, than he does that of Job, who demands an account of the evils overwhelming him; no more of Galileo—the ancestor, albeit despite himself, of all those who will answer to the hypothesis of God by this call from the heart: "but He does not really exist!"—than of the inquisitors who proposed that Galileo accept that his thesis was only a hypothesis and that it does not pertain to man to constitute the world as the respondent for his ideas. The freedom for the world to move, whatever Job and Cain, and Galileo and Bellarmin, and Whitehead and Nietzsche or Artaud may think, since its very movement has produced them all, the dissonant heirs of unforeseen possibilities of feeling and of suffering, of affirming and

destroying, of demanding accounts, reasons, and justifications, those possibilities that are our fate, that comment on us and render us thinking.
And if speculative philosophy has a meaning, it is in slipping among
these possibilities, of new modes of laughter, of cavalier creation, and of
humor: we ought not to exaggerate.

Freedom for what inherits! A refusal to raise the vibrant continuities,
the mandates accepted, the risks prolonged, to the power of metaphysical
or existential affirmation. A refusal to confer an excess of legitimacy on
what may have been taken up again, confirmed, echoed in multiple testimonies and adventures. A refusal to justify a lineage by ratifying the eminent quality it assumes, whose consequences it should loyally unfold. A
refusal to come to the aid of victory, blessing what has taken place, that
is, also kicking what might have been when it is down. For what we can
testify to has certainly found in us its proxies. But the importance of the
testimony does not consist in its fidelity, and above all, no testimony is
possible with regard to the crowd of what has cried in vain, of what has
found no other echo than a touch of worry, a certain something that silently testifies that something that might have been is not. Every perspective is cavalier.

Whitehead's cavalier perspective, whether he is addressing philosophers, the authors of concepts that have so often made reason rhyme
with power, or Christians, who, in the name of the power of Truth, have
destroyed what their words disqualified, is neither that of a righter of
wrongs nor of a denouncer. The present does not have to take charge of
what has been excluded, to become the guardian and spokesman of its
own culpability. Irresponsible, it cannot help but decide for the epoch to
which it belongs. The terrible question—to defect, or to assume a pain to
whose truth one no longer adheres—yields to the speculative problem:
"What might this epoch be capable of?" A humorous problem, because it
leaves undecided, and undecidable, the question of whether what this
epoch might be capable of belongs to it, or topples it into the past. Yet it
is also a technical problem, and it is up to Whiteheadian concepts to create its terms, to create the actual possibility of belonging to an epoch
without letting oneself be defined by it.

Here, speculative empiricism reencounters something of what Nietzsche called a "hammer-thought," supposed to crush and abolish what
cannot bear it. Whereas the hammer crushes things, Whiteheadian empiricism "makes things hold together," but it does so in a rather perverse
way, apt to demoralize the judgment that, as an excess of subjectivity,
never ceases to come in second with regard to all experience, and every
possible that is sensed, never ceasing its claim to submit what has hap-

pened to a measure authorizing its pronouncement. In both cases, the test is in the present. The Nietzschean eternal return: you who judge, you will return again and again, carried, produced, and nourished by what you think you can judge. Tender Whiteheadian perversity: the rights conferred upon you by the critical consciousness by which you authorize yourself are a wonderful illustration of creativity; they will be added to the many, and perhaps be articulated with what they claimed to disengage themselves from. What you claimed to judge once and for all will return in new contrasts.

The eternal return is indeed the Similar, repetition in the eternal return is indeed the Identical—but precisely resemblance and identity do not exist prior to the return of what returns. They do not initially qualify what returns, they are absolutely merged with its return. It is not the same that returns, it is not the similar that returns, but the Same is the returning of what returns, that is, of the Different, the similar is the returning of what returns, that is, of the Dissimilar (DR, 384).

CHAPTER EIGHTEEN

Feeling One's World

W E ARE NOW up against the wall. Enough of putting things in perspective: what demands to be thought will have to be populated with concepts. First of all, that which, in *Science and the Modern World*, had not succeeded in being thought: actuality, which is "the only value." As we recall, the Whiteheadian approach, following the lead of the "possibilities of value," had failed in the pragmatic sense. It was incapable of awakening the appetite for what abstraction left out of consideration. The "flight of experience" brought about by "eternal activity" did not cause a new sun to rise, germinating new questions. We must therefore forget this eternal activity and start all over again in another way; starting out this time from the only thing that, according to the ontological principle, is a cause for the ontological principle: the actual entity.

That the actual entity is a "feeling" of "its" world is what Whitehead tried to think from beginning to end of *Process and Reality*. And if there is one thing that must first be associated with "feeling," it is the notion of a vector. To feel is "to be affected by," that is, at the same time, to confer upon what is felt "there" the power to have an effect "here." The point is thus to take literally the common-sense statement "this thing is present in my experience insofar as it is elsewhere," and to construct its concept, even in its most phantasmagorical consequences. The temptation to escape this "immediate fact" of experience is inseparable from the misplaced concreteness associated with the notion of simple localization. It is this temptation which, for Whitehead, inspired the set of sleights of hand through which metaphysics becomes judgment, disqualifying what we sense in favor of what we judge reasonable, sleights of hand that are destined to wind up at what is, for once, a genuine phantasmagoria, that of the bifurcation of nature. In other words, the choice is between a conceptual deployment that exhibits the actually fantastic character of experience, of any experience, and a retreat of this experience to reassuring categories which are, above all, not to be followed too far in their consequences, for they lead straight to the absurd. That is to say that for Whitehead, there is no choice. This, moreover, is what is affirmed by the fourth category of explanation, introducing the "principle of relativity."

The principle of universal relativity directly traverses Aristotle's dictum, "A substance is not present in a subject." On the contrary, according to this principle an actual entity is present in other actual entities (PR, 50).

We had to begin by recalling this because this may be what is most difficult to accept in Whiteheadian metaphysics. We have, for better or worse, become accustomed to think that two bodies can interact "at a distance," that is, *qua* distant, but we are reassured by the fact that distance makes itself felt (at least in the definition of the gravitational interaction), and that the interaction responds to a regular mathematical function. Here, the conceptual scandal is fully deployed, irreducible to a redefinition of space-time as Einstein proposed it. If I feel something, this thing certainly enters into the definition of my experience: it belongs to my experience, and it is not forged by my experience. I sense it insofar as it testifies to something else. I produce myself *qua* feeling that which is not me.

"To feel," of course, insofar as it holds true both of an electron and of a mathematician contemplating a sunset, cannot answer the ironic questions that will arrive in throngs. Feeling is appropriate to every actual occasion, whereas the perceptions we might invoke as examples—and especially those that are apparently most simple, the most apt to found serious thought, the whiteness of that house I see out there, through the window—refer to the occasion *qua* belonging to a highly sophisticated social environment. The felt contrast between "here" and "over there," by which Whitehead characterized the "percipient event" in *The Concept of Nature,* is by no means generic. What is generic—and what this contrast requires if nature is not to bifurcate—is that the "sophisticated route" of occasions that gives meaning to the percipient event should nowhere be reducible to a construction that brings forth an illusory "there" for an experience that is in fact localizable, belonging only to the "here" of perception. The vectorial character of feeling translates the "delocalization" of every "here."

If the concepts constructed in *The Concept of Nature* are henceforth defined as relative to a highly sophisticated experience, because they designate the perceiving mind as ultimate, what will be taken as generic, belonging to the ultimate generalities, is the statement that there is the feeling of an "object" by a "subject." At the risk, of course, that "subject" and "object" may find themselves slightly redefined.

The philosophy of organism is the inversion of Kant's philosophy. The Critique of Pure Reason *describes the process by which subjective data pass into the appearance of the objective world. The philosophy of organism seeks to describe how objective data pass into subjective satisfaction, and how order in the objective data provides intensity in the subjective satisfaction. For Kant, the world emerges from the subject; for the philosophy of organism, the subject emerges from the world—a "superject" rather than a "subject." The word "object" thus means an entity which is a potentiality for being a component in feeling; and the word "subject" means the entity constituted by the process of feeling, and including this process [...] the process is the elimination of indeterminateness of feeling from the unity of one subjective experience* (PR, 88).

We have indeed left behind the "flight of experience" induced by eternal activity, for the contrast between potentiality and actuality no longer presupposes an "underlying" activity. Every object is defined as potentiality, calling for determination: feeling, well and good, but how? The atomic character of becoming is, however, preserved. Once an actual occasion has produced its own determination, once it has satisfied all of its obligations, it has simultaneously achieved and produced "its" specific satisfaction. All indeterminacy is consummated. *The many have become one.* Whitehead calls this fully actualized subjective unity "superject." The subject becomes so that a superject may be.

The many have become one ... and is augmented by one. The being-world, a veritable Leibnizian monad, a producer-product enjoying the adoption-of-a-position that has actualized "its world," can no longer be the syntactic subject of a process, since every process corresponds to a becoming-determined. Definition, the soul of actuality (PR, 223), has been produced. Henceforth, being what it is, the occasion perishes *qua* subject-superject, *qua* subjective immediacy, to become a "that which": that which others will feel.

This doctrine of organism is the attempt to describe the world as a process of generation of individual actual entities, each with its own absolute self-attainment. The concrete finality of the individual is nothing else than a decision referent beyond itself. The "perpetual perishing" (cf. Locke, II, XIV, 1) of individual absoluteness is thus foredoomed. But the "perishing" of absoluteness is the attainment of "objective immortality" (PR, 60).

Time, according to Locke, was "perpetual perishing," but Whitehead goes back beyond Locke toward the *Timaeus,* where Plato concludes that what is conceived by opinion with the help of sensations, and thus outside of reason, is in incessant becoming but never really "is." And he happily accepts this verdict.

Completion is the perishing of immediacy: "It never really is" (PR, 85).

Of course this borrowing ignores the Platonic intention, in a cavalier way. If what becomes "never really is," what traditionally designated the subject, the sense of self, the immediacy of subjective presence to oneself, never really *are* either. It is therefore not a matter, as in Plato, of casting doubt on the category of becoming, but of affirming that becoming as such is indeed ungraspable, since it is the grasp itself that "makes things become." What I can grasp, what I will say "is," is nothing other than what has become, what has achieved "satisfaction." It is bereft of meaning for itself, but it is henceforth "public," available for objectivation, which will make it an ingredient for new becomings.

In other words, Whitehead here takes up as a metaphysical principle what characterized the relation of cogredience explored in *The Concept of Nature.* Satisfaction marks the transition of the present to the past, and this means a radical change of nature. "That which" we feel belongs to the past. But this past is not in flight, inaccessible. Quite the contrary, it is what will *have to be felt.* Like a book as soon as it is published, however, it is incapable of stipulating how it should be felt; it is a potentiality for feeling. One can indeed say "my past belongs to me," but this is a tautology. What has achieved "objective immortality" belongs by definition to whoever feels it. My past belongs to you as much as to me, although you do not feel it in the same way.

In fact, it is well known that whoever endeavors to think of an experience as "truly hers" of course *ipso facto* makes it topple into the past. It may then no longer have any present existence except as a term for an anxious contrast, bringing into play the purely rhetorical hypothesis, suspicious or downright worrisome, that its property is only an illusion. And if I have to deal with a genuine project of questioning "my" experience, even this contrast can be eliminated, leaving to what I claim as mine only the abstract position of a pretext, a reference. I will then embark upon an adventure of panic, as uneven as shooting the rapids: the stereotyped pleasure of confrontation, the anticipation of traps and retaliations, impatience inspired by the feeling of being the victim of the other's bad faith or manipulative talents, the suspicion of an ungraspable misunderstanding, the fear of emerging victorious without having understood what the other meant, and so on. All of that collides and becomes entangled in a way that is so shaken up that I could very well say later: "I couldn't see heads nor tails in it any more." Sometimes, moreover, the only way to find one's bearings is a brutal break, an outright refusal, a transition into action. For Whitehead, however, these ambiguous experiences testify to the fact that each experienced continuity is a produced continuity, a veritable miracle of resurrection of what was "dead"—that is, "public"—available for something other than itself, beyond itself.

The concrescence, absorbing the derived data into immediate privacy, consists in mating the data with ways of feeling provocative of the private synthesis. These subjective ways of feeling are not merely receptive of the data as alien facts, they clothe the dry bones with the flesh of a real being, emotional, purposive, appreciative. The miracle of creation is described in the vision of the prophet Ezekiel: "So I prophesied as he commanded me, and the breath came into them, and they lived, and stood up upon their feet, an exceeding great army" (PR, 85).

The import of the "inversion of Kant's doctrine," which has here become the "miracle of creation," can never be overemphasized. Kant's problem was that of the "knowledge" of what presents itself as an "object" for a subject. As such, this problem was the heir of a long tradition of controversies, which, in the Middle Ages, caused the emergence of the notion of "objective reality," not in the sense of "as it exists," but in the sense of "that to which" thought refers. This problem, constantly relaunched, was that of the relation between objective reality and the thing "in itself," that is, its "essential" or "formal" being, as conceived and created by God. In other words, the problem of creation was above all a problem of knowledge, forcing us to think of the relation between the creative Intellect and man, the image of God, who knows "objectively," whereas God conceives/creates. Whitehead adopts a convergent line of approach with regard to this tradition: knowing is the name for a (particular) form of creation, and what is created is always inseparably creator and creature, making what it emerges from its own.

The fact that we have to do with a "miracle of creation" obviously does not imply a contrast between "natural" and "supernatural." Creativity is the ultimate. To talk about miracles is a way of recalling this, of recalling that nothing is capable of causing "naturally" or "by itself," that every efficacy presupposes that *the many become one* and renders it explicit, but without ever being able to explain why *the many* is capable of becoming *one*.

As we have seen, among the "causes" of the process is the subject itself. Determination cannot be assimilated to a consequence that could be deduced from initial data: as a mathematician, Whitehead knows that the problems that were able to find this kind of solution are part of the past of mathematics, but that a genuine problem, in the present, implies a face-to-face confrontation between mathematicians and their data. Mathematicians, however disarticulated may be their thought in this confrontation, are "purposive." Likewise, the subject is not only what determines itself, but what aims at its own determination, its completion as a superject. This means that the superject is not merely the end point of the process but is "already present," as a final cause, as that whose production orients the progressive determination. The separation between subject and superject is thus a simplification, and Whitehead will, moreover, make frequent use of the inseparable binome subject-superject.

Prehensions are not atomic; they can be divided into other prehensions and combined into other prehensions. Also prehensions are not independent of each other. The relation between their subjective forms is constituted by the one subjective aim which guides their formation. This correlation of subjective forms is termed "the mutual sensitivity" of prehensions [. . .] the prehensions in disjunction are abstractions; each of them is its subject viewed in that abstract objectification. The actuality is the totality of prehensions with subjective unity in process of concrescence into concrete unity (PR, 235).

Here, Whitehead uses the term "prehension," which, according to his categories, is more general than that of feeling. A feeling is always positive, including what is felt in a synthesis, whereas a prehension may be "negative." What is prehended will then be eliminated from the unified complex feeling in the course of determination. Yet what matters more generally is the impossibility of defining a prehension independently of the process of subjective determination. Prehensions do not explain the unity that comes into being, without being explained by it. No explanation is ever unilateral in Whitehead, none can abstract from what the ontological principle demands: among the actual entities entering into explanation appears the final cause that the entity in the course of constitution constitutes for itself. All explanations therefore set in motion a set of reciprocal presuppositions that designate what they all presuppose: creativity.

Concrescence thus implies a twofold convergence: the subjective forms (the "how" of feelings) converge upon a superject, while the multiplicity of data of these feelings converge upon one datum, the actual world of the "satisfied" entity. Here again, Whitehead is thinking like a mathematician, because for a mathematician, a well-defined function expresses and implies a convergence. If a series diverges, it does not define a mathematical object. When the mathematician becomes a metaphysician, however, convergence ceases to be the condition for a definition and becomes a process of determination; and the construction of convergence that brings to existence a single, well-determined world, as "what is felt," is just as much the one that brings to existence the "subject" for which there is convergence, the subject who feels this world. Satisfaction and determination coincide.

In *Science and the Modern World*, Whitehead had made up his mind to atomize becoming in order to make the possible exist in an irreducible mode, that is, in order to relegate to a specialized abstraction what mathematical physics regards as its great exploit: to reduce change to a function of well-defined variables. One of the ways of expressing the satisfaction that closes the process of the constitution of an actual occasion is to say that each felt entity, functioning as a datum for a feeling, belongs henceforth and ultimately to a quite determinate, functional actual world, to a community within which it has a well-determined function or role.

Calculemus, Leibniz had proposed, and here we may understand this exhortation in its fully deployed sense. It is no longer directed to rational human beings, already constituted and gathered together by an active "we," endowed with rights and duties, proposing to submit a situation to a consensual calculation. The "miracle of creation" calls for a double creation, strictly inseparable, of the "we" and of what is to be calculated. This is specified by categories of explanation XX, XXI, XXII, and XXIII.

(xx) That to "function" means to contribute determination to the actual entities in the nexus of some actual world. Thus the determinateness and self-identity cannot be abstracted from the community of the diverse functionings of all entities [...]

(xxi) An entity is actual, when it has significance for itself. By this it is meant that an actual entity functions in respect to its own determination [...]

(xxii) That an actual entity by functioning in respect to itself plays diverse rôles in self-formation without losing its self-identity. It is self-creative; and in its process of creation transforms its diversity of rôles into one coherent rôle [...]

(xxiii) That this self-functioning is the real internal constitution of an actual entity. It is the "immediacy" of the actual entity. An actual entity is called the "subject" of its own immediacy (PR, 25).

These categories of explanation by no means justify that we can make a state of affairs correspond to a function. They do, however, enable us to understand that this is (approximately) possible, as physics testifies, and to connect this possibility to endurance, both from the viewpoint of the person speaking or attributing and of the being to whom a role is attributed, or of the state of affairs to which a function comes to correspond.

To be able to attribute a role or to make a state of affairs correspond to a function is essential to what we call explaining, interpreting, telling a story; but all these exploits profit from a continuity they cannot justify. Prior to us, it is our words and our organs that already capture, exhibit, and select the invariants of all kinds, in relation to which their own functional role has been established, a role, moreover, that has no need of "consciousness." As Emile Meyerson pointed out, the dog who catches a stick thrown in the air shows himself able to "calculate" the trajectory which, since Galileo, mathematicians have learned to describe by a mathematical function. In no case, however, will the identification of the two meanings of "function"—the one that refers it to a continuous state of affairs, and the one that designates the role assumed by a prehension in the functioning of an actual entity—be justified. "To function" in the sense of categories XX, XXI, and XXII is absolutely not "to be defined by a function," and the same is true of the "actual world" of an entity, never to be confused with a "common world" that would preexist its appropriation.

Just as Descartes said, "this body is mine"; so he should have said, "this actual world is mine." My process of "being myself" is my origination from my possession of the world (PR, 81).

The "nexus" of actual entities that Whitehead calls the "actual world" is in no way a "state of affairs." It has no enduring identity of its own, no identity that does not come from its appropriation by a concrescent process. Does it even constitute "a" world independently of the taking possession of "its" world by each entity? As we shall see, this will be one of the sites of transformation of Whitehead's position. Let us recall already, however, that one of the formulations of the ontological principle specifies that there is no real togetherness that is not a being-together in the formal constitution of an actual entity. And in fact, when, in the fourteenth category of explanation, Whitehead must render explicit what the definition he has given of the nexus *qua* third category of existence can possibly mean ("nexus," or "public matters of fact"), he avoids using the term *together* or *togetherness*. Instead, he has recourse to the neutral and static term *set*. We may think of a set as a "collection" of objects that may well be united only by the common feature of having pleased the collector.

That a nexus is a set of actual entities in the unity of the relatedness constituted by their prehensions of each other, or—what is the same thing conversely expressed—constituted by their objectifications in each other (PR, 24).

The "miracle of creation" is then the transformation of a "set" into a "togetherness." Yet, as I will not tire of repeating, the term "miracle" permits no savings. We must now take up the question that remains pending, the question of what is required by this transformation of a set into a togetherness so that what is "ultimately" felt may not in any way be assimilated to a result in the sense of physics (summation) or of logic (deduction). Here again, it is perhaps the example of physicists articulating their functions that may guide us. The question physicists address to their subject-matter is not "what does the world look like," but "what variables and how should they be articulated," what to take into account, and how. The question is that of "what" and "how."

It is here, of course, that the eternal objects will be required. They are defined very briefly (the fifth category of existence) as "pure potentials of specific definition." The categories of existence, because they precede those of explanation, cannot "be explained." They will generally be rendered explicit by a category of explanation, in this case the seventh category.

That an eternal object can be described only in terms of its potentiality for "ingression" into the becoming of actual entities; and that its analysis only discloses other eternal objects. It is a pure potential. The term "ingression" refers to the particular mode in which the potentiality of an eternal object is realized in a particular actual entity, contributing to the definiteness of that actual entity (PR, 23).

We will encounter the question of eternal objects again and again. What matters, already at this stage, is not to attribute to them the responsibility that Plato attributes to his Ideas. The eternal objects are not determinant, but "potential for determination." They are what determination requires, the definition of the "how" of each feeling, but no particular "how" constitutes a privileged path allowing us to rise back up toward an eternal object. The eternal objects, as Whitehead repeats, "are what they are," and they tell no story about their ingressions (PR, 256): in other words, they explain nothing, justify nothing, guarantee nothing, privilege nothing, especially not intellectual operations in search of abstraction.

Correlatively, the term "ingression" is here again a primary term. This does not mean that Whitehead will not ask the question of which eternal objects make ingression into which actuality: quite the contrary. Yet the question of a "mechanism of ingression" is not to be asked, for this would imply that ingression is explained on the basis of eternal objects. Because ingression is ingression of an eternal object, it is mute. All reasons will have to fit with statements that take actual entities as their reason: actual entities are the only reasons.

In *The Concept of Nature*, Whitehead had placed the object's ingression into an event under the banner of a resolute refusal of all explanation: "The event is what it is because the object is what it is," but "objects are what they are because events are what they are" (CN, 144–145). Here, we may say that the ingression of an eternal object has the consequences it has because the actual occasion is what it is, but it must immediately be added that this occasion is only itself because it is determined as it is determined. This is what is affirmed by the ninth category of explanation:

That how an actual entity becomes constitutes what that actual entity is [...] *Its "being" is constituted by its "becoming." This is the "principle of process"* (PR, 23).

The process is reality, but reality is not pure flux, it is "realization," and the process must be just as much said to be a "process of determination." This is why eternal objects are required. One might be tempted to call them "abstract" because they are separate from all questions concerning actuality. And one can indeed do so, but on the condition that the term "abstraction" be divorced from the verb "to abstract," and be connected only to the adjectives "pure," "separate," "impassible." This is another way of saying that the question of realization must be radically separated from that of knowledge, and from all the distinctions we produce between abstract and concrete knowledge. Whitehead confirms this when he amuses himself by juggling with the concepts we have inherited from medieval philosophy, together with the link created by this philosophy between categories of existence and categories of knowledge.

The notion of a universal is of that which can enter into the description of many particulars; whereas the notion of a particular is that it is described by universals, and does not itself enter into the description of any other particular [...] *both these notions involve a misconception. An actual entity cannot be described, even inadequately, by universals; because other actual entities do enter into the description of any one actual entity* [...] *Thus every so-called "universal" is particular in the sense of being just what it is, diverse from everything else; and every so-called "particular" is universal in the sense of entering into the constitutions of other actual entities* (PR, 48).

The eternal object is exactly what it is, and as such, it is unknowable, unnamable. This is so, not in the manner of the God of negative theology, by his eminence, but because the verbs "to know" or "to name" refer to (sophisticated) modes of feeling, all of which presuppose the determination of the "how." If eternal objects have nothing to do with what we call an abstraction, in the sense of an "abstract characterization of a situation," it is because they characterize nothing, but are required by the "how" of each characterization. When physicists try to understand, wondering how to articulate their function, that is, what variables to choose, one will not address eternal objects in order to understand what they are trying to achieve, to justify the order they are trying to abstract from their data. Although every comparison is dangerous, however, the reference to eternal objects, whose ingression "contributes to the definiteness of an actual entity," can be more analogically adequate when what is at stake concerns physicists trying to understand, to "realize," the way in which their problem can (perhaps) be solved. For the adequate analogy is the one that enables the celebration of a process of co-creation of physicists and of their function. Indeed, what is in play is the twofold transformation of a perplexed, hesitant being, and of a mass of disparate, partially redundant information, indeterminate with regard to its meaning, into a being who knows how to take each item of information into account in a determinate way, the meaning of some of them being determined by their articulation, by the "how" of their taking-into-account, and others being defined as ultimately insignificant.

An eternal object, in abstraction from any one particular actual entity, is a potentiality for ingression into actual entities. In its ingression into any one actual entity, either as relevant or irrelevant, it retains its potentiality of indefinite diversity of modes of ingression, a potential indetermination rendered determinate in this instance. This definite ingression into a particular actual entity is not to be conceived as the sheer evocation of that eternal object from "not-being" into "being"; it is the evocation of determination out of indetermination. Potentiality becomes reality; and yet it retains its message of alternatives that the actual entity has avoided. In the constitution of an actual entity:—whatever component is red, might have been green; and whatever component is loved, might have been coldly esteemed (PR, 149).

As is specified by the principle of relativity stated by the fourth category of explanation, "it belongs to the nature of 'beings' to be a potential for each 'becoming'" (PR, 22). What has happened has happened, and will have to be felt as such. One may perhaps—Whitehead does so—speak of negative prehension with regard to beings, but this will not mean exclusion, only indistinction, or reduction to insignificant noise. When it comes to eternal objects, however, the notion of negative prehension will take on a decisive importance: by negative prehension, an eternal object *may be eliminated*. Even if its ingression had been determinant in the constitution of what the concrescence inherits as "having to be felt," it can itself be excluded from the synthesis that determines the way in which this concrescence will satisfy the obligation. A component that was loved can be inherited in the mode of indifference, and it will soon be submerged by the great noise of the world.

The actualities have *to be felt; while the pure potentialities* can *be dismissed. So far as concerns their functionings as objects, this is the great distinction between an actual entity and an eternal object. The one is stubborn matter of fact; and the other never loses its "accent" of potentiality* (PR, 239).

Because the eternal objects may be "excluded from feeling," actual worlds may diverge. The Leibnizian idea of a convergence among all viewpoints toward "the same world," with each monad including, in its way, the totality of the world, had already been abandoned in *Science and the Modern World*. For a decision to be concrete, it must not only reflect a finite viewpoint, which would be the case if the decision bore only upon what will be taken into account in a distinct way and what will be felt in a way that is merely obscure. It must be partial, in the sense of capable of eliminating the "how" that defined something that is being felt. The mirror must be broken and the metaphor of reflection abandoned. It must be possible to decide that one doesn't want to know about it, that one is not one's brother's keeper. In *Science and the Modern World*, this possibility was ensured both by the discrimination concerning being and not-being (the ideal situation) and by all the non sequiturs, "this far but no farther," that affirmed the limited character of the problematic horizon with regard to which a decision is taken (God as the principle of limitation). And all of this referred to the triple envisagement of eternal activity. It henceforth pertains to each entity to "explain itself" with regard to what it takes into account, and with regard to the way it will evaluate what it takes into account. Convergence is the work of the subject as it becomes a superject while it appropriates "its world," which did not preexist this appropriation *qua* "world" but *qua* nexus or set.

The actual world is thus what is expressed, whose expression is the subjective satisfaction, and it is categorically impossible to separate expression and expressed, to conceive the expression in contrast to what is expressed. This impossibility must even be stated twice. It derives, first, from the fifth category of explanation of the Whiteheadian scheme, which may recall the Leibnizian principle of indiscernibles, according to which no two identical viewpoints on the world exist, nor, therefore, do two similar blades of grass.

That no two actual entities originate from an identical universe [...] the nexus of actual entities in the universe correlate to a concrescence is termed "the actual world" correlate to that concrescence (PR, 22–23).

To this impossibility, which is "poor" because it is compatible with the fact that there are "nearly similar" viewpoints, or nexūs, another must be added. In fact, it is the very possibility of "comparing" that is in question when one distinguishes the initial nexus, as a set, from the actual world as a subjective "togetherness." The comparison abstracts from the "private" character of the subjective synthesis, designating what is compared in the mode of objectivity, and therefore implying its "public" character, available to be felt. In order to affirm the categoreal error constituted by any evaluation about the way an actual entity has evaluated its world, Whitehead has recourse to a term that comes straight from the medieval tradition.

I will adopt the pre-Kantian terminology, and say that the experience enjoyed by an actual entity is that entity formaliter. *By this I mean that the entity, when considered "formally," is being described in respect to those forms of its constitution whereby it is that individual entity with its own measure of absolute self-realization* (PR, 51).

The distinction between "formal" and "objective" belongs to pre-Cartesian philosophy and reflects the hiatus between the divine Intellect, which makes conception and creation coincide, on the one hand, and the human intellect, to which "objective reality" corresponds, on the other. Yet Whitehead, not without humor, takes this distinction from Descartes at the very moment when Descartes, in the responses to the *Objections* that follow his *Meditations,* tries to close the problem and to focus the philosopher's effort upon "objective reality" alone. Descartes, Whitehead affirms, expressed the very thesis of objectivation he himself defends, when he writes,

Hence the idea of the sun will be the sun itself existing in the mind, not indeed formally, as it exists in the sky, but objectively, i.e. in the way in which objects are wont to exist in the mind; and this mode of being is truly much less perfect than that in which things exist outside the mind, but it is not on that account mere nothing, as I have already said (PR, 76).

What neither Descartes nor the medieval thinkers had foreseen is that the distinction between "formal" and "objective" would be disengaged from the question of knowledge, to be extended to everything that happens.

Every actual entity, once it has determined itself, will be "objectified" by others: its "being" will be that it is to be felt. And if this "way of being" can be said to be "imperfect," this is because what will be objectified is not the indivisible unity of the actual entity for itself, its "formal" unity, *causa sui.* What will be objectified, called upon to participate in a new process, is an entity henceforth defined as analyzable, endowed with a "morphology" that articulates as its "parts" all the feelings that converged into a unique, nondecomposable satisfaction.

The peculiarity of an actual entity is that it can be considered both "objectively" and "formally." The "objective" aspect is morphological so far as that actual entity is concerned: by this it is meant that the process

involved is transcendent relatively to it, so that the esse *of its satisfaction is* sentiri. *The "formal" aspect is functional so far as that actual entity is concerned: by this it is meant that the process involved is immanent in it. But the objective consideration is pragmatic. It is the consideration of the actual entity in respect to its consequences* (PR, 220).

An entity will be objective *qua* prehended by another entity. It itself has, in one way or another, "satisfied its obligations": nothing more can happen to it; the consequences of what it has "made happen" concern entities other than it, that is, the entities that will prehend it. The entity prehended by others as a defined, obstinate, established fact imposing the question of its consequences, is not, as Descartes said, a "pure nothing." But its consequences will have to be produced, and it is up to what prehends it to produce them, to confer upon them their determinate identity, their pragmatic value.

In other words, objective consideration does not initially center around the question of knowledge, even if all knowledge is also pragmatically taking-into-account. It is generic: every actual entity in its process of constitution is obliged to take into account what has taken place, what is publicly imposed as having taken place but which is, as such, asignificant, waiting for the pragmatic significance others will confer upon it.

In contrast, when Whitehead "tells the story" of the way an entity decides for itself by itself, formally, proceeding to what he calls a genetic analysis or division, he is characterizing a "private" process. This means that such an analysis is obviously an abstraction, and more precisely, it abstracts from the fact that it cannot be carried out by anyone. It constitutes an ontological impossibility because there exists no possible "hold" on the process of concrescence. In fact, between *Science and the Modern World* and *Process and Reality,* we can say that Whitehead has "simply" switched abstractions. Eternal activity could only be characterized in abstraction from actuality, which is also impossible. The problem, however, was not that it is impossible but that the abstraction did not inspire any appetite for that from which it had abstracted: a failed framing of the problem. Genetic analysis—just as impossible—will, for its part, be a success if it obliges the reader, and Whitehead himself, to think.

In fact, the categories that deal with concrescence as such are called "categories of obligation." The point is neither to describe nor to explain, but to produce a set of constraints that impose on thought a regime of reciprocal presupposition. A "leap of the imagination" may answer these categories, but it is a vertical leap, conferring on words the capacity to evoke, not to designate. It is not that process "transcends" language, but what is appropriate to it is the component of stammering in language, the *"well, what I mean is . . . "* or the *"how should I say . . . "* in which what hesitates is not a set of potential statements but the very wording of the words, their articulation, together with the "I" who "should say."

The analogy is, of course, false from a twofold perspective. On the one hand, stammering refers to a "route" of occasions, each one of which has produced its own satisfaction for itself. Moreover, once "what one meant" has finally been said, the relief, the conscious impression of success, translates a message about the alternatives avoided, about the possibility of a stammering that aborts in a renunciation. Likewise, when physicists or mathematicians construct a function that converges, it is a genuine achievement against the background of possible failure, the conscious experience that one has succeeded in constructing what is required for a function to have a meaning. But the convergence as producing a unique, well-determined functional world, as realized by the subject "who feels its world," is not, for its part, a "success," in the sense that it never "misses."

No actual entity can be conscious of its own satisfaction; for such knowledge would be a component in the process, and would thereby alter the satisfaction (PR, 85).

In no case will an actual entity, as such, be able to become "conscious" of the role it assigns to what it feels, of the way it "functions." "Becoming conscious" is never "coincidence with oneself" but is always relative to a *de facto* continuity. Achieving convergence, for the actual entity, means to perish from immediacy, and it cannot be sanctioned by any "becoming conscious" which, as such, might be bequeathed to what follows it. Correlatively, consciousness, for instance, the feeling that one has more or less succeeded in saying what one "meant," does not refer to any dynamic of advent of the truth, but should rather evoke a mutation that affects its social environment, characterized by a new distribution between what is "mine" and "not mine," a mutation that we do not yet have the means to explore.

Let us return to concrescence, the site of the process of convergence. It cannot, for its part, give any meaning to an experience of success. What is more, it translates and renders explicit the fact that creativity, Whitehead's ultimate, is neutral with regard to the distinction between cosmos and "disordered" multiplicity. Whatever the individual satisfaction, it is always an exemplification of creativity. However, one cannot stop here. If incoherence is to be avoided, concrescence, as such, must provide the means for approaching the cosmic question. In itself, the ambition of metaphysical neutrality to which it responds presupposes in effect, by construction, a reference to the cosmos: it presupposes the possibility of correcting the awareness of its excess subjectivity.

As we saw when it came to characterizing evil, the destroyer of "greater" things: all satisfactions cease to be equal from a cosmological viewpoint, a viewpoint that makes a difference between the creation of new contrasts and the static chaos produced by the sempiternal clash between ways of inheriting characterized by the reiteration of the negative prehensions of what each has to deny in order to affirm itself. This cosmological viewpoint, like every genuinely cosmological viewpoint, whether it refers to Stoic thought or to that of Leibniz, puts us to the test. It designates a kind of truth access to which is at the same time a transformation of those who accede. Adjusted to metaphysical neutrality, the cosmological test may be so described: people who hate the world that clashes with their aims or hopes, hate their world, the one they have provided for themselves by producing themselves as hateful, denying or relegating to irrelevance all that might have been felt as worthy of love. Yet in order to function, this test must correspond to a possibility of feeling on the part of the person who hates.

In this process [of concrescence], *the negative prehensions which effect the elimination are not merely negligible. The process through which a feeling passes in constituting itself also records itself in the subjective form of the integral feeling. The negative prehensions have their own subjective forms which they contribute to the process. A feeling bears on itself the scars of its birth; it recollects as a subjective emotion its struggle for existence; it retains the impress of what it might have been, but is not. It is for this reason that what an actual entity has avoided as a datum for feeling may yet be an important part of its equipment. The actual cannot be reduced to mere matter of fact in divorce from the potential* (PR, 226–227).

Without negative prehensions and the scars they leave, Whitehead's system would be incoherent, since there would be an arbitrary disconnection between neutral metaphysics and the cosmological viewpoint. As we have already seen, the ingression of eternal objects gave meaning to what, in a sophisticated experience, might be called "experience of the possible": "Potentiality becomes reality; and yet it retains its message of alternatives which the actual entity has avoided." Of course, one will not say that a route of electronic occasions, for instance, can take such a message into consideration. Here, we must distinguish between what is generic and what matters. The message is generic, but it can matter only to routes of occasions that are highly sophisticated, those for which modes of experience dominated by the "subjective emotions" that we call resentment, hope, despair, hate, or trust have a meaning; those, therefore, for whom the difference between chaos and cosmos counts. And it is also for these routes of occasions that the "scars" left by a feeling's struggle for existence may matter. Their generic character makes it possible for nature not to bifurcate, and for consciousness not to be responsible for the feeling that something else was possible. They are required by the cosmos, if the difference between convergence by elimination and convergence by new contrasts is not to impose itself like a "divine judgment" falling upon indifferent beings. A contradiction must be able to be felt as a dead end, or as a defeat.

In the Whiteheadian universe, then, one is never even with regard to anything, although to consider oneself even is part of a perfectly legitimate way of inheriting. Of course, all of Whitehead's work bears witness to the possibility of transforming scars into data, into contrasts that are felt in the mode of an obligation. One must succeed in affirming together what has been felt, and what this feeling has excluded in order to occur. Underlining the traces testifying to the insistence of what philosophers have nevertheless eliminated as negligible, in the name of the coherence of their system—typically the unexpected affirmative emergence, at the hazard of one of his discussions, of what a philosopher intends to exclude—constitutes for Whitehead a principle of reading in the field of the history of philosophy. This is not to criticize the author but to constitute the protocol of his own undertaking: to include and affirm together what seemed doomed to contradiction. However, for the very principle of this work to be coherent with what it affirms, it had to be authorized categoreally. For speculative philosophy, which explodes the categories of empiricism and rationalism by adding enough reasons to save all the facts together, to be possible, negative prehensions had, by categoreal definition, to leave scars.

If, however, the eternal objects and the scars left by what has been avoided are required by the possibility of a cosmos, they by no means suffice to guarantee it. More precisely, they are neutral with regard to the possibility that evil may be overcome. In fact, the message concerning alternatives may add venom to the wounds; the decision to avoid may be intensified by resentment and find itself stabilized by that resentment. As for the possibility of inheriting in a way that integrates a feeling that has as its datum what was an emotional tone, that is, a feeling of the contrast between what has been and what might have been, it certainly testifies to a sophisticated experience, but it is not "good in itself." Justice-dealers can be public dangers: they can empower the "trick of evil," imposing the importance of a feeling at the wrong season, making the future of a society hesitate between regression and the creation of new contrasts.

More generally, the nine categories of obligation (the fifth of which will be, as we will see, eliminated in the course of writing) only detail what "obliges" inheritance, or the way an entity produces itself by inheriting from the past. They are neutral with regard to any idea of "moral" obligation. The "atomic" character of the entity is respected: it is "its" satisfaction that the entity pursues as its final cause, not cosmic harmonization. As we will see, even with regard to God, the atomic character of this pursuit will be maintained. Albeit barely: Whitehead will have to avoid that the "divine ordering" that "conditions creativity" be that thanks to which an entity, while pursuing its own end, contributes to the best of worlds, like a donkey urged along by a carrot. If he had failed on this point, God would have been, if not the creator, then at least responsible for the cosmic order, like the person holding the carrot is responsible for the donkey's progress.

In other words, the difference between cosmos and chaos has no direct translation into the categoreal scheme. It will, however, take on a more concrete meaning when it comes to the creative advance itself, that is, by and in the production of what makes a difference that matters, which Whitehead henceforth calls "society."

CHAPTER NINETEEN

Justifying Life?

N A MUSEUM the crystals are kept under glass cases; in zoological gardens the animals are fed. Having regard to the universality of reactions with environment, the distinction is not quite absolute. It cannot, however, be ignored. The crystals are not agencies requiring the destruction of elaborate societies derived from the environment; a living society is such an agency. The societies which it destroys are its food. This food is destroyed by dissolving it into somewhat simpler social elements. It has been robbed of something. Thus, all societies require interplay with their environment; and in the case of living societies, this interplay takes the form of robbery. The living society may, or may not, be a higher type of organism than the food which it disintegrates. But whether or no it be for a general good, life is robbery. It is at this point that with life morals become acute. The robber requires justification (PR, 105).

Only the "anti-specists," that new variety of saint, can assign themselves the goal of teaching their cats to appreciate vegetarian food. And unless they have recourse to genetic manipulations, they will not be able to transform the situation "in general," but will have to address each cat, one by one. The cat's mode of existence implies the death of mice and birds, and that of the least cell implies the destruction of sophisticated chemical edifices. Life is robbery, and the robber requires a justification. Not any specific robber, this cat eating this mouse, but the general principle that singularizes life, the link between order and destruction. Life therefore implies the cosmological question.

The distinction Whitehead proposes between crystals and "living societies" corresponds to the contemporary distinction, associated with the work of Prigogine, between "equilibrium structures" capable of maintaining themselves indefinitely, requiring only that the environment maintain itself more or less as it is, and "dissipative structures," the price of whose existence is "dissipation": "something" in the environment must be consumed to nourish the permanent processes whose structure expresses its articulation. Yet Whitehead does not intend to raise the general question implied by this distinction: for him, a cyclone, as a typical dissipative structure, would not have required a cosmological justification. The cosmological question arises with regard to "life," for in this case destruction is not merely a fact. The history of life is, among other things, that of an active invention of means for locating, grasping, seducing, capturing, trapping, and pursuing. A cyclone does not seek out the most heavily populated zone to feed on the ravages it causes. It goes where it goes. To tell the story of the evolution of living beings, by contrast, is to tell the story of an increase in the creation of ever more effective modes of destruction, inventing new preys for new predators.

That what is under discussion is the moral order, and with it the "cosmos," will be a shock for biologists. The celebration of the moral harmony of nature is part of their prehistory. Evolutionary biologists are proud of describing the history of living beings as essentially opportunistic, and therefore rebellious to everything that might resemble the unity of a project, an intentionality, or even a measure capable of defining progress. On this last point, Whitehead might perhaps speak of an excess subjectivity: a testimony, certainly, to a success of human consciousness—to have succeeded in not constituting itself as the norm and truth of the evolution of living beings—but a testimony that is mute about all that is implied by the very possibility of this success. A speculative position cannot, for its part, be content with the twofold, rather abstract satisfaction of having escaped both anthropocentrism and the morality of nature. As always, when we have to do with speculative philosophy, the point is to be concrete, that is, complete. And therefore, to render contrasts explicit, whereas scientists, in the name of evolutionary history and the unity of one nature, accentuate resemblances.

As an example of such contrasts, let us take the term "opportunity." When used by biologists, it allows the successful denial of the need to describe such-and-such a living being *qua* responding to a goal, or *qua* means for the realization of a project. Yet to characterize evolution as opportunistic, if it is not one abstraction denying another abstraction, in this case denying the characterization of evolution as finalistic, calls for a whole series of requisites. An opportunity does not exist without something capable of seizing it, that is, of inventing it *qua* opportunity, *qua* possibility "for" something new.

"Opportunity," possibility "for": these terms are not metaphysically neutral. They refer directly to the question of the cosmos, and hence to the question of God *qua* conditioning creativity. It is in fact the question of the "divine ordering" that may well "require a justification." However, Whitehead makes it clear that this ordering by no means implies a "project," a global vision, a finalized "order of nature." Hence the terminological choice on which I have already commented:

If we say that God's primordial nature is "vision," we suggest a maimed view of the subjective form, divesting it of yearning after concrete fact—no particular facts, but after some actuality. There is deficiency in God's primordial nature which the term "vision" obscures [. . .] "envisagement" is perhaps a safer term than "vision" (PR, 33–34).

Here again, Whitehead may have been thinking against Leibniz, against the image of a God able to "read" in the slightest state of a monad the total series of states it unfolds in the course of time, thus bringing to existence those monads whose harmonious totality will give meaning to a particular world, the best of all possible worlds. In that case, life would be justified without any particular question, together with the world, with everything referring to a single unknown, that of the definition God has given to the "best." Job's friends would be right.

God yearns after concrete facts, whatever they may be: the future, whatever its mode of existence in the divine "subjective form," will not appeal to the realization of a particular possibility but to the concrete fact as such: "some actuality" as *causa sui,* self-determining its own value. Otherwise, God would have a position analogous to that of Socrates, who, in the *Meno,* waits for the slave to say to him, "Yes, Socrates, you are right." That would be a caricature of the "yearning" Whitehead portrays. Socrates is not yearning after an answer, whatever it may be; he is waiting for the "yes" that will allow him to move on to the next stage in his argument.

With the question of life as requiring justification, we are thus beginning the maneuvers to approach a terrain that did not exist prior to the flight of speculative experience. What remained somewhat incoherent in *Science and the Modern World* will also be explored: on the one hand, eternal activity had no need of obstinate and destructive living beings; on the other, organisms were defined as "limited to being none other than themselves," that is, as being their own justification. Coherence, this time, must be satisfied in a positive way, without easy ways out or half-solutions. Thus, with regard to the way the divine envisagement is deficient, the rather poor idea should be proscribed that God conceives the future "in broad outline," and is therefore yearning after an actuality that should specify what he conceptualized only in a "vague" way. Such an idea would imply that Whitehead not only read Leibniz with the radical lack of indulgence that a mathematician may reserve for another mathematician because they both share the same ideal of the well-framed problem, but that he read him badly. For between a "vague" possible and a determinate reality, what interposes itself is the multiplicity of universes that diverge as radically as one may wish. For Leibniz, there is no opposition between "Adam the sinner" and "Adam who resists temptation," hence participating in the history of an eternal paradise, but a difference so minimal that precisely only God's vision could discern them. A God who coincides, in one way or another, with a mode of existence of the future *qua* "partially indeterminate" would, by contrast, be the God of a regular, stable universe, where Adam's role is robustly attributed, thus turning "our experience of responsibility, of approbation or of disapprobation, of self-approval or of self-reproach, of freedom, of emphasis" into an illusory construction. The reason Whitehead can be so hard on Leibniz is that they both affirm the same kind of world, a world that "bifurcates everywhere," although they affirm it by different means.

In Leibniz [. . .] the bifurcations, divergences of series, are veritable frontiers between worlds that are mutually incompossible; so that the monads that exist include the totality of the compossible world that comes into existence. For Whitehead (and for many modern philosophers), in contrast, bifurcations, divergences, incompossibilities, and disagreements belong to the same multicolored world, which can no longer be included among expressive units, but merely does or undoes following prehensive units and according to variable configurations, or changing captures (LP, 110–111).

The justification of life does not require a "higher freedom" that would see farther and wider than we. It requires "yearning" as such, a yearning directed both to what is done and to what is undone, in the "here and now" of decision: thus and not otherwise. Here, moreover, Whitehead meets Leibniz once again, for whether Leibnizian or Whiteheadian, the solution proposed to the question of the world's moral order will constitute a kind of "hammer-thought," according to the expression Nietzsche reserved for his hypothesis of the eternal return. Like this hypothesis, the Whiteheadian solution will pay no attention to the preservation of the particularities that are dear to us, which we associate with projects, disappointments, and even with our maintenance in existence through good and bad encounters. Yes, God "makes a difference," but for Leibniz as for Whitehead, this difference does not ratify the alternative between "being authorized to hope" or "having the right to despair"; it displaces it.

It is as if one told men: do your duty, and be happy with what will happen, not only because you could not resist divine providence or the nature of things (which may be enough to feel at peace, but not to be happy) but also because you have to do with a good master. And this is what might be called fatum christianum *(Th, 31).*

Yet how can one tell Job he has a "good master" without unleashing his fury? How can one tell a woman whose child has been eaten by a tiger that the "robbery" to which she has fallen victim has a justification? For Whitehead, the difference made by the hypothesis of God cannot evoke a secret harmony between a general justificatory principle and particular circumstances. It cannot ask Job to trust in God's justice, nor the woman to understand the loss of her child. Rather, it passes between despair as an eventual concrete fact—"*I can no longer find any reason to hope*" or "*life has made a hog out of me*"—and the ratification that would come to justify it—"*may the world that has betrayed my hopes be cursed!*" or "*well, then, a hog I shall be!*"—what Nietzsche called resentment. It implies the rather strange possibility of not despairing of the world, even when it crushes you or kills you.

The primordial appetitions which jointly constitute God's purpose are seeking intensity, and not preservation. Because they are primordial, there is nothing to preserve. He, in his primordial nature, in unmoved by love for this particular, or that particular; for in this foundational process of creativity, there are no preconstituted particulars. In the foundations of his being, God is indifferent alike to preservation and to novelty. He cares not whether an immediate occasion be old or new, so far as concerns derivation from its ancestry. His aim for it is depth of satisfaction as an intermediate step towards the fulfillment of his own being. His tenderness is directed towards each actual occasion, as it arises.

Thus God's purpose in the creative advance is the evocation of intensities (PR, 105).

"Evocation," the term chosen by Whitehead, is interesting: spiritualists do not command the spirits they "evoke": they only know how to call them, how to invite their coming. Likewise, one does not command memory, as Bergson showed when speaking of pure memory. Evoked memory emerges when consciousness becomes a "medium," passive and yet deliberate, the search not for a memory but for the way that memory allows itself to be approached, as it vacillates between expansion and flight. In both cases, the accent is placed not on a project but on a "here and now" on which everything depends, both suspension and opening up to a possibility of becoming. Yet although the term "evoke" is interesting, it does not authorize any analogy. There is no analogy between divine experience and those we can evoke; otherwise, it would lead us to what is obscene. While the groans of human suffering rise up, an indifferent God feeds on what, for him, corresponds to so many anonymous intensities.

And yet, God is indeed indifferent to what counts most for us: preservation. Divine evaluation is impartial and makes no distinction between a "new" occasion and an "old" one, deriving from a long ancestral line, while it is this difference that is implied by our complaints and our claims, our feeling of injustice and demands for justification. It is our life that is at stake and not some fundamentally anonymous "present," since as soon as I think of it as "mine," it will have slipped into the past, will have become objectively immortal, available for any objectification. If God is a "good master," it is not, as with Leibniz, because he has chosen the best of all worlds; but the test is analogous, for what his tenderness is directed to is deeply indifferent to us.

Correlatively, the justification of life does not imply, or at least not directly, what was the central notion of *Science and the Modern World*: the organism, whose success had to be defined as preservation or endurance. Yet this will not stop Whitehead from continuing to speak of his philosophy as a "philosophy of organism."

In the philosophy of organism it is held that the notion of "organism" has two meanings, interconnected but intellectually separable, namely, the microscopic meaning and the macroscopic meaning. The microscopic meaning is concerned with the formal constitution of an actual occasion, considered as a process of realizing an individual unity of experience. The macroscopic meaning is concerned with the givenness of the actual world, considered as the stubborn fact which at once limits and provides opportunity for the actual occasion (PR, 128–129).

According to this distinction between microscopic and macroscopic, the organism has lost what constituted its signification in *Science and the Modern World*. For there, it played the part of a key that allowed the question of the order of nature to be penetrated, in such a way that the diversity of cases was articulated to a unique definition. The organism and all the definitions it authorizes depend on a success: the organism exists insofar as it succeeds in enduring, that is, also, in infecting its environment with "patience." Yet the "microscopic" organism constituted by the actual entity no longer conjugates "endurance" and "success" at all. From now on, the organism articulates an "indivisible process of realization," on the one hand, which never fails because it always ends in what Whitehead calls "satisfaction," and, on the other hand, "objective immortality," what is given to be felt by others, an immortality being impartially accorded to everything that has satisfied its obligations, in whatever way, whether trivial or innovative. As far as this "macroscopic" signification of the organism is concerned, it seems to designate the role assumed by the environment. Yet it is only the actual world of an occasion as objectified by the ones that have to feel it. The dynamics of infection, in which the contrast between patience and impatience was played out in *Science and the Modern World,* has thus disappeared. The environment is "given," simultaneously limit and opportunity. It is no longer a "stake."

The organism is thus no longer anything more than a witness to the past, and yet, by its stubborn survival, it translates a continuity that is important to Whitehead. The "actual entities" are "final realities" or *"res verae"* (the first category of existence), as the organism was in *Science and the Modern World,* because they, like this organism, are a "unifying holding-together," and because, again like the organism, this holding-together cannot be described in the abstract mode of Aristotelian logic, in terms of a subject endowed with attributes. What the subject "attributes to itself" belongs to it only in the very act by which, as it constitutes itself, it attributes it to itself.

That which, in *Process and Reality,* "endures," a "mundane" success to which God is indifferent, has as its new name "society" or "nexus enjoying a social order." This is no longer a nexus *qua* "set," that which is correlated with every actual entity, where it is up to that entity to turn it into "its" world. It is a much more limited set, which includes actual entities having something in common.

A nexus enjoys "social order" where (i) there is a common element of form illustrated in the definiteness of each of its included actual entities, and (ii) this common element of form arises in each member of the nexus by reason of the conditions imposed upon it by its prehensions of some other members of the nexus, and (iii) these prehensions impose that condition of reproduction by reason of their inclusion of positive feelings of that common form. Such a nexus is called a "society," and the common form that is the "defining characteristic" of the society (PR, 34).

An abstract definition, to say the least, but we can understand its abstraction if we recall that the concept of society must succeed in what the organism sought to accomplish: to unite under the same definition all that "endures" in one way or another, whether electron or human person.

Two things are remarkable in this definition, which, of course, enables a rather clear relation with the eco-ethology associated by *Science and the Modern World* with entangled organisms. First of all, the "common form," felt positively by each member of the nexus. Then, the term "impose."

Form is the name Whitehead sometimes gives to the eternal objects, and it is important, here, to remember that the eternal objects do not dictate a particular mode for their ingression into an actual entity. Consequently, in the case of a society, the "positive feelings of that common form" does not mean that a form will be felt in the "same way" by each member. We thus are not dealing with a "social form." The defining characteristic does not in itself have the power to define: each occasion, as it includes positive feelings of the common form, has ensured the relevance of the defining characteristic, but each can confer a distinct role on what is in common. The only restriction is that this role must be positive. A society will not be defined by the fact that a form exists upon which none of its members confers a role. If one wished to define a "society" by a common positive reference to the truth, for instance, it could therefore include liars, if they know that they are lying, but not those to whom the difference between the true and the untrue is completely indifferent. And a common indifference cannot be the "defining characteristic" of a society.

The second remarkable feature is the link between ingression of the common form and the notion of imposition. The eternal objects, pure potentials, have no power to impose their ingression. If the fact that each member of a society includes a common element of form is imposed upon it, it is not imposed by a power associated with the form itself but by the other members of society: we have to do with a successful dynamics of infection.

It is thus society that inherits the link between endurance and success. Its endurance is not a right; there is no "common form" that imposes itself by itself on its members, but only the "fact" that the feeling of this form succeeds in imposing itself, infecting each new entity. Each, therefore, produces itself *qua* member of a society, because of its prehensions of the other members of this society; without any justification to transcend this fact. People to whom the difference between truth and lie is completely indifferent do not transgress anything, do not deny anything, do not break with anything. This is so even if they have to deal with others for whom this indifference must dissimulate a transgression, a negation, or a will to carry out a break, or even if it inspires on their part, as the case may be, the worst impatience: to insist on being born at the wrong season is the trick of evil.

Some commentators on Whitehead have regretted that "societies" did not receive the categoreal dignity of the *"res verae,"* or the actual entities which, according to the ontological principle, are "the only reasons." Life would then find a quite simple, even simplistic justification. It would be the process thanks to which ever more important beings, and therefore

reasons, would come into existence . . . including the State and the reason of the State? The anti-Dreyfusards would be right: the State is justified when it destroys the life of a simple private person.

This argument is a bit below the belt, I admit. But this is deliberate: the
point is not to denounce, but to call to the flight of experience. If societies
were to be *res verae,* all the terrains in which one could land would become swampy: experience would be bogged down in moral problems,
sometimes calling for operations of normative stabilization and discrimination. Such operations are the daily bread of sociology and political
philosophy (what is a sect?), but it does not pertain to speculative philosophy to simplify a difficulty that constitutes the daily bread of specialists. It is not up to it to propose to specialized undertakings, trying to
describe the variety of situations where what we have to deal with "holds
together," concepts on which these undertakings could rely, or rest, in
order to define "the proper way of approaching the situation"; all depend on what matters for them. The speculative aim is generic.

For instance, let us take as an example the classic question in sociology: should a human society be defined as a collective aggregate of preconstituted individuals, or as a collective whole, the subject of its own
adventures? For Whitehead, it is clear that it is no simple aggregate, for
an aggregate is made up of parts whose properties appear as susceptible
of being described and attributed, at least at a first approximation, independently of the situation of aggregation. Society as an aggregate would
presuppose that human beings are defined by "consciousness" independently of the collectivities in which they are born; that is, they would be
conscious in the same inevitable way as they breathe. Yet a human society is not a "whole" either, for if it were, human beings, defined as "parts,"
would be intelligible in terms of the kind of patience required for the
enduring success of that whole. This will seem to be an acceptable hypothesis only to sociologists who identify their knowledge with a disenchantment or demythification of the illusions of freedom—at the risk that these
sociologists may have to define how their science protects them from the
common lot. Specialized branches of knowledge have no need for rein-
forcement of what is their permanent temptation: to confer the power of
self-legitimatization upon some types of description.

The difficulty in defining a human society is obviously connected to
the fact that the project of definition matters to human beings, as is the
case for all the questions they can ask themselves with regard to what
they are, to what they belong to, to what they know, to what they owe,
or to what they think. And therefore, to what justifies them. "Whiteheadian sociology," because it raises the question of justification to its specu-

lative, cosmological power, cannot ratify any particular justification. If it were to construct a "good" definition of what matters, generic with regard to the specialized categories, a definition capable of specifying what justifies a society as such, this definition, whatever it might be, would become a weapon and raise the question of its own justification, of what justifies the destructions it will ratify in the name of what is then "cosmic progress." This is why Whiteheadian sociology will not involve definitions but "modes of thought," to take up the title of Whitehead's last book. What Whitehead proposes is the contrary of ready-to-think: instead, thought pluralizes itself in various modes according to the way it envisages the importance of the situation it is trying to characterize. To penetrate is to create.

To penetrate and to create, however, thought must be "equipped," and it is such an equipment that metaphysics offers it *qua* "neutral," that is, *qua* refusing to privilege a "specialization" of importance, in order to affirm creativity as an ultimate. In *Science and the Modern World*, Whitehead had thought that the notion of organism could "equip" thinkers, inspiring their aesthetic appetite for the order of nature *qua* variety of successes, to be described as such. But the organism gives no primordial meaning either to hesitation or to originality, or to doubt, or to the possible, without which thinkers themselves are inconceivable. The speculative equipment must enable resistance to all the "social reasons" that would relegate hesitation, doubt, and originality to mere psychology. This is why I choose to think, with Whitehead, that a society is not a reason, in the sense of the ontological principle, and does not enjoy any transcendence with regard to the entities who are its members. The "reason" of an entity's social belonging refers not to "society" but to other actual entities as prehended by that entity. The social nexus constitutes a more or less dominant environment for each entity that unifies itself *qua* one of its members. It is sometimes so dominant that the entity might seem to be explained on the basis of its belonging, which is the case each time we can define a nexus as a unique line of inheritance.

Such a nexus is called an "enduring object." It might have been termed a "person," in the legal sense of that term. But unfortunately "person" suggests the notion of consciousness, so that its use would lead to misunderstanding. The nexus "sustains a character," and this is one of the meanings of the Latin word persona. *But an "enduring object," qua "person," does more than sustain a character. For this sustenance arises out of the special genetic relations among the members of the nexus [. . .] These enduring objects and "societies," analysable into strands of enduring objects, are the permanent entities which enjoy adventures of change throughout time and space* (PR, 34–35).

What we have to deal with, in the sense that we can, if not explain it, then at least have the words to describe or characterize it, always refers to nexūs that "sustain a character," and that are, moreover, able to maintain it throughout the adventure our interest makes them undergo. Yet a character can always be transformed. The art of the Sophists, who had recourse to all the syntactic and semantic subtleties that language allows but also to that of the mathematicians, may be characterized as an exploration of transformations of character. The same holds true of contemporary models in biology and in ecology, which take us further and further away from the notion of "natural equilibrium" or the body's "wisdom" toward the exploration of the unimaginable and precarious sophistication of the roles, of the risky tinkering of functions, of the metastable assemblage of coexistences. In contrast, when a society is described as a "whole" made up of "parts," the description ratifies a stable assignation of roles, with the parts being measured and evaluated according to their service to the whole *qua* characterized by the function that articulates them. Biological macromolecules are then defined by their role in the metabolic concert, which enables the cell to be a functional part of an organ which . . .

The Sophists were denounced as immoral, veritable public poisoners who destroyed the adherence the citizens owe to the values of their society. Mathematicians are "amoral" in the sense that they adhere to their definitions only in a hypothetical way, and owe loyalty only to the adventure of mathematics. Consequently, it is particularly stupid to praise the "heroism" of mathematicians, if this term is to evoke the heroic sacrifice to which the part must, if the case may be, consent for the salvation of the whole, in the mode of the highest morality. Individual heroism responds to a successful social infection.

For example, consider the patriotism of the Roman farmers, in the full vigour of the Republic. Certainly Regulus did not return to Carthage, with the certainty of torture and death, cherishing any mystic notions of another life—either a Christian Heaven or a Buddhist Nirvana. He was a practical man, and his ideal aim was the Roman Republic flourishing in this world. But this aim transcended his individual personality [. . .] In this estimate, Regulus has not in any way proved himself to be exceptional. His conduct showed heroism that is unusual. But his estimate of the worth of such conduct has evoked widest assent. The Roman farmers agreed; and generation after generation, amid all the changes of history, have agreed by the instinctive pulse of emotion as the tale is handed down (AI, 290).

Regulus was a hero, but through the exemplary value of his choice, he inspires a mode of thought that celebrates the enduring value of an ideal capable of inspiring the sacrifice of those who henceforth adhere to the role that is assigned to them. The immediate assent inspired by his sacrifice may, of course, satisfy morality, but not a mode of thought that raises to the cosmic power the need to justify, not to praise, the "sacrifices" associated with maintaining living societies. And this is so, even when it is an ideal that demands this sacrifice in order to survive. The approval inspired by Regulus's choice belongs to the thought of the organism, not to the one that asks the question of the "justification of life."

Quite different is the perplexed silence inspired by the Original, and it is indeed this type of silence Whitehead produces for those who have approached his texts then moved away from them somewhat stunned, finding neither the possibility of adherence nor the incitement to become indignant and denounce. I have already risked, for Whitehead, the capital "O" that Deleuze reserved for those fictional characters, such as Bartleby, through whom one discovers "the power of an impersonal that is by no means a generality, but a singularity to the highest degree" (CC, 13). Here the circle closes. The need to think "with Whitehead" rather than "about Whitehead" is an example of the discrete efficacy that Whitehead himself associates with originality, such that it can infiltrate and, in this case, turn readers away from a reading that tries to "form an opinion" to which it can adhere.

Life lurks in the interstices of each living cell, and in the interstices of the brain (PR, 105–106).

For Whitehead, originality is the justification of the "robbery" that conditions the endurance of living societies. But no living society is original in itself. Every social success must be said to be "tradition," or successful reiteration. Life, for its part, "is the name for originality, and not for tradition" (PR, 104).

This contrast, however, does not imply an opposition, whether heroic or patient. One will not oppose living societies and novelty, habit and freedom, conformism and autonomy. Rather, one will ask the question of what social belonging makes possible. Is it not, in fact, this question that Whitehead explores when he constructs concepts that put to the test the rationalist tradition to which he himself belongs? Living societies are not opposed to life; they are what "shelters" the interstices in which life lurks; they constitute the environment needed by the "non-social" or "entirely alive" nexūs, which designate the ultimate social question: what may a given society become capable of?

The characteristic of a living society is that a complex structure of inorganic societies is woven together for the production of a non-social nexus characterized by the intense physical experiences of its members [. . .] *there is intense experience without the shackle of reiteration from the past* (PR, 105).

There is a typically academic snigger that consists of pointing out the limits to a thought's originality, all that it has borrowed, or accepted, without questions. But the events of thought associated with the names of the most "anti-social," or the most impatient thinkers, Nietzsche, Artaud, or Foucault, are neither placed in doubt nor diminished by all that they repeat, at the same time as they innovate. For if originality needs ūinterstices, it requires that with regard to which there is an interstice. Interstices do not even have to be defined against societies; they are just "to one side," as "non-social nexūs," correlated with experiences that are not adherence to the past, that are not intelligible either on the basis of the defining characteristic of a society, or, of course, on the basis of the rejection of that characteristic. But Whitehead is not celebrating what is nonsocial as such as if it were the justification of life. Originality is the justification of life.

Life is a bid for freedom: an enduring entity binds any one of its occasions to the line of its ancestry. The doctrine of the enduring soul with its permanent characteristics is exactly the irrelevant answer to the problem which life presents. The problem is, How can there be originality? And the answer explains how the soul need be no more original than a stone (PR, 104).

For Whitehead, a soul that would have both freedom and endurance is an unacceptable ontological setup, one of those setups that are proposed whenever too much confidence is accorded to an abstraction, accepted as such in spite of the dramatic bifurcation it leads to, between what would be free and what could be explained. One turns the soul into a "permanent characteristic," which means social conformity, and one attributes to it at the same time what contradicts that conformity: freedom. The logical contradiction, perfectly predictable, is transformed into a deep mystery.

Yet the same problem arises for any living society, insofar as it is envisaged from the viewpoint of the question that henceforth matters, that of the originality of its responses to its environment. The marvelous organization of living beings, with their strata and their functional hierarchies, does not answer this question.

We ask for something original at the moment, and we are provided with a reason for limiting originality (PR, 104).

One of the main effects of speculative thought is, in fact, to infect all the questions raised by living societies with the hesitations and uncertainties that are the lot of what we call "sociology." For Whitehead, it is always societies that we study. Everything is sociology, and human sociology, with all its difficulties, merely exhibits the questions, taken to their full exacerbation, that other sciences can neglect, insofar as they can neglect the question of originality, insofar as the way they study living societies does not impose upon them what constitutes the "justification of life." This is why Whitehead can no more tell us what a society is than Spinoza could say what a body is capable of. In both cases, "we don't know." We only know that the two opposite extremes, "my body belongs to me" and "I belong to my society," are both somewhat misleading simplifications.

No one ever says, Here I am, and I have brought my body with me (MT, 114).

I can, of course, say "my keyboard," "my fingers," "my body," "my tongue," "my text," and even "my reader," but the meaning of "my," marking possession, is obviously different each time. They are all mine, however, in the sense that they belong to "my" actual world, the one that requires the triggering of that chain of events of an indescribable complexity: to decide that there will be a "colon" here, introducing as an example the very situation in which, as I wrote, I make a whole world for myself of the question of how to use my experience as an example. An instant later, however, the reader on whom I have decided to "play this trick" has evaporated. Reader, you may well have smiled or become annoyed, and, if the straw broke the camel's back, you will perhaps have closed this book for good. That is no longer my problem, for it is the syntactic setup that has concerned me, as I hesitate between "my sentence" and "the sentence." It is this setup that had to be tamed, but it has also become the subject that now demands that "its author" show herself to be worthy of what, by her decision, that author has placed herself in a position of owing to it. Belongings are not only multiple but fluid and constantly entering into new assemblage. Between "that belongs to me" and "I belong to," the distribution never ceases being produced anew, while a subject, amazed to have been able to experience this, that, and that, never stops occurring and concluding. Likewise, belonging to societies of different types, endowed with different modes of endurance, is required to allow the production of that Cartesian affirmation—so original—"I think, therefore I am."

Far from constituting a "defining characteristic," my feeling of being "me," continuously, in a heterogeneous world in which my attention never ceases to vary, which the mutations of my interests, the permanent transformations of the "here" of my perception, never cease to recompose, is thus in itself an "exploit" requiring that the "chains of reiteration of the past" be constantly forged, tinkered with, and improvised. What is woven in this way is the thread of what Whitehead calls a "living person."

An "entirely living" nexus is, in respect to its life, not social. Each member of the nexus derives the necessities of its being from its prehensions of its complex social environment; by itself the nexus lacks the genetic power which belongs to "societies." But a living nexus, though non-social in virtue of its "life," may support a thread of personal order along some historical route of its members. Such an enduring entity is a "living person." It is not of the essence of life to be a living person. Indeed a living person requires that its immediate environment be a living, non-social nexus (PR, 107).

There is no reason to suppose that the kind of experience Whitehead associates with the notion of "living person" is reserved to human beings. In any case, it can designate all those living beings that have a sense of duration, that is, for whom the notion of "specious present," which Whitehead borrowed from William James, is relevant. Indeed, James's emphasis on the pseudo-continuous character of an experience made up of intervals and connections designates precisely what Whitehead defines as a thread of continuity, having a nonsocial living nexus as its immediate environment. A thinker does not think twice, a cat does not listen twice to an interesting rustle in a bush, but when one block of the present slips as such into the past, a thread of continuity, which is that of a process of appropriation, is woven. For the new present, the past becomes "its past," unless the strange experience of a hiatus should make itself felt. Thus, for instance, when I find myself at the wheel of my car on a habitual road that was not at all the one I had planned to take. Has the thread of a "living person" that had been "me" been broken, without anything having come to commemorate it, that is, to canalize it into a repetition that constitutes me as the owner of a memory? "Where" was I during that past, of which I cannot find the slightest memory? Was I paying attention, or was I distracted, and did I avoid a near disaster?

What I hope, in this case, is that the routines of my conduct were such that, in the case of something unforeseen, they would bring me back to myself in time, that is, that the entire social environment that explains what is meant by "driving a car" does not oppose "attention" to "routine." I hope, then, that the social routines of driving integrate that without which my distraction would risk being fatal. This particular hope may be misplaced, but it communicates with a more general question: how, from the viewpoint of the "justification of life," can we characterize social order in the sense that it is required by originality but does not explain it?

If we refer to that which, whether a work or the adoption of a position, is qualified, in our judgment, as "original," the relation between a society and the "interstices in which life lurks" first brings the "patience" of society into the spotlight. The "true professional" constitutes an environment that is impatient with regard to its interstices. When a society mobilizes for war, the interstices become imperceptible, and all originality is suspected of treason. Only a society that does not define the environment on which it depends as a threat can tolerate originals. And the fact that a state of emergency can, moreover, signify bracketing a large number of "traditional" usages, may perhaps confer an important meaning upon the term "tradition": one might say that only a tradition is liable to cultivate the interstices that make originality possible. And in that case, originality itself cannot be defined as antisocial, nor as asocial either: originals, even if they are solitary, have fashioned for themselves a world of habits, rhythms, objects, places, and distances that are carefully dosed with their contemporaries. If one can nevertheless say that they do not "belong," it is insofar as originals constitute their fellows, their contemporaries, as an "outside," which certainly obligates their own mode of existence, but according to a "how" that disconcerts any effort to make them a participant in a "we" by which they could be explained, including in terms of impatience with our routines (the trick of evil). A "how" that makes us feel the misplaced character of any characterization of originals as "exemplary." Whatever they finally may become, heroes, creators of epochs, openers-up of the world, great reformers, simple visionaries, traitors, prophets, public poisoners, martyrs, and so on, originality is not a virtue.

The fact that original humans require a society that does not denounce the person who escapes the "we" is an example of a general truth: for a nonsocial nexus to have original consequences, it must survive, and this requires protection. This is thus what justifies life, justifies the robbery that is the price of every living society. Such survival obviously has nothing to do with the question of the "survival of the soul." Far from designating the endurance of a lineage that is faithfully reproduced, it may evoke those experiences in which we must become "passive" in order to allow, within us and outside us, the prolongation of the process by which a thought searches for itself, in which what is often called an "intuition," fleeting and indecisive, takes shape, liable to evaporate at any moment, as if a gap were inexorably closing. In such experiences, it may seem that the universe itself holds its breath, which is perfectly correct from a Whiteheadian viewpoint, for these experiences exhibit the justification of life. They do not deny the social character of experience, but reflect a change in the mode of belonging. Everything we know, and can do, seeks to become an environment for something possible, which is not ours, because it is nonsocial, but whose eventual "socialization" depends entirely on "us," on the environment we constitute for it: a culture of interstices.

The culture of interstices is not the privilege of personal experience. It may also be a way of understanding ritual trances, divinatory utterances, and the objects manipulated by therapists, which open a human collectivity to an outside whose intrusion suspends habitual social functioning. However, interstices do not need to be deliberately cultivated. The fact that I can evoke such experiences, the fact that I know, and can think that my reader knows, what it means, for instance, to cultivate the type of attention to which a memory appeals, the fact that we can understand the mode of evocation Bergson analyzed in *Matter and Memory,* all these facts designate us as "conscious." But the interstices make themselves felt just as well without any "becoming aware": when a young child attempts her first steps, risks her first words, and bursts out laughing, when I learn a new type of gesture, when I stammer while trying to get to the end of a sentence, when I feel myself to be alive in a new world.

If life lurks in the interstices of each living cell, one may say just as well that the singularity of living societies, what justifies them as such, should be called a "culture of interstices." What belongs properly to human societies is the question raised by its interstices, at the risk that some social answers to this question may turn against their culture, for instance, when professionals are honored because they know how to refuse hesitation and adhere heroically to their role, or when freedom is set against determination, good against evil, order against disorder, subversive purity against recuperation. Words matter here, and the ones Whitehead uses first put to the test the oppositions that poison us.

Apart from canalization, depth of originality would spell disaster for the animal body. With it, personal mentality can be evolved, so as to combine its individual originality with the safety of the material organism on which it depends. Thus life turns back into society: it binds originality within bounds, and gains the massiveness due to reiterated character (PR, 107).

"Slowdown" is a term that may be just as fitting for Whitehead as for Bergson, to designate the socialization of the new—yet in different ways. Bergsonian *élan vital* is associated with a power that "falls back" or "becomes bogged down," with intuition disguising itself as reasoning. The slowdown associated with Whiteheadian life should rather be called "percolation": propagating from interstice to interstice until the flow itself becomes recognizable, describable, socialized, no longer interstitial but the thread of a living person. The sentence one begins while knowing (more or less) how it will finish, the self-assurance of the person who "knows" how to walk or to read, the experienced behavior that was, I hope, mine, when I took a wrong turn while distracted.

Correlatively, Whitehead will never oppose, as Bergson does sometimes, the "pure" to the interested, the busy, or the preoccupied. Jesus would have been one more visionary, destined, like a fleeting dream, to sink into oblivion, if his words had not subsisted inside a story, an institution that, to be sure, never ceased betraying them, but also never ceased being judged in the name of this betrayal. Every social inheritance is a betrayal, in the sense of "recuperation," but that which, as it makes society, inherits what was original, is transformed by what was betrayed, and creates the possibility of new interstices.

As far as "pure" originality is concerned, and the becoming that is irreducible to all explanation, they are, as such, neutral. Especially if the concern for having to remain pure comes to socialize them surreptitiously, if the pleasure of being the only ones to be right and contempt for the herd come to canalize them, they can be identified with what Whitehead calls evil. But "pure" originality, or life as nonsocial, is first and foremost erratic, as is moreover amply attested, since Whitehead, by experiments of so-called "sensory deprivation." When the "world" no longer provides a landmark, it is not that "I am another," as if this other assumed the features of a "foreign" personality, it is that without the possibility of "there," able to produce the invariants of recognition, the stable differentiation between "body" and "world" evaporates into the "non-social" saraband of a frenzied experience, impossible to narrate, and even impossible to reconstitute by means of memory.

The contrast between Whitehead and Bergson is thus rather obvious, and corresponds to the project announced as early as the preface of *Process and Reality,* to rescue the type of thought of Bergson, James, and Dewey "from the charge of anti-intellectualism, which rightly or wrongly has been associated with it" (PR, xii). Living societies, as the shelters for interstices, undo every binary opposition that might be transformed into a philosophical weapon of war. The distinction between living societies and life is not the one between intellectual reasoning and intuition. The effects of such a distinction are rather of a pragmatic type, and belong to the revision of our modes of abstraction, with which Whitehead associated philosophy.

"Living societies" are conceptual abstractions: we never have to deal with a living society as such, but rather with what requires that the social order not be the last word. The slightest cell, insofar as its reactions to external stimuli may be interpreted as adaptive—that is, as Whitehead emphasizes, original—requires what the social order as such cannot give meaning to. Even the worst professionals, the most insensitive with regard to what their judgments eliminate, may manifest a certain originality with regard to the way they reject objections. One may, of course, doubt this when one regularly hears physicists suggest that those who do not manifest the appropriate respect for the laws of physics, and thus believe that gravitation is a human invention, should throw themselves out the window. Yet we know that if those whom they address burst out laughing, and ask them if people confused doors and windows before Galileo and Newton, they would adapt their arguments without, for all that, changing their position. As Lewis Carroll's Red Queen said, it takes all the running one can do to keep in the same place. The fact that a living being can succeed in maintaining itself in a changing, uneven environment implies both a social order and interstices in which life lurks.

The conceptual distinction Whitehead proposes between living society and life thus does not confirm the opposition between repetitive, reproducible order and invention. In the case of living societies, reproduction itself requires invention, original approaches to an environment that is never the same twice; in short, it constitutes a social adventure. But this distinction matters when it comes to our modes of abstraction, and in particular the contrast between the way we address living and nonliving societies.

Today, it is no doubt the extremely sober version of this contrast proposed by Stuart Kauffman that fits best with the Whiteheadian difference. The success of physics and chemistry, as he emphasizes, is to define what they study as functions, involving a well-determined number of variables, that is, also, to describe the set of behaviors studied as belonging to the space of possibilities defined by these variables. The conservation of the number of relevant variables is an operative constraint, which is at work in the very definition of the object under study and the questions that will be asked of it. Reciprocally, it will be confirmed by the deductive character of the derived descriptions and explanations, whether deterministic or probabilistic. When it comes to the biosphere and the evolution of living beings, however, this constraint loses its relevance. Indeed, what matters henceforth is the expansion of the number of variables, that is, of the number of aspects of a situation that may come to matter, and that a relevant description must take into account.

Kauffman takes up the term "exaption," created by Stephen J. Gould, to designate the emergence of new meanings that come to associate themselves with a preexisting feature. The classic example is that of "proto-wings," whose adaptive role may have been associated with thermal regulation. The emergence of wings can then be described as a transformation of the meaning of the air, which ceases to be a mere factor of friction, to become a crucial ingredient of what we call "lift." A new possible has been created, modifying the definition of the biosphere, for this biosphere henceforth includes the multiple adventures of those beings who have a stake in flying.

If I am right, if the biosphere is getting on with it, muddling along, exapting, creating and destroying ways of making a living, then there is a central need to tell stories. If we may not have all the categories that may be of relevance finitely prestated ahead of time, how else should we talk about the emergence in the biosphere or in our history—a piece of the biosphere—of new relevant categories, new functionalities, new ways of making a living? (I, 134–135).

The interest of the Kauffmanian contrast is that it arises from a practice that pushes as far as possible the possibility of reproducing in biology the symbiosis with a formal language that characterizes physics. Kauffman is a specialist in the behavior of complex systems and in particular of connectionist networks, whose ambition is to construct a bridge between nonliving and living things. This is why what is put on stage is not a living order endowed with an intrinsic, inventive dynamic, but a pragmatic difference between the mode of abstraction appropriate for physics and chemistry and the one that is appropriate to living beings and the biosphere.

More generally, every scientist, but also every novelist, is, in Whitehead's terms, a "sociologist," for only societies can be characterized, only social adventures can be recounted. This also means that scientists, if they accept the Whiteheadian proposition, should know that their description, and, as the case may be, their explanations, require the social endurance of what they describe; in general, novelists are well aware of this. The distinction between nonliving and living societies reflects the difference between the pragmatic consequences of this knowledge. A living society may, of course, lend itself to descriptions in terms of stable categories, which claim to explain its workings in a mode analogous to the one that allows the modes of abstraction of physicists and chemists. Yet the sociologists whose description depends on the endurance of "living societies" cannot have the ambition of achieving the success of the physicist or the chemist, for what they have to deal with raises, in the first instance, the question of the relation that the social order maintains with its own interstices.

The primary feature of living societies is not a limitation on the power of our explanations, as it is the case, for instance, with a cyclone and its somewhat unpredictable behavior. Quite the contrary, they question our thirst for explanation, that is, our faith in explanation as what would suffice to define the attention they are due. Indeed, the "sociologists" who address such societies must learn to resist the temptation to explain their stability in the terms that this stability makes relevant. They have to learn to pay attention to the interstices, even if what lurks in the interstices has no significant consequences as long as the social order maintains itself. And when it comes to those who call themselves sociologists, that is, who address human societies, they must know that explaining their stability will merely ratify the categories and justifications produced by this society itself when dealing with what threatens its stability.

Thus, where we might be tempted to describe a static distribution between what matters and what does not matter, for instance, when we describe a society called "traditional," which perpetuates itself in a way that is apparently unchanged through a changing environment, perhaps we have to deal with a positive culture of interstices, with the adventure of a regime of original and permanent renewal, that ceaselessly re-creates what will be described as a relation of "traditional" belonging. As for a disciplined army, which is meant to obey like a single man in a terrifying environment, it cannot be explained by the soldiers' obedience to orders, or by training that would make them the parts of a single body. Here, novelists and filmmakers are better guides, as they echo the testimonies of soldiers at the front, and experiences that never cease creating interstices: doubts, nostalgias, a feeling of absurdity, questions dealing with life and death, lucidity with regard to the stupidity of the orders they must obey, even if those orders signify their probable death. "Enrolled" humans may well think more than those who busy themselves with their daily affairs. If the army "holds," it is to the extent that, in one way or another, these interstices lack the power to propagate themselves and to entail "original" behaviors, especially disobedience or desertion. It is possible that what "makes" a soldier, what prevents him from such "betrayals," but also often from objecting and denouncing when he sees his brothers in arms commit what he knows to be a crime, cannot be explained by the values inculcated by the army, nor by training. The stability of the society known as an army might depend on that which, brought into being by the unimaginable situation in which all soldiers find themselves, prevents the interstitial thoughts of each one from having consequences: *"you don't abandon your buddies."*

Correlatively, in the case of a "social catastrophe," when the soldiers flee in panic, every man for himself, or when the modes of reproduction of a tradition cease to function, the question will not be one of external causality, of which the catastrophe would be the effect, but of a society's relation to its own interstices. Obviously, this is not to deny the outside world, but to demand that we do not speak of external "causes." One should not speak of "social" causes either, for to speak of a "social" cause is to confer on a society the power to explain its own endurance. The point is then to try to tell stories, for only stories are capable of giving meaning to the way in which what seemed separated ceases to be so, in which what seemed to have the power to explain loses this power, in which what was required, what seemed to go without saying, reveals its role, in which what seemed insignificant becomes important.

Among "living societies," those that interest Whitehead most directly are certainly those one might call our "mental habits." This is why, for him, the paradigmatic "social science" was education, with its crucial element: the transmission of the abstractions without which we cannot think. These abstractions may be transmitted either as "living values," values that incite curiosity, the appetite for contrasts, in short, original responses to the situations of this world, or as "dead values," usually inciting compliant submission and the inhibition of what questions that compliance. Perhaps one of the most intense experiences that turned Whitehead into a philosopher was the power of these abstractions that demand submission. Speaking of the industrial revolution, he writes,

Ultimate values were excluded. They were politely bowed to, and then handed over to the clergy to be kept for Sundays [. . .] The workmen were conceived as mere hands, drawn from the pool of labour. To God's question, men gave the answer of Cain—"Am I my brother's keeper?"; and they incurred Cain's guilt (SMW, 203).

Whitehead does not denounce; he is terrified, for those who have given this answer, who have looked at the consequences of the industrial revolution with a "stone-blind eye," are not only the captains of industry—there was something in it for them—but also, as he emphasizes, the "best men" of the time. And, for instance, those honorable, disinterested, gentle, and educated men with whom he dined in the evening at the high table of his college. They are the men we know well today, and who we feel really do incur the guilt of Cain: that guilt that is first translated by an inability to accept the interstices of imagination and doubt. Or, more precisely, it is what they make us feel, when they infect us with the feeling that if they were to face up to that guilt, they would collapse.

Mental habits, insofar as what lurks in the interstices that they harbor can be said to be "danger" for them, thus intensify the question of good and evil dealt with in *Religion in the Making,* and taken up again in *Process and Reality* with the trick of evil. These honorable men, who "never doubted," reflect the instability of evil, for they held fast only by inhibiting, in them and around them, that which would make them doubt. As far as the good in a cosmological sense is concerned, it is what prevents us from defining a society on the basis of its mode of order. It is impossible to exclude what, for Whitehead, is the paradigmatic cosmic event: that evil be overcome, that is, that what was felt as intolerable be accepted, canalized, admitted to infect its social environment, making it capable of original responses.

Whitehead's cosmological perspective corresponds to the faith in progress that William James, in *The Moral Philosopher and Moral Life,* proposes to moral philosophers. For James, these philosophers must defend themselves against the temptation of trying to define a system of moral obligations that should be acceptable to all. Like Whiteheadian sociologists explaining the stability of a living society, moralists could not help but confer the force of law upon some of the categories of their own social environment. It can even be said that, justifying the elevation of an ideal to the highest status, whence the rest can be deduced, they might contribute to the trick of evil, that is, ratify the sacrifice of other ideals, demanding other obligations.

If we follow the ideal which is conventionally highest, the others which we butcher either die or do not return to haunt us; or if they come back and accuse us of murder, everyone applauds us for turning to them a deaf ear (MPML, 203).

James thus seems to condemn moral philosophers to relativism, to the admission that all moral ideals are of equal value. Yet this is not so, and the position James proposes, like that of the evolutionary biologists in the sense of Stuart Kauffman, and like those of the sociologist in the Whiteheadian sense, demands an attention to the interstices. For James, this first means to accept that the question is tragic. Philosophers should be able to resist the temptation to justify the sacrifice, the exclusion of other ideals. They should accept that the victims haunt the interstices of their adherence to an ideal. They should accept to let their experience throb with the complaint of those who were sacrificed in the name of what they define as moral.

This is not, however, the same thing as taking sides with the excluded, for we are not in the domain of the just and the unjust, but of the tragic: every definition of what is just and good produces victims. And it is against a tragic background that James defines his trust in a moral progress that cannot be reduced to relativism. Moral philosophers who trust this progress will situate themselves in the midst of an adventure, in which it may happen that new ways of satisfying an ideal, original ways that demand fewer victims, become socially acceptable or even obvious. Philosophers cannot foresee such events, for they are not the product of a tolerant relativism, of a general affirmation that no aspiration should impose anything upon anybody. They are "cosmic" events in Whitehead's sense, in which an evil is overcome, in which an apparently insuperable contradiction becomes a contrast.

The knowledge that such an event is possible, transforming the judgment of moral philosophers themselves about what is envisageable and what is not, implies an empiricism that is on alert. Philosophers should be attentive to the action of "thinkers" at work in their time, who create new moral "facts," and to original ideals that appear in the interstices but gradually modify social judgment, making it normal for it to accept what it was proud of rejecting.

Everywhere the ethical philosopher must wait on facts. The thinkers who create the ideals come he knows not whence, their sensibilities are evolved he knows not how; and the question as to which of two conflicting ideals will give the best universe then and there, can be answered by him only through the experience of other men (MPML, 208–209).

Yet philosophers who know how to wait for those other people, who will teach them what their own categories doomed them to exclude, are not mere spectators. If they are heard, if their words—themselves interstitial—are audible to the society to whose values they adhere, they may contribute to the event, to the socialization of the novel sensibility. Trust in the possible, the humor of a relation that does not try to justify what seems obvious to us, and does not disqualify it, for that matter, as arbitrary, but situates it in the midst of an adventure that no justification will constrain, can transform the relation between our modes of abstraction and their interstices. Ever since he became a philosopher, Whitehead did nothing but work for such a transformation.

This is what we will see now, with a new flight of experience toward the territory Whitehead first explored when, in *The Concept of Nature*, he questioned the specious clarity of perceptive experience, in which leaves are green, the sky is blue, and my body is "here."

CHAPTER TWENTY

The Adventure of the Senses

T HE RISE OF ANIMAL, *and then of human, consciousness is the triumph of specialization. It is closely connected with the evolution of clear and distinct sensory experience. There is abstraction from the vague mass of primary feelings, and concentration upon the comparative clarity of a few qualitative details. These are the sensa.*

Unless the physical and physiological sciences are fables, the qualitative experiences which are the sensations, such as sight, hearing, etc., are involved in an intricate flux of reactions within and without the animal body. These are all hidden below consciousness in the vague sense of personal experience of an external world. This feeling is massive and vague—so vague that the pretentious phrase, namely, personal experience of an external world, sounds nonsense. A particular instance can be explained more simply. For example, "I see a blue stain out there" implies the privacy of the ego and the externality of "out there." There is the presupposition of "me" and the world beyond. But consciousness is concentrated on the quality blue in that position. Nothing can be more simple or more abstract. And yet unless the physicist and physiologist are talking nonsense, there is a terrific tale of complex activity omitted in the abstraction (MT, 121).

Whitehead never tires of returning to the grey stone or the blue stain, and to the error of the philosophers who have accepted them as starting points that are both simple and assured. He never tires of describing and undoing the trap always set for philosophers by the search for a starting point, able to dictate the way it must be taken into account. The question is not what these philosophers affirm when they proclaim "*I (here) see a blue stain (there)*"; it is everything they deny when they act "as if" this were the faithful account of their incontrovertible experience. As if there were not, in addition to a "state of affairs" over there, for an "I" over here, at the very least an ingredient that requires precisely what they intend to deny. This ingredient is "causality," to which the blue stain gives no meaning, whereas it matters for both physicists and physiologists.

[. . .] *The "make-believe" character of modern empiricism is well shown by putting into juxtaposition two widely separated passages from Hume's* Treatise: *"Impressions may be divided into two kinds, those of sensation, and those of reflection. The first kind arises in the soul originally, from unknown causes." And "If it be perceived by the eyes, it must be a colour . . . "*

The earlier passage is Hume's make-believe, when he is thinking of his philosophical principles. He then refers the visual sensations "in the soul" to "unknown causes." But in the second passage, the heat of argument elicits his real conviction—everyone's real conviction—that visual sensations arise "by the eyes." The causes are not a bit "unknown," and among them there is usually to be found the efficacy of the eyes. If Hume has stopped to investigate the alternative causes for the occurrence of visual sensations—for example, eye-sight, or excessive consumption of alcohol—he might have hesitated in his profession of ignorance. If the causes be indeed unknown, it is absurd to bother about eye-sight and intoxication. The reason for the existence of oculists and prohibitionists is that various causes are known (PR, 171).

The freedom for Hume, and for so many other philosophers, to act as though the difference between "seeing something" and "hallucinating" depended on their verdict. The freedom for prohibitionists and oculists to quietly testify to this difference, whatever the philosopher may say. And the freedom, as well, for those who wonder how to tell someone they need glasses or how to ask someone to stop drinking. For Whiteheadian causality—we see "by the eyes"—does not, like the causes defined by experimentation, constitute the answer to a well-defined question. It refers to that "bodily life" that Whitehead, in *The Concept of Nature*, had associated with the "here" of the percipient event, a life associated not with the knowledge of scientists but with a feeling that is most often vague.

The first principle of epistemology should be that the changeable, shifting aspects of our relations to nature are the primary topics for conscious observation. This is only common sense, for something can be done about them. The organic permanences survive by their own momentum: our hearts beat, our lungs absorb air, our blood circulates, our stomachs digest. It requires advanced thought to fix attention on such fundamental operations (MT, 29).

It is thus not a matter of choosing between two accounts of experience that are just as abstract: that of purificatory empiricism, which acts as though causality could be eliminated from our experience like a parasitical belief, and that of science, which acts as if experience could be defined on the basis of a chain of causes. The point is to affirm them both as abstract and therefore highly interpretative, that is, also, to construct a more complete interpretation.

If we desire a record of uninterpreted experience, we must ask a stone to record its autobiography (PR, 15).

The description bereft of interpretation aimed at by the empiricists is chimerical: a pure testimony to the excess subjectivity that can affect conscious experience, denying its selective character while pushing selection to the extreme. What Whitehead chooses to underline, and to interpret speculatively, is the interpretative choice from which our experience has issued. We do not know how a bat, armed with its sonar, or a dog, capable of tracking by smell, perceive "their" world. We can identify the features they discriminate, but we can only dream of the contrast between "that which" they perceive and what they are aware of. All we "know" is that their experience is, like ours, highly interpretative, and that, like ours, it has solved an extraordinarily delicate problem: to give access, in a more or less reliable way, to what it is important to pay attention to. For Whitehead, what we know in this way suffices to engage speculative interpretation. The point is to think of an experience in which what is at stake is "realistic," that is, must propose an interpretation that is not adequate, but reliable with regard to what matters. This crucial element will communicate in a privileged way with the class of eternal objects Whitehead names "sensa."

Here, Whitehead prolongs the "logical" hierarchization of objects to which he had proceeded on the basis of perceptive experience alone in *The Concept of Nature.* He had shown that sense objects do not presuppose any other type of object, whereas all other types of objects presuppose sense objects. Likewise, the eternal objects Whitehead calls "sensa" (independently of whether or not they communicate with an experience that is "sensible" for humans, or even for any inhabitant of the earth) form the "lowest category," because their realization does not require any particular other eternal object. In this sense, the sensa are "simple."

Because the ingression of a sensum does not require that other eternal objects make ingression at the same time, the sensum is also that which does not require a particularly sophisticated process of concrescence in order to make ingression. Colors can enter into complex contrasts, make a child happy and drive a painter mad, but sensa can also make ingression into "simple physical feelings," into societies characterized by the thread of a "reproduction" in conformity, as privileged by physics. In other words, among all the ways of "feeling," those in which the sensa make ingression have the peculiarity of always being able to be taken into account, whatever the concrescence may be.

The singularity of a sensum is therefore the fact that it can play a role that is rather analogous to that of a trading currency among the members of a human society. A four-year-old child will, of course, not make the same use as you or I of a ten-dollar bill, and the possession of such a bill will take on a completely different significance for him and for me, or for a jobless person and a multimillionaire. Yet each person to whom the bill is transmitted can make use of it, and neither age nor social status presents an obstacle to its circulation from seller to buyer. From an abstract viewpoint, one may say it is "same" bill, whoever its possessor, and in a way that is much more relevant than if one speaks of this book in the hands of a reader or of a four-year-old child.

The reactivation of a sensum from occasion to occasion does not mean conformity of experiences between "electromagnetic" societies and a person contemplating a sunset. But the sensum's simplicity, the absence of presupposition that characterizes its mode of ingression, allows the satisfaction of the demands associated with the experiences whose "realism" is at stake. Realism demands that the blue of this coat designate, in one way or another, this coat as an "active condition." I am not hallucinating. You can tell it how you will, but I demand that what I call "coat" shall be actually implied in my perception. This does not mean, however, that I demand that the color I perceive be what is common to the coat and to my perception, that the coat be "intrinsically blue." Nor do I demand that what I perceive as a coat explain the sensation "blue." I do demand, however, that this color I perceive have a respondent different from me. It is precisely this demand that is satisfied by the ingression of a sensum. This ingression does not explain either this coat that exists on its own account, or the complex and entangled set of societies presupposed by "I who am looking at it." In fact, it is because this ingression cannot be invoked as a "cause" in any particular explanation that the ingression of this sensum can be what my perception owes to this coat: the sensum is a "same," indefinitely available for all significations, and of which each disparate society, both the "coat" and "myself," must, on its own account, produce the signification. It is the paradigmatic transmissible, since its reproduction, from occasion to occasion, does not require any other eternal object.

The realization of a sensum in its ideal shallowness of intensity, with zero width, does not require any other eternal object, other than its intrinsic apparatus of individual and relational essence; it can remain just itself, with its unrealized potentialities for patterned contrasts. An actual entity with this absolute narrowness has an ideal faintness of satisfaction, differing from the ideal zero of chaos, but equally impossible. For realization means ingression in an actual entity, and this involves the synthesis of all ingredients with data derived from a complex universe. Realization is ideally distinguishable from the ingression of contrasts, but not in fact (PR, 115).

Every contrast is, according to the eighth category of existence, "a mode of synthesis of entities in a single prehension." If the chaos Whitehead evokes here corresponds to the categorically impossible hypothesis of a "vacuous" satisfaction, the hypothesis of a satisfaction limiting itself to the realization of a sensum corresponds, for its part, to an abstract idea, a pure mental exercise. In other words, what is at stake in the sensum is not to privilege "pure" transmission: its realization can play the most different roles in the most diverse contrasts. *Qua* available without constraint to participate in various contrasts, and free in itself with regard to every contrast, the sensum does not communicate with the empiricist censorship that would ask us to restrict ourselves to the "common." It satisfies the demands of the freest empiricism, the one that intends to accept at the same time, and to place on the same plane, all the experiences that can oblige us to think.

As we recall, colors, sounds, and smells not only inhabit experience as perception, "that gray stain there," but they also communicate with a completely different version of "empiricism." For the painter or poet of *Science and the Modern World,* color haunts time, but is not in time; it surges forth somewhere, but does not stay anywhere. It does not emerge, does not occur, it is there or is not there, and, when it is there, it does not orient toward the past nor toward the future, and it is perceived in a way that affirms itself as independent of the person perceiving: it stands up on its own.

The goal of art, with the means of its materials, is to tear the percept away from the perceptions of objects and the states of a perceiving subject, to tear the affect away from affections like the passage from one state to another. To extract a block of sensations, a pure being of sensation [. . .] Memory plays a minor role in art (even, and especially, in Proust). It is true that every work of art is a monument, but here the monument is not what commemorates the past, it is a block of present sensations that owe their own conservation only to themselves, and give the event the compound that celebrates it. The act of a monument is not memory, but fabulation (QPh, 158).

The fact that we can, according to the expression of Deleuze and Guattari, tear the percept away from perception, that is, as Whitehead would say, produce an experience dominated by sensible contrasts *qua* sensible—the shimmering of colors celebrated by Shelley in *Science and Modern World*—is what obliges the artist's fabulation, and must oblige the philosopher's, but in very different ways.

For Whitehead, the "act of a monument" certainly matters, in a way that specifies art, but in a more generic way what matters is to liberate the green from abstraction, to refer it to the multiplicity of contrasts and experiences that make it intervene: whether this contrast is itself sensible, for the painter creating a complex, sensible composite, or for Shelley celebrating the forest; whether it belongs to a perception—this green leaf—or translates a doubt—*I was sure that your eyes were green;* whether it becomes an object of comparison—*what green should we choose for the door, this one or that one?*—or intervenes in a philosophical thought that defines it as a "secondary quality."

Of course, we are much more civilized than our ancestors who could merely think of green in reference to some particular spring morning. There can be no doubt about our increased powers of thought, of analysis, of recollection, and of conjecture. We cannot congratulate ourselves too warmly on the fact that we are born among people who can talk about green in abstraction from springtime. But at this point we must remember the warning—Nothing too much (MT, 38).

Congratulations become excessive when they make the poet responsible for the patterned, sonorous harmony of the nightingale's song, that song about which we know that the nightingale that produces it is also the first to enjoy it. What we should rather congratulate ourselves warmly for is the way in which animal experience, then human consciousness, have privileged and given an eminent role to the ingression of the "simple" eternal objects that enable sensible and perceptive experience to bear witness to the actual solidarity between disparate actual entities. What we should celebrate is the way each new apparatus for detection, each new prosthesis, comes to increase this solidarity.

It pertains to what Whitehead calls the "categories of obligation" to specify how a process of concrescence is "obliged" by its "causes," by what it inherits and by its final accomplishment. Yet it is interesting to emphasize that once an apparatus for detection is prepared, this relation between obligation and cause finds a direct exemplification. Such an apparatus is not, like a thermometer for instance, a physical process set up and calibrated in order to exhibit a functional relation that takes on the role of a measure. Its elaboration is intended to ensure it a sensibility that is extremely selective to "what must be detected," that is, to what can be designated, in a reliable way, as the "cause" of the signal it will emit. The final accomplishment, for its part, obviously refers to the person who carries out the elaboration. An apparatus that has finally been perfected may be defined as "synthesizing" what was previously disjointed: such beings as electrons or radioactive particles, which its perfecting presupposed but to which, once it is perfected, it testifies in a reliable manner, and human specialists who have become able to detect the presence of these beings. It is then inseparable, in the same sense as an organ, from an experience that it does not explain but that designates it as its respondent: no longer a coat, or a tiger ready to leap, but what was previously "unobservable." In other words, the perfecting of an apparatus for detection has as its goal to transform the "what it detects" into ingredients of human reasoning and action.

Although such an apparatus implies only physical processes, the assemblage of these processes cannot be completely described by physics, a science that is all the more relevant when what it describes exhibits its conformity. The assemblage, for its part, exhibits its finality; it is made to produce a "same" that did not exist prior to its selective abstraction. As such, it prolongs the invention of sense organs, conferring an eminent role upon the sensa. And as such an organ, it is silent with regard to the diversity of the adventures that require it, independently of which it would not have come into existence, but to which it pertains to produce the signification of what it testifies to.

In a sense, one could say that the research of artists and of technicians prolongs the animal invention of organs along divergent paths. Artists seek to bring to existence new sensations for the eyes or the ears, sensations that are, of course, much more complex than red or sweet, but capable, like red or sweet, of testifying in a fleeting way to eternity. Those who prepare an apparatus of detection, in contrast, create new organs for sensible experiences that have nothing particular in themselves—*there we go, it's sizzling*—but that may intervene, as culmination or denouement, in unprecedented and intense interpretative adventures. Only experimenters can waltz around singing in their laboratory because a detector has emitted the expected signal. And from that point of view, detection here involves, but cannot be reduced to, what Whitehead, following Bergson, calls "sense-reception."

The more primitive types of experience are concerned with sense-reception, and not with sense-perception. This statement will require some prolonged explanation. But the course of thought can be indicated by adopting Bergson's admirable phraseology, sense-reception is "unspatialized" and sense-perception is "spatialized." In sense-reception the sensa are the definiteness of emotion: they are emotional forms transmitted from occasion to occasion. Finally in some occasion of adequate complexity, the Category of Transmutation endows them with the new function of characterizing nexus (PR, 113–114).

The "unspatialized sense-reception" discussed by Bergson is by no means a typical case of primitive experience, in the sense that such an experience might be associated with an electron, or any other being described relevantly in terms of conservation or conformity. It is at the heart of the practical sphere of "psychophysics," on which Bergson comments at length in his *Essay on the Immediate Data of Consciousness*. Bergson's (critical) interest responded to the ambition of this field, that is, the articulation between the "objective," quantitative measure of a sensible signal, and the "subjective" evaluation of the intensity of that signal. Such an articulation obviously requires an experimental setup in which maximum homogeneity is realized, in which no difference can insinuate itself that refers to an interpretation, an interest, a doubt. This is why the experimental setup is dominated by passivity: it confers, as it were, upon the "subject" the role of detection apparatus for the scientist. The experimental subject "bears witness" to the intensity of the sound, the pain, the light, in an experimental context that is actively opposed to perceptive experience. The testimony concerns a sensation, for instance in terms of the threshold at which it manifests itself to consciousness, the threshold of saturation after which quantitative differences will no longer be sensible, and the estimation of the variations of intensity between these two thresholds. Like the invention of detection apparatuses, the "psychophysical measure" is thus a triumph of abstraction, providing itself with the means to name, if not to describe, components of experience that are usually "what goes without saying." Yet to describe this apparatus in a concrete, and therefore complete way, we must add that it presupposes the docility of a "witness" who accepts to submit to this kind of experiment. Just as the technical detection apparatus presupposes an assemblage whose finality is foreign to the assembled physical processes, the psychophysical apparatus cannot relate the objective measure of a signal and the subjective testimony to its intensity without exhibiting what is foreign to such a relation: the fact that the subject agrees to submit to a situation that is new for a human. Like technical detection, the psychophysical experience is creation, implying that scientists equip themselves with a new prosthesis.

What, then, of the experiences that can indeed be under the banner of an "unspatialized reception," those, for instance, that I have already attributed to insects, when, speculatively denying them perceptive experience,

I spoke of "detection" with regard to them? The analogy with technical detection has the interest of emphasizing that the category of "sensible reception" defined by Whitehead covers an immense social variety. From this viewpoint, there is no opposition between the processes studied by physics or chemistry, as long, of course, as they are technically articulated and stabilized enough to play a role in detection, and those physiologists discover when they study the functions of selective capture accomplished by an organ. In none of these cases, however, should "primitive experience" evoke the idea of an "automatism." For Whitehead, we certainly do not have any access to the type of enjoyment of occasions belonging to nonliving societies, to which we delegate detection and the production of a selective signal, but every experience is productive, enjoying the intensity it produces. The main difference between apparatus and organs is that laboratory apparatuses and prostheses exhibit their dependency on issues of knowledge and reliability that can be formulated independently of their functioning. If the experience in question is to be "primitive" as such, it must not exhibit such a dependence.

This is why if one can, as I have already risked doing, conceive the experience of a butterfly or a fly as "detection" rather than as "perception," it is by taking the term in its full sense. The sense in which, when experimenters exclaim *"there we go, it's sizzling";* their experience is not dominated by a contrast between a "here" and a "there" of a perceptive type. The experimenter is affected in a way that is first and foremost "emotional." "Detection" ought therefore to evoke rather the accentuation of what we live as "presence," giving rise to an irreversible, uncontrollable mutation of experience. We need only think of a feeling of fright or disgust, or else an attack of the giggles, and perhaps we can approach what a butterfly "feels" when it detects the odor of its female: to speak of "detection" implies that what is detected "makes a sensation" in a way that may be closer to a "trance" than to the identification "here" of something that is "there."

We now come to sense-perception, that is, to spatialized experience, implying a contrast between "here" and "there." Whitehead associates the emergence of this contrast with the sixth category of obligation, which defines "transmutation."

When [...] one and the same conceptual feeling is derived impartially by a prehending subject from its analogous simple physical feelings of various actual entities in its actual world, then, in a subsequent phase of integration of these simple physical feelings together with the derivate conceptual feeling, the prehending subject may transmute the datum *of this conceptual feeling into a characteristic of some nexus containing those prehending actual entities among its members, or of some part of that nexus. In this way the nexus (or its part), thus characterized, is the objective datum of a feeling entertained by this prehending subject [. . .] This category is the way in which the philosophy of organism, which is an atomic theory of actuality, meets a perplexity which is inherent in all monadic cosmologies. Leibniz, in his* Monadology, *meets the same difficulty by a theory of "confused" perception. But he fails to make clear how "confusion" originates* (PR, 27).

The category of transmutation, sixth of the nine categories of obligation, implies, because it requires the notion of "conceptual feeling," the fourth category, the "category of conceptual evaluation." Unlike transmutation, which corresponds to a possibility (the prehending subject "may" derive), this fourth category is generic. It concerns every actual occasion, from the most simple to the most sophisticated. At the initial phase of every process of concrescence, there is "conceptual evaluation."

From each physical feeling there is the derivation of a purely conceptual feeling whose datum is the eternal object determinant of the definiteness of the actual entity, or of the nexus, physically felt (PR, 26).

Let us recall that both physical feelings (that is, feelings initiating the concrescence, which have actual entities as their data) and conceptual feelings (feelings of an eternal object) belong to genetic analysis, and as such do not communicate with any experience. In particular, a conceptual feeling (or conceptual prehension) has nothing to do with an intellectual experience. Like the eternal object of which it is the feeling, it "tells no story." It is "evaluation" in the sense that it is the feeling of the eternal object, in its capacity to be realized *qua* determining the how of a physical feeling. Elsewhere, Whitehead asks (PR, 33) that it be understood in an absolutely neutral way, without admitting the slightest connotation suggesting a thought or an intellection. This must be the case, since conceptual feeling belongs to the initial phase of any concrescence and will also designate the divine feeling of eternal objects.

Transmutation, as defined by the sixth category of obligation, is not an intellectual operation either. What is transmuted is the datum of a conceptual feeling, which leads to a new mode of ingression for the eternal object, whose feeling has been impartially derived from a multitude of physical feelings. There is no need to think that the eternal object whose mode of ingression is transmuted is always a sensum. What can be affirmed, in contrast, is the particular importance, from our animal viewpoint, of the application of the category of transmutation to the sensa to which our sense organs testify. Correlatively, the simplicity of these eternal objects known as the sensa is particularly appropriate for transmutation, for their

conceptual feelings, which do not require the feeling of any other particular eternal object, lend themselves to the impartial derivation presupposed
by transmutation. Whether the blush that infuses your cheeks is of shame
or of anger, it is always such a colored nuance, offering a contrast with the
rest of your face.

If transmutation is not specifically linked to perception, it is certainly a
condition for perception. Only if it has issued from a transmutation can
what is felt be felt "there," that blue stain entering into contrast with
other colors in the midst of a colored world, or the great roar of that wave
crashing, there, against that rock. Or it may not be, like the confused multitude of little noises produced by the droplets presumed to compose that
roar, which I do not perceive "there," but which no doubt confer a definite character on the emotion inspired by the roar of the wave or that
slightly diffuse pain in my head. Transmutation makes spatialization possible, but does not operate it.

The transmutation that conditions a perception certainly has detection
as its own condition: it requires selective organs to give meaning to the
simple physical feelings from which it is possible to derive, in an impartial way, one and the same eternal object, one and the same sensum. For
Whitehead, however, it first constitutes the paradigmatic example of a link
between social success and simplification. We are amazed that the flight
of a butterfly can testify to the presence of a single "odoriferous" molecule, but Whitehead, for his part, celebrates as a much more sophisticated exploit the fact that we smell "an odor" or that we hear "a noise."

*The examination of the Category of Transmutation shows that the ap-
proach to intellectuality consists in the gain of a power of abstraction. The
irrelevant multiplicity of detail is eliminated, and emphasis is laid on the
elements of systematic order in the actual world* (PR, 254).

The simplification produced by transmutation is not in itself synonymous with intelligibility, as is attested by the difficulty in naming a pain,
but it conditions the "that which" of perception, marking the threshold
where, for us, experience will be exhibited not only as selective but also as
"original," exhibiting the "miracle of creation." It fact, it opens onto all
the experiences in which the questions raised in *The Concept of Nature*
assume meaning, those questions that all designated "mind" as ultimate.

We must, however, insist on the fact that transmutation does not by
any means open specifically upon consciousness, even though the conscious experience of a world of things existing at the same time as we do
implies transmuted feelings on a massive scale. Nor does it characterize
exclusively all the experiences that end up as localized perception. A "sonorous environment" does not designate its source, and a rabbit, if it

bolts at the slightest "worrisome" noise, switching to a desperate mode of existence in which it will be said to be "wholly in its flight," may be dominated by a "there" experience rather than by a felt contrast between here and there—it hasn't taken the time for that. Its mode of endurance had as its component an acute sensitivity to the highly specialized contrast "everything's OK/danger!" and the *how* of the transmuted sensation is then called "flee." Habit, instinct, intuition, reflex: many names—some pejorative, some laudatory—have been given to the variety of behaviors that attest no hesitation with regard to what is felt, and this is so whether these behaviors come before any learning (closing one's eyes if a moving object approaches them quickly), or are the fruit and crowning moment of a process of learning (to know how to drive or read). Whitehead would call them all "important," social successes proper to the bodily life and to the immense variety of experiences of which it is and becomes capable, successes that, as the case may be, will be the social environment proper for receiving other feelings that are even more complex.

Our intuitions of righteousness disclose an absoluteness in the nature of things, and so does the taste of a lump of sugar (MT, 121).

For a dog, smells may testify as much as colors to the localization that makes verification possible. As far as many human beings are concerned, there is something absolute about smell and taste, which leaves no room for the slightest hesitation. Yet the cry *"That's not right!"* also testifies to an absolute intuition that makes experience tip over. It has nothing to do with being made explicit: I judge that this experience, such as I perceive it, does not correspond to the definition of a just situation. The contrast between detection and perception is thus not the only one. Multiple contrasts inhabit all human experiences. Even a mathematician, after years of furious work, may be moved to tears when evoking a successful demonstration.

Between "bolting without asking for verification" and "asking for it," taking the time to pay due attention to what is worrisome, for instance, by turning one's head toward the source of the worrisome noise, the difference is important, and sometimes lethal. For humans, however, the difference can also become very important between "asking for a verification" and "wondering how one should ask for it," and it is here that consciousness comes into play.

How do you know that something is or is not just? A self-administered doubt, a situation of open controversy, a fleeting change in the interlocutor's physiognomy, it matters little: what may disappear is the "trust" that constitutes the common feature between the experience of the bolting rabbit and that of the rabbit turning its head. A predator is a predator, and "intuition" is absolute, even if it has proceeded to a verification. As for the disappearance or effective questioning of the absolute character of an "intuition," they are neutral in themselves: they may be deplored when our doctrines sap our trust in "what we know," but they are required to tell the difference between the professional, like a predator, who "never doubts," and Leibniz wondering how his perception of the great roar of the surf can be generated by a nondenumerable multiplicity of small noises.

The possibility included in the question *"how do you know that's just?"*—that the intuition of what is just may be challenged—has the eventual efficacy of brutally transforming the assertion "it is just" into an example of a theory that could be false, and the subject who inherits this transformation can say goodbye to any resemblance to a rabbit.

The general case of conscious perception is the negative perception, namely, "perceiving this stone as not grey." The "grey" then has ingression in its full character of a conceptual novelty, illustrating an alternative. In the positive case, "perceiving the stone as grey," the grey has ingression in its character of a possible novelty, but in fact by its conformity emphasizing the dative grey, blindly felt. Consciousness is the feeling of negation: in the perception of "the stone as grey," such feeling is in barest germ; in the perception of "the stone is not grey," such feeling is in full development. Thus the negative perception is the triumph of consciousness. It finally rises to the peak of free imagination, in which the conceptual novelties search through a universe in which they are not datively exemplified (PR, 161).

If the rabbit turning its head testifies to the possibility that a noise may not signify a predator, this does not mean that it is conscious, in the sense that Descartes is conscious when he meditates "I see a piece of wax there" (or anything else). The confrontation between the wax and an "extended substance" that no perceptual data exemplifies belongs to the summits of free imagination, like the multitude of tiny noises made by drops, envisaged by Leibniz. The difference, for Whitehead, does not consist in the superiority of consciousness over the feeling that we can attribute to the rabbit or over ourselves in most of our experiences. It testifies to a transformation of what is at stake. One of the ways to express the difference is to recall that the piece of wax does not really interest Descartes: for him, it is an "example." His experience is dominated by the question of having to construct a description of it that resists any possible challenge. One must refuse to the piece of wax everything whose "objective reality" could be denied. On the contrary, Leibniz's experiment is dominated by the possibility that we may refuse to the world the obscure multiplicity hidden by our clear perception of the roar of the surf.

From pedagogic goodwill *("I'll explain it to you")* to worried speculation *("he's going to judge me on the basis of my explanation"),* it is,
moreover, not certain that it is always judicious to leave behind the
domain of taste and colors, of trust in the nature of things, for that of the
adventure of arguments, as is attested by the doctrines that have made
nature bifurcate. The brutality of the passage from impersonal obviousness, *"that is just,"* to the personal position, *"that is what I felt, and now
I have to explain myself,"* opens the door to what was and remains one
of Whitehead's great concerns, the construction of reasons that, in order
to resist challenges, make a clean slate of what we nevertheless know.
This is why consciousness is placed under the banner of novelty, not of
any possibility of transcendence. And if it has something to do with the
question of truth, it is in terms of "attention to truth" (PR, 275): new
risks, new original possibilities of experience, new contrasts.

Attention to truth is primary with regard to "truth values." It refers
rather to the conscious mobilization of the question of "due attention."
We shall return to this point when we undertake to explore the positive
power of language, which can be an ingredient of every social environment in which such a question may be raised. What needs to be emphasized here is that attention to truth does not found, for consciousness, any
claim to a privileged access that would enable us to disqualify the experience of the rabbit turning its head. A habitual gesture does not "lack" anything, but it is different from a conscious gesture, runs other risks, translates
other urgencies than those, presupposing language, of having to account
for what one "means." The fact that the rabbit, when it turns its head or
bolts, is not equipped for the abstract "how can one recognize a predator?" does not, ultimately, deprive it of much, as Wittgenstein, moreover,
showed in a pretty way: most of our discursive definitions try to "follow"
what we "know," and if a definition contradicts this knowledge, it is the
definition that will be modified.

*Language was developed in response to the excitements of practical ac-
tions. It is concerned with the prominent facts. Such facts are those that
are seized upon by consciousness for detailed examination, with a view of
emotional response leading to immediate purposeful action. These prominent facts are the variable facts—the appearance of a tiger, of a clap of
thunder, or of a spasm of pain [. . .] But the prominent facts are the superficial facts. They vary because they are superficial; and they enter into
conscious discrimination because they vary. There are other elements in
our experience, on the fringe of consciousness, and yet massively qualifying our experience. In regard to these other facts, it is our consciousness
that flickers, and not the facts themselves. They are always securely there,*

barely discriminated, and yet inescapable. For example, consider our deri-
vation from our immediate past of a quarter of a second ago. We are
continuous with it, we are the same as it, prolonging its affective tone,
enjoying its data. And yet we are modifying it, deflecting it, changing its
purposes, altering its tone, re-conditioning its data with new elements.

We reduce this past to a perspective, and yet retain it as the basis for
our present moment of realization. We are different from it, and yet we
retain our individual identity with it. This is the mystery of personal iden-
tity, the mystery of the immanence of the past in the present, the mystery
of transience. All our science, all our explanations require concepts origi-
nating in this experience of derivation. In respect to such intuitions, lan-
guage is peculiarly inadequate (AI, 210).

Can you identify the grey of that stone that you have just mentioned in
this color chart? Even color can be taken up again in an experience that
testifies to the "mystery of personal identity." What I have just mentioned,
I suddenly discover to be rather different from a simple perception. This
color, suddenly belonging to the past, does not have much to do with the
shades presented in the paint-seller's color chart. When I mentioned it, it
was as if present, preserved, the immanence of the past in the present of
my experience. But when summoned to define itself in a public way, it
becomes mine, and just as much slips into the past, for it is in contrast
with the evocation of an experience *qua* past that I feel that none of the
shades presented in a way that allows them to be compared quite does
justice to that one, unique and incomparable, that I had loved. But this
conscious hesitation will probably be hard to remember when I face the
wall once painted: it is its color.

Inadequacy does not mean denunciation. The point is not to achieve a
"neutral" consciousness or to oppose the purity of sense evidence, or the
"mystery" of what is always there, to hesitant, fearful, perplexed, or passionate negotiation. Quite the contrary, it is the interest of this negotiation, the mutations of experience it brings about, that matter, that resitu-
ate consciousness, not at all as an avenue to the truth but as the product
and vector of an adventure.

In fact, Whitehead is far more interested in the adventure of free imagination than in the veracity of judgment. Freedom of imagination is not
indifferent to the question of truth but presupposes it in an original way.
To say "once upon a time," or "let's pretend," or even "let there be" (an
ideal triangle) presupposes critical judgment, since these utterances indicate the need for its inhibition. "Imaginative rationalization" also implies
the provisional bracketing of the question of the "true." Let us suppose
we can construct a coherent language, equally adequate whatever the

experience may be, and let us reserve for the applicable cases the attention to truth required by its verification. If speculative philosophy concerns the contrast between "true" and "false," it is only *via* the detour of that genuine triumph of free imagination that Whitehead associated with metaphysics, defined as a "dispassionate consideration of the nature of things." There is nothing indifferent about such an absence of passion, for it deliberately suspends "what we know well," that is, what our various ways of speaking—the one that is appropriate for describing me, the one that is appropriate for describing this keyboard—define as important. Artificially, experimentally, through the imperative of coherence, it demands that language take charge of the experiences compared with which it is most inadequate. This is why "attention to truth" in the sense of speculative philosophy does not presuppose critical consciousness, but the critical experience of consciousness. It does not presuppose becoming aware of the finitude of experience, but becoming aware of its social and therefore partial functioning. William James had suggested making consciousness a "function." Whitehead associates it with a social novelty, which, far from defining human experience, "flickers" intermittently.

Pluralism. The sensible, the intelligible, the problematic, all designate modalities of sense-experience which, although they are put on the same plane, must be carefully distinguished. The experiences that exhibit in a dominant way the relevance of the category of transmutation—"*Sweet!*" "*Run away!*"—must not be idealized, because they escape all hesitation, nor "overcome," because they escape all reason. We must recall that they testify not to the "concrete" but to what is carried out by transmutation: abstraction.

Apart from transmutation our feeble intellectual operations would fail to penetrate into the dominant characteristics of things. We can only understand by discarding (PR, 251).

However, the truth of the adventure of the senses is not the abstraction of transmutation. Already in *The Concept of Nature,* Whitehead emphasized the importance of what we call synesthesia, and which he called "conveyance of one sense-object by another." That flannel coat that is not a blue patch, which I sense in the mode of "wear" or "touch." The fact that I can be led to admit that all I see there is a blue form designates me as vulnerable to the imperative of having to give an account of my experience: that is, not as a human being in general, but as belonging to a social adventure, in which the questions that were created by philosophy have been taken up by the school institution that accustoms people to deny, or to pretend to deny, what they are aware of, although they cannot justify it.

The blue flannel coat was appropriate for Whitehead's project in *The Concept of Nature*, centered as it was around nature as what we are aware of in perception. The coat allowed the affirmation that what we are aware of is not a blue form. But the triumph of the adventure of the senses is not that I know that I could touch this coat that is here. What *The Concept of Nature* could only allude to is the experience of presence, the presence that affects us, makes us feel, much more than we perceive it.

In *The Spell of the Sensuous*, David Abram suggests associating this presence—presence of the word, presence of things—with a convergence of the senses that places what Whitehead calls conveyance under the banner of the event.

When the local tomcat comes to visit, I do not have distinctive experiences of a visible cat, an audible cat, and an olfactory cat; rather the tomcat is precisely the place where these separate sensory modalities join and dissolve into one another, blending as well with a certain furry tactility. Thus, my divergent senses meet up with each other in the surrounding world, converging and commingling in the things I perceive. We may think of the sensing body as a kind of open circuit that completes itself only in things, and in the world. The differentiation of my senses, as well as their spontaneous convergence in the world at large, ensures that I am a being destined for relationship: it is primarily through the engagement with what is not me that I effect the integration of my senses, and thereby experience my own unity and coherence (SS, 125).

When I associated the functioning of a detector with the ability to detect a being's presence, I dared to make a comparison with the experience of a butterfly "detecting" the odor of its female, which means that I denied the butterfly the experience described by Abram, that of sensing its female "as present." The fact that experimenters do not feel the presence, attested by their detectors, of radioactive atoms or neutrinos is the correlate of experimental practice, whose success is the creation of relations with beings that do not belong to "our" world. Yet to refuse the experience "of what is not me" to the butterfly is obviously much more risky, and only has meaning in order to try to give all its importance to the plurality of animal experiences against the hiatus between humans and animals. Some day, perhaps, for instance, if neurophysiology succeeds in associating an aspect of the brain with the achievement constituted by conveyance, we shall learn more about the contrast between our experience and that of butterflies. Yet whatever scientists and philosophers may say, we know, even if we cannot justify it, that the world is present for a cat, as it is for Thomas Nagel's famous bat.

The fact that David Abram took a tomcat as an example is nevertheless significant. Many of us have little experience with bats but will protest if we are told that we know nothing about what it is like to be a cat. Scientists will then denounce the temptation to anthropomorphize, to imagine, in particular, a reciprocity of attention, a cat that looks at us as we look at it. Instead, *The Spell of the Sensuous* raises the question of the rarefaction of such an experience in the midst of a world henceforth dominated by signs that claim a purely intellectual efficacy. A world in which the living and expressive presence of cats is an exception.

Direct, prereflexive perception is inherently synaesthetic, participatory, and animistic, disclosing the things and the elements that surround us not as inert objects but as expressive subjects, entities, powers, potencies. And yet most of us seem, today, very far from such experience. Trees rarely, if ever, speak to us; animals no longer approach us as emissaries from alien zones of intelligence; the sun and the moon no longer draw prayers but seem to arc blindly across the sky. How is it that these phenomena no longer address us, no longer compel our involvement or reciprocate our attention? If participation is the very structure of perception, how could it ever have been brought to a halt? To freeze the ongoing animation, to block the wild exchange between the senses and the things that engage them, would be tantamount to freezing the body itself, stopping it short in its track. And yet our bodies still move, still live, still breathe. If we no longer experience the enveloping earth as expressive and alive, this can only mean that the animating interplay of the senses has been transferred to another medium, another focus of participation (SS, 130–131).

The transformation of experience described by Abram corresponds to the experience of what, following Whitehead, I have called the "solitary consciousnesses," and to its mute, disenchanted world. It is what the bifur cation of nature turned into the only rational starting point for inquiry. But the originality of Abram's proposition, which places it within the Whiteheadian tradition, is to reject this idea of disenchantment, with all its connotations of a truth to be assumed by a humanity that has left its illusions behind. The enchantment of presence has not disappeared, but it has been displaced. In a dominant way, "our world," the world of most of this book's readers, is a world "to be read." Isn't reading a text, inseparably, to see it and to hear it, to feel it as a "presence" different from us? Don't philosophers, who refuse even to a cat the reciprocal attention that its presence nevertheless suggests, address a text as if that text "wanted" something from them? Aren't they forced to feel and to think "with" that text?

The fact that, as Abram suggests, reading inherited the achievement of synesthetic collaboration, and therefore belongs to the adventure of the senses, implies that the solitary consciousness does not mark the irreversible triumph of the intellectual over the sensible. It would be inseparable from an event, from the strange fact that written words, made up of alphabetic signs abstracted from any allusion to the world, have a power over us, speak to us, and make us feel in a way that captures our ability to feel "with." Those who write, but also those who read, would then be under the sway of a "spell" that comes before awareness because it concerns the senses. To consider oneself solitary would then be of the order of what Whitehead would have called a culturally bred exaggeration, a consequence of what would be, in the first instance, an etho-ecological mutation.

It is moreover, the question of this mutation that Whitehead addressed when, in *Science and the Modern World,* he called for an education that provides a habit of art, that is, the habit of enjoying living, expressive values, values which, he affirmed, are in the world, rather than mere products of our imagination. Abram gives this affirmation a radical expression, since he demands that what we know when we speak of the magic of a work of art, of a poem, or of a landscape be taken literally, to the letter.

If trees seldom speak to us, literate people, can we accept that written texts do without claiming it is "only a metaphor"? The solitary consciousness will snicker. Yet what is meant by the demand for a "literal" understanding if not the attribution to the written sign of a power over us? We shall certainly not learn how to cope with this power by affirming that it is "only a metaphor." What demands to be understood literally is not separable from the experience of "sheer disclosure" aroused by a text, since it is aroused by a presence upon which our senses converge. This is attested by the adventures of mathematics, of poetry, and also of philosophy, all the adventures in which one does not feel oneself to be the master of what one writes, but where writing forces one to think, to feel, and to create. And the very writing of *Process and Reality* not only belongs to this adventure but affirms it. When Whitehead writes that all the concepts that will be defined in it appeal, silently, to a leap of the imagination (PR, 4), he testifies to his experience as a writer but also warns his readers that they will have to make themselves available to the efficacy of the text, or else close the book.

In this perspective, the idea, current among contemporary philosophers, that it is language that has separated us from things, is one that could only be conceived by those who have the benefit of the powers of thought, analysis, memory, and conjecture that have been contributed by writing. Only the spell of writing makes intelligible the idea a discursive world closed upon itself, in which the meaning of all words could be explained by reference to other words. And when the thesis that there is no such thing as a "perfect dictionary" is celebrated as a major event of thought, the power of the spell is not broken, but rises to new intensity.

The account of the sixth day should be written, He gave them speech, and they became souls (MT, 41).

Writing in this way the account of the day when humans (after most animals) were created would mean giving to written words the poetic power to lead us back to what, for Whitehead, is specifically human: the power of spoken words over our experience. Humans are those whom words can inspire, or bewitch, enrage, or kill. This is why the tale of the sixth day should not tell the story of man's creation in the image of God, but of the efficacy of spoken language, which is "received" by every human offspring. And the souls humans became are not, primordially, rational ones. "Men are the children of the Universe, with foolish enterprises and irrational hopes" (MT, 30). The adventure of reason itself is a somewhat mad adventure.

This is why the adventure of the sensa is not over. Hasn't one of its prolongations, in the course of the somewhat mad history known as philosophy, been the somewhat irrational hope that the data of the senses might define a "pure" perception? It is in this capacity that "blue" was engaged by David Hume in a speculative adventure, which was to be taken up and prolonged in *Process and Reality* in a mode that would certainly have surprised Hume himself. I refer to the thought experiment involving the "case of the missing shade of blue."

Like all philosophical thought experiments, this case corresponds to a highly artificial situation, conceived to illustrate a philosophical abstraction, and unlike thought experiments in physics, it does not communicate with any conceivable experimental invention. Hume imagines a person familiar with all colors except a shade of blue, which she has never encountered. Suppose she is presented with a color chart featuring all the tones of blue, except that shade: she would, Hume supposes, perceive a "gap," a hiatus, discontinuity, or lack. The question is whether her imagination will enable her to fill that gap, and to positively imagine the shade of blue she has never seen.

If Hume's question is valid for Whitehead, it is because Whitehead has accepted as a constraint, in order to think of any concrescence, the thesis that integration draws all of its resources from its primary phase, conceived in terms of "physical feelings" and the conceptual feelings that derive from them. He even baptized this constraint "Hume's principle," as if he were repeating—in a slightly modified form, of course—Hume's central thesis that all our simple ideas, when they first emerge, are derived from simple impressions.

Conceptual feelings and simple causal feelings constitute the two main species of "primary" feelings. All other feelings of whatever complexity

arise out of a process of integration which starts with a phase of these
primary feelings. There is, however, a difference between the species. An
actual entity in the actual world of a subject must enter into the concres-
cence of that subject by some simple causal feeling, however vague, triv-
ial, and submerged. Negative prehensions may eliminate its distinctive
importance. But in some way, by some trace of causal feeling, the remote
actual entity is prehended positively. In the case of an eternal object,
there is no such necessity. In any given concrescence, it may be included
positively by means of a conceptual feeling; but it may be excluded by a
negative prehension (PR, 239).

That which, for Hume, served to question the pretentions of experiences to go beyond "empirical" data has become an experimental constraint for Whitehead. More precisely, "Hume's principle" is that thanks
to which the extent of the ontological principle, what it imposes and
what it forbids, will be able to unfold and measure itself against the demand of adequacy. The primary phase collects all the causes that can be
invoked for concrescence, except the cause that the latter will constitute
for itself. Its characterization, marked by the distinction between physical or "causal" feelings and conceptual feelings, gives a good translation
of the distinction between the "cause"—what will, in one way or another,
function as a "reason"—and the open question of *how* it will cause, or of
what determination it will become the reason.

Initial physical feelings, feelings having actual entities as their data, are
limited to reproducing themselves: what has been felt is to be felt again.
This is the "power" proper to objective immortality. The way it will finally be felt, however, is part of the subjective decision. The eternal objects that are the data of the initial conceptual feelings may be eliminated
by negative prehension. Conceptual feelings, because they enter into the
heritage without obliging it, thus reflect the problematic dimension that
is generally concealed by the notion of cause: to cause, of course, but
how? No cause has the power to prescribe the way it will cause. What
has been felt in this way might be felt otherwise, or might find itself bereft of any distinct importance.

Whoever says constraint also says "putting to the test." Ultimately, it is
adequacy that will judge. If "Hume's principle" were to lead to explanation by elimination, it would have to be abandoned, but it can be abandoned only after what it authorized has been fully deployed first. And it
is therefore here that the "case of the missing shade of blue" assumes its
speculative importance, for this case raises the question of "what was not
felt," and more precisely of an "unrealized eternal object" in the primitive
phase. How, without infringing the ontological principle that prescribes

that actual entities are "the only reasons," could such an eternal object make ingression?

This question should not make us think that, independently of the possibility, still in suspense, of such an ingression, there would only be a more or less selective transmission without true originality. If Whitehead had thought this, he would have thought like a poor mathematician, referring the essential aspect of the difficulty to a unique and obscure question after having defined as a "regular," unproblematic solution a rather uninteresting case in which creativity is only exemplified under the aspect of a possibility to neglect, not to take into account. Good mathematicians do not refer everything that causes problems to one vast undifferentiated category: they learn to discern the difficulty, that is, correlatively, to enlarge the class of "regular" solutions as broadly as possible. This is what Whitehead has done, by distinguishing between pure physical feelings and "hybrid" physical feelings in the gamut of physical feelings.

In a "pure physical feeling" the actual entity which is the datum is objectified by one of its own physical feelings [. . .] in a "hybrid physical feeling" the actual entity forming the datum is objectified by one of its own conceptual feelings (PR, 245–246).

Thanks to hybrid physical feelings, "Hume's principle" already authorizes by itself a great variety of cases connecting "inheriting" and "creating." As Whitehead remarks (PR, 246), the entities for which hybrid feelings are important designate societies for which the notion of energy, conserved and transmitted, loses not its validity but its relevance. The functioning of a living body conserves energy, of course, but a decomposing cadaver conserves it just as well. A bacterium swimming up a gradient of sugar concentration combines a movement with a contrast (more or less sugary), and it is this contrast as such that, together with its social repercussions, "explains" the movement for the biologist. In general, the originality of living beings with regard to their environment, attested by living societies, requires that the subjective form acquired by conceptual feelings in the course of an integration (an intensive evaluation, which Whitehead calls "adversion" if it is positive, and "aversion" if there is attenuation or elimination) may be felt as such. Since the most typical manifestation of originality is partiality, that is, adversion or aversion, the feeling of these subjective forms is part of what may crucially matter. Furthermore, for sophisticated experiences, what may come to play a role are "the scars" of what an entity's heritage has avoided, the subjective emotion associated with what might have been but is not.

Nevertheless, hybrid physical feelings do not solve the question of unrealized eternal objects any more than this question is solved by the category of transmutation, implying an initial phase in which the same conceptual feeling may be derived impartially from the feelings of multiple entities. What is new in transmuted feeling is the mode of ingression of the eternal object, but not the eternal object itself. The fact that the same eternal object is implicated is essential to realism—the green of this leaf does indeed belong to the leaf—but this is precisely what cannot be the case with the missing shade of blue, first perceived insofar as it is lacking, and then, eventually, experienced for itself.

This shade of blue is certainly not a spectacular case of conceptual innovation. Just as the sensa have as their primary interest the possibility of a transmission indifferent to the disparate character of social environments, so the sensum corresponding to that shade has as its only interest to give a simple illustration, debatable as such, of the question of the entry into the world of a new eternal object, not realized in the transmitted heritage.

But this question is crucial for Whitehead, since it is connected with that of relevance. If a nonrealized sensum can make ingression into experience, it is because the order of the color chart makes its absence "glaring," because its ingression responds in a relevant way to what is felt as a "lack." In Whitehead's thought, relevance is closely linked to the cosmological question. Novelty, in the cosmological sense, is always "relevant novelty." Therefore, wherever blue is "missing," God is not far, for God is precisely that thanks to which what has been realized is plunged into the possible, that thanks to which realization is not the last word.

The things which are temporal arise by their participation in the things which are eternal. The two sets are mediated by a thing which combines the actuality of what is temporal with the timelessness of what is potential. This final entity is the divine element in the world, by which the barren inefficient disjunction of abstract potentialities obtains primordially the efficient conjunction of ideal realization. This ideal realization of potentialities in a primordial actual entity constitutes the metaphysical stability whereby the actual process exemplifies general principles of metaphysics, and attains the ends proper to specific types of emergent order. By reason of the actuality of this primordial valuation of pure potentials, each eternal object has a definite, effective relevance to each concrescent process. Apart from such orderings, there would be a complete disjunction of eternal objects unrealized in the temporal world. Novelty would be meaningless, and inconceivable. We are here extending and rigidly applying Hume's principle, that ideas of reflection are derived from actual facts (PR, 40).

The author who wrote these lines could not raise the problem of the missing shade of blue, since this problem did not exist for him. In fact, this author was quite close to the one who, in *Science and the Modern World*, had defined the ideal situation as implying all the eternal objects. For him, the "primary phase" issued from an "ordering"—here, at last, is the "divine ordering"—implying a relation of relevance defined for all eternal objects. The fact that in other passages of *Process and Reality* Whitehead accepts the problem of the missing shade of blue thus indicates the metamorphosis undergone by the "cosmotheological" economy of *Process and Reality* in the course of its writing. For there to be a problem, the divine ordering, whatever its role may be, must no longer have an answer for everything, that is, the initial phase of a concrescence must contain feelings of all the actual entities (the principle of relativity), but its conceptual feelings must be limited exclusively to eternal objects that have been realized. Hume's principle, far from being able to be "extended and rigidly applied," then begins to raise the problem of what it excludes.

We do not know what determined Whitehead's transformation on this point. Perhaps it was a dynamic linked to the increasing importance he gave to the constraint of having to resist the slope of "great explanations" and their power to explain anything and everything. The fact that the "divine element in the world" can be responsible for the relations of relevance of all the eternal objects with regard to each process of concrescence, constitutes such an explanation. At the limit, the ontological principle did not yet need, on this hypothesis, to be formulated, for it would not have entailed any constraint: divine actuality satisfies it every time.

Correlatively, the divine ordering ran the risk of crushing the actuality of what is temporal. If eternal objects have received their degree of relevance prior to any subjective decision, the essential point has been decided. The idea that occasional becoming is "cause of itself" threatens to be a mere hypocritical witticism. In fact, it would rather be akin to a simple appropriation. The subject comes into existence where a perspective is already proposed, and this perspective includes unrealized possibles "ordered as a function of their relevance" by primordial evaluation. In other words, what is proposed to the subject already designates the way in which it will, eventually, be able to produce relevant novelty.

In fact, if what one inherits is already unified, the question of how one inherits is about as open as that of how to function for a functionary: there are ways to sabotage, to cheat, to let oneself be corrupted, to commit faults with incalculable consequences, in short, to poison one's environment, but not to play its meaning over again. Unity demands conformity. The relation between individuals and their language, it will be noted, is quite different. They inherit it, of course, and learning it fashions, one by one, each of the human offspring who accomplish that incredible *tour de force* of learning to speak. But it does not have a unity such that it would assign a role to human beings, since it also enables them, to a certain extent, to ask the question of this role. Is it not, moreover, this possibility of questioning that is required by speculative philosophy itself, as also by all the adventures in which people risk something other than their body?

The risk Whitehead faced can be stated on the basis of the contrast between language and grammar, in the sense that the latter demands conformity and claims to define the normal usages of a language. If one adheres to such a claim, each particular utterance becomes a simple case, and each locutor can be judged. Likewise, concrescence could be assimilated to a mode of realization of a preexistent possible and judged on the basis of the way this possible will be realized, the way the concrescence will produce, *qua* realized novelty, that whose pertinence has already been ideally defined.

The clarity with which I have just defined this risk is the retroactive product of the itinerary that led Whitehead to affirm the occasional becoming as "cause of itself," and the ontological principle as restrictive. These affirmations probably did not preexist in their capacity as constraints, but issued from the flight of experience, and probably coincide with the tipping point where Whitehead separates himself from his reference to an "eternal activity" and adopts creativity as an ultimate. And it is probably along multiple paths that the difficulty "percolated," quietly insisting through the silence cast over unformulated objections. Be that as it may, the case of the missing shade of blue allows us to follow a story in which the consequences of this "becoming aware" are played out.

Thus, Whitehead will first answer the question of the missing blue by the fifth category of obligation, the "category of conceptual reversion." This category authorizes a second source of conceptual feelings, not contained within the initial phase. New eternal objects could make ingression if their difference with objects already realized is relevant. This relevance, Whitehead specifies, is determined by the "subjective aim," by the concrescent subject *qua* aiming at its own self-determination. The divine ordering, *qua* implying the relevance for experience of all eternal objects, has already absented itself. No doubt, moreover, the categories of obligation were born from this mutation, for they answer the challenge of rendering explicit what "obliges" a concrescent process in a way that excludes all preliminary determination.

Thus, the first phase of the mental pole is conceptual reproduction, and the second phase is a phase of conceptual reversion. In this second phase the proximate novelties are conceptually felt. This is the process by which the subsequent enrichment of subjective forms, both in qualitative

pattern, and in intensity through contrast, is made possible by the posi-
tive conceptual prehension of relevant alternatives. There is a conceptual
contrast of physical incompatibilities [...] *But it does limit the rigid*
application of Hume's principle. Indeed Hume himself admitted excep-
tions [...] *This "aim at contrast" is the expression of the ultimate cre-*
ative purpose that each unification shall achieve some maximum depth
of intensity of feeling, subject to the conditions of its concrescence. This
ultimate purpose is formulated in Category VIII (PR, 249).

The eighth categoreal obligation, which deals with "subjective intensity," states that the subjective aim is at the origin of the evaluation (adversion and aversion) of conceptual feelings, and that what is aimed at,
what gives its ultimate meaning to the creation of the subject by itself, is
the intensity of a feeling. It is thus the subject's aim, bringing into existence a contrast, a new possibility of intensity, that satisfies the ontological principle. The fact that Whitehead refers explicitly in this regard to
Religion in the Making in a note gives a good indication of what is at
stake. Conceptual reversion makes possible the transformation of destructive oppositions into positively felt contrasts. And the very experience of the person who, faced by the "lack of a shade," imagines the
missing shade, is an abstract example of a properly cosmic event, when
the future possibility of a still-inconceivable contrast intervenes as a determining factor in the experience of a destructive conflict.

Everything thus seems to be taken care of. Except that the category of
reversion not only signifies a "limit" to Hume's principle but raises another problem, much more serious. The eternal objects, which must be
indifferent to their own ingressions, here run the risk of exhibiting themselves as nonindifferent, partial, correlated, and even endowed with the
ability to cause their own ingression. For what does "relevance" mean if
not a relation of intrinsic proximity between eternal objects? But if this
relevance is no longer mediated by God's divine ordering, if it intervenes
in one of the categoreal obligations that determine what every concrescence can and should do, doesn't this proximity become intrinsic? This
would mean that the realized eternal objects themselves explain and give
rise to feelings of unrealized objects. In that case, however, eternal objects
would no longer be a multiplicity, but should be characterized as togetherness, that is, endowed with intrinsic relations. They thus risk acquiring
the ideal power that the ontological principle explicitly denies them.
Eternal objects do not have the power to make a difference by themselves, even if only by relations of proximity: no ideal proximity can be
invoked as a cause or explanation for the creation of a "but then ..."
implying a relevant association. For eternal objects would then say some-

thing, if not about themselves then at least about their relations of proximity. They would no longer be "pure potentials." But if eternal objects "say" anything at all about their ingressions, the entire problem is turned upside down. No half-measures are possible, and they will be in command. Whitehead has thus moved from the Charybdis of an overly determinant God to the Scylla of insistent eternal objects.

And suddenly, at the end of a paragraph, the problem and the solution are made explicit at the same time, when Whitehead announces a rearrangement of the categories of obligation.

The question, how, and in what sense, one unrealized eternal object can be more, or less, proximate to an eternal object in realized ingression—that is to say, in comparison with any other unfelt eternal object—is left unanswered by the Category of Reversion. In conformity with the ontological principle, this question can be answered only by reference to some actual entity. Every eternal object has entered into the conceptual feelings of God. Thus, a more fundamental account must ascribe the reverted conceptual feeling in a temporal subject to its conceptual feeling derived, according to Category IV, from the hybrid physical feeling of the relevancies conceptually ordered in God's experience. In this way, by the recognition of God's characterization of the creative act, a more complete rational explanation is obtained. The Category of Reversion is then abolished, and Hume's principle of the derivation of conceptual experience from physical experience remains without any exception (PR, 249–250).

This is no doubt Whitehead's most famous insertion, because in its case his procedure leaps to the eyes. The category of conceptual reversion, whose abolition he announces, will continue to be used imperturbably in the pages that follow. Whitehead will limit himself to adding, a few pages before, the reasons for which what has just happened to him, the necessity that an actual occasion (physically) "feel" God, was obviously necessary . . . retroactively.

The limitation of Hume's principle introduced by the consideration of the Category of Conceptual Reversion [. . .] is to be construed as referring merely to the transmission from the temporal world, leaving God out of account. Apart from the intervention of God, there could be nothing new in the world, and no order in the world. The course of creation would be a dead level of ineffectiveness, with all balance and intensity progressively excluded by the cross currents of incompatibility. The novel hybrid feelings derived from God, with the derivative sympathetic conceptual valuations, are the foundations of progress (PR, 247).

David Hume would no doubt have been rather surprised that "the case of the missing shade" finds its solution in a feeling directly derived from God. As far as we are concerned, to speak with Leibniz, while we might have thought that we had almost reached port, here we are thrown back on the high seas, and even into a stormy ocean. For it is one thing to link, as was the case in *Religion in the Making,* the theme of progress, or the possibility that evil may be overcome, with a cosmology implicating God. It is quite another to attribute to an actual entity a "hybrid feeling" derived from God, and more precisely—otherwise we would rediscover a new version of the bifurcation of nature—to attribute such a hybrid feeling to every actual entity.

It is always hard, especially with Whitehead, to know to what extent creators are aware of the problems that they have not yet provided themselves with the means to solve. Did Whitehead tell himself "this will do fine like that," or "that ought to be enough"? Did he know, when he evoked the divine ordering, that a shadowy zone remained, loading down his own future with "I shall have to go back to that"? The fact that his later books preserved the conceptual construction of *Process and Reality* does not, moreover, prove that he was not feeling other silent, insistent dissatisfactions, felt scars of negative prehensions. Fatigue can mark the end of an adventure: it is up to others, if possible, to prolong it. Nevertheless, the "hybrid feeling of God," a triumph of the ontological principle, is calling for new conceptual articulations. In Christian theology, God's providential function never did get along very well with his eternity, and Whitehead criticized lame theologico-metaphysical compromises too strongly not to finally tackle the problem. Once he has finished with what Lewis Ford has called his "final revisions," God will be endowed with a consequent nature, that is, a "physical" pole derived from the temporal world: we will come to that at the end of our itinerary. As far as the process of concrescence is concerned, it will undergo, and it is to this that we turn now, a transformation that will definitively drive away the specter of a unification that could be called the realization of an ideal possibility.

CHAPTER TWENTY-ONE

Actuality between Physics and the Divine

F WE SUBSTITUTE THE TERM "energy" for the concept of a quantitative emotional intensity, and the term "form of energy" for the concept of "specific form of feeling," and remember that in physics "vector" means definite transmission from elsewhere, we see that this metaphysical description of the simplest elements in the constitution of actual entities agrees absolutely with the general principles according to which the notions of modern physics are framed (PR, 116).

When it comes to *Process and Reality*, we must be careful at every step. The absolute agreement with the general principles associated with modern physics that is claimed here refers us directly to an ancient hope, ceaselessly reinvented. In *The Concept of Nature*, Whitehead proposed the relation between the electron and its field as a simplified but important example of the ingression of an object into an event. The inseparability of the electron, characterized by scalar quantities such as energy, mass, and charge, and its field (vectorial and delocalized) constituted a typical example of the way physics itself denounces the misplaced concreteness of simple localization. Whitehead, at the time he was writing his Gifford lectures, the text of which, somewhat modified, would finally become *Process and Reality*, apparently thought he could maintain the terms of an agreement he had long envisaged.

It is on the basis of this obstinate continuity that one can understand the importance of the conceptual transformation I set forth in the context of the case of the missing shade of blue. This transformation could certainly not be inspired by the physicists' electron, for no situation studied by physics seems to require the ingression of unrealized eternal objects. The flight of speculative experience, reassembling the notion of actuality from top to bottom, had as its starting point the extremely sophisticated actual entities with regard to which the question of consciousness arises—for instance, philosophers asking the question of the hiatus in the color chart of blues. Yet Whitehead intends to produce an interpretation applicable both to thinkers and to electrons, to novelty and to conformity. The electron must therefore be dragged into the upheaval provoked by the thinker. The question can then be asked of whether the upheaval in question has finally destroyed what Whitehead attributed so much value to: the agreement of his metaphysics with the general principles of physics. The text is silent on this subject: Whitehead allowed the passages expressing the importance of this agreement to remain, but, here as elsewhere, he seems to have left it up to his readers to "fill in the blanks," at their own risks and perils.

Rather curiously, a path can indeed be constructed that maintains, throughout all its conceptual transformations, Whitehead's ambition of a metaphysics that generalizes physics while bringing to light the partial and selective character of its successes. This path, which I shall take, will proceed by way of what is called "second generation" quantum formalism, which many commentators have affirmed raises "explicitly metaphysical" problems, concerning the very existence of a "reality in itself." In fact, Whitehead's silence with regard to the speculations inspired by quantum formalism, which however began at the very time when he was writing *Process and Reality*, is rather remarkable. He never commented on the theses according to which it is henceforth impossible to speak of "objective" physical reality, definable independently of the measuring operation, even independently of the mind of the person for whom measurement has significance. We can understand this if we recall that he did not like to criticize, for the great alternatives deployed by these speculations are so many variations on the theme of the bifurcation of nature. Either this bifurcation is solved by an absolute triumph of the "secondary qualities" over the "primary qualities"—this is what is celebrated by those who have opted for the radical negation all "physical reality," the only "object" of quantum mechanics then designating the results of the measurements that we choose to carry out. Or else it is resolved by the apotheosis of dualism: quantum reality would then be theoretically well defined, *via* Schrödinger's equation, for instance, but defined *qua* unknowable, with knowledge, for its part, referring to us, to our "becoming aware," assimilated to so many fragmentations of what cannot be fragmented, producing answers that are purely relative to the mode of questioning that conditions them. Or else again, as Whitehead predicted would be the case every time mind and nature intervened together, speculation makes the whole powder magazine explode, since measurement would then signify the conscious mind's power of direct intervention upon matter.

Here it is important to recall that the distinction Whitehead makes as early as *Science and the Modern World,* between the mental and the physical, does not offer any analogy with what the interpreters of quantum mechanics distinguish as "mind" and "matter." Whiteheadian "physical feeling" includes the feelings of everything that has obtained immortal objectivity, be it an "electronic" occasion or an occasional thought. In other words, we must accept that among what constitutes a heritage for the electronic occasion, there are also the physicist's feelings. The difference between the practice of the physicist and that of the psychologist consists in the fact that an electronic occasion cannot create a relevant integration between what the enduring society to which it belongs offers to its feeling, and what is felt about it by the physicist. Unlike the relation of double capture constituted, for instance, by an operation of taming or seduction, the relation of knowledge between physicist and electron designates its terms as dominated by mutually incompatible modes of feeling. The stubborn endurance of the material societies that maintain the thread of their conformity has nothing to do with the physicists' doubts. But the physicists' questions, taking advantage of this conformity, just as much ignore what could testify to "mental pole" of the occasions whose "routes" they study, relegating, if need be, what escapes this conformity to the unknowable: it is impossible to explain why an unstable radioactive nucleus breaks apart at one moment rather than at another.

The privilege of physics, when it comes to understanding the "physical pole," that is, the first phase of a process of concrescence, thus does not designate physics as a "science of matter" as opposed to mind. Instead, it can be claimed that it designates physics as highly selective, since the articulation it risks between experimental research and mathematical creation makes full use of the conformity of inheritance of the processes it selects. The inventive, relevant, and rigorous definition of physico-mathematical notions is what interested Whitehead in *The Concept of Nature,* and it is the adventure of this definition that I will use as a guide to unfold the radical nature of the transformation that will affect the "physical pole" of the actual entity. This transformation will enable creativity to be defined as the ultimate, actuality as *causa sui,* and the ontological principle as restrictive. First, however, we must begin (again) with the beginning, that is, what Whitehead was thinking in 1927.

The first phase is the phase of pure reception of the actual world in its guise of objective datum for aesthetic synthesis. In this phase there is the mere reception of the actual world as a multiplicity of private centres of feeling, implicated in a nexus of mutual presupposition. The feelings are felt as belonging to the external centres, and are not absorbed into the private immediacy. The second stage is governed by the private ideal, gradually shaped in the process itself; whereby the many feelings, derivatively felt as alien, are transformed into a unity of aesthetic appreciation immediately felt as private [. . .] *in the language of physical science, the "scalar" form overwhelms the original "vector" form: the origins become subordinate to the individual experience. The vector form is not lost, but is submerged as the foundation of the scalar superstructure* (PR, 212).

In physics, forces and fields, which are vectorial, designate the interdependent character of a reality, in which everything that occurs refers to something else. As for energy, it is a scalar quantity, and is required by measurement: every act of measure implies an exchange of energy. In the correspondences Whitehead is suggesting here, physics, confronted by diverse experimental situations and the power and constraints of mathematics, has therefore created a distinction that can be generalized. In this generalization, what physics characterizes as an individual, defined as localizable by the role it plays in energetic exchanges, will designate "individuals *qua* feeling their world," or concrescence *qua* taking a determinate position with regard to what it has received or, more precisely, coming into existence *qua* this taking of position, and therefore inseparable from what has become "their" world.

The characterization of concrescence that results from this generalization could have been produced by the author of *Science and the Modern World,* or more precisely by the author who, having finished writing *Science and Modern World,* would have undertaken to render explicit the aspects left in the dark, and in particular the link between realization as "a gathering of things in the unity of a prehension"—a cavalier generalization of Berkeley's thesis—and the theme of the atomic nature of the world of becoming. Such a link had only been risked from the viewpoint of the envisagement of eternal objects, that is, from the viewpoint of possibilities of value, whereas the question of "event-related processes," and hence of value, had remained unexplored. All that remained would be to conceive of that value, the way the "scalar" form "overwhelms" the initial "vectorial" form.

It is impossible to deal with the "physical pole" (vectorial) without dealing at the same time with the divine. For here, of course, we encounter the objection I had raised with regard to the "triple envisagement" proposed in *Science and the Modern World,* that is, the possibility of reducing Whiteheadian concrescence to what Gilles Deleuze calls "realization," as opposed to "actualization." To what extent is private appropriation not reducible to a selection in the midst of what is already potentially well-defined? To what extent is the contrast between "possibility of value," corresponding to an ideal situation, and "value," an actual taking of a position, not reducible to the passage to existence of a possible that lacked only existence? The term "energy" is, from this viewpoint, highly compromising. It is precisely the great success of rational dynamics to have articulated "energy" and "difference in potential" in a complete and coherent way. Every measurement is, of course, intimately linked, directly or indirectly, to an exchange in energy, but in dynamics "actual energy," as it can be measured through scalar effects, bears witness in a way that is complete and without remainder to the vectorial potential of which it is the realization. This is what makes dynamics the ideal to which physicists refer when they call themselves "realists."

To illuminate the situation as it presented itself to Whitehead in 1927, let us address another fragment from the same period of composition. Here, Whitehead comments on the selective character inherent in the process by which multiple feelings are transformed into a unique aesthetic appreciation.

Again the selection involved in the phrase "selective concrescence" is not a selection among the components of the objective content; for, by hypothesis, the objective content is a datum. The compatibilities and incompatibilities which impose the perspective, transforming the actual world into a datum, are inherent in the nature of things. Thus the selection is a selection of relevant eternal objects whereby what is a datum from without is transformed into its complete determination as a fact within. The problem which the concrescence solves is, how the main components of the objective content are to be unified in one felt content with its complex subjective form. This one felt content is the "satisfaction," whereby the actual entity is its particular individual self; to use Descartes' phrase, "requiring nothing but itself in order to exist." In the conception of the actual entity in its phase of satisfaction, the entity has attained its individual separation from other things; it has absorbed the datum, and it has not yet lost itself in the swing back to the "decision" whereby its appetition becomes an element in the data of other entities superseding it. Time has stood still—if only it could (PR, 154).

In fact, what emerges in this text is that there are two "moments" of selection. The first, which transcends the actual entity, is here relegated to the "nature of things": it is the compatibilities and the incompatibilities inherent in this nature of things that determine what the "perspective" of the concrescence will be. In other words, this perspective will concern what is already defined as unifiable, appropriable, which corresponds to the notion of an ideal situation envisaged in *Science and the Modern World*. A certain "ordering" has taken place, incompatibilities have already been eliminated. A "datum" is proposed, and, to characterize this datum, we read elsewhere (PR, 150) of "settlement," which designates both an "establishment," an "agreement" between parties, and a "decision" solving a problem, founding a new departure. The matter is closed. In short, what the entity "finds" is not a multiplicity but a matter that is already settled, a heritage offering the "real potentiality" that the data that make it up be felt in a unified way, as a datum.

The final stage, the "decision," is how the actual entity, having attained its individual "satisfaction," thereby adds a determinate condition to the settlement for the future beyond itself. Thus the "datum" is the "decision received," and the "decision" is the "decision transmitted." Between these two decisions, received and transmitted, there lie the two stages, "process" and "satisfaction." The datum is indeterminate as regards the final satisfaction [. . .] The actual entity, in becoming itself, also solves the question as to what it is to be (PR, 150).

We have once again to deal with the problem left in suspense by the underlying eternal activity of *Science and the Modern World*. The "divine ordering," inherent in the "nature of things," corresponds to the envisagement of the "ideal situation," with regard to which entities will have to choose "by addition of the future" what they are to be. The "triple envisagement" has thus simply become the way in which God, envisaging the totality of eternal objects, settles the deal that will be allotted to the entity. It is on the basis of this deal that an entity must decide what it will be, in somewhat the same way that gamblers decide what their play will be on the basis of the cards they have been dealt, all of which are compatible with the rules of the game. Here, therefore, datum is not the singular of data, the datum of a particular feeling, to be unified with the others. The datum is the hand dealt, already characterized by a form of togetherness which the actual entity will have to appropriate.

The contrast between vector and scalar, as invented by physics, would then be what is generalized by the difference between the possibility of value and value. Before moving from this observation to the possibility of going further, whose necessity it confirms, it is appropriate to think, with Whitehead, about why this generalization seemed so promising to him.

It is first important to emphasize that we have to do here with an "imaginative rationalization," for Whitehead did not take up this contrast as such from physics. Instead, by means of the example of the electron and its field, Whitehead has given central importance to what rational dynamics allowed to be omitted when it identified energy and potential (energy) difference, the transition from potentiality to actuality. Yet it is precisely thanks to this identification that the dynamic designation seems to designate an "objective" world defined as intrinsically measurable, explaining by itself the scalar quantities in terms of which physicists carry out their measurements. Correlatively, by accentuating the irreducible contrast between scalar description and vectorial description, Whitehead adopts a position with regard to what became a critical problem for physicists, with the quantum model of the atom proposed by Niels Bohr. Bohr's atom articulates two types of components, whose heterogeneity is now exhibited: a dynamic type of description (and therefore vectorial) of the "stationary states," and a scalar characterization of the energetic exchanges to which this atom is liable when it "changes states" in a way that dynamics cannot describe (the famous "quantum jump"). Whitehead's generalization thus does not obey physics, but has as its starting point a physics in crisis: in one way or another, physicists know that, when interrogating an atom, they can no longer recount its adventures as if they were the simple description of a well-defined being, endowed with strictly functional behavior.

In my commentary on the triple envisagement, I emphasized that its defect was that it did not inspire any appetite for the question of actuality. I was right, but this reason needs to be reformulated: Whitehead thought he knew how to solve this question, and the appetite that his text did not inspire may perhaps reflect his tranquility in this regard. He had, in fact, made the opposite choice to the one that was to be made by the physicists who, inheriting this first quantum physics, would come later to speak of a reality "indeterminate independently of measurement" (a measurement thanks to which the overly embarrassing quantum leaps were to be "overwhelmed" by the fascinating question of measurement). For Whitehead, indeterminacy by no means characterizes "reality," as opposed to the determination brought about by measurement. What we address has always already determined itself, "thus and not otherwise," as a stubborn fact. If one can speak of indeterminacy, it is in reference to the impossibility in principle, for every determinate fact, of determining how it will be taken into account; that is, in the vocabulary of *Process and Reality*, to the need for a decision with regard to the initial datum.

As far as physics is concerned, the viewpoint proposed by Whitehead is deeply relevant. If we follow him, we will say that quantum physics "does what it can," continues to decipher the regularities it can, while the new experimental apparatuses that have enabled it to "reach" atoms have entailed the loss of the deceptive limpidity of dynamics. Indeed, these apparatuses, because they place measurement under the banner of detection, detach "scalar quantities" from their dynamic explanation. We do not demand that a measurement by detection be explained in the same terms as what it characterizes. We ask it to designate its respondent in a reliable way: it is an electron that is detected. But detection itself, a selective and finalized operation, is by no means sufficient to define the behavior of what is detected; it can only define it as responsible for its own detection. It captures scalar quantities, but these will have to be articulated with "vectorial reasons," and no longer deduced from these reasons. In other words, whereas classical dynamics might seem able to describe what the behavior of a dynamic system is "in itself," *qua* obeying well-determined interactions, the physics of detectors imposes upon physicists a difficult referral from the "consequences," attested by the apparatus, to the description of the detected entity "in itself," *formaliter* in the sense of Whitehead, for whom this referral will therefore never succeed in reestablishing deducibility.

When, in April 1925, Whitehead decided to atomize time, he was able to propose an irreducible distinction between the atomic, private character of the process of formal determination of an entity and the constructed, social, as we will say henceforth, character of all continuity. This amounts to rendering explicit why, in agreement with Bohr's atomic model, the difficult referral envisaged by the physicists is in fact impossible. A quantum leap, characterized by a difference that is energetic, that is, scalar, does not "take any time" in the physical, continuous sense of the term. As an "atomic individual event," it is indivisible, unanalyzable in terms of a succession of instants.

The actual entity is the enjoyment of a certain quantum of physical time. But the genetic process is not the temporal succession: such a view is exactly what is denied by the epochal theory of time. Each phase in the genetic process presupposes the entire quantum, and so does each feeling in each phrase [...] The problem dominating the concrescence is the actualization of the quantum in solido (PR, 283).

With this description of a "quantum" that is indivisible and yet extensive, in the sense that, as we shall see, it atomizes an extension that it presupposes and confirms, Whitehead has raised to a metaphysical power the characterization William James proposed of the specious present (a characterization that had interested Niels Bohr to the highest degree). The specious present is always evaluated from the viewpoint of its completion—it will have been of such-and-such a thickness—since every characterization "during" this interval would constitute an interference that would force the present to topple into the past. To express it in a way that evokes relativity: concrescence in the formal sense, as long as it is not completed, as long as it has not produced its own position, corresponds to an "elsewhere." It does not belong to the past of any other entity, and no other quantity can take it into account.

Physical time makes its appearance in the "coordinate" analysis of the "satisfaction" (PR, 283).

Physical time does not matter only to our objective descriptions of the world. The latter are always social, always presupposing a twofold endurance. As Bergson said, we must wait for the sugar to melt, and this waiting implies the continuity of an articulating relation, presupposing the endurance of Bergson, who waits, and that of what he calls "sugar," which is capable of existing in a crystalline form or of testifying to its liquid existence by the sugary taste taken on by tea. Yet these descriptions require an important cosmological feature: the fact of a solidarity between the world and ourselves in the unison of "at the same time." Simultaneity testified to this solidarity in *The Concept of Nature,* and it is what perception exhibits in an abstract mode by proposing to us an external world "out there" perceived by me "here." We must also ask this solidarity for an interpretation of the relevance of physical laws and the interactions these laws involve. What Whitehead calls the coordinate analysis of satisfaction must thus ensure the adequacy of his philosophy with the unison expressed by the "at the same time," and enable the justification of the (relative) relevance of physical laws, not, once again, because physics is the "fundamental science of matter" but because it has pushed to the farthest point the risks associated with the explanation of the solidarity to be interpreted.

Science is either an important statement of systematic theory correlating observations of a common world, or is the daydream of a solitary intelligence with a taste for the daydream of publication. But it is not philosophy to vacillate from one point of view to another (PR, 329).

Coordinate analysis associates "time" and, more generically, "extension" not with objectification in general but with the way an undivided satisfaction will be divided by what will become its consequences, with a particular aspect of that objectification. In terms of "coordinate division," the "position occupied" by an entity is considered (is the object of a feeling) apart from how it is occupied. This is reflected by the adjective "coordinate," which evokes a homogeneous characterization, the situation of each element being entirely defined by its relation to the others. What an entity has undivided enjoyment of is thus felt in an abstract, impartial mode as the "situation" of that entity, defined by its relations to other equally situated entities.

When we divide the satisfaction coordinately, we do not find feelings which are separate, but feelings which might be separate (PR, 284).

The adoption of a position, when it is felt in the abstract mode that only corresponds to the way in which the felt entity has situated itself, is placed under the twofold banner of separability and potentiality. Each entity felt in this mode is felt *qua* situated in the place where it is, and in such a way that it might have been elsewhere. *Qua* felt in the mode of co-ordinate analysis, entities can "propose" to or "impose" upon the entity that is feeling them a way of situating itself that ratifies its belonging to what Whitehead calls the "extensive continuum."

For Whitehead, to be situated in the midst of the extensive continuum by a unified feeling of the coordinate relations that have already been accepted and confirmed by the entities belonging to the nexus that is to be made "its world" designates the most generic social belonging. The extensive continuum itself is nothing other than the impartial articulation of all situations, that is, of all possible viewpoints on each other, an expression of the solidarity of all these viewpoints, of their belonging to a single "community." As an expression of an accepted solidarity, that is, a solidarity taken up as an ingredient of their identity by all actual entities (including, in another way, by God), the extensive continuum is "real." In itself, however, it has no power to impose itself, and exists only as it is confirmed. It is "real" only to the extent that it is prolonged, from decision to decision. Coordinate analysis objectifies the standpoint that the entity is supposed to occupy within the nexus, but it is up to this entity to ratify its situation in the continuum, that is, its belonging to the nexus. This is why Whitehead makes the continuum a "real potentiality," that is, makes it relative to an actual entity, or for an actual entity. By "atomizing" the continuum, every adoption of a position will carry out what the continuum cannot account for: the difference between the past, which it has inherited, and the future, which will inherit from it.

Actual entities atomize the extensive continuum. This continuum is in itself merely the potentiality for division; an actual entity effects this division [...] with the becoming of any actual entity what was previously potential in the space-time continuum is now the primary real phase in something actual. For each process of concrescence a regional standpoint in the world, defining a limited possibility for objectifications, has been adopted. In the mere extensive continuum there is no principle to determine what regional quanta shall be atomized [...] the factors in the actual world whereby this determination is effected [...] constitute the initial phase of the "subjective aim." This initial phase is a direct derivative from

God's primordial nature. In this function, as in every other, God is the origin of novelty, aiming at intensification (PR, 67).

In other words, if God, as is the case so far, is he who proposes to each entity its initial "datum," it is also God who proposes to it the standpoint that will characterize it, the way it will atomize the extensive continuum. Here, God is an "organ" in that, like any organ, he is associated with a social endurance and with its particular mode of canalization, but he is the organ of "novelty," aiming at intensification, for belonging to the extensive continuum as proposed by the canalization constitutes the condition for an actual occasion to provide this intensification. God is thus what makes possible an adventure marked by solidarity, a cosmological adventure, rather than the frank chaos of free-for-all positions.

In fact, Whitehead wondered whether he should attribute to the solidarity deriving from belonging to the extensive continuum the character of a metaphysical generality or that of a "social fact," as for all belonging. But we have here a limit on speculation: although it may not be metaphysically excluded for a process of concrescence to "escape" extensive social canalization, refusing the proposed socialization, it is, by contrast, impossible to imagine this case, since such a case would exclude all the stabilities presupposed and required by the intensification associated with imaginative experience.

Some general character of coordinate divisibility is probably an ultimate metaphysical character, persistent in every cosmic epoch of physical occasions [...] *but* [...] *it is difficult to draw the line distinguishing characteristics so general that we cannot conceive any alternatives, from characteristics so special that we imagine them to belong merely to our cosmic epoch. Such an epoch may be, relatively to our powers, of immeasurable extent, temporally and spatially. But in reference to the ultimate nature of things, it is a limited nexus. Beyond that nexus, entities with new relationships, unrealized in our experiences and unforeseen by our imaginations will make their appearance, introducing into the universe new types of order* (PR, 288).

Whether the extensive continuum is metaphysical or cosmic, it cannot, in any case, be confused with the spatio-temporal relations rendered explicit by physical laws. The relevance of these laws presupposes a world in which the intervals of space and time matter, while the coordinate character of situations within the extensive continuum does not, as such, provide either measurability or dimensionality. In other words, in the positive sciences we never have to do with relations that can be reduced to the consequences of "situations" in the midst of the extensive continuum. The latter is impartial articulation, whereas every position, including spatio-temporal position, is partial and refers to more specialized societies.

The various societies that designate solidarity as spatio-temporal have endurance in common. And as soon as interactions appear on the scene that articulate space and time in a specific way, we have to do with positions marked by partiality. If physical laws must involve distance, it is because all distances have henceforth ceased to be equivalent. This is what physical interaction affirms: distance matters.

Before going further, however, a pause is necessary, for contemporary physics invites us to go one step farther with regard to the relation of contrast proposed by Whitehead between the extensive continuum and physical laws. This is the opportunity for a twofold test: of the social conception Whitehead proposes of "physical reality," and of the contemporary physical scenarios that have the ambition of introducing the genesis of differentiated interactions on the basis of what would, like the extensive continuum, be the very embodiment of impartiality.

Physicists today invoke the hypothesis of a primordial field characterized by a perfect symmetry, that is, by perfect impartiality. The symmetry of scale that characterizes this field implies the generalized equivalence of all the "situations" it allows to be defined. This is certainly a physical field, inhabited by particles and interactions, but all the interactions in it have the infinite range that contemporary physics associates with particles of zero mass (like the photon): in their cases distance, that is, localization as well, does not matter. And the analogy with the extensive continuum becomes even more captivating with the reason the physicists give for the appearance of differentiated interactions, that is, also the reason why "material societies" exist. It would be the result of an event of "symmetry breaking."

Whitehead was right to trust the inventiveness proper to physics. In their own way, physicists, too, henceforth affirm that physically differentiated particles are inseparable from a "social," that is also, "epochal," fact. For "symmetry breaking" corresponds to a twofold correlative definition: that of differentiated "actors," which endure, perpetuate themselves, and preserve their identity through what happens to them, and that of the partial character of their respective behavior, of what makes a difference for them, and of what difference they make for others. Physics thus describes the appearance of "partial" actors, inseparable from the role they play in the "society" without which they would not exist. Defined in this way, these actors and their behavior can be assimilated to "collective effects," inseparable from the global event that constituted the symmetry breaking affecting the primordial field. We are very far from the localized entities that Whitehead denounced as the "fallacy of misplaced concreteness"!

Did physicists "discover" the extensive continuum? If this were the case, Whitehead's cosmology would be finished, because, for them, there is no need of God. Symmetry breaking is explained on the basis of the same kind of laws that allow the continuum to be characterized. Impartiality seems to be able to engender partiality "by itself," that is, by "spontaneous" breaking. Physics would indeed have become "the" fundamental science, which is indeed what many who participate in this adventure believe. This is attested by the speculative presentation that turns the work of contemporary physics into the accomplishment of the Pythagorean dream, the ascent toward mathematical-aesthetic principles, the symmetries of which everything we have to deal with would be mere deformed reflections.

This speculative presentation, which transforms the adventure of physics into an epic, also allows us to grasp where the difference lies between extensive continuum and primordial field. It is no coincidence that we hear of deformed reflections. In fact, what physicists explain is by no means a "symmetry breaking" but rather a "symmetry hiding." They do not explain how impartiality can generate partiality, how a new "social fact" has come into existence. They explain how impartiality can be both preserved and hidden by a reorganization of the primordial field.

For physicists, the conservation of symmetry is just as precious as the hidden character of this conservation. Certainly, without the latter there would be neither physics nor physicists, only the impartiality of perfect symmetry, which excludes any local adventure. Yet this dramatizing tremolo is a subproduct of the physicists' adventure, where perfect symmetry was not associated with questions like "why is there something rather than a symmetrical nothing?" The issue was rather the maintaining of a successful trick, "renormalization," in situations where it should fail. Both the primordial field and the "hiding of symmetry" of which it is the theater have the primary interest of eliminating the poisoning impossibility of "renormalizing," that is, in fact, the impossibility of defining, certain interactions of finite range (or, equivalently, of defining the massive mediating particles that the physics of fields associates with these interactions). Symmetry, as both conserved and hidden, eliminates the obstacle barring the way to the technique of definition by renormalization, as it will apply to the hidden zero mass/interaction of infinite range hidden "reality."

The physicists' proposition is thus indeed an exploit: they have, one might say, succeeded in having their cake and eating it, too: in maintaining the general validity of their technique of definition, and in "explaining" the apparition of the experimentally defined interactions, which present obstacles to this technique. Yet this proposition answers a problem produced by their own formalism. What is saved is an audacious setup, inseparable from the adventure of quantum field theory.

It is not a matter of "debasing" physics. Whitehead's God also responds to problems raised by the audacious setup that constitutes the scheme. The point is to affirm the positive divergence of the adventures and their respective importance so as not to fall into the very trap to be avoided. Nature bifurcates enthusiastically, and the powder keg blows up if symmetry breaking hides the truth of its conservation. This, moreover, is what is affirmed by some speculative physicists: no longer the common world alone, but also so-called physical reality would be mere manifestations of hidden primordial symmetries . . .

The affirmation of divergence is not a defensive one. It is rather a demanding one. Facing the enticing similarity between a physical and a metaphysical construct, the point is not to suspect that physicists have trespassed and to conclude that they must be led back to their own territory, but to connect the constructs to the respective problems to which they were an answer. This demands paying due attention to "technical details," with the trust that if there is an enticing similarity it is a bit like the case of the rabbit jumping out of the magician's hat: something is concealed. Not that physicists would willfully trick us. Rather, they themselves are captivated by the beauty of the answer, and may easily forget about the requisites of their question. In this case, indeed, the question of the "instability" of the primordial field, leading to the symmetry breaking event, requires (technical detail) a definition of the field energy that allows such a question, a definition that is slightly different from the one that enters into the definition of a field. No big deal, but the possibility of symmetry breakings is now included in the description of the "primordial field." No surprise, then, that the physicists have no need for God in order to have partiality "emerging" from impartiality. Their field is not as impartial as the extensive continuum. It describes an impartial situation, *including the possibility of a partiality.*

The divergence between Whitehead's metaphysical description and so-called "physical reality" concerns aesthetic appraisals and the questions they entail. Whitehead emphasizes "novelty," the appearance of new modes of partiality, as a condition for avoiding the bifurcation of nature. Theoretical physics privileges impartiality, and creates highly inventive ways to interpret "apparent" partiality as in fact deriving from something "more fundamental," that is, more impartial.

An angry man, except when emotion has swamped other feelings, does not usually shake his fist at the universe in general. He makes a selection and knocks his neighbour down. Whereas a piece of rock impartially attracts the universe according to the law of gravitation.

The impartiality of physical science is the reason for its failure as the sole interpreter of animal behaviour. It is true that the rock falls on one special patch of earth. This happens, because the universe in that neigh-bourhood is exemplifying one particular solution of a differential equation. The fist of the man is directed by emotion seeking a novel feature in the universe, namely, the collapse of his opponent (MT, 28–29).

Physics is not alone in privileging impartial explanation, making it the only "rational" path, as confirmed by the progress of knowledge. When biochemists discovered seemingly partial operations of detection among living cells and between such cells, such as activation, reception, inhibition, and so on, didn't they successfully "explain" this partiality in physico-chemical terms? It was the result of biochemical molecular interaction, nothing more! This, of course, leads straight to a bifurcating nature, at the risk of reducing biochemists themselves to a complicated concert of physico-chemical interactions.

Avoiding the bifurcation of nature thus means thinking of impartiality as a particular limit case, and the (partial) question of values as the generic question. Such was Whitehead's position when he began to write *Process and Reality*. And it is in these terms that one may think of the question of the divine "ordering." Each entity is not proposed only one situation in the midst of the extensive continuum. Its initial datum includes "possibilities of value," that is, possibilities whose realization will ensure both solidarity and partiality. When biologists identify biochemical operations with physico-chemical interactions like all the others, they are not wrong, for the molecules *in abstracto* are not different. What is different is their "role," as related to their belonging to a living society, and the questions biochemists will have to invent in order to identify them.

It is also here that we find, in a new way, the question of conceptual transformation that was to mark the composition of *Process and Reality*. The danger of the divine ordering may be related to the divergence between physics and metaphysics I have just proposed. Yet physicists construct their descriptions in such a way that what is defined as responsible for something will indeed enable an explanation of this something (which is not the case at all in other sciences!). But isn't Whitehead's God "spoon-feeding" concrescence? God, therefore, or more precisely the "nature of things" *qua* decided upon by his inexorable evaluation, would find itself to be what is primarily responsible. This divergence conceals a threatening convergence, as the link between explanation and responsibility is common. This may not be shocking when it comes to electrons or biomolecules, but the point is also to think of the partial and vehement lament of Job.

The agreement Whitehead sought with physics risks turning against him, for his conception, physical in its inspiration, admits for the moment, between the datum and the actuality, only the kind of hiatus, ultimately rather poor, that he himself had noted between the vectorial field and the electron, characterized by scalar quantities: the private appropriation of the datum. A poor figure of actuality, threatening to restore the figure of a God who is the "soul" of the world, the creator of all possibility of "taking" a partial or innovative position—the position would not be taken in that case, but rather "adopted."

I must now live up to my commitment, and explore what can be contributed to this difficulty by the conceptual transformation that turned physics upside down with the quantum formalism "of the second generation."

This formalism has, in fact, exacerbated the hiatus between vectorial and scalar, by opposing the continuity of a "functional reality" to the discrete character of measurements, and introducing the need for a "choice" of measurement. It has, in other words, given measurement a "decisive role," indicating a completely new articulation between the scalar qualities issuing from this measurement, and the "vectorial reality" with regard to which measurement is carried out. And to say "decisive role" is obviously to open up the possibility of conceiving an actuality whose value might not be the ratification of a previously settled choice. To risk this possibility, however, one must, of course, be situated as close as possible to physico-mathematical technical innovation, that is, as far as possible from controversies over the interpretation of formalism.

In fact, the very possibility of attributing a "decisive role" to measurement is associated with the introduction of the new physico-mathematical notion of an "operator." Paying due attention to this notion guarantees us against any untimely intrusion of speculation, for the relevance of operators has today been generalized to all physico-mathematical laws. I will therefore concentrate on this generalization first, before introducing the singularity of quantum mechanics.

Whereas the formulation of the usual physical laws defined their object as inseparably uniting the two features necessary to satisfy physicists— observable (scalar) definition and functional (vectorial) definition—the intervention of the notion of operator in the formulation of these laws presupposes that these two features be treated separately. Scalar quantities, defining possible observations, are henceforth relative to the action of an operator on a function, which means that the "functional being" to which measurement as an operant question is addressed is not defined "in itself" in the terms of the answer. The general character of the hiatus that Whitehead emphasized is thus inscribed within the formalism itself. The "physical reality" introduced by the language of operators is no longer what is to be described "in itself," but what "answers" the operant question.

It is not surprising that controversies over the interpretation of quantum mechanics have attained a degree of sophistication that recalls medieval quarrels, for reality as "answering" translates the impossibility of guaranteeing any kind of resemblance between the answer obtained and what it was supposed to have answered. Yet the physicists who created the physics of operators, and now use it even in "classical physics," did not frame the problem in terms of resemblance. The language of operators may well mark the renunciation of the ascent from what is detected toward the reasons of the being responsible for the detection, but it enables the satisfaction of a demand that defines the value of an "answer" in physics in another way. The answer obtained must be capable of being authenticated; that is, it must not be able to be disqualified as an "artifact," *qua* produced by an operation incapable of defining what it is addressing as the "reason" for its result. In other words, what "answers" must be a "respondent," in the sense of "guarantor" of the question's relevance. What the physicists have created is thus their own way to distinguish between a "good" and a "bad" question.

What is a "good" question in the formalism of operators? In general, an operator acting on a function produces another function. But the case in which the operator qualifies as "a question that has received its respondent" is the case where the result of the operator's action on a function or vector is limited to the reproduction of the same function or vector, multiplied by a determinate numerical quantity. These particular functions or vectors are called the eigenfunctions, or eigenvectors of the operator ("eigen" in German means "own," the operator's "own functions"). As for the numerical quantities, they are called its eigenvalues. And it is to such eigenvalues that the definition of the "answers" satisfying the physicists' demands for a respondent will correspond. If what a question addresses can be represented in terms of the eigenvectors of the operator corresponding to this question, the eigenvalue obtained will be the well-determined answer to the operant question. As a result, a physical being, if it can be represented by a set of the eigenvectors of an operator, can thus be taken as guaranteeing, answering for, the adequacy of the question corresponding to that operator.

We can understand this definition of a "good" or "adequate" question in the sense that the question addressed by the operator to one of its eigenfunctions (or vectors) is addressed to something defined as susceptible of answering it without being transformed by it. This is where a speculative generalization of the physico-mathematical innovation constituted by operators becomes possible. The great interest of this innovation with regard to the hiatus verified by operators, and which Whitehead had already speculatively generalized, is to display in an explicit way that it corresponds to a problem of knowledge: what is a good question? This may enable speculative generalization to display, in its turn, that the problem raised by metaphysics is not that of a reality to be known, but to be produced. The relation between operator and eigenvector, although it may still bear witness to the "absolute agreement" between modern physics and metaphysics, will thus nevertheless change the definition of the agreement, insisting on the divergence between the parties. In physics, the relation satisfies the physicists' demand for authenticating "good questions." In metaphysics, it might well designate satisfaction itself, the superject concluding itself from its henceforth unified heritage, having itself become the unified feeling of a unique felt content.

Such an adaptation implies that the point will be not to define the subject as "operative," as the one that raises the question, the one that decides how it will question the world, but to situate it on the side of what is to be produced: the subject is that for which the question of its own unification as a superject arises. The Whiteheadian subject thus does not operate but concludes itself from an operation which, when completed, will determine the operator, the actual world of the subject. In other words, whereas the physics of operators, as a scientific theory, designates a reality that must be interrogated in order to be known, the theory of concrescence, as a metaphysical proposition, may designate "reality" *qua* raising the question of the operations that must proceed in order for the subject to become the unified feeling of its (eigen) actual world. The "agreement" with the physics of operators will therefore be stated as: the superject is the subject that has become the "eigenfeeling" of that which, as "its actual world," has become the operator corresponding to this feeling. Correlatively, the world is not what answers to the subject, nor the respondent for what the subject "knows"; it is that which, vectorially, "operates" what the subject is to feel.

As we can see, unlike the old agreement Whitehead sought, the transposition I am attempting implies rendering explicit the difference between what satisfies the problem of knowledge and the problem of production. The physicists' satisfaction is when the system can be represented in terms of the eigenvectors of the operator that corresponds to their question. A satisfaction in Whitehead's metaphysical sense is the final co-production of the subject and "its" world in such a way that it is henceforth impossible to tell whether it is the subject's standpoint that determines the world, or if it is the site, the standpoint, that calls forth its subject. Once the process is completed, once the superject has defined itself, the operator, the henceforth actual world acting on the superject that is its "eigensubject," should reproduce it equal to itself, affected only with an eigenvalue. In all its details, experience is then one and individual: private.

This doctrine, that the final "satisfaction" of an actual entity is intolerant of any addition, expresses the fact that every actual entity—since it is what it is—is finally its own reason for what it omits [...] In other words, indetermination has evaporated from "satisfaction" [...] thus, in another sense, each actual entity includes the universe, by reason of its determinate attitude towards every element of the universe (PR, 45).

Final, fully determinate satisfaction is such that the "that" of *"that's what makes me feel"* is just as inseparable from the "I" of *"I feel"* as the intelligible, the intellect, and intelligence are inseparable in the philosophy of Plotinus. In the risky transposition that is guiding me, intelligence, obviously not an attribute of the intellect, could well be a name for the "eigenvalue" of the satisfaction, the scalar value that physics associates with the outcome of measurement, and which here becomes the "private," scalar response, inseparably enjoyment of "self" and of "what is felt." And this value would then be at the same time a "decision referring to what is beyond it": "what will have been felt," obstinate fact, "immortal object," one added to the many, whose consequences remain to be decided, whose effects will be "occasional," according to the role and the value that other occasions will confer upon it *qua* participating in their own satisfaction.

Yet what about the "initial phase"? How has the question of the "datum" been modified? It is here, not in the general physical language of operators, that we will finally confront the singularity of quantum mechanics. In quantum mechanics, the operators corresponding to the various measurable quantities have distinct eigenfunctions. If what is questioned can be represented in terms of the eigenfunctions of a class of operators, it is, by definition, incapable of being defined as a respondent for the questions corresponding to another class of operators. This is why physicists must define the choice of the question, that is, of the operator, as an ultimate. If the choice of a measurement, and hence of the corresponding operator, is addressed to a quantum system that is not defined in terms of the eigenvectors of that operator, we will say that the measurement "perturbs the system," is unable to designate this system as its "respondent." This means that, according to the preparation of a quantum system, it will be susceptible of giving a well-determined meaning to certain measurements, but will be "perturbed" by others.

What should we retain from this singularity? The term "perturbation" must be excluded, for it is relative to the ambition of knowledge. For physicists, it interprets the difference between a "good" question, that has found its respondent, and a question whose answer has no determinate meaning. What we should retain is that in quantum mechanics it is impossible to make all the questions that can be raised, all the physical quantities that can be measured, converge toward a being that would be guarantor for the relevance of them all. This is why, in quantum mechanics, operators are not just one mode of representation among others but a necessity. Physicists are forced to admit not only that there is no answer without a question, but also that no question is the "right one," independently of the means they have taken (preparation) to be able to receive a determinate answer to this question and not to another one.

The "agreement" between physics and metaphysics, if it is to be renewed, will not concern only operators, which mark the taking-into-account within the very syntax of the physical theory of the hiatus that had inspired Whitehead. It will require the abandonment of the "initial datum," because this datum had the power of proposing, if not of imposing, its perspective on the entity that appropriates it, and because, in terms of knowledge, it is precisely this power that quantum entities lack. They do not dictate how they are to be questioned, but they are a respondent in the authentic sense only insofar as the person framing the question has undertaken the means to "prepare" them to answer.

Of course, when it comes to metaphysics, one might say that God is the one who "prepares" the datum, but in this case the imbalance between the power attributed to God and the insignificant character of the appropriation becomes blatant. All the more so as another possibility of thinking has appeared: that the definition of the "datum" itself, *qua* operative, coincides with the final phase, when the subject has become a superject. God is then no longer a "preparer," because "preparation" designates concrescence itself. And indeed, when Whitehead abandons the thesis according to which concrescence has as its starting point an already unified "datum," which it is up to it to appropriate, when he fully deploys the "miracle of creation," entrusting unification to concrescence itself, God will have ceased to be an "orderer," to become the "object" of a hybrid feeling that initiates concrescence. As such, his role may be compared to that of an "instigator," operating as a "lure for feeling" for the nascent concrescence.

To God's role as an instigator responds the need to differentiate between what the physicists would call "good" questions, because they have a respondent, and the goodness that necessarily qualifies God's intervention. It may well be that what is to be contrasted are two meanings of the word "relevance." Relevance as an issue is always primary. In physics, the "good question" is the relevant one, the one that is able to designate what answers as its respondent. However, when relevance explicitly becomes a value, that value designates the way a question gives rise to its respondent. If I ask you a question at the right moment, in the right terms, with the right intonation, so that you suddenly see a way out where the situation was blocked, my question will have proved its relevance by its effects, by the way that your experience is transformed. In other words, your transformation is an answer, but it is by no means an answer "to my question": it answers for the relevance of the question as a lure that has initiated the process of which your experience is the truth.

The conceptual transformation that witnesses the disappearance of the initial datum as the source and explanation of relevant novelty may be interpreted as granting to relevance the meaning it receives in some of our most important experiences: when a gesture, a question, a suggestion give rise to their respondent without having "deserved" it. Not the frustrated insistence of the *"You ought to understand,"* but the true miracle, celebrated by the concord of two voices—*Okay, now I understand/now you understand*—in the most radical absence of guarantees that this concord designates something that is "the same." What was to be understood did not preexist the understanding, and belongs only to the person who understands.

As for the subject, it could be said that Whitehead's has passed from a rather literal interpretation of a saying of Pascal, "you would not seek me unless you had already found me," to a more complex one. In the literal sense, the subject has already found the unity it seeks to become, since its initial datum is derived from the divine ordering. But in the more complex version, "you" and "I" should not be able to be defined independently of the quest. In concrescent unification, feelings and what they aim at gradually co-determine each other, until the *"you found me!"* at the final stage, when feelings become the feelings of a subject that has become a superject, emerging from its unified feelings.

It is better to say that the feelings aim at their subject, than to say that they are aimed at their subject. For the latter mode of expression removes the subject from the scope of the feeling and assigns it to an external agency. Thus the feeling would be wrongly abstracted from its own final cause. This final cause is an inherent element in the feeling, constituting the unity of that feeling. An actual entity feels as it does feel in order to be the actual entity which it is. In this way an actual entity satisfies Spinoza's notion of substance: it is causa sui. *The creativity is not an external agency with its own ulterior purposes. All actual entities share with God this characteristic of self-causation. For this reason every actual entity also shares with God the characteristic of transcending all other actual entities, including God* (PR, 222).

If we recall the "miracle of creation" associated with the vision of the prophet Ezekiel, we may say that this vision has now become even more risky, that is, more complete. Whitehead has abandoned any distinction between settling the datum and appropriating it. Subjective unification no longer has as an "objective" lure the unity of the datum, those skeletons that are well-prepared and quite ready to come to life again. For the miracle of creation to take place, it is a multitude of dried bones, not skeletons in good working order, that must organize themselves, dress themselves in the flesh of real, emotional beings, and gather themselves together in the unity of an innumerable army. This is why skeletons are not what inspire the prophet. When Ezekiel spoke the word as he was commanded, it was words coming from elsewhere that he repeated, whose meaning he did not possess. At first, this meaning had no other locus than the quivering of dispersed bones. It is as the miracle occurs that the prophet Ezekiel will come into existence, as the person toward whom the eyes and ears of this "one" army, that owes him its existence, are turned.

The "subjective aim," the aim of the feelings that will bring to existence the subject whose feelings they are, thus has a divine endowment as its *initium*. It is no longer the datum that testifies to God, but the initial aim or lure, which is the activation of the many feelings *qua* "aiming at." As the process of concrescence proceeds, the "initial aim" will become a "subjective aim": the aim at a subject producing itself as it determines its world. But the initial lure does not constitute a final cause. It pertains to the feelings themselves to operate, that is, to produce the subjective convergence that will make them the feelings of a superject, each of them becoming correlatively the "feeling of an aspect of the actual world," a well-determined component affirming the inseparability of the world that makes itself felt, and the superject, the "eigensubject" of this feeling.

Each temporal entity, in one sense, originates from its mental pole, analogously to God himself. It derives from God its basic conceptual aim, relevant to its actual world, yet with indeterminations awaiting its own decisions. The subjective aim, in its successive modifications, remains the unifying factor governing the successive phases of interplay between physical and conceptual feelings. These decisions are impossible for the nascent creature antecedently to the novelties in the phases of its concrescence (PR, 224).

However, a question arises. If there is no longer any "initial datum" offering a ready-made perspective on the basis of which the entity would be a mere "adoption of a position," isn't concrescence confronted by a titanic task, in any case "unimaginable" in the sense that it would not constitute a "lure" for the imagination: to make a world on the basis of a chaos of disparate feelings?

This objection must be examined more closely. Is the multiplicity of felt data really chaotic? Or, more precisely, in what sense is it chaotic? To envisage this question, let us turn to the sixth category of explanation.

That each entity in the universe of a given concrescence can, *so far as its own nature is concerned, be implicated in that concrescence in one or other of many modes; but* in fact *it is implicated only in one mode: that the particular mode of implication is only rendered fully determinate by that concrescence, though it is conditioned by the correlate universe. This indetermination, rendered determinate in the real concrescence, is the meaning of "potentiality."* It is a conditioned *indetermination, and is therefore called a "real potentiality"* (PR, 23).

The multiplicity of data by no means signifies "pure chaos," a pure, disjointed multiplicity on the basis of which each concrescence would be "creation of order *ex nihilo.*" We do, of course, have to deal with a "nexus," a set, no longer a datum, still less a "togetherness." The way in which there will be a "togetherness" is henceforth the very question of concrescence. Yet the determination of the unique mode of implication of each of the elements of the collection is nevertheless "conditioned" by "the correlate universe." How are we to understand this conditioning without making a datum emerge once again? How are we to differentiate between what is really "pure multiplicity," the eternal objects which, for their part, are pure potentialities, and that whose "conditioned indeterminacy" nevertheless designates a "real potentiality"?

To make explicit this real potentiality, which is neither pure disjunction nor preordered, I will allow myself a reference that interprets the universe Whitehead qualifies as "correlate" on the basis of the notion of "correlation." I must emphasize that I mean "correlation" in the physico-mathematical not the statistical sense. Here again, the difference designates the invention and imperative of relevance that belong to physics, and does not by any means characterize purely statistical reasoning.

In physics, correlations are neither calculated starting out from collected data, of the kind statistical enquiries attempt to reveal, nor from actual relations between two terms, like interactions—for instance, the force of gravity. An interaction is defined by its effects, by the determinate way in which one being (or, more precisely, an enduring society) contributes to the determination of another, or by the way the behavior of each testifies to the existence of the others. Although gravitational interaction has been called "at a distance," it implies a localized definition of the beings that interact. In Whiteheadian terms, the interaction is "social"; it is part of the way societies that are said to "interact" integrate a stable reference to one another within their respective adventures. In contrast, correlations in physics enable an answer to questions that do not fit with this definition of physical behavior as mutually determined. Correlations may indeed be said to exist "between" the entities belonging to a population, but they have no meaning when it comes to the behavior of these entities taken individually. They only intervene when it comes to characterizing the population itself. In other words, if one followed (or, more exactly, if one could follow) the behavior of a molecule as a function of its interactions with all the others, the fact that correlations may exist between these molecules would never intervene in the calculation. The difference between correlated and noncorrelated takes on meaning for questions that can only be addressed to the population as such, because they bear upon what this population is capable of as such, not as an ensemble of interacting bodies.

Historically, correlations were introduced to characterize the effect of a hypothetical reversal of the direction of the velocity of each of the particles that constitute a population (gas). The operation of velocity reversal has been described as "creating correlations" between particles to justify the fact that this operation may result in "abnormal collective behaviour" of the population, in this case to move away from thermodynamic equilibrium instead of approaching it. More generally, the notion of correlation corresponds to the possibility of characterizing a population as such on the basis of a contrast with the most simple situation, which can be relevantly described by presupposing that what happens in one place has no definable consequence elsewhere. When this hypothesis of "generalized indifference" is relevant, one will say that the correlations are of zero intensity and range. This is the case with thermodynamic equilibrium, as is reflected by the eminent simplicity of its macroscopic description. In contrast, there is no longer any "indifference" when one speaks of "critical" situations. What occurs locally is said to have repercussions in the entire population: in the vicinity of the critical point, the range and intensity of the correlations undergo a dramatic increase.

To bring up a somewhat evocative analogy, let us take two (human) populations, apparently similar, in the sense that they allow themselves to be described similarly in terms of economic interactions, that is, exchanges defined in amnesiac terms of supply and demand. A remarkable difference might appear on the occasion of an event affecting these populations as such, like an earthquake or an invasion. To simulate this difference, however, modelizations will have to associate with their actants a

term of "memory," which has no influence on individual exchange behaviors, socially defined as amnesiac, but becomes dominant when it
comes to asking how the population will respond to the test. In this sense,
correlations are delocalized, since they characterize the mode of belonging to a population, not behavior that can be attributed to the members
of this population. And they are abstract, in the Whiteheadian sense, in
that they have no meaning in themselves but only from the viewpoint of
the event that "activates" them—we could say that the event "questions"
the population as such about the response it might become capable of.
According to the event, correlations may remain without consequence or
"make all the difference."

The fact that correlations, as physics has invented them, may give
meaning to what is neither pure multiplicity nor a system unified by interactions to which each individual behavior would be subject testifies to
what constitutes the strength of physics: its ability to introduce what is required by the relevance of a description. In the present case, what the description required is analogous to what the Whiteheadian crowd of initial
feelings requires, in that the question raised is what this crowd will be
capable of. One could therefore say that the initial phase of feelings designates the data as correlated, and even defines the divine lure as a "creator
of correlations," so long as creation is understood as "activation" and especially not as creation *ex nihilo*. In fact, the multiplicity of data is rich in
activatable correlations, for they constitute a "nexus," a "set of actual entities in the unity of the relatedness constituted by their prehensions of
each other or—what is the same thing, conversely expressed—constituted
by their objectifications in each other" (PR, 24). The correlated universe,
the universe as correlated, is thus an "activated nexus."

It can thus be said that the "correlated universe" is not unified, but
may be characterized by a multiplicity of "correlations," relations that
are "non-localizable," for they are not defined between terms but rather
by repercussions and repercussions of repercussions: a reciprocal immanence that entangles harmonies and dissonances, convergences and divergences, captures and diversions. Each element refers to others and is
a reference for others, but each time in a way that is particular, possibly
qualified only by the type of pattern or the "defining characteristic" that
designates a "social fact."

This is why to characterize the crowd of feelings Whitehead could use
the very term he had used to characterize the "initial datum": that of
"real potentiality." But more than physics, it would henceforth be languages one should address to accentuate what matters here: the fact that
the determination of the indeterminate is no more a simple adoption of

position with regard to a datum than it is a "demiurgic" miracle. A concrescence is no more of a "demiurge" than a statement, and no less, for every statement has as its "real potentiality" the correlated multiplicity of what could be called the "usages" that make a language, and is the producer of a use that does not preexist it as such. It can thus be said of every statement, whether it is produced in the manner of a watchword, redundant with regard to the situation, or like a poetic statement, actualizing a completely new usage, that it is conditioned by "the correlated universe" of the language, that it is the realization of a "real potentiality." But it must then be added that a language, *qua* real potentiality, raises the question of its "reality," which is not to be confused with any of its realizations. In other words, the "usages" are not cases among which one has to choose, like the various possibilities of translation presented by a dictionary. Instead, they should evoke what these possibilities are made to bring about, the perplexed and undivided nebula whence the choice emerges: *"this is the word that fits."*

Let us return to the ontological principle that will take on its full import at the end of this journey; that is, it will impose that God, who is a cause, must also be "explicable" in terms of causes. We will examine later the theological question that arises in this case, but we can show here that what has already been set aside is the threat of a God solely responsible for the partiality of an adoption of position, and therefore responsible both for "good" and for "evil."

According to the ontological principle there is nothing which floats into the world from nowhere. Everything in the actual world is referable to some actual entity. It is either transmitted from an actual entity in the past, or belongs to the subjective aim of the actual entity to whose concrescence it belongs. The subjective aim is both an example and a limitation of the ontological principle. It is an example, in that the principle is here applied to the immediacy of concrescent fact [. . .] In another sense the subjective aim limits the ontological principle by its own autonomy. But the initial stage of its aim is an endowment which the subject inherits from the inevitable ordering of things, conceptually realized in the nature of God [. . .] Thus the initial stage of the aim is rooted in the nature of God, and its completion depends on the self-causation of the subject-superject. This function of God is analogous to the remorseless working of things in Greek and in Buddhist thought. The initial aim is the best for that impasse (PR, 244).

We do not yet know how the "inevitable ordering," conceptually realized in the divine nature, communicates with the "initial aim" of a nascent subject. What we know is that this ordering does not correspond to global calculation, from which the "best of subjective endowment" could be deduced, but is "what is best for *that* impasse." Whitehead's God is not "Leibnizian," in the sense that the global and the local do not communicate in him, for him, and through him. Reality, says Whitehead, is "incurably atomic," and God is not assigned to the service of an ideal, placing what is local in the service of some global best. In fact, such an ideal would have brought to existence the sophism Whitehead denounced as early as *Religion in the Making:* the one everyone winds up with who tries to reconcile God's assumed general will for the good with his rather curious particular applications. The biblical God does not approve of the friends who advise Job to submit his pretensions to the impenetrability of the divine plan. Whitehead's God is the envisagement of "that" impasse, Job's lament or friendly advice, and not of their role in a universal economy. And this is so, not by choice, out of respect for individual "freedom," but by the necessity of the divine mode of functioning.

The divine endowment thus corresponds to an individual possibility, not to what individuals should accomplish in the name of interests that transcend them. Here we find the concern that had led Whitehead, in *Science and the Modern World,* to introduce God as the principle of limitation: only what is actual has value, what is actually taking a position, that is, what is refusing as well. Thus and not otherwise. Whitehead modifies, rearranges, inverts the relations, but never does he blame concrete experience, including those that have been celebrated as exhibiting notions he has abandoned.

In *Science and the Modern World,* the divine limitation made the difference between the ideal and the individual. The ideal situation, insofar as it resulted from an ordering of all the eternal objects, gave no meaning to any horizon, to any possibility of bringing to existence the individual decision to be a prehension of "this," rather than of everything presupposed by "this." If there were no limitation, each occasion should have "reflected" all the other events, the whole of nature. How, then, could it be called "decision"? Decision was thus associated with the "mental pole" of an occasion, in contrast to its "physical pole," with the former "breaking off" from the latter's actual illimitability. In *Process and Reality,* the distinction between physical and mental poles has been deeply modified, since the physical pole is no longer placed under the banner of illimitability but of (correlated) multiplicity. Yet this distinction can now be generalized to God himself, and it is, as we shall see, this characterization of the divine functioning that will make it possible to coordinate the "ordering" constituted by eternal envisagement with the local character, relative to "that" impasse, of the initial divine endowment. Correlatively,

God will no longer be a principle but will have to satisfy, in his distinct way, the categoreal obligations.

In the first place, God is not to be treated as an exception to all meta-physical principles, invoked to save their collapse. He is their chief exem-plification (PR, 343).

Like Whitehead himself, who reserves the fifth and last (rather brief) part of *Process and Reality* to this question, I will not try to approach the rather thorny question of the divine functioning until the end of our itinerary, after having explored what Whitehead has just created. We now leave physics behind; for the locus where the Whiteheadian concepts will have to be experienced is the one from which the demand that what exists must be the cause of itself has arisen. Not an electron, to be sure, but a thinker: Job, for instance, demanding that his "lament" be heard. It is therefore toward the adventures of consciousness that the flight of speculative experience must henceforth orient itself.

CHAPTER TWENTY-TWO

And They Became Souls

THE INITIAL AIM *is the best for that impasse. But if the best be bad, then the ruthlessness of God can be personified as Atè, the goddess of mischief. The chaff is burnt. What is inexorable in God, is valuation as an aim towards "order"; and "order" means "society permissive of actualities with patterned intensity of feeling arising from adjusted contrasts"* (PR, 244).

It is still with regard to "evil" that metaphysics' correction of the excess subjectivity of consciousness, here expressing itself in a religious image, is played out. From this viewpoint, the example taken by Whitehead when he announces, in a somewhat elliptical way, that "the chaff is burnt," is particularly formidable. The prophecy of John the Baptist, to which the ellipsis refers (Matthew 3:7–12) is a prophecy of anger. The time of patience is succeeded by that of impatience, of the good affirming itself in the destruction of what resists it, in the elimination of what impedes it. The prophet baptizes with water, with a view to repentance, but he announces the coming of He who was to baptize in the Holy Spirit, and also in fire, of He who would sort the grain, and would have the chaff burned.

But the worst is yet to come. The text to which Whitehead alludes not only contains the usual prophetic threats, but it proposes a formidable novelty: the prophet's anger appeals to the pitiless figure of a God who, as he announces, is liable not to be held by the covenant. Or, more precisely, by the covenant in the sense that it includes a divine commitment to maintain that covenant with the Jewish people. Those who hear him, thunders the prophet, must know that if God so wills, children for Abraham can come forth out of these stones!

Were the words attributed to the prophet those of a Jewish prophet possessed by impatience, or did they come later, inscribed in the Gospels by those who thought that they were the true and new children of Abraham, therefore capable of designating the chaff which had been, was, and would be delivered over to the fire of God's anger? In any case, even if the proposition comes from John, it introduces a terrible possibility, which was to be exploited by the Christians, that God, while faithful to the covenant, might be free from the election that seemed to be synonymous with it.

A formidable contrast has been produced. The continuity of the covenant with the children of Abraham remains a fact, but this fact suddenly leaves the "how" of this continuity indeterminate. Of course, from the viewpoint of Christian theology, it is the entire economy of the sacrament of baptism that is announced here, by which God transforms into a member of his people, a child of Abraham, not, perhaps, stones, but any human being, henceforth taken one by one. From the viewpoint of those who turn values of universality into an ideal that justifies all means, there is no doubt reason in this to praise God, History, or Humanity, for this proposition opens up the covenant to all human beings. Nevertheless, the proposition according to which no difference of origin counts when it comes to the universality of salvation was coupled with divine anger, or with the sorting process carried out in the name of the opposition between faithfulness and infidelity. In an attempt to avoid all excess subjectivity, one will limit oneself to saying that this new arrangement, which distinguishes divine faithfulness to the covenant as such from the commitment bearing upon the election of the Jewish people, is, inexorably, very interesting, liable to give rise to new contrasts, and a vector of intense feelings.

Whitehead's God is neither patient nor impatient, for these adjectives designate the adventures proper to societies. He is not at all constrained by any covenant whatsoever, for he "cares not whether an immediate occasion be old or new, so far as concerns derivation from its ancestry" (PR, 105). More precisely, this derivation matters only through the contrasts it has stabilized: the formidable innovation introduced by John would have no meaning without the lineage of prophets calling Jews to faithfulness, denouncing infidelity. That the long worry of the chosen people about the patience of its God could constitute a locus for a new family of propositions, transforming the contrast negotiable between faithful and unfaithful into an opposition, is a "fact" that we inherit, not the manifestation of a divine impatience or of a divine project. Yet, no more than the new propositions that would eventually allow the opposition to be overcome, this fact is not inscribed either in any divine plan dealing with the elevation of men or with the economy of Salvation. The initial moment of the aim was, of course, like any other, rooted in the nature of God, but it was so in response to a "local" question: what is the best for "that" impasse?

"To envisage" is the term proposed by Whitehead to describe a God who conditions creativity, who bends creativity into a cosmic adventure. Yet this term has henceforth received a more precise meaning. It is specified by the question: "what is the best for that impasse?" the question which, by the way, is that of Whitehead when faced by the impasses of thought, whether they refer to professionals, to the bifurcation of nature, or to the omnipotent God of theology. And it does indeed work in an inexorable way, in the sense that it has the eminently nonsocial character already assumed by life, as a justification of the robbery that is required by the regime of existence of living societies: nothing of what a society stabilizes *qua* important, *qua* justifying maintenance and imposition, can escape the possibility of a new contrast, transforming this importance into an impasse urging escape. Yet what is at stake is still "that" impasse: the divine envisagement, like life, is always local and interstitial. Nothing guarantees that the possibility of escaping the impasse, if it gains importance, will not actualize the trick of evil: to insist on being born at the wrong season.

The reference to God's inexorable valuation thus does not make him a judge. God does not justify any judgment. If he is a respondent, it is only for the trust of the person who dares to appeal against a judgment, since God responds for the fact that no reason has the power to define as impossible the new contrasts that would transform the range and the meaning of a judgment. The adventure of religions is thus indeed a social adventure. The names men give to God do not testify to him, but to the adventures of the human consciousness in search of its justifications.

Quite obviously, all this does not mean, from a metaphysical standpoint, that the names human beings give to God are pure fictions without any importance. It signifies the need for a severe sorting process between religious statements and metaphysical statements, with the former testifying to what human consciousness has made itself capable of at a given epoch, and the latter accepting themselves as obligated only by the imperative of coherence. Yet this sorting process, because it quite obviously proceeds from a highly conscious demand, must itself find a metaphysical meaning.

So far, we have primarily dealt with consciousness in an indirect way, with regard to something other than itself. This mode is dominant in Whitehead, and we will find it again in the following pages; but this time the point will be to go further, as we are of course obliged to do by a minimum of coherence. Although Whitehead constantly insists on the one-sided and especially partial character of what we call conscious experience, deploying all that is blindly presupposed by the most reflexive of such experiences, the vocation of speculative philosophy—the flight of experience—designates this conscious experience as its most crucial issue. Or, more precisely, it designates as its most crucial issue the possibilities of modifying the conscious experience of those who expose themselves to that flight.

The distinction is crucial. The wager of making conscious experience the crucial issue designates modern philosophical thought, as defined by what Whitehead calls the "subjectivist principle." He himself will adopt what he calls a "reformed" subjectivist principle in order to mark his belonging to modern philosophy and to designate its limitations. For the subjectivist principle has made conscious experience the central issue, to be sure, but this issue does not designate the question of this experience's modifications, it designates it itself *qua* unique source of certainty and justification. This is why the "subject" always deals with an "objective reality" with regard to which the question arises of what it can say about it, what pertains to this reality, and what pertains to itself.

The difficulties of all schools of modern philosophy lie in the fact that, having accepted the subjectivist principle, they continue to use philosophical categories derived from another point of view. These categories are not wrong, but they deal with abstractions unsuitable for metaphysical use [. . .] The notions of the "green leaf" and of the "round ball" are at the base of traditional metaphysics. They have generated two misconceptions: one is the concept of vacuous actuality, void of subjective experience; and the other is the concept of quality inherent in substance. In their proper character, as high abstractions, both of these notions are of the utmost pragmatic use. In fact, language has been formed chiefly to express such concepts. It is for this reason that language, in its ordinary usages, penetrates but a short distance into the principles of metaphysics. Finally, the reformed subjectivist principle must be repeated: that apart from the experiences of subjects there is nothing, nothing, nothing, bare nothingness (PR, 167).

In order to affirm that nothing exists independently of the experience of subjects, and that there is therefore no sorting process to carry out on the basis of the distinction between subjective experience and objective reality, one must overcome a terrible hesitation, a veritable "leap of death." This explains, no doubt, why modern philosophical doctrines have made nature bifurcate. For if a stable world is no longer there to confirm what we think, to propose the ideal of a well-founded agreement, everything seems to be reducible to mere fiction, interpretations that no arbitrage will enable to distinguish. And it is often by designating beliefs that are "offensive," in the sense of William James, that philosophers proceed: if we have no criterion defining "objective reality" against fictions, everything will be no more than a matter of taste and color. We will be forced to accept that the earth might just as well be flat, or fail to contradict the creationists when they maintain that God created each living species separately!

The common feature of all these "offensive beliefs" is that those who evoke them trust the interlocutor not to adhere to them more than they themselves do: a typically philosophical rhetoric. Yet with propositions evoking the judgment of God, which have literally "infected" Christian history, the case is completely different. Whereas philosophers often act as though the conscious subject could indifferently envisage all possibilities, and therefore needed a referee to carry out the sorting process between fictions that are equally envisagable, those who listened to John the Baptist may have felt their world tremble to its foundations. In this case, words are efficacious. They instill offensive doubt and demand conversion. Yet it would not occur to us to search for a referee or to speak of fiction. Conscious experience has been modified as such. A cry may rise toward the heavens, but those who utter the cry are aware that their experience is the only possible "referee," and even that the reasons they themselves will produce come only after the decision. Independent of the subject, there is nothing.

With regard to those who utter such cries, one will speak not of consciousness that is sure of its pretensions or demands certainties that have finally been given a foundation, but of a soul in distress. And the distress of these souls testifies to what will be one of the major inventions of Whitehead's philosophy, the invention of what he calls "propositions." If, on the sixth day, we became souls, it is not because language enables us to manipulate the pros and cons, to wonder whether the earth is flat or round. It is because language raises to its highest power the efficacy of what cannot be confused with it, the efficacy associated with what Whitehead was to define as a genuine existent. For propositions appear among the categories of existence of the categoreal scheme, just as actual occasions and eternal objects do (eight types of existent are defined).

(vi) *Propositions, or Matters of Fact in Potential Determination, or Impure Potentials for the Specific Determination of Matters of Fact, or Theories* (PR, 22).

No category of existence is intelligible as such, since the categories of existence are required by the categories of explanation and thus cannot be explained. In particular, no verb is possible, since verbs pertain either to explanation or to obligation; that is, they correspond either to what we seek to understand or else to the way what comes into existence is produced. But the sixth type of existent may seem quite particularly enigmatic. What are "theories" doing among existents? In fact, propositions are rather curiously absent from most Whiteheadian studies. Perhaps Whitehead's heirs are embarrassed to find in the midst of the metaphysical scheme a type of existent which, far from being appropriate to every occasion, seems to pertain to the theory of knowledge in the sense that it presupposes consciousness. In this case, they are "victims" of the casual Whiteheadian manner: appearing in the scheme among "existents," propositions then disappear, to reappear only after Whitehead has discussed "symbolic reference" and "judgment." They can therefore be taken, in the same sense, as a means of characterizing the experiences that imply perception, propositions, in this case, marking the appearance of consciousness. There is nothing coincidental about this: Whitehead very probably decided rather late to transform the problem, and to turn certain aspects of conscious experience into the privileged witness to a type of efficacy that would not be limited to consciousness. Not until the third part of *Process and Reality* will the "propositional feeling" be introduced, corresponding to the categoreal definition of the proposition as "impure potential."

How can we approach the difference between a statement corresponding to a perception or to a judgment, and a statement exhibiting propositional efficacy? Let us abandon prophecy, too dramatic an example, and take Descartes contemplating a piece of wax and applying himself to doubt, to separating the attributes that may pertain to the "objective reality" of the wax from those which, because they are variable or unreliable, do not. How can we describe Descartes's experience, as he conscientiously constructs the motivations of a verdict that should enable him to impose upon "anybody" a definition of "extended substance" that is exemplified nowhere in the world? Does he doubt, or isn't the "doubting self" instead a part of the data of the problem whose solution Descartes is constructing? Does the emotional tenor of his experience speak of the risk of refusing to the wax what belongs to it? Or else, doesn't the risk lie elsewhere? Perhaps with the possibility of founding his theory, of infecting his reader not so much with experience of doubt as with the mode of judgment that doubt will authorize? Every time an experience is questioned in this way, not on the basis of the words that present a theory but of the way that theory inhabits thinkers, of the issues that actually obsess them, of the risks to which their theory exposes them, the "reformed subjectivist theory" is activated. "Beliefs" no longer demand a referee, because what they propose makes the thinker think.

As the reader will have understood, the flight of speculative experience here returns to what had been at the origin of the flight itself, White-head's "cry": "That's absurd!" inspired by the philosophical and scientific statements that make nature bifurcate. The example he borrowed to criticize the use made in modern philosophical doctrines of the subjectivist principle, "I see a green leaf there," is the paradigmatic example of a statement that is clear from the viewpoint of consciousness and confused from the viewpoint of propositional efficacy. The question that imposes itself, in fact, is "so what?" Now, however, the point will no longer be to criticize. The contrast between "that which" we perceive and what we are aware of in perception will no longer constitute an argument without being interpreted, correlatively, in a positive way: an exploit of perception that will be named "symbolic reference." One will, of course, still have to "correct" the excess subjectivity attested by the privilege accorded to the "that which" as opposed to the "what," but this time language will no longer intervene as what explains this privilege: this argument is valid only when it comes to understanding the difficulty proper to philosophical language. Correcting the excess subjectivity of skeptical and critical philosophers, the point will be to celebrate what Whitehead will call a veritable "fortune."

If Whitehead's exposition situated propositions "after" "symbolic reference" and "judgment," it is because the point was to manifest that speech, or language, thanks to whose gift we have become souls, must be approached from two distinct angles. According to the first, language is "made to express" the reliefs of an experience that is not initially linguistic, and this is why things are then "easy to say," as if words referred to matters of fact that they limited themselves to describing. According to the second angle, however, the point will be to redescribe this experience by introducing "propositions." According to the first approach, language is marked, one might say, by redundancy and can therefore be reduced to an instrument of communication, *"there is an elephant,"* whereas according to the second one it will exhibit itself as designating creativity, which is the ultimate. The first angle of approach will become, retroactively, as inseparable from the second as the description of the living organism, imposing its obstinate values at the cost of the destruction of other societies, is inseparable from originality, which is the justification of life. If we wish to make the analogy explicit, we will say that the redundancy of language, insofar as it ratifies an elimination, is a robbery whose justification designates propositional efficacy.

Before we come to propositions as such, Whitehead has thus proposed a kind of genealogy of the experiences that language requires but does not explain. Such a genealogy is complementary to the "adventure of the senses," but here the emphasis will be on the importance of abstraction. This is why we will start from the trap represented by the misplaced concreteness associated with some of these abstractions. In particular, the two "errors" of construction noted by Whitehead in his critique of modern schools of philosophy testify to this error: that of vacuous actuality and that of quality as inherent in a substance. Vacuous actuality refers to what would be devoid of subjective experience. It is connected with the abstraction of simple localization, when we say, "This stone is where it is, and it just 'is.' " As far as the concept of a quality as inherent in substance is concerned, it corresponds to the influence of logical abstraction, which among all relations privileges the attributives ones: the leaf is green, and Socrates is mortal. Linguistic expression is appropriate to this twofold abstraction in a privileged way, designating a world in which things that are contemporary with one another, and with myself, appear, the bearers of sensible qualities but bereft of any relation with one another other than spatial.

This time, therefore, the point is no longer to criticize but to approach what sets the trap. The world "placed as a spectacle and as logic," the world that "appears to us," which we perceive in the way Whitehead was to call "presentational immediacy," is certainly a trap as soon as philosophers try to construct their concepts while profiting from the abstractions exhibited by the spectacle. Yet these abstractions have nothing to do with the categories we would project upon a mute reality. If this were the case, a science such as physics, which depends on the measures of distance and time, and therefore on the abstraction constituted by simple localization, would be "the daydream of a solitary intelligence with a taste for the daydream of publication" (PR, 329). We must think of the perceived world as an audacious and sophisticated montage, whose metaphysical generalities are to shed light on its selective and biased character, but in the sense that this selection privileges something important, testifying to important aspects of a systematic order, without which we would not survive for an instant.

Perception in the mode of presentational immediacy, because it proposes a world made up of things that exist "simultaneously," indifferent to one another, each one defined by its position relative to the others, would be a daydream without the solidarity that Whitehead has interpreted in terms of coordinate analysis, with each actuality confirming and prolonging the extensive continuum in which it situates itself. Yet we must not confuse the indifference of what coexists in the "now" of simultaneity with the impartial articulation of coordinated situations. Nothing is less impartial than presentational immediacy, than the experience of a "slice" of the world without past or future. This experience exhibits the importance of transmuted feelings (the attribution of color, for instance, to a nexus) as well as of the social mode of extensiveness that characterizes societies insofar as they endure. Neither simultaneity nor "colored things" exist outside of visual perception, but they translate a "cerebral" trust in a community of enduring beings that actualize a separation between "space" and "time" according to interdependent modes. That tiger I see, and that I see looking at me, may well be my way of inheriting the past: it is nevertheless prudent that I wager that the past has not had my vision as its sole heir, and that I think about running away. Nor is this trust peculiar to perception, for it is that without which detection would not have any meaning either. If the source of the smell that orients a butterfly's flight did not endure on its own account while the butterfly is flying toward it, there would be no butterflies.

The indifference of presentational immediacy to contemporary actualities in the environment cannot be exaggerated. It is only by reason of the fortunate dependence of the experient and of these contemporary actualities on a common past, that presentational immediacy is more than a barren aesthetic display (PR, 324).

Presentational immediacy obviously allows a resumption of the distinction Whitehead made in *The Concept of Nature* between what we are aware of in perception and what we perceive. The ultimate fact constituted by the mind's "foothold" in nature, the relation of cogredience between the percipient event that is "here" and the duration that is "now," is henceforth commented on in terms of "fortunate dependence." The fact that perception itself induces us to pay "due attention" to the tiger is our "fortune," the biased and selective wager we inherit with regard to what matters. However, speculative interpretation will accentuate what *The Concept of Nature* left in the shadows, since Whitehead limited himself to associating the percipient event with what he called, "roughly speaking," "bodily life." This dimension of experience obviously does not testify to the "real" world as opposed to the abstraction of immediacy. But it testifies in another way, which Whitehead will call "causal efficacy": we apprehend reality *qua* "making itself felt." In other words, the idea that what presents itself now in the mode of indifferent coexistence "has made itself felt" through a route of sophisticated experiences that ends up in a perception "there" is by no means, as some empiricists would maintain, an intellectual hypothesis. On the contrary, it is these empiricists who fall into the trap by denying what we know but what our linguistic statements can say only "roughly."

Whitehead never tires of crossing swords with Hume on the question of causality. In the name of his system, Hume has denied the obvious. He has denied what everyone knows: what "I see," I see "with my eyes," and the feeling this "with my eyes" corresponds to testifies to the primordial character of the "causal efficacy" that his system turns into a judgment derived from "habit," with no regard, as we have seen, for what oculists and prohibitionists would think about that. Yet there is not even any need for their testimonies. It is with an almost sadistic delight that White-head notes the absurdity in which Hume ends up when he undertakes to reduce to the constraints of presentational immediacy a case where bodily experience, instead of being inconspicuous and steady, makes it-self brutally felt: the experience of a man who blinks his eyes while a lightning bolt tears through the darkness.

The sequence of percepts, in the mode of presentational immediacy, is flash of light, feeling of eye-closure, instant of darkness. The three are practically simultaneous, though the flash maintains its priority over the other two, and these two latter percepts are indistinguishable as to prior-ity. According to the philosophy of organism, the man also experiences another percept in the mode of causal efficacy. He feels that the experi-ences of the eye in the matter of the flash are causal of the blink. The man himself will have no doubt of it. In fact, it is the feeling of causality which enables the man to distinguish the priority of the flash; and the inversion of the argument, whereby the temporal sequence "flash to blink" is made the premise for the "causality" belief, has its origin in pure theory. The man will explain his experience by saying, "The flash made me blink": and if his statement be doubted, he will reply, "I know it, because I felt it" (PR, 175).

Philosophers who have adopted the subjectivist principle, including Kant, who raises causality to the dignity of an *a priori* category, have exaggerated—the favorite sin of philosophy. They have ignored the crowd of vague feelings, which are hard to put into words but nevertheless bear a quite different message, that of a "presence," not of a "presentation." We may well describe the world as if it were given to us as a spectacle or a picture, and eliminate the notion of "cause," which does not belong to the picture: the "causes" nevertheless make themselves felt. Of course, they take on a meaning completely different from the well-defined "causes" of our reasoning: they designate the "efficacy" of those presences that testify, simultaneously and inseparably, to a body and to things.

The "causal feeling" according to that doctrine [n.b., that of Hume] arises from the long association of well-marked presentations of sensa, one precedent to the other. It would seem therefore that inhibitions of sensa, given in presentational immediacy, should be accompanied by a corresponding absence of "causal feeling" [...] Unfortunately the contrary is the case. An inhibition of familiar sensa is very apt to leave us a prey to vague terrors respecting a circumambient world of causal operations. In the dark there are vague presences, doubtfully feared; in the silence, the irresistible causal efficacy of nature presses itself upon us; in the vagueness of the low hum of insects in an August woodland, the inflow into ourselves of feelings from enveloping nature overwhelms us; in the dim consciousness of half-sleep, the presentations of sense fade away, and we are left with the vague feeling of influences from vague things around us (PR, 176).

The point is no longer to criticize, but to enunciate importance. Hume made the mistake of trying to separate the inseparable. Reducing perceptive experience to presentational immediacy, he could only reintroduce what he had first eliminated, in the guise of mere habits linked to our associations: "this then that" becoming "this, therefore that." As we have already seen, Whitehead also speaks of habits in *The Concept of Nature;* yet these are not the habits of an individual, but of experience. For him, these habits constitute not what should be diagnosed, or even denounced, but the veritable "fortune" of perceptive experience, what we all owe to a past of which we are not the author.

If perception is not a "daydream," it is because all perceptive experience is in fact made up of two distinct perceptive modes, one pertaining to presentational immediacy, and the other to causal efficacy. It is in terms of a particular, enduring articulation between these two modes that Whitehead names "symbolic reference." The perception of that yellow patch striped with black that I see over there is inseparable from a brutal emotional transformation, giving its meaning to what is perceived: *"a tiger!"* or rather, *"do I have time to run away?"* What Whitehead calls "symbolic" is not something referring to something else, inaccessible or not. It is what we have in common with all animals endowed with perceptive experience. The emotion that may seize Christians when the host is offered to them is, of course, more complex than the one that invades a rabbit at the sight of a predator, but if the Christians' faith approaches the ideal called "simple faith," it does not, as such, require any particular conceptual innovation. And when we "understand" a word, it is often in the mode of a meaning "that goes without saying." The word, as an audible object uttered "there," is a "symbol," whereas meaning, sometimes laden with emotion, refers to causal efficacy. We understand a word "because it has a meaning."

It is mistake to think of words as primarily the vehicle of thought. Language also illustrates the doctrine that in regard to a couple of properly correlated species of things, it depends upon the constitution of the percipient subject to assign which species is acting as "symbol" and which as "meaning." The word "forest" may suggest memories of forests; but equally the sight of a forest, or memories of forests, may suggest the word "forest" [. . .] but we do not usually think of the things as symbolizing the words correlated to them. This failure to invert our ideas arises from the most useful aspect of symbolism. In general the symbols are more handy elements in our experience than are the meanings. We can say the word "forest" whenever we like; but only under certain conditions can we directly experience an existent forest. To procure such an experience usually involves a problem of transportation only possible on our holidays. Also it is not so easy even to remember forest scenes with any vividness; and we usually find that the immediate experience of the word "forest" helps to elicit such recollections. In such ways language is handy as an instrument of communication along the successive occasions of the historic route forming the life of one individual. By an extension of these same principles of behaviour, it communicates from the occasions of one individual to the succeeding occasions of another individual (PR, 182–183).

For Whitehead, the word is not the murder of the thing, but an instrument of communication that helps things to prolong themselves, to make felt in our experience the causal efficacy associated with the past. Correlatively, language is here placed under the banner of redundancy, not of thought. Only our relative difficulty in resuscitating vivid memories makes the difference between the word *qua* symbol and what it evokes *qua* its meaning.

Symbolic reference has major pragmatic importance. The rabbit's intense experience is fortunate: without it, it would no doubt not have survived. The irrepressible relation between words and things is the daily bread of human experience: without it, no language. But to talk about fortune, or luck, is also to talk about possibility of misfortune. Symbolic reference is always a risk, and this risk is also first and foremost pragmatic, as is testified by all the lures (lures for feeling) produced by both preys and predators. Here, however, a problem arises: butterflies can also be "lured." There does not seem to be a frank distinction between what I have called detection and what Whitehead calls "symbolic reference." Except that, unlike detection, which I have risked associating with what is incoercible, symbolic reference, because it is an articulation between two distinct perceptive modes, opens up the possibility of hesitation and of learning. The bird that has, more or less at random, spotted a caterpillar imitating a twig will begin to test all the twigs in its vicinity. "Twig" henceforth signifies *"might be a caterpillar!"*

In fact, symbolic reference places us at a crossroad. In one sense, it constitutes a primary fact, the source of many perplexities for consciousness. If a thunderbolt is, rather indubitably, the cause of your (incoercible) blinking, it is not certain, in contrast, that the emotion that invades you, makes you tremble, is "caused" by what you see there, in front of you. One thinks of William James's undecidable question: am I moved because the world is moving, or does the world seem to me to be moving because I am moved? On the other hand, however, we must not exaggerate. We are not, as some claim, "imprisoned" in the network of our symbols and our meanings. What is true of the bird, who is able to learn, is even more true for us. We can learn more, even about what moves us. And we are (sometimes) able to question a symbolic reference as such, to verify the "correctness" of the articulation between symbol and meaning.

Symbolism can be justified, or unjustified. The test of justification must always be pragmatic [...] *The rightness, or wrongness, of symbolism is an instance of the symbolism being fortunate or unfortunate; but mere "rectitude"* [...] *does not cover all that can be included in the more general concept of "fortune." So much of human experience is bound up with symbolic reference, that it is hardly an exaggeration to say that the very meaning of truth is pragmatic. But though this statement is* hardly *an exaggeration, still it* is *an exaggeration, for the pragmatic test can never work, unless on some occasion—in the future, or in the present—there is a definite determination of what is true on that occasion. Otherwise the poor pragmatist remains an intellectual Hamlet, perpetually adjourning decision of judgment to some later date. According to the doctrines here stated, the day of judgment arrives when the "meaning" is sufficiently distinct and relevant, as a perceptum in its proper pure mode, to afford comparison with the precipitate of feeling derived from symbolic reference* (PR, 181).

If there is a privilege of consciousness, it does not consist in symbolic reference, which is attested just as well by the way chimpanzees scatter when an alarm signal sounds. Nor even in the deliberate manipulation of symbolic reference, as is attested by the extraordinary invention by that chimpanzee, observed by ethologists, who produced cries of alarm, then calmly went to flirt with a female abandoned by her fleeing male. Consciousness is surely in command, however, when ethologists determine what an animal's "symbolic reference" articulates, when they use lures not to trap an animal and feed upon it, but to correctly identify what percept is articulated with what affect. It is not that these scientists "escape" pragmatic justification. Yet in their case, success does not designate a hunger to be assuaged, but their concern to separate what concerns the animal from what they themselves feel. They are not hungry, but are concerned for truth.

The fact that the day of judgment may arrive—relative, of course, to the formulation of a doubt—implies that symbolic reference may be taken up into new adventures. Pragmatist philosophers exaggerate when, referring all our constructions to their success, they forget that we are also capable of putting these constructions deliberately to the test, that is, of seeking other types of success. Factual truth, for Whitehead, counts in a sense similar to the fallibilist sense of Popper: not because it opposes error, but because it presupposes the explicit awareness that "we might be wrong," which sometimes makes the "day of judgment" happen.

"*It is only a theory, and it might be contrary to the facts*" is a concern proper to intellectual life. The experience of a disappointed expectation, or of an ambiguous sign that "attracts an animal's attention," makes it turn its head, or prick up its ears instead of running away without further ado, already exhibits the feeling of a possible contrast between a "theory" correlated to a percept that belongs to the "immediately present" world, and this world insofar as it is or is not capable of "causing" that which, emotionally, the theory evokes: terror, attraction, appetite, and so on. The head that turns, the ears that stand up testify to a possible contrast, foreign to detection, between the world in the "causal" sense and the "theory" that interprets it. But it does not testify to the fact that the animal experiences a feeling of the theory *qua* theory.

But a felt "contrary" is consciousness in germ. When the contrasts and identities of such feelings are themselves felt, we have consciousness. It is the knowledge of ideas, in Locke's sense of that term. Consciousness requires more than the mere entertainment of theory. It is the feeling of the contrast of theory, as mere theory, with fact, as mere fact. This contrast holds whether or not the theory be correct (PR, 188).

Consciousness, as the "feeling of the contrast of theory, as mere theory, with fact, as mere fact," is all the more important in that our genuine "fortune," the multitude of our interpretations, exposes human perception to error. The two go together: this may be a reason why on the sixth day, receiving language, which makes interpretations and significations proliferate, we became souls, concerned with making a difference between the correct and the noncorrect.

The link between consciousness and theory, felt "as mere theory," announces, of course, the intervention of the propositions that Whitehead, as we know, baptized "theories." And we may understand here that propositions first intervened in Whitehead's thought "after" judgment, oriented toward the contrast between correct and incorrect. His goal was to emphasize that judgment constitutes only a small part of intellectual experience, and to provide himself with the means to venture toward imaginative experience, in which consciousness really makes a difference with regard to perceptive hesitations.

For example, consider the Battle of Waterloo. This battle resulted in the defeat of Napoleon, and in a constitution of our actual world grounded upon that defeat. But the abstract notions, expressing the possibilities of another course of history which would have followed upon his victory, are relevant to the facts which actually happened. We may not think it of practical importance that imaginative historians should dwell upon such hypothetical alternatives. But we confess their relevance in thinking about them at all, even to the extent of dismissing them. But some imaginative writers do not dismiss such ideas. Thus, in our actual world of today, there is a penumbra of eternal objects, constituted by relevance to the Battle of Waterloo. Some people do admit elements from this penumbral complex into effective feeling, and others wholly exclude them. Some are conscious of this internal decision of admission or rejection; for others the ideas float into their minds as day-dreams without consciousness of deliberate decision; for others, their emotional tone, of gratification or regret, of friendliness or hatred, is obscurely influenced by this penumbra of alternatives, without any conscious analysis of its content (PR, 185).

Perceptive experience, even if it has symbolic reference as its fortune, and the fact that we may be mistaken as its concern, does not suffice to describe our experience. It does not give meaning to the interest of the Battle of Waterloo for those who live themselves as the heirs of the history it has decided. The multiple ways we "feel" the past, be it in the mode of that which, settled once and for all, leaves us free in the face of an indeterminate future, or in that of a debt we will never finish paying, do not call for a deliberate, pragmatic putting-to-the-test. Whereas judgment seems to prepare the definition of truth in the logical sense, the imagination reflects the fact that theory cannot be felt as theory without the truth, in a logical sense, being recognized as important, to be sure, but pertaining to an extremely specialized interest.

In fact, propositions apparently intervened in Whitehead's thought in the same sense as symbolic reference and judgment, in the continuation of a battle against a logicist approach to thought. More precisely, the point was to show that the "theories" privileged by this approach, because they designate a well-determined state of affairs, which might or might not verify them, are characterized by the redundancy associated with symbolic reference. Verification, in the logical empiricist sense, has as its condition the definition of a state of affairs whose meanings have already been chosen by symbolic reference and considered as having successfully surmounted the test of judgment. The "truth" of a statement such as "Socrates is a man" does not raise the slightest problem: the statement comes at the end of the reasoning process, making explicit what has been decided well before it.

It is merely credulous to accept verbal phrases as adequate statements of propositions. The distinction between verbal phrases and complete propositions is one of the reasons why the logicians' rigid alternative, "true or false," is so largely irrelevant for the pursuit of knowledge (PR, 11).

Logicist philosophy assigns a primary importance to the question of the correspondence between a statement and a state of affairs, confusing "verbal phrase" and proposition, that is, the possibility of syntactically organizing a series of words in a way that might correspond to a state of affairs, and the felt contrast of theory, as mere theory, with a state of affairs *qua* mere state of affairs. This is why it marks a clear propensity to focus on chimerical or fictive beings, or on offensive beliefs, which, defined in a purely linguistic mode, cannot generate any true hesitation.

In *The Concept of Nature,* Whitehead had already distinguished between "demonstrative" and "descriptive" statements (CN, 11–12). A purely demonstrative statement exhibits the redundancy associated with symbolic reference. If I were to move, I could point out what I am talking about. In contrast, when I say that Homer is the author of the *Iliad,* my statement is descriptive, since we know nothing about him except that fact. If, however, I am talking about the *Iliad,* my statements will once again be demonstrative to experts, for their experience will integrate a contrast between what I say and such-and-such an aspect of their own reading experience. Yet the same might be true if I have read a novel or seen a film in which "Homer" was depicted so that I remember it as if I had known him. The fact that this Homer is a fictional character matters little: what matters is the contrast between the descriptive mode of verbal functioning, presenting itself as self-sufficient, and the demonstrative one, in which words activate symbolic reference.

The point to be emphasized is the insistent particularity of things experienced and of the act of experiencing. Bradley's doctrine—Wolf-eating-Lamb as a universal qualifying the absolute—is a travesty of the evidence. That wolf eat that lamb at that spot at that time: the wolf knew it; the lamb knew it; and the carrion birds knew it. Explicitly in the verbal sentence, or implicitly in the understanding of the subject entertaining it, every expression of a proposition includes demonstrative elements. In fact each word, and each symbolic phrase, is such an element, exciting

*the conscious prehension of some entity belonging to one of the catego-
ries of existence* (PR, 43).

Any verbal statement may function in the mode of a lure for feeling,
but a statement is incapable of defining how it will function. Thus, the
very famous statement "this stone is grey" may be produced in the absence of any stone, especially if it has been uttered in front of an audience
of logico-empiricist philosophers. Perhaps in the same discussion, the
statement "the king of France is bald" will sound forth, or "the moon is
a piece of white cheese," unless discussion turns to unicorns. The possibility of talking about a unicorn, about a king of France today, about
a celestial white cheese or an absent grey stone implies that the corresponding statements are not to be confused with the expression of propositions. Even fiercely Republican Frenchmen can hear talk about the
"present king of France" without flinching, if they are logicians. Nor do
these statements indicate any particular urgency with regard to the distinction to be made between what has never existed, what no longer exists, what is defined as false, and what is still available for designation.
There is no hurry, because everybody knows about that. The only question is how best to formulate this difference *generaliter.*

In other words, if the statement "this stone is grey" can "work" in this
case, if it does not inspire astonished looks on the faces of the listeners
as they wonder what stone the speaker could possibly be talking about, it
is because its production, in this mode, has a very particular environment
as its condition. "This stone," perhaps placed in contrast to "this unicorn,"
presupposes the existence of the community of specialists for whom the
contrast is a watchword, causing no unease, inspiring no worry, no thought:
pure communication, fully belonging to the routines of logicism. Neither
the stone nor its color is of interest to the specialists, but only the way
their attention may eventually be attracted to new formulations, important for them, of the relation between language and states of affairs. The
statement itself is often nothing more than the signal that the community
has to deal with one of its favorite problems, and the specialists will wait
patiently for the eventual appearance of what Whitehead would call
genuine propositions, which will seduce or horrify them, or at least give
rise to the feeling of a possible contribution to a controversy, or a contrast, with regard to the state of affairs that constitutes the consensus of
the community.

A vague impression of uneasiness, of a "felt contrary," on the part of
one of the specialists listening to a colleague talking about the grey stone.
Is the specialist conscious, or not? The matter is undecidable, since the
mere fact that she asks herself the question will produce consciousness

and its verification: *"I heard what was just said, therefore I was conscious."* In contrast, the question of consciousness no longer arises if our specialist's body suddenly freezes, while the diffuse uneasiness is transformed into the feeling of a contrast between a statement heard and what becomes a "fact." A specific aspect of Hume's position, which she had perhaps never thought of explicitly in that way, has become relevant in that it contradicts the statement she has just heard. The statement has done its job as a lure: listening has become fully conscious, with each new statement nourishing a process of verification of disagreement, while the renewed understanding of Hume becomes ever more explicit, produced in a way that did not exist prior to the disagreement, in a way that perhaps comes into existence for the first time. An epochal change.

Here we must pause, for the contrast I have just described leads us to associate propositions and thought, or consciousness, in a specific way. This, indeed, is how Whitehead first introduces them. But when, in the third part of *Process and Reality,* which is devoted to the "theory of prehensions," he moves on to generic considerations, independent of our particular modes of functioning, the contrast between conscious thought and symbolic reference will disappear. This contrast belongs to social adventures that designate us in our difference from rabbits. Other forms of experience, assigning other degrees of importance, might also have been conceivable. It is possible, for instance, to imagine beings endowed with another kind of memory, for whom an experienced scene imposes itself with the vividness of the present, and who use words as markers, not as "endowed with meaning." It would then be the word that would be associated with the past, with a past classificatory convention, and that should be evoked. The association between proposition and verbal consciousness is important, to be sure, but it should not be exaggerated.

When Whitehead introduces propositions in a generic mode, he will introduce them in relation to "propositional feelings," and these will concern both the routine use of words and words that turn an experience upside down: both the rabbit heading as usual for his lair and the one that flees when the silhouette of a predator suddenly appears. In short, propositions will no longer intervene in the discussion of the contrast between "symbolism" and "conscious thought." The question will be generalized to the role played by a propositional feeling in the experience of which it is an ingredient.

In order to recall the former distinction, I will call "propositional efficacy" the capacity of a propositional feeling to make a path of occasions bifurcate, to "mark an event" or to "mark an epoch." The difference is, of course, hard to discern, since as soon as I evoke "the Battle of Waterloo" as an example of what might be, in certain experiences, bereft of any efficacy, I feel that efficacy. The difference is thus relative to a "social environment," not to the "propositional feeling" as such. On the other hand, this difference also concerns the rabbit with its perceptive habits, the alfalfa field, the rabbit hole, a familiar tree, and the efficacy upon it of the sudden noise or of a silhouette appearing unexpectedly. The difference, in this case, is crucial for survival: it designates the rabbit "on the watch," "always ready to flee."

The point is not to affirm that every occasion is susceptible of admitting "propositional feelings." What is at stake certainly concerns the rabbit, probably not the electron. But it does impose a certain correction of the excess subjectivity associated with consciousness. We are so permeated by the opposition between objective statement and fiction that we must evoke decisive intellectual experiences—"*but that isn't what Hume says!*"—to make recognizable the efficacy proper to language, its function as a "lure for feeling." We need to recall that there are "words that kill" and "words that change everything." Yet once propositional efficacy has been recognized, it must be situated, and it must be admitted that the "propositional feeling" to which it testifies is just as relevant where we evoke habits of experience, that is, in any case, for the totality of experiences marked by awareness, or the contrast between what we are aware of in perception and what we perceive. In this case, of course, theory is not felt as theory, but a habit does constitute a "theory."

Whitehead's discovery of the generalizable character of propositional feeling, that is, of propositions *qua* lure for feeling, was no doubt one of the events that marked the writing of *Process and Reality*. As usual, he did not note the event, and left it up to the reader to draw all the consequences. This may be the reason why propositions are rather neglected in Whiteheadian studies. Yet the style of this event is typically Whiteheadian. When, in *The Concept of Nature*, Whitehead had dissociated recognition from any psychological or neurophysiological discussion, rather addressing what it requires, the object that is there "once again," he had already placed the Platonic "great question," the one that permits the invocation of the Ideas, under the banner of the greatest generality. Here, the generality that propositional feelings will allow us to conceive is the difference between the cases that Whitehead groups as "primitive," in which the categories of transmission and transmutation suffice, that is, in which "conformal" reproduction predominates, and the cases in which partiality matters, and we are led to speak of "recognition," of "interpretation," and even of originality and novelty. This is the generality Whitehead had designated when, in *Science and the Modern World*, he distinguished between "physical" occasions and "mental" occasions. In *Process and Reality,* every occasion has officially received a mental pole, and the generality must be reformulated. It is needed in order to express the rather radical contrast between the electron and the physicists who demonstrated the existence of the electron.

The low-grade organism is merely the summation of the forms of energy which flow in upon it in all their multiplicity of detail. It receives, and it transmits, but it fails to simplify into intelligible system (PR, 254).

The proposition will thus henceforth be linked to the question of abstraction as such, an abstraction that is not in the first instance cognitive, nor linguistic, for it already designates the "what" of perception, that is, the meaning associated with a symbolic reference as well. According to Leibniz, it is preferable to hear Socrates tell why he is drinking the hemlock, rather than to describe in all their details the corporeal, muscular, and physiological movements that would (ideally) reduce his gesture, from the cup to the lips, to the result of "physical causes." For Whitehead, even if it were completely described, Socrates' gesture could never be analyzed in terms of "impartial" causes. Yet this only enriches the Leibnizian contrast: in any case, being able to listen to Socrates' reasons constitutes a very fortunate simplification, and any simplification, fortunate or unfortunate, has its reason. This reason refers to the ingression of an eternal object into a feeling, in a mode associated with a selective and partial "how," abstracting from what does not matter to it.

With propositions, then, eternal objects will intervene in a way that is new, but as always perfectly distinct from the one they have been suspected of playing as Platonic ideas in disguise. Their ingression will be synonymous with novelty, originality, and partiality. Transmutation, which conditions perception, signals a new mode of ingression for an eternal object, but it cannot give meaning to the fact that "what is transmuted" may be endowed as such with a meaning, even with the simplest "being there." As for the suddenly perceived predator, it is not a simple contrasting composition of colored patches "over there." The colored "nexus," coexisting with the other components of my world in the indifferent mode proper to presentational immediacy, has suddenly been transformed into a testimony to their active condition: *"it's a tiger!"* In *The Concept of Nature,* Whitehead could only emphasize the importance of active conditions, the attention due to the role they play, for to go further would have required questioning the mind, which was the ultimate. Here, however, the sudden attention to what actively conditions this colored contrast reflects the fact that the eternal object that makes ingression with a proposition is new with regard to physical feelings, which will henceforth be defined as the "subjects of the proposition."

In fact, when Whitehead introduces propositions with the status of existents, his first problem will be to distinguish them from eternal objects. Every time he had evoked a concrete case requiring eternal objects, it was to an experience, of which a propositional feeling is an ingredient, that he had referred. *"This is a circle."* The major contrast defined by Whitehead between eternal objects and propositions is that, whereas eternal objects say nothing about their ingressions, propositions

[. . .] *are the tales that might perhaps be told about particular actualities* (PR, 256).

Eternal objects are "pure" potentials, that is, without particular reference to any actuality, any particular epoch. This is why conceptual feelings belong to any concrescence. In particular, they are required so that from physical feelings may derive feelings of "how" what was felt was felt. This means, correlatively, that they do not communicate as such with any particular experience, whether conscious or not. We never have the experience of an eternal object as such, for every experience is always "such-and-such" an experience, whereas the eternal object refers to "any" experience.

In contrast, every proposition is "impure," requiring the cosmic epoch in which the subjects of the stories that "might be told" exist. The color blue requires visual organs, at the least. Even a mathematical truth, such as "one plus one equals two," is linked to a cosmic epoch, Whitehead specifies, an epoch in which there exist societies enduring enough for the notion of two beings existing "at the same time" to have meaning.

There is no difficulty in imagining a world—i.e., a cosmic epoch—in which arithmetic would be an interesting fanciful topic for dreamers, but useless for practical people engrossed in the business of life. In fact, we seem to have been only barely rescued from such a state of things. For amid the actual occasions located in the wilds of so-called "empty space," and well removed from the enduring objects which go to form the enduring material bodies, it is quite probable that the contemplation of arithmetic would not direct attention to any very important relations of things. It is, of course, a mere speculation that any actual entity, occurring in such an environment of faintly coordinated achievement, achieves the intricacy of constitution required for conscious mental operations (PR, 199).

Whitehead defines a second important contrast between eternal objects and propositions, or, more precisely, a contrast that gives importance to the "perhaps" that appears in the first contrast, the tales that might perhaps be told. Unlike eternal objects, which cannot be said to be true or false, it belongs to the definition of proposition to have to be "true" or "false."

But its own truth, or its own falsity, is no business of a proposition. That question concerns only a subject entertaining a propositional feeling with that proposition for its datum (PR, 258).

It is crucial to emphasize that the proposition in itself cannot be said to be true or false, any more than the eternal objects: in itself, it is indeterminate with regard to the way it will be entertained. As a lure—"what might be" said, or felt, about particular actual entities—it raises a question. It is the decision with regard to the fact that the proposition will or will not be realized, whether or not the corresponding propositional feeling will be an ingredient of the entity's final satisfaction, that determines the "truth" of the proposition. The role that propositional feeling will play, the meaning that will be associated with it, the decision concerning the "might be," also depends on the prehending subject of the proposition.

Quite obviously, the truth of a proposition has nothing to do with logic. Logical truth belongs to consciousness, and we cannot have consciousness of the ingredients of our satisfactions. Nor does this truth designate the question of "attention to truth." A proposition, true because its feeling is the ingredient of an experience, may nevertheless be entertained in the mode of derision: *"No, you idiot, we're in Africa: that's not a tiger, it's a zebra."* The negation, as well as the affirmation, imply the entertainment or realization of a proposition. Entertainment merely means that the entities designated as its subjects by the proposition actually assume, in a feeling that is an ingredient of the entity's satisfaction, the role that the proposition assigns to them. Again, however, the role that the feeling will play in satisfaction is not itself determined.

The primary mode of realization of a proposition in an actual entity is not by judgment, but by entertainment. A proposition is entertained when it is admitted into feeling. Horror, relief, purpose, are primarily feelings involving the entertainment of propositions (PR, 188).

The truth of a proposition thus corresponds, more or less, to the meaning "true" that William James associated with pure experience: it is an adherence. But adherence must be separated from any psychological connotation. One adheres as soon as what is proposed "makes sense," independently of the meaning that will be conferred upon it. The pigeon that learns to tap with its beak on a circular form in order to be fed no doubt "entertains" a proposition, in the mode of a purpose. With propositions, Whitehead thus has the means to affirm the inadequate character of any description that would place perception under the banner of neutrality. Any "objective" concrete perception presupposes that a propositional feeling has been entertained, that the proposition is "true," but the entertaining of a proposition makes it a "lure" for other feelings: it "makes one feel," and always in a determinate mode.

Horror, relief, and purpose all imply "bodily life," the causal efficacy associated with the body. Are we committing an injustice against the butterfly, or on the contrary doing justice to its difference, if, refusing perception to it, we refuse it a propositional purpose, relief, or horror? And what about the eye that blinks when lightning flashes? That hesitation which speculative philosophy can make explicit, but not, quite obviously, decide, will intervene every time a being, unlike an electron or a falling stone, exhibits a partiality that seems to have to be associated with an experience entertaining a proposition, but we lack any imaginative access with regard to that experience. What properly characterizes detection is "I cannot imagine": I can, of course, evoke incoercible nausea, but this is precisely the contrary of an image.

Propositional feelings are not, however, specifically allied with what we can imagine, any more than conceptual feeling are. Instead, propositions are closely linked to what Whitehead generically calls "originality." Their feeling is the capture of a particular—that is, partial—relation between felt entities, and more precisely the capture of those entities *qua* articulated by a particular relation.

In the proposition, the eternal object, in respect to its possibilities as a determinant of nexus, is restricted to these logical subjects [. . .] this eternal object is the "predicative pattern" of the proposition [. . .] thus the physical feeling indicates the logical subjects and provides them respectively with that individual definition necessary to assign the hypothetic status of each in the predicative pattern. The conceptual feeling provides the predicative pattern (PR, 257–258).

Like all feelings, propositional feelings derive from an integration between conceptual feelings and physical feelings, but in this case conceptual feelings and physical feelings are articulated in a new way, which could be associated with a "mobilization." The question is no longer "how" to feel, but it also bears upon "what" is felt. The proposition signifies that the "how," of which the ingression of an eternal object is a determination, now designates particular "logical subjects." Propositional feelings eliminate from physical feeling everything that exceeds the role of logical subject, which felt entities are called upon to play. Even if it means, of course, that what is eliminated becomes the subject of other feelings, which can create the kind of dramatic contrast according to which "the word is the murder of the thing."

In a proposition the logical subjects are reduced to the status of food for a possibility. Their real rôle in actuality is abstracted from; they are no longer factors in fact, except for the purpose of their physical indication. Each logical subject becomes a bare "it" among actualities, with its assigned hypothetical relevance to the predicate (PR, 258).

The difficulty raised in *Science and the Modern World* by the question of whether eternal objects might not ultimately be "what" is prehended, transforming actuality into a kind of ratification of the ideal situation, is thus solved. The breaking off (SMW, 171) that Whitehead associated with "mental" experience is none other than the predicative pattern, and it does not *need* to refer to a principle of limitation: it *is* limited, and may infect experience with limitation. The modes of experience that give primacy to the abstraction (for instance, that of presentational immediacy), correspond quite precisely to the working of a propositional feeling. What is felt is literally placed in the service of the predicative pattern; it is henceforth felt only as what this pattern indicates as its terms. The proposition is *the* vector of abstraction.

When the cry *"a tiger!"* marks the horrified entertainment of a new proposition in perceptive experience, the delicate contrasts between colors are eliminated, the colored patch is no longer anything more than a logical subject. Yet, of course, the possibility of such a logical subject belongs to the epoch when animals endowed with perception came into existence on earth. Otherwise, the proposition would literally "have no meaning." When John the Baptist proposes that God could transform even the stones themselves into the children of Abraham, the stones that the prophet was probably designating did not tremble with hope; their endurance as stones was not disturbed, for the logical subjects with which the problem of belonging to the people of God arises were not included in their experience. For them, the statement of the problem has no meaning. Its efficacy is restricted to those who could say to themselves with regard to themselves: *"am I, or could I become, a subject of election?"* In fact, the very gesture that designates the stones excludes them. They are logical subjects of the proposition, in the sense that they are bereft of everything that makes them real stones. *"Even stones!"* None of the features that characterize the chosen people as the logical subject of the proposition of covenant constitutes a guarantee any longer, except perhaps endurance.

Evidently new propositions come into being with the creative advance of the world. For every proposition involves its logical subjects; and it cannot be the proposition which it is, unless those logical subjects are the actual entities which they are. Thus no actual entity can feel a proposition, if its actual world does not include the logical subjects of that proposition. The proposition "Caesar crossed the Rubicon" could not be felt by Hannibal in any occasion of his existence on earth. Hannibal could feel propositions with certain analogies to this proposition, but not this proposition (PR, 259).

One might as well be talking to a stone! This is the desperate exclamation of a mathematics teacher when a student does not produce the *"I get it"* that signals the entertainment of the propositional feeling required by mathematical definitions, even though they appear fully explicit to the teacher. Mathematical language, by the spectacular contrast between its intelligibility, when the logical subjects of a proposition belong to the experience of the person who hears a statement, and the radical perplexity of the person for whom "that makes no sense," strongly exhibits the relation between propositions and the creative advance of the world. Yet it can be said, more generally, that it is the proper character of all language to give their full importance to propositions, not insofar as they themselves have the power to cause, in the sense of the ontological principle, but in that their entertainment lures us into feeling, thinking, speaking, in short, becomes, in the most various ways, an ingredient of the experiences that will follow it.

What we call "memory" or "image" are, of course, saturated with propositions. During his multiple expeditions to many lands, Caesar had the opportunity to cross many rivers, but we remember that "Caesar crossed the Rubicon," and if we remember this, it is because when he and his soldiers, fully armed, crossed this river (which no Roman army could cross on pain of being declared outlaws), they knew they were crossing "the Rubicon": not a mere river, but a frontier/image that made them topple into an unforeseeable future. This is why the Rubicon was "what had been crossed" for all the soldiers, right from the first step taken by Caesar's horse. As far as the physical adventure of the encounter with the cold water of the river is concerned, it does not belong to the propositional image, except, perhaps, in the personal experience of a soldier, or for a novelist who might evoke the episode under the banner, for instance, of the contrast between the greatness of the moment and the prosaic character of the sensation.

One of Caesar's old soldiers may in later years have sat on the bank of the river and meditated on the assassination of Caesar, and on Caesar's passage over the little river tranquilly flowing before his gaze. This would have been a different proposition from the more direct one which I am now considering. Nothing could better illustrate the hopeless ambiguity of language; since both propositions fit the same verbal phraseology.

There is yet a third proposition: a modern traveler sitting on the bank of the Rubicon, and meditating on his direct perceptions of actual occasions can locate, relatively to himself by spatio-temporal specifications, an event which inferentially and conjecturally he believes to include a portion of the past history of the Rubicon as directly known to him [...] Then there is the proposition which might have been in the mind of one of the crowd who listened to Antony's speech, a man who had seen Caesar and not the Rubicon (PR, 196).

Every proposition, of course, is abstract, even the one that includes as its logical subject a "Caesar" whom the soldier sitting beside the river had known well, even the one that makes Caesar himself think, *"I, Caesar, have crossed the Rubicon,"* although his horse has barely begun its movement. Yet abstraction explains nothing. On the contrary, it is the proposition's regime of existence, the feeling of which it is the object, and the role this feeling will play in experience, that decide upon the abstraction and its role, even the simple descriptive statement that may float in schooltime memory: *"Caesar, that was the guy who crossed the Rubicon ... "* Is the statement still a lure for feeling? The question has become undecidable, in the sense that the proposition's efficacy, what it lures to, no longer implies the risk taken by Caesar, any more than "the moon is made of white cheese" implies an epoch when moon and white cheese were food for a proposition that designates and articulates them. Dead abstractions of scholastic knowledge, or of the "cases" of analytic philosophy.

With language, the propositional efficacy *"Caesar has crossed the Rubicon! The times are changing, and nothing will be as before!"* is exhibited, as well as redundant routine. But language does much more than "express" an epoch, that is, a society and the logical subjects that are part of an experience *qua* social. It is itself the operator of changes of epoch, on every scale. Such is, ultimately, the reason why we became souls when we received language. And what we call "souls" must therefore designate the multiple epochs that are entangled in a human person. The soul has no other identity than the propositional efficacies to which the innumerable habits of a particular human experience are vulnerable. Yet neither this multitude nor the vulnerability itself designates "language" as such, but each language, what makes sense for each language, what another language is often unable to translate.

Mathematics teachers must trust "mathematical language" *qua* translatable into all languages. This is why they persevere, hoping that their statement, in one of its particular versions, or else the effect of the contrasting succession of such versions will bring about a change of epoch for the student, the correlative realization of the logical subjects and of propositional feeling, *"So that's what you meant!"* As far as John the Baptist is concerned, he speculated on the propositional efficacy of his furious and oh-so-eloquent gesture: *"Even the stones!"* This gesture presupposed an epoch, that is, auditors whose language presupposes the possibility of entertaining the proposition that made them the logical subjects of the covenant. For this is what would make them vulnerable to the propositional efficacy of the proposed modification, of the inclusion of new logical subjects in the proposition "covenant," of the inclusion of anyone at all! And all those who "heard" the prophetic exclamation adhered, were infected, even if some of them subsequently refuted the statement, shrugged their shoulders, and forgot. The proposition is indifferent to its consequences, it does not say how it should be felt, and obviously, not every entertainment signifies a change of epoch, even at the level of an individual thread of experience. Nevertheless, the fact that the prophet himself could utter this terrible statement is inseparable from the vocation he entertained for it, a vocation which presupposes that, sharing the same language with his auditors, he was addressing their "soul." He intended to make an epoch topple, to infect with a previously inconceivable alternative the experience of the proposition that makes the Jewish people the subject of the covenant.

In *Science and the Modern World,* Whitehead had made what he called "abrupt realization" the source of error, truth, art, ethics, and religion. He takes up this passage explicitly in *Process and Reality,* while stating the importance of propositions (PR, 189). When Whitehead cites himself, it is not to cover his tracks, to create the impression of a false unity, but, quite the contrary, to celebrate a reunion: not with himself, but with what had already obliged him to think. He succeeded in "saving" a statement, as a mathematician must save, in the new formal language that he explores, all the relevant mathematical truths already acquired. In this case, then, "propositions" enable Whitehead to recuperate the thesis of the "great refusal" for which, in *Science and the Modern World,* he had needed God.

The abrupt realization of *Science and the Modern World* had been placed under the banner of limitation. To the importance of propositions "rendered not true" by a decision corresponded the necessity of an abstraction bearing upon what is actually decided. What Caesar's decision, when crossing the Rubicon, renders "not true" must be limited; otherwise, his decision could be assimilated to the behavior of an electron, blind with regard to what "really" determines it and to its many repercussions. As I have emphasized, it is impossible to know whether Whitehead had taken the measure of the risk he was running by making God intervene as a principle of limitation. The undecidable character of the question illustrates, moreover, the abrupt character of realization: "what seems to you to be an implicit consequence of my position, you may of course make me admit it, and you can even make me admit that I 'should have' known it, and even, if you are in the mood for torturing, that I in fact knew it; but whatever I may be led to admit subsequently, the fact is that I had perceived my position, or the problem, in that way and not otherwise." In any case, the risk has henceforth been avoided. The propositions rendered "not true" by a decision are significant insofar as another decision might, socially, have made them true. Did Caesar render "not true" the propositions that would have lured him into submission to the Senate or into flight, considering the offensive character of the act he was committing? Or did he just decide to cross the river in spite of them? Error, truth, art, ethics, and religion are so many examples exhibiting propositional efficacy in conscious adventures marked by risk, the possibility of failure, and the explicit call upon the future.

When, in the eighteenth century, the new proposition resounded: "all men are equal in right" (and not: all are equally the children of God), what was affirmed was the risk taken with regard to social states of affairs, and it was the future that was appealed to. This means, more technically, that it was indeed the future that was to be infected. Those who would actually be infected by it might very well deny human equality, limit its import to specific circumstances, negotiate its consequences, raise its problem. Nevertheless, if they are truly infected, if they belong to that epoch in which this proposition makes sense, the equality that designates all men as its logical subjects will be included in their experience, by way of contrast, when the word "man" or "human" is pronounced. It will be, in this sense, "true."

It is here that the "scars" (PR, 226–227) left by what negative prehensions have eliminated take on all their importance. I am not speaking of the "rendered not-true" that is a positive, conscious part of experience but of the many repercussions of the abstraction that are part of propositional efficacy—what is described afterward by means of sentences such as *"they should have known that . . . "* or *"how could they not understand that . . . "* The "emotional tone" associated with scars links the Whiteheadian notion of epoch to a radical historicism: the adventure of propositions "makes an epoch," but the way it makes an epoch allows us to understand that those who refute a statement are just as much part of the same "history" as those who affirm it or as those who echo the interstitial expression of what has been rendered not-true.

Oliver Cromwell's cry echoes down the ages, "My brethren, by the bowels of Christ I beseech you, bethink that you may be mistaken" (SMW, 16).

The obstinate insistence of a realized proposition is obviously neutral with regard to the difference between good and evil. If the proposition "all men are equal in right" opens up new possibilities of evil on the part of those who reject it, it also opens such possibilities for those who receive it in a positive sense. For once a propositional feeling has infected experience, nothing is harder to imagine than that experience might not entertain it. There will be evil consequences of the revolt of a furious mathematics teacher in front of her student, "deaf as a stone." This is why also it is so easy to "transcend one's epoch." From the difficulty each of us has in accepting that the way we think and feel belongs to an epoch may well follow *"they are all racists without even knowing it!"* uttered against those who do not belong to our particular epoch, in which each person is supposed to be the logical subject for a proposition of equality. Those who adhere can then become "hogs," that is, transform the proposed equality into a vector of legitimate destruction, judging "the others" *qua* needing, voluntarily or by force, to be educated toward the universal. Rendering "non-true" *(I know, but still!)* the propositions dealing with the historical character of equality between men, they are the designated prey for the trick of evil.

We require to understand how the unity of the universe requires its multiplicity. We require to understand how infinitude requires the finite. We require to understand how each immediately present existence requires its past, antecedent to itself; and requires its future, an essential factor in its own existence [. . .] Again we require to understand how mere matter-of-fact refuses to be deprived of its relevance to potentialities beyond its own actuality of realization (MT, 83).

Propositional efficacy is obviously required by speculative philosophy, whose speculation deals precisely with the possibility of "leaps of the imagination," without which its statements would not make sense. Of course, every statement is saturated with abstractions, and every abstraction, of course, works as a "lure for feeling," demanding, in order to assume meaning, an entertainment that it does not explain. Yet it is the singularity of speculative abstractions to exhibit this demand. "Social abstractions" translate symbolic references that are relatively stable, and propose themselves most often as designating a state of affairs or as deriving from consensual obviousness. John the Baptist's prophetic statement speculates on a change of epoch, but he was careful not to announce it; otherwise, that statement would be entertained as a witty remark or a "mere speculation." Speculative abstractions, for their part, wager on the interstices of our social abstractions, not to disqualify them but in order to activate what lurks in these interstices, the "feeling" of the abstraction as such. They are meant to disclose misplaced abstractions and their power, a power that may infect us to the point that we can read, with a straight face, that it is the sequential association between the lightning and the blinking of the eyes that makes us conclude that the lightning is cause of the blinking.

With the existents known as propositions, then, Whitehead has provided himself with the means for speculative philosophy to account for what is required by the efficacy it claims. A veritable "machine" for suggesting "non-conformal" propositional feelings, it is "epochal," of course, because the propositional efficacy it aims at designates the social abstractions of a language which, in multiple ways, has stabilized the bifurcation of nature. Its effects on different readers, who would not be infected by these abstractions, are unpredictable. Yet we can speak of it as if it were a language, in the same sense as the mathematical or physico-mathematical languages. Like them, it exhibits abstraction: Whiteheadian "applications" are abstract language machines that make the routine dimension of verbal statements, their redundancy with regard to perceived things, shrink to a minimum, and deploy propositional efficacy to the maximum.

Yet propositions open up still other questions. In particular, they may entail a new flight of experience toward the "order of nature," which has become a "cosmos," and open up some hypotheses with regard to the "lure for feeling" provided for each entity by "God."

The fact that propositions can play so many roles, in so many questions, is a good indication that their entertainment, or what Whitehead calls their "truth," is neutral with regard to their meaning. It is the role played by the propositional feeling in satisfaction that is not neutral, and is never neutral. Making sense is neutral, but it calls for a signification that is never such. A propositional feeling is, therefore, somewhat like the conceptual feeling of those eternal objects called "sensa," eminently available for the most disparate experiences. Unlike a sensum, a proposition is always relative to an epoch, but once that epoch is given, it may be engaged in the most diversified adventures or, more precisely, the most divergent ones.

Another way of talking about "what makes sense" is to say "that's relevant." And relevance is always what Whitehead has associated with God. Divine intervention—the answer to the question *"what is the best for this impasse?"*—is certainly not thereby clarified, but the concept of a proposition already creates the necessary distance between envisaging and actualizing. If God's answer is propositional, it is indeterminate with regard to the way it will be "entertained" by final satisfaction or even to whether, in the final analysis, it will be entertained at all. And this indeterminacy is definitional: if it is a divine proposition that initiates the subjective aim of a concrescence, God does not precede actuality, does not entertain an ideal conception of what it should produce, and therefore will not judge it by the standard of that conception. Here, the term "relevant" takes on its fully conjectural and limited value, thanks to which an occasion is indeed an "occasion," a singular moment, not a simple aspect of the world as it would be envisaged by God. What Whitehead affirmed, without quite being able to justify it, in *Science and the Modern World,* can now be understood: only actuality is value.

As for the efficacy proper to propositions for what Whitehead calls "cosmos" or "creative advance of nature," *Process and Reality* remains silent on the subject. Whitehead did not even find it appropriate to return to the set of texts written about perception before he elaborated the concept of propositional feeling. As Lewis Ford remarks, Whitehead was much more concerned with the difficulties of his theories than with the explanation of what no longer seemed to him to pose problems.

I shall therefore try, before finally turning to God, to render explicit certain "cosmic" perspectives opened up by propositions, making use above all of *Modes of Thought* (1938), Whitehead's last book. In this work, we no longer read of eternal objects or of propositions. Not that Whitehead had (once again) changed his position: quite the contrary, this is an instance of the freedom of an author who has henceforth gained the freedom to address questions that are concrete—that is, by definition, "sociological"—concerning societies and implying traditions of thought. Whereas eternal objects and propositions belong to the metaphysics of actual occasions, our modes of thought, for their part, bring to the forefront imaginative adventures centered on what matters to us. Yet the penumbra of metaphysical propositions will make itself felt in the way the question of the bifurcation of nature will be taken up once again: *Modes of Thought* is the most poetical of Whitehead's works. The point is no longer to resist or to affirm, but to celebrate what metaphysics has allowed to be constructed, the fact that "nothing can be explained as normal."

CHAPTER TWENTY-THREE

Modes of Existence, Modes of Thought

MPORTANCE IS PRIMARILY monistic in its reference to the Universe. Importance, limited to a finite individual occasion, ceases to be important. In some sense or other, Importance is derived from the immanence of infinitude in the finite.

But Expression is founded on the finite occasion. It is the activity of finitude impressing itself on its environment. Thus it has its origin in the finite; and it represents the immanence of the finite in the multitude of its fellows beyond itself. The two together, namely Importance and Expression, are witnesses both to the monistic aspect of the universe and to its pluralistic character. Importance passes from the World as one to the World as many; whereas, Expression is the gift from the World as many to the World as one (MT, 20).

Expression, in *Modes of Thought*, actively requires the two meanings we can give it, designating subjective satisfaction as a final decision—thus and not otherwise—and as a decision for one future instead of another. It is that which will make itself felt, that which, in one way or another, will have to be taken into account. It does not, therefore, by any means designate the Leibnizian idea that a subject expresses "the" world, in the sense of being its reflection, deducible from a certain viewpoint. Whitehead's association between expression and "gift" rather brings to mind the way William James characterizes the "chance act": *Its origin is in a certain fashion negative: it escapes, and says, Hands off! coming, when it comes, as a free gift or not at all* (DD, 154). Individual satisfaction fashions its own perspective, its own divergence, and as such it will give to the world the gift of a new expression of itself, of what might perhaps make a difference.

Yet the fact that Whitehead talks about importance before talking about expression is significant. When he wrote *Modes of Thought,* he no longer had to struggle to conceive of an occasion as *causa sui,* and could therefore give meaning to its correlate: to the world dependent on an individual decision—*"Hands off!"*—which will come like a gift. Individual expression is important.

Whereas expressions refer to creativity, to the many becoming one and being increased by one, importance, for its part, refers to the Universe as "one," that is, to the Universe in its cosmological perspective. Nor is this perspective foreign to individual experience, for, as Whitehead affirms, importance "passes" to the world as many.

The verb "to pass" is the verb that, as we shall see, Whitehead used on the last page of *Process and Reality* to characterize the dynamics of the relationship between God and the world. Yet God is not, of course, what explains: he is what is required, in terms of the conceptual scheme, by the cosmological perspective. "Passage" then means that this perspective belongs to experience, in the mode of feeling that a decision will not only have consequences beyond itself, but matters to something other than itself. Unlike a throw of the dice, indifferent to the consequences that depend on it, a free gift implies that the feeling of waiting is an ingredient of the occasion. The question *"what is expected of me here?"* is too important in human life to be ignored.

The full solemnity of the world arises from the sense of positive achievement within the finite, combined with the sense of modes of infinitude stretching beyond each finite fact. This infinitude is required by each fact to express its necessary relevance beyond its own limitations. It expresses a perspective of the universe. Importance arises from this fusion of the finite and the infinite. The cry "Let us eat and drink, for tomorrow we die" expresses the triviality of the merely finite. The mystic, ineffective slumber expresses the vacuity of the merely infinite (MT, 78–79).

"The full solemnity of the world" does not transcend the "fact" but is required by the fact as soon as the latter is experienced in the mode of positive accomplishment or—which amounts to the same thing—of defeat or betrayal. The fact itself then demands relevance beyond itself, and both cry and mystical slumber bear witness to this, even if, each in their own way, they testify to it in the mode of what Whitehead, in *Science and the Modern World,* called "the great refusal," a decisive mode because of the importance for them of the propositions they render "non-true."

Here, what is to be thought is no longer an order of nature, for a form of dualism always corresponds to the definition of such an order: that of statements of knowledge that cannot help but presuppose and ratify a contrast between those who learn the attention due to what they deal with and what they have to deal with. The point will be to attempt, experimentally and with my own means, to inhabit the cosmological perspective opened up by Whitehead in *Modes of Thought*. Like all experimentation, this one has a goal. What matters here is to explore the proposition that the question of the cosmos does not transcend positive knowledge any more than the solemnity of the world transcends positive individual achievement. It merely demands that attention be paid to this knowledge itself, to the way that, although it deals with societies, it testifies to the question of the importance, beyond itself, of individual expression.

What matters here is thus the plurality of modes of knowledge. Let us take this simple question as a starting point: why do biologists, in general, have no doubt that the order they are trying to understand is that of a living being, whereas the order that physicists are in the habit of baptizing "laws of nature" has given rise to such a doubt, to the opposition between reality as it supposedly is "in itself" and as we define it as an "object of knowledge"?

The laws of nature are large average effects which reign impersonally. Whereas, there is nothing average about expression. It is essentially individual. In so far as an average dominates, expression fades (MT, 21).

The enduring social continuity that physicists describe by a function requires and translates the dominant "impartial" character of the modes of taking-into-account called "interaction," which the physico-mathematical function characterizes in terms of articulations between well-defined variables. The exploit constituted by the production of a physico-mathematical function is thus radically asymmetrical. The techno-conceptual creativity of those who formulate it implies the most extreme partiality, the most extreme importance accorded to the struggle against any possibility of confusing scientific statements and "opinion." But the statement, for its part, renders explicit the way in which societies reproduce by respecting a median conformity that we baptize "laws" or "regularity": in their cases, the divergence always constituted by an individual expression has no importance. Correlatively, the "reality" of what physics baptizes as an "individual property" (of electrons, atoms, molecules maintaining themselves in conformity with themselves) can always be placed in doubt, identified with the functional articulation of experimental relations and thus made relative to the questions raised by the experimenter.

In contrast, a living society must be approached in terms of questions that render explicit its partial character: what is food or poison for it, what will allow it to reproduce, what will provide it the opportunity to survive, what will kill it. In other words, functional articulation in biology has as its respondent a society characterized not in terms of conformity, but of selective choices that are extremely partial, precise, varied, and sometimes unexpected with regard to what does and does not count, with regard to what is relevant and what may be neglected. With regard to what matters. Biologists cannot confuse the choices with which they deal with a translation of their own questions, an answer to their own demands. To take up Heisenberg's famous saying, they are neither actors nor spectators, but "inquirers." In one way or another, the "biological function" refers to beings for whom the logical roles it makes explicit matter.

Here, the point is no longer to "justify life" from a cosmological viewpoint, but to celebrate it. The contrast between life and nonlife does not, of course, designate the cosmic epoch in which the question of importance emerges. This contrast designates our mode of thought in the first instance, the full solemnity of the difference between those of our modes of description that presuppose and confirm the possibility of neglecting the relevance of individual expression, and those that must recognize it in the guise of partiality. "Life is robbery": every living society implies the creation of a way of enduring whose importance is paid for by an active differentiation between what its maintenance requires and what threatens it. Whereas nothing in the description of copper alludes to the fact that its encounter with sulfuric acid will have as its consequence a social catastrophe for the molecules of copper, the least cell or the slightest bacterium exhibit the partial character of their relation with other societies, prey or poison, in their environment. Whereas the physico-mathematical function refers to a homogenous world, to the environment of a society as described by the same variables as those that describe its own social behavior, the history of life tells the story of the creation of multiple, selective, and innovative articulations. In biology, functions are related to issues.

I will first turn to *Religion in the Making* to find the terms of that celebration in Whitehead, for it is here that the term "expression," associated with a rather unexpected reference that I have decided to take seriously, appears for the first time with properly cosmic echoes.

Expression is the one fundamental sacrament. It is the outward and visible sign of an inward and spiritual grace [. . .] There is then a community of intuition by reason of the sacrament of expression proffered by one and received by the other.

But the expressive sign is more than interpretable. It is creative. It elicits the intuition which interprets it. It cannot elicit what is not there. A note on a tuning fork can elicit a response from a piano. But the piano has already in it the string tuned to the same note. In the same way the expressive sign elicits the existent intuition which would not otherwise emerge into individual distinctiveness. Again in theological language, the sign works ex opere operato, *but only within the limitation that the recipient be patient of the creative action* (RM, 131–133).

In *Religion in the Making,* the emphasis was on human experience, and the expressive sign rather clearly implies "human intuition," as it can be exhibited for instance by the proliferation and reception of a grimace, a gesture, a word, or a sound. This sign thus refers to what Whitehead calls the "symbolic." And yet, the fragments cited may also describe what, in *Modes of Thought,* Whitehead decided to call "expression," the way each actuality "proffers" its divergence, which will have to be taken into account and will contribute to bringing forth what will inherit from it. In this case, however, the one and only fundamental sacrament would designate creativity, as attested by any given concrescence. Each initial feeling is an "expressive sign," giving rise to the creative process that will make it come into being as the feeling of a subject.

Taking seriously the reference to sacrament that Whitehead associates in *Religion in the Making* with what he calls "expression" by no means signifies conferring any kind of privilege upon the conception of the supernatural associated with the Catholic religion. The sacraments are interesting in that in Catholic doctrine they designate the question of a reproducible intervention of the supernatural within the natural. Such a question implies a "mode of thought" inhabited by the contrast between this type of intervention and a nature defined by its own regularities. In this sense, the sacraments allow the question to be raised of what we call "regularity." On the other hand, among Catholics the efficacy of the sacrament is said to be "objective." The sacrament must actually produce what it signifies; its signification cannot itself be reduced to a "secondary quality." The contrast is thus irreducible to a form of symbolic efficacy, as we say today, testifying only to human subjectivity. The sacraments demand a "realism" that is precisely what Whitehead subscribes to when he emphasizes, still and again, that all feeling is the feeling of an object, and that objects are what have to be felt.

Quite obviously, the way that, prolonging Whitehead, I intend to generalize the notion of sacrament transforms the meaning of the contrasts associated with it by Catholic doctrine. It is our modes of thought that are under investigation, not an actual opposition between natural and supernatural, or between "merely" subjective and objective. What is at stake is a farewell to a "nature" capable of defining itself, a farewell to the possibility of attributing to "natural entities" a behavior, properties, or capacities that would enable a general definition of what is meant by "it can be explained 'naturally.'"

The question of the conditions under which the sacraments are effective has provoked passionate theological discussions. On what does this efficacy depend? What is the share of divine grace, and what is that of man? What is the share of the person who administers, and that of the person receiving? With the theological formula *ex opere operato,* Whitehead adopts a position in this discussion: the sacrament is efficacious independently of the person administering it. The priest's sacramental words are valid as soon as he is a priest, independently of his state of sin or of grace. The only condition is that the person receiving the sacrament not present an obstacle. What is an obstacle? That is another delicate theological question.

For Whitehead, when he was writing *Religion in the Making,* the question of obstacles obviously implied what is called "social environment" in *Process and Reality.* The stones do not tremble with hope when John the Baptist designates them. However, this definition of an obstacle no longer holds if we take the risk of accepting that what is called "expression" in *Modes of Thought* is still valid as "one and only fundamental sacrament." For here, expression is that whereby each actual entity, whatever it may be, transcends all the actual entities from which it inherits, including God. And, in this case, the relation between sign and response has neither measure nor judge, and the notion of obstacle therefore becomes completely indeterminate. The efficacy associated with the sacrament of expression, the "one and only fundamental sacrament," cannot be refused to any creature of creativity, any more than Leibniz refused a soul to any monad.

The great line of difference does not separate the organic from the inorganic, but crosses the one and the other by distinguishing what is an individual being from what is a collective or mass phenomenon, what is an absolute form and what are massive, molar figures and structures. These are the two levels or two aspects of the calculus [. . .] individual beings are probably the last and sufficient reasons [. . .] But the lower level is no less irreducible, because it implies a loss of individuality among its components, and relates to different kinds of composite collections material or secondary forces of linkage. Clearly, one level is folded over the other, but above all each one conveys a very different kind of fold [. . .] What must be radically distinguished are the pleats of matter, which always consist in hiding some part of the relative surface that they are affecting, and the folds of form, which on the contrary reveal to itself the detail of an absolute surface that is copresent with all of its modifications (LP, 139–140).

To the Leibnizian contrast described by Deleuze between folds and pleats, between actualization in the soul and realization in states of affairs, corresponds the distinction constructed by Whitehead between the indivisible unit of subjective satisfaction and the pragmatic value it will assume as part of the many for other occasions. Objective immortality in itself signifies the loss of the individuality of what has been accomplished, and the relevance of physical laws testifies to the possibility that nothing then "counts" other than a transmission dominated by conformity. The loss of individuality does not, however, as in Leibniz, proceed from a contrast between two modes of description, two levels, two aspects of a calculus, but from the "perishing" that transforms individuality into a fact, whose value depends on future decisions. Objective immortality means that what follows is responsible for the new modality in which the gift of individual expression will be taken into account. What is certain is that no occasion will inherit the way the subject made the multiplicity of its feelings hold together, in all its details, the way it was co-present to each *qua* immediately its own.

Yet if the loss of individuality does not pertain to modes of description, but designates the "perishing" of the satisfied subject, the "one and only fundamental sacrament" constituted by expression does not suffice to ensure the difference between a disorderly universe and a "cosmos." For there to be a cosmos, what has been decided, what the individual has made of itself, and what it has unified as its datum must be able to "matter," that is, to succeed in infecting its environment with the consequences of the fact that it is this expression that was produced and not some other. From the piano responding to the tuning fork, to the understanding that responds to a word, the "expressive signs" we can evoke do not, in fact, correspond to the one and only sacrament, for all of them require societies capable of granting importance to individual expressions, or, in Leibnizian terms, of giving meaning to pleats of matter that certainly hide, but that also exhibit a selective and partial manner of pleating in one way rather than in another.

Obviously, what we are approaching is the question of what I have called the "culture of interstices," which I have associated with the "cosmological justification" of living societies. The term "culture" referred, beyond the "fact" of the interstices where life lurks, to their importance, that is, to the way living societies can simultaneously canalize and be infected by what lurks: originality. And we can henceforth give a name to what may well be specifically associated with this originality, what the efficacy of a "sign" as such testifies to. It pertains to propositional feelings to open up new possibilities of "folding one level over the other." The relations between levels, the gift of the individual expression, may then be multiple, adventurous, and capable of originality.

And of course, the most exacerbated example of adventures that relate importance and expression, social belonging and originality, is language. No one can be said to be responsible, guarantor, depository, or author of a language, for no individual expression has the power to modify it unless this modification is taken up by others: unless it infects them. Language exists only in a collection of individual expressions, but these expressions translate at the same time a social "fact," a "cosmic reality," without which neither language nor speakers would exist: the efficacy proper to these expressions capable of infecting human experience, that is, just as much the "patience" of human experience with regard to this infection.

The question of "sacraments" is thus not closed. To unicity, to the one and only fundamental sacrament, corresponds the indefinite multiplicity of entities. But the question of the importance of an individual expression must also be raised, and it can only be raised according to the essentially plural modes of what societies make possible and what they impede, what they are unable to entertain. The prophet's audience trembles, but not the stones.

The unique sacrament of expression might then call for a sacramental plurality: "the" sacraments, in the sense that each one corresponds to a different ritualization, that is, communicates with the social question raised by the "patience" of a society *qua* condition for the efficacy of a sign. In *Modes of Thought,* of course, Whitehead no longer speaks of sacraments, but the cosmic meaning he confers upon expression and importance translates the same obligation to think in a deliberately "antinaturalist" mode. Importance, which "passes from the World as one to the World as many," and expression, "the gift from the World as many to the World as one," testify, by the plurality of the ways that one passes and the other gives, to a cosmos, in contrast to the neutrality of creativity. As in *Religion in the Making,* then, the point is to propose a "mode of thought" that articulates what the scientific and religious modes of thought oppose, but the question of the "culture of interstices" obliges us to reunite: the possibility of descriptions that "explain" certain living societies, and the ineffable mystic sentiment that leads "living persons" themselves to live in immediate unison with the cosmos.

Let us take first the scientific achievement of biochemists, demonstrating that a specific interweaving of chemical processes produces an overall behavior analogous to a form of "calculation," assigning to the interacting elements roles of a quasi-logical kind. Even if the biochemist-modelizers announce that an apparently finalistic functioning has been reduced to molecular behaviors that are perfectly compatible with physico-chemistry, they are in fact celebrating the signal novelty constituted by an interweaving of chemical processes that become, as such, capable of being described as "working" in a way that is both intelligible and partial, giving original consequences to the presence or absence of certain ingredients in its environment, that is, giving them a signification.

The discourse on successful reduction will turn the analyzed case into the representative of a generality, and the person holding this discourse will often make common cause with other defenders of the same generality. Yet "Whiteheadian" biologists, for their part, would be more "concrete": their result, even if its site is a laboratory populated by a chemist's instruments, has issued from questions that differ from those of chemists. For chemists who wish to obtain a given type of synthesis and no other, what matters is the success of "their" synthesis. The result will belong to them, and they must deserve it. Biochemists, too, must succeed and deserve, but their questions are directed to a success that has already taken place: the chemical interweaving "holds," "works," and "functions" before them and without them. In one way or another, the state of affairs they study implies that the molecules play "roles" which it is, of course, their job to decipher, but each of which, as they know *a priori,* should be the partial expression of a function without which they would not exist as such. From the viewpoint of this function, each molecular behavior is required, but none of these behaviors explains the function: it is the function itself that explains itself through them.

Wherever there is a region of nature which is itself the primary field of the expressions issuing from each of its parts, that region is alive (MT, 22).

Once again, this is not a matter of "mystery" but of a transformation of the mode of description. In one way or another, it is as if the biochemists were not the first "interpretants," as if what they deal with was simplifying, or schematizing, or abstracting "on its own account," in a way that can be described, and that can even be "explained," but on condition that all the relations that matter in *this* case have been identified and articulated. The explanation is not reductive, because the question it answers is not that of the chemist—what molecules are present, and how do they interact?—but that of the biochemist: how do these processes manage to . . . ?

If one had to associate the intelligible, logical simplification presupposed and made explicit by biochemical models with the efficacy of a particular sacrament producing what it signifies, that is, in this instance, the importance of a partial articulation, distinguishing success and catastrophe, life and death, it would be to the efficacy of the sacrament of marriage. Each such articulation is an entreaty to the universe: "What God has united, let nothing break asunder." To this sacrament corresponds the efficacy of functional "signs" or "sensibilia," signs that must be felt in order for the roles required by the function to be articulated.

With the time for marriage, however, what also begins is the time of "marriage against nature," of articulations between heterogeneous things as such. The intense traffic of signs, the multiplicity of traps, mimes, lures, and poisons woven by the lives of plants, insects, and parasites, had fascinated Bergson, who, in *Creative Evolution,* turned the contrast between the perfect precision of instinctive action and the clumsy hesitations of intelligent action into the terms of a choice between two divergent directions carried out by life. What Bergson celebrated with instinct translates the original successes proper to "functional societies": what succeeds may be called "requisition," the "grasping" of a being *qua* "playing a role" in a function. The orchid that presents a mime of the sexual organs of a female wasp increases its chances of contact with the male wasp, which improves its own chances of reproduction. The parasite that affects the brain of an ant so that it goes to immobilize itself at the end of a blade of grass increases its chances that the infected ant may be grazed along with the grass by the herbivore, as is required by its own reproductive cycle.

It is very important, from the viewpoint of the modes of thought called for by living beings, to emphasize the extremely varied field of relevance of what is called a "model" in biology. Biochemical models exhibit highly complex functions, articulating a rather large number of variables, most often requiring computer simulations. But what also lend themselves very well to modelization are the multiple modes of etho-ecological definitions of living beings, according to the "functional" signs they give or are sensitive to, what those signs elicit, with what consequences, and so on.

I will therefore associate the efficacy of the "sacrament of marriage" with what is the privileged field for modelization in biology, exhibiting the efficacy of functional signs, whether they refer to functions that are internal (the quasi-technology of intra- and intercellular detections, captures, and regulations) or external, between wasp and orchid, or between ants, or between the butterfly and its female, whose smell it can detect at a distance of several miles. The model makes explicit the articulation of roles played by various, disparate actors, independently of their personal experience: whatever the butterfly's experience may be, the odoriferous molecule intervenes in the direction of its flight, and the female, source of the odor, may be at the arrival point.

Can we already speak of a propositional efficacy, in the sense that it designates a "culture of interstices"? A model renders a proposition explicit, but what entertains this proposition—with admiration, astonishment, or amusement—is none other than the biologist. This is why the relevance of such a modelization communicates, in our modes of thought, with "natural selection," the great sieve, indifferent to what it retains, as long as it improves the chances of survival and reproduction. The model defines, in Leibnizian terms, the modes of "pleating," or partial, pragmatically verified simplifications that constitute the success of living societies insofar as they endure and infect. But the model is mute about what we cannot imagine, the efficacy of the functional sign itself, what it "does" to the experience it infects.

What does the wasp that has been seduced by an orchid "feel"? The butterfly detecting the odor of a female? The ant rushing to attack an intruder? We cannot imagine, and the models do not tell us, but they are also—and this is highly interesting—completely neutral in this matter. This corresponds well to the definition of marriage: whatever you feel toward your spouse, you are united. Ethologists know that they must certainly not attribute to insects and parasites—the two types of living beings which, according to Bergson, embodied the triumph of instinct—experiences that would imply the possibility of a disappointed, furious, or frustrated wasp, of a butterfly looking forward to a delightful encounter, or of a heroic ant overcoming its fear. Perhaps one could say that for such beings, action must be stated in the infinitive: "copulate," "go," "attack," as close as one can get to an imperative without a subject. In any case, it is important to insist, once again, on the fact that impotence in imagining by no means signifies absence. The experiences of a wasp, a butterfly, or even a biological macromolecule are unknown to us, and they are certainly different. It is possible that, unlike a macromolecule, the wasp's experience includes the sense of a continuity of experience. It is possible that, in its case, the reception of a "functional sign" is the experience of a bifurcation of experience. Ultimately, we do not know what constitutes for us the experience of a word when we are not paying specific attention to it either. Nor is it an accident that Nathalie Sarraute has named the obscure multiplicity of tiny experiential bifurcations "tropisms," a term used for plants and butterflies, successfully conveying the extent to which such bifurcations populate the adventure that is both required and smoothed over by the continuous construction of a "living person." Our imagination presupposes and implies attention to the truth, and to all the contrasts articulated around this attention. It cannot therefore bear directly on "a word," "this word," without making it change its nature, without transforming its reception into an imaginative experience. But some writers and other artists may succeed, by reinventing the very meaning of attention to truth, in evoking something of experience "outside of personal requisition."

The fact that models are relevant, although they cease where we cannot imagine, translates the proper efficacy of the "sacrament of marriage," the disjunction between experience and requisition. The sacrament is efficacious, whatever the spouses feel about it. The model renders explicit the way that disparate beings are in a situation of correlative requisition, requiring one another, and its relevance consists precisely in the fact that here it is requisition alone that matters, independent of the question of expression or the experience that gives rise to the functional sign. With functional signs, biologists thus celebrate life as "imposition" in the sense Heidegger gave to this term, a functional, calculating taking-into-consideration. One might also say that it is here that the (Hegelian) notion of the proposition as the murder of the thing takes on a precise meaning. If the proposition in general implies and carries out a form of robbery, reducing its logical subjects to the status of food for a possibility (PR, 258) with no concern for their individuality, the properly biological proposition carries out this operation to the letter.

Everything changes, however, once we can associate the notion of proposition with its "entertainment" in an experience that is not that of the biologist. Everything changes when we enter into the domain of behaviors to which ethology owes its existence, because these behaviors have imposed the interest of describing animals in "their" environment, not in one that has been artificially prepared. We can speak, of course, in the broad sense, of the ethology of ants or spiders, but the difference between environments in this case is not crucial: we know, or we think we know, what ants and spiders need to behave in a "typical" way. In contrast, when we are dealing with a rat or a bird, the difference between a "natural" and an "artificial" environment becomes important, as is attested by the confrontation between the ethological and experimental modes of thought, and is also attested by the suddenly highly questionable character of models that interpret behavior from the viewpoint of its selective value alone.

Where is the change to be situated? Here I will follow the suggestion of Deleuze and Guattari, according to whom we can designate the kind of animals capable of obliging our modes of thought to take this change into consideration. The animals in question are the ones called "territorial":

Art may begin with the animal, or at least with the animal who marks out a territory and builds a home (the two are correlative, or even merge sometimes, in what is called a habitat). With the territory-home system, many organic functions are transformed: sexuality, procreation, aggression, food, but this transformation does not explain the appearance of territory and home, but rather the reverse; territory implies the emergence of pure sensory qualities, which cease to be merely functional and become expressive features, enabling a transformation of functions (QPh, 174).

This suggestion, fully developed in *A Thousand Plateaus,* fits admirably with the sociology of life that Whitehead demanded. The point is (obviously) not to attempt a reduction of art to territorial signs, but to celebrate the irreducible character of the event named "territory." Everything changes "with" territory, "with" the emergence of signs that are no longer merely "functional" but "expressive," that make sense or symbolic reference "for" the animal itself.

The case of the butterfly attracted by an odor, and that of an "intruder," recognizing by an odoriferous mark that he is penetrating into someone else's territory, do not have much in common. No biochemist will risk undertaking a model that actually articulates the way that the detection of the odoriferous molecule matters, its consequences for the animal that "smells": the intruder's unease, its hesitations, its attention on high alert. Here, indeed, "what" is discerned discloses other discernible things, for instance, the possible presence of the legitimate owner of the territory into which the hesitant intruder is venturing. The animal is "aware" of the fact that it is not at home.

We are entering the domain where reference to "molecules" becomes a byword, concealing the fact that here due attention must be paid to propositional efficacy as such. We are entering the domain where the "culture of interstices" must manifest itself, that is, the notion of "living person" as well, whose constantly reinvented continuity presupposes both infection and canalization—in short, originality.

The fact that models are fairly inoperative in this case does not by any means signify that we have reached a mysterious point at which behavior becomes "inexplicable," but simply that the framing of the explanation has changed. Independent of any hypothesis about animal consciousness, the reference to territorial behavior as such implies that a series of contrasts has a meaning "for" the animal, matters "for" it, and ethologists, like a piano string "responding" to a tuning fork, will be irresistibly induced to make the animal the subject of their description. Henceforth, the individual lives in "its" environment, or "milieu," and ethologists, when they describe the radical difference between the behavior of the "intruder" and that of the "legitimate owner," no longer reconstitute but accompany with their words the risks experienced as such by those they are describing. Here, imagination is not a vector of a misplaced anthropomorphism but a risk inspired by an irresistible "community of intuition."

In other words, upon the traffic of functional signs—which, of course, continues—the open question of possible communities is superimposed, with their rituals, distances, synchronizations, rhythms and jingles, their perceptions. And upon the risks evolution has sanctioned throughout biological evolution are superimposed, in our modes of thought, the risks experienced as such by the individual, by the intruder whose tense, nervous body hesitates, testifying to the fact that it "does violence to itself," by the rabbit that hesitates to flee, or by the monkey isolated in its cage, who gnaws on its tail while the experimenters discuss the possibility that animals may suffer.

Pursuing the theme of sacraments, one might celebrate the territorial event in the terms that define the sacrament of baptism. Just as baptism introduces the members of God's people one by one into their native land, so the "territorial" sign may be described not merely as the entertainment of a proposition as such, but as an entertainment implying a feeling of belonging: my territory, my male, my people, my habits, my discipline. With the territorial animal, the notion of a "common world" assumes a meaning, under the banner both of a contrast—the community to which one does or does not belong—and of the appearance of "symbolic reference"—expressive features that are perceived, there, in relation to our trembling, hesitant, appetitive, assured bodies, which are "here": the percipient event.

How far should we extend the consequences of this innovation if it gives meaning to the contrast between "me" and "not me," "mine" and "not mine"? The animal whose fur stands on end when it identifies an intruder could surely not experience the radical metamorphoses of the experience of itself and its world that must be traversed by what we call a butterfly, from larva to winged creature. If we refer here, once again, to the great bifurcation that Bergson observed in the history of life, between instinct and intelligence, we can then wonder whether another novelty might not be correlated with it: living as "having a body." For Bergson, intelligence can be identified by its hesitation, clumsiness, and approximate character, translating an interpretative distance that is foreign to the sensible certainties of a butterfly flying toward a female. Yet hesitation, clumsiness, and approximation cannot be stated without presupposing a feeling of the difference between "self" and "one's body," a feeling of the body as property, itself endowed with properties with which one has to make do. In other words, the association between "percipient event" and "bodily life" that Whitehead pointed out in *The Concept of Nature* can also be phrased as "having a body."

The sacrament I associate with "baptism" would thus celebrate a conjunction in experience among what we designate as "having a world," "having a body," "being able to hesitate," "taking risks," and so on. Its efficacy would have as its correlate the fact that learning *from* these animals may also mean learning *with* them, implying that a common world is possible with them. And this is indeed what is translated by the risks proper to ethology, risks that translate the full solemnity of the event that is indicated by the "ethological mode of thought."

The first risk is that of "psychologizing projection." To speak of a "community of intuition" is not to speak of any guaranteed adequacy of interpretation, truth, or intersubjective fusion. As is demanded by the objective efficacy of the sacrament, the risk, that of an "empathetic" ethology, translates the new stakes that take on meaning for ethologists, and which are those of "symbolic reference." Moved by your expression, I may also be as completely wrong about the consequences as I infer them, as the ethologist may be wrong about what this chimpanzee showing his teeth means. To speak of "community" is to speak of creation of the problematic space in which the question of interpretation assumes meaning—of what has been understood or misunderstood, of trust and of deceit, of hesitation and of verification. As Bergson said, it is when life makes the choice of intelligence compared with instinct that the notion of error itself may be formulated. Here, then, the expressive sign, as a vector of abstraction for a problematic experience, may be said to be fully and simultaneously lure and decoy, eliciting temptation, hesitation, frustration, or disappointment. In short, when a society is no longer "functional," but gives meaning to a "community," its interstices make themselves felt by all the propositions entertained, which are therefore "true," but whose meaning it is sometimes better to verify.

Another risk proper to ethology is that ethologists, unbeknownst to them, may observe behaviors that they themselves have brought about, that is, that they may have "domesticated" those they thought they were just describing.

Here again, risk indicates the objective efficacy of the sacrament. The members of the people of God are introduced one by one, and it is only one by one that animals can be domesticated, that is, in this case, led to admit a particular human into their "domus": a singular, important person, whose gestures and attitudes may be interpreted as "theirs," as the "significant other" on whom they are counting and with which (or whom?) they live. If domestication is possible, it is no doubt because human beings understand something of the importance of the hesitations, temptations, fears, approaches, and flights of the animals they seduce. How they interpret what they understand is a wholly different question: what domestication celebrates is that nether the seduced nor the seducer may be defined in terms of functional signs that make a social, specific world for the insect. The expressive sensibilia that are being invented between themselves, laboriously, painfully, indicate that this time the adventure of life designates the individual, or the living person, as an active, vibrant site of the negotiation that takes place within it among fear, curiosity, and attraction. A site that testifies both to the infection and to the canalization through which what is new becomes important.

Finally, in ethology, there arises the thorny question of the innate and the acquired. There is no debate about the "innate" character of the behavior of ants and butterflies, but the question arises of the "innate" character of human intelligence, homosexuality, or aggression and of birdsongs, or of the long, complex parades that precede and seem to condition that functional behavior known as copulation.

Intelligence, homosexuality, and aggression are categories that are too "coarse" for the question to be elaborated in an interesting way. The question becomes interesting, however, in those cases where it is clear that the behavior under discussion is closely linked to properly functional urgencies, that is, to matters of selection. Through the question of whether something that is "innate" and as such is supposed to be the direct product of selection, can "explain" the behavior and hence the experience of the individual, the question arises of the articulation between the two "sacraments," corresponding respectively to functional individuality and to the possibility of a common world.

The natal is the new figure assumed by the innate and the acquired in the territorial assemblage. The affect proper to the nata, as heard in the lied: to be forever lost, or refound, or aspiring to the unknown homeland. In the natal, the innate tends to become displaced: as Ruyer says [n.b., Raymond Ruyer, in *La Genèse des formes vivantes*], *it is in some way prior to or downstream from the act; it concerns less the act or the behavior than the matters of expression themselves, the perception that discerns and selects them, and the gesture that erects them, or itself constitutes them* [...] *This is not to say, however, that behavior is at the mercy of chance learning; for it is predetermined by this displacement, and finds rules of assemblage in its own territorialization. The natal thus consists in a decoding of innateness and a territorialization of learning, one atop the other, one alongside the other* (MP, 410).

Once again, it is William James who may help us to understand what Deleuze and Guattari borrow from Ruyer, and more precisely that aspect of William James that has incited the most controversy, the one that affirms that the truth, or importance, of an idea is nothing other than its process of verification, the creative process in which the eventual consequences of these ideas are produced and put to the test. Let us take as an example of "act" the well-known case of the sexual display that precedes copulation, when a couple of storks is constituted, for example. Copulation responds to a functional imperative that must be satisfied in order for there to be storks in this world. This imperative is not satisfied until the outcome of the display, "downstream," but can we say that the storks obey it from the beginning, that is, that this display behavior is "innate"? For Ruyer, it is more adequate to say that at the outset each stork is for the other an object that is "valorized": important and interesting, eliciting. It may be innate, but must be "decoded" in order to get at its functional meaning. The imperative to be satisfied would have the status of a kind of "fleeing ghost," becoming specified as the display unfolds, as a value that is more and more significant: "my male," "my female." The efficacy of functional sensibilia, of what must be felt in the mode of the infinitive "to copulate," would then be conditioned by a learning process resulting in the creation of an object henceforth discerned, selected, in short, "recognized." *"That's him," "that's her," "that's our home"* will then be celebrated in unison every spring, when the members of the stork couple find one another upon their return from a distant migration.

To follow Ruyer, Deleuze, and Guattari, it is precisely at the moment when perception, in the sense that Whitehead described it in *The Concept of Nature,* becomes relevant, that the innate loses its power to explain, can no longer explain behavior independently of the way it itself acquires a territorial meaning, the way it is "decoded." The innate no more explains territorial behavior—*"my place," "your place"*—than an idea speaks its truth independently of its process of verification. The innate is explained in, by, and for the being that produces itself *qua* belonging to a "community."

A mode of ethological thought celebrating the events that transform the meaning and the stakes of terms such as innate, acquired, world, environment, individual, group, congener, behavior, and so on can certainly not avoid the critical questions that ethologists ask themselves about their perceptions and their interpretations. It might, however, distance them from any nostalgia for the verification processes designating what physicists or chemists call "objectivity," as well as for the modelizations corresponding to what selectivist biology designates as the only good explanation: the power of natural selection. In this sense, such a mode of thought might be vital for our scientific ideals, distorted as they are by the conflicts between the imperative of "objectivity" and the insistence of relevance.

In fact, this last point gives us a typical example of what Deleuze and Guattari call the "territorialization of learning." When working scientists "learn," objectivity is the imperative idea, on which the possibility for knowledge to survive *qua* "scientific" depends. Yet learning is not explained by objectivity, which is only satisfied downstream once what is relevant in each case has been recognized, once the due type of attention has been determined. Then, and only then, will scientists have become what Kant wanted them to be: judges interrogating "their" object. With regard to the sciences in which the imperative of objectivity does not need to be "decoded," nor learning territorialized, where what the scientist deals with has an *a priori,* "methodical" definition of objectivity imposed upon it, they become the sad analogy of behaviors qualified as "purely instinctive," explicable by the imperatives they obey.

Correlatively, for scientific learning to conclude successfully, for the imperative of objectivity to finally be satisfied, the scientist's question must ultimately be able to designate its "respondent." Not, of course, in the same sense in which the female stork "responds" to the male's advances, but nevertheless in the sense that what has been discerned, selected, and erected by the question "is appropriate," does indeed address something that matters for the being under interrogation. Physicists have learned to interrogate the atom on the basis of its spectra of emission and absorption of light, and their success attests to the fact that electromagnetic radiation matters to the atom, and that it does not matter for the atom's nucleus. Physics is relevant and inventive in that it takes the greatest account of this contrast it has learned to recognize, and it therefore cannot, any more than any experimental science, inspire the dream of an "objective" ethology, transcending the diversity of animal behavior toward a common definition. A successful question, here as elsewhere, is the one that finds its respondent, that learns to discern what matters to what is interrogated. The mode of thought of ethologists studying a territorial animal can therefore not help but differ from that of biologists specializing in bacteria, because the fact of being here or there may make a major difference for an animal if a territorial boundary passes between "here" and "there" whereas it makes none for a bacterium, to which, however, the detectable difference "more or less sugary" matters. With regard to the imperative of having to make a difference between a "good question," finding its respondent, and a misplaced or arbitrary question, it designates humans, of course, and the imagination whose power is celebrated by their mistrust.

When we come to mankind, nature seems to have burst through another of its boundaries. The central activity of enjoyment and expression has assumed a reversal in the importance of its diverse functionings. The conceptual entertainment of unrealized possibility becomes a major factor in human mentality. In this way outrageous novelty is introduced, sometimes beatified, sometimes damned, and sometimes literally patented or protected by copyright. The definition of mankind is that in this genus of

*animals the central activity has been developed on the side of its relation-
ship to novelty [. . .] In animals we can see emotional feeling, dominantly
derived from bodily functions, and yet tinged with purposes, hopes, and
expression derived from conceptual functioning. In mankind, the dominant dependence on bodily functioning seems still there. And yet the life
of a human being receives its worth, its importance, from the way in
which unrealized ideals shape its purposes and tinge its actions. The distinction between men and animals is in one sense only a difference in degree. But the extent of the degree makes all the difference. The Rubicon
has been crossed* (MT 26–27).

Julius Caesar knew that crossing the Rubicon had nothing to do with
"crossing a river." The Rubicon had its own importance at the time of the
Roman Republic, and was the object of explicit utterances. The decision
to cross it was thus inseparable from an utterance. Julius brought an exclamation into existence—"*Caesar crossed the Rubicon!*"—in order for
it to fashion Caesar's destiny, for better or worse.

Verbal statements are obviously not the only "lures for feeling" that
we fashion for ourselves. In some circumstances, turning one's back or
shrugging one's shoulders can—and we know this the moment we do
it—render present the as yet unrealized possibilities of a relationship, a
breakup, for instance, or the delicate question of the repair of the irreparable. Not to mention the multiplicity of "things," talismans, fetishes,
lucky charms, sorcerers' objects, testaments, experimental apparatuses,
and all our writings: so many socially maintained and stabilized ways
for charging a being that we fashion to intervene in our lives and those
of others, to modify their course. The list is open and might even
include—why not?—the scan of his wife's brain exhibited by some fanatical theoretician, declaring to a dazzled audience that this is the genuine portrait of his beloved (who, fortunately, is just as fanatical). For
even the scan might, for someone able to endow it with expressivity,
cease to be mute with regard to what counts in a portrait. It is not the
tender laugh of a face that will have been eliminated in the name of
physical measurement, it is the physico-mathematical structure that will
laugh tenderly.

There is no sorting process to be carried out here, no distinction to be
made between apparent and legitimate efficacy. The efficacy of reading is
as mysterious for those who are not readers as is the efficacy of a talisman
or a pilgrimage for others. The fact that Galileo may be radically transformed while, like a child, he is rolling balls along an inclined plane requires an entire epoch, as does the fact that a Catholic may share the body
of Christ, "his" body, where others would perceive "a" piece of bread.

If the distinction between animal and human is initially marked by the proliferation of belongings that are territorial—that is, also epochal—this proliferation does not explain novelty. It is rather that by which this novelty "explains itself," that is, inseparably, is socialized and causes social divergence. Galileo's experience includes the knowledge that others might compare him to a child while he himself discovers the power of "facts." Catholics, when not defined by an "animal faith," or "blind faith," know that one must belong to the community of believers to accept the piece of bread in the way that is appropriate to the body of Christ. There is a proliferation of belongings, but some belongings are produced under the banner of a contrast, confronting belonging with the real possibility of nonbelonging. And it is here, of course, that we also find the theme of the "great refusal": all the propositions rendered nontrue by a decision link importance and divergence irreducibly.

The efficacy proper to the sacrament of the Eucharist, that is, the miracle of transubstantiation, may be appropriate for characterizing the Rubicon crossed by humanity, for it is precisely with regard to it that a contrast is proposed that is addressed, not to a living person, but to a decision as such. And here, adhesion, marking the entertainment of a proposition, causes divergence: the community of Christians adheres to the proposition *"this is my body"* in the mode of a "scandal of faith," not with the child's beatific happiness, *"this is my mother."* Here, too, a difference may be introduced between animal "faith" and the professionals' adherence to their categories, when this adherence boasts of its obviousness "without qualms." To take up the Leibnizian distinction between "the pleats of matter" and the "folds of the soul," here we can no longer ignore the "soul" in favor of "matter," and our descriptions can no longer limit themselves to celebrating the invention of a "folding over" according to the contrast between what is mine and not mine, or the production of the expressive signs that give meaning to a community.

The specificity of human experience is not defined by its limitations, but rather by "leaps of the imagination" that respect no limitation. Of course, community of intuition still rules and even proliferates. But it may also be experienced as such. In addition, the entertainment of a new proposition is felt as an event. Our modes of thought, as soon as they concern humans, have this specificity as their question, including, perhaps above all, the doctrines that make nature bifurcate, with their explicit or implicit dualism. For both their "subject," claiming a freedom that does not belong to any creature, and their "objective reality," defined by a highly exaggerated coincidence between explanation and submission, testify to the great refusal. Hesitation, the felt risk of error, may be replaced by terror in the face of the somewhat inflated risk of the production of chimaeras and arbitrariness. If no difference can be made between objective and subjective, everything is permitted!

With the experience Whitehead was to call "intellectual," risk itself henceforth becomes material for propositions, turning experience into a logical subject, reduced to the status of food for a possibility. And it is this risk, rather than any "defining characteristic," that best designates how souls matter for us: they are what we risk losing, what might be captured, reduced to wandering, enslaved. Between "self-righteous people," who know what the good is (a case of community adherence), and hogs, clever territorial animals, the difference is trivial. Correlatively, losing one's hold becomes, in a somewhat exaggerated way, what will be identified with the paradigmatic disaster, or else with the precondition of any initiation or any spiritual transformation.

In other words, we have to deal here with the exorbitant novelty of societies implicitly exhibiting the importance of the possible, or of what might have been, and producing the means to raise the partiality of perspectives to its pinnacle. For the difference between what will and will not be recognized as legitimate, what will or will not be recognized as valid, is no longer a "social fact," but what is at stake: a problem whose terms are, of course, socially defined, but in a way that makes interstices proliferate. This is shown just as much by the minutiae of moral casuistry and examinations of conscience as by the ferocity of scientific controversies. Attention to truth demands sensitivity to new signs and the production of new tests. The devil is in the details, the difference between artifact and correctly established experimental fact demands passionate interest, the devious imagination of competent colleagues.

The fact that Whitehead, apparently quite innocently, calls this novelty "intellectual feeling" may mean that the point is not to describe all our "spiritual" adventures. Instead, it is to designate with great precision, so as to correct any excess subjectivity, the Rubicon that has been crossed. What "might be" is no longer declared by hesitation demanding verification but becomes what matters as such.

In an intellectual feeling the datum is the generic contrast between a nexus of actual entities and a proposition with its logical subjects members of the nexus [. . .] This contrast is what has been termed the "affirmation-negation contrast." It is the contrast between the affirmation of objectified fact in the physical feeling, and the mere potentiality, which is the negation of such affirmation, in the propositional feeling. It is the contrast between "in fact" *and* "might be," *in respect to particular instances in* this *actual world. The subjective form of the feeling of this contrast is consciousness* (PR, 266–267).

The cry of the solitary consciousness, its refusal to conform, its heroic affirmation that it is possible to be right, even one against all, suffice to show that there is nothing neutral about "intellectual feelings." An intellectual feeling may be a vector of heroism, to the point of martyrdom; a vector of stupid arrogance, to the point of the opposition between the future science of neurons and the opinion that "believes" in motives, reasons, and intentions; a vector of eradicative passion, to the point of the systematic persecutions of peoples who cultivate it otherwise. Yet it is also what some ethologists know how to cultivate. They know with lucidity, when performing as the advocates or active protectors of baboons, chimpanzees, or gorillas, that the ability of these beings to inspire our sympathy or our love may be what they will owe their survival to, but they also know that it is not what defines these beings' proper value. Or again, it is what is demanded of his readers by Michel Foucault, who designates himself as a positivist historian and undertakes to describe the social power at work not only in the repression, but also in the production of the feelings we associate with what is true, just, and interesting.

In any case, the fact objectified in "physical feeling" is not a simple percept. It may designate physical feelings that are as sophisticated as possible, but it always designates them by introducing an operation of transubstantiation that de-territorializes them: "my gorillas," for whom I would give my life, are also "gorillas," who, for their part, confer a wholly different sense upon our attachment. "My" most authentic "feelings" about the difference between good and evil, the true and the illusory, cannot be disentangled from social habits induced by the apparatuses of power.

Yet we must not exaggerate. The feeling of such contrasts matters, but only intermittently, and the import of each contrast is limited.

Consciousness flickers; and even at its brightest, there is a small focal region of clear illumination, and a large penumbral region of experience which tells of intense experience in dim apprehension (PR, 267).

The question that begins with intellectual feelings is that of exaggeration, the power granted to the abstractions derived from the "clear" zone to define a situation. As Leibniz said, Buridan's ass, confronted with two fields similar from every viewpoint, would not remain stumped: the slightest detail, the cry of a bird, a fragrant breath of air, apprehended in a confused way, would make the difference. Yet it is quite possible that "Buridan the philosopher" might, because there are no good reasons to choose, confer such power upon intellectual feeling as to affirm that only a violent decision, the expression of a freedom identified with arbitrariness, can decide the question. This is why Leibniz's moral advice, *Dic cur hic*, does not demand that a decision be justified but intends to induce the development of a sensitivity to the concrete of *this* situation, *hic*, against the generalities authorized by conscious abstraction, against the excess differentiation between the limited zone of clear thought and the penumbra of physical feelings accepted without question. Leibniz himself did not rely on his abstractions, ceaselessly testing his system in his encounters with his numerous correspondents, experiencing what they demanded to see recognized, what he was capable of recognizing, what formulation could satisfy them.

Each occasion is an activity of concern, in the Quaker sense of that term. It is the conjunction of transcendence and immanence. The occasion is concerned, in the way of feeling and aim, with things that in their own essence lie beyond it; although these things in their present functions are factors in the concern of that occasion. Thus each occasion, although engaged in its own immediate self-realization, is concerned with the universe (MT, 167).

The concern of the Quakers, or the Friends, which Whitehead evokes, is not the disquiet—*inquiétude* or *Unruhe*—that allowed Leibniz to gather in the same register the disquiet of the thinker, the hesitation of Buridan's ass, or the readiness of a rabbit on alert, but also that of the pencil standing on its tip, which the slightest solicitation would make fall to one side or the other. Whereas the person who follows Leibniz's advice must resist the power of what imposes itself as clear, what makes the Quakers tremble is not to have been silent enough to feel what obscurely demands to be felt. In both Leibniz's and the Quakers' cases, however, the point is to address, by means of distinct intellectual feelings, an excess subjectivity that itself exhibits the efficacy of intellectual feelings, to address the way we ask the zone of clear illumination in which our reasons are formulated to define what a situation demands, and to silence the interstices in which alternatives lurk.

The contrast between the means used by Leibniz and Whitehead reflects a contrast between their respective epochs. Although the Leibnizian analogy, allowing the soul's disquiet to belong to the same plane as the instability of the pencil, could be effective in the seventeenth century, it became dangerous in the twentieth century. In Leibniz's time, it could make a breath of humor waft over statements laden with hatred and polemics, over a theology haunted by the dark question of grace, in whose name Protestants and Catholics were killing one another. Today, power is on the side of the specialists of the pencil, and the instability of the pencil poised on its tip is destined, almost inevitably, to appear as the "finally objective" explanation of the soul's disquiet.

As for the proposition according to which every entity is "concerned," in the Quaker sense of the term, it inspires the most surprising contrast with all our territorial physical feelings, with all our social judgments concerning what is "ours" and what pertains to an unstable pencil. It acts as a revelator: what appears clearly is the contrast between the seriousness with which every proposition intended to assimilate us to an unstable physical system is entertained and the outlandish character, inspiring only irony, of a proposition that would inaugurate the inverse movement, associating with a cosmic suspense each process of self-determination, be it that of the slightest electronic occasion or that of a painter adding the last touch to her work, on which its success or failure may depend.

The soul may certainly be said to be "disquiet" when it refers to a living person. But what emerges with the soul is the possibility, among others, of the Quakers' "concern," that is, the experience of the "full solemnity of the world." This is why Whitehead could integrate the Quaker sense of the term "concern" into his cosmological, speculative thought. What Quaker concern brings into existence cannot be reduced to a worried hesitation, for it escapes all final appropriation: the Quaker God will never be "their" God. The same holds true for the regime of thought induced by the Whiteheadian scheme, whose singularity is to provide an explicit disclosure of the efficacy of the sacrament of transubstantiation. For this regime of thought, which can be said to be deliberately speculative, includes within it a speculation on the possibility that it might become a habit, a mode of thought. Not in the sense of an "uprooting" from every community, a devaluing the living person, but rather in the mode of the "humor of thought": a stable articulation between two regimes of signs, the "territorial" signs that give rise to a "community of intuition," and the "speculative" signs, bringing about the experience of what "might be thought": "facts" as witnesses to a cosmos. Fully deployed intellectual feeling, exhibiting the justification of life as a "culture of interstices," does not coincide with critique, or with a break, but it has trust as its condition: letting go does not mean losing one's hold.

Here, then, with the circle closed, we have once again encountered the function Whitehead attributed to his categories, each application of which was to coincide with a leap of imagination: for we have to do with a culturalization of the "miracle of transubstantiation" itself. Each experience, always initially objectified according to the propositions of a specialized territory, must be able to be called upon to undergo a transformation that gives its importance to the conscious contrast "affirmation/negation," but that does not appeal to the "last judgment" of a critical operation, productive of new territorialities that could be opposed to others. Quite the contrary, the speculative character of thought is marked by the impossibility of constituting "applications" into appropriable states of things, "my" world designated in "my" language. Speculative language will never be "my" language, in the sense that it will never have to end up in the formation of judgments, whether they have the form of an affirmation, a negation, or even of a suspension of what is pronounced. It does not enable a pronouncement, but it pronounces, and this is its efficacy: its expressions bring into existence a "might be" that no art of consequences can transform into a verified "state of affairs." Yet it nevertheless matters, as did the appearance of expressive signs transforming, without denying them, the imperatives corresponding to functional signs, by displacing them downstream.

The question inspired by this analogy might be: what about downstream? Does an imperative of truth finally find satisfaction in it? If this were the case, there would no doubt be an analogy with Spinoza's third genre, or with a certain version of Nietzsche's will to power, or else with peace according to Leibniz. I shall return to this point at the end of our itinerary. What must be emphasized already is that there will certainly be no question of celebrating God as truth. Divine envisagement—*what is best for that impasse?*—does indeed belong to the "speculative regime" of thought. God is its logical subject, and the feeling of the proposition does not require a judgment concerning the existence of God, in the social sense, implying the possibility of a "last judgment." Its verification depends on its effects, and these designate the person who entertains such a proposition *qua* aware of the contrast between a given judgment and the way in which, immersed in the cosmological hypothesis, this judgment might be "transubstantiated."

In other words, every "*that's true*," every adherence to a proposition concerning God, constitutes a fact that, in the "inevitable ordering of things," is just as much a participant in an impasse. Whitehead's God does not "judge" the propositional feelings that take God as their subject, according to any kind of truth value that would transcend their entertainment. For speculative thought, he is not associated with truth but with relevance. Just as, in *Science and the Modern World*, God's power was defined by the "worship" he inspires, in *Process and Reality*, the importance of the propositions that take God as their subject refers to the difference they make for the experience that entertains them, to their efficacy in the transubstantiation of individual experiences.

Whitehead's metaphysical God does not recognize his own, he does not read in our hearts, he does not understand us better than we do ourselves, he does not demand our recognition or our gratitude, and we shall never contemplate him in his truth. None of these negative propositions denies its positive as factually inexact; it denies it as pertaining to the fallacy of misplaced concreteness. All belong to the mode of thought that celebrates my relation to my self and my belongings, to my body, to my feelings, my intentions, my possibilities of perception. No thinker thinks twice. It is the risks of thought that are exhibited as such with speculative propositions, and if an imperative of "truth" exists that is satisfied downstream, it cannot be separated from the exercise of thought itself.

Thinking promotes general indifference. It is a dangerous exercise nevertheless. Indeed, it is only when the dangers become obvious that indifference ceases, but they often remain hidden and barely perceptible, inherent in the enterprise. Precisely because the plane of immanence is prephilosophical and does not immediately operate with concepts, it implies a sort of groping experimentation and its layout resorts to measures that are not very respectable, rational, or reasonable. These measures belong to the order of dreams, of pathological processes, esoteric experiences, drunkenness, and excess. We head for the horizon, on the plane of immanence, and we return with bloodshot eyes, yet they are the eyes of the mind. Even Descartes had his dream. To think is always to follow the witch's flight [. . .] Usually these measures do not appear in the result, which must be grasped solely in itself and calmly. But then "danger" takes on another meaning: it becomes a case of obvious consequences when pure immanence provokes a strong, instinctive disapproval in public opinion, and the nature of the created concepts strengthens this disapproval (QPh, 44).

We know nothing of the "measures" to which Whitehead, the most amiable of philosophers, had recourse, except perhaps for the strange frenzy of his insertions, implying a highly unreasonable strategy of communication. Yet the result, taken in itself and calmly, that is, a labyrinth of propositions deliberately fashioned to "induce" the "sheer disclosure" proper to a speculative regime of thought, can indeed have "a strong, instinctive disapproval" as its consequence. For the question, crucial for philosophical opinion, *"is this really serious?"* will always be answered only by a double series of consequences, which never cease being revived, like the zigzag of a witch's flight: those that make being exist as importance, and those that make thought exist as expression.

CHAPTER TWENTY-FOUR

God and the World

T HE FINAL SUMMARY can only be expressed in terms of a group
of antitheses, whose apparent self-contradictions depend on neglect of the diverse categories of existence. In each antithesis there
is a shift of meaning which converts the opposition into a contrast.

It is as true to say that God is permanent and the World fluent, as that
the World is permanent and God is fluent.

It is as true to say that God is one and the World many, as that the
World is one and God many.

It is as true to say that, in comparison with the World, God is actual eminently, as that, in comparison with God, the World is actual eminently.

It is as true to say that the world is immanent in God, as that God is
immanent in the World.

It is as true to say that God transcends the World, as that the World
transcends God.

It is as true to say that God creates the World, as that the World creates God.

God and the World are the contrasted opposites in terms of which
Creativity achieves its supreme task of transforming disjoined multiplicity, with its diversities in opposition, into concrescent unity, with its diversities in contrast (PR, 347–348).

Anyone might think that the philosopher who wrote those lines, three
pages before the end of Process and Reality, is summarizing a careful
argumentation in which he will have demonstrated how it is possible to
affirm antithetical statements at the same time, in the mode of "it is as

true . . ." And my reader is no doubt preparing for a new flight of experience, for the new leaps of imagination that should be brought about by taking into account the categories of existence whose neglect, Whitehead affirms, explains why the antitheses take on a contradictory character. As usual henceforth, the circle that announces the leap seems to be there: that a series of oppositions may be transformed into so many contrasts testifies to a cosmos, and it is the difference between cosmos and neutral creativity that requires Whitehead's God. The way Whitehead is going to oblige us to think of God and the World should in itself constitute a testimony to the role of God in the World.

[. . .] *There is no meaning to "creativity" apart from its "creatures," and no meaning to "God" apart from the "creativity" and the "temporal creatures," and no meaning to the "temporal creatures" apart from "creativity" and "God"* (PR, 225).

We know what to expect: we will be obliged to think of God and the World in a regime of reciprocal presupposition, affirming creativity as the ultimate. God and the actual occasions will be described in a mode that makes them both the creatures of creativity and the conditions of creativity. A new flight of speculative experience will begin.

And yet, in this case, the leap of imagination did not take place. Whitehead's interpreters have remained perplexed and even "appalled," and in any case rooted to the soil of their disagreements. The divergent interpretations and hypotheses with regard to the manner of "modifying," "prolonging," or "completing" *Process and Reality* succeed one another. As if, in this case, the conceptual assemblage could not suffice, could not become a matter of "sheer disclosure."

In fact, the triumphalist character of Whitehead's "final summary" should not impress us overmuch. On November 11, 1947, that is, a few weeks before his death, Whitehead, speaking of *Process and Reality,* fragments of which were perhaps going to be reedited, affirmed the true credo of his research to Lucien Price:

"In the preface to it," said he, "I wrote something which ought to have been repeated in the opening sentence of the first chapter, and repeated at frequent intervals all through the book: namely, how impressed I am with the inadequacy of any human being's attempt to express such philosophical ideas at all; how utterly beyond our scope are these universal processes. All one can do, in venturing on such subjects, is to offer suggestions" (DANW, 359).

However, one must not turn the inadequate character of human thought into the specific explanation of the difficulties encountered by readers when it comes to divine experience. When Whitehead speaks of the inadequacy of human attempts, he is not talking about God in particular but about all the ideas proposed in *Process and Reality*. What is more, precisely in the case of God it was most important for him that the attempt should not end in defeat, in the thesis of a "learned ignorance," an experience of the impotence of human intelligence in the face of an infinite perfection that makes the categories appropriate for finitude pass to their respective limits and collapse together. Whitehead knows that many of his readers will be Christians, or at least "infected" by Christian theological notions. And Lucien Price reports the brutal judgment Whitehead pronounced in this regard: "I consider Christian theology to be one of the great disasters of the human race" (DANW, 171).

The theological figure of a creator God, omnipotent, perfect, paternal, omniscient, providential, and judge, never inspired anything but the strictest disapproval in Whitehead, right down to the end. Constructing a concept of God, he could not, of course, envisage repairing the historical disaster humanity had undergone, but he certainly undertook to create the means to fight against its consequences where this was possible for him: in philosophical thought.

The secularization of the concept of God's functions in the world is at least as urgent a requisite of thought as is the secularization of other elements of experience. The concept of God is certainly one essential element in religious feeling. But the converse is not true; the concept of religious feeling is not an essential element in the concept of God's function in the universe. In this respect religious literature has been sadly misleading to philosophic theory, partly by attraction and partly by repulsion (PR, 207).

It must therefore be accepted that the "suggestions" Whitehead offers about God should, for him, satisfy the demands of thought. In contrast, the fact that the concept of God, which he has to construct, may, as previous ones, be an essential element in religious feeling rather expresses *Science and the Modern World*'s trust in the religious vision recurring "with an added richness and purity of content." In such a purified vision, however, this concept will be "one" essential element, but it will not be "the" essential element. Whitehead's attempt at secularization is not meant to prescribe the new content of an eventual religious vision, even if this vision may benefit from consciousness' self-correction of its own initial excess of subjectivity, which is the subject of philosophy.

Was the attempt successful? As I have said, for many of Whitehead's readers the answer is no. They considered that *Process and Reality* should either be rewritten with no God, or else that it alluded to a book that Whitehead could not or did not wish to write, in which the concept of

God would certainly have gained the coherence which, according to them, is missing.

Yet it so happens that I think it possible to construct this coherence on the basis of the text as it was written. And I can attempt, already at this point, to convey the reason why the absence here of the "disclosure" usually associated with a Whiteheadian construction may well be a coherent consequence of that construction. For what is at stake in this case is "the secularization of the concept of God's functions in the world," and in order to succeed in such an operation of secularization, one must first succeed in not thinking of Man in the image of God; that is, reciprocally, in not constructing a God who would be in the image of Man, all the singularities that enable mankind to be opposed to beasts or electrons, passing to infinity to converge toward the inconceivable divine perfection. Mankind, beasts, and electrons designate societies, and even thought and its concepts refer to adventures conditioned by societies. But God is indifferent to societies. In other words, not only did God not make Man in his image, but above all, our image of ourselves as a living continuity, demanding to be acknowledged and appreciated, finds no respondent in God.

And this is what makes divine experience, properly speaking, "unimaginable." Imagination cannot "leap" in this case for it too is intimately linked to social adventures. It is only when something of our own experience enters into resonance with what our words formulate that imagination leaps. Our experience cannot enter into resonance with that of God: such, it seems to me, is the first meaning of the statement that "the concept of religious feeling is not an essential element in the concept of God's function in the universe."

In any case, let us think of the term "function" that Whitehead used to define what is to be understood. The point is not to set forth a "perfect being" in concepts but to characterize a function or a role. How better to prohibit the mystical élan that the leap of imagination would constitute here than by this characterization? Yet we can go further. Whitehead was a mathematician, and for a mathematician the term "function" typically designates what belongs to the solution of a problem. If the following pages do not inspire a flight of experience, it is precisely because the question of the relation between God and the World is raised, for Whitehead, as a problem that demands a solution, that is, it also refers entirely to the responsibility of the person who has raised the problem. The point is no longer to set out from what we in fact "know," from the common sense that the multiple versions of the bifurcation of nature conspire to silence. The point is to contribute a keystone to the conceptual edifice, and every keystone is characterized by a rather special role as compared with the building's other stones. In this case, the rather special character designates precisely the need for taking up his conceptual categories in a way that separates them from what elsewhere constitutes their truth, the leap of imagination toward applications. They will not permit any "leap" toward God, for the hope that God will come to meet us is precisely what secularization must imperatively counter.

Before defining the problem for which I believe the concept of the divine functioning is a solution, I must specify the challenge my hypothesis will have to answer and the interpretative choice to which it responds.

The challenge consists in the fact that the fifth part of *Process and Reality*, devoted to the question of God, is literally saturated by "familiar" images. God "understands," "saves," "leads," is the "great companion," the "poet," and so on. I will have to show that the influx of these religious images is part of the verification of the solution: in the case of a positive verification, each will have to undergo a "speculative twisting" that counters the type of religious emotion usually associated with it. To counter does not mean to prohibit: nothing would give rise more effectively to the flight of experience that is to be countered than the prohibition defining it as an infraction. According to my hypothesis, it is thus by taking up, deliberately and systematically, the images associated with Christian theology and mysticism that Whitehead has chosen to put his solution to the test, and it is the success of this test that will have to be verified. This cannot happen, however, until the end of our itinerary, when we will have reached its solution.

As far as the interpretative choice is concerned, it concerns the problem, and must therefore be deployed already at this point. The definition of the problem which, according to my hypothesis, Whitehead tries to solve, presupposes a decision about the way we may understand the variety of the characterizations of the divine functioning that figure in the pages of *Process and Reality*. In this case, my decision subscribes to Lewis Ford's genetic interpretation, since I will suppose that Whitehead, here as elsewhere, did not take the trouble to rewrite his text, although, at the end of his redaction, the subject he was envisaging was undergoing a drastic mutation. The question that must then be raised is that of the modifications that he "should have" made.

As we know, at the beginning of *Process and Reality*, God was endowed exclusively with conceptual feelings, and conceived as "nontemporal primordial actuality." At the point of arrival, what was a pure, nontemporal act of envisagement will have become God's "primordial nature," initiating divine experience, and God, having become a "creature of creativity," will have been endowed with a "consequent nature," an addition whose consequences Whitehead characterizes by a rather spectacular contrast.

One side of God's nature is constituted by his conceptual experience. This experience is the primordial fact in the world, limited by no actuality which it presupposes. This side of his nature is free, complete, primordial, eternal, actually deficient, and unconscious. The other side originates with physical experience derived from the temporal world, and then acquires integration with the primordial side. It is determined, incomplete, consequent, "everlasting," fully actual, and conscious. His necessary goodness expresses the determination of his consequent nature (PR, 345).

Whitehead is not fooling around. If what he describes is faithful to his solution, and if the latter holds, one could even say that this solution passes precisely where Christian theology has appropriated philosophical concepts in a "disastrous" way. For God's conceptual experience, as it is characterized (except with regard to its "deficiency," that is, its thirst for actuality, which is the only value), corresponds quite well to the Greek concept of "unmoved Prime Mover," who moves without being moved and hence is not moved emotionally either, who orients without being affected by the way that beings respond to his orientation. Whitehead himself does not hesitate to emphasize this point (PR, 344). Yet this superb concept, if it is adequate for a celebration of divine perfection, of its difference from all creatures, has nevertheless raised a terrible problem for the Christian theologians who have appropriated it. It corresponds to a divine figure incapable of that relation to history required by a providential religion. God, the unmoved First Mover, may be He to whom the prayers of mankind rise up, but not He to whom these prayers are addressed if mankind requires that their prayers be addressed to a being capable of hearing them. But the physical experience Whitehead attributes to God seems to be the answer to this problem, and even affirms itself to be capable of integrating the goodness demanded by the religious idea of providence. If Whitehead's solution were to hold, one could say that he would have "taken the problem by the horns," creating not a concept of the divine in general but the finally coherent concept—the bad construction of which, according to him, was a disaster—of the God of the Christians: a tinkered solution which, as the case may be, has been celebrated as designating the unthinkable that must nevertheless be thought. In short, he will have speculatively eliminated the central mystery of Christian theology.

At this point, however, a question of reading arises. What Whitehead describes in this text as the two sides of God's nature, he often defines elsewhere as two "natures," primordial and consequent. In fact, he even spoke here of "two experiences," which has no meaning according to his concepts: *one* or *many*, not two. The only genuine conceptual implication of "two" is the duality of poles, physical and mental, of an experience that is in itself undivided. Does "two" translate a specificity of God? This hypothesis seems to me all the less necessary in that Whitehead will also come to speak, in these same pages, of "two experiences" for an actual occasion.

I am therefore going to run the risk of admitting that, in any case, we have to do with a "manner of speaking." When Whitehead speaks of God's two natures, or of two divine experiences, he is simply prolonging the little ruse that has allowed him to avoid tedious rewritings. It was enough for him to note—and even then not always—in the passages where he had spoken of God as "nontemporal" that he was obviously talking about God's "primordial nature." By so doing, he unfortunately set a trap for his readers, who were subjected to the temptation to attribute to this "primordial nature" as such the responsibility for the aspect of functioning that Whitehead had initially attributed to nontemporal actuality. This has very serious consequences, as we shall see on the basis of a typical example.

In what sense can unrealized abstract form be relevant? What is its basis of relevance? "Relevance" must express some real fact of togetherness among forms. The ontological principle can be expressed as: All real togetherness is togetherness in the formal constitution of an actuality. So if there be a relevance of what in the temporal world is unrealized, the relevance must express a fact of togetherness in the formal constitution of a non-temporal actuality (PR, 32).

From beginning to end of *Process and Reality,* one invariant remains: the fact that if God's intervention is necessary, it is in order to think of relevance. In this passage, the subject is the ingression of eternal objects that are not realized but "relevant." Yet to ensure that mental decisions are "relevant" was already the function of God as the principle of limitation in *Science and the Modern World,* and if this function is henceforth attributed to primordial nature alone, what is the function of consequent nature? It is that thanks to which God "feels" the world *qua* temporal, of course, but what are the consequences of this feeling for the world? Moreover, if relevance pertains to primordial nature alone, that is, to the infinite envisagement of all eternal objects, how can this envisagement end up in the definition of "what is best for that impasse," while itself remaining "eternal," not affected by the temporality implied by this impasse *qua* associated with a subjective satisfaction, thus and not otherwise?

It is perhaps because the notion of "Unmoved Prime Mover" constitutes an attractor too powerful for the conceptual imagination that so many Whiteheadian philosophers have acted as though they could treat each of God's "two natures" separately, instead of attributing to divine experience two poles that can only be distinguished abstractly. My reading choice will be the reverse: the point is to accentuate the inseparable character of the two "poles" of divine experience, the pole called mental and the pole called physical, and therefore to go right to the end of what Whitehead proposed when he made God an actual entity (almost) like the others.

Every actual entity is "in time" so far as its physical pole is concerned, and is "out of time" so far as its mental pole is concerned. It is the union of two worlds, namely, the temporal world, and the world of autonomous valuation (PR, 248).

Consequently, I propose to read the statements in which Whitehead speaks of a "non-temporal actuality" in a way that actively differentiates between what mathematicians call "necessary" conditions and "necessary and sufficient" conditions. When a statement refers to the nontemporal actuality, or to the primordial nature of God, as if one could speak of it in isolation, this is a "necessary condition": the envisagement of eternal objects is necessary; otherwise, it would be impossible for nonrealized eternal objects to make ingression, since the notion of relevance cannot explain without being itself explained. But is this envisagement sufficient to explain relevance passing into the world? In the fifth part of *Process and Reality*, by contrast, when Whitehead moves from divine conceptual envisagement, defined as a necessary condition, to that envisagement in the midst of the economy of divine experience, the question of necessary and sufficient conditions is raised. It is then a matter of taking fully into account the undivided nature of divine experience, the inseparable character of the two poles.

However, a Whiteheadian scholar will probably come up with a very serious objection to this reading choice. If the "divine endowment" constituted by the "initial aim" of each nascent subject must be referred to God as an actual entity, and not to his eternal primordial nature, it can be assimilated to a "conclusion" of divine experience with regard to "what is best for that impasse." But if God concludes each time, he can no longer be neither everlasting nor eternal: his experience is "atomic." What is given for the hybrid physical feeling from which an occasion will derive its initial aim is what has acceded to objective immortality, what marks the perishing of the divine subject who therefore "never really exists." Are we to imagine that a "divine occasion" could be reborn from each worldly satisfaction, from each feeling of an impasse? This is not Whitehead's solution, but it is the possibility accepted by Charles Harts-horne when he suggested making God a "society," a lineage of occasions that inherit from themselves and from the world as it has decided itself each time, according to the verdict of an occasional new "worldly" satis-faction. Hartshorne's suggestion has raised problems for those who insist on agreement with physics, in this case relativistic: in this interpretation, the divine feeling would correspond to a "true" definition of the world *qua* simultaneous with itself. Yet the definition of a "divine society" gives rise to many other difficulties, because turning God into a society means placing him under the banner not only of a continuity but of a confor-mity. This risks making him topple immediately toward the side of reli-gion, for this conformity will enable him to be characterized, allowing the definition of his "defining characteristic," and it will be hard to stop once one gets going and not to deduce from him the divine projects for the world. Such a characteristic is, moreover, ready-made, since White-head speaks of his "necessary goodness" as expressing "the determination of his consequent nature." But if "God is good" through his own, cease-lessly confirmed continuity, why is he indifferent to our own continuities? Job's cry rings out.

This is the defect of the idea of God as society: it has just given rise to a misplaced "leap" of the imagination. God's experience is social, "like ours," therefore . . . My reading hypothesis will thus go in the reverse di-rection. The goal will be to accentuate what makes God an actual entity "unlike the others," and, on my hypothesis, this difference can, as we shall see, justify a divine temporality that allows us to escape from the threat of the atomization of God.

Whitehead is very clear on the subject of how God differs from actual occasions. What differs is the fact that divine experience implies a "pole reversal" with regard to occasional experience. This, it seems to me, is the genuine problem to which divine functioning constitutes the solution, a problem that can be avoided by those who describe the two natures as if they could be separated. The solution Whitehead seeks is the character-ization of an experience that is literally "unimaginable," because the ini-tial pole of this experience is characterized by the envisagement of eternal objects that say nothing about themselves, nor about what their ingres-sion requires. They are not affected by the decisions that have conferred upon them one or another role, nor by the multiple epochs that succeed and become entangled with one another, punctuated by the appearance of new contrasts and new propositions. Obviously, we cannot attribute a satisfaction of the occasional type to such an experience, since this type of satisfaction would imply that everything that was indeterminate in the initial pole has found its determination. And therefore, we can suggest, already at that point, that God is he who is unable to "conclude," to arrive at a determination that is "thus and not otherwise." Yet how can we construct the positive definition of an experience that we cannot imagine?

According to my hypothesis, Whitehead "thinks by the middle." He will not try to conceive of God "in himself," but to affirm, by means of the correlated twofold definition of God and the actual occasions, the equal dignity of both poles, the physical pole that affirms that what has occurred has occurred, and the conceptual pole, by which nothing of what has occurred constitutes the last word. This is why the final chapter of *Process and Reality* does not deal with God without at the same time dealing—rather implicitly, it must be admitted—with actual occasions, that is, without submitting the coherence of the metaphysical scheme to a new test.

An actual entity in the temporal world is to be conceived as originated by physical experience with its process of completion motivated by consequent, conceptual experience initially derived from God. God is to be conceived as originated by conceptual experience with his process of completion motivated by consequent, physical experience, initially derived from the temporal world (PR, 345).

Whitehead never formulated in so technical a way as in these few lines the contrast which, according to my hypothesis, he wishes to construct, and it is this programmatic statement (involving the imperative "is to be") that will guide me from here on. This, according to my reading hypothesis, is the problem to which Whitehead must bring a solution.

In fact, this problem presents itself in the manner of two distinct "mathematical formulas," about which it must be determined how the different terms they connect are to be defined in order to make the formula work. And it is the contrast between the two formulas that obviously acts as a constraint. Whitehead's statement prescribes that the pole reversal should be thought in a mode that exhibits a partiality in favor of symmetry: both formulas propose an identical threefold articulation, "originated by," "with its/his process of completion motivated by," and "consequent [. . .] experience initially derived from." These three identical articulations must be understood as together forming a complex function, with the rest being variable. How should we interpret the variables in a way that satisfies and renders intelligible their articulation, allowing us to imagine that the two formulas are in fact one and the same, endowed with different variables?

Here, instead of the leap of the imagination, it is the laborious work of mathematicians constructing their solution that imposes itself. For we shall have to proceed as one does in mathematics: starting out from what may be considered "known," the functioning of actual occasions, to explore the way in which the first formula, supposed to define what is known, in fact obliges us to make explicit, and even to modify what we know, and use what has been acquired as a starting point toward the unknown. We shall therefore begin with the actual occasion, "conceived as originated by physical experience" and as endowed with "process of completion motivated by consequent, conceptual experience initially derived from God." I suggest that the reader who, having now understood my approach, hesitates to engage in this hypothetical exploration, skip directly to the next chapter, in which the construction I shall attribute to Whitehead will have to be evaluated on the basis of what it gives rise to: new leaps of the imagination.

As we recall, the question of the "physical experience" in which an actual occasion has its origin was marked by a major event: the abandonment of the idea that "physical feelings" are the feeling of an already unified datum. The demand answered by this abandonment is clear: the "initial phase," the physical feelings of the data but also the conceptual feelings that derive from them (according to the fourth categorical obligation), must always be already those of a subject, always be already inseparable from the process of completion whose superject to be determined constitutes a final cause.

Since the point is to "get to the bottom of things," one could ask the question "where does the subject 'come from'"? Rather remarkably, the "formula" does not say. Of course, the actual entity has its origin in physical experience, but this experience, once it has been referred to a nexus instead of a datum, has conferred its full meaning upon the "miracle of creation." The many that will have to be felt are, like dried bones, on vacation with regard to what will give them life, what will constitute them as multiple physical feelings. And if Ezekiel speaks as he was commanded, the very fact that he speaks implies that, one way or another, the command requires a proto-subject to listen and enact. Or that there is a relation of reciprocal presupposition between a germ of subjectivity and what answers to it, a multiplicity henceforth correlated, the shudder of the dispersed bones becoming data for physical feelings aiming at their subject. These would be two aspects of the same "origin" of the actual entity. And therefore, the "initial endowment," the hybrid physical feeling of God from which, according to the fourth obligation, the initial aim derives, requires and does not explain its subject.

In this regard, let us take up a fragment whose beginning has already been cited, and which describes how the initial aim is modified, becoming, according to the terms of the formula, the conceptual experience that motivates the process of completion. Its end, which I have not cited, gave the reason why the hybrid feeling of God was introduced.

Each temporal entity, in one sense, originates from its mental pole, analogously to God himself. It derives from God its basic conceptual aim, relevant to its actual world, yet with indeterminations awaiting its own decisions. This subjective aim, in its successive modifications, remains the unifying factor governing the successive phases of interplay between physical and conceptual feelings. These decisions are impossible for the nascent creature antecedently to the novelties in the phases of its concrescence. But this statement in its turn requires amplification. With this amplification the doctrine, that the primary phase of a temporal actual entity is physical, is recovered [. . .] *the primary phase is a hybrid physical feeling of God, in respect to God's conceptual feeling which is immediately relevant to the universe "given" for that concrescence. There is then, according to the Category of Conceptual Valuation, i.e. Categoreal Obligation IV, a derived conceptual feeling which reproduces for the subject the data and valuation of God's conceptual feeling. This conceptual feeling is the initial conceptual aim* [. . .] (PR, 224–225).

When Whitehead notes that a statement requires amplification, it is usually because he is making an insertion into a text written previously. In this case, the "amplification" has enabled him to affirm that the origin of an actual occasion is indeed a physical experience, answering to "Hume's principle." God's hybrid physical feeling thus enables agreement with both Hume's principle and the ontological principle, which demands a reason for the ingression of unrealized eternal objects. Yet as its name indicates, this feeling also presupposes its subject, albeit nascent.

In other words, the expression "initially derived from God" alludes to the derivation of a conceptual feeling from a hybrid physical feeling, but does not in the very least explain the "subject" that is presupposed in both cases. And a supplementary problem arises with regard to the second formula, which concerns divine experience, for in its case, the origin of the experience is defined as "conceptual." Coherence, in this case, implies that whatever may be its modalities that are still to be determined, divine experience must be initially conceptual. As a result, what Whitehead in this case calls "derivation" (God's process of completion as "motivated by the consequent physical experience initially derived from the temporal world") requires that the initium for God—what "activates" a divine experience—be the derivation of a physical feeling from a conceptual one, the latter involving moreover, one way or another, the temporal world. But there is no category that defines this possibility.

Here we face an initial difficulty of Whitehead's formula, and a decision becomes necessary. Insofar as the term "derivation" involved in the expression "initially derived" cannot be used in a strictly technical sense in the case of the divine, it is not necessary to think that it has the technical meaning conferred upon it by the fourth obligation in the other case. Thus, the formulas do not confer upon the term "derivation" that appears in it the categoreal meaning of "derivation of a feeling from another feeling." This is coherent, for when it comes to the delicate question of the "matching conditions" (as physicists call the operation of connection between two different registers of descriptions) between God and the world, and between the world and God, the categories of obligation can only remain silent, for they presuppose concrescence and concern the latter's process of self-determination. In order to emphasize the importance of this technical point, I will allow myself to use, instead of the henceforth opaque expression "initially derived," a new "name" that points out the problem where we were lured by a feeling of familiarity. This name will be added to the series of Whiteheadian names, that is, of the concepts that matter primarily by their relevance to other concepts, which is precisely what their name does not state.

The goal is to name the "beginning" to which corresponds the question "Whence comes the subject?" but also the "end"; the fact that, in a way that is still indeterminate, occasional experience can "make God physically feel" in such a way that God's consequent experience may be "relevant" for "that impasse." And we must choose a term that is indeterminate enough to escape the demand for reasons associated with the ontological principle. Not in order to introduce something arbitrary, but because the "reasons" associated with the ontological principle always include among those reasons the "final cause," the subject-superject: subjective feelings *qua* aiming at the superject that will be the subject of their unified feeling. Further, the reversal of poles makes the application of the ontological principle to God a problem. Should it be "no eternal object, no reason"? We must name what is demanded by creativity that is ultimate when it comes to the twofold "making-feel," that is, to what is required both by the hybrid physical feeling of God (which requires a subject to feel it), and by the divine feeling "about" the actual occasion as an impasse (which requires that the occasion make God feel).

"At the beginning of beginnings, there is induction." I have chosen the term "induction" for two reasons. First, the term evokes an operation of "passage" between two heterogeneous things: one thing induces something different. Then, when we have to deal with what is called hypnotic induction, the term is laden with indeterminacy. Hypnotized subjects seem to raise their arm against their will, "as they were ordered." Yet hypnotizers are well aware that they are not the ones who have given the order. If they have a role, it is rather that of indicating a path, or authorizing an experience. Those who induce hypnosis are thus quite unable to explain what they are bringing about, but they know that they are not its "reason."

One of the ways to specify that hypnotizers are not really in command is to say that they give rise to what did not exist before the induction, a new "you" to whom it is suggested "you must be able to raise your arm against your will." The "you must be able" is not an order, for an order supposes the preexistence of the person to whom it is addressed. It must be understood more in the mode of a diagnosis or of a hypothetical observation. In fact, this is a path suggested to the new "you" made to emerge by the addressing, by which the corresponding "I" will verify its own existence. The order corresponds to a "making felt," whence the subject of this feeling emerges, initiating, as the case may be, the raising of the hand "as ordered."

To choose the term "induction" is thus to give rise to the "leap of imagination" in a case that does not correspond to a religious feeling but has constrained scientists who seek reasons to acknowledge indeterminacy. I will take advantage of the flight of experience thus brought about to take up the second part of Whitehead's formula concerning the actual entity "with its process of completion motivated by consequent, conceptual experience," and to try to make it alive with regard to the adventure of human experience described by the French philosopher Étienne Souriau under the name "work to be done."

This is indeed a leap of the imagination, for the differences are just as remarkable as the common features. Thus, unlike occasional completion, the trajectory of completion of both work and worker requires consciousness, and more precisely a properly "non-social" mode of consciousness, since, as we shall see, none of the ingredients to be "set to work" can boast of a stabilized role, none can be felt independently of the contrast proper to intellectual feeling between "in fact" and "might be." Moreover, unlike the accomplishment constituted by a work, the accomplishment constituted by every occasional satisfaction cannot, as such, be associated with the contrast between success and failure. Every concrescence produces its satisfaction, however trivial the way in which the many have become one on this occasion may be.

The common features, for their part, indicate that those who have used the expression "work to be done"—that is, Étienne Souriau, and after him Gilles Deleuze—sought to depersonalize the experience of the work as it is carried out, that is, also to divest it of the reasons, whether psychological or social, that claim to account for it. The result has been a characterization of that experience that could indeed be read as a testimony in favor of the Whiteheadian genetic process, somewhat as in physics, the (social) properties of superconducting bodies testify in favor of the relevance of quantum mechanics. Perhaps, moreover, this characterization converges with what Whitehead himself understood by "wholly living nexus," for the "non-social" mode of consciousness of creators at work situates them in the interstices of the habits, slogans, and judgments proper to discursive consciousness, fashioning step by step a thread of continuity that may be broken as soon as trust is stratified into assurance, or dissolves into fatigue.

The "work to be done" is, with the "task to be fulfilled" and the "problem to be solved," one of the ways in which Gilles Deleuze (DR, especially pp. 253 and 274) characterizes the "reality" of the virtual, distinguishing it from the potential, which lacks only existence. This, in fact, is how the correlated multiplicity of primary physical feelings can be described, feelings which appeal, as to their final cause, to the "solution" that will celebrate the correlative determination of the superject and its actual world: satisfaction. Yet the Deleuzian virtual does not state explicitly that it requires, in order to assume its imperative meaning, "to be done," "to be fulfilled," "to be solved," someone who hears and accepts. No problem can, of course, insist "in general," or demand its solution "in general," independently of the person experiencing this insistence, who will be mobilized by this demand. Thus, Fermat's conjecture is, for the non-mathematician, a proposition that is plausible but "dead," "the kind of thing whose eventual demonstration may excite mathematicians." And for most mathematicians, this conjecture was accompanied, before its demonstration, by all the discouraging stories about the failures that succeeded each another for centuries: a problem to be solved, perhaps, but those who attacked it had to think they were capable of succeeding where so many others had failed. The conjecture only became "alive" for those who, at their own risks and perils, felt themselves able to inherit not the repeated failures but the possible, the "it should be possible *to demonstrate it*." For them, the conjecture assumed the imperative character of the question that would devour a life.

In this "it should be possible," one will of course recognize the "making felt" that corresponds what I have called "induction." The imperative of the problem to be solved has made itself felt, which also means that the subject of these feelings is born, for whom the correlated multiplicity of known mathematical theorems and relations is now what the solution "should come" from.

Yet what happens next also illuminates the process of completion which, for Whitehead, has the character of a quantum *in solido,* that objective analysis can only decompose in a way that abstracts from its undivided character. A problem can only be divided when it is in fact solved, when mathematicians have succeeded in giving it a formulation that constitutes them as "masters" of their procedure, allowing them to proceed to the verification of their solution. They can then make the ordered stages succeed one another, and proceed to the progressive determination of the landscape, where, finally, the solution should swoop down like an eagle on its prey: QED. Yet verification is preceded by rovings, zigzags, dreams, and nightmares, in which the dissolved self of the mathematician and the indeterminate fragments of what might be the solution affect one another in an entanglement that is impossible to recount. For this entanglement, on the one hand, creates ever more singular relations between the initial data—all the mathematical theorems that might be relevant—and, on the other, the enrichment of the "final cause" that motivates the mathematician: the abstract "it should be possible" gradually becomes half-formulated hypotheses, hesitant conjectures. As if the solution were in some way more and more "present," motivating an effort that is more and more singular, but without it being possible for this presence to be, for all that, the object of an appropriation enabling a narration: *"and then I said to myself that . . . "* It is not that creation is ineffable, but those who narrate it divide the indivisible, transforming what had put them to the test into questions they would have asked themselves. Creation is a "private" process, but "private" has nothing to do with a psychological form of intimacy, the refusal to show something until it is finished. It is because, strictly speaking, there is nothing to see, nothing to show, nothing to discuss, nothing to share, except by allusion, and only with those who—and the private can clearly be collective—also expose themselves to be inhabited by a question to enter into a process of creation.

The "inappropriable presence" that motivates the work, the idea that flees if one tries to make it explicit, for its only clarification will coincide with the work produced, is called by Étienne Souriau the "spiritual form" of the work to be done, or again the "Angel of the work."

You realize, of course, that I only propose this word while accompanying it with all the appropriate philosophical "as it weres." No doubt, for this comparison of spiritual form and the Angel, I could take shelter behind the authority of William Blake. In fact, and to speak a more severe and more technical language, I do indeed say that the work to be done has a certain form. It is a form accompanied by a kind of halo of hope and wonder, whose reflection is a kind of Orient for us. All these are things than can obviously be commented upon by a comparison with love. And in fact, if the poet did not already love the poem a bit before writing it, if all those who think of a future world that is to be brought to life did not find, in their dreams on this subject, some amazed premonition of the presence called for, if, in a word, the waiting for the work was amorphous, there would no doubt be no creation. Here, I am not letting myself be swept along by a kind of mysticism of the creative effort, but I simply observe that the creator can scarcely escape this kind of mysticism, by which his effort is justified" (MEOF, 14–15).

"Spiritual form" means neither "model" nor goal. On the contrary, Souriau's Angel plays a role analogous to that of consequent conceptual experience, "motivating" the process of accomplishment, for that of which it is the omen or "lure" is inseparable from the work in the making: not a fixed form to be achieved but an insistence, ceaselessly relaunched, whose enigma puts creators to the question, turning them into the creatures of their question. The Angel neither suggests nor inspires an answer, he demands it from creators, and the creators alone are responsible for the way they respond: either a success or a failure.

If the question of the work to be done can traverse all the registers of a life in Étienne Souriau (and in Deleuze), from the poem to life itself, then raised to the anonymous power of "a life," it is because it is irreducible to the continuity instituted by any positive description: a creator endowed with habits, projects, and ideas. And it is no doubt because Whitehead was a man at work that he instituted in metaphysical terms, that is, in the very structure of the categoreal scheme, what the work to be done demands to see recognized: the radical difference between obligation and explanation. All explanation, because it is division, attributing causes and responsibilities, distributing reasons and circumstances, takes advantage of a social stability that it confirms, or of an accomplished work that it verifies. An obligation cannot be explained but must be respected, and there is nothing moral about the term "respect," either when Souriau's Angel makes the worker hesitate or when it comes to an actual occasion. It must be understood as close as possible to the expression "respect of specifications," which leaves open the question of how it will be so.

I can now return to my own specifications, that is, turn toward Whitehead's second formula, the one that characterizes the functioning of divine experience. The preceding allows the problem of this formula to be raised on the basis of the question of "matching conditions," that is, of the way in which the motivation of divine experience may be "initially derived from the temporal world." The first goal will be to understand the meaning, in this case, of the translation I have given of this initial derivation: "there is induction." Not, of course, in order to explain induction, but to ask in what way the "temporal world" may "induce" a divine experience.

But God, as well as being primordial, is also consequent. He is the beginning and the end. He is not the beginning in the sense of being in the past of all members. He is the presupposed actuality of conceptual operation, in unison of becoming with every other creative act. Thus, by reason of the relativity of all things, there is a reaction of the world on God. The completion of God's nature into a fullness of physical feeling is derived from the objectification of the world in God. He shares with every new creation its actual world; and the concrescent creature is objectified in God as a novel element in God's objectification of that actual world (PR, 345).

Whereas occasions inherit "stubborn facts," God shares "his" world with each new creation. We will thus have to play close to the vest, for the term "share" seems to imply that God physically feels the actual world correlated with the entity, that is, just as much that he feels the entity itself, since the entity and its world are in fact the two sides of one coin, as I have previously tried to illustrate by bringing up the inseparability between the operator, the actual world that has become well-determined, and the "eigensubject" who is its feeling. But the hypothesis that God feels the world "physically" is excluded by the first part of the formula, defining as the "origin" a mental pole that must be expressed in terms of feelings that are uniquely conceptual. Here, the decision I have taken to let myself be guided by "the formula" will impose a risky interpretation. We will have to succeed in "placing at the origin" everything that will have to be mobilized by the process of divine completion, a process that will shed light on what Whitehead calls "sharing."

In addition, a supplementary question arises, inspired by the term "sharing." Can God share his process of completion with an occasion? In this case, God would transcend the distinction between the "private" and the "public." He would therefore become quite close to the God of Leibniz, able to read in the slightest state of the least monad "what occurs everywhere, and even what has occurred and will occur." Whitehead has, of course, rejected the idea of a "divine reading" that refers our experience of choice, hesitation, decision, and novelty to the "as if." Yet the opposition is perhaps not as irreparable as he thought. A Bergsonian reader of Leibniz like Gilles Deleuze was able to take up, in an almost Whiteheadian way, the Leibnizian metaphor of God as reader, thereby overcoming the "evil" always constituted by an irreparable opposition.

Here, it seems that the present loses its privilege, and that determinism is reintroduced as predestination. But in what sense? Is it because God knows everything beforehand? Is it not, instead, rather because He is, always and everywhere? [. . .] *Yet to say that God is always and everywhere is to say, strictly, that he goes through all the states of the monad, however small they may be, such that He coincides with it at the moment of action "without any distance." Reading does not consist in concluding from the idea of a preceding state the idea of the following state, but in grasping the effort or the tendency by which the following state itself comes out of the preceding one "by a natural force." The divine reading is a genuine passage of God into the monad (somewhat like Whitehead speaks of a "passage of nature" locally). What is more, each monad is nothing other than a passage of God: each monad has a viewpoint, but this viewpoint is the "result" of a reading or a view of God, which passes through it and coincides with it* (LP, 98–99).

God is certainly "passed through" Deleuze reading Leibniz, and the opposition overcome by a "grasp" of Leibniz's effort trying to think of God "reading the world" would no doubt have made both Leibniz and Whitehead rejoice. In no case, therefore, will one say that "the ways of God" are impenetrable, for it is the very idea that God could trace paths that contradicts what is to be affirmed first and foremost: for Leibniz, if we follow Deleuze, the effort or tendency of each monad, which God cannot foresee but only accompany, without any distance; for Whitehead, the creative independence of each concrete occasion, the absence of any viewpoint from which the choice it produces by itself could be said to be a function of something else.

However, the opposition does not, it seems to me, disappear in favor of an agreement, but of a contrast. For the case proposed by Deleuze with regard to Leibniz corresponds to the one I evoked when I noted that the private may be collective. It must simply be restricted to those who allow themselves to be inhabited by the question, who share the question of completion. Yet Whitehead speaks of the new creature "objectified in God," *qua* "new element of God's objectification of that actual world." The fact that he uses the term "objectification" is important, for, since this distinction was available to him, he could have attributed to God the possibility of knowing an entity formally, from the viewpoint of its own enjoyment, which would correspond to the "passage" of God evoked by Deleuze. And the expression *"qua* new element of that actual world" confirms that Whiteheadian "sharing" respects the strictly private character, *causa sui,* of concrescence: God's consequent experience is about the actual world of the occasion, not about the privacy of the creature "in the making." Whitehead thus rejects a God who, prehending "without any distance" how the subject determines itself, would then find himself in a position somewhat comparable to that of a hidden voyeur, seeing without being seen, that is, without his seeing having the slightest effect on what he sees. Nothing is hidden in the world of Whitehead, and if the occasion as *causa sui* were not to transcend God, the whole economy of the system would have to be revised.

In other words, it seems that a distance should vibrate where Leibniz enunciated a coincidence "without any distance." This distance by no means signifies nostalgia, the impossibility of plenitude, or exile. In front of his students, Whitehead, searching for the situation that would make them feel what he wanted to make them understand by "reality," one day invoked rugby: "to be in the middle of the pack." Reality never situates us as contemplative spectators, but always in the middle of the pack, where there is pushing, shoving, and mutual constraint. Likewise, the affirmation that reading is never "to take cognizance," in the sense of coinciding with what is written, is not a cause for lamentations. "Reading" is, still and yet again, creating. And since the impossibility of a knowledge that "coincides" with its object is not a matter of mourning, it is valid for God as for everybody else.

If God, as Whitehead sometimes says, is "in unison of becoming" with each creative act, this does not mean that such a unison signifies contemporary community. If God is to "share," this sharing is part of the process of completion initially derived from (induced by) the temporal world. Yet a new problem arises, almost immediately. Since this is an experience that is, strictly speaking, unimaginable, we cannot get very far with what induction means when it concerns the "beginning" of an actual occasion. But Whitehead says a bit more when the induction involves God as its addressee. In any case, this is what seems to be meant by the way he will answer a question suddenly asked, just before the chapter devoted to God: the question of "ultimate evil."

The ultimate evil in the temporal world is deeper than any specific evil. It lies in the fact that the past fades, that time is a "perpetual perishing." Objectification implies elimination. The present fact has not the past fact with it in any full immediacy. The process of time veils the past below distinctive feeling [...] "He giveth his beloved—sleep" (PR, 340–341).

The increasingly confused character, from objectification to objectification, of what was decided on the occasion of an individual completion, and its gradual forgetting, would thus be the "ultimate evil." This definition comes as somewhat of a surprise in *Process and Reality*, since nothing has prepared the reader for it. Yet it prepares for one of the functions which, thanks to the intervention of the consequent nature, Whitehead will associate with the divinity, "the tender care that nothing be lost."

Confronted by this image, we must bear in mind that Whitehead wished to succeed in "secularizing" God's function. The point is thus to take great care that our interpretation of the question of ultimate evil does not communicate with a function of the religious type, in particular, with God as associated with the "survival of the soul." In fact, if "thanks to God" nothing is lost, nothing, even so, will "survive" as such. What "is not lost" will not be "saved" as such, but in the mode of the unimaginable divine experience. Moreover, neither the question nor its answer gives any particular importance to death in the usual sense, mine or yours. The question of ultimate evil may be understood as a supplication, which it raises to its cosmic power: "May what I have gone through not sink, purely and simply, into insignificance, under the banner of an abstraction that is ever poorer as it is taken into account successively and in divergent ways!" But what I experienced one day ago, one hour, or one minute has already undergone this fate. This is why the question of ultimate evil is not the religious one of the survival after death of a "living person," but it arises for each occasion, whose determination also means "perishing."

God's conceptual realization is nonsense if thought of under the guise of a barren, eternal hypothesis [. . .] Again this discordant multiplicity of actual things, requiring each other and neglecting each other, utilizing and discarding, perishing and yet claiming life as obstinate matter of fact, requires an enlargement of the understanding to the comprehension of another phase in the nature of things. In this later phase, the many actualities are one actuality, and the one actuality is many actualities. Each actuality has its present life and its immediate passage into novelty; but its passage is not its death (PR, 349).

"Its passage is not its death": unfortunately, no more precise indication is to be found in the text, but this one is precious. The unison of becoming might well imply that the "perishing" of an occasion concerns only the temporal world. Of course, the subject-superject perishes, from the viewpoint of its inheritance, and in a twofold sense. First, its process of completion cannot, as such, be evaluated, even by God, in the sense that evaluation would imply the possibility of "putting oneself in another's place," and replaying what has occurred, a possibility excluded by the fifth category of explanation, according to which "two actual entities never derive their origin from an identical universe" (PR, 22). Second, what has been decided, having acceded to "objective immortality," is categorically incapable of appealing against the use other occasions will make of its decision. Yet Whitehead does not talk about "resurrection" in

God, preferring to distinguish between "perishing" and "dying" as far as actuality itself is concerned. It is thus here, through this distinction, that the question can finally be raised of induction, or the way in which a satisfied occasion is able to "make God feel."

Whatever "making feel" may mean, it is a vector. And in fact, the argument according to which the vectorial dimension of feelings disappears with satisfaction may be repeated with this new question: what if its disappearance were not its death? For nothing demands that the multiplicity of vectorial feelings that have attained what they aimed at, their concrete unity for a subject that will answer for its world, be suppressed upon satisfaction. Their disappearance means that all has been determined, that, as far as the process of completion is concerned, there is nothing left to aim at. Yet we must note that their elimination has no meaning in the physico-mathematical language with which Whitehead tried to remain in harmony: in physics, vectors may counterbalance their effects and hence disappear *qua* "having an effect," but no conceivable physical process can "eliminate" them in favor of a scalar quantity. Only the act of measurement can accomplish this exploit, but in an abstract way, because the measured quantity is there for whoever measures it, for whoever, in other words, is affected by it: a vector. If satisfaction coincides with the production of a value, which every actual occasion will henceforth have to take into account, there is no reason to believe this is the end of the story.

There is a beautiful theory in Leibniz, articulating the vectorial powers of the soul with those studied by dynamics: the theory of *conatus*. In both cases, *conatus* means that there is never any rest. Rest evokes a state that is indifferent to time, which is an impossibility for Leibniz. That is why every quiet soul and every immobile body are in fact "animated" by a *"conatus,"* an effort toward the future to which no quantity may be assigned, and which cannot in itself have any effect. The *conatus* is "effort toward," perpetual disquiet. In physics, if a body is maintained at equilibrium, its *conatus* is the beginning, at each instant, of a movement that aborts in that instant, to be reborn in the following one. If equilibrium is broken, however, the *conatus* unfolds into motion. More generally, *conatus* designates the vectorial power insofar as it can never be "eliminated," but insofar as it does not have within itself the means to develop, since its development depends upon circumstances.

The contrast associated with the *conatus,* the deployment or absence of any assignable effect, is appropriate for the question of the becoming of the occasional subject, and its perishing. The vectorial dimension depends "on circumstances." It is deployed when feelings aim at their unification and disappears in the "circumstance" in which there is no longer anything to aim at, in which all has been accomplished. Yet the analogy with the *conatus* allows us to say that its disappearance is not its elimination: if the subject/superject perishes, it is as "cause of itself," in the sense that it pertained to it to start out from its own circumstances, *in solido,* to determine in and for itself its own production. It is henceforth up to others, given other circumstances, to decide on the meaning of the unit produced.

Here, the analogy enables something new. As Whitehead never ceases to repeat, the subject/superject's determination with regard to itself is just as much a position with regard to the future. The occasion's "perishing" then means that in this perspective the position will have no assignable consequence. Actual occasions will take the "position" into account, but they will remain deaf to the vectorial dimension of the position's "appeal to the future," and, more precisely, deaf to the imperative dimension of that call, which demands to be heard for itself. This deafness is crucial for their own freedom of self-determination. "Am I my brother's keeper?" asks Cain, and rightly so in this case, according to Whitehead. In this sense, the superject does indeed have the features of a *conatus,* a vectorial appeal to a future that it does not have within itself the means to make heard by its successors. And it may be this appeal that finds its addressee in God, he whose experience will be induced by the vectorial imperative. Yet induction is not identical with sharing. God would be what the superjective *conatus* aims at, the appeal to the future that no occasion will inherit, but the deployment of the *conatus* always depends on the circumstances: the definition of the way the appeal will be heard depends on the "circumstances" of divine experience.

What I have just proposed does not appear anywhere in *Process and Reality,* but the proposition is technically acceptable. And it allows us to approach the question of the object of the "induced" conceptual feeling, a feeling which, on my reading, belongs to the "mental origin" of divine experience. The fact that the superjective appeal to the future may "make itself felt" means, at the same time, that the divine process of completion will give its answer to the plea that what the subject/superject has become for itself may not sink into oblivion. That which, from the categoreal viewpoint (the ninth category of explanation: "how" an actual entity "becomes" constitutes "what" that actual entity "is") implies that what will be initially objectified is a "how," the "completed how." Yet it is precisely this "how," a quite determinate articulation of a limited group of eternal objects, that no actual occasion can inherit as such, for the articulation will become undone, dismembered, and replayed by each new process of determination. If the divine feeling that is induced is a conceptual feeling of this "how," there is as yet no question of sharing, for the articulation of the eternal objects, quite obviously, does not tell any story about itself. It nevertheless constitutes the full determination of its satisfaction, a complete but silent version of what has been accomplished.

Thus, God would not "resuscitate what is dead," but "feel" a "how" that may have no addressee but him. What will become of what has been felt, the mode of deployment of the *conatus,* does not depend on the appellant but depends on the "circumstances" of divine experience, and it is God's answer that is to be defined as "sharing." In other words, "in the beginning," God does not "share" the actual world of the satisfied entity. This actual world will be "objectified" in the sense that this term designates the fact of "being felt" by something other than oneself, according to a pragmatic value that belongs to the formal constitution of that other thing. When it comes to God, this pragmatic value will allow us to speak of "sharing," since God is he for whom every occasion, even the most tenuous, "matters," insofar as it is new. In this sense, divine pragmatics will not be decisional, for every decision means taking a partial position, thus and not otherwise, instrumentalizing what it takes into account for its own ends. It will, however, be "inexorable," adding a new element to what was initially felt. If there is sharing, it will not only be in the full deployment of what is the "proprium" of the fully determined entity, in the full, singular coherence of its appeal: the appeal will finally be heard, but in a way that plunges it into the eternal divine ordering. That is, as we shall see, in a way that inexorably articulates this appeal with everything about which it has drawn a blank.

However, before we move on to the divine process of completion, we must obviously pause for a moment over what has become, on this hypothesis, of the infinite envisagement of all eternal objects, that is, the primordial nature of God. According to my hypothesis, Whitehead's two formulas must have an obligatory value. If divine induction is required by the first, primary phase of occasional concrescence, we must conclude, in parallel, that although the divine envisagement of eternal objects may well be "eternal," "free," or "primordial," it nevertheless requires, in order to be "this" envisagement, the induction produced by a superject's appeal to the future. In other words, divine conceptual realization, even if it includes all the eternal objects, and as such is therefore not affected by any new fact, would not for that reason be static.

This hypothesis does not appear in the Whiteheadian text, and it might seem to contradict the ceaselessly repeated theme of the unique, complete, and eternal character of divine conceptual realization. In fact, however, it obliges us instead to specify this character: this theme is the correlate of the way the multiplicity of eternal objects is characterized, indifferent to their ingressions, to the difference between realized and unrealized. God's primordial nature is thus not constrained by the selection of eternal objects realized, nor is it limited by the "world's creative progress": it is eternally complete, without exclusivity or exception, the realization of all eternal objects. Yet this does not necessarily mean that it is the invariant realization of all possible relations between all eternal objects. Quite the contrary, the hypothesis of such an invariance would imply that any articulation between eternal objects realized by an occasion could never be anything other than a case in an eternally preexistent totality, just as every particular combination is a mere case in the predefined set of all possible combinations. Yet if God is a creature of creativity, he must exemplify, more than anything else, the reason why Whitehead confers the status of ultimate upon creativity: he is what will spell out and illustrate all novelty *qua* irreducible.

If the divine conceptual realization is, as I suppose, "induced" by the superjective appeal, if it includes the conceptual feeling of the complex of eternal objects corresponding to "how" an occasion has determined itself, this realization must be interpreted as fully deploying this "how," that is, deploying it in a way that completely determines the differentiated relevance of each eternal object with regard to this particular complex. Such a realization could be said to be one and eternal, because any "grouping" of all eternal objects holds for all others. Once again, Whitehead never wrote this, but it would shed light on the import of some of his utterances.

The endeavour to understand eternal objects in complete abstraction from the actual world results in reducing them to mere undifferentiated nonentities. This is an exemplification of the categoreal principle, that the general metaphysical character of being an entity is "to be a determinant in the becoming of actualities." Accordingly the differentiated relevance of eternal objects to each instance of the creative process requires their conceptual realization in the primordial nature of God. He does not create eternal objects; for his nature requires them in the same degree that they require him. This is an exemplification of the coherence of the categoreal types of existence. The general relationships of eternal objects to each other, relationships of diversity and of pattern, are their relationships in God's conceptual realization. Apart from this realization, there is mere isolation indistinguishable from nonentity (PR, 257).

Whitehead seldom renounces a concept, but rather recycles it. Thinking with Whitehead, I have just carried out such a recycling, for if primordial conceptual experience is, as I propose, experience of all eternal objects in the kind of relation determined by the finite complex of eternal objects grouped in an "occasional" relationship, it corresponds to the "ideal situation" proposed in *Science and the Modern World,* which also implied all the eternal objects. And this correspondence may guide us in the question that remains to be solved. If God does not "physically" feel the satisfied occasion and its world but only the complex ideal articulation that defines both the subject and its world, what about his consequent nature, that is, the process of completion that is "motivated" by a consequent "physical" experience?

In *Science and Modern World,* God was a principle of limitation, categorically determined by the difference between the implications, unlimited in principle, of all realization, *qua* realization of an ideal situation, and the abruptly limited character of the meaning of a decision. If conceptual divine realization is free, unconstrained by the differentiation between realized eternal objects and those that have not been realized, a physical experience can indeed derive from it, in the sense that every physical experience is the experience of something that has been determined thus and not otherwise. God's initial "physical" experience, since it "derives" from its mental origin, is not a "direct prehension" of the occasion. It is the feeling of the contrast between the unlimited character of the ideal situation and the limited character of the occasional, finite complex of eternal objects. And the divine process of completion will then be initially motivated by the physical experience of the determinate, selective, partial, and exclusive character of occasional completion. Thus and not otherwise.

The wisdom of subjective aim prehends every actuality for what it can be in such a perfected system—its sufferings, its sorrows, its failures, its triumphs, its immediacies of joy—woven by rightness of feeling into the harmony of the universal feeling, which is always immediate, always many, always one, always with novel advance, moving onward and never perishing. The revolts of destructive evil, purely self-regarding, are diminished into their triviality of merely individual facts; and yet the good they did achieve in individual joy, in individual sorrow, in the introduction of needed contrast, is yet saved by its relation to the completed whole. The image—and it is but an image—the image under which this operative growth of God's nature is best conceived, is that of a tender care that nothing be lost (PR, 346).

Despite the images that populate it, this is a technical text. It describes the way in which divine experience is "motivated" by a physical feeling that is itself consequent. The initially abstract physical feeling, "this" limitation, or "this impasse," becomes the feeling of what the entity has done with itself, "its sufferings, its sorrows, its failures, its triumphs, its immediacies of joy"; but the process motivated by this physical experience is not that of a partial actuality, closed to its incompatibilities and its refusals, an obstinate appeal to the future that will verify it, whatever the cost may be. The process is feeling "with a rightness that weaves" physical experience "into a harmony," for the negative prehensions that were the price of the decision are also felt positively. Just as much as what the entity has decided, what it has rejected is a part of the decision. And the image of the "tender care," God's reaction to the superject's appeal to the future, drives away the threatening one of condescension. Divine experience is the experience of limitation *qua* completion, not of completion *qua* limited. Whitehead has not changed his mind since *Science and the Modern World*: actuality, and therefore limitation, are the sole value, even when it comes to God.

It remains to define the "final cause" of the process of divine completion.

This final phase of passage in God's nature is ever enlarging itself. In it the complete adjustment of the immediacy of joy and suffering reaches the final end of creation. This end is existence in the perfect unity of adjustment as means, and in the perfect multiplicity of the attainment of individual types of self-existence. The function of being a means is not disjoined from the function of being an end. The sense of worth beyond itself is immediately enjoyed as an overpowering element in the individual self-attainment. It is in this way that the immediacy of sorrow and pain is transformed into an element of triumph. This is the notion of redemption through suffering which haunts the world. It is the generalization of its very minor exemplification as the aesthetic value of discords in art (PR, 349–350).

If divine experience can be said to be conscious, it is precisely to the extent that it can have the value of "induction" for a new occasional subject. Divine experience is, of course, accomplished by sharing what the subject/superject has decided, but in a way that just as much transforms this decision into a "means." The appeal of the occasional superject to an addressee for whom it would be, as such, value will have been heard, but according to the circumstances of conscious divine experience, which integrates the fact, the physical experience of all that has been affirmed and all that has had to be rejected, in an inexorable way that turns this fact into an impasse, entering into a contrast with the feeling of this impasse envisaged as a means. In this sense, divine experience is conscious, but also incomplete. God is not the envisagement of what might be; his experience neither precedes nor prefigures the decision to come. His envisagement is a thirst for a novelty that this thirst will induce, but which, by definition, will transcend him.

Whitehead's two formulas can thus be placed in parallel, and this parallel has allowed me to make explicit a twofold deficiency: that of occasional completion, which appeals to the future, but in the mode of the *conatus,* and that of divine completion, a thirst for actuality that will give its consequences to envisagement. A twofold dehiscence thus corresponds to what I have called "induction": God and the occasion, each calling for what transcends it, for what will answer the call, but according to its own circumstances. But there is also a major difference between God and the occasion, which allows us to understand the "reversal of poles": divine consciousness, unlike human consciousness, is not placed under the banner of "blinking," but is constantly growing (everlasting).

The thirst for a new actuality cannot be assimilated to a superjective vectorial dimension, insisting by means of a "conclusion" that would have satisfied God's "consequent nature," for no conclusion can transform primordial divine conceptual experience, the envisagement of all eternal objects, into a well-determined unity. What we call God cannot be separated from the multiple feelings that aim at him, any more than any other occasional subject; but when it comes to him, the vectorial dimension of these feelings will never be submerged by a (scalar) enjoyment, by the "eigenvalue" corresponding to the full determination of what operates as an "actual world." The divine feeling "never perishes"; it is experience "together," perpetually increasing, of contrasts, each of which implies the feeling of an individual completion in its living immediacy, that is, *qua* appeal to the future, and the feeling of this completion *qua* means. Each new contrast, as it is added, will be integrated into harmony in the form of what it has made possible, the feeling of what was "best" for that impasse. An inexorable ordering.

From the viewpoint of his consequent nature, God may thus be said to be conscious because he is experience of the contrast between the "impasse" that is and a possibility that turns this impasse into a "means" for new realizations. He can be said to be fully actual, for the evaluation of each particular experience, *qua* feeling of what it has accomplished and what it has refused, corresponds to a complete determination of that experience as it is woven into the "eternal ordering." But what emerges from this weaving, the feeling of what would be best "for that impasse," does not correspond either to a transcendent knowledge or to a determinate anticipation. Instead, this feeling has the features of a question of the "what if?" type. That is, more technically, of a proposition entertained in the mode of the thirst for an answer, which would have as its logical subjects the subject to be born and its situation in the extensive continuum. The fact that divine experience has the features of a question brings us back, moreover, to the only invariant that ever defined God's role for Whitehead: relevance. Only questions—not adequacy, nor speculation about "what" might be, or prediction—make relevance their highest value.

It is as true to say that God is perpetually satisfied as to say that he is perpetually unsatisfied, and in this respect he constitutes a unique concrescence, without a past, in perpetual becoming, in unison with a world that transcends him as much as he transcends it. And the series of "as true" that inaugurated this chapter, if the reader looks back to it, may henceforth be read as a "verification" of the operation undertaken by Whitehead. The "different categories of existence," whose neglect he deplored, are those that his twofold formula has articulated, although, it must be admitted, in a rather condensed way.

The operation of secularization seems to me to have succeeded: the "hybrid physical feeling of God" is anything but a religious feeling. It does not make God the being to whom one may say "Thou," for he has no other value than the difference he will make in the occasional experience that will derive from him its initial aim. God, insofar as he is felt by the budding occasion whose emergence is induced by his thirst, is felt under the aspect of "how" he might constitute a relevant resumption of an impasse, but this "how" conceals no secret. The ways of God are thus not inscrutable, because the hybrid physical feeling is not the enigmatic sign of a "way." They are not "trail-blazing signs," or an indication offered by God to the world in the hope that the world might take the path that he himself envisages as the best. Divine induction has no other import than the emergence of the respondent for whom it thirsts, of the occasion which, in one way or another, will confer an actual meaning upon what is "proposed" as eventually relevant. And therefore, if God is in unison with the world, it is because the enlargement of his consciousness depends on the world, not as workers depend on their tools to carry out the work they have planned but rather as what must transcend him in order to "make him feel."

In the course of these last pages, the fragments of Whitehead cited have been populated by images of a religious type, as the reader will have noted. I hope that my reading will have satisfied the announced test, that the operation of secularization will have succeeded in stripping these images of all religious connotations other than those celebrated by Whitehead himself in *Modes of Thought* when he tried to make his reader feel the "full solemnity of the world." Yet the test, when fully deployed—that is, addressed not only to religious hopes but also to the hopes that haunt all our appeals to transcendence, whatever this transcendence means—will resume in the next chapter. To conclude this one, here is a fully developed sample of what will put us to the test.

The consequent nature of God is his judgment on the world. He saves the world as it passes into the immediacy of his own life. It is the judgment of a tenderness which loses nothing that can be saved. It is also the judgment of a wisdom which uses what in the temporal world is mere wreckage.

Another image which is also required to understand his consequent nature is that of his infinite patience. The universe includes a threefold creative act composed of (i) the one infinite conceptual realization, (ii) the multiple solidarity of free physical realizations in the temporal world, (iii) the ultimate unity of the multiplicity of actual fact with the primordial conceptual fact. If we conceive the first term and the last term in their unity over against the intermediate multiple freedom of physical realizations in the temporal world, we conceive of the patience of God, tenderly saving the turmoil of the intermediate world by the completion of his own nature. The sheer force of things lies in the intermediate physical process: this is the energy of physical production. God's rôle is not the combat of productive force with productive force, of destructive force with destructive force; it lies in the patient operation of the overpowering rationality of his conceptual harmonization. He does not create the world, he saves it: or, more accurately, he is the poet of the world, with tender patience leading it by his vision of truth, beauty, and goodness (PR, 346).

Shall we accept to be "saved"?

CHAPTER TWENTY-FIVE

An Adventure of Ideas

RADUALLY, SLOWLY, STEADILY the vision recurs in history under nobler form and with clearer expression. It is the one element in human experience which persistently shows an upward trend. It fades and then recurs. But when it renews its force, it recurs with an added richness and purity of content. The fact of the religious vision, and its history of persistent expansion, is our one ground for optimism (SMW, 192).

If the propositions bearing upon divine experience cannot, as such, inspire a speculative flight of experience, the same does not hold true of the contrasts that derive from it. These contrasts, when they concern the "religious vision," even aim rather clearly at participating in what Whitehead, in *Science and the Modern World,* called our "one ground for optimism."

When he was writing the lines I have just cited, Whitehead no doubt did not yet know that he was soon going to attempt the paradigmatic leap of death: to construct a proposition capable of participating in the adventure of the religious life. He was, however, perfectly explicit about the barbarous brutality of traditional religious statements, and particularly outspoken on the subject of the despotic role attributed to the monotheistic God. In fact, the God who closes the pages of *Process and Reality* might be said to "save" the world, but he constitutes just as much an attempt to save God himself from the role assigned to him by the theological propositions that make him the respondent to the religious vision.

Here, it is not enough to have an intellectual appreciation of how Whitehead succeeded in carving out the keystone concept that ensures the speculative edifice its conceptual coherence. This edifice and its keystone are dry bones, unless they participate in what is for Whitehead the "one ground for optimism": the return of the religious vision, endowed with a nobler form, a clearer expression, and a renewed force. And we might guess that the force that must return is that of worship, or feeling the world in its "full solemnity." Yet the way that Whitehead undertook to participate in the adventure of the religious vision, that is, in its expansion, confirms the position adopted in *Religion in the Making*: the only true identity of the good is evil *qua* capable of being overcome. It is therefore first by putting to the test our ideas about what is "good," by creating possibilities of "overcoming" the destructive oppositions they bear within them, that Whitehead participates in the adventure and undertakes to "save" it. The "good," the new eventual expansion of his vision, will be nothing other than this vision, henceforth capable of being entertained without entertaining at the same time all the propositions in the name of which, today more than ever, crusades are being launched.

The various modalities of the Whiteheadian test will all turn around the term I have just used, "to save." The test is already under way at this point, for the very fact that, to "save" the adventure of the religious vision, Whitehead was able to undertake to "save God" *qua* liable to "save the world," will be effective only if we can succeed in making two apparently incompatible meanings of the verb "to save" converge. Both meanings belong to our history, one to the history of knowledge and the other to the theology of salvation, and both are laden with an intensity that, in different ways, connects them with destructive oppositions.

"The point is to save the phenomena": we have inherited this utterance from Greek astronomy, which devoted all its skill to translating observational data into the language of circles, and affirmed, by this utterance, that these data by no means dictated the undertaking but on the contrary received their signification from it, then exhibiting themselves as belonging to the eternal perfection that alone is fitting for the heavens. Yet the term assumed new, intense resonances with the "Copernican revolution." It then designated, in a pejorative mode, the "cautious, timid cowards" who affirmed diplomatically that the heliocentric system was never anything other than a different way of "saving the astronomic phenomena." This was in opposition to those who, like Galileo, "dared to affirm" that the sun *really* was that around which the earth rotated, without retreating before the possibility that the "new science" might go to war with the religious authorities. If this pejorative value is preserved, if the courage of truth remains opposed to the compromises that blunt the verdict of facts or deck out its hard nudity in reassuring finery, Whitehead's God will obviously appear as a "pure intellectual fabrication," just good enough to fudge the difference between those who "believe" in God and those who do not need this hypothesis.

As far as the paths of salvation are concerned, they lead quite obviously to a multiplicity of utterances about which it is rather hard to affirm that they have, historically, contributed to the creation of contrasts that overcome destructive oppositions. Whether it is the solitary conscience's appeal to Him who will defend it against mediocre judgments, or the anguish of that consciousness when besieged by the world's temptations, the question of salvation has not ceased to be the vector of an appeal to transcend the values called mundane, and the reference ratifying the destructions carried out in the name of this radical transcendence. "One does not fool with divine judgment": this formidable platitude may lead not only Protestants but also atheists and even Catholics to agree with Luther and Calvin against the "Roman whore" who allowed herself to sell indulgences and guarantee that expensive masses would ensure the salvation of the souls of the dead. What does the anguish of the survivors matter? As far as the "cosmologico-progressive" utterances are concerned, in which God does not initially make the difference between the good and the bad, but pilots the world as a whole toward some Omega point, they may be just as formidable in their consequences, and in fact they have not prevented their author, Teilhard de Chardin, from diagnosing the divine path, even when this path entailed the violent conquest of Abyssinia. In any case, if salvation remains associated with he who will separate the wheat and burn the chaff, the way that Whitehead's God saves the world without condemning anything, accepting with infinite patience everything that occurs, will appear as an insult to the victims, an outrage to the hope of the good.

The way Whitehead proposes to save a God about whom it can be affirmed that he saves the world may thus be subject to a double disqualification. For some, it will be a purely intellectual compromise position, suitable only for those who are, in any event, indifferent to the question. Scientists need to think that their constructions have a "true" respondent, that they are addressing a reality that is "truly" able to make the difference between the questions that are addressed to it. Why wager that, when it comes to God, this same need would not make itself felt? For others, it will be a position that undermines what it pretends to satisfy, as is attested by the deliberate duplicity of the images Whitehead mobilizes.

God is the great companion—the fellow-sufferer who understands (PR, 351).

This could be Whitehead's answer to Job, but the biblical Job runs the risk of rejecting whoever answers him in this way among the false friends whose soothing discourses infuriate him. What Job demands is that He who understands understand him in a mode that makes Him his defender. Yet if Whitehead identifies God's "consequent nature" with his judgment on the world, that judgment would never end up in a verdict. He will never agree with Job against his false friends. God "suffers" and "understands" in the sense that all suffering, every refusal, and all limitation are comprised, "taken together," with the same impartial tenderness, into his experience, in the sense that all the ways of addressing him, denying him, ignoring him, or of blessing him and trusting him are evaluated in the same inexorable way, without any other finality than the emergence of new, intense contrasts. This may, moreover, suggest another image, rather worrisome: the great companion, whom Whitehead also calls the "poet of the world," may recall Nero, singing while Rome burns.

If this worrisome image is out of place, it is so to the same extent that it is just as misplaced to transform all the words Whitehead uses concerning God into divine "virtues": justice, tenderness, patience, goodness, wisdom, rationality, and so on. To praise God's virtues is just as inappropriate as to attribute an "altruistic" character to an ant that "sacrifices itself" for the group. In this case, neither God nor the ant can do anything other than what they do. God is patient, but he cannot be anything other than patient. He does not refuse to use productive or destructive force, but they are not at his disposal. He does not leave up to what is free the possibility of making use of its freedom, whatever the risks may be: neither risks nor freedom have any meaning for the impasse, always *that* impasse, that he saves. In short, what we call virtue, what we associate with the passion of the "work to be done"—all that implies the possibility of a hesitation, a betrayal, a risk—are alien to his own experience, even if he "understands" them.

A God whom it is impossible to praise, bless, or curse, in whose name none can say, *"Have faith, God knows best"*: this is the result of the operation of secularization carried out by Whitehead. Must we therefore conclude that he has abandoned the definition of God he gave in *Science and the Modern World*: God's power is the worship he inspires? As such, that is, in abstraction from the world, his God may well no longer inspire this leap of the imagination, that flight of religious experience that is called "worship." Yet Whitehead's proposition cannot be reduced to what, in non-Whiteheadian terms, one might call "purely intellectual rationalization," a rationalization that would purify the religious vision not only of its barbarous elements but also of any particular efficacy. The person who wrote the end of *Process and Reality* has been transformed by his writing. God may well no longer be that to which "worship" is addressed, but he nevertheless intervenes in it. This, moreover, is why Whitehead gave the name God to what was initially an answer to the need to think about the possibility of relevant novelties in the coherent way.

The non-temporal act of all-inclusive unfettered valuation is at once a creature of creativity and a condition for creativity. It shares this double character with all creatures. By reason of its character as a creature, always in concrescence and never in the past, it receives a reaction from the world; this reaction is its consequent nature. It is here termed "God"; because the contemplation of our natures, as enjoying real feelings derived from the timeless source of all order, acquires that "subjective form" of refreshment and companionship at which religions aim (PR, 31–32).

However, the "contemplation of our natures" should not be identified with a finally universally acceptable, purified definition of religion's aim, at least if we maintain the definition of religion as "what the individual does with his own solitariness" (RM, 16). Like all the constructions of *Process and Reality*, the concept of God's function in the world is meant for the "solitary consciousnesses," whose excess of subjectivity is expressed by both philosophy and religion. Here as elsewhere, therefore, Whitehead's proposition will have to be evaluated by its pragmatic effects, by the way it puts to the test the judgments of the "solitary consciousness," and, in this case, the way it can "correct" the excess of subjectivity that leads this consciousness to define itself "against" what it denounces as opinion, tradition, social belief. In short, against the reasons set forth by the false friends of Job.

In the Bible, God proved Job right: he condemned all the appeals to acceptance and wisdom of those who tried distract Job from the non-negotiable alternative he had enunciated: either his Defender lives, and will silence those who construct socially acceptable reasons for his misfortune, or else life is delivered over to what is arbitrary, to injustice, to lies. The worship that defines God's power has thus legitimized the condemnation of what might be an obstacle to the experience of this power. It has been a vector of evil, defining itself against what contradicts it. My hypothesis is that the possibility of overcoming this evil, of proposing to the solitary consciousness a respondent that separates this consciousness from its propensity to worship the sword, is what Whitehead experienced at the time he was writing the last part of *Process and Reality*.

One of the definitions of the solitary consciousness is its mistrust of the world. The corresponding religious feeling, according to the description Whitehead gives of it in *Religion in the Making*, defines the appeal to the "possible" as appealing against the "socially probable" or "herd-psychology." The intervention of "God" as a logical subject, that is,

"God's power," corresponds to the correlative need to think of something beyond the blind, smothering facts, behind them and within them, to think in terms of the possible and not only of the probable. God is then the respondent to the ultimate ideal, and the quest without guarantees. Yet this purely factual world, thematized by the solitary consciousness, a world subject to routine, to the arbitrary, to relations of force, a world that is deaf to its complaint, to its appeal, to its hope, is the work of this consciousness. The religious feeling is thus an appeal to a transcendence capable of restoring what was first denied to the world by the solitary consciousness, an appeal to the interstices in which new possibilities of relevance lurk. And if the Whiteheadian God is not to be worshiped, and is thus separated from the power of worship that religious Gods inspire, it may be because the point is to restore to the world what it had been stripped of at the outset.

What Whitehead calls "God" is thus baptized relative to the territories covered by the judgments of the solitary consciousness. Only solitary consciousnesses, experiencing themselves as "alone in the world," are liable to celebrate the fact that "our natures" are able to enjoy real feelings, that is, feelings that are not reducible to relations of force or social habits. Only they can feel the threat of this possible "sociological" answer to Job: what you "felt" when you lived as a righteous man means nothing; your notion of justice is only the result of what is defined as such in your social environment. It is thus *qua* an author who has issued forth from a determinate social environment, nourished on the words and contradictions proper to this environment, that Whitehead first experienced the worship that confers upon God his power. The modification he proposes is confined to adding that this power does not belong to God but is strictly relative to the difference that will be made, in the experience of the person who entertains them, by the propositions that articulate God and the World.

Yet this addition changes everything. For the infinitive "to trust" henceforth accepts obstate facts no longer as crushing, but as preconditions for creativity. It is to this "to trust," moreover, that Whitehead's proposition testifies in itself. For judged in terms of a socially defined situation, a situation described in a way that would claim the power of defining it, Whitehead's proposition would have no chance of modifying the judgment of solitary consciousnesses. In particular, it will disappoint the expectations nourished by the Christian religion, from which he deliberately borrows his vocabulary. The God constructed by Whitehead lurks in the interstices of the Christian religious experience, and his eventual efficacy will not testify to the power of the worship he inspires, but rather to the impossibility for a social environment to determine what that environment nevertheless conditions: the disqualification of the world to which "God's power" responds may be overcome.

We do not have the slightest reason to think that the modes of existence need transcendental values to compare them, select them, and declare that that one is "better" than the other. On the contrary, the only criteria are immanent, and a possibility of life is evaluated through itself by the movements it traces and the intensities it creates on a plane of immanence: what does not trace or create is rejected. A mode of existence is good or bad, noble or vulgar, complete or empty, independently of Good or Evil, or any transcendent value: there are never any criteria other than the tenor of existence, the intensification of life. Pascal and Kierkegaard, who were familiar with infinite movements, and who extracted from the Old Testament new conceptual personae able to stand up to Socrates, were well aware of this [. . .]

The problem would change if it were another plane of immanence. It is not that the person who does not believe God exists would gain the upper hand, since he would still belong to the old plane as negative movement. But, on the new plane, the problem may now concern the existence of the person who believes in the world, not even in the existence of the world but in its possibilities of movements and intensities, to give birth once again to new modes of existence, closer to animals and rocks. It may be that believing in this world, in this life, has become our most difficult task, or the task of a mode of existence still to be discovered on our plane of immanence today. This is the empiricist conversion (we have so many reasons not to believe in world of men; we have lost the world, worse than a fiancée, a son or a god [. . .] The problem has indeed changed (QPh, 72–73).

To believe in the world, but not in a world that would be confined to existing, at the same time backdrop, resource, and land of conquest, that world in which Job and Socrates confront one another over the vocation of human beings, and what it is permissible for them to hope. For Job and Socrates are united in their common scorn for those who ignore what divides them, salvation by faith or by reason. To believe in this world, already existent in the passionate becomings where mathematicians become functions, affected by what they define as variables, where the wolf becomes a pack, a part, ceaselessly redefined, of a multiplicity without fixed hierarchy, and where we ourselves know something about what it is to run in a pack, or else to walk noiselessly, a solitary hunter, where nothing is a slogan, for everything can become an sign. This world that Whitehead the educator, in *Science and the Modern World*, already designated when he affirmed the necessity of art, that is, of the habit of enjoying living values.

Here we reencounter the question of that God whose function is to "save" the world, and the test designated by the term "to save." If God "saves" the world, it is precisely because he is the impartial feeling of all values *qua* living, in their discords, their incompatibilities, their partialities. He is not the "domus" in which they find their unity, but the unison in which each is the movement it has traced, the intensity it has created, in which each affirms itself "for the world," as the condition and creature of creativity. Nor is it in his power to save the world: this is his function, and nothing but his function.

Will Job be able to accept the test constituted by the "wisdom" of a God who "saves" by relegating to the triviality of individual facts the difference he demands between the just and the unjust? Will he be able to accept that his cry be "purged" of what is, in this way, defined as destructive, demanding the condemnation of the unjust in order that the just may triumph? Will he be able to accept divine impartiality, that, is, also his radical indifference to who recognizes him and who denies him? In short, will he be able to accept seeing his cry "saved" as the religious images mobilized by Whitehead may be "saved": in a way that strips the religious address of any possibility of earning or of deserving in any particular way a tenderness, an approval, a recognition that is, in any case, unconditionally, impartially, and inexorably the destiny of every occasion?

Yet the test is addressed just as much to Socrates's descendants, who, since Plato, have concluded to the urgent need for "truths" capable of silencing the plurality of the partial and discordant opinions of the irrational populace. Will Socrates be able to accept that it is his own questions about justice, the good, or love that have given rise to the discordant character of the answers? Will he be able to accept that those who have answered did not simply express "what they thought," but assumed a stance with regard to the situation that was proposed to them? Will he be able to accept that it is the situation he created that produces the contradictions on which he bases himself, whereas Pericles, the politician he disqualifies, might perhaps have given rise to other responses, addressed to him in order that he might create their unlikely agreement?

And the scientists, who demand that what they deal with must be capable of proving a view right or wrong, not of lending itself to the possibility of being saved in multiple ways: will they accept that what they call the "objective world" is what satisfies this demand? Will they accept, not the utterance, despairing but somewhat facile by the eminent lucidity it attributes to its utterer, that "everything is relative," but the one—more difficult, because addressed to them more specifically—that their "objective" world is just as much fabricated by the polemical opposition between truth and appearance as the irreconcilable opinions of Athens's inhabitants are "fabricated" by Socrates?

And those, heirs to the same story, who would turn this fabrication into the confirmation of their denunciation of "science" as blind and calculating: will they accept to celebrate the multiple and relevant technical knots, neither objective nor subjective, that scientists sometimes succeed in creating with what they deal with? And will they be able to accept that the authentic experience of which they wish to be the defenders also required an adventurous fabrication?

There is nothing universal about the test proposed by Whitehead, and this is its primary quality. It requests no mourning, no renunciation that is not addressed specifically to the "excess of subjectivity" attested by the adventures of faith, and of the rationality in which speculative philosophy itself takes its place. Nor does it demand either the renunciation of the "thou" required by prayer, or of the respondents, molecules and neurons, required by the scientists who undertake to study the brain of people who pray. It simply proceeds to add a divine experience, "including everything without restriction," not limited by the abstractions that doom neurons and prayer to enter into conflict. Infinite divine experience "saves" what has determined itself thus and not otherwise, but in the mode of conceptual realization that transforms every contradiction, every disjunctive alternative "either ... or" into so many consequences of "thus and not otherwise." This does not mean that the incompatibilities are nullified, but neither are they ratified. They acquire the problematic status that propositions never lose, the "perhaps" with regard to which every entertainment is determination, true or false, but whose exhibition pertains to intellectual feeling.

The fact that Whitehead can identify the divine intervention that "saves the world" with a "patient operation of the overpowering rationality of his conceptual harmonization," moreover, gives his intervention its signature. Although Whitehead's God is neither the God of the missionaries, nor the God of the martyrs, nor the God of the scientists, he might well satisfy the appetite of those who take part in the adventure of mathematics. Divine feeling, which "saves" individual accomplishment in such a way that its value includes what has been rejected, eliminated, or vaguely felt so that the accomplishment may be what it is, will not shock mathematicians, for a theorem previously demonstrated has a living value for them, even if the theorem is now understood in terms of the restrictive conditions that had enabled its demonstration. The mathematicians' appetite may be aroused by the identification of these conditions, but their appetite does not mean that they already know how one could "do better" than this demonstration, that they are anticipating the path to follow in order to transcend the limitation that the conditions confer upon the theorem. They sense the conditions insofar as, conditioning a success, they make this success exist as a problem, giving rise to the question of the possibilities of generalization.

Of course, to describe the divine appetite on the basis of the mathematical appetite for generalizations to be constructed is completely inadequate, as is every imaginative proposition that deals with divine experience. A mathematician envisages a new theorem, a new kind of solution, whereas God makes a question emerge from every solution. Yet the interest of the analogy with mathematics is to divest of all painful connotations the description of divine experience as perpetual and incomplete, not liable to be accomplished in a satisfaction that would make intellect, intelligence, and the intelligible coincide. The analogy allows us to avoid the image of a God who is perpetually dissatisfied, tragically separated from himself, that is, at the same time, to give imaginative flesh to creativity as the ultimate, that creativity exhibited, more than any other, by the adventure of mathematics.

Correlatively, the analogy with mathematics may shed light on the brutal introduction, on the final page of *Process and Reality*, of a new theme: "God's love for the world."

In the fourth phase, the creative action completes itself. For the perfected actuality passes back into the temporal world, and qualifies this world so that each temporal actuality includes it as an immediate fact of relevant experience. For the kingdom of heaven is with us today. The action of the fourth phase is the love of God for the world. It is the particular providence for particular occasions. What is done in the world is transformed into a reality in heaven, and the reality in heaven passes back into the world. By reason of this reciprocal relation, the love in the world passes into the love in heaven, and floods back again into to the world (PR, 351).

Here, love is certainly not what is understood by the Christians, for whom God's love must be addressed to the human person. Rather, it evokes the Eros of the Greeks, because of its impersonal character. It is addressed to each particular occasion, that is, impartially, to the slightest electronic occasion, to the least of our immediate experiences. One might say that it is addressed much more to the tissue our dreams are made of, which flee as soon as we try to transform them into reasons, than to us, who demand that love be addressed to us, *qua* living continuities. However, if the Greek Eros has heirs in the European tradition, it is the mathematicians, who "love the truth" with a love that owes nothing to the polemical power attributed to truth. Only the adventure of mathematics admits, as a fully positive value, that the truth can bring about a convergence between saving, bringing to existence, and creating, and mathematicians would be liable to understand that God's love for the world can designate the incessant relaunching of a question with no regard for the security of persons, beliefs, or traditions. For their own love of mathematics depends on the fact that a question ceaselessly relaunched, such for instance, as "what is a circle?" or "how can we define the value of p?" was able to inspire so many answers, so many creations, each one involving a new problematic space, bringing new stakes into existence without the new disqualifying the old. For mathematicians, every mathematical creation has its perfection, which is to be appreciated as such.

As a mathematician, Whitehead was able to make all the words used when it comes to God—judgment, tender patience, inexorable fatality, impartiality, the aim at new, intense contrasts, and finally, "love"—converge toward so many descriptions of the divine appetite for the world, without fear of falling back into a Christian theology of a personal God, because he knew that the question that engages the hand-to-hand confrontation with a problem finally raised in a promising way is not addressed to a person. Instead, it is what will transform a person into that through which a problem will be defined. This is why Gilles Deleuze can, on this subject, speak of "chance" in the way James spoke about it, which comes as a "free gift, or not at all."

This decisional power at the heart of problems, this creation, this launching that makes us members of the race of the gods, is nevertheless not ours. The gods themselves are subject to the laws of Ananke, that is, to chance-heaven. The imperatives or the questions that traverse us do not emanate from the I, which is not even there to listen to them. The imperatives are being, every question is ontological, and distributes "what is" into problems (DR, 257).

And love, therefore, becomes relevant to all of creation, "on earth as it is in heaven," without hierarchy, without any privilege conferred on what endures, with no demand for reciprocity, guarantee, or permanence. The same love, particular every time for each particular occasion, the eternal return of an imperative question responding to the cry of experience against ultimate evil. The call is heard: what your experience has accomplished will not have only partial, deaf heirs as its addressees, those who, occupied with their own business, will dispose as they see fit of what you propose to them. Who you have been is inscribed in another register, for another experience. But if the call is heard, it is just as much "saved," saved from the demand for an addressee who not only "understands" but justifies. For "God's judgment" will not follow up the complaint, will not pursue the crime, will not share the refusals, and will not ratify the eliminations. What will be saved is not the authentic prolongation of yourself, with the treasure-house of your sufferings, your refusals, your passions. Instead, it is their humorous double. Divine experience saves by neutralizing, making what has been affirmed and what the affirmation has denied return at the same time. What will be saved at the same time as you, woven together with you, is what you have excluded to become what you have become, and what will not be saved, will not be able to be saved, is the continuity of the construction that links your identity with the disqualifications you have carried out, the judgments in terms of which you have justified yourself, the legitimacies you have claimed.

This inexorable divine functioning can take its place, rather obviously, in a Stoic tradition, for if there is a love that can respond to this divine love, it is *amor fati,* a love that is not addressed either to the world as we can understand it, nor to a divine person who understands us, but to a cosmic destiny indifferent to what Deleuze calls our "birth in the flesh": what attaches us and leads us to say "me," "my" story, "my" sufferings, "my projects," I who was born in this world, of this world, who knows she will die and who wonders whether life is worth living.

One can say nothing more, and never has anything more been said: to become worthy of what happens to us, therefore to wish for and extract its event, to become the offspring of one's own events, and to be thereby reborn, to get oneself a new birth, to break with one's fleshly birth (LdS, 175).

Whitehead, however, is no philosopher of detachment and asceticism, and *Process and Reality* was not written to point out the path of a Stoic *askesis,* or, more generally, to provide a philosophical justification for the spiritual disciplines intended to liberate experience from the illusions of the self. The God of *Process and Reality* belongs to the adventure of reason, to the deliberate, constructed undertaking of saving "all experiences" together, and it is important that this undertaking not privilege any one experience, nor claim to appropriate those other adventures in which what matters is the question of the meaning and the obligations of daily life. Speculative philosophy does, of course, allude to religion, as it alludes to science, but it does so under the constraint of creativity, and what is at stake here, still and again, is to revise our modes of abstraction. What is directly at stake here is thus not religious experience but the theological modes of abstraction which, after blessing accusations of heresy and wars of religion, have not been able to avoid that in the modern period the Christian religion has degenerated into a decent formula, embellishing a comfortable life (SMW, 188).

However, it might be objected that Whitehead is also the one who, in *Science and the Modern World,* at a time when his God was still to come, described religion as one of the fundamental experiences of humanity, and God's power as the worship he inspires. One might accept that, as I have argued, the deliberately visionary and religious vocabulary Whitehead uses in the last part of *Process and Reality* constitutes, to be sure, a test of the ability of speculative concepts to "save" the religious vision from the solitary consciousness' excess of subjectivity. But it might perhaps also be, simultaneously and without contradiction, the very expression of such a vision, "returning with a content that is richer and more pure." The philosopher, having done his job, would experience the way in which the new modes of abstraction he has constructed become ingredients of his religious experience.

The question "Is Whitehead a theistic philosopher?"—raised in the United States but not in Europe—is not to be too easily dismissed. Whitehead presents himself as the philosopher who comes after William James. It is thus permissible to wonder to what extent Whitehead is not also the heir to James's God. However, this hypothesis entails an initial test. To inherit James's God also means to inherit the struggle William James fought against any confusion between the theistic viewpoint and what he called the Gnostic siren song, the philosophico-mystical temptation to situate mankind's fate and vocation in the perspective of a final cosmic reconciliation

[. . .] *in which the reality to be known and the power of knowing shall have become so mutually adequate that each exhaustively is absorbed by the other and the twain shall become one flesh, and in which the light shall somehow have soaked up all the outer darkness into its own ubiquitous beams* (RAT, 139).

The ideal sung by the Gnostic sirens corresponds rather precisely to the satisfaction of the Whiteheadian occasion, and it may also evoke the moment in which a mathematician "understands," when a problem is finally formulated in a way that exhibits its solution. The Whiteheadian God, however, has taken on meaning in a speculative construction that may be seen as a humorous version of the Gnostic vision. His construction does indeed accomplish the Gnostic ideal of "reconciliation," but it accomplishes it by rendering it "trivial" in the mathematical sense, for it is an ideal realized by every occasion, whatever it may be. One might say that in so doing Whitehead aims at revising our modes of abstraction, not at reaching a truth that would be the vocation and the salvation of the human experience.

But the question is insistent: If the speculative God, derived from the adventure of rationality, is not able to satisfy the vital need that James's God answered, how does Whitehead inherit this need?

For William James, theistic faith was inseparable from a conception of life not as reconciliation but as a battle, a life woven together from contradictions, rifts, and destructions. His faith was not intellectual but vital, for it found its meaning in what, for James, was the dramatic choice imposed by this life: to consent to this world, to engage in the battle, or to refuse. This choice is a test, and it forces us to turn our backs on any perspective that adulterates this test. It must be carried out, on pain of obscenity, in the "presence" of all those who have been crushed by life and of the immense army of suicides evoked in "Is Life Worth Living?" One might certainly say that there is a common point between James's cruel and deceptive life, and Whitehead's living order as robbery: both need justification. William James needed God in order for the battle to be worthwhile, and Whitehead needed *Process and Reality* to be an *Essay in Cosmology*.

Yet the difference matters: as human beings, we cannot commit ourselves to the Jamesian battle of life in the name of the Whiteheadian cosmological perspective. Correlatively, James's God must lend himself to the experience of encounter; he must hear the cry we utter as *our* cry, and not in a mode that includes it within his own perfection.

[. . .] *God's personality is to be regarded, like any other personality, as something lying outside my own and other than me, and whose existence I simply come upon and find. A power not ourselves, then, which not only makes for righteousness, but means it, and which recognizes us,— such is the definition which I think nobody will be inclined to dispute. Various are the attempts to shadow forth the other lineaments of so supreme a personality to our human imagination [. . .] But the essence remains unchanged. In whatever other respects the divine personality may differ from ours or may resemble it, the two are consanguineous at least in this,—that both have purposes for which they care, and each can hear the other's call* (RAT, 122).

For me, it is crucial that Whitehead did not speak of his God as a person or a personality, and that the reversal of the physical and mental poles suppresses any possible relation of consanguinity between him and us. Otherwise, his concepts would certainly have "saved" James's God, and James's need that his cry be heard, but in a way that would have silenced what James wanted to make us feel, what he needed in order to consent to this world: life as a (solitary) battle to which we can consent only if we believe that it demands our commitment, that is, also, that God needs us to fight it because the outcome is not already decided, "in the hands of God," because, albeit in a minimal way, that outcome depends on us.

This is not a matter of psychology. The question is not whether White-head felt the need that gives reality to the God of William James but to specify the link between the adventure of rationality, to which White-head's speculative philosophy belongs, and the "*adventure of the spirit*" (SMW, 192), which he associated with the worship of God. The way James defines his God, who is real because his effects are real, because without him the battle would not be worth fighting in a world that gives us every reason to despair, is very likely, to the same extent as the faith of the Quakers, what Whitehead was thinking about when he spoke of the religious vision which, when it returns, returns with content that is richer and more pure, freed, in particular, from the belief in a justice-dealing, all-powerful God. Yet the speculative God that Whitehead himself con-structed is not the respondent to such a vision. He belongs to a distinct adventure, even if both adventures aim at correcting the excess of subjec-tivity of the solitary consciousness. If Whitehead's God is required, it is by the metaphysical scheme, and it is to affirm what, it seems to me, claims Whitehead's own worship, the "full solemnity of the world" he mentioned in *Modes of Thought*.

Whitehead does not, of course, refute theism, nor the empirical impor-tance of the need to which it testifies. He simply asks, as the worthy heir of William James, that the theists abstain from addressing metaphysical compliments to the God of faith, or from dreaming of a fusion between the demands of reason and those of faith. The power of this last dream may rather explain why Whitehead's most audacious conceptual inven-tion, the reversal of the poles that shatters any relation of resemblance between divine experience and ours, has often been neglected by theistic interpreters. As James emphasized, in order to answer the cry of the reli-gious soul, "is life worth living?" a theist must require that God be expe-rienced as "present," that he be the object of a possible encounter, which requires an analogy between his experience and ours. But in *Modes of Thought*, where God is no longer named, we may hear the cry of a distinct soul, the Whiteheadian soul, with other requirements.

We require to understand how the unity of the universe requires its multiplicity. We require to understand how infinitude requires the finite. We require to understand how each immediately present existence requires its past, antecedent to itself; and requires its future, an essential factor in its own existence (MT, 83).

I would conclude that the God of *Process and Reality* differs from the theist God of William James because they communicate with distinct experiences of "sheer disclosure." Whitehead's God alludes to a religious vision, but, no more than the other Whiteheadian allusions, it does not give a particular meaning to a truth that would be the horizon of human life, or would testify to a vocation of human consciousness as such. The experience of disclosure does not concern human privilege, rather the requisites without which human adventures could be reduced to forms of illusion. The efficacy of the Whiteheadian allusion would then be: you who are engaged in an adventure, whatever it may be, do not forget what this adventure requires, in the name of the reasons that justify it; do not give to these reasons the power to make the full solemnity of the world, to which your commitment testifies, be forgotten; do not rob the universe of the importance that you demand be accorded to your reasons.

It is because they are situated at the level of requisites, not of passionate reasons that commit us, that when it comes to human destines Whiteheadian descriptions always feature a certain platitude, sometimes humorous. Platitude is necessary to succeed in what the judgment of the solitary consciousness cannot help but miss: not only to put everything on the same plane, but to avoid that this plane be oriented by the impassioned question of what is demanded by the accomplishment, or the authenticity, of human experience. The plane must affirm adventure, not progressive elucidation.

For instance, in many a philosophy since Kant, the starting point would be an eloquent dramatization of human responsibility, or even of the drama of Man, who is born free and "responsible for everything before everyone," as the Existentialist tradition would have it. Yet from a Whiteheadian viewpoint, we must limit ourselves to recognizing that the question of responsibility is part of human adventures, whatever the answers to this question may be. What matters, from the point of view of the adventures of ideas that take shape around what we call responsibility, is that the question not be illusory, for irresponsibility, as an ultimate metaphysical generality, would be, as Whitehead reproached Leibniz, inadequate.

The feelings are what they are in order that their subject may be what it is. Then transcendently, since the subject is what it is in virtue of its feelings, it is only by means of its feelings that the subject objectively conditions the creativity transcendent beyond itself. In our own relatively high grade of human existence, this doctrine of feelings and their subject is best illustrated by our notion of moral responsibility. The subject is responsible for being what it is in virtue of its feelings. It is also derivatively responsible for the consequences of its existence because they flow from its feelings (PR, 222).

The notion of moral responsibility is thus a testimony to a generic, neutral fact. A partial testimony, to be sure, since this notion introduces a "person who is responsible," who should be able to detach herself from her own feelings in order to be able to judge them. This transforms responsibility into an "ultimate," on the basis of which it is possible to formulate, in a deductive way, everything the solitary consciousness may see fit to demand: freedom, autonomy, reflexivity, and so on. The metaphysical interpretation makes this partiality stammer, but what this interpretation alludes to is not a truth that would enable us to escape partiality. The stammering is that of humor, the mode of intellectual feeling that exhibits the possibility of affirming what matters, without, for all that, having to affirm that it *must* matter.

Whiteheadian humor thus thwarts the temptation of making a big deal of the cosmological perspective. There are enough dramatic scenes in human lives; there's no need to add more. And in the process, it points out, in a rather salutary way, that no Idea will defend the person who is possessed by it from the insensitivity and rigidity that can degrade good people, and great creators, into pigs. The fact that what lurks in the interstices may come to be translated in terms of a hostile or contemptuous stance against the societies that condition these interstices, and that social norms may lead a battle against the creatures of creativity to whom it gives shelter, are the risks of the adventure. Whitehead's singularity, the very meaning of the circular workings of his thought, may be attention to that risk. "Nothing in excess!" Such attention forbids nothing, but constrains us to consider at the same time the arrow that leaves the ground of our habits and that ground that will confer its meaning, without appeal, upon what escapes it.

Unseasonable art is analogous to an unseasonable joke, namely, good in its place, but out of place a positive evil. It is a curious fact that lovers of art who are most insistent on the doctrine of "art for art" are apt to be indignant at the banning of art for the sake of other interests. The charge of immorality is not refuted by pointing to the perfection of art. Of course it is true that the defence of morals is the battle-cry which best rallies stupidity against change. Perhaps countless ages ago respectable amoebae refused to migrate from the ocean to dry land—refusing in defence of morality. One incidental service of art to society is in its adventurousness (AI, 268).

Adventure: this is the term Whitehead proposes, where apocalyptic visions haunt our imaginations, where "art for art" or "the defense of society" clash in titanic combats that make the foundations of the earth tremble as their imprecations rise toward heaven. To combat pious, conformist, or hateful opinion is part of the risks of philosophy, but the test Whitehead proposes for philosophy is to fight it by "saving" it, by addressing it as if it were capable of participating in the adventure. Christians, Stoics, Nietzscheans, Kantians are all accepted together, with the co-presence of the others being part of the test for each. The irresponsibility of Cain, the creature of creativity, when he refuses to be his brother's keeper, and the responsibility that makes Quakers tremble when they live each of their acts as what conditions cosmic becoming: the point is not to oppose them, but to situate them in a mode such that their coexistence may be not a contradiction to be resolved but a fact to be celebrated.

There is a greatness in the lives of those who build up religious systems, a greatness in action, in idea and in self-subordination, embodied in instance after instance through centuries of growth. There is greatness in the rebels who destroy such systems: they are the Titans who storm heaven, armed with passionate sincerity. It may be that the revolt is the mere assertion by youth of its right to its proper brilliance, to that final good of immediate joy. Philosophy may not neglect the multifariousness of the world—the fairies dance, and Christ is nailed to the cross (PR, 337–338).

Heaven dances with the fairies, and rips open when Christ dies. And if philosophy needs God, it is precisely to resist the passion of taking sides in this regard. The neutrality of metaphysics is not an imitation of divine impartiality, for it has no relation of resemblance with the latter. It is an audaciously concocted antidote, not a functional definition. And like any antidote, it designates how it matters. In fact, the way in which the reversal of poles, which is Whitehead's great invention in theology, defines God and the World, completes the circuit begun by the link between metaphysics and neutrality. The fact that Whitehead speaks of function, not of freedom, with regard to God, of inexorable evaluation and not of enjoyment, of patience and not of decision, "simply" brings about a passage to the limit of the imperative of nonconfusion of categories between our "living values," what we care about, and importance as a generic category. Dance is important to fairies, and the salvation of mankind to Christ, but God does not let himself be described in terms of importance, only of appetite, which is perpetual and ever-renewed. The experience entertaining this last proposition would have to be characterized by the most determined lack of appetite for relating adventures and apocalyptic values. And, correlatively, it should signify the importance of learning, and of saying, which living values each adventure embodies. Whitehead meets up with Leibniz: *dic cur hic.*

I am suggesting that Protestant theology should develop as its founda-
tion an interpretation of the Universe which grasps its unity amid its
many diversities. The interpretation to be achieved is a reconciliation of
seeming incompatibilities. But these incompatibilities are not hypotheti-
cal. They are there on the stage of history, undoubted and claiming inter-
pretation [. . .] The last book in the Bible illustrates the barbaric ele-
ments which have been retained to the undoing of Christian intuition
[. . .] Finally, the book only states, more pointedly and more vividly,
ideas spread throughout the Old Testament and the New Testament,
even in the Gospels themselves. Yet it is shocking to think that this book
has been retained for the formation of religious sentiment, while the
speech of Pericles, descriptive of the Athenian ideal of civilization, has
remained neglected in this connection. What I am advocating can be
symbolized by this shift in the final book of the authoritative collection
of religious literature, namely, the replacement of the book of the Revela-
tion of St. John the Divine by the imaginative account given by Thucydides
of the Speech of Pericles to the Athenians. Neither of them is history: St.
John never received just that revelation, nor did Pericles ever make just
that speech (AI, 170–171).

We can always count on Whiteheadian humor for a formula that interrupts prophetic momentum. We had started out from the interpretation
of the Universe, and we wind up with Pericles. Yet no Whiteheadian formula can be attributed to mere occasional humor or to wit. Understanding the Whiteheadian adventure also means accepting that Whitehead
was indeed much less interested in the Stoic *fatum* as a test against our
attachments than in the promises included in the success—concrete and
important to him—attributed to Pericles.

According to Thucydides, Pericles addressed the Athenians as free citizens, that is, animated by divergent priorities, values, goals, all this without asking them to strip themselves of these attachments in the name of
what transcends them. At the same time, however, he addressed them as
Athenians, on whose action the life of the city depends. Athens will only
be saved by its citizens, all together. And because he believed in the Athenians in their diversity, and not in Athens insofar as it transcends the
freedom of its inhabitants, Pericles enabled them to rise to the height of
the occasion. He interpreted them as attached but not defined by, or subject to, what attaches them, and therefore susceptible of a new type of
unity that would be Athens. And indeed, they became what they were
from the cosmic viewpoint: incompatibilities demanding an interpretation to reconcile them, not in general, but here and now, for the Athens
they henceforth brought into existence in a new mode.

The Periclean ideal is action weaving itself into a texture of persuasive beauty analogous to the delicate splendor of nature (AI, 51).

If Pericles, a politician who succeeded in persuading the crowd of undisciplined Athenians to act together without being constrained by violence or legal coercion, should have the last word in the formation of the religious spirit aimed at by biblical literature, it is because his success is the paradigmatic example of what is meant, for Whitehead, by evil as what may be overcome. Lack of discipline is not an evil in itself but designates the multiplicity of individual enjoyments that constitute the primordial truth of the world. Pericles does not deny this when he addresses the crowd of Athenians, but he trusts in what "his" world is capable of, that is in "his" fellow citizens *qua* able to feel, each in their own way, the need for common action.

For Whitehead, Plato, who despised democracy, is nevertheless an heir of Pericles, whose trust he turned into a philosophical generalization. This is why there is not the slightest contradiction in the fact that this philosopher whose affinities with the Stoics, Nietzsche, or Deleuze I have emphasized had, for his part, defined the European philosophical tradition as "footnotes" to Plato's text (PR, 39). What "saves" Plato, for Whitehead, making him the first philosopher, is the affirmation that the divine element in the world must be conceived in terms of action that is persuasive or erotic (lure), not coercive. This implies, correlatively, that human beings are defined by their susceptibility to the attraction of the true, the beautiful, and the good.

The fact that the power of the true, the beautiful, and the good over human souls is that of Eros thus constitutes, in the cavalier perspective typical of Whitehead, a properly philosophical generalization of what was first attested by Pericles, persuading the Athenians to unite without threats or reference to transcendent values to force them to it. Consequently, whatever may be the restrictive conditions, normative judgments, and unnecessary oppositions produced by the Platonic statement, Plato is, for Whitehead, the first philosopher, because he defined the human being as "capable of the Idea."

Philosophy as footnotes ... and indeed, the most misanthropic or the most subversive philosophers, because they are philosophers, may well denounce the pettiness of humans, the stupidity of opinion, the nastiness and cowardice of conformism: they will still inherit, albeit in a critical form, an ideal based on the intrinsic possibilities of the human. And all this for the simple reason that what makes them live and think is called "an idea," and that it belongs to the very concept of an idea to affirm that humans are capable of accepting what ideas demand, without being constrained by any force other than that of the idea itself. You who denounce voluntary servitude, people refusing to come out of their cave, *dic cur hic*.

Plato conceived the notion of the ideal relations between men based upon a conception of the intrinsic possibilities of human character. We see this idea enter human consciousness in every variety of specialization. It forms alliances with allied notions generated by religion. It differentiates its specializations according to the differentiations of the diverse religions and diverse scepticisms associated with it. At times it dies down. But it ever recurs. It is criticized, and it is also a critic. Force is always against it. Its victory is the victory of persuasion over force. The force is the sheer fact of what the antecedent volume of the world in fact contains. The idea is a prophecy which procures its own fulfill-ment (AI, 42).

While fairies dance, and fetishists have commerce with their divinities, and mystics undertake to die to the world, Whitehead, for whom what matters is above all the Adventure of Ideas, fabricates a "self realizing prophecy" to "save" that adventure. Like Pericles' speech, this prophecy is addressed to the "solitary consciousnesses" who define themselves as humans and testify to the powers of ideas through the divergent and con-flicting adventures of religion, philosophy, and science, but also of the arts and of politics. And the common feature made manifest in this way, turning the discordant multiplicity of adventures into a singular, problem-atic one, is also a transformation of this common feature. The definition associating the adventure of ideas with "solitary consciousnesses" may also correct the exaggeration inherent in this experience of solitariness. Solitude is not the last word.

What is the last word, the one that closes the circle, and includes Whitehead in the adventure? God is obviously not the ultimate, but nei-ther is creativity in this case, for it is only the ultimate of Whitehead's philosophical construction, referring to his responsibility as a thinker, not to what makes him think. The ultimate of adventure, the only thing that really matters, is the question that inhabits this adventure of ideas: the question of what those who define themselves as "capable of ideas" are capable of. This is the question that always returns. It unites Job, whose solitary cry rises up to God; Protagoras, who turns the gods into fabrications of which man is the measure; Pericles, who knows that all that matters is the greatness to which the undisciplined crowd may rise; Jesus, who announces the victory of love over death, but also those mer-chants who Jesus drove from the Temple, insofar as their practice wagered on mutual persuasion and not on force; and finally Nietzsche, whose hammer-thought undertook to destroy that Temple.

Whitehead's God is thus an idea, derived from the adventure of Ideas, and its non-power, its functional character that excludes all coercion, designates the way Whitehead tries to save this adventure, addressing it like Pericles addressed the crowd of Athenians. Pericles supposed this crowd to be capable of actually becoming what they were abstractly: all inhabitants of Athens. He supposed his auditors to be capable of accepting the proposition "we are Athenians," in an experience henceforth likely to contribute to saving Athens. Whitehead supposes that we are capable of transforming the proposition that we have all set forth on the same adventure into a feeling likely to transform it. And to transform, by so doing, our own experience as solitary consciousness. This transformation has a Whiteheadian name, and the final pages of *Adventures of Ideas* are devoted to "Peace."

The Peace that is here meant is not the negative conception of anaesthesia. It is a positive feeling which crowns the "life and motion" of the soul. It is hard to define and difficult to speak of. It is not a hope for the future, nor is it an interest in present details. It is a broadening of feeling due to the emergence of some deep metaphysical intuition, unverbalized and yet momentous in its coördination of values [. . .] The experience of Peace is largely beyond the control of purpose. It comes as a gift. The deliberate aim at Peace very easily passes into its bastard substitute, Anaesthesia. In other words, in the place of a quality of "life and motion," there is substituted their destruction. Thus Peace is the removal of inhibition and not its introduction. It results in a wider sweep of conscious interest. It enlarges the field of attention [. . .] Amid the passing of so much beauty, so much heroism, so much daring, Peace is then the intuition of permanence. It keeps vivid the sensitiveness to the tragedy; and it sees the tragedy as a living agent persuading the world to aim at fineness beyond the faded level of surrounding fact. Each tragedy is the disclosure of an ideal:—What might have been, and was not: What can be. The tragedy was not in vain [. . .] The inner feeling belonging to the grasp of the service of tragedy is Peace—the purification of the emotions (AI, 285–286).

What Whitehead is describing may be what Spinoza called "knowledge of the third kind," and this is a mode of experience that does not belong to any particular human tradition, and which all no doubt celebrate in their own language. Among "our" words, which the imperative question, or the Idea, has launched into divergent adventures, haunted by the question of the "intrinsic-possibilities-of-the-human," it is perhaps, purifying an overly emotive relation to the truth, Leibniz's *"Calculemus"* that best expresses the kind of habits in whose interstices Whiteheadian peace lurks.

The commitment to the risk of calculation does not spell the end of disputes, or reconciliation in the name of a higher truth—and especially not the truth of "calculability." It is the deliberate affirmation of what, for "us," is not an object of deliberation, since it is what has launched us into adventure, a trust we attest even in our denunciations and our angers. "That which may be," the possibility of saving our tragic and singular adventure, is not a matter of transcendence, but it belongs to the "non-power of God," to the worship whose possibility is saved by the God constructed by Whitehead, but which is not addressed to him, of transforming each of the ingredients of this adventure into an unknown, calling for additions and condensations. To transform the interstitial laughter of Nietzsche, the prophesy of Jesus, and the submission of Regulus to the social institution of the promise into so many explorations testifying to the same adventure.

There is an iteration in calculus, just as there is a repetition in problems which reproduces that of the questions or the imperatives from which it proceeds. Here again, however, it is not an ordinary repetition. Ordinary repetition is prolongation, continuation, of that length of time which is stretched into duration: bare repetition [...] However, who is prolonged in this way? A singularity, as far as the vicinity of another singularity? On the contrary, what defines the extraordinary power of that clothed repetition, more profound than bare repetition, is the resumption of singularities in one another, the condensation of singularities one into another, as much in the same problem or Idea, as between one problem and another or between one Idea and another (DR, 259).

Speculative philosophy as clothed, adequate repetition, perhaps as a vector of peace, of the discordant adventures of the Idea.

Word of a Dragon, Word of Trance

Philosophy begins in wonder. And, at the end, when philosophic thought has done its best, the wonder remains. (MT, 168)

THE FACT THAT wonder remains at the end, not as a residue, as that which resists reasons, but "once and for all," in the very place where our reasons are constructed, becoming enriched by every reason, is the properly Whiteheadian fall into the classical definition according to which philosophy has its starting point in wonder. And this, as it were, is Whitehead's last word, the one that appears at the end of *Modes of Thought,* the book in which John Gardner, the author of *Grendel,* discovered what could be a "dragon word," an ageless word uttered by a being for whom the succession of epochs boils down to the gloomy repetition of naivetés, arrogances, and blind pretenses to illusory meanings.

The young Grendel cannot understand the dragon's words, as the latter well knows. Yet what does that matter to him? There would have been no story to tell if Grendel had not produced himself as a creature of resentment, hating the humans who live off the illusions suggested to them by the Shaper and to which he himself cannot adhere. He has only found enjoyment, bitter and repetitive, in terrorizing them, killing them, humiliating their heroes and demonstrating the impotence of their gods. Until he once again comes across Whitehead's words, this time uttered by a blind priest, a word of trance that speaks of God and routs him. The critical spirit, denouncer of all idols, interested in verification alone, exciting but trivial in the sense of the mathematicians, of the possibility of destroying, has fled, in full disarray.

A homage of fiction to the philosopher who conceived of philosophical thought as the Shaper himself conceives of history—as fabulation—and who has succeeded in making converge what should have diverged. For the blind prophesy does not contradict the dragon's cynical knowledge: it does not add to it any hope, any guarantee, any transcendence that would inevitably have given Grendel a reason to kill. The blind man merely separated this knowledge from the consequences, futility and destiny, with whose implacable truth Grendel, for his part, identified himself. Yet the dragon does not draw any consequence from this: he counts his gold and jewels. Perhaps, eventually, he will go so far as to sort them into piles. The prophesy would not have affected him precisely because, from what he knows, there does not follow any of the "and therefores" that the blind priest's word of trance transmutes in the mode of fabulation. Whitehead's cosmology has nothing to add to the dragon's words, for the latter has retreated from the order of consequences, which are all that matters cosmologically. It addresses those who, in one way or another, are struggling with the "adventure of hope" and therefore, when hope is transformed into disappointment, anger, and suffering, with the passion of despair. This is why what it repeats are the "and therefores" in a way that exhibits that outside of logic: nothing follows logically. Every consequence is a creation of consequence.

Dragon's word or word of trance, it is indeed a strange language which, perhaps, the reader who has followed me this far, in the course of the preceding pages, may have learned to understand. A language whose efficacy does not derive from its power to denounce, to criticize, to vanquish objections, and to constrain us to agree but, quite the contrary, from its radical absence of power in this sense. For no utterance in this language has the power to construct an argument, and every argument repeated in this language loses its power, for it loses what such power presupposes. The argument that demands to be taken into account presupposes that the words used may be defined independently of the account in the process of formation, in order to be instruments for the confrontation of viewpoints or their mutual measurement. And it is precisely this possibility of definition that is dissolved by speculative repetition.

In this sense, each speculative utterance functions somewhat like the proverbs that endlessly punctuate discussions under the African palaver tree: words that do not belong to their speakers, do not express their point of view, but, on the contrary, turn the speaker into the *expressum* of what they express. Then, and for no transcendent reason referring the utterance to an intention (I meant to say . . .) whose means it would be. And yet, these utterances matter. The Africans know what they are doing. Their efficacy does not derive from any kind of "presentification" of that which, because it is sublime, transcends the divergences about which the discussion is being held. Neither Grendel nor any reader of *Grendel* has bowed down before the blind man's profession of faith, as before the expression of what transcends rational argument. If Grendel had felt the sublime, he would have killed or would have converted, but he would not have felt distress.

When all is said and done, the sublime goes rather well with rational calculation. Critical thinkers have long since admitted into the heart of the city the interstitial presence of poets, and of all those who renounce critical discussion and the constraints of communication, to bring into existence, in one form or another, that which reasons cannot board and inspect. The most "materialist" doctors will grow proud in those moments when they feel a soul within them, in communion with the music that elevates them or with the suffering that recalls them to common humility. The most ardent supporter of a "purely technical" rationality may cite Heidegger, if only to affirm that indeed "we assassinate to dissect," and to conclude to the impossibility of a rational knowledge that is not reductive . . . and therefore to the vanity of all criticism of knowledge *qua* reductive. And the most "reductionist" physicists will affirm that they are sensitive to the splendor of the sunset. Even neurophysiologists, who occupy the very site where reduction should be carried out, can call themselves lovers of art . . .

Yet the marriage of the sublime and the rational has as its strictest principle the separation of assets. Woe to whomever is suspected of confusing them! Thus, those who plead for the objectivity of physical laws have the very curious habit of proposing to whomever seems to them not to have enough respect for these laws to jump out a window, some from the sixth floor, some, if they are really angry, from the fifteenth: the miscreant will thus be able to verify that the "law of gravity" is indeed universal. In general, the miscreant declines this kind invitation, and, we may remark in passing, quite rightly. For what her fall would verify is nothing other than a "consensual" fact, suitable to be accepted by all sufficiently heavy terrestrial animals, all of whom, except birds and bats, would tend to resist if one wished to push them through one of these infamous windows. The importance of not falling is part of the animal's mode of existence. In contrast, as Paul Valéry has written, it is rather the audacious hypothesis that the Moon never ceases falling toward the earth, like a vulgar apple, that singularizes the passion of modern physicists since Newton.

In any case, it is precisely the principle of this couple, placed under the regime of the separation of assets, that Whitehead comes to confuse. There is nothing sublime in his texts, for the poetic moments that abound in them are most often interrupted by a technical specification, a comic comparison, or a terminological reflection. The text exhibits an omni-presence of reasoning, of demonstration, of critical questioning of the meaning and range of phraseology, in short, an ostentatious will to sub-mit himself to the norms of rational communication. Yet never does rea-soning, or critical questioning, wind up in a judgment ratifying a separa-tion. Grendel, who transformed critical thought into a devastating weapon, who wanted to be the scourge of human shapers, flees.

If critical thought, which had assigned itself the task of ensuring the separation of assets, is put to flight, it is because its most certain hold becomes redundant here. As Bruno Latour has so well diagnosed, this hold works by the identification of other people's beliefs, the denuncia-tion of the fetishism that makes them bow in the face of what they or their fellow-humans have fabricated, a veritable sin of thought. Thought will be iconoclastic or enslaved, it will smash the images that captivate it or will forget itself in the barbarism of all fanaticisms. Yet Whitehead fabricates, composes, constructs—deliberately, technically, artificially—a universe whose facticity and fictional character cannot be denounced, because they are obvious. And it is this factitious construction, exhibiting the traces of the hand-to-hand fight with the problems raised for him by his own construction, that he proposes *qua* participant in the adventure of reason, as liable not to smash but to save the daring abstractions in which critical thought places its faith.

Citing Kant's famous statement, in the name of which the critical Tri-bunal has passed so many of its judgments, "thoughts without content are empty, intuitions without concepts are blind," Whitehead confines himself to adding the premise which, according to him, Kant has sup-pressed: "Intuitions are never blind" (PR, 139). Intuition is never "with-out concepts," because it is always decision, the unification of the many, thus and not otherwise. Every intuition is "consequent," and the concepts invoked by Kant are nothing other than the mode of unification that has prevailed, which, moreover, constitutes as such what is at stake in every flight of speculative experience. Kant, making himself the vector of the somewhat excessive pretenses of conscious, discursive experience, de-manded of concepts that they designate the object of possible knowledge that is communicable, capable of being abstracted from the fact consti-tuted by a concrete experience. Whitehead, in contrast, for whom intu-itions are never blind, addresses his demand not to experience but to critical consciousness itself. It pertains to consciousness not to verify ti-tles of legitimacy but to accept a creation of concepts that exposes it to adventure, making it capable of providing a thought content to what is felt. It then becomes "verification" in James's sense, experiencing what is imposed by its abandonment of its position as judge. If "the concept of 'God' is the way in which we understand this incredible fact—that which cannot be, yet is" (PR, 350), this concept must not be dissolved in a *mise en abyme* or a paradox, but modify the conscious distribution of the believable and the unbelievable.

Not to judge, to criticize, perhaps, but to transform critique into an instrument of modification. To abstain even from telling anyone what would be "better," as Leibniz did, for instance, when he confronted the claim that Socrates's gesture of raising the poisoned cup to his lips could be explained by a chain of mechanical actions: Leibniz noted that although this movement may doubtless be explained from a muscular viewpoint like any other, nevertheless, to describe it and explain it, it is better to listen to Socrates's reasons than to address his muscles. The Leibnizian "better" inspires the impatience of specialists, who ask "in the name of what" one undertakes to limit their questions, who demand that one define that which, in Socrates's gesture, could indeed have the power to present an obstacle to a mode of explanation conceived so as to have none. And the Leibnizian argument will disappoint just as much the partisans of human freedom, who do not find in this "better" the guarantee of a radical freedom, without which Socrates's morality would be an empty word.

In this case, the weakness of the Leibnizian "better" is that what it tries to limit is a practice that is also oriented, in its way, toward the formulation of the best description—according to the problem that matters for this practice. And this problem does not, as such, admit of a limitation in the name of questions to which it can give no formulation. One might as well ask a tiger on the prowl to spare that young gazelle, who is so charming, remarking that the situation here is even more serious. For the tiger will remain indifferent and will simply kill the gazelle, whereas the history of our modern disputes testifies to the solidarity between the intensity of an appetite and what undertakes to limit it. Scientists and those who wish to "domesticate" them, restricting them to their "domus," are inseparable, the appetite of the ones being excited by the scandal they know how to stir up among the others. On another level, moreover, this is what the dragon warned Grendel, who did not understand: by wanting to be the scourge of men, he would in fact be the one who would instigate them to "shape" the blind brutality of his own predations, that is, to create all that he himself abhors, science, poetry, religion. Grendel and the men he persecutes are "as inseparable as the mountain-climber and the mountain" (Gr, 62).

This is why it is important to emphasize that Whitehead's speculative intervention does not by any means intend to propose "better" descriptions, instead of those that actually succeed. Here, one may return to the regret formulated by some of Whitehead's heirs with regard to the fact that societies have not received the status of "existent," of "*res vera,*" that no principle of emergence or act of unification has a place in the categoreal scheme. How can we satisfy a minimum of realism, they ask, if we cannot confer its own ontological unity upon a composite entity, an irreducible unity upon the way individual beings enter into the composition of other individual beings? How can we do without the categories that authorize us to speak of a being that endures as of a subject "to whom" things happen, as a veritable actuality endowed with the power of unifying its component parts? After all, why should an author who, as we have seen, does not hesitate to have recourse to the doctrine of sacraments to do justice to the multiplicity of our modes of thought deprive himself of the sacrament that would give consciousness what it demands, when it affirms the unity of its experience, its legitimacy to claim its past and its future as its own?

If Whitehead had sought plausibility, or the possibility of proving his description to be "better," the "incurably atomic" character of his metaphysical definition of what is real would indeed have been a weakness, justifying the reexamination of the edifice. Yet according to what constraints should one proceed to this reexamination? How can we avoid ending up with a kind of "rational psychology," authenticating certain claims and rejecting others? How can we affirm, on the same level, the adventures of Kant and those of a shaman, the passion of the mathematician Cantor, feeling the categories of his thought dismembered by the question of the continuous infinity of numbers, and the decision of the mathematician Hilbert, postulating the axioms that domesticate the Cantorian infinite? In short, how can we avoid a normative sociology, prescribing the right way to frame the problem, what dictates its solution, what sorts out beings according to whether they do or do not have the ontological right to exist? How, also, can we avoid a confrontation between rival endurances: is time the number of motion, designating the great regularities of nature, or is it the subjective condition of our human intuition, with the great natural regularities then becoming relative to the endurance of the subject of knowledge? To rule in favor of the claims of continuity also means being obliged to institute a court capable of judging and sorting out these claims.

For Whitehead, it goes without saying that the "bests" as defined by these social adventures that we call knowledge are doomed to divergence. For they are inseparable from those adventures, themselves divergent, adventures in which modes of endurance and specific definitions of importance—which, for Whitehead, are so many living values—have invented themselves, each time on their own account. Speculative philosophy is not about giving a plausible account of what exists but about approaching each society with the question of what it might be capable of, and this capacity designates not its judgments but the interstices to which it provides shelter. The question is then no longer how to "stop" physicists, rather how to modify their dreams, that is, as well, how to infect them. This is the meaning of what I would call "speculative presence."

The heavy, ancient presence of the mountains, already evoked by Whitehead in *Science and the Modern World.* Those who feel it can always shake themselves, come back to earth, and laugh at what they have experienced. We have ready-made words—imagination or daydreaming—to cancel the interstitial experience rejected by our impatient certitudes, our specialized criteria, correlates of the abstractions that matter socially for us. Nevertheless, for a time, before the interstice closed, the mountain, ancient and heavy, was no longer "there" for the subjects perceiving it "here," a colorless, motionless form which they could approach if they chose. English humor was required to give a technical definition of what others celebrate as ineffable, and define it as "infection." And to comment on infection itself in terms of "causal efficacy," that is, to associate with the notion of cause not a transparent relation with a well-defined effect, but the hold over us of what we perceive.

To the efficacy of speculative presence as infection corresponds a conception of the "sociality" that separates it from the moral features of the cooperation of the parts toward the maintaining of the whole, and a conception of the commitment that separates it from the power of the cause that commits. What "belongs" to a society and what it excludes never correspond to a generality, for instance, to the generality that would attribute to the whole the power to define its own parts, or to the parts, conceived separately, the power to explain the whole. Belonging is always factual, mutual inclusion rather than participation, a field of emergence, no doubt, but whose differentiated expressions make society exist as the *exprimatum* of the emergent correlation or inter-reference. For Whitehead, the dynamics of possession, obsession, and capture must not be explained in a specific way, as would be the case if autonomy were the norm. They exhibit, in a somewhat exacerbated mode, a generality that refers both to the order of nature and to the regimes of production of conscious experience. No experience can be separated from the play of partial, selective repercussions that it unifies on its own account.

This, of course, does not entail any apocalyptic consequences with regard to the illusory nature of our experiences, but it broadens the spectrum in such a way that speculative infection may slip in without demanding any rift or exceptional status. Everyone can remember those moments, testifying to an obstinate, almost obsessive insistence of the "others in oneself," in which we catch ourselves having smiled, accepted a role, adopted a position, almost despite ourselves. Yet this is no terrible truth, although at times it may have terrible consequences. In fact, even when we feel ourselves, quite justifiably, to be more or less the authors of our choices, the causes we might invoke to justify them will be a mere translation, often redundant, of what has a "hold" on us. And speculation itself would remain a dead letter if it did not succeed in "getting a hold," were not liable to infect, in its specific way, those whom it addresses.

The efficacy associated with speculative philosophy is thus not based in the least on a principle that transcends what it has the ambition of infecting. Nor will it have any character of generality, as would be the case if the point were to make divergent social adventures converge. What is aimed at can, of course, be defined in a general way: it will be a transformation of the way these adventures diverge. Yet the transformation itself cannot, of course, be deduced from what provokes it. The singularity of speculative efficacy is, moreover, from this viewpoint, to exhibit this indeterminacy, that is, not to propose any norm, any rule, or any imperative identifying what a "right" thought would be.

One may nevertheless define the efficacy associated with speculative thought as a Whiteheadian version of the therapeutic vocation which philosophers often assign to their work. In this case, however, it is a rather original version of this vocation, for "healing thought"—Plato and his myth of the cave is the prototype of this, Wittgenstein a good example, and perhaps even Bergson may be one—has usually designated the idea of a "return to health." Whether philosophers diagnose error, illusion or stupidity, or a deforming screen, parasitical questions, or misplaced confidence in words and reasons, the operation of diagnosis then has the consequence that philosophers become "masters of thought," possessing a knowledge that enables them to define what health is and to deduce therefrom a prognosis with regard to the possibility of its return, even if it means deploring the "voluntary slavery" that constitutes an obstacle to that return.

This is the position Whitehead escapes as early as the diagnosis of the harmful absurdity of the "bifurcation of nature" when he did not lay claim to any particular conception of the relations between mind and nature, but embarked upon the adventure of a construction that "saves" by adding new obligations, new artifices, new stakes. Whitehead neither denounced nor pursued the power of abstractions, but tried to metamorphose their efficacy. But this is precisely what non-modern therapists do, as Tobie Nathan proposes that we interpret them. They give a name to what is persecuting a patient, a name by which the persecutor can be convoked so that one can negotiate with it the conditions of its inscription within a context where the victim may connect with what was persecuting her. One might therefore say that Whitehead, like those therapists, has fashioned statements capable of convoking to conscious experience powers with which one may enter into viable relations. These powers are not gods, ancestors, or genies, but those of our own rationalist tradition.

In a sense, then, Whitehead meets up with the "non-modern" art of therapy, an art that does not separate diagnosis, prognosis, and healing process, but includes them in a becoming whose secrets therapists do not possess, because there is no secret. The therapist is an operator, but the objects with which she operates are neither a response to an independent diagnosis (as medications claim to be), nor symbols of something else. They neither explain, nor are they explicable in any sense other than that which constitutes becoming, or metamorphosis, as a touchstone. In Whiteheadian terms, evil, its cause, and the becoming to which it obliges are explained in the very process by which evil may be actually "overcome." This is why healing is never a "return to health," but rather a "social transformation," implying the event of an articulation of experience with beings that the person "in good health" can do without.

If we follow this parallel, the theme of the bifurcation of nature becomes a diagnosis. It holds true for all the divergences that dismember modern thought, because these divergences present themselves in the mode of the "either/or" which, whatever the choice may be, imposes the need for a mourning that can only be carried out by mutilating thought itself. This is why "true professionals," be they scientists, technicians, philosophers, or others, are both the products and the vectors of bifurcation, those for whom it will pose no problem whatsoever, and those who will propagate its infection, in the name of a thought that is finally serious. Yet no prognosis responds to this diagnosis, affirming the need for a return to the kind of unity that has been destroyed by modern times, for such a unity, already placed under the banner of the monotheist-rationalist adventure, may have imagined Christ on the cross but not the dance of the fairies (PR, 338). To have the ambition of a return to the type of unity that has been destroyed would mean, just as much, to ratify what that unity had already destroyed.

What the prognosis proposes is a "social transformation" of the rationalist adventure itself, that is, the production of a separation between the divergent adventures it never ceases to inspire and their respective justifications. Whitehead's prognosis therefore does not derive its authority from the truth of the diagnosis, but is, identically, a commitment to the future. If the speculative infection is to be efficacious, this will depend on the leap of imagination enabling both a departure, without mourning or drama, from any claim to a legitimacy that transcends the facts and a full appraisal of each fact as never to be parted from the living value it discloses. There are no sheer facts. Speculative presence does not carry out any convergence, but suspends the retranslation of the divergent terms into a contradiction such that it seems possible to affirm the one only if the other is denied.

However, the healing process Whitehead proposes to thought does not oblige us to renounce any kind of demand whatsoever. Freedom for Galileo, for his adversaries . . . and also for the earth. Nor is this a matter of relativism. The historicist or positivist undertakings that speak in the name of "facts," to identify what is "merely" relative to human invention, have much to learn from biologists: the latter would be very surprised to see the extraordinary co-invention of living beings and their world reduced to a critical discourse involving the way in which animals allow themselves to be deluded, lured, seduced, or manipulated by their own invention (fetishism!). The fact that aerobic living beings invented oxygen as a resource, whereas it was poison for their predecessors, does not inspire any judgment concerning the relativity of biochemistry but rather the celebration of an event that resounds throughout the history of Gaia.

Whitehead does not deconstruct anything. Quite the contrary, he takes every construction to its cosmological power. And therefore, there can be no question of excluding as illusory the references to what transcends history—the true, the beautiful, the good—or to what exceeds the observable—quarks, the unconscious, the ancestors. Neither the insistence of truth nor the obligations due to the ancestors, including the latter's power to ensure that such obligations are respected, neither the dance of the fairies nor Christ nailed to his cross may be judged, that is, disqualified, as relative to "our" historically variable ideas. They may be destroyed, no doubt, but not criticized "in the name of the facts," for they are constitutive of them, as affirmed by all those who, consciously or not, in the mode of habit, perplexity, fear, incredulousness, wonder, or demand, take up a position with regard to them.

Thus, speculative thought does not deny the possibility that a society may explain the reasons why it endures a given way and not otherwise, or that it demands that others recognize the well-foundedness of these reasons. Yet it turns such a possibility into an aspect of the endurance in question. This is why speculative thought is presence rather than argument, a presence whose efficacy is to infect every justificatory argument with the adventurous questions of what is demanded by the position whose legitimacy it expresses, of what it recruits to endure or propagate, and of the way it is liable to be affected by the encounter with another position.

These kinds of questions, and the humorous effects they produce, may, of course, inspire the rage of those who wish, in one way or another, to demonstrate that they differ in a different way, capable of relegating all the other differences to the same indistinctness. Yet this is the risk of every therapeutic process, pharmacological in the sense that the "remedy" does not contain within itself the means to guarantee that it may not have, in certain circumstances, the effect of a poison. And this is the risk that also defines "the good" in the sense of *Religion in the Making,* that is, the possibility of overcoming the exclusive disjunction, "either . . . or," when the realization of one thing demands the destruction of something else. This possibility, if it presents itself at the wrong time, can be the trick of evil. As I have emphasized, healing, the possibility of affirming a position without multiplying fact by right, is not a "return to health" or to normality, which is why it is, by definition, a risky process.

At a time when every position is infected by the summons, applied to everyone, that it must justify itself according to a "logical" type of argument, or admit that it is merely "taste and color," with the accusation of "intolerant dogmatism" coming, if need be, to intensify the infection, it is as well to specify that the operation of "healing" with which speculative philosophy can be associated has nothing to do with that general, genteel virtue called "tolerance." The virtue of tolerance, exhibited by the thought that presents itself as postmodern, if it is not simple hypocrisy, in fact translates rather well what Whitehead described when he spoke of the instability of evil. Evil may disappear with the disappearance of what makes one suffer. The transformation of the modern conflict for legitimacy into a civilized conversation, to speak with Richard Rorty, may be said to "turn into pigs" those who happily converse, for they agree on avoiding any serious conflict. They indulge in well-bred—that is, without consequence—language games, for they have renounced everything that might compromise their belonging to the same world. If the "cure" is to take place, if the contradiction can be metamorphosed into a contrast, it will not be by the path of ironic renunciation. On the contrary, this contrast will have to be celebrated in the manner of a new existent, adding a new dimension to the cosmos. In other words, evil, eventually overcome, is a cosmic event, excluding all skepticism that is well-bred because it is cynical. To affirm the irreducibility of this event, to propose that we think in its presence, and not to use it as an argument, it was necessary to shake the heaven and earth of our certainties: this is what Whitehead attempted when he came to propose the double dehiscence of the world and of God.

The point is thus, above all, not to renounce the rationalist adventure but to free it from what hides its originality, from what allows it to appear as neutral, a common destiny for all humans. For it is this neutrality which, generalizing the power of logical argumentation, confers upon this adventure the destructive character that Whitehead associates with evil. What is generalized is the power to define a situation in a way that makes agreement rhyme with submission. Those who claim to have logic (and the facts) on their side claim to be able to put themselves in the place of the person they are addressing—*"But don't you see that . . . "*, *"Everyone will admit that . . . "*—that is, they lay claim to a legitimacy with regard to which they themselves are mere spokespersons, and which, in principle, defines speaker and auditor as interchangeable. Divergence is thus reduced to a misunderstanding, or what could be dispersed by a little goodwill. Or to ignorance, which a bit of knowledge would suffice to repair. Or to a lack of tolerance, which could be reasoned with thanks to a bit of relativism. All are negations of the living values of divergence. Divergence is never a misunderstanding, but has the actuality and necessity of every position, "thus and not otherwise."

Obviously, the point is not to deny that an argument is logical or compelling, but simply to restrain its power to the homogeneous spaces in which the presumed interchangeability is affirmed by all concerned protagonists. To that extent, it is similar to interaction in the physical sense. Interaction implies terms that make a difference for one another, but a difference that does not modify their identity. Two masses that interact are still masses: what varies is their speed and relative positions. Likewise, if your arguments convince me, I am supposed, unless I admit I have undergone an "irrational" influence, an undue suggestion, to be able to define what my position had not taken into account, which explains why, although preserving my autonomous identity, I have been led to change my mind.

Argumentation, interaction, and rational conversation bet everything on homogeneity, that is, the possibility of putting oneself in the other's place. Roles are ideally interchangeable: *"let there be two charged bodies,"* but also *"you should realize that . . . "* or *"if I were you, I would . . . "* And above all, *"and therefore . . . ,"* to the import of which nothing must present an obstacle: from my viewpoint, what interests you is illusory, and the progress of knowledge will be sure to demonstrate that. Conversely, speculative presence, and the eventual efficacy associated with it, constitutes the wager of the interstice, or, as Deleuze would say, of what "grows out from the middle." What it aims at is above all not homogeneity and hence conversion, but only a slight modification, about which, what is more, it cannot foresee how it will come about, what causes, resources, and what consequences it will invent for itself. The vector of an infection never explains its efficacy; viruses tell about the animals they will kill only by indirect allusions, which biologists decipher laboriously, while the morbid process propagates virulently. The infection is "without reason," in the sense that its reasons depend on the fact of its success.

Perhaps we may take the risk of calling what designates the field of speculative ambition "ethics." Every time we use the term "ethics," we must obviously distinguish it from the term "morality," for this distinction does not exist prior to its respective users. William James's "moral philosophy," for instance, refers to what I call here ethics. Etymologically, in fact, the two terms are related. Since morality refers to the Latin "mos" (custom), and ethics to the Greek "ethos," both can be used to designate "good" behavior, "good" conduct; they can even be generalized to customs in general, both animal and human, which is what "ethology" does. It so happens that Whitehead often used the term "morality," with various meanings, but seldom the word "ethics," which therefore remains available in the context of his vocabulary. I take advantage of this, with all the more pleasure in that by so doing I concur with the reading Deleuze has suggested of ethics in Spinoza's sense, a reading which, referring the question of good and evil to that of what is good or bad, is of a hygienic rather than a normative type.

If the speculative ambition can be expressed in ethical terms, then, it will be in the sense in which "ethical" is linked to "ethos," and is therefore connected with the great theme of habit, in a way I have already mentioned with regard to Whitehead's educational project. The habits Whitehead calls "aesthetic" have as their correlate the question of presence, in the generic sense. In contrast, one may call "ethical" the habits that concern a social identity such that it accepts, or does not accept, the test constituted by the encounter with other, divergent identities.

Physicists may be imbued by the beauty of a sunset, yet relegate a poet's work to subjectivity, whereas their work, by contrast, is objective. This judgment, which makes nature bifurcate, is a very bad habit from an ethical viewpoint. The social identification of physics with objectivity may seem acceptable to poets who have acquired the (bad) habit of accepting this distribution of honors, but it communicates directly with the denunciation of all that cannot be subjected to this distribution. What is aimed at by an "ethical modification," in this case, is not "modified" physicists, having become able to reconcile what has bifurcated. It is simply physicists capable of celebrating the adventure they inherit in its singularity, without turning the "physical reality" of the electromagnetic waves emitted by the sun into "the" objective version, in opposition to which all the other versions must be defined. Such physicists may, in the trajectory that gave them this capacity, have been the fundamentally anonymous site of experiences that testify to evil, *qua* liable to be overcome. And they may, of course, by the example they provide, be accused by their peers of "demoralizing" the community. This happened, for instance, to Henri Poincaré and Pierre Duhem. Yet their "ethics" remain indeed those of physicists, as do their dreams, their doubts, their hopes, and their fears. They have "simply" acquired the good habit of dreams that do not turn them into the thinking head of humanity, taking charge of the questions that "men" have allegedly asked themselves forever, and which physics would recently have learned to answer.

Unlike reflexive or critical practices, which seek to persuade everyone to recognize the limits of their knowledge and adjust their claims to what these limits authorize, the ethical question, as I define it here, has as its stake not the passage from dogmatic slumber to critical wakefulness, but the difference between dream and nightmare. It does not aim at bringing forth heroic beings who have stripped themselves of the habits that enslave others. It does not produce a new version of the myth of the cave, with the invariant in all versions being the need to leave behind one's neighbors, the variable ingredient being what is waiting "outside the cave." There is no speculative figure of the cave in Whitehead, no overall judgment emitted against the partial and divergent interpretations that are supposed to predominate in it: if you wish to have an experience free of all interpretation, ask a stone for its biography . . .

The Whiteheadian adventure does not aim at awakening, leaving the cave. It is itself a dream, a storytelling: to learn "inside" the Platonic cave, together with those who live and argue within it. Not in the hope that the false appearances will gradually yield their secrets, but in the hope that these "appearances," if they are appreciated in their affirmative importance, might be articulated into fabulous contrasts.

The singularity of the Whiteheadian dream of learning inside the cave is that the person infected by it, who is lured by Whiteheadian propositions, is not mandated to become a missionary and propagate the infection. To be sure, this book tries to do so, but in a way to which only a very benign and limited infection may correspond, not a galloping process. Instead, this dream obliges the person it infects to address the dreams of others, for only dreamers can accept the modification of their dream. Only dreams and stories, because they are the enjoyment of living values, can receive the interstices without the panic effect of people who believe themselves to be in danger of losing hold.

Every philosophy endeavoring to lead people "out of the cave" has a direct connection to the universal, in which respect it is akin to therapeutics in the modern sense: the first refers to a use of thought that is finally adequate, or moral; the second to a return to health, to the morality of parts reconnecting with the possibility of a healthy cooperation in the service of the whole. This is why the paths they both propose are by right open to all. In contrast, speculative efficacy—the word of a dragon or of a trance, not of a counselor—is addressed to dreams, to doubts, to fears and ambitions, not to perplexity, confusion, to qualms in search of landmarks. No doubt the young Grendel suffered too much for the dragon's words to infect him in a speculative mode. Thus, as the trick of evil, it had the effect of transforming its feeling of loneliness into contempt and hatred.

Speculative philosophy is thus not addressed to everyone, but to others, insofar as they are "in their element," insofar as their habits constitute a world for them, into which they admit no free trespassing. To others, then, insofar as one cannot claim to "put oneself in their place." That these habits may be inflected, for instance, that laughter may resound testifying to the entertainment of a proposition that transforms what was accepted as an unavoidable alternative into a badly posed problem, such is the success that is dreamt of.

I will take the risk of giving a name to the "modification of others' dreams" that is the aim of speculative philosophy. That name is "politeness." In the first instance, such a name expresses the restriction of the address. The trick of evil will take advantage if the possibility of politeness is suggested to someone who has no choice left other than despair or anger. And this name also expresses the specific character of the antidote concocted by Whitehead. It does not concern those populations for whom politeness is already a synonym for civilization. It is addressed to the "moderns," who will confirm the relevance of this address by denouncing such politeness as artificial, even hypocritical, in any case far removed from any authenticity. Or, at the least, they will answer that it is only a secondary character. Thus, one may be a very good physicist and completely impolite, and the naive arrogance of the physicists' disqualifications is often even celebrated as their mark of genius, of the power of the dream that makes them "sleepwalkers." The Whiteheadian antidote is thus coherent with the absurdity that turned him into a philosopher. The ones it addresses, that is, also the ones who would snigger, are those who have made themselves the vectors of modern passions, adhering to one or another conflicting version of the bifurcation of nature.

To turn the Whiteheadian "scheme" into a matrix, whose applications would be thinkers who may be somewhat eccentric but are vectors of a disarming politeness, will surprise more than one reader. In general, philosophers are no more polite than physicists or sociologists, and much less so than some ethologists, who learn from what they observe how to address it. The critical interpellation "remember the conditions that set limits to your knowledge," a descendant of "remember that you are going to die," is not polite. It shocks those it addresses, as it to be expected, since the point is to wake them up. The need for awakening presupposes the legitimacy of "making someone lose hold," of shaking up routines and shattering certainties. Speculative interest, in contrast, respects the importance of the hold. The critical interpellation *"remember . . . "* is then replaced by the questions *"what is required by your hold?" "from what wager does your success proceed?"*—polite questions that one creature may address to another creature. And if the exchange is possible, if sometimes—an essentially anonymous event—one dream may induce the modification of another or evoke another, it is insofar as their point of junction is always a tangent point: neither a frontal clash between rival powers nor being swallowed up in the other's dream, not confusion in a banal dream of power but a local resonance, designating past tenses of divergent accomplishments and future tenses responding to distinct tests.

"What is required by your hold?": such a question affirms and presupposes that the others' dreams, like yours, are created according to the means of their own adventure, and to this extent this question constitutes a test: it is a question that beings of power will have difficulty tolerating, proceeding as they do in the name of an intangible right that must be satisfied everywhere, which recognizes no difference between here and there, other than that of the parasites to be eliminated so that they themselves may be confirmed. Yet it is a question that one dreamer can address to another dreamer, for dreams do not abstract from the means, but rather dissolve the dreamer's identity in adventures that restore to the "means" their mode of actual existence: that of propositions that possess individuals far more than individuals possess them. This is why, when philosophy has succeeded doing what it can do, not only is wonder still there, but it henceforth infects all the statements whose vocation was to explain the world, that is, to disenchant it.

The Whiteheadian scheme is a work of politeness because it seeks to be "adequate," refraining from insulting any living value. Yet if it is effective, it owes this to its fabrication, to the articulation of constraints that oblige thought, an "asignificant" matrix whose truth is the events of "disclosure" it may induce, modifying a being's relations to its environment, and, in this case, the relations of a statement to its consequences. Whitehead made coherence the vector of this efficacy, and it is coherence that demanded the twofold production of Whitehead as speculative thinker and of that strange object, the speculative scheme. Whitehead fabricated this scheme in order that the scheme might fabricate him, that it might oblige him to undergo the becomings of thought demanded by coherence.

As a thinker, Whitehead is thus not so much the author of the scheme and the concepts he articulates as he was obliged by them, in a process of empirical experimentation-verification that is akin to trance, because in it thought is taken, captured, by a becoming that separates it from its own intentionality. A "mechanical" becoming in the sense of Deleuze and Guattari, in the sense that thinkers can produce this thought only because they have themselves become a piece, or gear, of what has captured them, much more than they have created it. Thought is then no longer the exercise of a right but becomes an "art of consequences," consequences that leap from one domain to another, or, more precisely, that make interstices zigzag where a homogeneous right had seemed to reign, and make connections proliferate where *"this has nothing to do with that"* had prevailed.

That is why I had to "think with Whitehead," that is, accept the capture and become a gear.

Index